Cost Estimator's
Reference Manual

COST ESTIMATOR'S REFERENCE MANUAL

Rodney D. Stewart
Richard M. Wyskida

A Wiley-Interscience Publication

John Wiley & Sons

New York • Chichester • Brisbane • Toronto • Singapore

Library of Congress Cataloging-in-Publication Data:

Cost estimator's reference manual.

    "A Wiley-Interscience publication."
    Bibliography: p.
    Includes index.
    1. Engineering—Estimates. 2. Costs, Industrial—
Estimates. I. Stewart, Rodney D. II. Wyskida,
Richard M., 1935-
TA183.C64   1987   658.1′552   86-15884
ISBN 0-471-83082-8

Printed in the United States of America

10 9 8 7 6 5 4 3 2 1

PREFACE

Welcome to the world of cost estimating! This handbook on cost estimating has been two years in the making and contains expert advice from a team of 11 well-qualified and experienced professionals who have been practicing for a total combined time of about 200 person-years in cost estimating and related professions. The handbook is designed to permit a thorough cover-to-cover study of cost estimating or to permit quick reference to specific areas and disciplines for those who have encountered trouble spots in a cost-estimating situation. You will be told *how* to develop a credible and accurate cost estimate; *where* to get supporting information and data; *what* tools and techniques are available; and *whom* to contact about being certified, obtaining publications and information, and gaining education and training in the profession.

The editors themselves have contributed to early chapters in estimating fundamentals and statistical techniques and have solicited chapters from estimating professionals and practitioners on a smorgasboard of subjects representing a cross section of the disciplines and fields needed to address the varied aspects of cost estimating. As in any smorgasboard, there is something for everybody even though every estimator may not need *all* the information provided. Estimating techniques such as cost allocation, discounted cash flow analysis, learning curves, parametric estimating, risk analysis, and the use of microcomputers in cost estimating are presented in detail in individual chapters. Estimating in selected fields such as high-technology projects, construction, government procurement, and software development is addressed by experienced practitioners who have had hands-on positions in industry and government related to the subjects discussed in these specialized chapters. Advanced subjects such as the emergence of cost estimating as an established profession and the use of artificial intelligence in cost estimating are presented in two final chapters.

The novice or beginner in cost estimating should study thoroughly Chapter 1, "Fundamentals of Cost Estimating." This chapter walks the reader through the 12 basic steps of cost estimating, starting with development of the work element structure and ending with publication and use of the estimate. The beginner should also review in depth each of the chapters on estimating methods and techniques and study selected chapters that relate to his or her specific work activity or work output.

The apprentice or experienced professional estimator will find a wealth of in-depth data on techniques, methods, and approaches to estimating in Chapters 2 through 15. These chapters serve as a ready reference or refresher to help in the solution of specific cost-estimating problems or as a basis for an in-depth study of one or more of the detailed aspects of cost estimating. The chapter on the use of microcomputers for cost estimating will introduce the reader to the methods of employing these low-cost, high-technology tools to the job of estimating projects, products, processes, or services.

As can be seen by the content of this manual, estimating is a truly multidisciplinary field. The field involves engineers, accountants, manufacturing planning personnel, mathematicians, statisticians, economists, engineering managers, and many other professions. There is virtually no business, commercial, or public sector activity that is not touched at one time or another with the need to apply excellent cost-estimating methods, procedures, tactics, and strategies. As a result of the far-reaching effects of cost estimation on all work activities and outputs, it is important to outline everything one needs to know about the subject in one volume. The authors have been successful in describing the methods used and in telling where to get additional information and data for further study, analysis, and synthesis into cost estimates. The editors have endeavored to provide a well-rounded manual with a balanced set of topics that will apply to the widest possible array of cost-estimating situations. The extensive bibliography at the end of the book lists more detailed publications relating to the cost-estimating field. There are many other books, manuals, and articles on cost estimating being published every day: keep your eyes peeled for these emerging publications in an important and growing profession.

In the meantime, adhere to the advice of these experienced practicioners, and you will benefit greatly by both the derived and inherent professional, technical, and business benefits of excellent cost estimating.

RODNEY D. STEWART
RICHARD M. WYSKIDA

Huntsville, Alabama
November 1986

Contents

CHAPTER 1. **FUNDAMENTALS OF COST ESTIMATING**
Rodney D. Stewart

CHAPTER 2. **COST ALLOCATION**
Richard H. Shuford, Jr.

CHAPTER 3. **STATISTICAL TECHNIQUES IN COST ESTIMATION**
Richard M. Wyskida

CHAPTER 4. **DISCOUNTED CASH FLOW ANALYSIS**
Joseph W. Hamaker

CHAPTER 5. **LEARNING CURVES AND PROGRESS FUNCTIONS**
Leon M. Delionback

CHAPTER 6. **DETAILED COST ESTIMATING**
Rodney D. Stewart

CHAPTER 7. **PARAMETRIC ESTIMATING**
Joseph W. Hamaker

CHAPTER 8. **COST / SCHEDULE / TECHNICAL PERFORMANCE RISK ANALYSIS**
Nona M. Whatley

CHAPTER 9.   THE USE OF MICROCOMPUTERS FOR
              COST ESTIMATING
                  Ann L. Stewart

CHAPTER 10.   CONSTRUCTION COST ESTIMATING
                  James D. Stevens

CHAPTER 11.   COST ESTIMATING IN MANUFACTURING
                  John N. Lovett, Jr.

CHAPTER 12.   SOFTWARE COST ESTIMATING
                  Rodney D. Stewart

CHAPTER 13.   ASPECTS AFFECTING COST ESTIMATION
              IN GOVERNMENT PROCUREMENT
                  Richard H. Shuford, Jr.

CHAPTER 14.   COST ESTIMATING AS A PROFESSION
                  Raymond H. Croninger

CHAPTER 15.   ARTIFICIAL INTELLIGENCE IN COST
              ESTIMATING
                  James D. Johannes

BIBLIOGRAPHY
DICTIONARY OF ESTIMATING TERMS
INDEX

DETAILED CONTENTS

CHAPTER 1. FUNDAMENTALS OF COST ESTIMATING   **1**

1.1. Organizing for Estimating, 2
1.2. Developing Ground Rules and Assumptions, 3
1.3. The Work Element Structure (or Work Breakdown
      Structure), 4
      1.3.1. Work Element Numbering System, 5
      1.3.2. Development of the Structure, 6
      1.3.3. Designations of Work Element Levels, 9
      1.3.4. Treatment of Alternate, Parallel, or
             Recurring/Nonrecurring Costs, 10
      1.3.5. More About Work Element Coding
             Conventions, 10
      1.3.6. Work Element Dictionaries, 11
1.4. Scheduling, 11
      1.4.1. Precedence/Successor Relationships and
             Dates, 12
      1.4.2. Techniques Used in Schedule Planning, 12
1.5. The Retrieval and Use of Historical Cost Data, 15
1.6. Cost Estimating Relationships, 17
      1.6.1. Removing and/or Accounting for the
             Effects of Inflation, 17
      1.6.2. Removing the Effects of Labor Rate
             Fluctuations, 18
      1.6.3. Adjusting Historical Data to Account for
             Past Inefficiencies, 19
1.7. Develop and Use Production Learning Curves, 21

1.8.   Identification of Skill Categories, Skill Levels, and
       Labor Rates,   21
       1.8.1.   Skill Categories,   22
       1.8.2.   Skill Levels,   22
       1.8.3.   The Dynamic Skill Mix,   22
       1.8.4.   Static and Dynamic Skill Mix
                Examples,   23
1.9.   Developing Labor and Material Estimates,   27
       1.9.1.   Motion and Time Method (MTM),   30
       1.9.2.   Industrial, Shop, or Office Standards,   31
       1.9.3.   Staffing and Shoploading Estimating,   32
       1.9.4.   Material Estimating,   32
1.10. Develop Overhead and Administrative Cost
       Estimates,   32
       1.10.1.   Direct Costs: Definition,   33
       1.10.2.   Indirect Costs: Definition,   33
       1.10.3.   Other Costs: Definition,   33
1.11. Applying Inflation and Escalation (Cost Growth)
       Factors,   34
       1.11.1.   Dealing with Inflation,   35
       1.11.2.   Dealing with Escalation,   36
1.12. Pricing or Computing the Estimated Cost,   37
1.13. Analyzing, Adjusting, and Supporting the
       Estimate,   38
1.14. Publishing and Presenting the Cost Estimate,   39
       References,   40

CHAPTER 2.   COST ALLOCATION   42

2.1.   Cost Classifications and Concepts,   42
       2.1.1.   Accounting Structures and Systems,   42
       2.1.2.   Patterns in Cost Behavior,   46
       2.1.3.   Traceability of Costs,   49
2.2.   The Nature of Product Costing,   50
       2.2.1.   Product Cost Flows,   51
       2.2.2.   Job Order Costing,   51
       2.2.3.   Process Costing,   56
2.3.   Indirect Cost Allocation,   59
       2.3.1.   Allocation to Jobs,   60
       2.3.2.   Allocation of Service Department
                Overhead,   63
       2.3.3.   Allocation in Process Costing Systems,   65
2.4.   Cost Control Utilizing Standards,   66
       2.4.1.   Material Standards,   66
       2.4.2.   Labor Standards,   67
       2.4.3.   Flexible Budgeting,   69

2.5.   Analyzing Performance by Cost,   70
          2.5.1.   Variance Analysis,   70
          2.5.2.   Break-Even Analysis,   73
          2.5.3.   Differential Analysis,   76
          2.5.4.   Profit Relationship of Segments,   79
          2.5.5.   Profit of the Company,   81

CHAPTER 3.   STATISTICAL TECHNIQUES IN COST
                 ESTIMATION   85

   3.1.   Introduction,   85
          3.1.1.   Historical Data Collection,   85
          3.1.2.   Statistical Inference,   86
          3.1.3.   Parametric versus Nonparametric,   86
   3.2.   Basic Concepts Regarding Statistical Tests,   87
          3.2.1.   Statement of Hypotheses,   87
          3.2.2.   Choice of Statistical Test,   88
          3.2.3.   Level of Significance,   89
          3.2.4.   The Sampling Distribution,   91
          3.2.5.   The Region of Rejection,   91
          3.2.6.   The Statistical Decision,   92
   3.3.   Parametric Statistical Tests,   92
          3.3.1.   The Treatment of Outliers,   93
          3.3.2.   Large Sample Goodness of Fit Testing,   95
                   3.3.2.1.   Graphic Methods,   96
                   3.3.2.2.   Chi-Squared Test,   96
          3.3.3.   Transformations,   99
          3.3.4.   Predictive Methods,   101
                   3.3.4.1.   Linear Regression,   102
                   3.3.4.2.   Sampling and Regression
                              Analysis,   107
                   3.3.4.3.   Multiple Regression,   108
                   3.3.4.4.   Selection of Independent
                              Variables,   112
   3.4.   Nonparametric Statistical Tests,   115
          3.4.1.   Kruskal-Wallis *H*-test,   115
          3.4.2.   Kolmogorov-Smirnov One-Sample
                   Statistic,   117
   3.5.   Concluding Remarks,   119
          References,   119

CHAPTER 4.   DISCOUNTED CASH FLOW ANALYSIS   120

   4.1.   Introduction,   120
          4.1.1.   The Time Value of Money Concept and
                   When It Applies,   120
          4.1.2.   Cash Flows,   121

4.2.   Structuring the Discounted Cash Flow Analysis,   125
        4.2.1.   Multiple Levels of Investment,   125
        4.2.2.   Exclusion of Common Cash Flows and
                 Sunk Costs,   125
        4.2.3.   Equal Capabilities between
                 Alternatives,   126
        4.2.4.   Equal Economic Lifetimes,   126
        4.2.5.   Income Tax Considerations,   127
        4.2.6.   Disregard Payment Schedules Due to
                 Financing Arrangements,   128
        4.2.7.   Uncertainties and Risk,   128
4.3.   Decision Criteria,   129
        4.3.1.   Present Value,   129
        4.3.2.   Equivalent Annual Amount,   132
        4.3.3.   Assumption of an Infinite Horizon,   133
        4.3.4.   Internal Rate of Return,   134
        4.3.5.   Example of the Present Value Method,   137
4.4.   Selection from Multiple Alternatives,   141
4.5.   The Relationship between Interest and Inflation,   145
4.6.   Choosing a Discount Rate,   154
4.7.   Summary,   155
        References,   156

CHAPTER 5.   LEARNING CURVES AND PROGRESS
              FUNCTIONS   157

5.1.   Introduction,   157
        5.1.1.   Objectives/Purpose,   157
        5.1.2.   Problem Statement,   158
5.2.   Applied Learning Curve Theory,   161
        5.2.1.   Assumptions,   161
        5.2.2.   Constraints,   162
        5.2.3.   Approaches,   162
                 5.2.3.1.   Wright System,   162
                 5.2.3.2.   Crawford System,   164
5.3.   Preliminary Considerations,   165
        5.3.1.   Theoretical First Unit (TFU) Cost,   165
        5.3.2.   Learning Curve Slope Ranges,   167
5.4.   Analytical Techniques,   168
        5.4.1.   Mathematical Relations,   169
        5.4.2.   Solution Procedures,   171
                 5.4.2.1.   Graphical Solutions,   171
                 5.4.2.2.   Algebraic Solutions Using
                            Established Equations,   171
                 5.4.2.3.   Tabular Solutions,   174
                 5.4.2.4.   Composite Learning
                            Curve,   175

                              5.4.2.5. Solution of Learning Curve
                                        Problems by Use of
                                        Microcomputer, 176
        5.5. Effects of Design Changes on the Learning
              Curve, 177
        5.6. Factors Affecting Learning Curve Slope, 177
        5.7. Other Information on Learning Curves, 178
                    5.7.1. Learning Losses Due to Production
                            Interruptions, 178
                    5.7.2. Learning in Small Lots, 178
                    5.7.3. Learning Curve/Complexity
                            Relationships, 179
                    5.7.4. Incentives During Learning, 179
                    5.7.5. Misapplications of the Learning Curve
                            Concept, 179
                    5.7.6. Learning in Manual Operations, 180
                    5.7.7. Learning Curves from Standard Time
                            Data, 180
                    5.7.8. Learning in Mechanical Assembly
                            Tasks, 180
              References, 180

CHAPTER 6. **DETAILED COST ESTIMATING**   **182**

        6.1. The Anatomy of a Detailed Estimate, 182
                    6.1.1. Time, Skills, and Labor-Hours Required
                            to Prepare an Estimate, 185
        6.2. Discussion of Types of Costs, 186
                    6.2.1. Initial Acquisition Costs, 186
                    6.2.2. Fixed and Variable Cost, 187
                    6.2.3. Recurring and Nonrecurring Costs, 187
                    6.2.4. Direct and Indirect Costs, 187
        6.3. Collecting the Ingredients of the Estimate, 187
                    6.3.1. Labor-Hours, 187
                    6.3.2. Materials and Subcontracts, 189
                    6.3.3. Labor Rates and Factors, 189
                    6.3.4. Indirect Costs, Burden, and Overhead, 190
                    6.3.5. Administrative Costs, 190
                    6.3.6. Fee, Profit, or Earnings, 190
                    6.3.7. Assembly of the Ingredients, 190
        6.4. The First Questions to Ask (and Why), 191
                    6.4.1. What Is It?, 192
                    6.4.2. What Does It Look Like?, 192
                    6.4.3. When Is It to Be Available?, 192
                    6.4.4. Who Will Do It?, 193
                    6.4.5. Where Will It Be Done?, 193

6.5.   The Estimate Skeleton: The Work Element
        Structure,   193
6.6.   The Hierarchical Relationship of a Work Element
        Structure,   194
6.7.   Functional Elements Described,   194
6.8.   Physical Elements Described,   196
6.9.   Treatment of Recurring and Nonrecurring
        Activities,   196
6.10.   Work Element Structure Interrelationships,   198
        6.10.1.   Skill Matrix in a Work Element
                  Structure,   198
        6.10.2.   Organizational Relationships to a Work
                  Element Structure, 199
6.11.   Methods Used Within the Detailed Estimating Process,
        6.11.1.   Detailed Resource Estimating,   200
        6.11.2.   Direct Estimating,   200
        6.11.3.   Estimating by Analogy (Rules of
                  Thumb),   200
        6.11.4.   Firm Quotes,   200
        6.11.5.   Handbook Estimating,   201
        6.11.6.   The Learning Curve,   201
        6.11.7.   Man-Loading Methods,   204
        6.11.8.   Statistical and Parametric Estimating as
                  Inputs to Detailed Estimating,   205
6.12.   Developing a Schedule,   208
6.13.   Techniques Used in Schedule Planning,   209
6.14.   Estimating Engineering Activities,   211
        6.14.1.   Engineering Skill Levels,   211
        6.14.2.   Design,   211
        6.14.3.   Analysis,   211
        6.14.4.   Drafting,   212
6.15.   Manufacturing/Production Engineering,   212
        6.15.1.   Engineering Documentation,   214
6.16.   Estimating Manufacturing/Production and
        Assembly,   214
        6.16.1.   The Process Plan,   214
6.17.   Manufacturing Activities,   217
6.18.   In-Process Inspection,   217
6.19.   Testing,   218
        6.19.1.   Special Tooling and Test Equipment,   218
6.20.   Computer Software Cost Estimating,   219
6.21.   Labor Allowances,   220
        6.21.1.   Variance from Measured Labor-Hours,   221
        6.21.2.   Personal, Fatigue, and Delay (PFD)
                  Time,   221
        6.21.3.   Tooling and Equipment Maintenance,   221

6.21.4. Normal Rework and Repair,   221

6.21.5. Engineering Change Allowance,   222

6.21.6. Engineering Prototype Allowance,   222

6.21.7. Design Growth Allowance,   222

6.21.8. Cost Growth Allowance,   222

6.22. Estimating Supervision, Direct Management, and Other Direct Charges,   223

6.23. The Use of ''Factors'' in Detailed Estimating,   223

6.24. Summary,   224

CHAPTER 7. PARAMETRIC ESTIMATING   225

7.1. Introduction,   225

7.1.1. An Overview of Parametric Estimating,   225

7.1.2. Origins of Parametric Estimating,   227

7.1.3. Applicability of the Parametric Method,   228

7.2. Data Base Development,   229

7.2.1. Data Collection, Organization, and Normalization,   229

7.2.2. Bookkeeping Normalizations,   230

7.3. Model Building,   233

7.3.1. Common CER Equation Forms,   233

7.3.2. Choosing the Right Equation Form for the CER,   242

7.3.3. Measures of Goodness of Fit,   245

7.3.4. Multiple Regression,   247

7.4. Model Application,   247

7.4.1. CER Stratification,   249

7.4.2. Cost Adjustments and Complexity Factors,   251

7.4.3. Number of Developmental Units,   252

7.4.4. Design Inheritance,   252

7.4.5. Design Complexity,   252

7.4.6. Production Rate Effects,   253

7.5. Trends and Directions,   254

7.5.1. New Applications and Broader Scopes,   255

7.5.2. Parametrics and Risk Analysis,   255

7.5.3. Computers and Parametric Cost Estimating,   256

7.5.4. Commercial Cost Models,   257

7.5.5. Professional Societies,   257

7.6. Summary,   257

References,   258

**CHAPTER 8. COST / SCHEDULE / TECHNICAL
PERFORMANCE RISK ANALYSIS   259**

8.1.   Risk Analysis, 259
8.2.   Aspects of Risk Analysis, 260
      8.2.1.   Probability Theory and Expert
            Opinion, 261
      8.2.2.   Methods for Quantifying Expert
            Opinion, 262
            8.2.2.1.   The Modified Churchman-Ackoff
                  Method, 262
            8.2.2.2.   The Normalized Geometric
                  Mean Vector Method, 263
            8.2.2.3.   Gamble Method, 264
            8.2.2.4.   Diagrammatic Method, 264
            8.2.2.5.   The Delphi Technique, 264
8.3.   Risk Analysis Techniques, 264
      8.3.1.   Network Analysis, 265
            8.3.1.1.   Network Analysis
                  Technique, 271
            8.3.1.2.   Critical Path Method
                  (CPM), 272
            8.3.1.3.   Program Evaluation and Review
                  Technique (PERT), 274
            8.3.1.4.   ARTEMIS Probabilistic Analysis
                  of Network (PAN), 275
            8.3.1.5.   Risk Information System and
                  Network Evaluation Technique
                  (RISNET), 278
            8.3.1.6.   Venture Evaluation and Review
                  Technique (VERT), 285
      8.3.2.   Decision Risk Analysis Method, 295
      8.3.3.   Cost Estimating Risk Analysis
            Technique, 297
            8.3.3.1.   Stochastic Aggregation Model
                  (SAM), 299
            8.3.3.2.   Example Case: Project X, 302
                  8.3.3.2.1.   SAM Input Form for
                        Project X, 302
                  8.3.3.2.2.   SAM Output for
                        Project X, 303
            8.3.3.3.   SAM Technical Notes, 304
                  8.3.3.3.1.   How SAM Handles
                        CER Risk, 304
                  8.3.3.3.2.   Interpretation of
                        SAM Output, 304
      8.3.4.   Risk Factor Method, 305

8.4. Application of Risk Analysis Technique, 306
     References, 309

CHAPTER 9. THE USE OF MICROCOMPUTERS FOR COST ESTIMATING   **311**

9.1. Approaches to Cost Estimating with Microcomputers, 311
     9.1.1. Combining Word Processing with Number Processing-Rationale, 311
     9.1.2. BASIC Programs, 313
     9.1.3. Spreadsheets, 313
     9.1.4. Integrated Software Packages, 313
     9.1.5. Vertical Market Systems, 313
     9.1.6. Estimating Interfaces with Accounting and Design, 314
9.2. Microcomputer Use Throughout the Estimating Process, 314
9.3. Developing the Work Element Structure, 315
     9.3.1. Multiplan™ Template, 316
     9.3.2. Lotus 1-2-3™ Templates, 317
     9.3.3. The Sixteen Construction Divisions, 319
     9.3.4. Work Structure Correlation with Scheduling, 321
9.4. Scheduling the Work Elements, 330
9.5. Retrieval of Historical Cost Data, 333
9.6. Development and Use of Cost Estimating Relationships, 340
9.7. Development of Production Learning Curves, 343
9.8. Identification of Skill Categories, Levels, and Rates, 345
9.9. Estimating Labor Hours and Material Quantities, 349
9.10. Estimating Overhead, Administrative Costs, and Fee, 352
9.11. Inflation, Escalation, and Cost Growth , 354
     9.11.1. Inflation, 354
     9.11.2. Escalation, 355
     9.11.3. Other Allowances, 357
9.12. Synthesizing and Publishing the Cost Estimate, 359
     9.12.1. Microcomputer Graphics Outputs, 361
     9.12.2. Cost Summaries by Work Element, 362
     9.12.3. The Estimate Report, 365
9.13. Microcomputer Hardware for the Estimator, 367
     9.13.1. The Microcomputer, 367
     9.13.2. The Printer and Plotter, 369
     9.13.3. Software, 371
     9.13.4. Peripheral Devices, 372

9.14.   Summary and Final Advice,   372
        References,   372

CHAPTER 10.   CONSTRUCTION COST ESTIMATING   373

10.1.   Introduction,   373
        10.1.1.   Overview,   373
        10.1.2.   Consideration of Construction Type,   374
                  10.1.2.1.   Building Construction,   375
                  10.1.2.2.   Heavy Construction,   375
        10.1.3.   Consideration of Contract Form,   375
                  10.1.3.1.   Cost-Plus Contracts,   375
                  10.1.3.2.   Lump-Sum Contracts,   376
                  10.1.3.3.   Unit-Price Contracts,   376
        10.1.4.   Degrees of Cost Estimating,   377
        10.1.5.   Bidding Strategy,   378
10.2.   Preliminary Cost Estimating,   378
        10.2.1.   Overview,   378
        10.2.2.   Preliminary Cost Estimating for Building
                  Construction,   378
                  10.2.2.1.   Area and Capacity
                              Estimates,   379
                  10.2.2.2.   Systems Estimates,   380
                  10.2.2.3.   Comparable Facility
                              Estimates,   380
                  10.2.2.4.   Time Estimates,   385
        10.2.3.   Preliminary Cost Estimating for Heavy
                  Construction,   385
                  10.2.3.1.   Estimating Highway
                              Construction,   386
10.3.   Detailed Cost Estimating,   388
        10.3.1.   Overview,   388
        10.3.2.   Building Construction,   389
                  10.3.2.1.   Quantity Takeoffs,   389
                  10.3.2.2.   Labor Rates,   390
                  10.3.2.3.   Equipment Rates,   391
                  10.3.2.4.   Subcontracts,   392
                  10.3.2.5.   Indirect Costs,   395
        10.3.3.   Heavy Construction,   395
                  10.3.3.1.   List of Pay Items,   396
                  10.3.3.2.   Unit Prices,   396
                  10.3.3.3.   Distribution of Indirect
                              Costs,   397
                  10.3.3.4.   Unbalanced Bids,   397
        10.3.4.   Cash Flow Analysis,   397

10.4.   Time Schedules in Cost Estimating,   403
          10.4.1.   Overview,   403
          10.4.2.   CPM Schedules,   404
                    10.4.2.1.   Arrow Diagramming,   405
                    10.4.2.2.   Precedence Diagramming,   406
                    10.4.2.3.   CPM Calculations,   407
                    10.4.2.4.   Least-Cost Scheduling,   411
                    10.4.2.5.   Payment Progressing,   415
                    10.4.2.6.   Resource Leveling,   415
          10.4.3.   PERT Schedules,   418
          10.4.4.   Monte Carlo Simulation Schedules,   422
10.5.   Summary of Construction Cost Estimating,   425
          References,   426

CHAPTER 11.   COST ESTIMATING IN MANUFACTURING   427

11.1.   Introduction,   427
11.2.   Labor Costing,   429
          11.2.1.   Engineering and Design,   429
          11.2.2.   Standard Time Data,   433
                    11.2.2.1.   Direct Time Study,   434
                    11.2.2.2.   Predetermined Systems,   438
          11.2.3.   Labor Rate Schedules,   445
          11.2.4.   Indirect Labor,   446
11.3.   Materials Costing,   447
          11.3.1.   Bill of Material,   447
          11.3.2.   Master Production Schedule,   448
          11.3.3.   Inventory/Order Costs and Policy,   449
11.4.   Equipment and Tooling Cost Estimating,   456
          11.4.1.   Cost Models,   456
          11.4.2.   Standard Data Tables,   458
11.5.   Quality Control, Reliability, and Test
          Estimating,   460
          11.5.1.   Inspection,   460
          11.5.2.   Analysis,   460
          11.5.3.   Scrap and Rework,   461
11.6.   Other Costs,   461
          References,   462

CHAPTER 12.   SOFTWARE COST ESTIMATING   463

12.1.   Types of Software,   463
          12.1.1.   Processing Software,   463
          12.1.2.   Monitoring Software,   464
          12.1.3.   Control Software,   464
12.2.   Types of Software Cost Estimates,   464

12.3.   Detailed Software Cost Estimating,   464
    12.3.1.   Software Development Phases,   465
        12.3.1.1.   Information Processing
                    Analysis,   468
        12.3.1.2.   Information Processing
                    Design,   468
        12.3.1.3.   Computer Program
                    Design,   469
        12.3.1.4.   Computer Program Coding and
                    Checkout,   469
        12.3.1.5.   Computer Program Functional
                    Test,   469
        12.3.1.6.   Information Processing
                    Integration Test,   470
        12.3.1.7.   Information Processing
                    Installation and
                    Implementation,   470
    12.3.2.   Factors Affecting Detailed Software Cost
              Estimates,   470
        12.3.2.1.   Computer Equipment
                    Configuration and
                    Performance,   470
        12.3.2.2.   Software Product
                    Characteristics,   471
    12.3.3.   Establishing Skill Categories, Skill Levels,
              and Labor Rates,   472
    12.3.4.   Estimating, Pricing, and Publishing the
              Estimate,   473
12.4.   Parametric Software Cost Estimating,   474
    12.4.1.   The COCOMO Model,   474
    12.4.2.   The PRICE S Parametric Cost Model,   477
    12.4.3.   The SLIM Parametric Software Cost and
              Schedule Estimating Model,   479
    12.4.4.   JPL Software Simulation Model,   479
    12.4.5.   ESD Parametric Software Cost Estimating
              Model,   481
    12.4.6.   Other Software Cost Estimation
              Models,   484
12.5.   A Case Study: A Software Cost Estimate for an
        Estimating System,   484
    12.5.1.   Definition of the Work,   484
        12.5.1.1.   Overview,   485
        12.5.1.2.   The User Interface,   485
        12.5.1.3.   The Module Design,   487
    12.5.2.   Estimation of Resource Requirements,   492
    12.5.3.   Cost Estimate Outputs,   496

12.6. Summary, 496

References, 497

CHAPTER 13. ASPECTS AFFECTING COST ESTIMATION IN GOVERNMENT PROCUREMENT 498

13.1. Federal Government Philosophies and Policies, 498

    13.1.1. Governmental Perspective, 498

    13.1.2. General Statutory Requirements, 499

    13.1.3. Broad Policies, 499

13.2. Procurement Planning Requirements, 501

    13.2.1. Agency Acquisition Plans, 501

    13.2.2. Annual Budget Cycle, 502

    13.2.3. Multiyear Procurements, 502

13.3. Cost Estimation in Government Contracts, 504

    13.3.1. Firm-Fixed-Price Contracts, 505

    13.3.2. Fixed-Price Contracts with Economic Price Adjustment, 505

    13.3.3. Fixed-Price Incentive Contracts, 506

    13.3.4. Fixed-Ceiling-Price Contracts with Retroactive Price Redetermination, 507

    13.3.5. Fixed-Price Contracts with Prospective Price Redetermination, 508

    13.3.6. Firm-Fixed Price, Level-of-Effort Term Contracts, 508

    13.3.7. Cost-Sharing Contracts, 509

    13.3.8. Cost-Plus-Incentive-Fee Contracts, 509

    13.3.9. Cost-Plus-Award-Fee Contracts, 510

    13.3.10. Cost-Plus-Fixed-Fee Contracts, 511

    13.3.11. Indefinite-Delivery Contracts, 511

    13.3.12. Time-and-Materials, Labor-Hour, and Letter Contracts, 513

    13.3.13. Federal Supply Schedule Contracting, 514

    13.3.14. Facilities Contracts, 514

    13.3.15. Construction and Architect-Engineer Contracts, 514

    13.3.16. Contracts with Educational Institutions, 515

    13.3.17. Contracts with State and Local Governments, 515

13.4. Cost Accounting Standards and Principles, 516

    13.4.1. Applicability of Government Standards, 516

    13.4.2. Special Cost Terms, 516

    13.4.3. Standards, 517

    13.4.4. Cost Principles, 518

13.5.   Cost Grouping and Structures,   519
        13.5.1.   Five-Year Defense Plan,   519
        13.5.2.   Program Management,   519
        13.5.3.   Contracting,   523
13.6.   Separate Cost Principles,   523
        13.6.1.   Compensation for Personal Services,   523
        13.6.2.   Special Contracts and Grants,   523
13.7.   Constraints Outside the Cost Estimate,   524
        13.7.1.   Limitation of Costs Clause,   524
        13.7.2.   Practices and Decision Precedents,   524
13.8.   Other Considerations in Cost Estimating for Contracts
        with the Federal Government,   525
        References,   526

CHAPTER 14.   COST ESTIMATING AS A PROFESSION   528

14.1.   Cost Estimating Defined,   528
14.2.   Evolution of Cost Estimating,   528
14.3.   Movement into the Industrial Age,   529
14.4.   Estimators Seek Professionalism,   530
14.5.   Educational Disciplines,   530
14.6.   Education/Training,   531
14.7.   Personal Qualities and Qualifications,   532
14.8.   Functional Derivatives,   532
14.9.   Professional Certification,   534
        14.9.1.   National Estimating Society,   534
        14.9.2.   Institute of Management Accounting,   535
        14.9.3.   American Association of Cost
                  Engineers,   536
        14.9.4.   National Contract Management
                  Association,   537
        14.9.5.   Institute of Cost Analysis,   537
        14.9.6.   American Society of Professional
                  Estimators,   537
        14.9.7.   Society of American Value Engineers,   537
        14.9.8.   International Society of Parametric
                  Analysts,   537
14.10. A New Changing Environment in Cost
        Estimating,   537
        References,   538

CHAPTER 15.   ARTIFICIAL INTELLIGENCE IN COST
              ESTIMATING   539

15.1.   Introduction,   539
15.2.   Knowledge-Based Cost Estimation Paradigm,   542

15.3.   Formal Models,   545
15.4.   A Frame-Based System,   545
        15.4.1.   Building Work Element Structures,   546
        15.4.2.   Skill Category and Skill Mix
                  Determination,   547
        15.4.3.   Scheduling and Resource Adjustments,   547
        15.4.4.   Cost Growth and Contingency
                  Estimates,   548
        15.4.5.   Parametric Estimating,   548
        15.4.6.   Cost Factor Development and Use,   549
        15.4.7.   Make-or-Buy Criteria and
                  Determination,   549
        15.4.8.   Determining Mix and Magnitude of
                  Independent Research and
                  Development,   550
        15.4.9.   Profit and Profitability Determination and
                  Planning,   550
        15.4.10. Purchasing Decision Making (Source
                  Evaluation and Selection),   551
15.5.   Summary,   551
        References,   551

Bibliography   **553**
Dictionary of Estimating Terms   **555**
Index   **615**

Cost Estimator's
Reference Manual

1

FUNDAMENTALS OF COST ESTIMATING

RODNEY D. STEWART, PE, CPE, CCA

To begin the study of cost estimating, one must understand that there is an inseparable relationship between cost *estimating* and cost *analysis* (see Figure 1.1). Even though the two disciplines are functionally separate, they are interrelated so that each depends on the other. *Cost Estimating*, the process of predicting or forecasting the cost of a work activity or work output, depends on inputs from *cost analysis*, the process of studying and organizing past costs and future estimates. Likewise, *cost analysis* often depends on the ability to make good preliminary *cost estimates*. This is the reason why most books on cost estimating contain much information on both disciplines: cost estimating is principally a look forward into future occurrences, and cost analysis is principally a view into the past with an eye toward the future. This book takes no exception to that past tradition of treating the two disciplines but views the subjects from the cost estimator's standpoint. Each step of the cost-estimating process requires some pure analysis and some pure estimating, with the completion of one triggering the start of the other, and the start of the one triggering the need for the other. References [1] and [2] provide in-depth discussions, data, methodologies, and examples for cost estimating and cost analysis.

In this chapter the cost-estimating process is divided into 12 basic steps that represent the principal jobs the cost estimator must perform to produce a completed cost estimate. The 12 steps are as follows: (1) develop the work element structure; (2) schedule the work elements; (3) retrieve and organize historical data; (4) develop and use cost-estimating relationships; (5) develop and use production learning curves; (6) identify skill categories, skill levels, and labor rates; (7) develop labor hour and material estimates; (8) develop overhead and administrative costs; (9) apply inflation and escalation (cost growth) factors; (10) price or compute the estimated costs; (11) analyze, adjust, and support the estimate; and (12) publish and present the estimate so that it can be *used* effectively. Figure 1.2 shows sche-

1

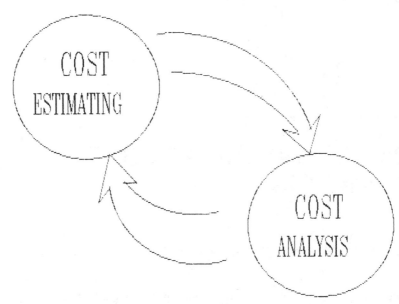

Figure 1.1. Relationship between cost estimating and cost analysis.

matically these 12 steps leading to the development of an effective cost estimate that can be used for bidding, negotiations, cost tracking, and cost analysis. Following the systematic and structured approach to cost estimating shown in this diagram will assure the estimator that each required step has been accomplished and that each will build upon the previous step in a way that will create a solid foundation of rationale, backup material, and supporting data.

1.1 ORGANIZING FOR ESTIMATING

Like any process that involves the synthesis of information, thoughts, or material into a completed product, the cost-estimating process requires implements or tools that must be available or collected to perform the estimating function. The four principal tools are (1) information, (2) methods, (3) a plan or recipe for the estimate itself, and (4) skills. In estimating small tasks, a correspondingly small amount or number of tools are required. Larger estimating tasks require organization and collection of these tools prior to starting the estimating process. Estimating *information* that must be collected includes historical data or recent information on similar work, professional and reference materials (books, magazines, presentations, and reports), knowledge of the shop or office operation, and the results of market and industrial surveys. *Methods* include those techniques, procedures, policies, and practices discussed in this manual. The recipe or plan of action is a schedule for the estimating activity itself. The same planning techniques used for estimating the cost of a work activity or work output can be used to plan

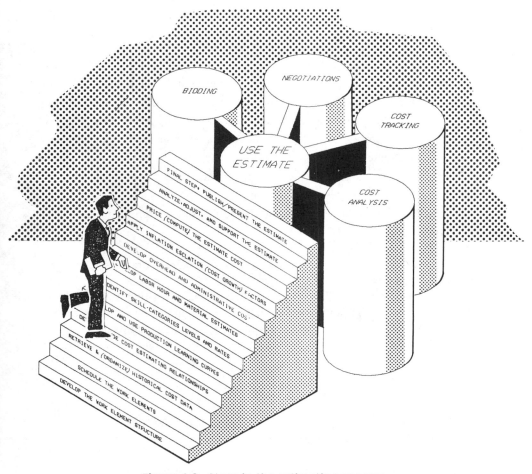

Figure 1.2. Steps in the estimating process.

the estimating activity itself. The skills needed in estimating mirror the complexity and content of the work being estimated and include business and finance skills, engineering and technical skills, manufacturing and assembly skills, mathematical and statistical skills, and production planning or industrial engineering skills. Several or all of these skills can be manifested in either a single estimator or an estimating team. An organization that is embarking on an estimating mission needs to identify, collect, organize, and activate these principal estimating implements.

1.2 DEVELOPING GROUND RULES AND ASSUMPTIONS

Many of the pitfalls that cause inaccurate or misleading cost estimates can be avoided if the estimator or estimating team will spend some time in the detailed development of ground rules and assumptions prior to starting the cost-estimating process. Typical questions that should be asked are:

1. What is the start date assumed for the project?
2. What are the principal deliverable hardware items?
3. What are the principal deliverable software and documentation items?
4. What is the location of the work and where will the deliverables be shipped?
5. Will nonrecurring costs be estimated separately from recurring costs?
6. What warrantees will be provided?
7. What spare parts or service will be provided?
8. Are engineering or test models required?
9. What are the product/service quality and reliability requirements?
10. And many more.

As the cost-estimating process gets into full swing, many more questions of this nature will inevitably arise. For each question that arises, an assumption must be made or a ground rule established to proceed with the estimating process. All of these assumptions and ground rules are then recorded and documented as *part of* the cost estimate, lest there be any later confusion as to the pedigree and basis for the estimate. References [3–5] provide detailed assumptions and ground rules by which to establish the elements of costs throughout the entire life cycle of a work activity or work output.

1.3 THE WORK ELEMENT STRUCTURE (OR WORK BREAKDOWN STRUCTURE)

The fiber or reinforcing cloth that holds a cost estimate together and is used to collect or allocate resources or costs is the work element structure. It has also been called the ''work breakdown structure'' principally because of the way the work element names and relationships between them are initially developed: by breaking down the work into its major tasks, then breaking down the major tasks into minor tasks, the minor tasks into subtasks, and so forth. The term *work element structure* is preferred because it is really a hierarchical structure of work *elements*, tied together with relationships and definitions (a work element structure dictionary) that defines the full family tree of a work activity or work output's contents. The work element structure is the first, vital, indispensable step in producing a cost estimate because it produces a solid framework on which the estimate can be built. The character, personality, and format of the job is established during the formulation and definition of the work element structure, and the discipline required in developing it forces the estimator to identify all parts of the work. It is an indispensable agent in reducing or eliminating duplications, overlaps, or omissions of vital work segments.

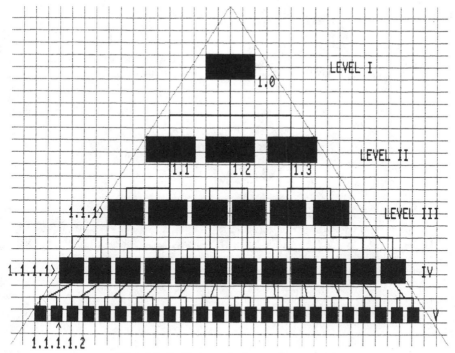

Figure 1.3. The work element pyramid.

The work element structure is built from the top down, but the resulting estimate takes form when elements at the bottom are given substance, combined to produce higher elements in the structure, and recombined with other combined elements to produce a pyramidlike structure where each higher level element is comprised of the lower level elements below it. Figure 1.3 shows a typical five-level work element structure pyramid. The elements in each level identify the work (and resources required to do the work) in the elements below. The pyramid shown in Figure 1.3 is symmetrical, with Level V tasks supporting all Level IV tasks, and with only two tasks making up each higher task up to Level III (three Level II tasks make up the Level I or total project resources in the example).

1.3.1 Work Element Numbering System

A commonly used numbering system for work element structures is also shown on Figure 1.3. Notice that the number of sets of digits between decimals in each work element number coincide with the *level* of the element (1.0 is read as merely ''1''). Hence, element number 1.2.2 is a Level III element, element number 1.3 is a Level II element, element number 1.1.1.1 is a Level IV element, and so on. This numbering system is practical and useful because one can readily determine the level wherein the work element resides by observing its code number. As is shown later, a work element code can contain more than one digit between each decimal: that is, 10.1.12.4 is a Level IV element.

1.3.2 Development of the Structure

The technique used to develop a work element structure is first to subdivide the work activity or work output into its major Level II work elements. These Level II work elements can be either *physical* or *functional* work elements, or a mixture

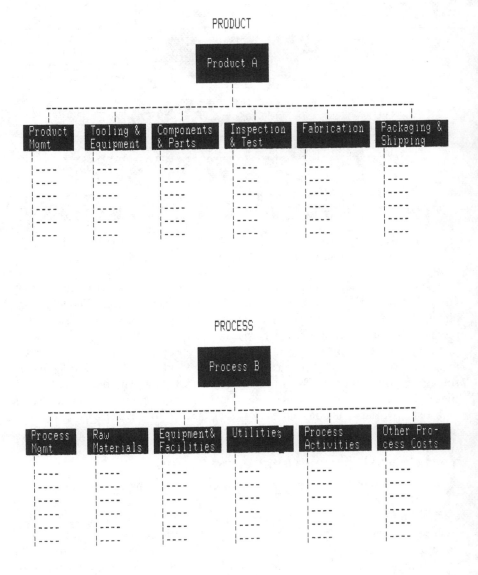

Figure 1.4. (*a-d*) typical work element structures.

of both and can number from two to more than 10 depending on the type and complexity of the work. It is preferable to keep the number of work elements under each subsequent element in each level to five or six where possible so that the work can be subdivided into not-too-many bite-sized pieces. Figure 1.4 shows sample work element structures, with Level II elements identified, for a typical

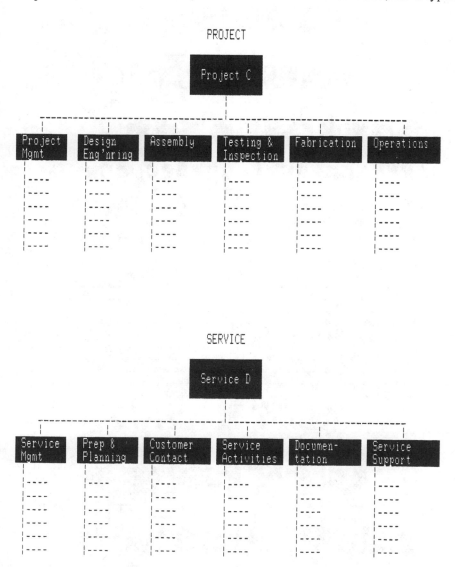

Figure 1.4. (Continued)

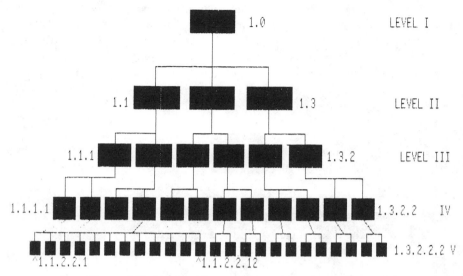

Figure 1.5. Varying the number of Level V elements.

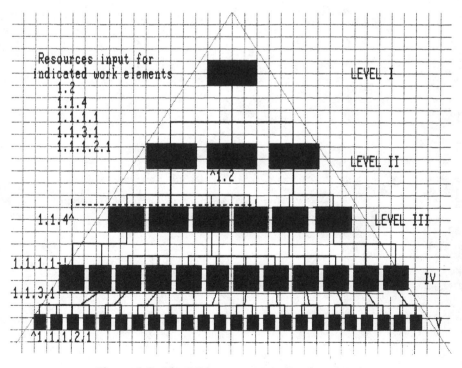

Figure 1.6. Inputting resources at various levels.

product, a typical process, a typical project, and a typical service. The definitions and examples of products, processes, projects, and services are found in references [1] and [2]. The next step is to subdivide each of these Level II elements into their principal or important Level III tasks, and so on. Degree of importance and impact on the project is more of a breakdown criterion in this process than is the size of the anticipated resources or costs because the work element structure is used not only to collect resource estimates, but also to provide management visibility into the distribution of resource expenditures in the important facets of the overall work output or work activity. As we proceed downward into the work element structure, the tendency is to increase the number of elements that feed into the next higher level element. Unsymmetrical pyramids are created when the number of elements, say at Level V as shown in Figure 1.5, varies; or when elements cannot be further subdivided as shown in Figure 1.6. Notice in Figure 1.5 the use of two-digit designators between decimals in the work element code number.

1.3.3 Designations of Work Element Levels

As shown in the figures in this section of the manual, Level I is usually the top level of the estimate, although some organizations start with higher level numbers (say Level II or III) because their work is part of a hierarchy imposed by the customer. Nonetheless, a handy way of looking at work element levels can be seen by the following table:

Level Number	Breakdown	Common Terms
I	Total job	Project, product, process, service
II	Major subdivision	System or primary activity
III	Minor subdivisions	Subsystem or secondary activity
IV	Tasks	Major components or tasks
V	Subtasks	Subcomponents, parts, or subtasks

The common terms shown are for a typical work activity or work output. A five-level cost estimate based on a five-level work element structure will usually involve estimating the smallest parts in a hardware assembly or the smallest subtasks in a job. In many instances, estimates will only require subdivision to Level II or III. Only in the most complex jobs, usually multidisciplinary undertakings such as a major space or weapons system project, will it be necessary to proceed past Level V to Levels VI, VII, and VIII. A computer code that will accommodate an eight-level work element structure will handle virtually any estimate conceivable. One that will accommodate four levels will suffice for most work activities and work outputs.

1.3.4 Treatment of Alternate, Parallel, or Recurring/ Nonrecurring Costs

Many times it is desirable to produce one or more *mirror-image* estimates that use basically the same work element structure as the original estimate. This is particularly true when there is a requirement to subdivide costs into recurring and nonrecurring costs, to present or propose alternate approaches or designs, or where parallel activities at two or more locations are planned. A third dimension can be added to the work element structure to accommodate these duplicate or near-duplicate structures as shown in Figure 1.7. The first digit in the structure is changed for each alternate approach; and all other digits in all other work element codes, as well as the work element names or titles, remain the same. Using single-digit designators between decimals will provide up to nine parallel work element structures, double-digit numbers will permit up to 99 parallel work element pyramids. For example, nonrecurring costs could be estimated under a work element structure labeled ''1.0,'' while recurring costs could be collected under a mirror-image structure labeled ''2.0.''

1.3.5 More About Work Element Coding Conventions

Because computers do not recognize more than one decimal in a numerical representation, numerical sorting cannot be used for the conventional multiple deci-

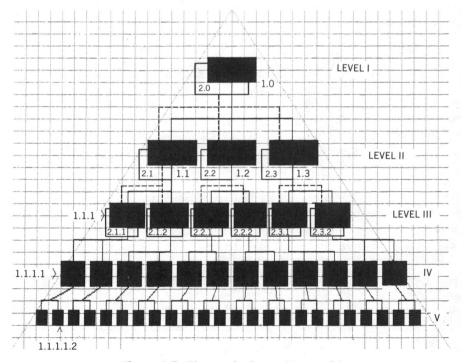

Figure 1.7. The work element pyramid.

mal point code numbers that have been used for designating work elements, specification paragraphs, and sometimes part numbers and drawing numbers. However, computers do a good job of sorting alphanumeric codes if they are put in an alphabetical or alphanumeric rather than numerical format. The sorting of work element codes is essential in any computer software program that attempts to add up resources in a hierarchical arrangement. Therefore we suggest a code starting with an alphabetic character followed by numerical characters separated by dashes or decimal points. Dashes are required if the resources are to be filed under a computer file name. Thus the alphanumeric work element code for a Level III element might be "A-2-1." This convention has the added convenience of permitting single-character representation of the first level with 26 (the entire alphabet) rather than nine (1 to 9) characters and works well in sorting work elements in most spreadsheet and data base applications computer software programs (see Chapter 9 of this reference manual, "Microcomputers in Cost Estimating").

In using the alphanumeric work element coding recommended for computer use, two-digit codes must be used for any level where a two-digit code is anticipated between hyphens or dashes. For example, the designator A-01-08 will provide for up to 99 boxes at Levels II and III. The zero in front of single-digit codes is required to effect proper sorting once the first digit of the two is nonzero.

1.3.6 Work Element Dictionaries

To provide sufficient work definition prior to starting the estimating process, it is important to develop a work element structure dictionary. This dictionary describes the work to be done under each work element in detail, describes the interfaces between related work elements, and lists work that is specifically included or excluded from each work element where appropriate. Each work element definition should define adequately the nature of the work to be accomplished under that particular work element and its relationship with other work elements. The estimating process cannot be started until the job is adequately defined. The work element structure dictionary helps the estimator and the company or organization doing the estimate to define the work in sufficient detail for estimating. If sufficient detail for estimating is not available at this point, design, analysis, engineering, and study work should proceed at once to provide sufficient rationale, backup information, and criteria to describe the work activity or work output in depth.

1.4 SCHEDULING

The second major step in cost estimating (as shown in Figure 1.2) is to schedule the work elements. So far, in our three-dimensional representation of a work activity or work output there has been no mention of time.

Because timing of work activities is important in (1) determining personnel, facilities, and resource requirements, (2) applying inflation and escalation ground rules, and (3) arranging for resource availability, development of a schedule for the work to be estimated is vital. Although many projects have been planned, estimated, and successfully carried out where the schedule elements differ from the work elements, the job of planning, estimating, and management is much more efficient when the schedule elements coincide with the work elements. The total job is already subdivided into convenient elements that are coded, named, and organized into a hierarchy that generally represents their importance and position in the overall activity: the work element structure. Now each work element must be placed on a time base to permit later determination of *when* the resources to be estimated will be needed in performance of the work. Scheduling is particularly important in the estimation of life cycle costs of a work activity or work output. Life cycle costs are discussed extensively in references [3–5].

1.4.1 Precedence/Successor Relationships and Dates

There are many techniques in developing project schedules; several are discussed in more detail in later chapters of this reference manual. Most of these techniques are based on precedence/successor relationships where each work element requires that certain other work elements be completed before it can be started or that the given work element must be completed before others can be started. Occasionally there is a specific calendar date on which a given work element must be started or completed, as would be the case when an item or document must be delivered to the customer. Specific calendar dates may exist representing times before which a work element cannot be started, perhaps due to the availability of resources, a facility, or manpower on that given date. The skills to be acquired and used in scheduling a work output or work activity for later estimating involve and provide a systematic and organized method of sequencing precedence, successor, and date relationships to permit the overall job to be completed on time and with the most efficient use of resources. The following example from *Cost Estimating* [1] is provided with permission of the publisher to give the reader a simplified example of the scheduling of work elements. A more detailed exposition of critical path methods, program evaluation and review techniques, and precedence diagramming is contained in reference [6].

1.4.2 Techniques Used In Schedule Planning

There are a number of analytical techniques used in developing an overall schedule of a work activity that help assure the correct allocation and sequencing of schedule elements. Among these techniques are the use of precedence and dependency networks, arrow diagrams, critical path bar charts, and PERT (program evaluation and review technique). These scheduling techniques use graphical and mathematical methods to develop the best schedule based on the sequencing of schedule activities in a way that each activity is performed only when the required prede-

Calendar year

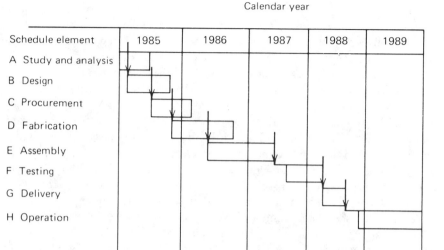

Figure 1.8. Scheduling a project.

cessor activities are accomplished. A simple example of how these techniques work is shown on Figure 1.8.

In this schedule, eight schedule elements have been chosen, the length of each schedule activity has been designated, and a relationship has been established between each schedule activity and its predecessor activity as follows:

SCHEDULE RELATIONSHIPS

Schedule Element	Title of Schedule Element	Time Required for Completion (months)	Percent Completion Required[a]
A	Study and analysis	6	$33\frac{1}{3}$
B	Design	8	50
C	Procurement	8	50
D	Fabrication	12	$66\frac{2}{3}$
E	Assembly	12	100 plus 2 months
F	Testing	8	100
G	Delivery	4	100 plus 4 months
H	Operation	36	100

[a]Percent completion required before subsequent activity can be accomplished.

Notice several things about the precedence relationships: (1) some activities can be started before their predecessor activities are completed; (2) some activities must be fully completed before their follow-on activities can be started; (3) and some activities cannot be started until a given number of months after the 100% completion date of a predecessor activity. Once these schedule interrelationships are established, a total program schedule can be laid out by starting either from a selected beginning point and working forward in time until the completion date is reached, or by starting from a desired completion date and working backward in time to derive the required schedule starting date. In many instances you will find that both the start date and completion date are given. In that instance, the length of schedule elements and their interrelationships must be established through an iterative process to develop a schedule that accomplishes a job in the required time period. If all schedule activities are started as soon as their prerequisites are met, the result is the shortest possible time schedule to perform the work.

Most complex work activities have multiple paths of activity that must be accomplished in parallel with each other. The longest of these paths is called a "critical path," and the schedule critical path is developed by connecting all of the schedule activity critical paths. Construction of a schedule such as that shown on Figure 1.8 brings to light a number of other questions concerning a schedule. The first of these is, "How do I establish the length of each activity?" This question strikes at the heart of the overall estimating process itself since many costs are incurred by the passage of time. Labor costs of an existing work force, overhead costs (insurance, rental, and utilities), and material handling and storage costs continue to pile up in an organization whether there is a productive output or not. Hence it is important to develop the shortest possible overall schedule to accomplish a job and to accomplish each schedule element in the shortest time and in the most efficient method possible. The length of each schedule activity is established by an analysis of that schedule activity and the human and material resources available and required to accomplish it. Manpower and material estimating techniques are used extensively by the estimator in establishing the length of calendar time required to accomplish a schedule activity as well as the work-hours and materials required for its completion.

A second question is, "What do I do if there are other influences on the schedule such as availability of facilities, equipment, and manpower?" This is a factor that arises in most estimating situations. There are definite schedule interactions in any multiple-output organization that must be considered in planning a single work activity. Overall corporate planning must take into account these schedule interactions in its own critical path chart to assure that facilities, labor, and funds are available to accomplish all work activities in an effective and efficient manner. A final question is, "How do I establish a credible 'percent-complete' figure for each predecessor work activity?" This is accomplished by breaking each activity into subactivities. For instance design can be subdivided into conceptual design, preliminary design, and final design. If the start of the procurement activity is to be keyed to the completion of preliminary design, then the time that preliminary design is complete determines the percentage of time and corresponding design activity that must be completed prior to the initiation of procurement.

1.5 THE RETRIEVAL AND USE OF HISTORICAL COST DATA

Boehm [7] states that "The most valid historical cost data is that which is developed by the organization that is doing the estimating." A number of excellent handbooks and data bases are available or becoming available in several disciplines; some are discussed in this manual, but because each company's operations are unique, the rapid development of in-house historical cost estimating data is also a necessity for continued excellence in cost estimating. Too often, estimates are performed with little precollection of in-house historical and actual data. Initiation of estimate requirements is often accompanied by the frantic search for existing data which turns out to be only marginally applicable to the project at hand. Competitors are not willing to provide help in building up one's data base, particularly if they have preengineered cost advantages designed to help them win in the marketplace. Data gathering and consulting companies provide industry averages normalized in such a way that specific competitive advantages of any specific company are not readily visible. So it is up to the estimator's own organization to add to its externally derived cost data base sound historical data that is continually upgraded to account for emerging improved efficiencies, economies, and innovations that lower cost.

Organized and systematic collection and continual updating of labor hour and cost data used in estimating requires a disciplined approach to accounting and recordkeeping. A computerized data base will usually be required because of the sheer volume of data that must be stored and available for rapid retrieval. A complicating factor in most cost estimating data bases is that accounting and finance departments seldom accumulate all of the data required for a comprehensive cost estimating data base. Often, the accounting department is interested only in data that are required to pay the employees and bill the customer. These data may not include the nuances the estimator needs to adapt the data to specific estimating situations. The estimator, for example, will be interested in not only the cost of an item but also in the quantity purchased at that cost, the delivery date or schedule, a full product description, and any special requirements placed on the subcontractor. In labor-hour data, the estimator will want to know which skill categories and/or skill levels were used to produce the item rather than just the total labor hours. Therefore the very first job the estimating department must accomplish after developing the work element structure and the work schedule is to track down and record pertinent historical cost data from *both internal and external sources*, and then to organize these data into a format that will be easy to use during the estimating process.

The very best approach in collecting and organizing historical cost data is to assign this function to a department or group of individuals separate from the estimating function. Since historical data collection should precede the estimating process, this function should be in operation long before there are requirements for estimates, and should continue in operation parallel to ongoing estimating activities. The function of this department or group of individuals is the *cost analysis* function mentioned earlier in this chapter and shown on Figure 1.1. A typical data base form used for historical cost analysis might appear as follows:

I. Name of item or operation
II. Physical description
   1. Model number
   2. Manufacturer
   3. Address of manufacturer
   4. Phone number of manufacturer
   5. Weight
   6. Length
   7. Width
   8. Height
   9. Power requirements
   10. Channels
   11. Memory
   12. Speed
   13. MTBF (mean time between failures)
   14. Other pertinent performance data
III. Resource/schedule information
   1. Purchase cost (at what production or purchase quantity)
   2. Labor hours
   3. Delivery date
   4. Maintenance costs
   5. Training costs
   6. Lead time
   7. Support equipment costs
   8. Operating costs

Purchasing, finance, and accounting functions in the company should be aware of the need for these data for estimating and should be chartered to collect and record these data for organization by the cost analysis function and then use by the cost estimating function. Use of a rapid retrieval (probably computerized) data base will permit quick access to any item if any one or more of its characteristics are known. A computerized data base could permit the retrieval of a list of all microcomputers purchased with a memory capacity of 256K or greater, all generators produced by a given manufacturer, all motors of 2.0 horsepower or greater, and hundreds of other combinations. The data base by itself will be a valuable tool to the estimator *provided that it is updated and corrected periodically!* The next step, then is to develop cost estimating relationships from the data base to even further enhance the estimator's capability of easily applying historical cost data.

1.6 COST ESTIMATING RELATIONSHIPS

Cost estimating relationships can be anything from simple rules-of-thumb to complex relationships involving multiple variables. The statistical techniques used to develop cost estimating relationships are covered in detail in Chapter 3. The development and use of cost estimating relationships in parametric estimating are explored in Chapter 7.

The principal function of cost estimating relationships is to provide equations or graphs that summarize historical cost or resource data in a manner that will allow the equations or graphs to be used in estimating future costs. There are several pitfalls that must be avoided in developing cost estimating relationships. The first is the failure to use data that are truly correlatable. Care must be taken, for example, to be sure that the work activities and work outputs being used to develop the estimating relationship are of the same type, complexity, duration, state-of-the-art, or geographical makeup—if a parameter such as product weight or volume is being correlated with cost or labor hours. Care must be taken to assure that the cost estimating relationship is used only to estimate work activities and work outputs whose characteristics are like those from which the historical data were derived. The effect of past inefficiencies must be taken into consideration in developing cost estimating relationships. Failure to ensure that expected productivity improvements are taken into account in development of the cost estimating relationship will propagate the policy of accepting past performance as the best that can be done and will result in an estimating relationship that will not produce a competitive cost estimate.

Before historical data are used in developing cost estimating relationships, the effects of known variables such as inflation indices, geographical location, labor rate variations, and special cost-driving factors should be removed from the data.

1.6.1 Removing and/or Accounting for the Effects of Inflation

The first factor to remove in normalizing a data base for use in cost estimating relationships is the inflation factor. Each year the United States Government publishes a set of inflation indices that indicate the average increase in the price of goods and services as compared to the previous year. Some government economic reports even go so far as to forecast the effects of inflation in future years. Actual or predicted price indices have not been published at this writing for the years 1987 through 1990, but a hypothetical set of indices follows for purposes of illustration:

Calendar Year	Assumed Inflation Index
1987	5.5%
1988	7.2%
1989	6.8%
1990	9.1%

The inflation index is the percent increase in the average cost of equivalent goods and services above the previous year's costs. If the product, for example, a special precision shop machine tool, cost $7500 at the end of 1987, the cost of the same item at the end of 1990 can be computed as follows: First convert the percentage to decimal form and add one (1) to develop a multiplier for inflation compounding:

Year	Index (%)	Decimal Form	Compounding Factor
1987	5.5	0.055	1.055
1988	7.2	0.072	1.072
1989	6.8	0.068	1.068
1990	9.1	0.091	1.091

To find a predicted inflated cost of the identical item at the end of 1990, the compounding factors for 1988, 1989, and 1990 are used as follows:

$$\text{Predicted price of the new item} = \$7500 \times (1.072 \times 1.068 \times 1.091)$$

$$= \$7500 \times (1.249)$$

$$= \$9367.50$$

Using this technique, the effects on price of inflation alone are brought to the current date. Similar techniques can be used to reduce all costs to any given "base" year costs. This technique, and its accompanying equations, are covered in greater detail in Chapter 4 of this manual.

1.6.2 Removing the Effects of Labor Rate Fluctuations

Because labor rates (wages) vary significantly from one area of the country to another, and from one time period to another, it is often desirable to remove the effects of labor rates on costs by determining the labor hours used to produce the product. Labor hours (rather than labor dollars) provide a more nearly universal quantity measurement because, at least theoretically, an individual or team with the same skills and equipment will take the same number of labor hours to perform the same job wherever they are located geographically or whenever they perform the work. If the cost of the machine tool under discussion consisted of 70% labor, and the composite labor rate of the production team was $26.00 per hour in 1986, then the labor hours can be computed as follows:

$$\text{labor dollars} = 0.7 \times \$7500 = \$5250$$

$$\text{labor hours} = \$5250/26.00 = 201 \text{ hours}$$

Reduction of historical costs to labor hours wherever possible will enhance the development of credible cost estimating relationships since the units being utilized

TABLE 1.1. Typical Salary Relationships for Selected Skills

City	Brick. (B)	Carp. (C)	Elect. (E)	Paint. (Pa)	Plast. (Pl)	Plumb. (Pb)
			Skill Category			
Albuquerque, NM	0.99	0.99	0.92	0.90	0.95	0.99
Anchorage, AK	1.52	1.45	1.62	1.67	1.57	1.45
Baltimore, MD	0.85	0.84	0.88	0.87	0.81	0.81
Chicago, IL	1.00	1.01	1.07	0.97	1.00	0.96
Dallas, TX	0.83	0.84	0.85	0.84	0.86	0.79
Evansville, IN	0.93	0.90	0.95	0.85	0.89	0.99
Fresno, CA	1.16	1.28	1.15	1.07	1.09	1.23
Grand Rapids, MI	0.81	0.84	0.83	0.74	0.93	0.94
Huntsville, AL	0.78	0.70	0.85	0.76	0.78	0.83
Indianapolis, IN	0.95	1.03	0.97	0.92	0.97	0.93
Jacksonville, FL	0.76	0.77	0.85	0.77	0.63	0.88
Kansas City, MO	1.03	0.99	1.04	1.03	1.03	1.04
Las Vegas, NV	1.01	1.11	1.20	1.18	1.11	1.25
Manchester, NH	0.76	0.73	0.84	0.64	0.81	0.83
Nashville, TN	0.75	0.76	0.77	0.72	0.75	0.79
Oklahoma City, OK	0.86	0.80	0.88	0.81	0.82	0.90
Philadelphia, PA	1.04	1.05	1.06	0.98	1.10	0.93
Raleigh, NC	0.57	0.70	0.67	0.62	0.57	0.70
Salt Lake City, UT	0.93	0.85	0.95	0.88	0.90	0.93
Topeka, KS	0.89	0.82	0.97	0.87	0.87	0.93
Wilmington, DE	0.92	0.97	0.96	0.88	0.94	1.00
Youngstown, OH	1.00	0.99	0.99	1.06	1.01	0.97

are proportional to work content. Hence, the use of labor hours (or labor weeks, months, or years) rather than labor costs removes geographical and time effects from labor resources. Material prices should remain in dollar form in the historical data base but be adjusted for inflation as previously described.

Typical geographical variations in labor rates are shown in Table 1.1. This table shows *wage adjustment factors* for bricklayers, carpenters, electricians, painters, plasterers, and plumbers for 22 different cities. The wage adjustment factor is the number that when multiplied by the national average wage for that skill category, produces the average wage for that given city of all skill levels within that category. The relationships of the wage adjustment factors for six skill categories are shown graphically on Figure 1.9 for four selected cities. One can see from this chart the large variation that can be encountered in costs due to geographical influences on wage rates.

1.6.3 Adjusting Historical Data to Account for Past Inefficiencies

If the plant's labor efficiency in 1987 was judged to be 80%, and if it is projected to increase to 92% in 1990, then the projected efficiency increase should be taken

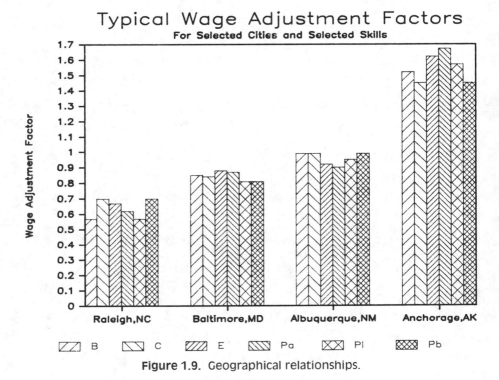

Figure 1.9. Geographical relationships.

into account in the future labor estimate as follows: Assume the shop measured time is 201 hours. The equation for efficiency is:

$$\text{Efficiency} = \frac{\text{actual hands-on labor time}}{\text{measured total shop labor time}}$$

Therefore

actual hands on labor time = efficiency × measured shop labor time

Actual hands-on labor time estimated to produce the product in 1987:

201 hours × 0.80 = 160.8 hours (actual hands-on labor)

Projected measured total shop labor time estimated to produce the product in 1990:

160.8 hours/0.92 = 174.78 hours (measured shop labor time)

Likewise, new inefficiencies that have been introduced into the process or plant since the historical data was collected should be taken into account in making adjustments to be used for cost estimating relationships. For example, if a union contract has just been signed that permits each employee to spend 1% of his or her time on union activities, then the new labor-hour figure would be computed as follows (100% − 1% = 99%, in decimal form = 0.99):

$$174.78 \text{ hours}/0.99 = 176.56 \text{ hours}$$

The chapter on statistical techniques shows that sufficient data points are required to develop a trend in a cost estimating relationship. If historical cost data are properly adjusted for inflation, geographical location, labor rate effects, and efficiency effects, credible cost estimating relationships can be developed.

1.7 DEVELOP AND USE PRODUCTION LEARNING CURVES

Chapter 5 demonstrates how to use learning curves in projecting labor hours and costs when several or many identical items are being produced. When organizing and correlating historical data before producing a learning curve percentage based on those data, the same considerations as those already discussed must be taken into account. All historical costs could be normalized to a given year and a specified plant efficiency and location if desired. To develop a credible learning curve, experience must be available from a normal production run. One can also develop an average learning curve from a number of production runs of various lot sizes. These lot sizes should encompass those for which production costs or hours are to be estimated.

The theory of learning curves, that production efficiencies increase with the number of units produced, is based on the fact that repetition and uniformity of operations decrease the labor hours required for each successive unit of production and that this decrease in labor hours per unit *itself* decreases with the number of units produced. Where large quantities of identical operations are anticipated in providing a work output or work activity, the learning curve is a useful tool for forecasting resource requirements.

1.8 IDENTIFICATION OF SKILL CATEGORIES, SKILL LEVELS, AND LABOR RATES

Since labor costs are a large part of the controllable costs of most work activities and outputs, it is important to identify the skill categories and skill levels required to perform the job being estimated to establish realistic labor rates for each skill category and skill level and to *adjust the mixture of skill categories and skill levels as the work progresses* to enhance cost effectiveness and to increase the competitive posture of the resulting cost estimate.

1.8.1 Skill Categories

Skill categories are the trades or disciplines required to perform the work. Typical skill categories in construction projects would be bricklayers, carpenters, electricians, painters, plasterers, or plumbers. For high technology research and development projects, the categories might be engineering, manufacturing, testing, tooling, and quality, reliability, and safety engineering. Every industry has a typical set of skill categories needed to perform its unique set of tasks. In the grouping of skill categories, the various trades or disciplines are characterized by employees with like types of backgrounds, training, tools, and work methods.

1.8.2 Skill Levels

Skill levels represent the various degrees of proficiency, training, or seniority *within* a cost category, and these degrees of experience, proficiency, or training are usually accompanied by wage rates or salaries that are commensurate with the level of competence, training, and/or seniority. Typical skill levels within the overall skill category of machinist, for example, might be: trainee, apprentice, journeyman, machinist, and master machinist. In engineering design the skill levels could be: technician, draftsman C, draftsman B, draftsman A, junior design engineer, associate design engineer, design engineer, senior design engineer, and design engineering supervisor. Estimating can be accomplished by determining the number of labor hours required for each skill level within each skill category or by estimating total hours for an engineering or manufacturing crew or shop as shown in the following section on the development of labor hours and material estimates.

1.8.3 The Dynamic Skill Mix

The use of a dynamic skill mix will provide a competitive edge in bidding. A dynamic skill mix is a skill mix that changes during the performance of a job and adjusts to varying skill category and skill level needs as the work progresses. A static skill mix is one where the skill categories and skill levels and the percentages of each skill category and skill level remain constant throughout the performance of a work activity or production of a work output. Many estimators and managers propose static skill mixes because (1) estimates are easier to develop using a static skill mix; (2) the static skill mix conforms closely to the composition of a team that will see the project through from start to finish; and (3) a static skill mix is easier to manage throughout the job's lifetime because there will be fewer staffing changes.

The use of the dynamic skill mix, however, permits the development of a more competitive bid. The price of labor will be more attractive when a dynamic skill mix is used because high-cost skill categories are phased out as the need for them is reduced during job performance; and, even more important, skill levels (and their corresponding labor rates) are reduced as more team experience is gained and as the need for more highly skilled personnel is reduced. The use of a dynamic skill mix in an estimate assumes that there are or will be other jobs starting or peaking during the lifetime of the job being estimated, and that personnel with the highly paid skill categories and skill levels needed to get the project off to a good start can be transferred to a new job as the jobs progress. One can see that the decision to use a dynamic skill mix involves some courageous management decisions because failure of the new work to materialize would result in no fruitful work to assist in the care and feeding of some available but not gainfully employed high-level (and highly paid) skills. The results could be the dismissal of some experienced people. This is a risk that some estimators and managers choose to take to gain a competitive advantage.

1.8.4 Static and Dynamic Skill Mix Examples

The spreadsheet shown on Table 1.2 shows the use of a *static* skill mix. The example shown is for an engineering project that spans a period of nine years. A nine-year project is rather long, but this span of time is used to assist in graphically showing trends and demonstrating the effects of inflation on costs. Notice that both the skill mix and the total labor hours remain constant throughout the project. Estimators and managers are often tempted to use this approach because the skill mix may be one that exists in the shop or office that is going to do the work, and the manager wants the shop or office to be gainfully employed throughout the lifetime of the project. This approach may be useful in retaining an existing staff, but as can be shown, it is not cost competitive. Notice that the cost of this initial approach is $6.052 million. The labor hour mix for each year is plotted graphically on Figure 1.10. Notice that no attempt has been made to distribute work throughout the time of the project, which would be a more realistic approach. Any job of this magnitude usually takes some start-up time and some buildup phase, as well as a taper-off period to phase out the staff to enable the transfer of personnel to the next job or jobs.

Table 1.3 shows a dynamic spread of the same total labor hours (354,367 hours) over the nine-year period using a *beta distribution* curve that spreads the labor hours so that 80% occur within the first half of the project time, a typical spread for an engineering project. The result of this redistribution of labor hours is shown in Figure 1.11. Note the smooth buildup and phase-down of the project. Notice also in Table 1.3 that the total cost has reduced to $5.55 million, a reduction of 8.3% from the original estimate. This reduction is brought about by the earlier labor loading because labor rates for the earlier years are slightly lower. Hence there has been an 8.3% savings in costs *with no decrease in labor hours, labor rates, or skill levels.* We are now beginning to see how a competitive advantage can be increased by dynamic spreading of work over the project duration.

Another step that can be taken to further reduce costs *with no sacrifice* in labor hours or labor rates, is to adjust the skill mix each year to (1) provide a well-rounded team approach to the job each year and (2) decrease the highly paid skills while increasing lower skills as the job progresses. Providing that a skill redistri-

TABLE 1.2. Engineering Project Using a Static Skill Mix

Name of Skill Level		1986	1987	1988	1989	1990	1991	1992	1993	1994	Total
Draftsman	Hours	7,280	7,280	7,280	7,280	7,280	7,280	7,280	7,280	7,280	65520.00
	Rate	$8.50	$9.04	$9.60	$10.21	$10.85	$11.54	$12.26	$13.04	$13.86	
	Labor cost	$61,880	$65,778	$69,922	$74,328	$79,010	$83,988	$89,279	$94,904	$100,883	$719,972
Designer	Hours	3,120	3,120	3,120	3,120	3,120	3,120	3,120	3,120	3,120	28,080.00
	Rate	$10.75	$11.19	$11.65	$12.13	$12.62	$13.14	$13.68	$14.24	$14.83	
	Labor cost	$33,540	$34,915	$36,347	$37,837	$39,388	$41,003	$42,684	$44,434	$46,256	$356,405
Eng. assistant	Hours	10,920	10,920	10,920	10,920	10,920	10,920	10,920	10,920	10,920	98,280.00
	Rate	$12.62	$13.28	$13.97	$14.69	$15.46	$16.26	$17.11	$18.00	$18.93	
	Labor cost	$137,810	$144,977	$152,515	$160,446	$168,789	$177,566	$186,800	$196,513	$206,732	$1,532,149
Junior engineer	hours	4,576	4,576	4,576	4,576	4,576	4,576	4,576	4,576	4,576	41,184.00
	Rate	$14.85	$15.86	$16.94	$18.09	$19.32	$20.63	$22.04	$23.54	$25.14	
	Labor cost	$67,954	$72,574	$77,510	$82,780	$88,409	$94,421	$100,842	$107,699	$115,022	$807,211
Engineer	Hours	9,734	9,734	9,734	9,734	9,734	9,734	9,734	9,734	9,734	87,606.40
	Rate	$16.20	$17.35	$18.58	$19.90	$21.31	$22.83	$24.45	$26.18	$28.04	
	Labor cost	$157,697	$168,887	$180,878	$193,720	$207,474	$222,205	$237,981	$254,878	$272,975	$1,896,695
Senior engineer	Hours	3,744	3,744	3,744	3,744	3,744	3,744	3,744	3,744	3,744	33,696.00
	Rate	$19.75	$20.26	$20.79	$21.33	$21.89	$22.45	$23.04	$23.64	$24.25	
	Labor cost	$73,944	$75,867	$77,839	$79,863	$81,939	$84,070	$86,256	$88,498	$90,799	$739,075
Total	Hours	39,374	39,374	39,374	39,374	39,374	39,374	39,374	39,374	39,375	354,367
	Rate										
	Labor cost	$532,825	$562,998	$595,011	$628,974	$665,011	$703,253	$743,842	$786,927	$832,667	$6,051,507

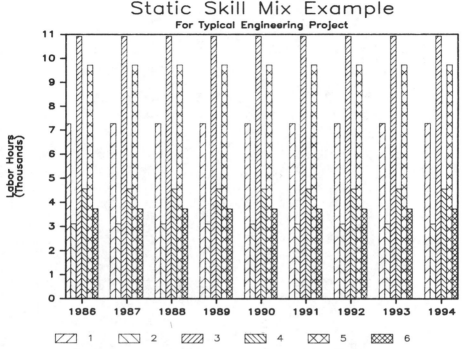

Figure 1.10. Skill dispersion versus year: Static Mix.

bution can be accomplished each year (and a thorough understanding of the work to be performed and its corresponding skill level needs for the particular job is required to do this), a labor spread similar to that shown in Table 1.4 can be achieved. The graphic representation of this dynamically spread and adjusted skill mix is shown in Figure 1.12. Notice in Table 1.4 that the total project cost has decreased to $5.286 million, which is 87.3% of the original $6.052 million, or a cost reduction of 12.7%. This reduction could very well represent the capability to win a price competition. And all of these reductions have been achieved with no reduction in person power (labor hours) allocated to do the job: a criterion that the customer will be very interested in when evaluating a cost proposal. Of course, it is up to the organization and management proposal to demonstrate that jobs can be phased in to lower skill levels as the work progresses. The skill level changes and profiles are more clearly shown in Figure 1.13, and the cost (price) reductions made possible in the three steps are shown in Figure 1.14.

Notice that cost reduction in the project is accompanied by reallocation of the skills. Some of the cost reduction is brought about by using lower paid skills while some results from mere judicious time-phasing of labor hours.

Companies who have used dynamic skill mix techniques have been successful in capturing more work that is doable within the original cost estimate. These companies have had the foresight to avoid the tendency to cover all existing em-

TABLE 1.3. Engineering Project Using a Dynamically Spread Skill Mix

Name of Skill Level		1986	1987	1988	1989	1990	1991	1992	1993	1994	Total
Draftsman	Hours	6,209	13,412	14,838	12,836	9,277	5,550	2,567	757	74	65,520
	Rate	$8.50	$9.04	$9.60	$10.21	$10.85	$11.54	$12.26	$13.04	$13.86	
	Labor cost	$52,780	$121,181	$142,512	$131,058	$100,686	$64,033	$31,475	$9,868	$1,025	$654,618
Designer	Hours	2,661	5,748	6,359	5,501	3,976	2,379	1,100	324	32	28,080
	Rate	$10.75	$11.19	$11.65	$12.13	$12.62	$13.14	$13.68	$14.24	$14.83	
	Labor cost	$28,608	$64,323	$74,080	$66,716	$50,194	$31,261	$15,048	$4,620	$470	$335,319
Eng. assistant	Hours	9,314	20,117	22,257	19,255	13,916	8,325	3,850	1,135	111	98,280
	Rate	$12.62	$13.28	$13.97	$14.69	$15.46	$16.26	$17.11	$18.00	$18.93	
	Labor cost	$117,545	$267,084	$310,849	$282,906	$215,096	$135,378	$65,855	$20,433	$2,100	$1,417,245
Junior engineer	Hours	3,903	8,430	9,327	8,069	5,831	3,489	1,613	476	46	41,184
	Rate	$14.85	$15.86	$16.94	$18.09	$19.32	$20.63	$22.04	$23.54	$25.14	
	Labor cost	$57,961	$133,701	$157,976	$145,962	$112,664	$71,987	$35,551	$11,198	$1,169	$728,168
Engineer	Hours	8,302.60	17,932.52	19,839.32	17,163.42	12,404.46	7,421.27	3,431.65	1,012.11	98.89	87,606.25
	Rate	$16.20	$17.35	$18.58	$19.90	$21.31	$22.83	$24.45	$26.18	$28.04	
	Labor cost	$134,502	$311,133	$368,656	$341,576	$264,393	$169,411	$83,899	$26,502	$2,773	$1,702,844
Senior engineer	Hours	3,193	6,897	7,631	6,602	4,771	2,854	1,320	389	38	33,696
	Rate	$19.75	$20.26	$20.79	$21.33	$21.89	$22.45	$23.04	$23.64	$24.25	
	Labor cost	$63,070	$139,766	$158,647	$140,818	$104,419	$64,095	$30,409	$9,202	$922	$711,348
Total	Hours	33,584	72,537	80,250	69,426	50,176	30,019	13,881	4,094	400	354,367
	Rate										
	Labor cost	$454,467	$1,037,187	$1,212,720	$1,109,035	$847,452	$536,165	$262,236	$81,822	$8,459	$5,549,542

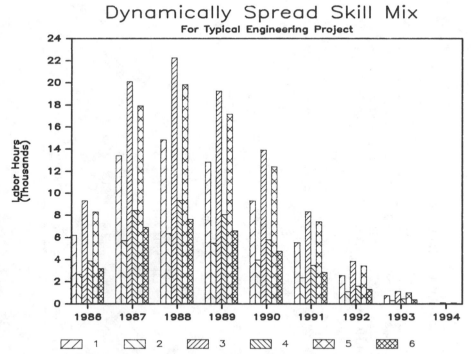

Figure 1.11. Skill dispersion versus year: Dynamically Spread Mix.

ployees with work on ongoing projects in order to provide high employee retention and utilization. Smaller, more flexible companies which are entreprenurial in makeup can more readily adopt the dynamic skill mix estimating technique, but large companies can also take advantage of this practice if they carefully schedule the personnel transition and exchange between work activities. The message here is to avoid an "overskill" (and resulting overpricing) condition during the conduct of the job by systematically shifting personnel to the right job at the right time.

1.9 DEVELOPING LABOR AND MATERIAL ESTIMATES

Since the key links between performance and cost are labor and materials, the credibility of the estimate hinges on the accurate estimation of these two quantities. Of the two quantities, the most difficult to estimate is labor. Labor is difficult to estimate because it is measured by different time increments, and allowances are treated differently in the various estimating methods. The following discussion presents an overview of these differences and tells where you can get more information on each method. Much more about labor estimating in the specific fields of construction and manufacturing are found in Chapters 10 and 11 of this manual.

TABLE 1.4. Engineering Project Using a Dynamically Spread and Adjusted Skill Mix

Name of Skill Level		1986	1987	1988	1989	1990	1991	1992	1993	1994	Total
Draftsman	Hours	3,358	11,606	12,840	16,662	13,548	6,904	4,303	2,293	192	71,706
	Rate	$8.50	$9.04	$9.60	$10.21	$10.85	$11.54	$12.26	$13.04	$13.86	
	Labor cost	$28,546	$104,865	$123,325	$170,119	$147,032	$79,654	$52,772	$29,887	$2,661	$738,861
Designer	Hours	4,366	12,331	13,643	13,191	10,035	6,304	3,193	737	40	63,839
	Rate	$10.75	$11.19	$11.65	$12.13	$12.62	$13.14	$13.68	$14.24	$14.83	
	Labor cost	$46,934	$137,996	$158,929	$159,969	$126,689	$82,847	$43,678	$10,495	$593	$768,130
Eng. assistant	Hours	6,045	13,057	16,853	14,579	8,530	5,704	2,776	614	20	68,178
	Rate	$12.62	$13.28	$13.97	$14.69	$15.46	$16.26	$17.11	$18.00	$18.93	
	Labor cost	$76,289	$173,343	$235,372	$214,214	$131,846	$92,744	$47,490	$11,051	$379	$982,730
Junior engineer	Hours	7,388	14,507	18,458	11,802	8,028	5,103	2,082	205	20	67,594
	Rate	$14.85	$15.86	$16.94	$18.09	$19.32	$20.63	$22.04	$23.54	$25.14	
	Labor cost	$109,719	$230,084	$312,638	$213,507	$155,106	$105,300	$45,884	$4,818	$503	$1,177,558
Engineer	Hours	9,068	13,782	13,643	9,025	7,526	4,503	972	123	8	58,649.33
	Rate	$16.20	$17.35	$18.58	$19.90	$21.31	$22.83	$24.45	$26.18	$28.04	
	Labor cost	$146,896	$239,121	$253,506	$179,618	$160,421	$102,790	$23,756	$3,216	$224	$1,109,547
Senior engineer	Hours	3,358	7,254	4,815	4,166	2,509	1,501	555	123	120	24,400
	Rate	$19.75	$20.26	$20.79	$21.33	$21.89	$22.45	$23.04	$23.64	$24.25	
	Labor cost	$66,328	$146,985	$100,106	$88,855	$54,906	$33,703	$12,792	$2,903	$2,910	$509,489
Total	Hours	33,584	72,537	80,250	69,426	50,176	30,019	13,881	4,094	400	354,367
	Rate										
	Labor cost	$474,713	$1,032,396	$1,183,876	$1,026,281	$775,999	$497,039	$226,372	$62,370	$7,270	$5,286,316

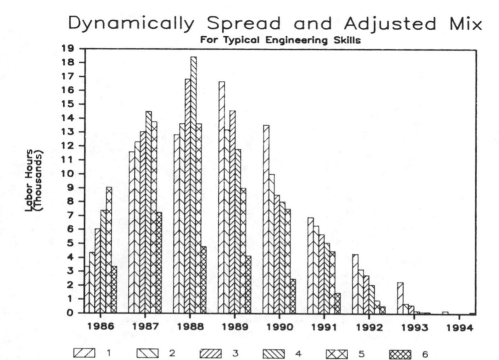

Figure 1.12. Skill dispersion versus year: Dynamically Spread and Adjusted Mix.

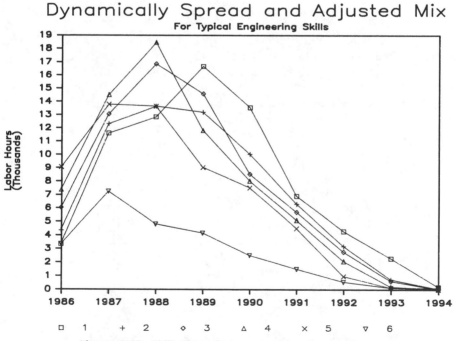

Figure 1.13. Skill dispersion versus year: Comparisons.

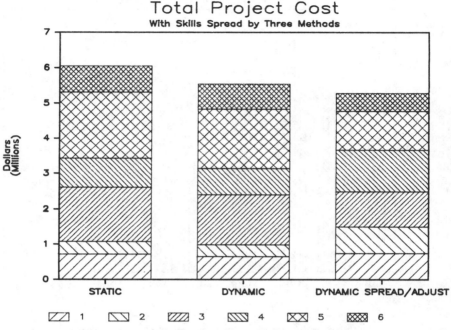

Figure 1.14. Skill allocation method: Price Reductions.

1.9.1 Motion and Time Method (MTM)

The motion and time method is based on a buildup of the "microscopic" time increments required to perform a task. This method of evaluating and estimating labor required is most applicable in industrial manufacturing and mass production with highly repetitive tasks. Industrial production tasks are broken down into basic body, hand, and eye movements. Measurements are made in seconds, tenths of seconds, or hundredths of seconds. A sample listing of just a few of these basic movements, along with a measured time for each, follows:

Action	Time (sec)
Manually reach	0.32
Manually grasp	0.25
Manually move	0.45
Manually turn ($\frac{1}{4}$ turn)	0.12
Stand up (from seated position)	1.05
Sit down (from standing position)	1.85
Visually check alignment	0.82
(And many more)	

As can be seen in the preceding list, these are some of the basic body movements that occur while performing work, and a day's work can include many thousands or even tens of thousands of such movements. It is also obvious that the actions required to produce work do not include allowances for time variations encountered by all humans (such as scratching, sneezing, distractions, fatigue, and errors) to say nothing of the larger allowances for personal, and administrative reasons. Hence, allowances are usually not included in an initial motion and time study and must be included as a significant factor once experience has been gained in a specific office, shop, or industrial setting. Detailed data bases and computer programs are avalable to help collect historical motion and time data, to generate detailed job instruction sheets, and to estimate labor hours using this method. More information on MTM estimating methods can be obtained from the MTM Association, 1001 Broadway, Fair Lawn, New Jersey 07410.

1.9.2 Industrial, Shop, or Office Standards

Industrial, shop, or office standards for labor estimating are usually stated in terms of minutes, hours, or tenths of hours for larger specific tasks that comprise work. For example, time in minutes or hours may be measured for installing a bit in a machine, maintaining the machine (oiling, removing chips, changing cutting fluid, etc.), typing a page of manuscript, or creating an engineering sketch or drawing. In this type of labor estimating, labor time is usually divided into setup time and run time. Setup time is the time required at the beginning of the day or production lot to get prepared for a routine run of several units. Run time is the time required to process each piece of material, batch of product, or piece of paper (as in printing). Industrial, shop, or office standards are usually derived from historical data that has been normalized to remove inflation, geographical location, efficiency, and labor rate differences, and this data is usually highly proprietary because each company develops its own standards. Occasionally, however, handbooks such as those used for construction or automobile repair are available to provide industry-wide averages of the labor time to perform various tasks. These handbooks give the estimator a good start in developing in-house estimating standards but should not be relied upon solely in the competitive bidding environment.* Many trade and industry associates publish labor standards for their industries. Look up the specific trade association that covers the product or service you are estimating, and chances are they will provide some excellent help in supplying the same initial industrial, shop, or office labor standards.

---

*An excellent book of estimating standards used in the electronics industries, *Electronics Industry Cost Estimating Data,* by Theodore Taylor has been published by John Wiley & Sons of New York. Standards for construction estimating are available in the Dodge cost manuals published by McGraw Hill, New York; cost handbooks published by the R. S. Means Company of Duxbury, Massachusetts; and in building estimating data published by Craftsman Book Company of Solana Beach, California. Automobile repair labor and materials estimating manuals are available from Mitchell Manuals, Inc., of San Diego, California, and others.

1.9.3 Staffing and Shoploading Estimating

Estimating of staffing and shoploading are *macroscopic* methods of determining the labor hours required to perform a job. Staffing a job with a certain number of people for a given time period is a commonly used method of developing labor estimates when detailed motion and time methods or labor productivity factors are not available. As discussed in the previous section on the identification of skill categories and levels, care must be taken to adjust the skill mix of the staff as the work progresses to avoid using more highly qualified (and more highly paid) individuals than are really necessary to get the job done.

In the shoploading method, the estimator assumes that a certain proportion or percentage of a given office or shop is available to do the work. The labor hours within this percentage and within this time period in the shop are included in the labor estimate. Allowances are most likely *included* in staffing and shoploading estimates because estimating is being done on a macroscopic or team basis, and the estimator envisions just how many people or what part of the shop or office is required to do a job during a given time *including* allowances. Reference [7] contains excellent information on labor estimating for software development, including allowances for growth.

1.9.4 Material Estimating

Estimating the basic materials required to do a job usually involves an accurate computation of the material quantities, determining the price of the material at that quantity (including a scrap or waste allowance), and calculating the total material costs. Accurate drawing takeoff methods or prespecified bills of material are required to estimate material costs effectively. Historical data and an industrial materials utilization analysis are required to predict scrap and waste accurately. Scrap and waste can result in significant estimating errors if not predicted with precision. Chapter 6 discusses industrial engineering labor and material-based estimating techniques and methods in detail.

1.10 DEVELOP OVERHEAD AND ADMINISTRATIVE COST ESTIMATES

Most companies incur costs that cannot be attributed or charged to a specific ''direct'' project or work activity but that must be budgeted and allocated to perform the work (see Chapter 2 for a discussion of cost allocation). These costs are usually grouped into two categories: (1) *overhead* or *indirect* costs and (2) *general and administrative* costs. To provide a distinction between the various types of costs, the following is a listing of direct costs, indirect costs, and other costs.

1.10.1 Direct Costs: Definition

1. *Labor*
   Engineering
   Manufacturing
   Tooling
   Quality and reliability assurance
   Testing
   Planning
   Tool design
   Tool maintenance
   Packaging
2. *Materials and Subcontracts*
   Raw Materials
   Partially finished materials
      (forgings)
   Parts, sheet stock, fuels and
      lubricants
   Tool materials
   Equipment and supplies
3. *Other Direct Costs*
   Travel costs
   Shipping
   Transportation
   Computer services
   Reproduction services
   Training costs

1.10.2 Indirect Costs: Definition

1. *Labor Burden*
   Bonuses
   Health insurance
   Paid holidays
   Paid vacations
   Social security
   Supervisor's salary
   Pensions
2. *Material Burden*
   Handling
   Inventory control
   Purchasing costs
   Storage
3. *Overhead*
   Amortization
   Claims
   Communications
   Custodial
   Depreciation
   Heating and cooling
   Industrial relations
   Insurance
   Lighting
   Maintenance
   Operating supplies
   Power
   Rental of buildings
   Waste disposal
   Water

1.10.3 Other Costs: Definition

1. *General and Administrative*
   (G&A) Expenses
   Administration
   Advanced design
   Bid and proposal costs
   Independent research and
      development
   Advertising
   Corporate expenses
   Executive salaries

1. (*Continued*)
   Finance
   Marketing
   Personnel department
   Research
   Training department
   Corporate taxes
2. *Furnished Equipment*
   Fuels and lubricants
   Subassemblies
   Facilities
   Equipment

   Spare Parts
   Experiments
   Selected services
3. *Other*
   Warrantee costs
   Hazardous pay
   License fees
4. *Fee (Profit or Earnings)*
   Return to stockholders
   Reinvestment
   Capital equipment and tooling

To arrive at an overhead percentage, divide the total overhead costs for a given period by the direct costs incurred or expected to be incurred for that same period. It is not uncommon for overhead costs to exceed 100%. This means that every dollar that is estimated to be required to do the job must be accompanied by another dollar of overhead. Labor burden and material burden are commonly included in overhead costs, and the entire category of indirect cost is called overhead cost. The general and administrative expense percentage is derived by dividing the general and administrative costs for a given period by all other costs (direct and indirect). General and administrative expenses range from just a few percent to 20 or 25% of total costs for some companies—a not insignificant figure when added to all direct and indirect costs.

Development of credible indirect or overhead costs, and *control* of these costs, are vital steps in becoming and remaining competitive in any business environment. Overhead and administrative costs and their related functions are essential to any business activity because employees and equipment must be given adequately heated, cooled, and lighted office space provided with telephone communications, furnished adequate comfort and safety facilities and features, and furnished with a host of equipment, supplies, facilities, and benefits to keep them working as an efficient team. It is important for the cost estimator to (1) recognize the need for overhead and administrative functions and their related costs, and (2) distinguish between direct and indirect costs and their effects on cost estimates. The estimator must be sure (1) not to include the costs that are slated to be in the indirect category as direct costs and (2) to identify all project-related costs as direct that are not indirect.

1.11 APPLYING INFLATION AND ESCALATION (COST GROWTH) FACTORS

One of the most difficult questions confronting the cost estimator is how to deal with and understand inflation and escalation. Although inflation and escalation have often been treated as one, they are two distinctly different phenomena and are driven or created by altogether different forces. Inflation is the time-oriented increase in costs brought about by rising prices and rising costs of materials, subcontracts, parts, supplies, goods, and services. It is caused principally by the injection of funds into the economy that unbalance the law of supply and demand for money. The distribution by the government of more money than is collected through taxes and other income causes economic growth, but it also decreases the amount of work or goods that can be purchased with the dollar because the *value* of the dollar is thereby decreased.

Escalation, on the other hand, can be defined as the time-oriented increase in costs brought about by increases in labor hours required to do given amounts of work, increasing the skill level and corresponding wage level to accomplish given tasks, and in nonproductive labor encountered in providing work activities and work outputs. Both escalation and inflation have been difficult to predict and control because very little has been known about their makeup and the factors that influence their magnitude.

1.11.1 Dealing with Inflation

Control of inflation is a multinational task that is entwined with political, geographical, and social policies and trends. It is an almost unanimous opinion among economists that the inflation rate in this country can be more successfully controlled by holding Federal spending down to the level of Federal income than by any other means. The law of supply and demand works for money just as it does for other goods. The more money there is, the less value it has, the less there is, the more value it has. As long as there remains a conscious decision to print more money and to inject it into the economy to stimulate growth, inflation will stay with us. It is evident from this, then, that it is more in the purview of the cost estimator to recognize, predict, and account for inflation than to try to do something about it.

Inflation can be accounted for and dealt with by the cost estimator in two ways. First, the price trends of the specific work elements being estimated can be observed, recorded, and used in estimating the costs of the new work activity or work output. The sensitivity of each work element and each cost element to inflationary trends must be determined, and historical information and projection rationale must be developed for predicting the course of price changes for that element. In doing this, overall company production, purchasing, investment, and financing decisions can be made to gain strategic cost advantage over competitors. As an estimator, you should know enough about the work output, its components, and the historical and forecasted economic influences on the resources required to predict or forecast a cost that is compatible with inflationary trends.

Second, the cost estimator, in cooperation with company management and the contract negotiators, can develop economic price adjustment clauses for the contract. Contract cost adjustments can be tied to one of the several cost indices formulated and periodically published by the U.S. government. Other strategies to avoid the effect of inflationary prices are (1) to purchase raw materials in quantity and either to have these materials on hand or to have a firm quote in hand prior to bidding the job; (2) to judiciously use in-house production to avoid purchasing items at a too-high cost; or (3) to negotiate contracts in which the customer provides the materials.

1.11.2 Dealing with Escalation

Escalation is caused by one or more of the following factors:

Inaccuracy of the original cost estimate

Incomplete definition or design at the time of estimation; bidding design changes

Unforeseen increases in labor burden

Unanticipated and excessive customer involvement

Increased government regulation and control

Inflexibility of the work force

Inability or failure to hire new personnel at lower labor rates

Unanticipated failure of suppliers or subcontractors to deliver on time and within original cost estimates

Escalation can be nipped in the bud early in the estimation process by providing a sufficient allowance for cost growth. When job definition is hazy or incomplete, cost growth is a certainty and not a contingency. Allowances for cost growth should be imbedded in each work element of the cost estimate, with each allowance proportional to the amount of change expected in that work element. Cost growth allowances added at the lowest level of the cost estimate permit each work element or work package manager to predict and to subsequently respond to cost growth influences as they occur. Company management must make the courageous decision to allow unit and subunit managers to retain adequate cost growth allowance amounts, even in the face of stiff cost or price competition. Removal of all cost growth allowance amounts as a means of becoming cost or price competitive is a major pitfall or mistake that causes companies to ''win'' jobs that cannot possibly be done within the contracted cost. In these instances the winner is actually the loser because the ''overrun'' must either come out of profit or be recouped through sometimes agonizing adversary conflicts with the customer. Neither of these outcomes is acceptable from a standpoint of continued prosperity and customer goodwill.

Design definition deficiencies at contract initiation must be accommodated by sufficient allowances at the outset, and a clear understanding of which changes, if any, are the responsibility of the supplier should be spelled out in detail. The customer must know beforehand that the customer will have to pay for customer-directed or requested changes.

Increases in labor burden brought about by increases in social security taxes, retirement benefits, paid holidays, sick leave, medical and dental insurance contributions by the company, and paid vacations should be anticipated to the greatest extent possible by surveying business trends, union contract projections, and socioeconomic demographics. Increases in these employee benefits are caused by new government legislation, renegotiation of union contracts, and changes in employment policies required to stay in competition for highly qualified personnel. Although these contributions to escalation are difficult to control, some positive steps can be taken to restrain them. For example, the hiring and training of younger personnel with less seniority and the retirement of older employees will reduce the average paid vacation time, sick leave, and other company-paid employee benefits.

The degree of customer involvement should be anticipated during the estimating process, with anticipated or built-in cost impacts or schedule delays accounted for and added to total cost. Here, the estimator must know something about the whims and desires of the specific client or customer and make internal estimate adjustments accordingly. A customer who is flexible and understanding when it comes to approving minor changes in work content or schedule can go a long way toward helping to hold costs in line, whereas one whose reviews and demands become increasingly frequent may cause the work to slip in schedule or to increase in cost. Likewise, a knowledge of one's subcontractors and suppliers and their reputation for delivering on schedule and within cost will help in establishing internal cost growth allowances.

Government regulation and control must be accounted for in establishing schedules and costs for commercial work as well as for government-related work. The increasing numbers of socioeconomic laws, procedures, and regulations dealing with equal opportunity, human rights, occupational safety and health, geographic dispersion of work, purchasing and using American products, and other government criteria and their effects on productivity, must be taken into account in the estimating process.

These are some of the more intangible, subjective, and difficult to quantify factors that confront the estimator in combatting, or at least accommodating the phenomenon of escalation. Increased innovation, productivity, and adaptability and flexibility of the work force will help to counteract or at least partially nullify the effects of both inflation and escalation.

1.12 PRICING OR COMPUTING THE ESTIMATED COST

The number of tools available to the cost estimator for performing the more routine job of pricing or computing the estimated costs, once the basic resource estimates and allowances are established, are increasing at a rapid rate. Chapters 6, 7, and 9 of this manual cover industrial engineering, parametric, and computer estimating tools and methods that are now available and becoming increasingly available in the age of high technology.

In the past, most companies have been forced to develop their own mathematical and computer tools to create price extensions, add up costs, and develop detailed cost proposals. The 1980s were marked by the emergence of a number of firms, consultants, and specialists in cost estimating and analysis who supply mathematical cost models, computer programs, and expert advice in the synthesis, correlation, assembly, adjustment, analysis, and publication of detailed cost estimates. Further, commercial software companies have developed easy-to-use computer application programs for job costing, scheduling, cost analysis, pricing, and graphics which take the drudgery out of the process of assembling and analyzing large amounts of resource and cost data.

In the 1990s and beyond, cost estimators will be continuing to rely on the computer as an indispensable tool in rapidly producing accurate cost estimates from raw resource data. Many estimators who have previously had limited or no access to computers are now finding that microcomputers and their related cost estimating software are sufficiently inexpensive and easy to use to permit integration into even the smallest estimating office. Even one-person or part-time estimating functions are finding that the microcomputer is a good investment and even an indispensable tool. A wide variety of microcomputer systems and software is now available for cost estimating (see Chapter 9 of this reference manual and the book, *Cost Estimating with Microcomputers*, Stewart and Stewart, McGraw-Hill Book Company, New York, 1986). Vertical market systems, electronic spreadsheets, data base programs, scheduling/costing systems, and customized systems are available for cost estimating. With the low-cost computerized cost estimating systems now on the market, it would be inappropriate for cost estimators to continue spending hours of time on the calculator or adding machine merely to sum up a detailed cost estimate. The newest automatic data processing machines have the added advantage of low-cost letter-quality outputs that can be used as is for bids or proposals; sophisticated graphics that can be produced in minutes from numerical data; and large storage capacities to hold many estimates that can be accessed immediately for use in similar or modified estimates. With these sophisticated tools, the estimator can spend more of his or her time in performing the creative tasks in estimating rather than in routine calculating. This creativity can be directed toward the construction of improved cost models, the development of more credible cost estimating rationales, and the formulation of improved methods of extracting and using valid historical cost and labor hour data for future estimates.

1.13 ANALYZING, ADJUSTING, AND SUPPORTING THE ESTIMATE

With the advent of the computer the calculation of price often triggers another step in the estimating process—the fine-tuning of the estimate through the process of analysis, adjustment, modification, and supporting the estimate. The iterative process shown in Section 1.8 on identification of skill categories and skill levels shows one example of how adjustments can be made to bring cost into line with a competitive environment. The development of a first-cut cost or price through the initial calculation process is often the starting point for a *design-to-cost* iteration that develops a slightly different product or service with a slightly different cost. Design-to-cost exercises require an initial or baseline cost because the design-to-cost situation usually results from a budget or target figure that cannot be exceeded because of fund availability. The job first needs to be structured and estimated to produce a data base of resource information related to a product or service specification, which can then be tailored to a given budget.

When a computed estimate has been analyzed and found to be in excess of the budget allocation or market price objective (and, for some reason, the estimated cost usually *exceeds* objectives rather than underrunning budget or market price objectives), the adjustments must be made through a reestimating process where cost reductions are accompanied by corresponding decreases or changes in labor hours, unit quantities, schedules, or performance specifications. Across-the-board cuts in each work element are an all-too-often used remedy for an excessively high cost estimate. Arbitrary reductions in any part of a cost estimate without corresponding changes in the work content is, of course, unacceptable if a properly funded, manageable end product or service is desired. Cost reductions should be allocated with some knowledge of their impact on schedule, quality, or performance. Then, the element being cut must be adjusted by combining work functions, decreasing performance, using lower skill levels (see the previous section on this subject), or developing innovative design or work-planning methods that end up using fewer or less expensive labor hours or materials.

Thus any adjustment to a cost estimate must consist of an iterative process in which the job to be performed is adjusted commensurate with the desired cost reductions. This will permit the retention of traceability and rationale that is needed to tie cost credibly to a given product or service and will give the managers of the would-be work activity or work output at least a satisfactory chance of holding costs within the budget when the work is performed. As adjustments and changes are made to costs, schedules, and/or performance to meet target cost goals, the rationale and backup material that supports the estimate must be altered and updated accordingly. The finished cost estimate, then, which is recomputed to develop a "best and final offer," should be as supportable and credible as the initial estimate. The details of what is included and what is excluded in each work element, which are part of the work element structure dictionary, should be updated to a point where they solidly support the cost. These details then must form the basis of an agreement between supplier and customer that will permit rapid identification of any desired changes that are outside of the scope of the estimated costs.

1.14 PUBLISHING AND PRESENTING THE COST ESTIMATE

Do not underestimate the value of a well-organized, cohesive, supportable, attractive, and easily understood cost estimate report. Whether the cost estimate is to be used as a cost volume for a bid or proposal or merely as an internal document that sums up the results of a cost study, it is important to bind together the assumptions, ground rules, basic specifications, and other vital related information with the cost estimate details, rationale, and cost summary. A problem with many cost estimates is that they represent cost information only and that they do not adequately describe that which has been estimated. A cost number without its accompanying product or service description is of little value. A good stand-alone cost estimate report should contain as many as possible of the following elements.

   I. Introduction, background, and date
  II. Ground rules and assumptions
 III. Description of the work activity or work output that was estimated
    1. Schedule
    2. Specifications
    3. Quantities
    4. Location
    5. And so on
 IV. Detailed cost breakdown
    1. By work element
    2. By cost element
    3. By schedule element
  V. Summary cost estimate
 VI. Pricing factors
    1. Labor rates for all skill categories and skill levels
    2. Inflation rates used
    3. Material prices
    4. Overhead, G&A, and fee rates and rationale
 VII. Estimating team names, telephone numbers, and assignments
VIII. Detailed rationale and backup material

Finally, the cost estimate should be put together into an easily understandable, attractive, well-written, and organized document. A few niceties like tabs and subtabs for quick reference, a detailed table of contents, and an index are helpful. Final publication of the cost estimate opens the door for effective *use* of the cost estimate in functions like bidding, negotiating, cost tracking, or cost analysis. A well-prepared cost estimate will be an invaluable tool to management in making bid-no-bid decisions, make/buy decisions, plant location decisions, and new product decisions. The hard and dedicated work by the cost estimator deserves to be represented by an attractive, organized, and easy-to-use document.

REFERENCES

1. Stewart, R. D. *Cost Estimating*. John Wiley, New York, 1982.
2. Ostwald, P. F. *Cost Estimating*. Prentice-Hall, Englewood Cliffs, N.J., 1984.

3. Blanchard, B. S. *Design and Manage to Life Cycle Cost.* M/A Press, Portland, Or., 1978.

4. Seldon, M. R. *Life Cycle Costing.* Westview Press, Boulder, Co., 1979.

5. Earles, M. E. *Factors, Formulas, and Structures for Life Cycle Costing.* E/E Press, Concord, Ma., 1978.

6. Moder, Joseph J. et. al. *Project Management with CPM, PERT, and Precedence Diagramming* 3rd Ed. Van Nostrand Reinhold Company, New York, N.Y., 1983.

7. Boehm, B. W. *Software Engineering Economics.* Prentice-Hall, Englewood Cliffs, N.J., 1981.

2

COST ALLOCATION

RICHARD H. SHUFORD, JR., DBA

2.1 COST CLASSIFICATIONS AND CONCEPTS

Throughout business and government there is, and has been, recognition of the need to allocate the various costs incurred in relation to products, services, and objectives. This recognition has led to development of concepts, principles, classifications, structures, standards, and systems for the accounting of costs.

2.1.1 Accounting Structures and Systems

Accounting for costs within any organization takes place after the decision to incur the cost. Therefore the fundamental and underlying foundation for all accounting is the historical (it has already happened) nature of costs. Historical costs are thus structured (accounted) for a variety of purposes to serve needs of the several groups that may have an interest or need to know about the organization's performance. In this sense, the allocation of costs to the organization's products, services, and objectives constitutes a system for the measurement of costs. The system embraces the process of recording, summarizing like transactions, analyzing relationships, and interpreting what has occurred. The American Institute of Certified Public Accountants' Committee on Terminology has defined accounting in this manner:

> The art of recording, classifying, and summarizing in a significant manner and in terms of money, transactions and events which are, in part at least, of a financial character, and interpreting the results thereof.

Within our society two groups have a basic interest in an organization's performance. Managers inside the organization need accounting information structured for decisions about costs that fall within their jurisdiction or functional area, for example, manufacturing, research and development, advertising, and asset management. Other managers outside the organization need information on which to base decisions that may affect their relationship with the organization, for example, stockholders, creditors, governmental agencies, organized labor, and financial analysts. The different needs of these two groups has led to such terms as *managerial accounting* for the former and *financial accounting* for the latter. It should be noted by cost estimators that both managerial and financial accounting deal with historical costs.

Most organizations adopt as a standard a classification system for the recording of financially oriented transactions. This system is designed to serve the needs of both insiders and outsiders within a single structure. The classification structure is generally called a chart of accounts. In most cases the chart of accounts is a detailed listing of the individual accounts to which like transactions are to be summarized. The design of the structure tends to be tied to financial reports appropriate for the outsiders' needs, and other classifications are added as insider needs are made known.

In building the chart of accounts, the organization is guided by the nature of its products, services, and objectives, plus the accepted practices within its industry and the precise requirements of regulatory agencies. For the private, publicly held organizations there is the need to accommodate the regulatory requirements of the Securities and Exchange Commission, Internal Revenue Service, State Securities Commissions, and similar organizations.

Charts of accounts follow requirements established for financial reports. Two financial reports guide the chart of accounts cost structure. The first focuses on financial position and is a static report called the balance sheet, based upon the equation:

$$\text{assets} = \text{liabilities} + \text{owner's equity} \qquad (2.1)$$

Assets represent costs of properties owned. Liabilities are claims against those properties where some form of credit has been extended or payment deferred, such as periodic taxes, compensation, and the like. Owner's equity is the residual value of assets accruing to the owners after claims and deferred payments have been satisfied.

The preceding first-level classifications—assets, liabilities, and owner's equity—are exploded into additional classifications, principally these:

☐ *Current Assets.* Cash or other assets (e.g., temporary money market funds, accounts receivable, inventory) which may be realized in cash or consumed in the normal operating cycle of the business (assumed to be the next 12 months in the absence of special circumstances.

☐ *Plant and Equipment or Property and Equipment.* Assets that are used in the normal operations of the business, have an economic life longer than one operating cycle, and will not be sold in the normal course of business; for example, machinery, buildings.

☐ *Investments.* Permanent investments of the organization, such as land for development.

☐ *Other Assets.* Those properties having economic value that have not been previously classified; for example, goodwill, patents, licenses.

☐ *Current Liabilities.* Claims to be paid within the next accounting period (one year assumed); for example, accounts payable, wages payable, notes payable, taxes payable.

☐ *Long-Term Debt.* Claims that are not due within the next accounting period (one year assumed); for example, notes payable in year 2000, mortgage payable, bonds payable.

☐ *Stockholder's Equity or Owner's Equity.* A corporation's original investment by shareholders plus earnings retained in the business; for example, preferred stock, common stock, retained earnings.

```
Cost Allocation


                    December 31, 1984

                         Assets
                     (in thousands)

Current Assets:
      Cash and Marketable Securities         $162,800
      Accounts Receivable                     101,379
      Inventory                                89,607
      Other Current Assets                     39,517
                                              --------
      Total Current Assets                   $393,303

Plant and Equipment less depreciation         107,214
Investments                                    67,939
Other Assets                                   40,295
                                              --------
                                             $608,751
                                              ========


         Liabilities and Stockholder's Equity
Current Liabilities:
      Accounts Payable                       $177,104
      Wages Payable                            23,812
                                              --------
      Total Current Liabilities              $200,916

Deferred Income Taxes                          17,318
Mortgage Payable                               35,921
                                              --------
      Total Liabilities                      $254,155

Stockholder's Equity                          354,596
                                              --------
      Total Liabilities and
         Stockholder's Equity                $608,751
                                              ========
```

Figure 2.1. SDE Corporation balance sheet.

The SDE Corporation's balance sheet for the year 1984 is shown in Figure 2.1. Notice that the balance sheet bears a single date, a specific point in time at which historical costs have been summarized. Assets are totaled and are equal to the sum of the total liabilities and the stockholder's equity.

The second financial report guiding the structure in the chart of accounts is in the income statement. This statement focuses on the earnings performance within a time period and is a dynamic report. To measure the overall performance, the income statement concentrates on flows and is based on the equation

$$\text{revenue} - \text{expenses} = \text{net income} \qquad (2.2)$$

Revenue equates to income from the sale of products and/or services and income from other sources. Revenue is an inflow and tends to be reflected in the balance sheet in increases to cash, accounts receivable, inventory, and other assets. Expenses, on the other hand, constitute an outflow that, within a given period, are costs for creating the revenue generated. Net income is the difference between revenue and costs for the period and can be measured not only as a differential, but by examining the changes in accounts between the balance sheet periods.

SDE Corporation's income statement is shown in Figure 2.2.

```
Cost Allocation


              Year Ended December 31, 1984
                    (in thousands)


    Revenues
         Net Sales                               $245,583
         Other Income                                 789
                                                 _____

                                                  246,372


    Expenses
         Cost of Products Sold                    163,285
         Product Delivery                          21,009
         Selling, advertising
            administrative and general             19,635
                                                 _____

                                                  203,929


    Earnings Before Interest and Taxes             42,443
    Interest Expense                                  962
                                                 _____

    Earnings Before Taxes                          41,481
    Income Taxes                                    18,391
                                                 _____

    Net Earnings                               $  23,090
                                                 ========
```

Figure 2.2. SDE Corporation income statement.

2.1.2 Patterns in Cost Behavior

Understanding what creates profitability or reaching the objective is central in cost estimation. Managers responsible for decisions of this class find that they consistently ask themselves the following question: How do the changes in overall performance volume affect the behavior of costs?

Achievement of objectives and profits generally are managed. They do not just happen. Most organizations develop profit plans or budgets to think through and to establish for future control the factors that limit or promote the desired goals. As seen in Figure 2.2 the net earnings are derived by subtracting all costs (including taxes) from available revenues. Information in Figure 2.2 was developed as a report after all the events, activities, and transactions had occurred—the historical cost approach. On the other hand, to manage the achievement of objectives and profits, estimates must be developed on projected revenues and projected costs.

Estimating costs for planning purposes requires recognition that all costs do not behave alike. Because of differences in behavior, a single approach to cost estimation for all types of costs is impractical. Through analysis of volume relationships, categories of costs with behavior can be determined, thus facilitating the estimating process.

Certain costs can be identified directly with the product being manufactured or the service being rendered. Materials incorporated into the product or labor hours expended in the development of a standard computer software routine are representative examples. The number of products planned for production will determine the amount of material needed, and the number of standard routines will determine the number of labor hours required. These costs can be said to vary directly with volume and are called *variable costs*.

On the other hand, certain costs are incurred on the basis of an amount in each time period. For example, the real estate taxes and depreciation of the plant and office building will generally be the same each year. Other costs such as executive salaries not tied to profit arrangements tend to remain fixed or constant for each time period. Such costs do not change regardless of the number of units produced. These costs are thus called *fixed costs*.

A third group of costs may vary somewhat in relation to volume but their percent of change is not the same as the percent of change in volume. Since these costs behave differently from either variable costs or fixed costs, they are known as *semivariable* costs or mixed costs. A portion of these costs are fixed and another portion of these costs are variable. For example, sales salaries may have a base amount plus a commission (percentage). The base amount will be paid to the salesperson regardless of the volume sold; thus it is the fixed component of the semivariable cost. The commission amount will vary with the volume of products or services sold and thus constitutes the variable component of the sales salary semivariable cost.

Figure 2.3 shows graphically the general behavior of variable, fixed, and semivariable costs.

In classifying individual cost elements according to behavior, it is important to

Cost Allocation

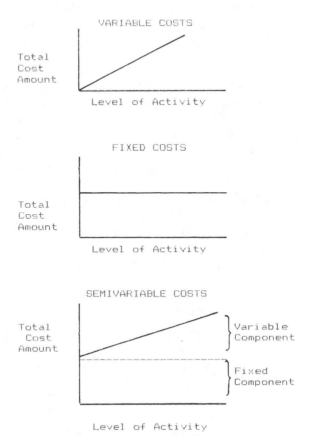

Figure 2.3. Variable, fixed, and semivariable costs.

ascertain if the behavior pattern is the same for all levels of activity. Or does the cost element have a relevant range in which it behaves in a certain manner? Power costs are typically thought of as a variable cost associated with machine operating activity levels. Most power costs, however, are tied to rate schedules which show different costs per kilowatt hour for usage within a *relevant range*. This type cost should be estimated in accordance with planned usage and in consideration of the price breaks per kilowatt hour as the activity level increases or decreases, passing from one relevant range to another.

Certain fixed costs sometimes may alter their behavior as the activity level moves from one relevant range to another. These are called *step-fixed costs* and depending upon their magnitude in the cost estimate can be treated as a semivariable cost.

The cost estimator will benefit in making estimates if semivariable costs are broken down into their fixed and variable components. There are three basic methods for segregating the components. All three methods assume that there is a linear relationship between the amount of the cost element and volume.

When the estimator has a good history of the amount of expense for various operating levels, a simple plot of these on a graph will serve to identify the fixed and variable components. Procedurally, the points are plotted from cost/volume data, and a scattergraph is created such as in Figure 2.4. Next, the estimator constructs by "freehand" a line by having half of the points above and half of the points below the line. The line is extended to intersect the level of fixed expenses. The difference between the total expense for a given volume and the fixed expense is the variable component of the semivariable cost element.

The scattergraph can be used when semivariable history is readily available and only an approximation is needed because of the costs to be included in the estimate.

A second method for breaking down semivariable is called the "high-low points" method. This method is useful when only limited historical data is available. For the new organization, data for semivariables may have to be obtained from consultants or trade associations. Assume that office expense is a semivariable and that trade data indicates the following:

Level of Operations	Operating Hours	Total Cost
High point	6200	$52,200
Low point	3800	37,800
Difference	2400	$14,400

Cost Allocation

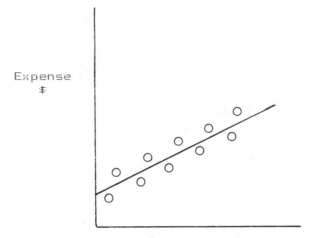

Figure 2.4. Scattergraph.

Variable costs can be computed by dividing the cost differences for the two levels by the hour differences: 14,400/2400 = $6 per hour. The fixed cost can be computed by selecting either the total cost at the high or low point and subtracting the variable cost. The residual amount is the fixed cost component. Selecting the low point total cost of $37,800 minus (3800 hours @ $6) results in a fixed cost of $15,000 for office expense in the foregoing situation.

The third method is called the "least squares method," and it requires a reasonable history of cost for operating volumes. The method is based on the equation for a straight line. Typically, the equation for a straight line is:

$$Y = mX + b \qquad (2.3)$$

where Y = total semivariable cost
  b = fixed component
  m = variable cost component
  X = volume or activity level

Using a mathematical criterion to fit a straight line to the data observed about the semivariable and activity levels, the estimator minimizes the difference between the plotted and the straight line. In the scattergraph method, the straight line was freehand, whereas in least squares, the line is fitted to the plotted data. Details of how to fit a straight line are included in the next chapter.

Equation 2.3 is highly useful for the estimator once the fixed and variable proportions are established. Estimates of power costs are generally performed using the equation. A basic cost for power is charged regardless of the level of operations. This is the fixed component. The per kilowatt hour rate can be substituted as the variable component and several operating levels assumed.

Another approach to classifying costs is the timing aspect of when costs enter the income statement. Costs incurred in the manufacturing process that add value are referred to as *product costs*. These costs are shown in the income statement under headings such as inventory and cost of products manufactured and sold. Costs adding value are accumulated and deducted from revenue as the products are sold. Costs are thus released as expenses are matched against their associated revenues.

Costs incurred that are not involved in the manufacturing value-added process are deducted from revenue on a time period basis. These *period costs* are not influenced by the level of activity, rather by the passage of time. Building rent, leases, and depreciation of office machines are common examples of costs that are tied to periods of time.

2.1.3 Traceability of Costs

To establish an accurate data base for cost estimation, it is desirable to be able to relate those costs that can be considered as *direct costs* and *indirect costs*. *Direct costs* can be traced to a specific unit of product or service—for example, a piece of sheet metal that is formed as a side for a file or storage cabinet. Costs not directly traceable to the product or service are referred to as *indirect costs*.

Since cost elements may be classified as either direct or indirect costs, a specific cost element may change classification as it moves from one department of the organization to another. Material classified as indirect costs in Production Department A may become direct costs as the output from Department A is transferred to Department B for further processing. The concept of traceability is founded on the purpose for which the cost is used. Direct and indirect costs incurred by service departments which are subsequently allocated or prorated to revenue producing departments become indirect costs for the revenue producing departments.

When two cost elements, direct materials and direct labor, are grouped into a single summary cost element, the combined costs are referred to as *prime costs*. Another combination frequently used is the grouping of direct labor and manufacturing overhead into a single summary cost element which is called *conversion cost*.

The use of summary cost elements such as prime cost and conversion cost has become fairly standard as a convenient way of aggregating major components of manufacturing or product costs. Since manufacturers typically possess three types of inventories—raw materials, work-in-process, and finished goods—there is a continuing requirement at the end of each reporting period to identify the amount of costs necessary to convert those partially processed products (work in process) into finished goods. Thus conversion cost estimates are a common necessity in planning for future periods.

Traceability of costs is also important as the organization seeks to assign responsibility for the control of costs. Most all costs, product or period, are controllable to a certain degree by someone in the organization. This fact has led to a different cost classification system which generally is superimposed over the classification system used in the development of the financial statements. This often divides costs into those that are controllable by the activity unit and those beyond the control of the activity unit. Logically then, costs that are capable of being controlled are called *controllable costs*. Costs incurred beyond the control of an activity are *uncontrollable costs* to that unit but generally are controllable costs by another, often higher level, activity unit.

The concept of using a cost control classification system helps to relate organizational structure and authority for decisions to specific activity units, sometimes called *responsibility centers*. It is always desirable from the cost estimator's viewpoint that individual managers who provide data for the cost estimate also be responsible for decisions on costs as the products or services are produced. Postmortem analysis of the validity of the cost estimate is essential in maintaining a realistic data base of costs.

2.2 THE NATURE OF PRODUCT COSTING

In the manufacturing process, product costs are inventoriable costs. They are accumulated, summarized, and reported as assets until they are sold. Raw materials purchased and held for immediate or subsequent use represent one class of inventoriable costs. As they are transferred from stores to the production process, most of the materials will be traceable direct to the product and become *direct materials*. Other raw material purchases may be used in the production process but are not directly traceable to a product; these are *indirect materials*. Note that the terminology changes slightly to drop the word "costs."

2.2.1 Product Cost Flows

As the manufacturing process continues, labor is applied to the materials to transform them into finished products. A portion of the labor costs called *direct labor* is directly traceable to the product. Another portion, for example, first-line supervisor salaries, is *indirect labor* since these labor costs cannot be directly traced to the product.

Cost of the raw materials and conversion costs (direct labor plus manufacturing overhead) that do not result in finished goods at the end of the reporting period remain as *work-in-process inventory*. Costs incurred in producing the finished goods are transferred to an account called *finished goods inventory*.

A summary account is used to collect all costs used in the production process except for direct materials and direct labor. The account is called *manufacturing overhead*. Such indirect costs as indirect materials, indirect labor, plant depreciation, and machine rental, are grouped under the manufacturing overhead title. The pool of manufacturing overhead costs must later be divided to allocate a portion of the costs to the partially completed products remaining in the work-in-process inventory at the end of the period and the remainder to the finished goods manufactured.

Most manufacturers develop a schedule to itemize the costs of goods manufactured. Figure 2.5 shows the buildup of costs by the typical manufacturer in development of the cost of goods manufactured schedule.

Figure 2.6 shows the flow of costs in a typical manufacturing firm and their relationship to the balance sheet and income statement accounts. The ability to trace the flow of costs is essential to the cost estimation process because the inclusion of inappropriate costs, or the omission of appropriate costs, quickly invalidates the cost estimate and its use for pricing, profit planning, and similar purposes.

2.2.2 Job Order Costing

Manufacturing firms do not all function alike. The differences have resulted in the need to capture cost data in accordance with the productive or marketing methods used. One of the product cost accumulation systems is called the *job order costing system*.

The title itself helps to define the job order costing system. Its characteristics include the following:

1. Accumulation of manufacturing costs for specific contracts, jobs, or batches of products.

SDE CORPORATION

COST OF GOODS MANUFACTURED

```
Direct Materials:
    Raw Materials Inventory Dec. 31, 1983    $38,625
    Purchases                                 27,138
                                             _____

    Cost of Direct Materials Available
        for Use                               65,763
    Raw Materials Inventory Dec. 31, 19484    30,217
                                             _____

Direct Materials Used                                   $ 35,546

Direct Labor                                              74,921

Manufacturing Overhead:

    Indirect Materials                         8,171
    Indirect labor                             5,386
    Power                                      1,712
    Depreciation Plant & Equipment             9,374
    Machine Rental                               620
    Miscellaneous Expenses                     1,398    26,661
                                             _____    _____

Total Manufacturing Costs
    Incurred During 1984                                137,128

Add: Work-in-Process Inventory
    December 31, 1983                                    53,714
                                                        _____

Manufacturing Costs to Account for                      190,842

Less: Work-in-Process Inventory
    December 31, 1984                                    27,557
                                                        _____

Cost of Goods Manufactured                             $163,285
                                                       ========
```

Figure 2.5. SDE Corporation cost of goods manufactured.

2. Reporting periods do not control the starting or stopping of cost accumulation. The orders (quantity, quality, and delivery date) control cost accumulation.

3. The work-in-process inventory summary account is supported by a subsidiary ledger for each job. The ledger is supported by cost sheets reflecting material, labor, and the amount of manufacturing overhead allocated to the job.

4. The system is usable for many industries where one-of-a-kind production is common practice, for example, custom aircraft, die molds, spacecraft, custom furniture.

Figure 2.7 illustrates the several cost flows incident to a job order costing system.

Cost Allocation

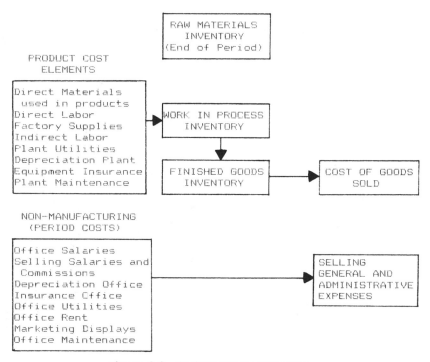

Figure 2.6. Cost summary accounts.

The cost estimator will recognize that in a job order costing system, the cost data for direct materials and direct labor are readily available from the material requisition forms and the payroll tickets. The other job cost component, manufacturing overhead, must be approached differently.

Jobs can be completed at any time in the accounting period. Job estimates may be needed prior to the sale. Overhead costs must be included in the estimate prior to pricing the job, and billing must be based on the actual cost of the job (including overhead) if pricing is cost plus a profit margin. Both these common conditions result in establishing a predetermined rate for overhead costs. That is, the total estimated manufacturing overhead costs are divided by a suitable base for allocation. Common bases used are total direct labor hours, total machine hours, tenths of miles of paving completed, total cubic feet, and the like. The ratio used for computing the predetermined overhead rate is illustrated as follows:

$$\frac{\text{estimated total manufacturing overhead costs}}{\text{estimated total units in base (machine hours, etc.)}} = \text{predetermined rate.} \quad (2.4)$$

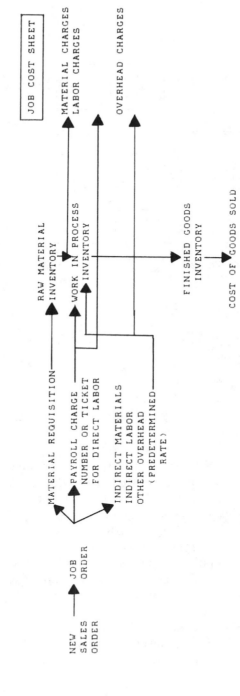

Figure 2.7. Job order costing system cost flows.

The concept of a predetermined rate for allocating overhead costs to specific jobs provides a convenient mechanism for estimating in connection with sales and for pricing jobs completed prior to the end of the accounting period when actual costs are known. The mechanics of using a predetermined rate, however, does create a problem when actual costs are different from the total manufacturing overhead costs allocated.

The cost estimator can solve this problem of difference between actual overhead costs and costs applied to jobs by using the technique of a control or "clearing" account for manufacturing overhead. All manufacturing overhead cost elements would have separate subsidiary accounts in which actual costs are collected as they are incurred. At the end of the accounting period these accounts are closed into a clearing account. During the accounting period costs are applied to jobs using the predetermined overhead rate, and at the end these costs are summarized into the clearing account as an offset to actual costs incurred. Any difference between these cost totals (actual and applied) represents under-or-overapplied overhead. The concept is summarized in Figure 2.8.

At this point the condition of underapplied or overapplied overhead can be disposed of by adjustment to actual accounts for the amount of the difference. The preferred method for adjustment is to prorate the difference between the work in

Cost Allocation

	CONCEPT	TERMINOLOGY
1.	Individual cost elements which are not directly traceable to products are estimated. The cost estimate is accomplished prior to the accounting period and a predetermined overhead rate established.	Estimated Overhead Cost ——— Allocation Base = Overhead Rate
2.	Actual costs incurred during the period for each cost element included in overhead.	Actual Overhead Cost
3.	The total amount of dollar charges using the predetermined overhead rate approach which have been added to job cost sheets and the work-in-process inventory account during the period.	Applied Overhead Cost
	The difference between 2 and 3 represents costs not yet fully accounted for.	Underapplied Overhead or Overapplied Overhead

Figure 2.8. Overhead descriptions.

process, finished goods, and cost of goods sold accounts. The basis of proration is the percentage relationship existing at the end of the accounting period. The balances in the three accounts are summed and a percent for each computed. The percentage is multiplied by the overhead difference and the result added to, or subtracted from, the respective account, depending upon whether the overhead was underapplied or overapplied. The rationale for this adjustment method is its accuracy. The final result is to assign the overhead costs to their proper place if there has been no difference between estimated and actual costs for the period.

A simpler method for adjusting the difference is frequently utilized. This method adjusts only the cost of goods sold account by the amount of the difference, increase or decrease.

There is widespread use of a single, predetermined overhead rate. The cost estimator should not restrict thinking to its use when the organization's activities are so diverse that jobs do not have a common flow pattern as they progress through the organization. In these situations, it is more realistic to consider establishing multiple departmental and divisional overhead rates. A labor-intensive department may have its own overhead rate, and a machine-intensive department a different rate, to equitably allocate the total group of overhead cost elements.

Regardless of whether a single or multiple overhead rate structure is used, it is highly desirable to compare the actual costs of each overhead cost element with its estimated costs at the end of the accounting period. This is necessary to determine whether or not an estimated cost element should be revised for the next accounting period so that overhead rates will be more accurate. In periods of fluctuating production levels, the impact of fixed costs in the overhead estimate is significant. When production is low, the fixed costs are spread among a smaller base than when production is high; therefore rates would reflect these activity levels. Organizations experiencing significant fluctuation in production prefer, however, not to adjust overhead rates for each accounting period; instead, they seek to normalize the overhead rate by computing an average overhead rate based on averaging costs and activity levels.

2.2.3 Process Costing

When manufacturing production occurs on a continuous, regular basis and products are mass produced for immediate shipment or warehouse stock, a different costing approach called *process costing* is utilized. Industries such as bakeries, oil refineries, steel, textile yarns, and plastic injection molders usually manufacture standardized products, and the identity of the customer is unknown at the time of manufacture. Characteristics of process costing are as follows:

1. A specific product with continuous or long production runs is typical.
2. Costs are accumulated on a process or departmental basis without regard to job, batch, or customer.

3. Costs are measured for specific time periods.
4. Each production department or process has its own work in process account.
5. Production typically is a sequential process where partially completed units move from department to department.

Figure 2.9 illustrates the general model of process costing using sequential processing found in the typical commercial bakery operation.

In Figure 2.9 raw materials are shown as being added in each department. The nature of some production processes is such that materials may be added only in the first production department.

It is important to recognize in process costing that departmental costs in any accounting period generally consist of units in three distinct levels:

1. Units that were started in prior periods and completed during the period.
2. Units started and also completed during the period.
3. Units started and incomplete at the end of the period.

The various stages of completion require that measurement of the department's output be based on equivalent units of production. *Equivalent units of production* are the number of units that could have been manufactured from beginning to

```
Cost Allocation

Departmental Production                          Costs


                                      Raw Materials (flour, yeast, etc)

   Mixing Department                  Direct Labor (Time)
      Work in Process
                                      Departmental Overhead (machine
                                         depreciation, utilities, etc)


                                      Raw Materials (glazings)
   Baking Department                  Direct Labor (Time)
      Work in Process                 Departmental Overhead (oven
                                         depreciation, utilities, etc)

                                      Raw Materials (wrapping paper,
                                         etc)
   Packaging Department               Direct Labor (Time)
                                      Departmental Overhead (machine
                                         depreciation, utilities, etc)

   Finished Goods Inventory

   Cost of Goods Sold
```

Figure 2.9. Bakery process costing.

completion during the period. The computation of equivalent units for our bakery process would be determined for the Mixing Department assuming this data:

Inventory, April 1	10,000 loaves completed
Completed and transferred to Baking during April	170,000 loaves completed
Inventory, April	3,000 loaves, 40% completed
Equivalent units or production computation:	
To process loaves in inventory on April 1	10,000 loaves × 75% = 7,500
To process loaves started and completed during April	170,000 − 10,000 = 160,000
To process loaves in inventory on April 30	3,000 × 40% = 1,200
Equivalent units of production in April (loaves)	168,700

In the Mixing Department equivalent units of production computation, there is an assumption that material costs and conversion costs are applied uniformly throughout the period. When these costs are not uniformly applied within the period, it is then necessary to establish a separate estimate of the stage of completion for materials and a second stage of completion estimate for conversion costs. The foregoing computational method follows the principle of "first-in, first-out" flow. Units in the beginning inventory are assumed to be completed and transferred out first and to carry their own unit cost.

To establish the Mixing Department's unit cost for the period, total direct material, direct labor, and predetermined manufacturing overhead costs are summed and divided by the equivalent units of production. Unit costs are needed for performance evaluation, audit, and for valuing the work in process inventory at the end of the period, and thus the beginning work in process inventory for the next period.

Figure 2.10 illustrates a cost of production report for the Mixing Department. This report provides an accounting for all units and all costs. Unit costs are based on equivalent units of production. The unit cost for March was slightly higher than for April. March unit cost can be determined from the April report by dividing the April 1 in process cost, $790, by the equivalent units in production, 10,000 loaves at 25% complete.

Although there are significant procedural differences in cost allocation and estimation between the job order system and the process costing system, there are many similarities. Particular cost elements and their purposes provide for different treatment between similar organizations. The manufacturing process may cause one company to reflect costs as direct, whereas another company would charge the same costs to indirect. Most of the differences between companies and industries fall in the area of allocating indirect costs for cost estimation and for financial accounting.

MIXING DEPARTMENT
FOR THE MONTH ENDING APRIL 30, 19__

Quantities (Loaves)

Charged to Production:
In process, April 1   10,000
Units started   163,000

Total Units to be accounted for   173,000

Units accounted for:
Transferred to Baking Department   170,000
In process, April 30   3,000

Total Units accounted for   173,000

Costs

Charged to Production:
In process, April 1 $ 790
April costs:
Direct Materials   17,910
Direct Labor   22,738
Manufacturing Overhead   11,312

Total Processing Costs   51,960

Total costs to be accounted for $ 52,750

Cost allocated as follows:

Transferred to Baking Department
10,000 loaves @ $0.3100   3,100
160,000 loaves @ $0.3080   49,280
In process, April 30
3,000 loaves X 40% @ $0.3080   370

Total costs accounted for $ 52,750

Unit costs April:
$51,960 $\div$ 168,700 = $0.3080

Figure 2.10. Southern Bakers cost of production report.

2.3 INDIRECT COST ALLOCATION

Overhead rates have been discussed earlier as the summation of indirect costs divided by an appropriate base. In many cases the development of overhead rates will require recognition that some overhead cost elements are variable and others are fixed.

Examples of variable overhead costs could include such cost elements as fuel and power, scrap, rework, receiving costs, factory or departmental supplies, premium pay for overtime, and temporary office salaries. Fixed factory overhead could include these cost elements: insurance for plant, property taxes, depreciation of plant and equipment, salaries for plant superintendent and production supervisors, and compensation for indirect labor.

In addition to variable and fixed overhead costs, a third category of overhead costs is semivariable. Examples of these overhead cost elements could include utilities, employer's portion of payroll taxes, maintenance and repair, quality control services, the fringe benefits of employees, and the costs from service departments. Considerable care must be taken by the estimator in the selection of which indirect cost elements are appropriate to each producing department, each service department, and those appropriate for general administration and marketing.

2.3.1 Allocation to Jobs

From the chart of accounts, the indirect cost elements can be determined. The ability to trace the costs incurred and where the costs were incurred inside the organization provides the rationale for assigning overhead cost elements to particular departments. Typical departmental overhead rates would be determined by the analysis of historical costs and designing a predetermined overhead rate for each department. The following table shows how to calculate overhead rates, assuming that the Byers Manufacturing Company has three production departments.

ESTIMATED OVERHEAD

Cost Element	Total	Dept. A	Dept. B	Dept. C
Indirect labor	$ 44,300	$24,100	$12,500	$ 7,700
Depreciation equipment	39,600	28,200	10,000	1,400
Heat, light, power	15,800	12,500	2,400	900
Factory maintenance	11,250	9,250	1,000	1,000
Insurance expired	2,500	1,750	600	150
Factory supplies used	3,900	900	3,000	—
Miscellaneous factory expense	2,650	200	400	2,050
Estimated total factory overhead	$120,000	$76,900	$29,900	$13,200
÷ Estimated direct labor hours	87,000	50,000	32,000	5,000
= Overhead rates		$ 1.54	$ 0.93	$ 2.64

The base for computing the Byers overhead rate was direct labor hours. The selection of direct labor hours was considered appropriate because of the operating characteristics of the departments. It is possible to select a different base for each department. For example, an analysis of the estimated overhead cost elements at Byers shows that depreciation of equipment constitutes approximately 37% of the factory overhead for Department A and 33% for Department B. Depreciation of equipment costs in these percentage amounts could have suggested that machine hours may also be an appropriate base for computing overhead rates.

When the Byers Manufacturing Company's overhead costs are examined and traced, the basis for distribution of each cost element must be determined. In the following table are typical bases for departmental distribution:

Overhead Cost Element	Distribution Factors	Departments A	B	C
Indirect labor	Direct labor	57%	37%	6%
Depreciation equipment	Machinery cost, fraction	2%	2%	1.5%
Heat, power, light	Square feet occupied	79%	15%	6%
Factory maintenance	Maintenance worker hours	82%	9%	9%
Insurance expired	Asset value	70%	24%	6%
Factory supplies used	Quality control hours	23%	77%	—
Miscellaneous factory expense	Number of grade 50 employees	8%	15%	77%

As indicated earlier, the job cost sheets provide a record of the costs for the job. Assume the following data are available:

Direct Materials Placed in Production	A	Departments B	C	Total
Jobs 601	$ 4,000	$14,000	$ 5,000	
602	9,000	8,000	6,000	
603	12,000	9,000	2,000	
604	2,000	7,000	12,000	
605	6,000	2,000	6,000	
Total	$33,000	$40,000	$31,000	$104,000

Direct labor costs				
Jobs 601	$ 7,000	$14,000	$ 5,000	
602	2,000	8,000	3,000	
603	10,000	—	2,000	
604	3,000	10,000	9,000	
605	—	17,000	5,000	
Total	$22,000	$49,000	$24,000	$ 95,000

Assume average rate = $5.00 to convert to direct labor hours

Overhead applied				
Jobs 601	$ 2,156	$ 2,604	$ 2,640	
602	616	1,488	1,584	
603	3,080	—	1,056	
604	924	1,860	4,752	
605	—	3,162	2,640	
Total	$ 6,776	$ 9,114	$12,672	$ 28,562
Department rate used	$ 1.54	$ 0.93	$ 2.64	

If all the jobs started during the period were completed, total costs for each job can now be determined and a job cost summary report prepared as follows:

	Cost Categories			
	Material	Labor	Overhead	Total Job
Jobs 601	$ 23,000	$26,000	$ 7,400	$ 56,400
602	23,000	13,000	3,688	39,688
603	23,000	12,000	4,136	39,136
604	21,000	22,000	7,536	50,536
605	14,000	22,000	5,802	41,802
Total	$104,000	$95,000	$28,562	$227,562

In the previous report it was assumed that actual overhead costs amounted to the same as the estimated overhead costs. This is rarely the case in the real world, and adjustment is generally required.

	Computation		
	Dept. A	Dept. B	Dept. C
Applied overhead	$6,776	$9,114	$12,672
− Actual overhead cost	7,000	9,000	13,000
= Underapplied or (overapplied) overhead	$ 224	$ (114)	$ 328

Since these cost differences are small and represent less than 1% of any job of any department's total cost, the simplest and easiest method is to adjust the cost of goods sold for these differences.

Sometimes the difference between departmental actual overhead costs and estimated costs can be significant. In costing jobs where the departmental overhead is a major portion of total cost, the predetermined overhead rate must be adjusted to align costs more properly to jobs.

Large differences between actual and estimated overhead should be adjusted by prorating the difference and allocating the prorated amounts to work in process, finished goods, and cost of goods sold. Assume that a difference of $5000 is underapplied at the end of an accounting period. Proration might be accomplished as follows:

	Account Balance	Percent of Total		Underapplied		Allocation
Work in process	$ 27,000	27	×	$5,000	=	$1,350
Finished goods	33,000	33	×	$5,000	=	1,650
Cost of goods sold	40,000	40	×	$5,000	=	2,000
Total	$100,000	100				$5,000

When jobs are not complete at the end of the accounting period, their material, labor, and overhead costs are shown on the job cost summary report, but the report is annotated to reflect incomplete jobs. The total cost of all incompleted jobs should be equal to the total cost shown in the work in process inventory account after the cost of completed jobs has been transferred to finished goods inventory, in other words, the ending balance.

The job summary report must be modified slightly when there are incomplete jobs carried into the next accounting period. The modification is to add a beginning of month column showing those costs charged in the previous accounting period.

2.3.2 Allocation of Service Department Overhead

Most of the methods previously discussed are applicable in the allocation of overhead for service departments. The service department will have its own direct materials, direct labor, and indirect costs such as utilities, indirect materials, repairs, depreciation, and taxes. Indirect or overhead costs would be distributed to service departments using the same basis for distribution as used for producing departments. For example, if the basis for distribution of utilities is square feet of space occupied, the service department would be allocated its portion of the total utilities cost based on the amount of square footage occupied.

It is important to recognize that some service departments may provide support only to the factory portion of the organization. Other service departments may serve both the factory and the general administration and marketing offices.

In either case, the basis for allocating the total costs (direct or indirect) of a service department should be the relative usage made of the service department. Another way of expressing this is that the allocation should be based on the level of activity in the service department created by the departments served. For example, the Purchasing Department at Byers Manufacturing provides acquisition and contract administrative services for factory requirements of three departments: marketing department, controller's department, and the administrative office.

Assume that the Purchasing Department has direct and indirect costs for the month of August of $30,000. During the month the department processed a total of 300 procurement requirements at an average cost of $100 per procurement. The Purchasing Department's activity report shows which segments of the organization received their service. Using the average procurement cost for August, they would allocate their total costs to the departments served:

Department Served	Activity Level	Monthly Rate	Monthly Allocation
Factory Dept. A	125	$100	$12,500
Factory Dept. B	115	100	11,500
Factory Dept. C	40	100	4,000
Marketing	10	100	1,000
Controller	3	100	300
Administration	7	100	700
Total	300		$30,000

The cost estimator will note that the Purchasing Department's allocation of its cost is a first tier in the allocation of service department costs. Marketing, controller, and administration are also service departments, but second tier. Their costs must be reallocated to producing departments.

If a solid basis can be found for allocating each of the second-tier department costs, then activity levels may be used to reallocate the second-tier costs. Generally, it is difficult to find suitable bases for using activity levels appropriate to the service being provided. This difficulty results in costs for the marketing, controller, and administration departments being pooled into a common overhead cost center and the pooled costs reallocated to production departments. A unit of production or sales units may be used.

Here we assume Byers costs were: Marketing, $48,000; Controller, $27,000; Administration, $25,000. This service overhead cost pool totals $100,000.

Units of Production	August Rate	Cost Pool Allocation to Departments
1700	$20	$ 34,000
1800	20	36,000
1500	20	30,000
Total 5000		$100,000

At this stage all of the costs, direct and indirect, have been allocated and assigned to production departments, and at the end of an accounting period the production departments prepare a production cost report. The report used by Byers illustrates a usable format:

PRODUCTION COST REPORT

MONTH: AUGUST 19_____

DEPARTMENT A

Cost summary:		
Direct materials		$225,000
Direct labor		$387,500
Production department overhead		
Indirect materials	$29,000	
Indirect labor	12,000	
Utilities	4,900	
Depreciation	8,500	
Taxes	1,600	
Allocation from purchasing	12,500	68,500
Allocation from cost pool		34,000
Total monthly costs		$715,000

2.3.3 Allocation in Process Costing Systems

The nature of the process costing system creates requirements for special cost methods in certain situations. For sequential process organizations, any indirect cost will be assigned to the department incurring the cost or allocated to the process department using a rationale basis. At the end of an accounting period, the total costs of the process department are either (1) assigned to the work in process inventory or (2) transferred out to the next process department. The division of the total costs is based on equivalent units of production discussed earlier.

Although a general characteristic of process manufacturing is sequential processing, a single processing department might find that at a definite point in manufacturing it is practical to splitoff and create two or more *individual products.* *Joint product costs* are the costs accumulated before the split-off point. Industries where this is common are dairies, chemicals, petroleum refining, and flour milling.

Up to the split-off point, all the costs are costs common to the separate products created after the split-off point. To determine the cost of products, it is necessary to allocate the joint product costs between the several products, and then to add any costs incurred by further processing of the products. A lumber mill processes timber initially by removal of the outer bark from logs. Additional processing creates one-, two-, four-, six-, eight-inch thicknesses of varying lengths. The bark removal process is a joint product cost for creating one-inch shelving, 2×4's, 4×4's, and similar products.

The most common method used for allocating joint product costs is the sales value of the final products created. MacFarland Mill in November had joint costs of \$90,000 in producing 10,000 units of Product Sloan and 50,000 units of Product Terry. Sloan sells for \$5 per unit and Terry sells for \$2 per unit. The allocation would be as follows:

$$\text{Product Sloan} \quad \frac{50,000}{150,000} \times \$90,000 = \$30,000$$

$$\text{Product Terry} \quad \frac{100,000}{150,000} \times \$90,000 = \underline{\$60,000}$$

$$\text{Total joint product costs} \; \underline{\underline{\$90,000}}$$

A lumber mill typically has leftover materials from its processing. Sawdust and wood scraps are common. These items may have little value in relation to the principal wood products. Such products are called *by-products.*

The cost assigned to a by-product is the sales value. When additional processing is required to create the salable by-product, such as transforming scrap wood into wood chips for waferboard, these costs must be added to any cost estimate.

Assume that only sawdust is created as a by-product. The work in process inventory should be reduced by the sales value, now cost value, of the sawdust. The work in process account is decreased, and the finished goods inventory account is increased.

Some industries find that changes in technology and market factors cause by-products to become principal products. Under these circumstances, cost estimation must be adjusted to the organization's purposes.

2.4 COST CONTROL UTILIZING STANDARDS

The job order and the process costing systems are designed to determine for estimators, managers, and auditors the actual unit and total cost of products and services. Such cost data are useful in controlling costs and seeking to achieve the highest possible profit level.

Another type of cost system is used that links budgeting procedures with detailed estimates of the various cost elements in manufacturing. The accounting mechanism of these systems calls for the establishment of a standard for each cost element, called a *standard cost*.

Budgets are constructed using standard costs, which helps managers to determine the amount a product should cost. At the end of the accounting period, the standard costs are compared with the actual costs and variances are analyzed. Standard costs can be used in conjunction with job order and process costing systems.

2.4.1 Material Standards

Material cost standards are developed by first establishing the specification for each item of direct material to be incorporated into the product. Organizations selecting certain materials for product use typically use specifications designed by industry or professional groups. In other cases, material specifications may be established by the customer. For example, a military standard, MIL-STD, may be designated for materials used in a Department of Defense (DOD) contract. The MIL-STD may specify that the materials be able to withstand certain temperature extremes, and so on.

The cost estimator should recognize that the requirements in a material specification are especially important since each requirement generally adds cost to the material. Unnecessary requirements included in material specifications can increase costs, make acquisition (procurement) more difficult, and restrict the use of substitute or alternate materials.

Once the material specifications are decided, the product design will dictate the amount of each material to be used in a single unit or product. When the product is complex, a complete *bill of materials*, or listing of all product materials and amounts for each material item in each subassembly, is indicated.

Material budgets will typically be constructed by working backward through the budgetary process. The sales estimate will show the number of units and dollar amounts projected for the budget period. A decision will be made for the desired level of ending inventory. These two factors will determine the number of product units needed. The quantity to be produced is determined by deducting the quantity on hand at the beginning of the period. Byer Manufacturing budgets its materials on a quarterly and annual basis as follows:

MATERIALS PURCHASE BUDGET

Material: Product Sloan 2A Cloth	1Q	2Q	3Q	4Q	Year
Desired ending inventory	6,200	7,250	4,650	4,200	4,200
Material usage—Prod. Sch. V	9,500	27,000	32,250	19,250	88,000
Total needs	15,700	34,250	36,900	23,450	92,200
Beginning inventory deduct	5,000	5,200	7,250	4,650	5,000
Purchase requirements unit	10,700	29,050	29,650	18,800	88,200
Estimated unit standard price	$ 0.50	$ 0.50	$ 0.50	$ 0.50	$ 0.50
Total purchases	$ 5,350	$14,525	$14,825	$ 9,400	$44,100

From the bill of materials, one can determine that two yards of cloth are required for each unit of Product Sloan. Using standard costs, the direct material quantity and price standard can be constructed by consulting the production budget to determine the quantity to be produced. Assume the following data:

material quantity standard:

number production units $\times$ standard quantity/unit

$$44,000 \times 2 = 88,000 \text{ yards}$$

material price standard:

standard quantity/unit $\times$ standard price/unit $=$ standard cost product unit

$$2 \times \$0.50 = \$1.00$$

In the establishment of direct material quantity standards, consideration should always be given to allowances for unavoidable waste, but caution should be used in providing allowances for avoidable waste since this would increase total cost. Similarly, in the establishment of the direct material price standard, purchasing department experience, overall economic conditions, and the number of qualified suppliers would all be considered in estimating a standard price for the future period. Both standards must be reviewed periodically to validate their accuracy and reasonableness. All items in the standard should be carefully selected to increase the accuracy when standard costs are projected into future periods.

2.4.2 Labor Standards

When considering the establishment of standards for direct labor, the human dimension of work requires inclusion of time for more than actual work time. Generally, some level of operating efficiency is assumed, and actual work time is enhanced by reasonable time allowances for work breaks, shift changes, safety meetings, and similar activities essential to recognized available operating time.

Efficiency levels for individual skills are frequently determined by periodic industrial engineering studies called MTM (methods–time measurement). Such studies may be supplemented by work sampling. Also important in establishment of labor standards are the labor specifications. Labor specifications indicate the job requirements for individuals. Job requirements would include physical requirements, mental abilities needed, physical coordination, specific skill, and speed performance required.

Many manufacturing processes are performed by groups of individuals. In these cases the labor standards will specify the skill mix necessary for completing the part or product.

Different skills are typically costed at rates of pay commensurate with the skill level. Organizations tend to establish pay scales and thus labor rates based on comparable skills. Union pay scales in a particular trade may be different from nonunion pay scales. Frequently the pay scale may be set for the organization by the prevailing wages paid for similar work by other manufacturers or service companies in the local area.

The cost estimator will find the direct labor standards, called labor rate standards (price for wages), and the labor efficiency standards are more sensitive to local conditions than are generally thought. The skill mix of a competitor may be different because the competitor can achieve an acceptable efficiency with lower-skilled individuals.

Using the labor efficiency data from previous studies, it is possible to establish what output can be expected per unit of labor. A unit of labor in this instance may be a single individual or a group. Costing the unit of labor by application of a standard rate serves to establish the dollar labor standard per unit of output. For example, if three direct labor hours are required per product, and the standard labor rate is $5 per hour, then the unit labor standard would be $15.

The direct labor budget is basically a schedule, similar to the one that follows:

BYERS MANUFACTURING
DIRECT LABOR BUDGET
DIRECT LABOR HOURS (DLH)

Product	Std Hours	1Q	2Q	3Q	4Q	Total
A	3.0	7,000	9,000	12,000	10,000	38,000
B	2.5	14,000	18,000	37,000	22,000	91,000
C	4.0	11,000	13,000	17,000	12,500	53,500
Total DLH		32,000	40,000	66,000	44,500	182,500
Total dollars ($5/DLH)		$160,000	200,000	330,000	22,500	912,500

Where the labor skills involve group performance per unit of product versus individual skill rates, the labor rate is called a *composite rate*.

2.4.3 Flexible Budgeting

Most of the discussion thus far has been toward formulation of estimates for budgetary purposes, and the implication has been that a single one-time budget or static budget is prepared. The static budget with a standard cost system would be based on a *standard volume of activity*. The standard volume of activity typically is set below the activity level utilizing the full capacity of the organization.

Organizations rarely plan to full capacity because managers recognize that operating at the 100% level for extended periods of time is not always the most efficient and profitable. A standard volume of activity below 100% is the rule rather than the exception. The planning may visualize a volume of activity at 85% of capacity as its standard volume of activity for budget and cost standards. Such a level recognizes that performance evaluation should be based on the capability to sustain performance rather than measuring wide peaks and valleys.

The use of the standard volume activity level as a budgeting tool generally results in organizations establishing flexible budgets instead of static ones. A *flexible budget* recognizes several possible activity levels and adjusts the manufacturing overhead cost elements based on different activity levels. If the semivariables have already been separated into their fixed and variable components, then only the variable costs in the manufacturing overhead will need adjustment.

A flexible budget can be constructed by preparing a series of fixed budgets for projected possible activity levels that the organization might attain (1000, 1200, 1400, 1600 machine hours, etc.). Another approach to flexible budgeting is to change the base in the predetermined overhead rate equation. The estimated cost base is changed to adjust the variable cost to a series of discrete levels or to an equation consisting of manufacturing overhead fixed costs plus a variable cost rate per unit utilized.

Byers Manufacturing finds its executives prefer that departments use discrete levels for flexible budgeting:

BYERS MANUFACTURING
DEPARTMENT—OVERHEAD BUDGET

Machine Hours	1000	1100	1200	1300	1400	1500
Variable costs	3,500	3,850	4,200	4,550	4,900	5,250
Fixed costs	6,500	6,500	6,500	6,500	6,500	6,500
Total budget	$10,000	10,350	10,700	11,050	11,400	11,750

At the end of each accounting period the budget for the activity level attained is compared with the actual costs incurred. This is performed for each cost element included in manufacturing overhead. A simple four-column report showing the cost element, the budgeted amount, the actual amount, and the differences is commonly used.

2.5 ANALYZING PERFORMANCE BY COST

Standard cost systems carry with their use the obligation to compare actual cost performance with the performance established by the standard. Differences between standard costs and actual costs are called *variances*. The total variance in a period is often a composite of several individual variances.

2.5.1 Variance Analysis

To illustrate variance analysis, assume that Byers Manufacturing has the following standards:

    Product Sloan
       Material: 2 yards per product unit at $0.50 per yard
       Labor: 3 direct labor hours at $5 per hour
       Overhead: $1.25 per direct labor hour
       July production: 8000 units

Actual costs for the 8100 units produced in the month of July were: material purchases of 17,000 yards for $8840; material issued to production, 16,500 yards; labor, 25,000 hours costing $126,250; and overhead costs amounted to $31,000. Variance computations are as follows:

    Material price variance:

$$
\begin{array}{lll}
\text{actual quantity} \times \text{actual price} & & \\
\text{17,000 yards} \times & \$0.52 & = \$8840 \\
\text{actual quantity} \times \text{standard price} & & \\
\text{17,000 yards} \times & \$0.50 & = \underline{8500} \\
\text{material price variance} & & \$\ 340
\end{array}
$$

Note: The material price variance is based on the actual quantity purchased. Generally, the purchasing department is responsible for the material price variance.

Material quantity variance:

$$
\begin{array}{lll}
\text{actual quantity} & \times \text{ standard price} & \\
16{,}500 \text{ yards} & \times \qquad \$0.50 & = \$8250 \\
\text{standard quantity} & \times \text{ standard price} & \\
(8100 \times 2 \text{ yds}) & \times \qquad \$0.50 & = \underline{\quad 8100} \\
\text{Material quantity variance} & & \$ \ 150
\end{array}
$$

Note: Actual production units were used, thus adjusting amounts under flexible budgeting. Under static budgeting, the planned production of 8000 units would be used.

Labor rate variance:

$$
\begin{array}{lll}
\text{actual hours of input} & \times \text{ actual rate} & \\
25{,}000 \text{ hours} & \times \qquad \$5.05 & = \$126{,}250 \\
\text{actual hours of input} & \times \text{ standard rate} & \\
25{,}000 \text{ hours} & \times \qquad \$5.00 & = \underline{\quad 125{,}000} \\
\text{labor rate variance} & & \$ \ 1{,}250
\end{array}
$$

Labor efficiency variance:

$$
\begin{array}{lll}
\text{actual hours of input} & \times \text{ standard rate} & \\
25{,}000 \text{ hours} & \times \qquad \$5.00 & = \$125{,}000 \\
\text{standard hours for output} & \times \text{ standard rate} & \\
(8100 \text{ units} \times 3 \text{ DLH}) & \times \qquad \$5.00 & = \underline{\quad 121{,}500} \\
\text{labor efficiency variance} & & \$ \ 3{,}500
\end{array}
$$

Overhead spending variance:

$$
\begin{array}{lll}
\text{actual DLH} & \times \text{ actual overhead rate} & \\
25{,}000 \text{ hours} & \times \qquad \$1.24 & = \$ \ 31{,}250 \\
\text{standard DLH for output} & \times \text{ standard overhead rate} & \\
(8100 \times 3 \text{ hours}) & \times \qquad \$1.25 & = \underline{\quad 30{,}375} \\
\text{Overhead efficiency variance} & & \$ \quad 875
\end{array}
$$

The computation of the individual variances is the beginning point of understanding why the actual total costs exceeded the planned costs using standards. The differences to be analyzed and explained are as follows:

Cost Element	Budgeted Standard Cost	Actual Cost	Total Variance
Direct material	$ 8,100	$ 8,840	$ 740
Direct labor	121,500	126,250	4,750
Manufacturing overhead	30,375	31,000	625
Total manufacturing	$159,975	$166,090	$6,115

The total cost variance is unfavorable since it exceeds standard costs for the budget period. This unfavorable variance (U) after analysis can be explained from the cost data as follows:

Material price variance	$ 340 U
An additional two cents above standard was paid for the 17,000 yards purchased.	
Material quantity variance	150 U
Usage exceeded standard by 300 yards at $0.50 standard price.	
Labor rate variance	1250 U
An average of five cents above standard was paid for the 25,000 DLH used.	
Labor efficiency variance	3500 U
An additional 700 DLH above standard was used in production at $5.00 standard rate.	
Overhead spending variance	250 F
Actual costs for overhead averaged one cent less than standard for the 25,000 DLH allocation base.	
Overhead efficiency variance	875 U
The increase of 700 DLH added to overhead costs at the predetermined rate of $1.25/DLH.	
Inventory change	250 U
Inventory increased 500 yards at standard cost, $0.50/yard.	
Total cost variance	$6115

Normally, the production departments would provide detailed analyses of the material quantity variance, labor rate variance, and the labor efficiency variance. Material quantity variances could arise for a variety of reasons, such as malfunction of equipment, improperly marked rolled yardage, end-of-roll losses because of nonstandard lengths, rejection of material not up to the quality standard. Labor rate variances are in the hands of production supervisors where labor skill mix in actual production increases cost. Absenteeism may require substitution of higher-skilled individuals for lower-skill jobs. The labor efficiency variance may result from lower production caused by the introduction of new employees to the production line. The morale of employees could result in a "slowdown" in performance. The lack of proper training, quality control rejects and rework, and the inexperience of first line supervisors can all contribute to increased direct labor hour usage.

2.5.2 Break-Even Analysis

Each organization has the requirement to determine, through cost estimation, the point at which its projected revenues and those costs expiring during the period are exactly equal. This point is known as the *break-even point*. Operating volumes below this point will result in a loss, and volumes above this point will result in profit.

The break-even point can be determined by several approaches. Figure 2.11 illustrates a graphical approach to break-even. Operating data in terms of costs and sales revenues are shown on the vertical axis. The various production volumes or capacity levels are spread along the horizontal axis. Fixed costs for the relevant

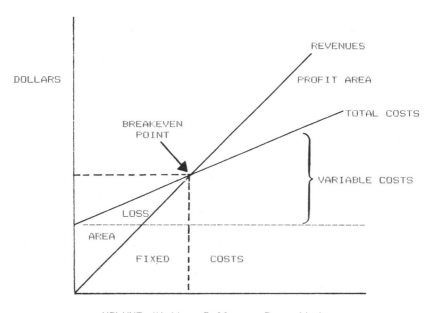

Figure 2.11. Break-even chart.

range are entered as a straight horizontal cost line. The variable costs are plotted above the fixed costs line, thus creating a total cost line, since graphically these variable costs for each volume level are being added to the fixed costs. The revenue or sales for the volume levels is then plotted from the point of origin. Where the revenue line intersects the total cost line is the break-even point. Costs at break-even can be read by projecting a horizontal line to the vertical axis from the break-even point, and volume can be read by dropping a perpendicular to the horizontal axis.

Again, in the graphical approach to break-even, only fixed and variable costs are plotted. This approach assumes that any semivariable costs incurred or anticipated have been broken down into their fixed and variable components, and these components have been added to other truly fixed and variable costs.

A simple mathematical approach can also be taken to determine the break-even point. The concept of total costs being exactly equal can be restated as follows:

$$\text{revenue} - \text{variable costs} - \text{fixed costs} = \text{zero} \tag{2.5}$$

(as a perecentage
of revenue or
total for the
revenue level)

The preceding equation will yield a result in dollars. To determine break-even units, the dollars must be divided by an average unit sale price.

The simplicity of this mathematical approach to break-even gives it widespread usage. The equation also serves as a computational method for estimating the sales volume required to produce a specific operating income objective. Instead of using zero in the equation, the operating income dollar amount is used, and the equation is changed slightly to read:

$$\text{revenue} = \text{variable costs} + \text{fixed costs} + \text{operating income} \tag{2.6}$$

A third approach to break-even uses an analytical technique called the contribution margin or marginal efficiency. *Contribution margin* (CM) is the excess of revenues over the variable costs. It is the amount of dollars available to cover the fixed costs and to produce profit. Mathematically it is:

$$\text{CM} = \text{revenue (R)} - \text{variable costs (VC)} \tag{2.7}$$

Break-even can be determined utilizing CM on a unit basis or a dollar basis. On a unit basis, this equation is used:

$$\text{break-even} = \frac{\text{sum of fixed costs}}{(\text{unit sales price}) - (\text{variable costs per unit sold})} \tag{2.8}$$

or algebraically:

$$BEP_u = \frac{FC}{p - VC} \quad \text{or} \quad \frac{FC}{\text{unit CM}} \qquad (2.9)$$

On a dollar basis, the contribution margin is converted to a CM ratio. The *CM ratio* is contribution margin expressed as a percentage of revenue:

$$\text{CM ratio} = 1 - \frac{VC}{R} \qquad (2.10)$$

Break-even point in dollars is determined by the equation:

$$BEP = \frac{\text{fixed cost}}{\text{CM ratio}} \qquad (2.11)$$

It is now obvious to the cost estimator that tools such as the various approaches for determining break-even permit the estimator to solve numerous problem situations found in the typical organization. The impact on break-even of changes in price, additions to fixed costs, and volume adjustments can be quickly measured.

When an organization receives its revenue from two or more products or services, the break-even point will vary with the proportion each product or service contributes to the whole. The relative proportion is frequently called the *sales mix*. To compute a break-even for this type organization, a weighted average CM is developed.

Assume that the organization has two services provided on a time basis.

	Programming	Systems Analysis
Price	$38.00	$40.00
Variable cost	20.00	28.00
Unit CM	$18.00	$12.00
Sales mix	75%	25%

The weighted average unit CM is computed as:

$$\text{unit CM} = (\$18)\,(0.75) + (\$12)\,(0.25) = \$16.50$$

If the organization has monthly fixed costs of $99,000, then the break-even point is:

$$\$99,000 \,/\, \$16.50 = 6000 \text{ time units}$$

These time units can be divided by the sales mix proportion to determine the unit break-even points:

programming: 6000 units $\times$ 75%   = 4500 time units

systems analysis: 6000 units $\times$ 25% = $\underline{1500}$

6000 time units

The cost estimator in the multiproduct organization recognizes that approaching break-even as just described carries the assumption that the sales mix is not going to change during the planning period. If the sales mix changes in actual operations, the break-even will also change.

All estimators and managers recognize that the best estimate can result in differences when measured against actual results. A common concern in the use of cost and revenue data for budget preparation and determination of break-even is the degree to which the planning can be in error before losses will occur.

Estimators can use the *margin of safety* method to answer this type of concern and to measure the degree of risk. The margin of safety is the difference between budgeted revenue and break-even revenue expressed as a percent of budgeted revenue. The equation is

$$\text{margin of safety} = \frac{\text{budgeted revenue} - \text{break-even revenue}}{\text{budgeted revenue}} \quad (2.12)$$

If budgeted revenue were $25,000 and break-even revenue is $20,000, the margin of safety is 20%:

$$\frac{\$25,000 - \$20,000}{\$25,000} = 20\%$$

Stated differently, budgeted revenues could decline by 20% before the organization would experience operating losses.

2.5.3 Differential Analysis

Many of the decisions requiring cost estimation are those in which there must be a choice from among alternatives, for example, weapon system A or B, manufacture the part in-house or purchase from a vendor, sell the product at this stage of processing or process it further. Fundamentally, these problem situations are common to many organizations but do not recur regularly. They are nonroutine, and, because they are nonroutine, only those costs that are relevant should be considered in the decision. *Relevant costs* are any costs that are present under one alternative but are absent, either in whole or in part, under another alternative. Relevant costs are frequently called *differential costs*. Differential costs present both the cost increases and cost decreases between alternatives.

To perform a proper analysis of alternatives, the estimator will need to gather the cost data appropriate to each alternative. The data collected should then be analyzed and two types of cost data removed or discarded. Costs that are the same for each alternative do not contribute to the decision because they provide no comparative difference. Costs that have already been incurred and cannot be changed by the decision currently or in the future are *sunk costs*. These costs are not relevant since they provide no differential and should be discarded. The residual cost data will show clearly the true differences in alternatives and provide a sound basis for nonroutine decisions.

Consider the problem of whether to manufacture a part or to buy the part from a vendor. SDE Corporation has identified a vendor who will supply the part for $7.80. SDE has the following costs:

Direct costs:		
Material	$2.28	
Labor ($\frac{3}{4}$ hour)	2.90	
		$5.18
Indirect costs:		
Fixed manufacturing overhead	$1.80	
Variable		
Manufacturing overhead—		
50% of direct labor	1.45	
		3.25
Total cost		$8.43

In comparing the vendor price we would want first to eliminate any irrelevant cost from the SDE data. The fixed manufacturing overhead cost of $1.80 will be incurred whether the part is purchased or manufactured. Eliminating the fixed manufacturing overhead cost because it is identical for each alternative (make or buy) results in the following:

Cost if purchased	$7.80
Incremental costs, if manufactured	6.63
Cost savings, if manufactured	$1.17

Manufacturing the part provides a $1.17 contribution toward SDE Corporation's fixed costs. If the part were purchased, the contribution would be lost.

SDE managers also must decide if they should sell Product Terry as it is manufactured at present or process the product further and sell the enhanced version at a higher price. The initial sale price is $300, and the enhanced version commands a price of $345. Differential revenue is $45 per unit. The sales volume estimate is 5000 units, regardless of which version is produced. Further processing costs are as follows:

Additional material ($20 per unit)	$100,000
Additional labor ($10 per unit)	50,000
Additional variable manufacturing overhead (50% of direct labor)	25,000
Additional fixed manufacturing overhead—equipment depreciation four-year life	25,000
Imputed interest Special equipment $100,000 at 12% interest	12,000
Total further processing cost	$212,000

The final analysis requires comparing the differential revenue with differential (additional) costs:

Total further processing cost	$212,000
Differential revenue	200,000
Loss if further processing is accomplished	$ 12,000

Differential analysis can also be used in pricing decisions. By comparing the price for each practical production volume, the point that differential revenue equals differential cost is the production level affording the highest net income. Examine the following table:

Production Level (units)	Average Price	Unit Cost	Total Revenue	Total Cost	Differential Revenue	Differential Cost	Net Income
4,000	$30	36	120,000	144,000			(24,000)
6,000	28	28	168,000	168,000	48,000	24,000	0
8,000	26	24	208,000	192,000	40,000	24,000	16,000
10,000	24	21	240,000	210,000	32,000	18,000	30,000
12,000	22	19	264,000	228,000	24,000	18,000	36,000
14,000	20	18	280,000	252,000	14,000	24,000	28,000

At a production level of 12,000 units, net income reaches its highest point. Above the 12,000 unit level, net income declines. When the average price is $22 and volume is 12,000 units, conditions are at their optimum.

SDE Corporation has been approached by a foreign company to purchase 1000 units of Product Terry at a price of $225 per unit. At this time, the company has unused capacity and could accept the order. The price offered by the foreign company is below SDE's regular price. The problem is should SDE accept the order when its costs are as follows:

> Product Terry: unit cost
>
> | | |
> |---|---|
> | Direct materials | $ 89.00 |
> | Direct labor | 60.00 |
> | Variable manufacturing overhead cost | 30.00 |
> | Fixed manufacturing overhead cost | 50.00 |
> | $250,000 ÷ 5,000 units | |
> | Total unit cost | $229.00 |

In this special order problem, differential analysis using the contribution margin is desirable as follows:

> | | |
> |---|---|
> | Foreign order unit price | $225 |
> | Variable costs: | |
> | (DM, $89; DL, $60; OH, $30) | 179 |
> | Contribution margin | $ 46 |

SDE should accept the foreign company order since the offering price covers all variable costs and makes a $46 contribution to fixed costs. The fixed manufacturing costs are not relevant to this decision, and only the direct costs should be considered.

2.5.4 Profit Relationship of Segments

Cost allocation in the decentralized organization requires the analysis of portions or segments. In the multiproduct company, costs are presented by product lines or divisions depending on the organizational structure.

The preferred method for allocating costs in these organizations is the contribution margin approach. SDE has two divisions representing its major marketing territories. Assume the following data are available for the division:

	Divisions		
	Eastern	Western	Company Total
Revenue	$200,000	$250,000	$450,000
Less: variable manufacturing expenses	−80,000	−100,000	−180,000
Manufacturing margin	$120,000	$150,000	$270,000
Less: variable selling expenses	20,000	30,000	50,000
Variable administration expenses	25,000	30,000	55,000
Total	−45,000	−60,000	−105,000
Contribution margin	$ 75,000	$ 90,000	$165,000

| | Divisions | | |
	Eastern	Western	Company Total
Less: direct fixed expenses			
Manufacturing	$ 20,000	24,000	44,000
Selling	18,000	20,000	38,000
Administrative	5,000	6,000	11,000
Total	–43,000	–50,000	–93,000
Divisional margin	$ 32,000	$ 40,000	$ 72,000
Less common expenses:			
Manufacturing			$ 16,000
Selling			17,000
Administrative			14,000
Total			–47,000
Net income before interest and taxes			$ 25,000

Earlier in the contribution margin approach all variable costs were lumped together and deducted from the revenues to determine the contribution margin. With segment reporting of costs, it is necessary to expand the presentation to reflect (1) the manufacturing margin, (2) total variable selling and administrative costs directly traceable to the division, (3) fixed expenses directly traceable to divisions, and (4) isolation of those common costs beyond the control of divisional managers. These later costs must be controlled at the company level.

The Eastern and Western divisions both provide a divisional margin of 16% of revenues. The Western division has revenue 25% higher than Eastern's. Its variable costs are 1.5% higher than Eastern, and its direct fixed expenses are 1.5% lower than Eastern's. The cost differences may merit closer examination with the idea of increasing profitability by establishing cost objectives associated with the lower cost percentages achieved by one of the divisions.

If Western division could lower its variable costs to 62.5% of revenue, and if Eastern could lower its direct fixed costs to 20% of revenue, the company net income would increase to $31,750, representing a 27% increase.

Segment reports are useful when the organization is considering whether to discontinue a product, territory, or profit center. The contribution margin approach provides the format for computation of the product margin, territory margin, or profit center margin.

In the computation of the product margin, it is more difficult to identify and isolate the direct fixed expenses traceable to a product. Direct fixed expenses at the divisional level may not be direct fixed expenses at the product level. The general operating expenses of the division will generally be common to all products. With product level segment reporting it will be normal for a significant portion of total costs to be classified as common costs. Any costs that benefit two or more segments at a lower level are common costs, unless amounts can be directly traced to a particular segment.

When an organization is considering discontinuing a product, division, or territory, the segment margin becomes significant. Consider the following hypothetical situation:

HILL & COMPANY
INCOME STATEMENT (PARTIAL)

	Product Segments			Company Total
	A	B	C	
Revenue	$60,000	$40,000	$20,000	$120,000
Variable costs	30,000	20,000	10,000	60,000
Contribution margin	30,000	20,000	10,000	60,000
Depreciation expense	10,000	8,000	15,000	33,000
Segment and company income	$20,000	12,000	(–5,000)	$ 27,000

Product C produces a loss of $5000, and initially the cost estimator may wish to recommend discontinuance. However, if the cost element depreciation expense allocated to Product C will be present even if Product C is discontinued, then Product C should be retained. Stated differently, unless the $15,000 depreciation expense charged to Product C is no longer applicable, this amount will have to be absorbed by Products A and B, and overall company income will drop from $27,000 to $12,000.

Segment reports are primarily for internal management use. There is, however, for the diversified multidivisional organization, a trend to show segment data in the annual reports of publicly held companies.

2.5.5 Profit of the Company

Profit performance of individual segments is measured by their segment income in relation to assets utilized to generate that amount of income. Assume that divisional SDE's Eastern and Western division margins were $32,000 and $40,000 as shown in the earlier table.

	Total Company	Divisions	
		Eastern	Western
Divisional and company income	$25,000	$32,000	$40,000
÷ Asset base	485,000	225,000	260,000
= Return on investment	5.15%	14.22%	15.38%

The performance of divisions for a single period should be compared to those of prior periods to determine if performance is on a positive trend. At the company level it can be expected that total company performance will be lower than an average of the divisions because of the significant amount of common costs that cannot be traced to a particular division.

Segment and company performance may also establish a standard of performance such as a minimum acceptable rate for the return on investment. An organization's cost of capital frequently is used as the minimum standard. An excess of net income (divisional margin) over the minimum acceptable rate is called *residual income*. Residual income levels are sometimes used to designate "superior performance" and to trigger added compensation for managers. Using the earlier data, residual income would be calculated as follows:

	Total Company	Divisions	
		Eastern	Western
Asset base	$485,000	$225,000	$260,000
× Minimum acceptable rate	5%	12%	12%
= Minimum acceptable income	24,250	27,000	31,200
Actual income	25,000	32,000	40,000
= residual income	$ 750	$ 5,000	$ 8,800

On the basis of these figures, SDE's Western division's performance may be considered "superior performance," and the Eastern division could be rated as "above average performance." For the company as a whole, the low residual income would result in management concentrating attention on the common costs. Any minor increases in the components of the common costs could accumulate and result in the company's not meeting its minimum acceptable income level.

Return on investment (ROI) is defined as operating revenues divided by operating costs. Alternatively, return on investment is also margin multipled by asset turnover, where

$$\text{margin} = \frac{\text{operating income}}{\text{revenue}} \qquad (2.13)$$

and

$$\text{turnover} = \frac{\text{revenue}}{\text{operating assets}} \qquad (2.14)$$

Therefore a particular ROI can be achieved by a variety of combinations of margin times turnover, as follows:

Possible Performance	Margin (%)	×	Turnover	=	ROI (%)
(1)	6	×	2	=	12
(2)	5	×	2.4	=	12
(3)	4	×	3	=	12
(4)	3	×	4	=	12
(5)	2	×	6	=	12

Recognition that a weak margin can be offset by strong turnover is an essential element in judging the profit performance of an organization. For the cost estimator there must be an awareness that margins can be increased by reducing expenses, increasing sales at a faster pace than expenses, or reducing costs. Margin is a measure of efficiency or profitability, whereas turnover measures how well the organization utilizes (manages) its assets.

Many organizations budget to achieve a profit objective by establishing a desired rate of return and cost-plus pricing. Assume that SDE anticipates a normal annual volume of 60,000 units for one of its products. The product unit costs are $30, the estimated operating assets to be utilized are $800,000, and the estimated costs for selling and expenses total $140,000. SDE would establish its selling price using this method, assuming a desired rate of return of 20%:

Desired rate of return	
(20% × $800,000)	$ 160,000
Estimated selling and administrative	
expenses	140,000
Total	$ 300,000
Cost to manufacture	
(60,000 units × $30)	$1,800,000

Required markup = $300,000/1,800,000 = 16\frac{2}{3}\%$

Pricing:

Cost to manufacture	$ 30
Markup ($30 × $16\frac{2}{3}\%$)	5
Target selling price	$ 35

Where all costs are included in the pricing decisions, the organization is said to employ *full cost pricing*. In the earlier example of whether the company should accept the foreign order, only the direct costs were considered in determining whether the offering price was satisfactory. The contribution margin approach to pricing can be used only for short-run price decisions where fixed cost can be temporarily ignored.

When an organization possesses unused capacity and is considering additional production, it can price the additional units below the price necessary to cover total costs and desired profit. Initial production will cover the fixed costs, and profit may be maximized by selling additional units at a price less than full cost pricing. Market conditions will dictate whether the additional units can be disposed of in a manner so as not to jeopardize the initial production price. Pricing by this method is *differential cost pricing*, where only variable costs are considered as the levels of activity change beyond the initial full cost absorption production level. Periodically, organizations will make decisions that result in capital expenditures with the view that the inflow from such expenditures will exceed the investment cost. Capital expenditures could be new product lines, more efficient equipment, additional production capacity, or quality improvements of existing products. All of these types of expenditures are intended to increase the net income for the organization. The cash inflows from these expenditures are expected to extend over a fairly long time.

Since cash flows are estimates, the reliability of the estimated flows is an important factor in judging whether or not to undertake the investment. Over time, it is the sum of the various capital investment decisions that increases or decreases the organization's profitability.

The real measure of profitability is the ability of the organization to add increments of profit annually. These increments show profit growth, but the estimator should regularly compare profit levels of the organization with levels achieved by other companies in the same industry. An organization could be regularly increasing profits but falling behind when compared with similar companies offering like products or services.

In a free enterprise economy, it is the duty of managers to earn the highest possible profit level in relation to overall goals and objectives. Profit is essential to the well-being of the organization and to the society it serves. Profit levels over time in a society determine its standard of living and the savings rate, which permits reinvestment to sustain continued existence. The development of rational cost allocation processes allows the cost estimator to play a major role in the long-term survival of the organization.

3

STATISTICAL TECHNIQUES IN COST ESTIMATION

RICHARD M. WYSKIDA, PHD, PE

3.1 INTRODUCTION

Statistical methods are a very ancient means of treating information. However, analytical statistical techniques, together with the breadth of data collected, are recent developments. Statistical techniques can be said to parallel the general procedures of the scientific method. However, misconceptions about statistical techniques abound, largely because practitioners have not been exposed to the scientific method on a continuing basis.

In general, statistics deals with the description, analysis, and interpretation of data that are subject to errors of measurement and prediction. The cost estimation arena is a prime user of statistical techniques, since data analysis and data interpretation precede the development of any meaningful and valid cost estimate.

3.1.1 Historical Data Collection

The collection of historical data for cost estimation purposes is very time-consuming, and in some isolated instances, impossible. The methods by which records of past projects have been maintained are, in many instances, difficult to comprehend. In general, government agencies are somewhat consistent in record keeping from the standpoint of providing conversion codes when changing from one method of record maintenance to another. Industry is considerably less consistent when comparing record maintenance of a particular corporation with government or other corporations. Each corporation structures its record keeping to top management's desires or old-line company policies. Consequently the collector of historical data for cost estimation purposes is confronted with unique challenges concerning comparability of the collected data.

3.1.2 Statistical Inference

Two types of problems are addressed by statistical inference, namely:

1. Estimation of population parameters
2. Tests of hypotheses

Webster [1] states that the verb *to infer* means "to derive as a consequence, conclusion, or probability." When an individual observes a moving automobile with the windows down in 110°F temperature, one may infer that the automobile does not possess air conditioning.

In statistical inference one is concerned with how to draw conclusions about a large number of events on the basis of observations of a reasonable sample of them. The procedures for drawing conclusions are formalized and standardized by the tools of statistics.

Statistical inference procedures introduce order into any attempt to draw conclusions from the evidence provided by samples. The procedures dictate some of the conditions under which the evidence must be collected, whereas statistical tests identify the magnitude of observed differences before one can have confidence that the few sampled events represent real differences in the parent population.

A common statistical inference problem is to determine, in probability terms, whether observed differences between two samples signify that the populations sampled are themselves really different. The cost estimator must be assured that the samples from different populations possess the same probability distribution form. Since differences occur simply based upon the operations of chance, it is necessary that conclusions be drawn about the observed differences. The procedures of statistical inference permit us to determine, in terms of probability, whether the observed difference falls within the range that could likely occur by chance, or whether it is outside the specified range and signifies that the two samples are probably from two different populations.

Another common problem faced by the cost estimator is to determine whether a sample of cost data is from some specified population. The collection of cost data from several different program/project sources causes one to legitimately question whether the cost data differs among the programs/projects. This chapter addresses each of these statistical inference aspects.

3.1.3 Parametric Versus Nonparametric

In modern statistical methods, the first techniques of inference that appeared were those that made several assumptions about the nature of the population from which the data was acquired. Statistical techniques based on population values are called parametric, since population values are "parameters." Frequently, an inference technique is based on the assumption that the collected data was acquired from a normally distributed population. Another assumption may be that two sets of data are acquired from populations possessing the same variance σ^2. The resulting conclusions must obviously be prefaced by the invoked assumptions to assure that the results are not misinterpreted.

A large number of inference techniques exist that do not make numerous or stringent assumptions about parameters. These techniques are called *distribution-free* or *nonparametric*, resulting in conclusions that require fewer qualifications.

This chapter addresses both parametric and nonparametric techniques, depending upon the data source, sample size, and desired robustness of the final result.

3.2 BASIC CONCEPTS REGARDING STATISTICAL TESTS

The development and use of cost estimation techniques requires the acquisition of historical data on which to base the cost estimate. These historical data must be analyzed statistically to determine their validity as a predictive data base. This analysis occurs in the context of hypothesis testing.

As a means of determining whether a particular hypothesis is confirmed by a set of data, an objective procedure for accepting or rejecting that hypothesis must be available. The scientific method requires that one arrive at conclusions by methods that are public and may be repeated by other competent individuals. Consequently the objective procedure is outlined as follows in the order of performance:

1. State the null hypothesis H_0 , and the alternate hypothesis H_1.
2. Choose a statistical test for evaluating H_0.
3. Specify a significance level α.
4. Identify the sample size n.
5. Identify the sampling distribution of the statistical test under H_0.
6. Define the region of rejection.
7. Calculate the value of the test statistic, utilizing the sample data.
8. Reject H_0 or accept H_1 based on the calculated test statistic.

3.2.1 Statement of Hypotheses

The initial step in the hypothesis testing procedure is to state the null hypothesis H_0 and the alternative hypothesis H_1. The null hypothesis is a mathematical statement of no difference, usually written for two sample means as

$$H_0: \bar{x}_1 = \bar{x}_2$$

The null hypothesis is usually formulated for the precise purpose of being rejected. If the null hypothesis is rejected, the alternative hypothesis H_1 may be accepted. The alternative hypothesis is a mathematical statement indicating a difference exists and is usually written for two sample means as

$$H_1: \bar{x}_1 \neq \bar{x}_2$$

The alternative hypothesis is the operational statement of the cost estimator's belief.

When one wants to make a decision about differences, H_0 is tested against H_1. The rejection of H_0 implies the acceptance of H_1.

Additional insight into the development of alternative hypotheses is in order. The previous alternative hypothesis specified that the sample means were different without specifying the direction. If the direction of difference can be ascertained prior to setting up the test statistic, then the alternative hypothesis may be stated as

$$H_1: \bar{x}_1 < \bar{x}_2$$

or

$$H_1: \bar{x}_1 > \bar{x}_2$$

Only one of these alternative hypotheses may be utilized when actually performing the testing procedure.

3.2.2 Choice of Statistical Test

The cost estimator must select an appropriate statistical test for evaluating the historical data collected. A statistical test is said to possess good power if it has a small probability of rejecting H_0 when H_0 is true, but a large probability of rejecting H_0 when H_0 is false. If two statistical tests have the same probability of rejecting H_0 when it is true, the cost estimator is inclined to select the test that has the larger probability of rejecting H_0 when it is false.

There are considerations other than power that enter into the choice of a statistical test. The manner in which the data were collected, the characteristics of the population from which the data were acquired, and the type of data measurement, are all matters that enter into the determination of the most appropriate test statistic.

The most powerful tests are those that have the strongest or most extensive assumptions. Parametric tests, such as the t or F tests, encompass several strong assumptions. When those assumptions are satisifed, these tests are the most likely of all statistical tests to reject H_0 when H_0 is false.

The conditions necessary to make the t test the most powerful are at least these:

1. The collected data observations must be independent. This means the selection of any observation from the population must not bias the selection chances of any other observation.
2. The data observations are acquired from normally distributed populations.
3. The normally distributed populations must have the same variance, or in special cases must have a known ratio of variances.

All of these conditions are elements of the parametric statistical t test. Ordinarily, these conditions are not tested while performing a statistical analysis. However, the meaningfulness of the probability statement arrived at by the parametric test depends on the specified conditions being satisfied. The cost estimator would be well-advised to perform statistical tests on the collected data to ascertain that the stated conditions are satisfied prior to conducting any parametric test.

3.2.3 Level of Significance

After the null and alternative hypotheses have been stated and the appropriate statistical test identified, the next step is to specify a level of significance α and to select a sample size n.

The significance level of a statistical test is an expression of our reluctance to give up or reject the null hypothesis. If a "stiff" significance level is adopted, such as 0.01 or 0.001, one is implying an unwillingness to reject the null hypothesis unjustly. A consequence of this ultraconservatism will be a large probability of not rejecting the null hypothesis when it is really false unless the actual deviation from the null hypothesis is large. This is an acceptable situation if one is satisfied with the status quo and interested in making a change only if the change represents a very substantial improvement.

Objectivity requires that α be identified prior to collection of the historical data. The level should be determined by the cost estimator's evaluation of the importance or possible practical significance of his results.

In basing decisions on the outcomes of statistical tests, one runs the risk of making either of two types of error. If one rejects the null hypothesis when it is true, for example, proclaim a difference that really does not exist, then one commits an "error of the first kind" or a Type I error. The probability of committing a Type I error is given by α. The larger the α value, the more likely it is that H_0 will be rejected falsely, or the more likely it is that the Type I error will be committed.

If one fails to reject a null hypothesis when it is false, for example, fails to detect a difference when a difference exists, then one commits an "error of the second kind," or a Type II error. The Type II error is represented by β.

In Figure 3.1, if μ_0 is the true value of μ under H_0 and μ_a is a specific alternative value of interest, then the area to the right of K under the normal curve centered at μ_0 is α. The area to the left of K under the curve centered at μ_a is β. The location of K is determined from reference [2] and the equation

$$K = \mu_0 + Z_\alpha \left(\frac{\alpha}{\sqrt{n}} \right) \tag{3.1}$$

where: μ_0 = population mean
Z_α = test statistic table value for a large sample
σ = population standard deviation
n = sample size

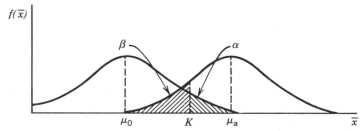

Figure 3.1. α and β for a statistical test.

Figure 3.2 illustrates the relationship that exists between the decision rendered with regard to H_0 and the reality of the situation. The relationship between the confidence level $1 - \alpha$ and the significance level α also becomes apparent.

An inverse relationship exists between the likelihood of making the two types of errors; that is, a decrease in α will increase β for a given n. The only means available to reduce both types of errors is to increase the sample size n.

It should be clear that in any statistical inference a danger exists of committing one of the two alternative types of error. Therefore it is desirable to reach some compromise that optimizes the balance between the probabilities of making the two errors. In attempting to achieve this balance, the notion of the power function for a statistical test becomes pertinent.

The power function of a statistical test gives the probability of rejecting the null hypothesis when the null hypothesis is false [2]. Equation (3.2) identifies the manner in which the power function is calculated:

$$\text{power} = 1 - \text{probability of Type II error} = 1 - \beta \qquad (3.2)$$

In general, the power of a statistical test increases with an increase in sample size.

		DECISION	
		ACCEPT H_0	REJECT H_0
Reality	H_0 TRUE	correct decision Prob $= 1 - \alpha$ $=$ confidence level	Type I error Prob. $= \alpha$ $=$ level of test
	H_0 FALSE	Type II error Prob $= \beta$	correct decision Prob $= 1 - \beta$ $=$ power of test

Figure 3.2. Possible results of a hypothesis test.

3.2.4 The Sampling Distribution

In the process of making an inference from a sample to a population, one ordinarily calculates one or more statistics. Since the samples are randomly selected, the resulting value of the calculated sample statistics may vary from sample to sample. Consequently the sample statistics are random variables themselves, and their behavior can be modeled by probability distributions. The probability distribution of the sample statistic is called a sampling distribution [3].

The selection of a particular statistical test for collected historical cost data requires the identification of the sampling distribution. If the sample size is large ($n \geq 50$), and a goodness of fit test has been selected to determine if the data are normally distributed, the obvious sampling distribution is normal. However, the sampling distribution could be Poisson or binomial, and the goodness of fit test would still be proper. Many of the statistical tests are appropriately utilized with several different distributions, depending on the user's ability to ascertain the underlying collected data distribution.

3.2.5 The Region of Rejection

The region of rejection is a portion of the sampling distribution. Since the sampling distribution includes all possible values a test statistic can possess under H_0, a subset of these possible values constitutes the region of rejection. Furthermore, the region of rejection is defined as the occurrence of a test statistic having a value that is in the subset identified as α. In other words, the region of rejection consists of a set of possible values that are so extreme that when H_0 is true, the probability α is very small that the sample actually observed will yield a value that is among them.

The location of the region of rejection is affected by the structure of H_1. If H_1 does not indicate the direction of the predicted difference, a two-tailed test is required, as shown in Figure 3.3. If H_1 indicates the predicted direction of the difference, then a one-tailed test is in order, as shown in Figure 3.4. The region of rejection differs in location (but not in size) for one-tailed and two-tailed tests. In a one-tailed test the region of rejection is entirely at one end, or tail, of the sampling distribution. In a two-tailed test the region of rejection includes identically sized ends of the sampling distribution.

The level of significance α identifies the size of the region of rejection. If $\alpha = .05$, then 5% of the entire space included under the curve in the sampling distribution represents the region of rejection (Figure 3.4) for a one-tailed alternative.

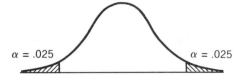

$\alpha = .025$ $\alpha = .025$ **Figure 3.3.** Two-tailed test region of rejection.

$\alpha = .05$ **Figure 3.4.** One-tailed test region of rejection.

The two-tailed alternative shown in Figure 3.3 depicts the difference in location for the rejection since $\alpha/2$ is located at each end of the sampling distribution.

3.2.6 The Statistical Decision

If the calculated test statistic yields a value located in the region of rejection, one rejects H_0. The rationale behind this decision process is very straightforward. One attempts to explain the actual occurrence of a value in the region of rejection by the following:

1. Deciding the null hypothesis is false
2. Deciding that a rare and unlikely event has occurred

The structure and logic of our decision process encourages the selection of the first explanation. Occasionally the second explanation will be the correct choice. The probability that the second explanation is correct is given by α, for rejecting H_0 when in fact it is true represents a Type I error.

When the probability associated with an observed value of a statistical test is equal to or less than the previously determined value of α, one concludes that H_0 is false. Under these conditions the observed value would be identified as significant. The null hypothesis H_0 is rejected whenever a significant result occurs.

Examples to illustrate the use of the material presented in this section are provided in parametric and nonparametric statistical techniques for cost estimating.

3.3 PARAMETRIC STATISTICAL TESTS

This section outlines a number of statistical test procedures in which very definite assumptions are made about the nature of the population distributions. The most common assumption is that the data are derived from an underlying normal distribution. For large sample sizes, the χ^2 goodness of fit test may be invoked to test the hypothesis of data normality. Small sample sizes would utilize the nonparametric Kolmogorov-Smirnov (KS − 1) one-sample statistic for a test of data normality. This section considers several different parametric statistical tests that have been found useful in cost estimation studies.

3.3.1 The Treatment of Outliers

When a set of cost data is collected or derived from historical records, it sometimes occurs that one or two data points fall way out of the range of the rest of the data. The question arises—does this data point come from the same population as the rest of the data, or was an error made in recording or typing the data? An unscrupulous person might just throw the data point out without any justification, if it did not conform to his desired results.

The test for outliers gives justification for keeping or rejecting one or two data points. The test is based on the range where values are arranged in ascending order. It is assumed that the collected observations come from a single normal population with mean $\bar{x}$ and standard deviation σ. However, the population mean and the population standard deviation are unknown. The sample in hand is the only source of available information.

The test considers one or two outliers on the left (the small numerical end of the data set) according to the following equations [4]. r_{10} and r_{11} test for one outlier on the left where:

$$r_{10} = \frac{x_{(2)} - x_{(1)}}{x_{(n)} - x_{(1)}} \qquad \text{for } 3 \leq n \leq 7 \qquad (3.3)$$

$$r_{11} = \frac{x_{(2)} - x_{(1)}}{x_{(n-1)} - x_{(1)}} \qquad \text{for } 8 \leq n \leq 10 \qquad (3.4)$$

r_{21} and r_{22} test for two outliers on the left where:

$$r_{21} = \frac{x_{(3)} - x_{(1)}}{x_{(n-1)} - x_{(1)}} \qquad \text{for } 11 \leq n \leq 13 \qquad (3.5)$$

$$r_{22} = \frac{x_{(3)} - x_{(1)}}{x_{(n-2)} - x_{(1)}} \qquad \text{for } 14 \leq n \leq 25 \qquad (3.6)$$

and $x_{(1)}$ denotes the smallest point and $x_{(n)}$ the largest point.

To detect outliers on the right, all four previous equations can be transformed by replacing $x_{(i)}$ by $x_{(n-i+1)}$ and reversing the sign of each term.

For example, transform r_{21} to r'_{21} where r'_{21} is 2 outliers on right.

$$r_{21} = \frac{x_{(3)} - x_{(1)}}{x_{(n-1)} - x_{(1)}} = \frac{x_{(n-3+1)} - x_{(n-1+1)}}{x_{(n-n+1+1)} - x_{(n-1+1)}} \qquad (3.7)$$

$$r'_{21} = \frac{x_{(n)} - x_{(n-2)}}{x_{(n)} - x_{(2)}} \qquad (3.8)$$

The null hypotheses for the two possible situations (left or right) are given as:

H_0: $x_{(1)}$ belongs to S for points on the left.

H_1: $x_{(1)}$ does not belong to S.

where S is the set of sample points from the population.

H_0: $x_{(n)}$ belongs to S for points on the right.

H_1: $x_{(n)}$ does not belong to S.

It should be noted that the test is one-tailed, since it is testing at the lower end of the data when testing on the left, while testing at the upper end of the data when testing on the right.

H_0 is rejected when $r_{ij} > r_{crit.}$, where $r_{crit.}$ is taken from readily available tables for the rejection of outliers.

Consider Table 3.1 which displays program data collected on three programs for each of eight effort categories. The collected data are assumed to be independent.

If we utilize the historical program man-hour data presented in Table 3.1, it is possible to initiate the outlier test by placing the data in ascending order, as shown in Table 3.2.

Evaluating the data in Table 3.2, we ask, "do $x_{(n)} = 26020$ and $x_{(n-1)} = 25730$ belong to the collected set of data?" Since these are data points at the upper end of the data set (the right side), the null hypothesis becomes:

H_0: $x_{(n)}$ and $x_{(n-1)}$ belong to S.

H_1: $x_{(n)}$ and $x_{(n-1)}$ do not belong to S.

The level of significance is $\alpha = 0.05$.

Since $x_{(n)}$ and $x_{(n-1)}$ are two data points on the right with $n = 24$, use r'_{22}.

$$r_{22} = \frac{x_{(3)} - x_{(1)}}{x_{(n-2)} - x_{(1)}} \tag{3.9}$$

$$= \frac{x_{(n-3+1)} - x_{(n-1+1)}}{x_{(n-n+2+1)} - x_{(n-1+1)}}$$

$$= \frac{x_{(n-2)} - x_{(n)}}{x_{(3)} - x_{(n)}}$$

Therefore,

$$r'_{22} = \frac{x_{(n)} - x_{(n-2)}}{x_{(n)} - x_{(3)}}$$

$$r'_{22} = \frac{26020 - 19646}{26020 - 1137} = \frac{6374}{24883} = 0.256 \tag{3.10}$$

TABLE 3.1. Manhours for Selected Programs

		Program 1	Program 2	Program 3
Effort categories	A	6800	4554	1066
	B	9457	10313	1353
	C	19646	6248	1137
	D	16386	6692	1111
	E	12404	12344	1731
	F	17603	17479	2311
	G	14168	10639	2185
	H	25730	26020	7115

From the table of critical values,

$$r_{\text{crit.}} = 0.413$$

Since $r'_{22} < r_{\text{crit.}}$, accept H_0.

This means that $x_{(n)}$ and $x_{(n-1)}$ are legitimate data points within the given data set, from a statistical standpoint, even though visual inspection indicated a potential problem. This analysis should point out the dangers associated with drawing conclusions without performing the necessary statistical analysis.

3.3.2 Large Sample Goodness of Fit Testing

Many statistical tests are based on the assumption that the universe from which a sample is drawn is normally distributed. It is prudent, therefore, to test this assumption of normality. Various procedures are available for making such a test. The first procedure to be presented is graphic in nature and requires few calculations. The second procedure requires considerable mathematical manipulation but is much more precise.

TABLE 3.2. Man-hour Data in Ascending Order

i	$x_{(i)}$	i	$x_{(i)}$
1	1066	13	9457
2	1111	14	10313
3	1137	15	10639
4	1353	16	12344
5	1731	17	12404
6	2185	18	14168
7	2311	19	16386
8	4554	20	17479
9	6248	21	17603
10	6692	22	19646
11	6800	23	25730
12	7115	24	26020

3.3.2.1 Graphic Methods. Assuming that the sample is large enough to construct a histogram, we can plot a normal curve with the same mean and same standard deviation as the given data with the histogram to see how well the normal curve fits. This method is a nonnumerical comparison and relies on visual inspection for a decision. A visual comparison of this type provides no criterion on which to base a decision.

A more promising graphic method involves plotting the cumulated distribution on normal probability paper and then observing how well it is fitted by a straight line. Consider the historical data provided in Table 3.3. It is desired to plot this information on normal probability paper in the form of a cumulative distribution. Table 3.4 places the 75 data points into intervals of size 0.53, resulting in seven distinct intervals, and identifies the number of occurrences within each interval. This permits the calculation of the cumulative number of data points, from which the cumulative distribution can be developed.

Figure 3.5 shows a plot of the cumulative distribution associated with the 75 R&D program ratios on normal probability paper. The solid line represents the cumulative distribution; the dashed line represents the normal distribution. The plot shows the data depart from the straight line, but whether this is significant cannot be determined from the graph. Only a very gross decision can be made with this method.

3.3.2.2 Chi-Squared Test. A more commonly utilized method of testing normality is to conduct a χ^2 goodness of fit test. The χ^2 test compares a set of sample frequencies with a set of frequencies that would be expected on the basis of some null hypothesis. If the two sets compare favorably, the null hypothesis is accepted; if they compare poorly, the null hypothesis is rejected. The distribution on which the decision to accept or reject is based on the χ^2 distribution, from which

TABLE 3.3. R&D Program Ratios

0.63	1.75	1.96	2.36	2.52
0.73	1.75	2.00	2.38	2.53
0.78	1.82	2.04	2.39	2.54
0.78	1.84	2.04	2.40	2.56
1.25	1.85	2.11	2.40	2.57
1.34	1.86	2.13	2.41	2.58
1.35	1.87	2.14	2.42	2.58
1.37	1.87	2.15	2.43	2.59
1.53	1.88	2.17	2.44	2.61
1.55	1.90	2.17	2.44	2.66
1.56	1.92	2.28	2.46	2.89
1.67	1.92	2.28	2.46	2.90
1.73	1.93	2.28	2.49	2.96
1.74	1.94	2.29	2.51	3.02
1.74	1.96	2.36	2.51	4.31

TABLE 3.4. Cumulative Distribution of R&D Program Ratios

Upper Class Limit	Number	Cumulative Number	Cumulative Distribution
1.16	4	4	0.0533
1.69	8	12	0.1600
2.22	28	40	0.5333
2.75	30	70	0.9333
3.28	4	74	0.9867
3.81	0	74	0.9867
4.34	1	75	1.0000

the test is called the χ^2 test. The χ^2 test can be utilized to test the fit of a large set of sample data to any frequency distribution.

The conditions necessary for the proper application of the χ^2 test are as follows:

1. $n > 50$.
2. Each expected cell frequency should exceed 5. When cell frequencies are too small they may be grouped.

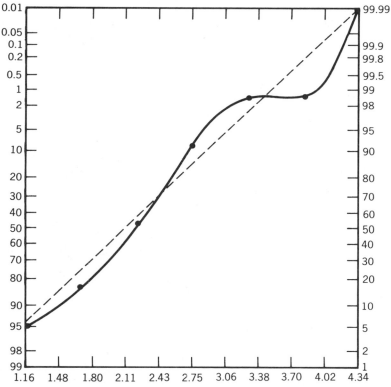

Figure 3.5. R&D program ratio data on normal probability paper.

3. The number of classes or cells should be neither too large nor too small. Usually in the range of $5 \leq m \leq 20$.

4. The number of classes is m, but the degrees of freedom is $m - 3$. The fitting process thus imposes the following constraints:

$$n = \sum_{i=1}^{m} f_i x_i \tag{3.11}$$

$$\bar{x} = \frac{1}{n} \sum_{i=1}^{m} f_i x_i \tag{3.12}$$

$$s^2 = \frac{1}{n} \sum_{i=1}^{m} f_i (x_i - \bar{x})^2 \tag{3.13}$$

Returning to the R&D program ratios given in Table 3.3, we now perform the χ^2 test on the provided data. It is possible to utilize some of the information contained in Table 3.4, namely, the identification of the class intervals. In setting up the material necessary for the χ^2 test, it is noted that $\bar{x}$ and s are required. These values have been calculated in the usual fashion and found to be:

$$\bar{x} = 2.12$$

$$s = 0.57$$

The null hypothesis and the alternative hypothesis are as follows:

H_0: sample data distribution = normal distribution
H_1: sample data distribution $\neq$ normal distribution
Let $\alpha = 0.05$

The calculations shown in Table 3.5 identify the steps necessary to perform the

TABLE 3.5. R&D Program Ratios χ^2 Test Calculations

Upper Class Bound x_i	$\dfrac{x_i - \bar{x}}{s}$	Area to Left of Z $(-\infty$ to $Z)$	① Class Interval Level	Exp f_i $n \times$ ①	Observed f_i	$\dfrac{(o_i - e_i)^2}{e_i}$
1.16	−1.68	0.0465	0.0465	3.49 ⎫ 17	4 ⎫ 12	1.47
1.69	−0.75	0.2266	0.1801	13.51 ⎭	8 ⎭	
2.22	0.18	0.5714	0.3448	25.86	28	0.18
2.75	1.11	0.8665	0.2951	22.13	30	2.80
3.28	2.04	0.9793	0.1128	8.46 ⎫	4 ⎫	
3.81	2.96	0.9985	0.0192	1.44 ⎬ 10.01	0 ⎬ 5	2.49
∞	∞	1.0000	0.0015	0.11 ⎭	1 ⎭	
					$n = 75$	$\chi^2 = 6.94$

χ^2 test. It should be noted that the expected frequency column is acquired by multiplying the appropriate class interval area by the sample size n. The observed frequencies are the same as those shown in Table 3.4. However, it is noted that the first interval possesses only four observations. Since this violates the second condition specified ($f_i \geq 5$), the first two intervals are combined. A similar combining is necessary with the last three intervals. After making these adjustments, the value of χ^2 is calculated: If

$$\chi^2_{cal} < \chi^2_{table}, \text{ accept } H_0$$

$$\chi^2_{table} = 3.84 \quad \text{with 1 d.f.}$$

$$\chi^2_{cal} = 6.94$$

Since

$$\chi^2_{cal} > \chi^2_{table}, \text{ reject } H_0$$

3.3.3 Transformations

Real-life data frequently do not conform to the conditions required for the strict appropriate techniques of statistical analysis. When this situation occurs, a transformation applied to the raw data may put the data into a form so that the appropriate conventional analysis can be performed validly.

The χ^2 test performed in Table 3.5 on the R&D program ratio data resulted in the conclusion that the sample data are not normally distributed. This conclusion prohibits the use of parametric statistical techniques on these data since the assumption of normality is not satisfied. This means one must resort to nonparametric statistics unless a transformation can be found that would place the sample data in the proper form resulting in a normal distribution.

Observing the original sample data, it has been decided to transform the original data into a set of data where each data point is multiplied by itself (square each data point). The result of this transformation is Table 3.6. The range of the data is seen to be from 0.40 to 18.61. Consequently seven intervals result in a range of 2.6 units per interval. The resulting $\bar{x}$ and s are

$$\bar{x} = 4.80$$

$$s = 2.52$$

The null hypothesis and the alternative hypothesis are:

H_0: transformed sample data distribution = normal distribution
H_1: transformed sample data distribution $\neq$ normal distribution
Let $\alpha = 0.05$

Table 3.7 provides the calculations for the χ^2 test on the transformed data. Once

TABLE 3.6. Transformed R&D Program Ratios

6.29	5.99	9.12	1.56	4.00
6.36	3.00	8.43	0.40	3.33
6.47	2.44	1.82	0.53	3.78
6.41	3.47	1.79	0.61	4.54
6.56	2.34	5.19	1.89	3.42
6.61	2.39	3.85	2.79	3.05
6.68	3.05	4.63	3.04	3.04
6.20	3.48	3.71	5.75	3.40
5.83	3.70	3.52	3.51	3.62
5.75	6.69	8.33	3.67	3.86
5.58	6.68	5.96	4.59	4.16
5.71	6.81	6.32	4.69	4.44
5.89	5.88	8.77	5.18	4.72
5.94	5.67	18.61	5.25	5.19
6.07	7.10	0.61	4.17	5.56

again it is necesary to combine class intervals to satisfy one of the constraints of the χ^2 goodness of fit test. After making these adjustments, the value of χ^2 is calculated. If

$$\chi^2_{cal} < \chi^2_{table}, \text{ accept } H_0$$

$$\chi^2_{table} = 3.84 \text{ with 1 d.f.}$$

$$\chi^2_{cal} = 2.61$$

Since

$$\chi^2_{cal} < \chi^2_{table}, \text{ accept } H_0$$

It is obvious that the transformation has caused the original sample data to be

TABLE 3.7. χ^2 Test on Transformed R&D Program Ratios

Upper Class Bound x_i	$\dfrac{x_i - \bar{x}}{s}$	Area to Left of Z $(-\infty \text{ to } Z)$	Class Interval Level	Exp. f_i	Observed f_i	$\dfrac{(o_i - e_i)^2}{e_i}$
3.00	−0.71	0.2389	0.2389	17.92	13	1.35
5.60	0.32	0.6255	0.3866	29.00	33	0.55
8.20	1.35	0.9115	0.2860	21.45	24	0.30
10.80	2.38	0.9913	0.0798	5.99 ⎫	4 ⎫	
13.40	3.41	0.9997	0.0084	0.63 ⎬ 6.64	0 ⎬ 5	
16.00	4.44	1.0000	0.0003	0.02 ⎭	0 ⎭	0.41
∞	∞	1.0000	0	0	1	
						$\chi^2 = 2.61$

cast into a normal distribution. Since the transformed data are now normally distributed, further parametric statistical tests may be performed as necessary, as long as the data remain in the transformed state.

The selection and identification of a transformation is a trial and error procedure which relies on the cost analyst's experience and intuition. Patience and persistence appear to be the necessary attributes when searching for a transformation.

3.3.4 Predictive Methods

Early in any cost estimation study, it is recognized that the establishment of relationships between various cost parameters is essential for an analytical approach to the cost estimating problem. Therefore the relationship between a single independent variable (such as dry weight) and a dependent variable (such as engineering hours) is investigated. The method of least squares or regression analysis technique is utilized for such an investigation.

The collection of additional, and refinement of existing historical data, combined with the analysis and evaluation of relationships involving two variables, leads to the investigation of the multivariable relationship. It is recognized that to consider a dependent variable, such as total hours or hours per pound, in terms of a single independent variable may not account for all variations in the dependent variable. After analysis and evaluation of the regression technique, it may be felt that the dependent variable can, in most cases, be estimated with greater precision if the estimate is based upon several independent variables rather than on only one.

When more than two variables are involved, their joint distribution cannot easily be represented by a graph. Therefore, in the discussion of specific categories analyzed by more than two variables (multiple regression analysis), the resultant equation will be of the form

$$y = b_0 + b_1 x_1 + b_2 x_2 + \cdots + b_m x_m \qquad (3.14)$$

where

$$y = \text{dependent variable}$$

$$b_0 = \text{constant term}$$

$$b_1, b_2, \ldots, b_m = \text{regression coefficients}$$

$$x_1, x_2, \ldots, x_m = \text{independent variables}$$

Many parameters can be considered as independent variables. The number of independent variables is restricted by the number of paired data points. The multiple regression technique requires one degree of freedom, that is, one less variable than the number of data points considered. Therefore, the selection of the independent variable is critical in establishing estimating relationships. The following paragraph from reference [5] points out the logic of variable selection:

If the several independent variables in the multiple regression study had been selected by considering a large number of possible independent variables, and by retaining only those which showed the highest gross or net correlation with y, there is a much larger possibility of the correlation in the sample exceeding the true correlation in the universe by a wide margin. In fact, it is almost certain to be erroneously high. If error calculations are to be used to judge the sampling significance of the correlations or regressions observed, the variables must be selected purely on logical or deductive grounds rather than on any such basis of empirical selection as those which show the apparent closest relation [5].

It should always be remembered that, if the choice is purely empirical, the next time the order of apparent importance of the several variables might readily be reversed.

Since the regression analysis technique is utilized for establishing estimating relationships, the conditions necessary for a valid regression analysis, together with the development of the normal equations utilized in simple and multiple regression are presented in the next section. A method to determine the validity of the final result is also presented.

3.3.4.1 Linear Regression.
In linear regression analysis, the first step is to express the relationship between the two variables as a line or mathematical equation. The variable to be predicted is designated as y, the dependent variable. The other variable x is the independent or predicting variable. The dependent variable is then expressed as some function of the independent variable, that is, $y = f(x)$.

Let us first treat the case where the regression of y on x is linear, that is, where for any given x, the mean of the distribution of the y's is given by $\beta_0 + \beta_1 x$. In general, an observed y will differ from this mean, and one denotes this difference by ϵ, writing

$$y = \beta_0 + \beta_1 x + \epsilon \tag{3.15}$$

Note that ϵ is a value assumed by a random variable and that one can always choose β_0 so that the mean of its distribution is equal to zero. The value of ϵ for any given observation will depend on a possible error of measurement and on the value of variables other than x that might have an influence on y.

Assume that one has collected man-hour data on seven projects together with the corresponding power requirements as shown in Table 3.8. A plot of this data is given in Figure 3.6. One now faces the problem of using the data plotted in Figure 3.6 to estimate the parameters β_0 and β_1 of the assumed regression line of y on x. Note that these parameters completely determine the regression line, and the estimation of β_0 and β_1 is equivalent to finding the equation of the straight line that "best fits" the data points. To handle problems of this kind, one must seek a nonsubjective method for fitting straight lines, which also has some desirable statistical properties.

To state the problem formally, one has n paired observations x_i, y_i for which it

TABLE 3.8. Historical Data

Man-hours (y)	Power Requirements (x_i)
1.07	0.58
1.35	1.07
1.14	1.19
1.11	1.35
1.73	1.88
2.31	7.19
2.18	9.94

is reasonable to assume that the regression of y on x is linear, and one desires to determine the line (that is, the equation of the line) that in some sense provides the best fit. There are several ways in which one can interpret the word "best," and the meaning given here may be explained as follows. If one predicts y by means of the equation

$$y' = b_0 + b_1 x \qquad (3.15a)$$

where b_0 and b_1 are constants, then e_i, the error in predicting the value of y_i corresponding to the given x_i, is

$$y_i - y_i' = e_i \qquad (3.16)$$

Note that Equation 3.15a provides an estimate of the equation of the regression line whose actual, but unknown, value is given by Equation 3.17 as

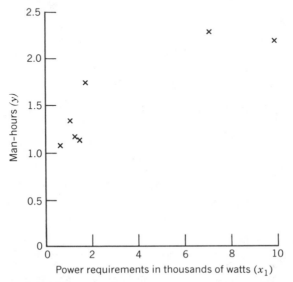

Figure 3.6. Man-hours as a function of power requirements.

$$y = \beta_0 + \beta_1 x \qquad (3.17)$$

The actual error in predicting y_i is ϵ_i, and this error is estimated by the quantity calculated in Equation 3.16. One attempts to determine b_0 and b_1 so that the estimated errors are in some sense as small as possible.

Since one cannot minimize each of the e_i individually, it may be feasible to try to make their sum, $\Sigma_{i=1}^n e_i$, as close as possible to zero. However, since the sum can be made equal to zero by many choices of totally unsuitable straight lines for which the positive and the negative errors cancel, one should instead minimize the sum of the squares of the e_i. In other words, choose b_0 and b_1 so that

$$\sum_{i=1}^n [y_i - (b_0 + b_1 x_i)]^2 \qquad (3.18)$$

is a minimum. Note from Figure 3.7 that this is equivalent to minimizing the sum of the squares of the vertical distances from the points to the line. This criterion, called the criterion of least squares, yields values for b_0 and b_1 (estimates for β_0 and β_1) that have many desirable properties.

A necessary condition for a relative minimum is the vanishing of the partial derivatives with respect to b_0 and b_1. This results in Equations 3.19 and 3.20,

$$2 \sum_{i=1}^n [y_i - (b_0 + b_i x_i)] (-1) = 0 \qquad (3.19)$$

$$2 \sum_{i=1}^n [y_i - (b_0 + b_i x_i)] (-x_i) = 0 \qquad (3.20)$$

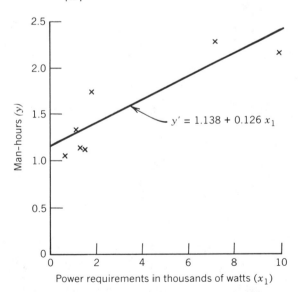

Figure 3.7. Regression equation for Table 3.8 data.

which can be rewritten in a somewhat more convenient form resulting in the normal Equations 3.21 and 3.22.

$$\sum_{i=1}^{n} y_i = nb_0 + b_1 \sum_{i=1}^{n} x_i \tag{3.21}$$

$$\sum_{i=1}^{n} x_i y_i = b_0 \sum_{i=1}^{n} x_i + b_1 \sum_{i=1}^{n} x_i^2 \tag{3.22}$$

The normal equations are a set of two linear equations in the unknowns b_0 and b_1; their simultaneous solution gives the values of b_0 and b_1 for the line that provides the best fit to the given data according to the criterion of least squares. Note that they can easily be remembered as follows:

1. Write down the equation

$$y_i = b_0 + b_1 x_1$$

2. Multiply both sides of the equation in 1 by x_i resulting in

$$x_i y_i = b_0 x_i + b_1 x_i^2$$

3. Sum each term on both sides of each of these equations.
4. The two normal equations result.

To illustrate the method of least squares as it is used to fit a straight line to a given set of paired data, let us apply it to the data given in Table 3.8 pertaining to the power requirements and manpower for several projects as given under x and y. Here the x's are the power requirements in thousands of watts and the y's are the man-hours in thousands of hours. The basic calculations necessary for input into the normal equations are given in Table 3.9.

TABLE 3.9. Linear Regression Calculations

y	x_1	$x_1 y$	x_1^2	y^2
1.07	0.58	0.62	0.34	1.14
1.35	1.07	1.44	1.14	1.82
1.14	1.19	1.36	1.42	1.30
1.11	1.35	1.50	1.82	1.23
1.73	1.88	3.25	3.53	2.99
2.31	7.19	16.60	51.70	5.34
2.18	9.94	21.67	98.80	4.75
10.89	23.20	46.44	158.75	18.57

The normal equations become

$$10.89 = 7b_0 + 23.20\, b_1 \tag{3.21}$$

$$46.44 = 23.2\, b_0 + 158.75\, b_1 \tag{3.22}$$

Solving these two equations simultaneously results in

$$b_0 = 1.138$$

$$b_1 = 0.126$$

Thus the equation of the straight line that provides the best fit in the sense of least squares is

$$y' = 1.138 + 0.126x_1 \tag{3.23}$$

This equation can be utilized to predict the man-hours required to design a system with power requirements specified as x_1.

A summary of the characteristics of a straight line fitted by the least squares criterion is as follows:

1. It gives the best fit to the data in the sense that it makes the sum of the squared deviations from the line smaller than they would be from any other straight line. This property accounts for the name "least squares."
2. The deviations above the line equal those below the line, on the average. This means that the total of the positive and negative deviations is zero.
3. The straight line goes through the overall mean of the data $\bar{x}$, $\bar{y}$.
4. When the data represent a sample from a larger population, the least squares line is a "best" estimate of the population regression line.

The variance σ^2 is usually estimated in terms of the vertical deviations of the sample points from the least squares line. The ith such deviation is

$$y_i - y_i' = y_i - (b_0 + b_1 x_i) \tag{3.24}$$

The estimate of the population variance σ^2 is provided by

$$s_e^2 = \frac{1}{n-2} \sum_{i=1}^{n} [y_i - (b_0 + b_1 x_i)]^2 \tag{3.25}$$

where s_e is traditionally referred to as the standard error of estimate.

For ease of calculation, an alternate form of the same equation is

$$s_e^2 = \frac{\sum\limits_{i=1}^{n} y_i^2 - b_0 \sum\limits_{i=1}^{n} y_i - b_1 \sum\limits_{i=1}^{n} y_i x_i}{n - 2} \tag{3.26}$$

For this example, upon substitution of the appropriate values, one acquires

$$s_e^2 = \frac{0.33}{5} = 0.066$$

3.3.4.2 Sampling and Regression Analysis.
Up to this point the regression line and standard error of estimate have been considered as descriptions of the average relationship between two variables and of the goodness of fit. However, the regression results are not looked upon solely as a description of a particular sample. Almost without exception one is looking for a relationship that will permit the control or prediction of new values of the dependent variable within limits of accuracy estimated from the original set of data.

Thus regression analysis must be approached from the standpoint of statistical inference from a particular sample to a "parent population" that includes the given sample, and also such future or additional observations as one wishes to control or predict. Both the given sample analyzed and the actual future values to be controlled or predicted represent only a fraction of all of the possible values that might conceivably be drawn from the population in question. The application of statistical inference to regression analysis leads to the discovery and verification of relationships between variables. This is one of the most challenging and basic problems of scientific research.

The regression line for a sample is only one of a family of regression lines for different samples that might be drawn from the same population. That is, regression measures are subject to sampling error. Nevertheless, one can estimate within what limits the "true" regression line in the population is likely to fall.

To make valid inferences from sample data about population relationships, certain assumptions must be satisfied as follows:

Assumption 1. When one fits a straight line to sample data to estimate the true or population relationship, the latter must also be linear. This is the property of linearity.

Assumption 2. The standard deviation of the errors is the same for all values of x. This means that there is a uniform scatter or dispersion of points about the regression line. This property is called *homoscedasticity*.

Assumption 3. The errors are independent of each other. This means that the deviation of one point about the line (its error value) is not related to the deviation of any other point. This assumption of independence is not valid for most time series data. Time series move in cycles rather than randomly about the trend, so that adjoining values (e.g., in two boom years) are closely related.

Assumption 4. The distribution of the points above and below the regression line follows a roughly normal curve. This means that the error values are normally distributed.

When these four assumptions are satisfied, the linear regression coefficients and standard error of estimate computed from a sample are efficient, linear, unbiased estimators of the true population values.

3.3.4.3 Multiple Regression.

Frequently it is necessary to utilize more than one independent variable to acquire a valid regression equation. The normal equations for two variables may be extended to three variables in the following manner:

1. Write the regression equation of y on x_1 and x_2.

$$y = b_0 + b_1 x_1 + b_2 x_2 \tag{3.27}$$

2. Acquire the new normal equations by multiplying both sides of the foregoing equation by 1, x_1, and x_2 successively, and summing on both sides.

$$\sum y = n b_0 + b_1 x_1 + b_2 \sum x_2$$

$$\sum x_1 y = b_0 \sum x_1 + b_1 \sum x_1^2 + b_2 \sum x_1 x_2 \tag{3.28}$$

$$\sum x_2 y = b_0 \sum x_2 + b_1 \sum x_1 x_2 + b_2 \sum x_2^2$$

where y is the dependent variable and x_1 and x_2 are the independent variables.

3. It is possible to extend the original equation to any desired number of independent variables in this fashion.

Adding another independent variable x_2 to the basic data provided in Table 3.9 results in the first three columns of Table 3.10. The remaining six columns rep-

TABLE 3.10. Multiple Regression Calculations

y	x_1	x_2	x_1^2	x_2^2	$x_1 x_2$	y^2	$x_1 y$	$x_2 y$
1.07	0.58	2.11	0.34	4.45	1.22	1.14	0.62	2.26
1.35	1.07	2.68	1.14	7.18	2.87	1.82	1.44	3.62
1.14	1.19	2.10	1.42	4.41	2.50	1.30	1.36	2.40
1.11	1.35	2.10	1.82	4.41	2.84	1.23	1.50	2.33
1.73	1.88	2.87	3.53	8.24	5.40	2.99	3.25	4.96
2.31	7.19	2.89	51.70	8.35	20.77	5.34	16.60	6.68
2.18	9.94	2.47	98.80	6.10	24.55	4.75	21.67	5.39
10.89	23.20	17.22	158.75	43.14	60.15	18.57	46.44	27.64

resent the calculations necessary for determining the coefficients of the normal equation terms. Substituting into the normal equations results in

$$10.89 = 7b_0 + 23.20b_1 + 17.22b_2$$

$$46.44 = 23.2b_0 + 158.75b_1 + 60.15b_2 \qquad (3.29)$$

$$27.64 = 17.22b_0 + 60.15b_1 + 43.14b_2$$

Solving for b_0, b_1, and b_2 results in:

$$b_0 = -0.489$$

$$b_1 = 0.100$$

$$b_2 = 0.696$$

Thus the equation of the multiple regression equation becomes

$$y' = -0.489 + 0.100x_1 + 0.696x_2 \qquad (3.30)$$

The equation necessary to calculate the sample variance associated with this multiple regression problem is

$$s_e^2 = \frac{\sum y^2 - b_0 \sum y - b_1 \sum x_1 y - b_2 \sum x_2 y}{n - 3} \qquad (3.31)$$

In general, the equation for calculating the sample variance for n independent variables in a multiple regression is

$$s_e^2 = \frac{\sum y^2 - b_0 \sum y - b_i \sum x_i y}{n - 1 - i} \qquad (3.32)$$

For the preceding example, on substitution of the appropriate values one acquires

$$s_e^2 = \frac{0.02}{4} = 0.005 \qquad (3.33)$$

All of the components are now present to conduct an analysis of multiple regression variance. This analysis has important implications since it is a means to evaluate the effect of the independent variables on the dependent variable, from a statistical point of view.

The numerator of Equation 3.33 is equivalent to the *sum of squares about regression* SS_{about}. The total variation SS_{total} is provided by

$$\Sigma \, (y_i - \bar{y})^2 = \Sigma \, y_i^2 - \frac{1}{n} \left(\Sigma \, y_i \right)^2 \tag{3.34}$$

The variation attributable to the regression itself is acquired from the following equation:

$$SS_{\text{total}} = SS_{\text{due to reg}} + SS_{\text{about}} \tag{3.35}$$

Placing this information into Table 3.11 results in a general format for conducting an analysis of multiple regression variance. Since the total variation is given by Equation 3.34, on substituting the appropriate values from Table 3.10, one acquires

$$SS_{\text{total}} = 1.61$$

As stated earlier, the numerator of Equation 3.33 is the value for SS_{about}. Consequently it is possible to place this information in a table according to the format of Table 3.11. However, prior to observing these results, it is necessary to state the associated hypothesis.

H_0: x_i have no effect upon y

H_1: x_i have an effect upon y

Let $\alpha = 0.05$

The F test is the appropriate test for determining whether the null hypothesis is accepted or rejected.

$$F = \frac{MS_{\text{due}}}{MS_{\text{about}}} \tag{3.36}$$

If $F_{\text{cal}} > F_{\text{table}}$, reject H_0. Placing the results for this situation into the proper format results in Table 3.12.

The SS column has been explained previously. The d.f. column indicates two degrees of freedom associated with "due to" variation since there are two inde-

TABLE 3.11. Analysis of Multiple Regression Variance Table

Source	S.S.	d.f.	M.S.
Due to	$\Sigma y_i^2 - \frac{1}{n}(\Sigma y_i)^2 - [\Sigma y_i^2 - b_0 \Sigma y_i - b_1 \Sigma x_1 y - b_2 \Sigma x_2 y]$	2	$SS/2$
About	$\Sigma y^2 - b_0 \Sigma y - b_1 \Sigma x_1 y - b_2 \Sigma x_2 y$	$n - 2 - 1$	$SS/n - 3$
Total	$\Sigma y_i^2 - \frac{1}{n}(\Sigma y_i)^2$	$n - 1$	

TABLE 3.12. Multiple Regression Analysis of Variance for Two Independent Variables

Source	S.S.	d.f.	M.S.	F_{cal}	$F_{0.05}$	Decision
Due to	1.59	2	0.795	159.00	6.94	Reject
About	0.02	4	0.005			
Total	1.61	6				

pendent variables. Since the sample size is $n = 7$, "total" d.f. is six since $n - 1 = 6$. The calculation of "about" d.f. is $n - 2 - 1 = 4$. The MS column reflects the MS calculations according to Table 3.8. The calculation of F_{cal} is simply MS_{due} divided by MS_{about}. This value is compared to an F_{table} value at the level of significance $\alpha = 0.05$. Consulting an F_{table} in any statistics book, with two and four degrees of freedom, $F_{2,4} = 6.94$. Since $F_{cal} > F_{table}$, the null hypothesis is rejected. Consequently it has been determined that the independent variables have a significant effect on the dependent variable.

If x_1 and x_2 had no effect on y, one would expect

$$\frac{MS}{MS} \leq 1 \tag{3.37}$$

Remember, MS contains all remaining sources of error. If x_1 and x_2 have an effect on y, one would expect the ratio to be greater than 1, the exact value depending on how strong the effect actually is in total.

A statistical procedure now exists to determine whether the overall regression results are significant. One may want to determine if the addition of another variable causes a significant reduction in the variation. The significance of the additional variable may be determined by reworking the analysis of variance (ANOVA) table.

Returning to our original problem considering only one variable, we find that x_1 results in

$$y' = 1.138 + 0.126x_1$$

with $SS = 1.61$
$SS = 0.33$
$SS = 1.28$

It is now possible to construct the ANOVA table, Table 3.13, including the appropriate elements of Table 3.12.

From Table 3.13 it is very apparent that the addition of x_2 increases the predictive ability of the regression equation considerably. Furthermore, since x_1 was a satisfactory predictor alone, the analysis to determine the effect of x_2 on the predictive ability of a multiple regression equation is very important. If x_2 did not

TABLE 3.13. Detailed ANOVA on Two Independent Variables

Source	S.S.	d.f.	M.S.	F_{cal}	$F_{0.05}$	D
Due to x_1 and x_2	1.59	2	0.795	159.0	6.94	SIGN.
Due to x_2	1.28	1	1.280	19.4	6.61	SIGN.
Due to addition of x_2	0.31	1	0.310	62.0	7.71	SIGN.
About x_1 and x_2	0.02	4	0.005			
About x_1	0.33	5	0.066			
Totals	1.61	6				

contribute in a significant manner to the predictive equation, it would be eliminated from the analysis and a search initiated for a different independent variable.

3.3.4.4 Selection of Independent Variables.
The small number of data points ordinarily available for cost estimation purposes presents a problem concerning the number of independent variables that may be utilized. Few general rules can be given for the handling of problems involving many variables, and a good deal of reliance must usually be placed on informed opinion of the relative importance of the variables concerned [6]. A method based purely on logical or deductive grounds is not necessarily the best solution to the independent variable selection procedure.

Where the number of independent variables is so large that it is preferable to avoid the fitting of a regression on all variables simultaneously, it is common practice to begin by fitting a regression on that single variable thought most likely to be related to the dependent variable, and then to introduce other variables in turn, retaining those that significantly increase the regression sum of squares.

Hence when the number of data points is small, it is necessary to consider each independent variable separately and select the best from an explained variation and an intuitive standpoint. Then consider each remaining independent variable in conjunction with the initially selected variable and retain that combination resulting in a minimum unexplained variation.

To illustrate the procedure, data were collected on eight R&D programs which have a total of 11 potential independent variables. It is desired to develop a significant estimating relationship. The data associated with the eight R&D programs are given in Table 3.14. Selecting x_1 as the initial variable, and utilizing procedures discussed previously results in

$$SS_{due} = 1.697$$

$$SS_{about} = 0.576$$

It should be noted that the values in Table 3.14 were transformed to natural log prior to performing any calculations.

Statistical theory indicates the smaller the standard error of estimate, the better

TABLE 3.14. Variable Values for Selected R&D Programs

P	Y	1	2	3	4	5	6	7	8	9	10	11
A	4,554	5,800	74,000	107,000	0.9367	1,105	46	578	211	28.5	110	59
B	10,313	10,700	76,000	45,000	0.9084	4,483	171	298	268	20.7	69	82
C	6,248	11,900	222,000	323,000	0.9630	3,360	70	780	210	32.7	143	63
D	6,692	13,500	187,000	255,000	0.9473	2,907	58	980	210	29.5	114	83
E	12,344	18,800	208,000	155,000	0.9341	11,883	190	502	287	21.0	71	86
F	17,479	71,900	900,000	955,000	0.9450	44,797	346	791	289	21.0	72	97
G	10,639	99,400	857,000	1,459,000	0.9158	13,482	207	763	247	19.4	73	78
H	26,020	283,900	4,297,000	7,455,000	0.9377	68,373	346	1457	289	20.8	73	92

TABLE 3.15. Variable Selection

x_1 Constant		x_1 and x_8 Constant		x_1, x_8, and x_9 Constant	
Variable	SS_{About}	Variable	SS_{About}	Variable	SS_{About}
x_8	0.0890	x_9	0.0407	x_2	0.0093
x_5	0.1230	x_{10}	0.0553	x_3	0.0132
x_6	0.1595	x_7	0.0570	x_4	0.0199
x_{11}	0.2386	x_2	0.0610	x_{11}	0.0249
x_3	0.3126	x_4	0.0648	x_{10}	0.0291
x_{10}	0.3229	x_5	0.0652	x_5	0.0396
x_9	0.4018	x_{11}	0.0678	x_7	0.0406
x_7	0.4068	x_3	0.0791	x_6	0.0406
x_2	0.5358	x_6	0.0865		
x_4	0.5534				

the estimating equation. Hence the combination with the lowest standard error of estimate should logically be selected. Table 3.15 illustrates how the variables are selected. It should be noted that each successive iteration results in smaller values of SS_{about}. Each iteration has a corresponding predictive equation. Table 3.16 provides a summary of the various calculated values, including the four predictive equations and the corresponding sum of squares, sample standard deviations, and the correlation coefficients.

As an example of a detailed ANOVA involving four independent variables, consider Table 3.17. The analysis is to determine if the addition of variables x_9 and x_2 to the regression that included variables x_1 and x_8, is a significant contribution.

The hypotheses to be tested are as follows:

H_0: The addition of x_9 and x_2 does not improve the x_1 and x_8 regression.
H_1: The addition of x_9 and x_2 does improve the x_1 and x_8 regression.
Let $\alpha = 0.05$.

The test of the null hypothesis that adding x_9 and x_2 to the regression does not improve the fit is given by the variance ratio 0.0398/0.0031. Comparison of the

TABLE 3.16. Summary Values

Regression Coefficients	b_0	Independent Variables				SS_{About}	$SS_{due\ to}$	s_e	r
		x_1	x_8	x_9	x_2				
		b_1	b_8	b_9	b_2				
Iteration 1	12.392	0.366				0.576	1.697	0.310	0.864
Iteration 2	1.481	0.209	2.270			0.089	2.184	0.133	0.980
Iteration 3	−6.541	0.227	3.193	0.863		0.041	2.233	0.101	0.991
Iteration 4	−22.448	1.361	4.720	3.490	−0.978	0.009	2.264	0.056	0.998

TABLE 3.17. Detailed ANOVA on Four Independent Variables

Source	S.S.	d.f.	M.S.	F_{cal}	$F_{0.05}$	D
Due to x_1, x_8, x_9, x_2	2.2642	4	0.5560	182.58	9.12	SIGN.
Due to x_1 and x_8	2.1845	2	1.0922	61.36	5.79	SIGN.
Due to addition of x_9 and x_2 to x_1 and x_8	0.0797	2	0.0398	12.84	9.55	SIGN.
About regression on x_1, x_8, x_9, and x_2	0.0093	3	0.0031			
About regression on x_1 and x_8	0.0890	5	0.0178			
Totals	2.2735	7				

calculated variance ratio with $F_{0.05}$ ($n_1 = 2$, $n_2 = 3$) = 9.55 from an F_{table} indicates the regression is significant at the 95% confidence level. The test of the hypothesis, that the regression due to x_1, x_8, x_9, x_2 does not significantly explain the variation with respect to the considered variable, is given by the variance ratio 0.5660/ 0.0031. From an F distribution table, $F_{0.05}$ ($n = 4$, $n_2 = 3$) = 9.12. Hence the regression is a very significant explanation of the variation of manufacturing effort, with respect to the considered variables.

The variance ratio 1.0922/0.0178 = 61.36 is a measure of the significance of x_1 and x_8 in explaining the variation in y. From an F_{table}, $F_{0.05}$ ($n_1 = 2$, $n_2 = 5$) = 5.79. Hence the regression due to x_1 and x_8 is an adequate expression for the variation. However, the predictive equation that incorporates all four independent variables would be a superior equation for predictive purposes.

3.4 NONPARAMETRIC STATISTICAL TESTS

This section outlines a number of test procedures in which very little is assumed about the nature of the population distributions. The population distributions are *not* assumed to be normal. Consequently these tests are often called ''nonparametric'' or ''distribution-free tests.'' The only assumptions made are that the individual observations are independent and that all observations have the same underlying distribution (whatever it is).

If the underlying populations are indeed normal, a nonparametric test is not as good as a parametric test. When nonparametric tests are applied to normal data the probability of the second kind of error (β) is larger for a given α and n.

3.4.1 Kruskal-Wallis H-test

When collecting cost data on different programs, the question frequently arises as to whether the various programs are derived from the same or similar populations. Almost invariably samples will differ, and the question is whether the differences signify differences among the populations or are merely the chance variations to be expected among random samples from the same population. When this problem arises, one tends to assume that the samples are of approximately the same form, in the sense that if they differ it is merely due to shift or translation.

Freidman [7] states that the *method of ranks* can be applied to data classified by two or more criteria to determine whether the factors used as criteria of classification have a significant influence on the variate classified. Hence the "method of ranks" tests the hypothesis that the values of the variate, corresponding to each subdivision by one of the factors, are homogeneous, that is, from the same universe.

Method of ranks utilizes information based solely on order and makes no use of the quantitative values of the variate as such. Therefore an assumption need not be made about the nature of the underlying universe. Thus a nonparametric *rank test* will provide the necessary information to make a determination of sample population similarity.

An excellent rank test is the Kruskal-Wallis *H*-Test [8]. The *H*-test requires that all the observations be ranked together, that is, to array the *N* observations in order of magnitude and replace the smallest by one, the next to the smallest by two, and so on, the largest being replaced by *N*, and then, the sum of the ranks obtained for each sample. The test statistic to be computed, provided there are no ties, is

$$H = \frac{12}{N(N+1)} \sum_{i=1}^{c} \frac{R_i^2}{n_i} - 3(N+1) \tag{3.38}$$

where c = number of samples

n_i = number of observations in the ith sample

$N = \Sigma n_i$, the number of observations in all samples combined

R_i = sum of the ranks in the ith sample

The null hypothesis associated with the *H*-test is that the samples all come from the same or identical populations with respect to averages. When the n_i are not too small, and the samples come from continuous populations, H is distributed as χ^2, permitting the use of readily available tables of χ^2.

TABLE 3.18. H-Test on Program Data

		Program 1	Program 2	Program 3	R	n	R^2/n
Effort	A	11	8	1	20	3	133.33
categories	B	13	14	4	31	3	320.33
	C	22	9	3	34	3	352.00
	D	19	10	2	31	3	320.33
	E	17	16	5	38	3	481.33
	F	21	20	7	48	3	768.00
	G	18	15	6	39	3	507.00
	H	23	24	12	59	3	1160.33
					Σ	24	4042.65

Placing the program data from Table 3.1 into the H-test format results in Table 3.18. The null hypothesis and alternative hypothesis are as follows, with $\alpha = .05$:

H_0: All samples come from the same or identical populations (no difference in sample populations).

H_1: Samples come from different populations.

Substituting into Equation 3.38 results in

$$H_{cal} = \frac{12(4042.65)}{24(25)} - 3(25)$$

$$= \frac{2021.32}{25} - 75$$

$$= 80.85 - 75. = 5.85$$

The degrees of freedom (d.f.) associated with the H-test are $c - 1$, where c is the number of effort categories. Therefore, for the sample provided, d.f. $= 8 - 1 = 7$. Entering a χ^2 table with 7 d.f. and $\alpha = 0.05$ results in

$$\chi^2_{table} = 14.07$$

The comparison is between the test statistic, H_{cal} and the corresponding χ^2_{table} value. If $H_{cal} < \chi^2_{table}$, the null hypothesis is accepted [8]. Since the calculated H value is less than the table H value, one accepts the null hypothesis. It is concluded that the program data are not significantly different from one another.

If the programs are, in fact, from different populations, this difference in population sources is not detectable from the sample data, at the specified value of α. Hence, from a statistical point of view, one is confident that the programs possess similar characteristics and attributes.

3.4.2 Kolmogorov-Smirnov One-Sample Statistic

The Kolmogorov-Smirnov (KS-1) One-Sample Test is a test of goodness of fit. It is concerned with the degree of agreement between the distribution of a set of sample values and some specified theoretical distribution. This test assists in determining whether the sample values reasonably can be thought to have come from a population represented by the theoretical distribution. The test involves specifying the cumulative frequency distribution that would occur under the theoretical distribution and comparing that with the observed cumulative frequency distribution. The point at which the theoretical and observed distributions show the largest divergence is calculated. The calculated value is compared with critical values of D from the sampling distribution, at the appropriate level of α. The significance of a given value of D depends on the sample size n. The method of the test is outlined as follows:

1. A sample of size n is taken from a population with a cumulative distribution $F(x)$. This will give a cumulative sample distribution of $F_n(x)$, where $F_n(x)$ is a step function. Calculate

$$F_n(x) = \frac{k}{n} \quad \text{for} \quad x_i < x < x_{i+1}$$

where k = number of observations equal to or less than x and, $x_1, \ldots, x_n$ denotes the sample values in ascending order.

2. The test statistic is D where

$$D = \max |F_n(x) - F(x)|$$

3. Acquire $D_{\text{crit.}}$ from readily available critical values of D.
4. Reject H_0 if $D_{\text{max}} > D_{\text{crit.}}$

Assume Table 3.19 represents the number of man-hours utilized in a specific skill on eight different R&D programs. Is the data compatible?

H_0: Observed frequency distribution = theoretical frequency distribution.
H_1: Observed frequency distribution ≠ theoretical frequency distribution.

The calculations follow with $\bar{x} = 15.274$ and $s = 5.98$.

From Table 3.20, it is seen that $D_{\text{max}} = 0.105$. Entering the Table of Critical Values of D shown in Appendix D with $n = 8$ and $\alpha = 0.05$, the value of $D_{\text{crit.}}$ = 0.457. Therefore $D_{\text{max}} < D_{\text{crit.}}$, and the null hypothesis is accepted. In other words, there is no reason to suspect the data are not compatible.

The KS-1 test is especially appropriate for small sample sizes where parametric statistics, such as the χ^2 statistic, cannot be utilized owing to the requirement that n be at least 50.

TABLE 3.19. Man-hours by Program

Program	Manhours $\times 10^6$
A	6.800
B	9.457
C	12.404
D	14.168
E	16.368
F	17.603
G	19.646
H	25.730

TABLE 3.20. KS-1 Test Calculations

Program	$x_i(10^6)$	$\dfrac{x_i - \bar{x}}{s}$	$F(x_i)$ = Normal Area $(-\infty$ to $Z_i)$	$F_n(x_i) = \dfrac{k}{n}$	$\lvert F_n(x_i) - F(x_i) \rvert$
A	6.800	-1.41	0.0793	0.125	0.046
B	9.457	-0.97	0.1660	0.250	0.084
C	12.404	-0.48	0.3156	0.375	0.059
D	14.168	-0.18	0.5286	0.500	0.029
E	16.386	0.18	0.5714	0.625	0.054
F	17.603	0.39	0.6517	0.750	0.098
G	19.646	0.75	0.7704	0.875	$0.105 \leftarrow D_{\max}$
H	25.730	1.75	0.9599	1.000	0.040

3.5 CONCLUDING REMARKS

The material presented in this chapter is the result of the author's involvement in various cost estimation studies. The limited availability of historical data causes the cost estimator to rely on relatively small samples. Consequently it is imperative that initial statistical analyses be based upon nonparametric statistics to reduce the number of confining assumptions necessary.

In many cases predictive capabilities are required in the cost modeling stage. Transformation of the historical data may be necessary prior to the utilization of the desired parametric statistic in this situation.

The ability of the cost estimator to speak in statistical terms concerning the final result greatly enhances the acceptability level of the derived cost estimate to higher management. The influx of quantitatively oriented decision makers in the higher management of U.S. industrial and governmental organizations implies that future cost estimators will be expected to develop and defend cost estimates from a statistical perspective. It is hoped that this chapter provides a framework for initiating statistical cost estimation.

REFERENCES

1. *Webster's New Collegiate Dictionary*, Merriam-Webster, Springfield, Mass., 1973.

2. Wine, R. L. *Statistics for Scientists and Engineers*. Prentice-Hall, Englewood Cliffs, N.J., 1964.

3. Scheaffer, R. L. and J. T. McClave. *Statistics for Engineers*. Duxbury Press, Boston, Mass., 1982.

4. Natrella, M. G. *Experimental Statistics*. National Bureau of Standards, Handbook 91, Washington, D.C., 1963.

5. Ezekiel, M. and K. A. Fox. *Methods of Correlation and Regression Analysis*, 3rd ed. *Wiley*, New York, 1967.

6. Davies, O. L. *Statistical Methods in Research and Production*. Hafner, New York, 1961.

7. Freidman, M. "The Use of Ranks to Avoid the Assumption of Normality Implicit in the Analysis of Variance." *Journal of American Statistical Association*, Vol. 32, 675–701 (1937).

8. Kruskal, W. H. and W. A. Wallis. "Use of Ranks in One-Criterion Variance Analysis." *Journal of American Statistical Association*, Vol. 47, 583–621 (1952).

4

DISCOUNTED CASH FLOW ANALYSIS

JOSEPH HAMAKER, CCA

> . . . Tom and me found the money that the robbers hid in the cave, and it made us rich. We got six thousand dollars apiece—all gold. It was an awful sight of money when it was piled up. Well, Judge Thatcher, he took it and put it out at interest, and it fetched us a dollar a day apiece, all year round—more than a body could tell what to do with.
>
> MARK TWAIN IN *ADVENTURES OF HUCKLEBERRY FINN*

4.1 INTRODUCTION

This chapter covers the most common analytical techniques used in discounted cash flow studies to account for the time value of money when choosing between alternatives. The underlying logic of the concepts is explained and the techniques of present value, equivalent annual amount, and internal rate of return are presented. Special coverage is included for cases involving the choice between multiple alternatives, the relationship between interest and inflation, and the choice of the proper discount rate.

4.1.1 The Time Value of Money Concept and When It Applies

All money has time value. Borrowed money has the time value equal to the interest payments made on the loan, whereas invested money has a time value equal to the returns or income that accrue from the investment. Money that is held as cash or in noninterest bearing accounts has time value because the money is forgoing either profits or interest that could have been earned if it had been invested in some other way.

120

Whenever an organization is contemplating an investment that involves more than one option, the time value of money will potentially affect the decision. This is true regardless of the source of the funding. It is not necessary that borrowed funds be involved, or is it necessary that the funds are visibly forgoing interest because they are being taken out of some interest bearing account. Equity money raised by the sale of stock has time value even though there is no guarantee made to the stockholder that a return will be earned or even that the original investment can be retrieved intact. The stockholder's investment has a time value because there are other uses to which the money could be put that would earn a return. By forgoing these alternate uses, the money is given a time value.

Thus it is advisable for the cost analyst to consider the time value of money whenever the costs of two or more alternatives are being compared that have disbursements and/or receipts distributed over time. Only if one alternative has lower disbursements and higher receipts in each period of the analysis, or in studies involving first costs only with no differences in cost or receipts in later periods, can the time value of money be safely ignored. In both cases there is still a time value associated with the money but not one that would affect the choice.

Before the time value of money can be considered it is necessary to first estimate the life cycle cost and revenues of options being compared excluding any interest effects. Stopping here, however, and comparing the total life cycle value of alternatives without considering interest effects may lead to a selection that is not the most cost-effective choice. Similarly, relying solely on payback period or return on investment (ROI) criteria, which, as normally calculated, do not recognize the time value of money, is inadvisable.

4.1.2 Cash Flows

The techniques for analyzing the time value of money are generally referred to as discounted cash flow analysis techniques, a cash flow being the expected life cycle costs and revenues of a contemplated investment presented as a time series of dollar disbursements and receipts. Many analysts utilize a cash flow diagram to visually present the flow of dollars. Figure 4.1 shows two cash flow diagrams for a study comparing the cash flows of two machines. Machine A is an existing machine with 3 years left in its design life of 5 years, an annual operating cost of $67,000, and a residual value (say, in this case, the scrap value after deducting the cost of dismantling the machine) of $500, and a value of $3000 if sold now. Machine B is a proposed replacement costing $30,000, with an annual operating cost of $63,000, and a residual value of $3000 at the end of its operational life of 8 years. Because Machine A has 3 years of service left and Machine B would last 8 years, the assumption is made that Machine A would be replaced with an identical machine at the end of 3 years which would give 5 more years of service, thus equalizing the service of the two machines at 8 years each. The cash flow diagrams of Figure 4.1 follow the convention of using down arrows to represent cash outflows such as investments and operating costs and up arrows to represent cash inflows such as residual values. The $5000 replacement cost of Machine A in year

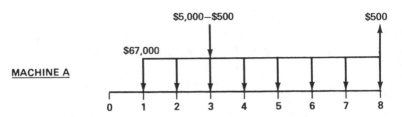

MACHINE A

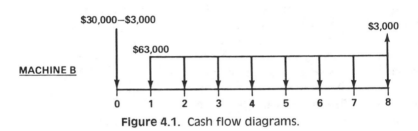

MACHINE B

Figure 4.1. Cash flow diagrams.

3 is offset to some extent by the cash inflow of $500 residual value, as shown in the diagram. The yearly operating cost of $67,000 is shown as cash outflows, and in year 8 another $500 cash inflow for residual value is shown for Machine A. Machine B's purchase cost of $30,000 is shown in the diagram reduced by $3000 which represents the cash inflow which would accrue from selling Machine A if Machine B is installed. The $63,000 annual cost of Machine B is shown over the 8 years with a residual value cash inflow in year 8 of $3000.

It is useful to recognize that discounted cash flow analysis applies to several different cash flow situations the cost analyst might encounter. The problem may involve only cash outflows such as an equipment selection, which is comparing alternatives that have identical output capability (like our preceding example). Because the revenue is the same for all options, only the life cycle costs need be considered in the time value of money analysis. Sometimes the problem might be an investment decision analysis between options that have not only different initial purchase and operating costs but also have different expected revenues as well. In such cases the cash flows carried into the time value of money analysis will need to include these revenue differences.

All such situations, if they are capable of being represented by a time series of dollar flows over time, are capable of being analyzed using the same basic time value of money concepts. The first situation (comparing the cost of equipment options with identical revenues) can be represented by an all negative cash flow for each of the options under consideration. (Here we follow the convention of assigning a negative algebraic sign to costs and any other cash outflows or disbursements and a positive sign to cash receipts, revenues, savings, or other cash inflows.) Figure 4.2 represents the same cash flows shown in the diagrams of

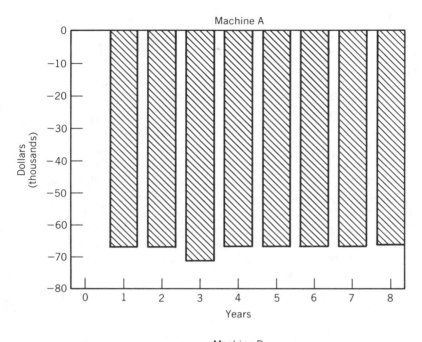

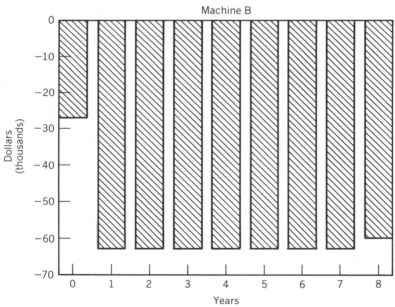

Figure 4.2. Cash flows.

Figure 4.1 but in the form of bar charts using our sign flow convention. The discounted cash flow analysis would be concerned with determining which of the options has the *least* negative cost after the time value of money is taken into account.

For cases in which the cash flows of each alternative include different revenue effects, the identical comparative techniques are applied, but the analyst would be interested in discovering which alternative resulted in the *most positive* result after taking into account the time value of money (presuming, of course, that the revenues or other cash inflows of the investment exceed the costs).

It is equivalent, and the preference of some analysts, to work with net cash flows. The net cash flow between two alternatives is simply the difference between the two cash flows. Net cash flows will typically show a differential initial investment (negative cash flows) followed by later differential returns (positive cash flows). The net cash flow of our example comparison of two machines is bar charted in Figure 4.3. The extra cost, which would be incurred in year zero, to purchase Machine B ($27,000) gives us our net investment, while the lower operating cost of Machine B and the fact that Machine A must be replaced in year 3 are responsible for our net savings. Using the net cash flow approach, the cost analyst would be interested in determining if the value of the cash flow was *at all positive* after taking into account the time value of money. Any net positive value would indicate that the savings of Machine B justify the extra cost of Machine B.

Commonly, therefore, the analysis will involve choosing between (1) one or more alternatives that have relatively high initial costs followed by relatively high

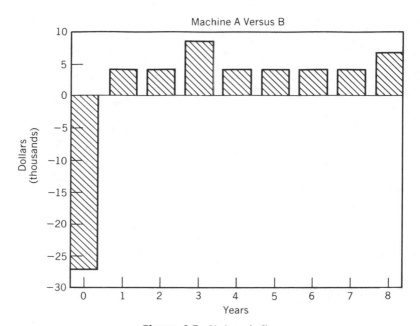

Figure 4.3. Net cash flow.

savings or revenues later in the life cycle compared to (2) one or more alternatives that have more modest initial costs but also have lower savings or revenues later (usually including the existing method). In cases where one option has lower negative cash flows and higher positive cash flows than any of the other options in each and every time period, then it is clear that this option is the most desirable (all other things being equal), and no time value of money considerations are necessary. Otherwise, when cash flow data that will be used to decide among alternatives have different magnitudes over time, then it is necessary for the estimator to consider the time value of money before the estimating job is truly complete.

4.2 STRUCTURING THE DISCOUNTED CASH FLOW ANALYSIS

Use of the discounted cash flow analysis method requires that there be at least two alternatives. Frequently there will be several. Often one of the alternatives in an investment analysis is to do nothing; instead, simply continue with the present system. Other options may involve minor modifications to the present method to make it more efficient. There may be alternatives that require major modifications to the present system and other options that involve replacement of the existing method with totally new methods. Discounted cash flow analysis is a tool for selecting the best from among those cash flows defined. It is obviously important that all viable options be considered. Additional discussion concerning the proper structuring of the cash flow analysis is provided in references [1 and 2].

4.2.1 Multiple Levels of Investment

Some of the options may have multiple levels of investment with incremental costs bringing incremental levels of performance. To the extent practical, such options should be broken down such that each marginal investment can be evaluated against its marginal return. There are sometimes alternatives that, on the whole, have attractive cash flows when compared to the competing alternatives but that actually contain subelements that, if separately analyzed based on the subelement's incremental investment versus incremental return, might be unattractive. The elimination of such subelements will enhance the overall alternative's performance. Although it is desirable to identify individually each of the potentially viable alternative courses of action, this must be balanced against the analytical advantages of holding the number of alternatives to the minimum necessary. It is perfectly acceptable to eliminate any options that may be determined to be nonviable based on preliminary analyses, and then concentrate on relatively fewer alternatives in a detailed analysis.

4.2.2 Exclusion of Common Cash Flows and Sunk Costs

It is only necessary to quantify and consider the cash flow differences between alternatives. Cash flows common to all options should be excluded. Likewise, sunk costs are of no consequence. The fact that one option (usually the existing method) has had a large previous sum of money invested in it should not bias the analysis. What is important is to identify, from the current moment onward, which of the alternatives is most economical.

4.2.3 Equal Capabilities between Alternatives

The cash flow analysis should be structured so that all alternatives are compared on an equal basis. The job of the cost estimator often includes making some analytical adjustments in the raw cash flows of the alternatives in such a manner as to compensate for nonequalities in capability. For example, it is usually the case that newer alternatives being considered have a higher performance than the old method. If this higher performance manifests itself as lower operating costs or higher revenues, then it will be taken into account when the cash flows are estimated for the alternative methods. Sometimes however, synthetic adjustments must be made to cash flows to equalize the capability between alternatives. One alternative may have certain capabilities that other alternatives do not possess. In such cases, the scope of the study can be expanded to include the services provided by the most capable alternative. Augmentations are then defined and costed that would bring the less capable alternatives up to the higher level of performance. Such augmentations do not necessarily need to be actions that are actually planned for the less capable alternatives in the event of their selection; however, they do need to be reasonable and viable augmentations that, to the extent possible, reflect the accurate worth of the additional capability.

Although it is desirable to assure that all expected and relevant cash inflows and outflows are captured in the analysis, and that any inequalities in capability are normalized by adjustments to the scope of the analysis and cash flows as discussed, there are sometimes fundamental differences in capability that cause inequalities that are extremely difficult to capture in the cash flows. At some point, adjustments to the cash flows of the systems being compared reach the point where any remaining differences must be treated in a nonquantitative manner. Any such considerations should be clearly documented and explicitly presented in the cash flow analysis. Not only does such documentation help decision makers in understanding the cash flow analysis structure, but also it becomes a potential discriminating factor in cases where quantifiable differences only in the cash flow analysis are not consequential enough to allow a confident selection.

4.2.4 Equal Economic Lifetimes

Alternatives with unequal economic lifetimes represent another common situation in discounted cash flow analyses because it is often the case that a new method will have a longer useful life than the old method. This can be compensated for by assuming that the shorter-lived options are replaced at the end of their lifetimes with an identical replacement. Thus an analysis comparing an alternative with a 5-year life to one with a 10-year life would require a 10-year cash flow and the inclusion of the replacement cost at the end of year 5 in the cash flow for the 5-year option. However, it still may be difficult to construct cash flows that end simultaneously for all options. Consider the case of an alternative with a 9-year life compared to an alternative with an 11-year life. The least common multiple of life cycles would be 99 years—an unwieldy length for a cash flow. In such cases a residual value approach can be used wherein the remaining value is included as a positive cash flow for any options that are not at the end of their lifetimes when the cash flow analysis terminates.

4.2.5 Income Tax Considerations

If the alternatives under consideration do not all have the same tax impact on the firm, then the cash flow analysis should be structured as an after-tax study by quantifying the tax differences in the cash flows in the appropriate time periods. Note that it is only necessary to calculate the *tax differences*, not the total tax effects of each alternative. Although it would involve a major accounting study to precisely quantify the different tax consequences among alternatives, it will often suffice to consider the differences in taxes due to the net deduction on capitalized (depreciable) assets and the net deduction due to operating expenses. For example, consider a comparison between option A, an existing manufacturing operation with an annual operating cost of $10,000, and option B, a 10-year lifetime capital equipment improvement that would cost $16,000 but reduce the cost of operations by $3000 annually. The existing operation can be assumed to result in a yearly operating expense tax deduction of $10,000 which, after taxes, at a rate of, say, 40%, would yield $4000 of tax savings. Option B would result in a depreciation deduction of $1600 per year (assuming straight-line depreciation), which would convert to a tax savings of $640, and an operating expense deduction of $7000, which would be worth $2800, for a total annual tax savings of $3440. Therefore option B would result in $560 additional tax each year, and this amount should be included in either option B's annual cash flow as a cost (negative) or included in option A's cash flow as a savings (positive). For studies in which the alternatives involve different expected revenues, then the cash flows must include these revenues and the estimated tax on the revenues. Perhaps only one of the alternatives being considered has an eligibility for a specific tax credit. Then this credit should be included as a savings for that alternative and included in the cash flow in the time period when the credit would be expected.

The preceding use of straight-line depreciation was a simplifying assumption for illustrative purposes which, in actual practice, should be replaced by whatever depreciation method (e.g., ARCS) is appropriate for the capital equipment being considered. Also, in light of some tendency among cost estimators to occasionally think otherwise, perhaps it should be stated explicitly that depreciation is not part of cash flow to an organization—it is simply an intermediate calculation leading to the calculation of taxable income. The inclusion of the purchase cost itself in the cash flow in the time period of its purchase fully accounts for the initial cost of the capital equipment. This point is well presented in reference [3].

4.2.6 Disregard Payment Schedules Due to Financing Arrangements

A point of confusion in cash flow analysis similar to the erroneous inclusion of depreciation in the cash flow is that of formulating cash flows that correspond to the payment schedule on the loan for an investment, as opposed to constructing cash flows that correspond to the cash flow obligation. Whether an investment that is being analyzed is to be financed by borrowed money or paid for either totally or in part by cash is not relevant to the timing of money in the cash flow analysis. The fact that the organization is financing an investment and will be making principal and interest payments over a period of time will be implicitly accounted for by the time value of money techniques to be introduced. The cash flow should therefore include the total purchase cost in the period or periods in which the purchase is expected to be made. This is usually the beginning time period in the cash flow. In instances in which investment is expected to to be made in several increments (as in the case of progress payments to a contractor), such payments do represent actual cash flows and should be timed accordingly in the analysis.

4.2.7 Uncertainties and Risk

Differences in perceived risk (both technical risks, such as the probability of a new method working as predicted, and economic risks, such as the probability of cost overruns or market uncertainties) can be handled in several ways.

The most straightforward way to account for risks is to add contingencies to the cost estimates of the alternatives. The alternatives with the highest risk would receive the highest contingency. It is, of course, sometimes difficult to decide the relative risk among options with sufficient confidence to establish the appropriate level of contingency. Also, the contingency method is limited in reflecting uncertainties in the revenue side of the cash flow.

Another method used to analyze risk is sensitivity analyses. In this approach, the cost analyst identifies the variables in the cash flow that are the least certain and then calculates the effects on the cash flows of allowing these variables to take on either lower or higher values.

A third common approach to the problem of risk is to include an allowance for risk in the discount rate used. As is shown later, the choice of the discount rate is an important consideration in the cash flow analysis, and the higher the discount rate used, the more difficult it is for new methods that require new expenditures to demonstrate cost-effectiveness against existing systems which require more modest up-front expenses. When there is some risk that the proposed new method may not mature as handsomely as projected, including a risk premium in the discount rate is a way to raise the minimum acceptable rate of return and make it more difficult for contending proposals to win.

Two more statistical, although also more complicated, approaches to risk analysis are Monte Carlo simulation and decision tree analyses. The simulation approach requires a cash flow model that will accept probability distributions for each variable in the analysis instead of single deterministic values. These distributions are then sampled a large number of times to build up a statistical data base that gives the cash flow as a function of probability. Decision makers can thus be presented not only the estimated cash flow but also the confidence associated with the estimated cash flow as well. Decision tree analysis is an approach used to analyze the uncertainties in investment analysis by laying out (usually in a tree-oriented structure) the various alternatives available to the decision maker. The probabilities of the events along the paths are estimated, and statistical methods are used to calculate the overall economic expectations of the investment.

4.3 DECISION CRITERIA

Once cash flows have been developed for each alternative, there are several time value of money decision criteria available to the cost analyst to apply to the problem of choosing between cash flows. These include present value comparisons (sometimes called net present value analysis or present worth analysis), equivalent annual amount comparisons (also called uniform annual amount and other similar names), and internal rate of return (sometimes called discounted rate of return, interest rate of return, and other names). As we show, these techniques, properly applied, are essentially equivalent and give consistent results.

4.3.1 Present Value

The most fundamental of these criteria, and probably the most commonly used, is the present value. The present value of a series of future cash flows is the value that it would be necessary to invest at the present time at a specified interest rate to be able just to make the future cash disbursements and receipts of the cash flow and completely exhaust the investment balance. The present value of $1000 one year from the present time at 10% interest is $909.09. That is, if one had $909.09 earning 10% for a year, then a $1000 payment could be made leaving a zero balance. This is easily verified because $909.09 invested at 10% for one year will have a future value of $909.09 multiplied by 1.10, which does indeed equal $1000. For this simple cash flow, the value $909.09 is the present value of the cash flow, and $1000 is the future value of the cash flow; both values represent the very same economic worth at 10% interest, and, other things being equal, a rational person would be totally indifferent in choosing one over the other. Thus present value is the reciprocal of future value and is found by dividing the future value by one plus the periodic interest rate raised to the power n where n equals the number of periods separating the present and the period of the amount. The present value of $1000 ten years from now at 10% interest is $385.54 ($1000 divided by 1.10 to the power of 10). Again, both values, $385.54 now and $1000 ten years from now are exactly equivalent at 10% interest.

The present value of a *series* of cash flows is calculated by summing the present values of each of the individual present values of the cash flow. For example, the present value of the following cash flow:

Year 0	Year 1	Year 2
−$1000	$800	$800

can be calculated as:

$$PV = [-1000/(1.10)^0] + [800/(1.10)^1] + [800/(1.10)^2]$$
$$= -1000 \qquad\qquad + 727.27 \qquad + 661.16 \qquad\qquad (4.1)$$
$$= 388.43$$

In this example, $388.43 is said to be the discounted present value of the given cash flow. The word *discount* relates to the fact that dollars in the future are not worth as much as dollars now, and the value of future dollars must be discounted both as a function of the interest rate and as a function of how far they are into the future.

In the context of present worth, the fact that future dollars are worth less than current dollars has nothing whatsoever to do with price inflation—a separate economic phenomena that is discussed in Section 4.5 of this chapter, "Relationship Between Interest and Inflation." Future dollars have less worth only because they have less time to draw returns. A dollar in hand can be invested today, whereas a dollar not in hand until a later period forgoes the potential to earn its owner returns until it is in hand. The future $800 in year 2 in the previous example are only worth $661.16 at the present time. Because having $661.16 today to invest at 10% interest is equivalent to waiting 2 years and receiving $800, one is theoretically indifferent about the choice.

Mathematically, as we have seen, a cash flow is discounted to its present value by calculating the present worth of each of its periodic amounts at the time selected as the present. It does not matter what instant in time is selected as "the present" as long as each cash flow being compared is discounted to the same "present." The present may be defined as the year 1914. Or it can be defined just as well as the year corresponding to the first cash flow, which is the normal convention in discounted cash flow analyses. It could also be defined as some "future present" such as the year 2121 or, say, the year of the last cash flow in the analysis. In this case the calculations would utilize negative exponents. Let us say we want to repeat our discounting example but define the present to be the end of year 2. The resulting present value would be:

Year 0	Year 1	Year 2

$$PV = [-1000/(1.1)^{-2}] + [800/(1.10)^{-1}] + [800/(1.10)^{-0}] \qquad (4.2)$$
$$= -1000\,(1.1)^2 \qquad + 800\,(1.10)^1 \qquad + 800\,(1.10)^0$$
$$= -1210 \qquad\qquad + 880.00 \qquad\quad + 800.00$$
$$= 470.00$$

This $470.00 value is the present value of our cash flow because we have temporarily defined the end of year 2 to be the present. It should be apparent from the second line of this calculation that we are performing an operation that is equivalent to what we would do if asked to calculate the future value of the cash flow at the end of year two. That is, $470.00 is also the future value of the cash flow, or the worth of the cash flow at 10% interest at the end of year 2. The same result for future value could be obtained by calculating the future value of the $388.43 that we initially calculated as the year zero present value. The future value of $388.43 two years hence is

$$FV = \$388.43 \ (1.10)^2 = \$470.00 \tag{4.3}$$

Thus the present value at the end of year zero of $388.43 is equivalent to the future value of $470.00 at the end of year two, both of which are equivalent to the original three-year cash flow of −$1000, $800, $800. In fact, there are an infinite number of other equivalent values because there are an infinite number of periods that we could define as present or future. Thus present value and future value are equivalent concepts, both of which collapse a time series of dollar amounts into a single dollar amount. This amount represents the worth of the entire cash flow it replaces taking into account the time value of money.

Therefore the general equation for present value is

$$P = F \frac{1}{(1 + i)^n} \tag{4.4}$$

where P is present value, F is the future cash flow amount, i is the discount rate decimal equivalent (e.g., 0.10 for 10%), and n is the number of periods separating the present and the future time periods. Most textbooks on engineering economics contain tables of the function for discount factors at various interest rates for any number of years. Today, most discounted cash flow analyses are performed on computers, which simplifies the mathematics of discounting cash flows. Many of the software packages that are popular among cost estimators (such as spreadsheets) have time value of money functions such as present value.

In comparing two alternatives, using present value as the decision criterion in discounted cash flow analysis, the alternative that enjoys the highest positive present value or the lowest negative present value is the preferred option (still following the algebraic sign convention of negative dollars for costs and positive dollars for savings, revenues, and other cash inflows). As was mentioned previously, the instant in time chosen as the present in the discounting procedure does not matter at all as long as each alternative is computed to the same present. It is common to define the present as the period where the cash flow with the earliest outlays begins. Some cost analysts prefer to use future value as a decision criterion. This is equivalent to defining some future time period as the present and is perfectly valid. Instead of calculating the value of a cash flow at a period of time close to the outset of the activity, the analyst calculates the value of all the cash flows closer to the end period of the cash flows. The equation, which again is in tables in most engineering economy textbooks, is just the reciprocal of present value:

$$F = P (1 + i)^n \qquad (4.5)$$

The avowed advantage in using future instead of present value in discounted cash flow analyses is that future value is easier to explain because it is the same as calculating the ultimate balance if one borrowed each invested (negative) amount in a series of future cash flows and continually refinanced both principal and interest until the time of the last cash flow (e.g., an arrangement like a construction loan for a new house) and *also* reinvested each (positive) return and its associated interest until the time of the last cash flow (e.g., like a compound interest savings account). Presumably some decision makers are more capable of identifying with the future worth of a cash flow than the discounted present worth. In any event, both present value and future value will give consistent results when they are used as decision criteria to choose between alternatives.

4.3.2 Equivalent Annual Amount

Another technique used as a criterion for selection in discounted cash flow analysis is the equivalent annual amount. In this approach, the cash flows being compared are all converted to a constant annual amount over a specified time period that has the same present value as the original cash flow. In other words, the original cash flow, which may have periodic amounts varying in magnitude from period to period, is converted to a uniform cash flow (one with the same dollar magnitude in each period) that has a present value equivalent to the original cash flow. Mathematically, the procedure is composed of two steps: The first calculates the present value of the series of cash flows just as in the present value technique. The second step uses what is generally called a capital recovery factor to calculate what constant amount of money spread over n periods at i interest rate would have the original present value. Therefore, to calculate the annual equivalent over n periods at i interest of a cash flow with a present value of P, use:

$$A = \frac{P[i(1 + i)^n]}{(1 + i)^n - 1} \qquad (4.6)$$

where A is the equivalent annual amount, and the parenthetical expression being multiplied by P is the capital recovery factor. For example, a cash flow that has been found to have a present value of $10,000 can also be represented over 5 years at 10% interest with an equivalent annual amount of $2637.97. The capital recovery factor equation is the same equation that lenders use to calculate the payment on a loan; $2637.97 is the same value one would be quoted by a banker as the annual payment on a $10,000.00 loan for 5 years (while for monthly payments n would be entered as the number of months over which the loan was to be financed and i would be entered as one-twelfth of the annual interest rate). Once two or more cash flows have been thus annualized, the preferred choice is the one with the highest positive present value or lowest negative present value.

One advantage of the equivalent annual amount approach is that in applications where the analysis is choosing the most cost effective production method for a product, the equivalent annual amount can be calculated over a period of time corresponding to the product's revenue life cycle, and the results of the analysis can be presented as a unit cost for the product. For example, if the production is 1000 units per year, the cost per unit in the preceding example could be quoted at $2.64 per unit. Said another way, to realize a 10% rate of return, the products must be sold for $2.64 apiece. For the next alternate production method, the cash flow could also be converted to a cost per unit and compared to the $2.64 value. A lower cost would cause the corresponding method to be selected whereas a higher cost per unit would cause its rejection.

A second advantage to the equivalent annual amount technique is that in many cost analyses the recurring annual cost (of a production method for example) is known. Since this cost is already "annualized" there is no need to perform any other time value of money calculations on these amounts. All that is required is to annualize any costs that are not on an annual basis (nonrecurring capital cost for example) using the appropriate capital recovery factor and to add the result to the known annual cost. Let us say that a proposed alternate method to produce our product involves the purchase of a $5000 machine and a $1000 annual operating cost made up of materials, labor, and all other recurring production costs. Assuming a 5-year life for our machine, the same capital recovery factor as used before would be applied to get a $1318.99 equivalent annual amount for the machine cost (0.2638 × $5000). This could be added directly to the other known annual costs of $1000 to get the total equivalent annual amount of $2318.99, which works out to $2.32 per unit. Since this is less than the $2.64 cost per unit of the former method, the new method is preferred.

4.3.3 Assumption of an Infinite Horizon

Although most cash flow analyses do set a limit on the length of the life cycle that is considered, limiting the economic horizon to one or more multiples of the service lives actually understates the value of the preferred alternative. The justification for this statement is that if two or more alternatives for future investment are compared in a discounted cash flow analysis, and one alternative is chosen because it demonstrates economic benefits over the other alternatives, then this benefit stream will likely extend indefinitely into the future. Why indefinitely and not just to the end of the alternative's useful life? Because at the end of the useful life of the chosen alternative, the alternative will either be replaced with yet another alternative that is at least as, and probably more, cost-effective. That is, a rational decision-making organization will never choose to return to any of the original contending alternatives which were proven to be less cost-effective, or will they ever again accept any alternative that is less cost-effective than the chosen alternative—instead they will either continue forever with the exact replacements of the chosen alternative or something even more cost-effective. Thus the benefits of the chosen alternative will continue forever at a level as great as that shown for it in the original analysis.

This concept, also called perpetual worth or capitalized costs, can be used in the comparison of alternatives by first calculating the equivalent annual amount of each alternative and then dividing the result by the interest rate. For our preceding cash flow, with an equivalent annual amount of $2637.97 over 5 years at an interest rate of 8%, the present value of an infinite horizon annual amount would be $2637.97 divided by 0.08 or $32,975. That is, the present value of a series of $2637.97 annual cash flows stretching into the future forever is $32,975. Although this idea overwhelmed Huck Finn, a moment's reflection will illuminate the principle because $32,975 put into an 8% bearing investment now would yield an annual interest income of $2637.97 forever without ever touching the principal. Incidentally, Huck's and Tom Sawyer's $6000 put out at interest by Judge Thatcher earning a dollar a day works out to be about 6% interest, apparently the going rate in the time of the novel (the mid-1800s).

Once an infinite horizon present worth has been calculated for two or more alternatives, the one with the most positive or least negative value is the preferred choice. The difference between two such infinite horizon present worths represents the preferred alternative's economic benefits with infinite horizon when compared to the other alternative.

Introducing infinite horizon into a comparison of alternatives will not change the choice that would have been made with either the present value or the equivalent annual amount methods using a finite horizon. It is simply another equivalent method. However, infinite horizon assigns a more encompassing measure to the ultimate economic benefits that will be obtained from an investment. Thus it is sometimes favored in applications such as those dealing with the justification of research and development funds when it is considered useful to remind decision makers that the approval of such investments might lead to far greater ultimate benefits than are indicated by simply calculating the benefits through the first life cycle of some potential improvement made possible by the R&D funding.

For discounted cash flow analyses of relatively long life cycles (say 30 years or longer) and/or relatively high interest rates (say 15% or more), the assumption of infinite horizon may not yield present value quantities significantly higher than those that would have been obtained without infinite horizon. This is because discount factors decrease over time and do so more rapidly at higher discount rates, as shown in Figure 4.4. For all practical purposes, discount factors approach zero after three decades or so for interest rates above 15%. Any cash flow extending beyond this (including one going to infinity) is essentially zeroed out by the discounting process.

4.3.4 Internal Rate of Return

Present values, future values, and equivalent annual amounts are all really just extensions of the same basic concept. Properly applied, they all give consistent

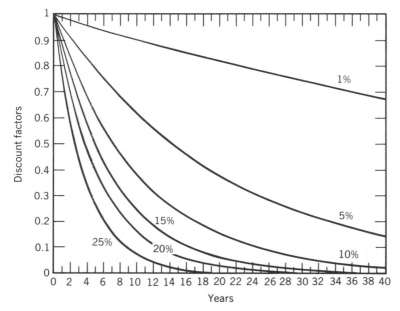

Figure 4.4. Discount factors decrease over time.

and reliable results when choosing among alternatives. A fourth technique often used as a decision criterion in discounted cash flow analyses is the internal rate of return (IRR). Assuming that a new method is being compared to an existing method, in a nondiscounted analysis one would say that an incremental investment of, say, $1000 that results in returns of $200 per year is a 20% rate of return. This simple return on investment (ROI) calculation fails to take into account that each dollar in the $200 returns flowing in each year are not worth, in the time value of money sense, the same as the dollars in the $1000 invested at time zero. The internal rate of return is a discounted rate of return that *does* correct for the differing time values of the dollars in the cash flows.

The internal rate of return for a given cash flow is defined as the discount rate that results in a present value of zero. Thus the IRR method finds the interest rate that equalizes the present value of the investment and the present value of the returns. For our ROI cash flow example, the IRR is 15.098%. (This can be verified by discounting the cash flow—a negative $1000 followed by 10 positive $200 amounts—by 15.098%. A net present value of zero will be found). Since the simple ROI result of 20% does not take into account the time value of money, it is to be expected in this case that IRR should be less than ROI.

The usual method for calculating the IRR is a trial and error procedure to discover just what discount rate will yield a zero present value for the cash flow. Sometimes this is combined with graphic interpolation. Figure 4.5 shows the net present value of the above cash flow over a range of discount rates. Because net present value goes negative at rates just above the internal rate of return, the IRR can be surmised from the graph to be very near the value of 15%. The use of a

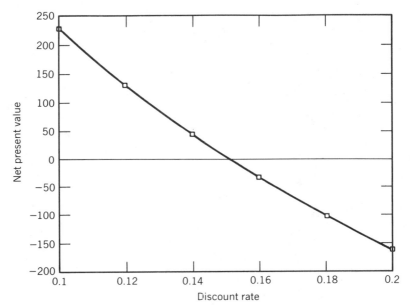

Figure 4.5. Internal rate of return = 15%.

computer and some iterative programming logic obviously facilitates such a procedure. Again, many popular software packages such as spreadsheets have built in IRR functions which make the calculations easy, fast, accurate, and eliminate graphic interpolation.

Once IRR is known for a cash flow, it is compared to the minimum acceptable rate of return, and the investment is either accepted or rejected accordingly. Considerations involved in specifying the minimum acceptable rate of return are discussed in Section 4.6, "Choosing A Discount Rate." Presuming that the minimum acceptable rate of return is known, the use of IRR as an investment decision criterion has a certain appeal because of this straightforward manner in which the investment decision is made—as long as the contemplated investment meets the organization's minimum rate of return requirement, then it is considered acceptable.

A potential problem with the use of the IRR as an investment decision criterion can occur in certain circumstances. Because the calculation of IRR involves finding a solution to a complex function, certain cash flows that are not well behaved may cause either multiple solutions or no solutions. A cash flow that begins negative and then turns positive will generally cause no problems in the IRR calculation. Cash flows with multiple sign changes can, however, result in multiple mathematically valid solutions, a disturbing outcome in investment analysis. In such an event, the cost estimator can rely on the criteria of present value and/or equivalent annual amount.

4.3.5 Example of the Present Value Method

Table 4.1 demonstrates the present value method for a problem involving the comparison of three alternatives. The first two alternatives are the two machines described earlier in the cash flow diagram of Figure 4.1 and the bar-charted cash flows of Figures 4.2 and 4.3. Machine A is an existing machine which had a purchase cost 2 years ago of $5000. The machine is designed for a life of 5 years, and thus has remaining 3 years of useful life. If sold now, its value would be $3000, and its residual value at the end of its life is $500. At the anticipated production rate, the machine has an annual operating cost of $67,000. Machine B is a proposed replacement. Machine B has a purchase and installation cost of $30,000, an 8-year life, a $3000 residual value at the end of 8 years, and a yearly operating cost of $63,000. This problem adds a third option, Machine C, another proposed replacement for Machine A, with an initial cost of $40,000, an 8-year life, a $4000 residual value and an operating cost of $60,000 yearly.

TABLE 4.1. Example of the Present Value Method

Assumptions: End of period cash flows
Negative cash flows shown in parentheses
Discount rate used 10%

		Cases		
		(A) Existing Machine A	(B) Proposed Machine B	(C) Proposed Machine C
Purchase cost		$5,000	$30,000	$40,000
Design life		5	8	8
Remaining life (years)		3	8	8
Value if sold now		$3,000	NA	NA
Residual value at end of life		$500	$3,000	$4,000
Annual operating cost		$67,000	$63,000	$60,000
	Year	Total Cash Flows		
(Present value at end of year 0)	0		($27,000)	($37,000)
	1	($67,000)	($63,000)	($60,000)
	2	($67,000)	($63,000)	($60,000)
	3	($71,500)	($63,000)	($60,000)
	4	($67,000)	($63,000)	($60,000)
	5	($67,000)	($63,000)	($60,000)
	6	($67,000)	($63,000)	($60,000)
	7	($67,000)	($63,000)	($60,000)
	8	($66,500)	($60,000)	($56,000)
Undiscounted total		($540,000)	($528,000)	($513,000)
Present value		($360,588)	($361,701)	($355,230)

This problem is the classic case of proposed new alternatives with incremental initial investments that promise later savings in operational costs. Machines B and C cost $30,000 and $40,000, respectively, but offer $4000 and $7000 savings, respectively, when compared to the existing machine. The total cash flows are shown in Table 4.1 (negative cash disbursements shown in parentheses) based on the data for each of the three alternatives. Table 4.1 (and all further examples in this chapter) follow the convention of assuming end of year cash flows. That is, it is assumed that each cash disbursement or receipt occurs on December 31. Thus in Table 4.1 the present is defined as December 31 in year zero. Both Machine B and Machine C are placed in service on December 31 of year zero with their purchase costs entered in the cash flow at that time and their first annual operating cost placed at the end of year 1. Notice that the $5000 original cost for Machine A is a sunk cost and is not included in year zero. Years 1 through 8 contain the respective operating cost for each of the machines. In addition, because Machine A has only 3 years of remaining life it must be assumed that Machine A must be replaced at the end of year 3 to provide the continuing service of the two proposed alternatives. Therefore year 3's cash flow for Machine A contains an additional negative cash flow of $5000 for replacement. In year 8 of the cash flows each alternative is given credit for its residual value (a positive value which reduces the net cash outflow as shown).

The discount rate for the problem of Table 4.1 is assumed to be 10%. The last row of Table 4.1 gives the discounted present value of each of these three cash flows. These happen to be present values as of December 31 in year zero, but as discussed earlier, they could just as well have been calculated at any other time defined as present provided that all three alternatives were discounted to the same time period. Because Machine C has the least present value of costs ($355,230) at our specified discount rate of 10%, it is the preferred alternative. The present values were calculated by summing the discounted values for each year's cash flow using our equation for present value:

$$P = F \frac{1}{(1 + i)^n} \tag{4.7}$$

which for year zero's cash flow for Machine C would be

$$P = \$37,000 \left[\frac{1}{(1.10)^0} \right]$$
$$= 37,000 \tag{4.8}$$

and for year 1's cash flow for Machine C would be

$$P = \$60,000 \left[\frac{1}{(1.10)^1} \right]$$
$$= 54,545 \tag{4.9}$$

and for subsequent years would be:

$$P = \$60,000 \left[\frac{1}{(1.10)^2}\right] = \$49,586 \text{ for year 2}$$

$$P = \$60,000 \left[\frac{1}{(1.10)^3}\right] = \$45,079 \text{ for year 3}$$

$$P = \$60,000 \left[\frac{1}{(1.10)^4}\right] = \$40,981 \text{ for year 4}$$

$$P = \$60,000 \left[\frac{1}{(1.10)^5}\right] = \$37,255 \text{ for year 5} \qquad (4.10)$$

$$P = \$60,000 \left[\frac{1}{(1.10)^6}\right] = \$33,868 \text{ for year 6}$$

$$P = \$60,000 \left[\frac{1}{(1.10)^7}\right] = \$30,789 \text{ for year 7}$$

$$P = \$56,000 \left[\frac{1}{(1.10)^8}\right] = \$26,124 \text{ for year 8}$$

which totals to a present value of $355,230 (ignoring rounding errors).

Table 4.2 adds additional rows to the previous example to demonstrate the selection between the same three alternatives using the equivalent annual amount method. The equivalent annual amount is shown in the table for each alternative just under the previously calculated present values. As can be seen, Machine C has the lowest annualized cost ($66,586) at our 10% rate of interest and would be chosen by this criterion as well. The $66,586 is calculated by multiplying the previously determined present value by the capital recovery factor for 8 years at 10% interest:

$$A = \frac{P\left[i(1 + i)^n\right]}{(1 + i)^n - 1}$$

$$= \$355,230 \, (0.187444) \qquad (4.11)$$

$$= \$66,586$$

As shown in the bottom portion of Table 4.2, 8-year cash flows of the annual amounts have the same present value as their respective original cash flows. For Machine C, for example, a uniform cash flow of $66,586 each year for 8 years has the same $355,230 present value as the original cash. Thus either present value or equivalent annual amount capture the worth of the entire cash flow in a single value that can be compared directly to the present value or equivalent annual amount of another cash flow.

TABLE 4.2. Example of the Equivalent Annual Amount Method

Assumptions: End of period cash flows
Negative cash flows shown in parentheses
Discount rate used 10%

		Cases		
		(A) Existing Machine A	(B) Proposed Machine B	(C) Proposed Machine C
Purchase cost		$5,000	$30,000	$40,000
Design life		5	8	8
Remaining life (years)		3	8	8
Value if sold now		$3,000	NA	NA
Residual value at end of life		$500	$3,000	$4,000
Annual operating cost		$67,000	$63,000	$60,000
	Year	**Total Cash Flows**		
(Present value at end of year 0)	0		($27,000)	($37,000)
	1	($67,000)	($63,000)	($60,000)
	2	($67,000)	($63,000)	($60,000)
	3	($71,500)	($63,000)	($60,000)
	4	($67,000)	($63,000)	($60,000)
	5	($67,000)	($63,000)	($60,000)
	6	($67,000)	($63,000)	($60,000)
	7	($67,000)	($63,000)	($60,000)
	8	($66,500)	($60,000)	($56,000)
Undiscounted total		($540,000)	($528,000)	($513,000)
Present value		($360,588)	($361,701)	($355,230)
Equivalent annual amount		($67,590)	($67,799)	($66,586)
	Year	**Equivalent Cash Flows**		
(Present value at end of year 0)	0			
	1	($67,590)	($67,799)	($66,586)
	2	($67,590)	($67,799)	($66,586)
	3	($67,590)	($67,799)	($66,586)
	4	($67,590)	($67,799)	($66,586)
	5	($67,590)	($67,799)	($66,586)
	6	($67,590)	($67,799)	($66,586)
	7	($67,590)	($67,799)	($66,586)
	8	($67,590)	($67,799)	($66,586)
Present value		($360,588)	($361,701)	($355,230)

4.4 SELECTION FROM MULTIPLE ALTERNATIVES

The discussion to this point has been limited to selecting the most cost-effective investment from only two or three alternatives. Extending the present value and equivalent annual amount methods to the problem of selecting from a large number of alternatives is straightforward—the alternative that presents the most positive (or least negative) present value or annual equivalent cost is the most economical choice. The IRR method can also be used, of course, to select from a large number of contending investments. There is, however, a potential pitfall when using IRR as the decision criterion when comparing multiple alternatives. It is not necessarily correct to calculate the IRR independently on each alternative cash flow and choose the option with the highest IRR. Instead, the investment options are placed in ascending order (the alternative with the lowest investment cost is put first, followed by increasingly more costly alternatives, with the alternative having the highest investment cost put last). The incremental cash flow of the second compared to the first alternative is then subjected to the IRR method. If the resulting rate of return exceeds the minimum acceptable rate of return, the second alternative becomes the new defender. Otherwise, the first alternative is retained as the defender. The incremental cash flow of the third alternative compared to the defender is then developed, and the resulting marginal rate of return is compared to the minimum acceptable rate of return just as was done before. Either a new defender is found or the previous defender is retained, depending on whether the IRR is higher or lower respectively than the minimum acceptable IRR. This pair by pair incremental cash flow comparison approach is continued until all alternatives have been completed. The next highest investment is always selected as long as it meets or exceeds the minimum IRR. The justification for this approach is that an alternative is attractive if the incremental investment results in sufficient incremental returns to meet our minimum requirements. This is not necessarily the same as selecting the alternative that yields the overall highest IRR.

There can be alternatives that yield overall rates of return that are higher than the competing alternatives but that are unable to absorb our total available investment capital. Other alternatives that may cost more initially and yield a lower overall rate of return may actually be the wisest choice because they are able to put more of our capital to work at rates higher than our minimum rate of return. As we discuss later when we explore the proper choice of discount rates, the minimum acceptable rate of return is defined by the other opportunities that are available for investment. As long as a contemplated investment is able to give a rate of return that exceeds this opportunity it should be made.

The example problem in Table 4.3 demonstrates the foregoing premise. Six alternatives are compared; the first three are the same as in our previous problems using present value and equivalent annual amount. First of all, the total cash flows of these alternatives are used to calculate present value and equivalent annual amount. These two criteria had already been calculated for Machines A, B, and C. Although previously we selected C based on its lowest present worth of costs

TABLE 4.3. Example of the Internal Rate of Return Method for Selecting from Multiple Alternatives

Assumptions: End of period cash flows
Negative cash flows shown in parentheses
Discount rate used 10%

			Cases			
	(A) Existing Machine A	(B) Proposed Machine B	(C) Proposed Machine C	(D) Proposed Machine D	(E) Proposed Machine E	(F) Proposed Machine F
Purchase cost	$5,000	$30,000	$40,000	$45,000	$50,000	$55,000
Design life	5	8	8	8	8	8
Remaining life (years)	3	8	8	8	8	8
Value if sold now	$3,000	NA	NA	NA	NA	NA
Residual value at end of life	$500	$3,000	$4,000	$4,500	$5,000	$5,500
Annual operating cost	$67,000	$63,000	$60,000	$58,500	$57,500	$56,800

Year			Total Cash Flows			
0		($27,000)	($37,000)	($42,000)	($47,000)	($52,000)
1	($67,000)	($63,000)	($60,000)	($58,500)	($57,500)	($56,800)
2	($67,000)	($63,000)	($60,000)	($58,500)	($57,500)	($56,800)
3	($71,500)	($63,000)	($60,000)	($58,500)	($57,500)	($56,800)
4	($67,000)	($63,000)	($60,000)	($58,500)	($57,500)	($56,800)
5	($67,000)	($63,000)	($60,000)	($58,500)	($57,500)	($56,800)
6	($67,000)	($63,000)	($60,000)	($58,500)	($57,500)	($56,800)
7	($67,000)	($63,000)	($60,000)	($58,500)	($57,500)	($56,800)
8	($66,500)	($60,000)	($56,000)	($54,000)	($52,500)	($51,300)

(Present value at end of year 0)

Undiscounted total	($540,000)	($528,000)	($513,000)	($505,500)	($502,000)	($500,900)
Present value	($360,588)	($361,701)	($355,230)	($351,994)	($351,426)	($352,458)
Equivalent annual amount	($67,590)	($67,799)	($66,586)	($65,979)	($65,873)	($66,066)

Net Cash Flows

Year					
(Present value at end of year 0) 0	($27,000)	($37,000)	($5,000)	($5,000)	($5,000)
1	$4,000	$7,000	$1,500	$1,000	$700
2	$4,000	$7,000	$1,500	$1,000	$700
3	$8,500	$11,500	$1,500	$1,000	$700
4	$4,000	$7,000	$1,500	$1,000	$700
5	$4,000	$7,000	$1,500	$1,000	$700
6	$4,000	$7,000	$1,500	$1,000	$700
7	$4,000	$7,000	$1,500	$1,000	$700
8	$6,500	$10,500	$2,000	$1,500	$1,200
Undiscounted total	$12,000	$27,000	$7,500	$3,500	$1,100
Net present value	($1,113)	$5,358	$3,236	$568	($1,032)
Equivalent annual amount	($209)	$1,004	$607	$107	($193)
Internal rate of return	8.87%	13.79%	25.56%	12.93%	4.36%

equal to −$355,230, we can now see that the new proposals for Machines D through F offer even lower cost alternatives. Because E's present value of cost at −$351,426 is lower than either D or F, we favor Machine E as the most attractive of these options. The same selection is confirmed by the equivalent annual amounts tabulated just below the present values.

Now let us apply internal rate of return as the decision criterion in this problem. First, the internal rate of return calculation requires a cash flow with an investment (i.e., negative dollars) and a return (i.e., positive dollars). The total cash flows in Table 4.3 for our six alternatives are all negatives since they represent the expected costs of six different machines. Therefore we must develop the net cash flows between these total cash flows because we are interested in knowing if the extra investment required by the increasingly more expensive options as we progress toward the right side of the table are worth the extra savings.

The net cash flow of our first proposal, Machine B, is calculated at the bottom of Table 4.3 in column B by subtracting the cash flow of Machine A from the cash flow of Machine B. Thus we obtain a net cash flow with an initial outlay of $27,000 followed by savings of $4000 for 2 years (the difference in operating cost), $8500 in year 3 (due to the replacement of Machine A), $4000 again for years 4 through 7, and finally $6500 in year 12 (due to the difference in residual value in the two machines). The net present value and net equivalent annual amount are displayed at the bottom of Table 4.3. Both criteria tell us Machine B is not a very good alternative when compared to Machine A. (Remember that we are now dealing with net cash flows in which it is to be hoped that the positive return exceeds the negative investment.) The internal rate of return of 8.87% is less than our specified minimum acceptable rate of return of 10%. Just as was the case when we examined the total cash flows with present value and equivalent annual amount, Machine B is to be rejected and Machine A continues as the defending alternative.

The net cash flow of the second proposal, Machine C, is calculated in column C by subtracting the cash flow of the defending alternative, Machine A, from the cash flow of Machine C. The net cash flow shows an investment of $37,000 followed by returns of $7000 for 2 years, $11,500 in year 3, and $7000 each year until the last year, when the marginal return is $10,500. For this alternative, both the net present value and net equivalent annual amount at 10% are positive, indicating that the option will give a return greater than the minimum required rate. Just how much more is indicated by the internal rate of return—exactly 13.79%. Thus Machine C becomes our new defender, supplanting the existing machine.

Column D gives the marginal investment and return profile for Machine D—another $5000 invested will get us an additional $1500 per year and $2000 in the final year. The net present value and net equivalent annual amount are positive at 10%, and the internal rate of return is 25.56%.

Column E gives us the marginal profile for Machine E—another $5000 invested will return $1000 for 7 years and $1500 in the final year. But is it worth it? The IRR is only 12.93%—not nearly as good as alternative D's 25.56%. Or is it? The answer is that Machine E does offer a better opportunity than D even though the rate of return is considerably less. How can this be? It is because the 12.93% is the marginal return only on the $5000 of extra investment, and since 10% represents our next best opportunity for putting our capital to work, if we do not choose to invest it in Machine E at 12.93%, then we will be able to earn only 10% elsewhere on our $5000. It is our choice—put the $5000 out at 12.93% or put it out at 10%. But if we succumb to this notion of picking E because its marginal return is greater than our minimum acceptable rate, will we not be loosing the opportunity of getting the 25.56% rate of return of Machine D? Not at all. Remember that E shows more savings per year than D (generally $1000 per year more). Alternative E offers us all the savings of D, plus some.

Finally, the net cash flow of Machine F in Table 4.3 results in all three criteria being undesirable, indicating that this alternative is not attractive. The additional investment of $5000 over the current defender, Machine E, yields $700 per year in returns and $1200 the final year, but the internal rate of return calculation indicates that this is only a 4.36% rate of return on the extra $5000. Our 10% opportunities offer us much more than that, and thus alternative F is rejected.

For those still troubled by the choice of alternative E and its 12.93% rate of return over D, look back at the top portion of Table 4.3 where the present value and equivalent annual amounts both indicated that Machine E is clearly the most cost-effective choice. As was said before, properly applied and interpreted, all three decision criteria give consistent results. Given the dangers of internal rate of return, would it not be better to stick with present value or equivalent annual amounts as more reliable decision criteria? Present value and equivalent annual amount will provide the correct choice every time with relatively low risk, but internal rate of return offers advantages at times. As was demonstrated in the example of Table 4.3, rate of return is an attractive criterion in choosing among multiple alternatives because it not only indicates the best alternative, but also perhaps gives the analyst and management a better intuitive feel for the degree of goodness through the comparison of the rate of return of the alternatives under consideration and the firm's other opportunities for rates of return. Present value and equivalent annual amount, on the other hand, convey less of a direct corollary meaning to the decision maker. Given the availability of computers in solving for each of the decision criteria that have been discussed, it is not infeasible to calculate each. An excellent treatment of the proper use of the various time value of money decision criteria is offered in reference [2].

4.5 THE RELATIONSHIP BETWEEN INTEREST AND INFLATION

A common mistake in discounted cash flow analysis is incorrectly accounting for the relationship between interest and inflation. Interest and inflation, although related in many ways, are totally different economic phenomena. Interest is a rent paid to the owner of money by the borrower of that money, or equivalently, is a rate of return earned (or lost) on an investment. Thus interest, by having the power of making capital either grow or shrink over time, gives money a time value.

Inflation also causes money to either increase or decrease in value over time, but this change in value is due to changes in the value of money as a standard unit of measure. The worth of a laborer's day may be put down in a cost estimate, but in periods of either inflation or deflation the value used will soon be out of date because laborer's are no longer being paid the same amount for a day's work. Inflation then, is not the same thing as interest. Inflation is instead a change in the measuring system—a change in the value of the dollar due to many reasons that have nothing to do with changes in value due to interest. (This disavowal of any connection between interest and inflation is, of course, only true in the micro-economic environment of engineering economics—the economics of a single firm for instance. In macroeconomics, interest and inflation are not so unrelated.)

Although interest and inflation are two different things, they are related to each other in fairly constant and predictable ways. Money that is earning a return (for example, money in an interest bearing account in a bank) is growing by an amount that can be calculated using compound interest equations, as we have already seen. For example, a $1000 principal amount invested at a 10% annual compounded interest rate grows in the following manner:

Year 1	Year 2	Year 3	Year 4
$1000	$1000(1.1)^1$	$1000(1.1)^2$	$1000(1.1)^3$
$1000	$1100	$1210	$1331

However, if inflation is some positive rate (say 6%), then those earnings are also decreasing in value at a rate equal to the inflation rate. This can be calculated as follows:

Year 1	Year 2	Year 3	Year 4
$1000	$1100/(1.06)^1$	$1210/(1.06)^2$	$1331/(1.06)^3$
$1000	$1038	$1077	$1118

This second calculation yields a cash flow that includes the effects of interest after correcting for inflation.

Since, as the previous example demonstrated, interest is calculated by multiplying the principle amount by the interest rate, and inflation is calculated by dividing by the inflation rate, the estimator can save a step by first adjusting the interest rate:

$$\text{adjusted interest} = \frac{1 + \text{interest rate}}{1 + \text{inflation rate}}$$

$$= \frac{1.10}{1.06}$$

$$= 1.038 \qquad (4.12)$$

and then the previous two-step operation becomes one step by using the adjusted interest rate:

Year 1	Year 2	Year 3	Year 4
$1000	$1000(1.038)^1	$1000(1.038)^2	$1000(1.038)^3
$1000	$1038	$1077	$1118

Economists call this interest rate after correcting for inflation the *real* rate of return or the *real* rate of interest. Over the long term, the rate of inflation and the rate of interest in the economy track each other and in fact the real rate of interest tends to remain fairly constant. Figure 4.6 shows this tracking trend in the inflation and interest rates in the United States from 1958 to 1986. As can be seen from the figure, when inflation is high, interest rates tend to rise as well because the holders of capital in the economy resist lending their money out at rates that result in small real gains. As we discussed, the real interest rate is the market interest rate divided by the inflation rate. Performing this arithmetic on the data of the previous figure results in Figure 4.7. Until the 1980s real rates tended to remain under 4%. After 1980, inflation decreased dramatically while federal budget deficits kept the market rate of interest high, resulting in real rates of interest that were double the recent historical average.

There are, incidentally, a number of sources for indices of historical interest rates and inflation rates available for the cost analyst to consult. Historical interest and inflation data for the United States are available from the *Department of Commerce Statistical Abstract of the United States* [4], an annual publication available in most libraries or for sale by the Superintendent of Documents, U.S. Government Printing Office in Washington. Historical as well as forecasted indices are available from several econometric forecasting firms such as Data Resources, Inc. in Lexington, Massachusetts [5]. These sources publish a number of specialized indices for specific sectors of the economy and specific industries as well as the more general indices such as the GNP deflator and prime interest rate.

The choice of the proper interest rate to use in a discounted cash flow analysis is discussed at more length in the Section 4.6, entitled "Choosing a Discount Rate." It is sufficient to say, for now, that the choice tends to be highly company specific depending on each company's cost of capital and other investment opportunities.

The proper choice of an historical inflation index is usually somewhat less company specific and more tied to the sector of the economy in which the company participates. The so called GNP deflator of Figure 4.6 is a very general measure of inflation in the overall output of the economy. Familiar indices such as the Consumer Price Index and Producer Price Index measure aggregate consumer and wholesale prices respectively. More applicable to the cost analyst are the detailed breakouts of these aggregate indices which are published by the previously mentioned sources. Lacking accurate company records on what historical inflation has been for their specific sector, the cost analyst would generally find such indices as those published by the government and the private econometric firms very useful.

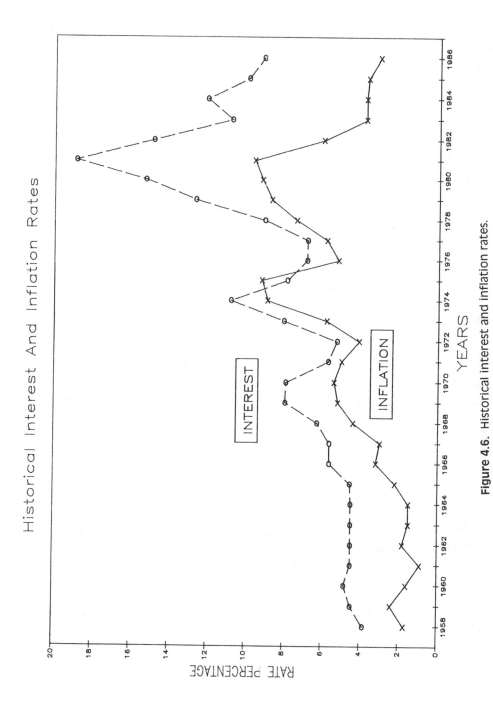

Figure 4.6. Historical interest and inflation rates.

148

Real Interest Rates

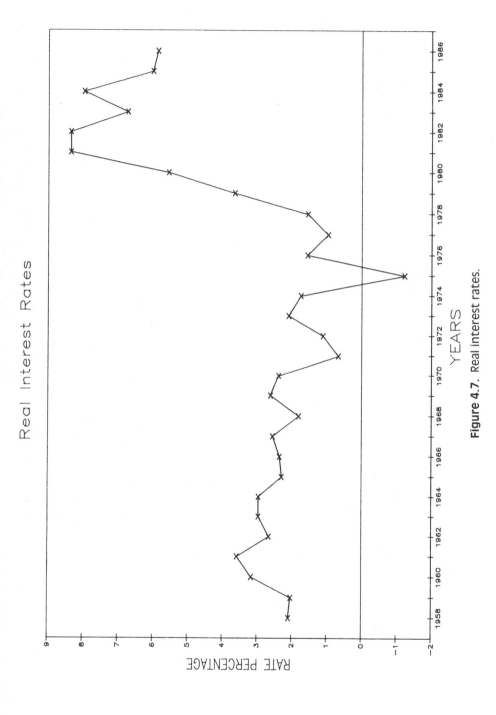

Figure 4.7. Real interest rates.

149

Although historical inflation data are essential to the cost analyst for adjusting old cost data to more current price levels for use in an analysis, the value of including an allowance in cash flows for future general price inflation is open to argument. First of all, predicting future price increases is an inexact process at best. Such predictions are seldom reliable in any absolute sense, and frequently are inaccurate in even relative terms. Second, unless there is some overriding requirement for including general future price inflation in the cash flow estimate, it should be omitted, because the inclusion of inflation usually adds no useful information to an analysis of competing alternatives when all the alternatives will be affected equally by the general inflation adjustment. Such justifications for including general escalation include the case of the cash flow that is going to be used directly in a bid proposal or in some other budgetary manner. Budgetary inputs usually need to include inflation. However, if the cash flow analysis is to be used solely for the comparison of alternative investments such as equipment selection, there is probably no need to try to include the effects of future inflation unless— and this is a big unless—there is some component of the cash flow that is expected to inflate or deflate differentially with respect to the other components of the cash flows. Good examples of differentially inflating components might be labor or energy costs. For any such components where the cost analyst has evidence that differential inflation is likely, the anticipated escalation should be included in the cash flow. Note that including differential inflation does not change the price level of the analysis. The dollars of the cash flows are still in the base-year prices (usually termed "Constant 19XX Dollars") and should be clearly labeled as such in the documentation of the analysis.

The foregoing argument for performing nonbudgetary cash flow analyses in constant rather than inflated dollars affects the choice of the discount rate to be used in the analysis. The rule is: Use a real discount rate for discounting cash flows that are in constant, noninflated dollars and use a market discount rate (i.e., one that includes inflation) for discounting cash flows that have been inflated into future-year price levels.

There is some confusion in terminology in this area. The term "current" is used by economists to refer to data that are in then current dollars. For example, a table tracking the nation's GNP from 1950 through 1980 and labeled "current dollars" would mean that the 1950 data are in 1950 dollars, the 1951 data are in 1951 dollars, and so on. If the table is in some constant-year dollars it would be labeled constant 19XX dollars. We follow this convention, using current to mean a cash flow that is in the price level of the year of the flow, and constant to mean a cash flow that excludes this allowance for general price inflation.

Either the constant-dollar approach or the current-dollar approach will give identical results in the typical application of selecting among alternatives. The following example demonstrates this fact as well as showing how differential inflation should be included in a cash flow analysis.

Let us consider an equipment selection problem involving any number of cash flows being compared. For one such cash flow, exactly the same present value will be obtained for both the constant-dollar and current-dollar approaches. Assume a purchase cost of $100,000 followed by a labor operating cost of $20,000 for each year of a three-year operating life. There are no other expected costs. Let us further assume that the cost analyst, on checking with the personnel office, discovered that owing to already negotiated labor contracts, operating cost for the equipment can be expected to increase at the general inflation rate plus 2% annually. The cost analyst consulted the company financial managers and determined that the appropriate market discount rate to use as the discount rate in the analysis is 12%. Consulting with economic seers, he determines that future general price inflation will be 8% annually.

Figure 4.8 shows a cash flow analysis of the given problem performed in current dollars (i.e., including general inflation) leading to the calculation of both present value and equivalent annual amount. In Figure 4.8 all dollars are in thousands. The cash flow profile is shown with the operations cost inflated by 10% annually, which includes both general inflation at 8% plus the expected escalation in operating cost of 2%. Thus the operating cost grows from $22 (thousand) in year 1 to $26.62 by year 3. Because this cash flow includes general inflation, a 12% discount rate which includes inflation is used to obtain a present value of $157.88. The application of a 12%, three-year capital recovery factor yields an equivalent annual amount of $65.73 in current dollars. As a check, the uniform cash flow of $65.73 is assembled at the bottom of Figure 4.8 and the present value calculated to insure that the same $157.88 is obtained.

Figure 4.9 repeats the analysis but in constant-dollar terms. First, a real interest rate is calculated by dividing the 12% market rate by the expected rate of inflation of 8%. As shown, this results in a real discount rate of 3.7%. Also, a differential inflation rate is calculated for operations cost by dividing the 10% operations inflation rate by the general price inflation rate of 8%, resulting in a differential operations cost escalation rate of 1.85%. Now general price inflation can be ignored. The operations cost profile is inflated by the 1.85% rate, which results in the operations cost growing from $20.37 in year 1 to $21.13 in year 3. The cash flow is then discounted by the real discount rate to obtain the present value of $157.88 (which is the same present value obtained in Figure 4.8 working in inflated dollars). A real capital recovery factor of 0.3583 is calculated, as shown, and applied to the present value to obtain an equivalent annual amount of $56.57. As a check, the uniform cash flow of $56.57 is assembled at the bottom of Figure 4.9 and the present value calculated to insure that the same $157.88 is obtained.

The equivalent annual amounts obtained by the two methods, $65.73 and $56.57, are also equivalent in terms of real value because uniform cash flows of these amounts discount back to equal present values. The only difference between the two values is the inclusion of an allowance for inflation in the $65.73 value. In other words, the $65.73 is in current dollars (over the year 0 to year 3 period), and the $56.57 is in constant year 0 dollars. The next step in this equipment selection problem would be to calculate the present values and/or equivalent annual amounts of the other alternatives. Consistent use of either constant or current dollars would result in the same relative ranking between the alternatives.

This above example demonstrates that a cash flow analysis can be done either

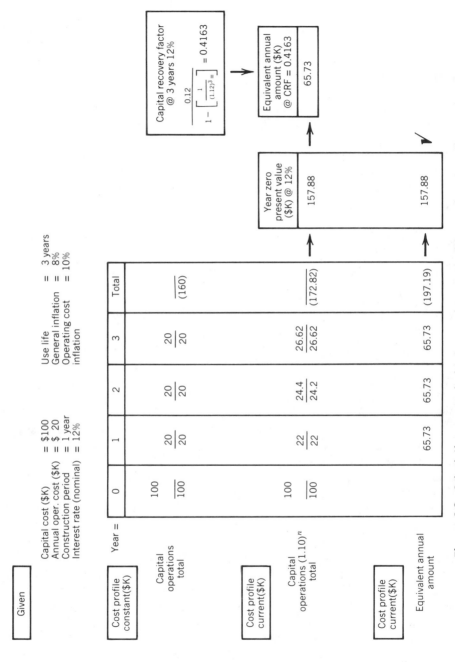

Figure 4.8. Calculating an equivalent annual amount with growing operating cost and inflation.

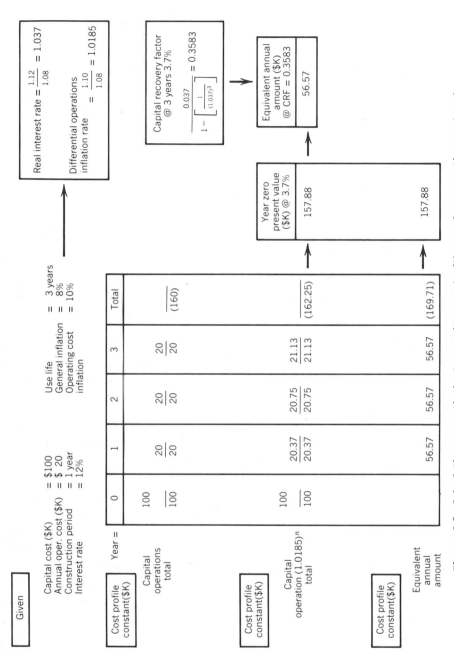

Figure 4.9. Calculating an equivalent annual amount with growing operating cost and constant dollars.

in inflated dollars using an interest rate that also includes inflation, or it can be performed using a real rate of interest and uninflated (constant-year) dollars. As the example shows, the two approaches are identical in the net result. The key point is that the cash flows and the interest rate must be in the same terms; inflation must either be put in both or put in neither. This Golden Rule of Engineering Economics—do unto the discount rate as thou hast done unto the cash flow—is quite often violated. Usually the mistake is that constant-dollar cash flows are discounted with market discount rates, which in fact overstates the opportunity cost of capital to the firm and tends to cause attractive proposals to be rejected.

4.6 CHOOSING A DISCOUNT RATE

The interest rate chosen for discounting obviously has a great effect on which potential investment among alternatives will demonstrate the greatest worth. High discount rates will cause options with large initial investment costs and/or long payback periods to look comparatively less attractive than they would appear if the analysis had assumed a lower rate of interest. Lower discount rates will, conversely, make these same options appear more attractive. Improperly setting the discount rate can cause an organization either to forgo investment opportunities that should have been pursued or to commit to projects resources that could have been used elsewhere to more beneficial effect.

In personal financial decisions the discount rate might be thought of as simply the going interest rate on loans at the local bank. For the individual trying to analyze, say, an electric versus gas-powered heating system for his house, and whose savings are tied up in not very liquid investments earning less than the rate at which the individual can borrow, then the loan interest rate is the correct discount rate. For business organizations, however, the cost of borrowed money is almost always too low to use as the discount rate in analysis of new investment opportunities. First, using the cost of borrowing for the discount rate theoretically can result in the choice of investment alternatives that yield no more return than the cost of the borrowed investment capital. A profit-making body that chooses ventures with no better possibilities than making just enough to pay the banker and bond holder has serious problems. (Although in fact regulated industries, such as utilities, theoretically might set their discount rates not much above their weighted cost of capital, taking into account borrowing, bonds, and equity stock. Governments, too, are quite apt to set discount rates at very low levels for other reasons. This discussion, however, is primarily concerned with discount rates for more traditional business organizations.) Second, as mentioned before, almost all investment projects have some element of risk—setting the discount rate too near the borrowing rate might leave insufficient reserves for unpleasantries that sometimes occur. Therefore, generally speaking, a firm's cost of capital is too low to use as the minimum attractive rate of return.

When an organization's money is committed to an investment, the opportunity to use that money for gains in some alternate investment is forgone. The time value of money, then, is a result of forgone opportunities. This way of thinking about interest is known as the opportunity cost of capital concept. The following example may help to make the notion more clear. Assume that for the coming year a firm has a pool of investment funds—a capital budget, if you will—of $1 million. It might be that this particular business has a product line that is extremely profitable, and the demand for this product exceeds the company's present production capabilities. If an investment in additional production capability could reap a rate of return of 40% for instance, then any alternate investment should be required to at least meet this rate of return potential (all other considerations being equal). We can say, therefore, that the opportunity to make 40% establishes this rate as a minimum when considering alternate investments. At some point however, say, after half of our $1 million budget has been committed, we have enough production facilities to meet the market demand for our star product. What is the opportunity cost of capital for the next increment of our investment pool? It depends on the next best opportunity. It may be that our second most profitable product can get us a yield of 25%, and it too can accommodate some increase in production. Our minimum acceptable rate of return is now 25% because we would obviously not want to invest in any project offering less, as long as the 25% is available. Once the investment in this second product has been committed, and assuming there are still available funds in our budget, we find the next best opportunity in our list of potential projects, and this defines our new minimum acceptable rate of return. This process can be continued until the capital budget is exhausted.

It should be noted that the list of possible investments should not be limited necessarily to the stable of products in our hypothetical company. It could be that the capital budget is large enough that we would begin to spend money on projects that result in a rate of return less than what could be obtained by investing outside the company or by declaring the excess capital as dividends to the stockholders (who could in turn invest the money).

Ideally, then, the rate of interest used in a discounted cash flow analysis should reflect the organization's minimum acceptable rate of return as defined by the other available potential investment opportunities. Proposed investments yielding returns higher than this minimum rate would therefore be accepted, and projects yielding less would be rejected.

4.7 SUMMARY

When the cost estimator is developing data that will be used to select alternative investment opportunities that have expenditures or receipts over time, the time value of money must be considered. Cash flows for each of the alternatives should be developed reflecting these expected disbursements and receipts. Each marginal level of investment should be individually compared to its marginal return. Any sunk costs or cash flow common to all alternatives should be excluded. The cash flows should represent investments of equal capability to the investing organization and have equal economic lifetimes. If it is expected that the alternatives will have relatively different income tax effects, then these effects should be included in the cash flows and the study performed as an after-tax analysis.

There are several decision criteria available for selecting between the alternative cash flows. The primary criteria are present value, equivalent annual amount, and internal rate of return.

The discounted cash flow analysis can be done either in constant dollars (ignoring future general price inflation) or in terms of cash flows inflated to their current price levels. Either method will result in the same preference between alternatives. Constant dollar analysis is generally preferred unless the cash flow data are to be used directly for budgetary planning. Care should be taken that the discount rate chosen for the analysis is real if constant dollar cash flows are involved or a market rate (including inflation) if the cash flows are inflated. The discount rate should reflect the organization's opportunity cost of capital as defined by other available investment opportunities.

REFERENCES

1. Fisher, G. H. *Cost Considerations in Systems Analysis*. American Elsevier, New York, 1971.

2. Grant, E. L., W. G. Ireson, R. S. Leavenworth. *Principles of Engineering Economy*, 7th ed. Wiley, New York, 1982.

3. Swalm, R. O. "Economics of Equipment Selection," *Industrial Engineering Handbook*, 3rd ed. H. B. Maynard, Ed. McGraw-Hill, New York, 1971.

4. U.S. Bureau of the Census, *Statistical Abstract of the United States*. Department Of Commerce, Washington, D.C., 1984.

5. *U.S. Long-Term Review*. Data Resources, Lexington, Mass., Winter 1984–1985.

5

LEARNING CURVES AND PROGRESS FUNCTIONS

LEON M. DELIONBACK, PhD, PE

5.1 INTRODUCTION

The *Learning Curve Phenomenon* had its beginning in the aircraft industry in 1936 when T. P. Wright [1] published an article in the February 1936 *Journal of Aeronautical Science*. Wright described the basic theory and provided equations for use in obtaining cost estimates based on repetitive production of airplane assemblies.

The learning principle can be applied liberally to dozens of situations in the real world, all the way from completing a simple job, like tuning up a car, to such a complex job as manufacturing a space shuttle. In other words, it is universal in its application for all hands-on, or combination of hands-on and mental activities.

The same mathematical equation applies both to learning situations for a person individually completing a job and to larger production-oriented organizations completing a unit or group of units.

5.1.1 Objectives/Purpose

Questions are frequently asked concerning the application of learning curves or "progress functions," as they are also called. A typical question might be: "What should be the learning function slope for an electronics subsystem?" One would need more information to give an intelligent response to such a question. The information would be acquired through such questions as:

1. How many units or subassemblies are involved?
2. What is the production rate?
3. Is the new design state-of-the-art or a brand new concept?

4. What is the program phase: design and development, or production?

5. What learning theory are we planning to use—Crawford, Wright, or others?

Often this information is readily available for projects being studied, but such answers are needed before any meaningful reply can be given. Currently available learning data do not break down research information to a specific subsystem and/or component level of detail. Stated succinctly, the objective of this chapter is as follows: ''Provide general guidelines for use by anyone seeking a ready reference on the application of learning or progress function information.''

The purpose of this chapter, then, is to provide a technique to estimate the serial time or cost to produce a unit of production for a product that is being repetitively produced by an individual, or by a production organization that produces many units of a particular product. When an individual is involved, the function is usually referred to as a *learning function* or *learning curve* and when an entire organization is involved it is called a *progress function*. Also, the progress function may be used to describe a situation involving innovations introduced in a production environment such as changes in material or design, tooling, machinery or equipment, or management system. The mathematics for both, learning curve or progress function, are identical, and solved example problems utilizing the theory are included.

5.1.2 Problem Statement

Learning or progress functions are expressed in the following format and are basically the same for either function:

$$Y = AX^b \tag{5.1}$$

where Y = the time or cost per cycle or unit
A = time or cost for the first unit or cycle
X = the number of cycles or units
b = exponent of the function (Table 5.1), constant for a given set of conditions.

A plot of Equation 5.1 for a 90% Wright-based learning curve on Cartesian coordinates is shown as Figure 5.1. The exponent b which is a negative value causes the dependent variable of the function to decrease from left to right.

The learning curve concept is one of the principal techniques used in the high technology industries to project costs of production units for space vehicles, aircraft, electronics, computers, or support equipment. The learning curve is an approximation of a geometric progression that forecasts the cost reduction from one unit of production to its succeeding unit. The units of production are assumed to be essentially identical from one production unit to the other, and the operation is repetitive. The job content of the operation varies over a wide range of activities,

TABLE 5.1. Exponent Table for the Negative Learning Curve Exponent
b **in the Equation** $Y = AX^b$

Slope (%)	Exponent b	Slope (%)	Exponent b
99	−0.0145	80	−0.3220
98	−0.0290	79	−0.3400
97	−0.0440	78	−0.3580
96	−0.0590	77	−0.3770
95	−0.0740	76	−0.3960
94	−0.0890	75	−0.4150
93	−0.1050	74	−0.4340
92	−0.1200	73	−0.4540
91	−0.1360	72	−0.4740
90	−0.1520	71	−0.4940
89	−0.1680	70	−0.5150
88	−0.1840	69	−0.5350
87	−0.2010	68	−0.5560
86	−0.2180	67	−0.5780
85	−0.2340	66	−0.5990
84	−0.2510	65	−0.6210
83	−0.2690	64	−0.6440
82	−0.2860	63	−0.6670
81	−0.3040	62	−0.6900

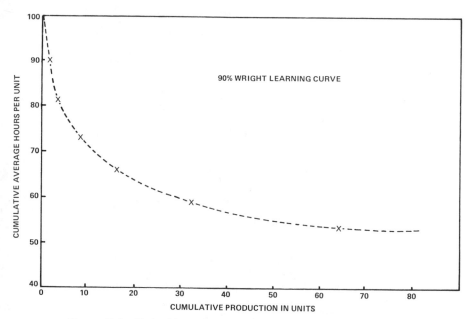

Figure 5.1. Plot of learning curve on Cartesian coordinates.

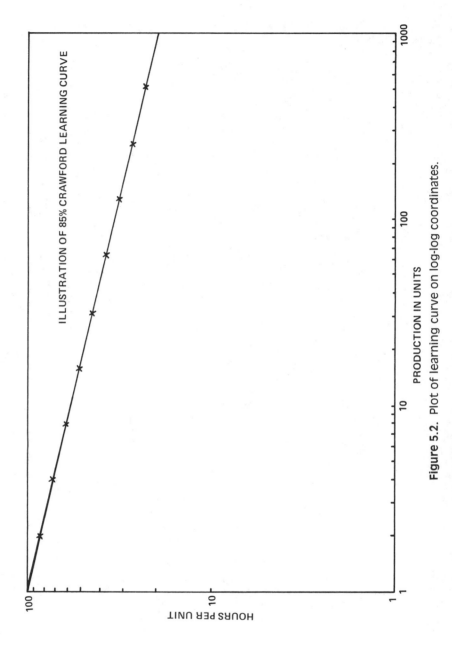

Figure 5.2. Plot of learning curve on log-log coordinates.

from a pure hands-on operation to jobs that are primarily mental exercises. A learning curve as plotted will forecast the cost reduction from one article or cycle to the next successive unit or cycle. The amount of decrease will be less with each successive unit. Labor hours can be substituted in place of cost for one of the curve parameters. The slope of the curve as plotted on logarithmic graph paper approximates a straight line and is used as the principal parameter to gauge the effectiveness of a particular learning curve. The slope is usually expressed in percent, that is, 80%, 85%, 90%, and so on (see Figure 5.2). This slope can be used to express the ratio of the cost of any unit value to the cost of twice the unit value. For example, if the cost of the initial unit value of a 90% curve is 100 hours, the curve will predict that the second unit will take 90 hours, and the cost for the fourth unit will take 81 hours.

Another way of looking at learning curve theory is to express the cost reduction in terms of a percentage of reduction, that is, for an 80% learning curve the reduction will be 20% of the direct labor or cost. Each time the number of articles is *doubled* the reduction in direct labor or cost will be 20%, and for a 90% curve it would be a reduction of 10% each time the quantity is doubled. For example:

$$\begin{array}{ll} \text{If the number of units per lot} = & 1 \quad 2 \quad 4 \text{ and so on} \\ \text{Direct hours for 80\% curve} = & 100 \ 80 \ 64 \text{ and so on} \\ \text{Direct hours for 90\% curve} = & 100 \ 90 \ 81 \text{ and so on} \end{array}$$

5.2 APPLIED LEARNING CURVE THEORY

It is necessary for the cost estimator to have a working knowledge of learning curve theory to project accurately resources required to produce multiple units of a product or service. The following discussion provides a basis for this working knowledge.

5.2.1 Assumptions

The application of the learning or progress function theory to real-world examples requires consideration of the following types of factors which normally contribute to the stated time or cost reductions of a learning or progress function curve:

1. Operator learning
2. Improved methods, processes, tooling, machines, and design improvements for increased productivity
3. Management learning
4. Debugging of engineering data
5. Production rates
6. Design of the assembly or part, or modifications

7. Specification or design of the process
8. Personnel factors such as fatigue, personal break times, employee morale

5.2.2 Constraints

From a myriad of reports, manuals, and books there has evolved a multiplicity of terms to describe essentially the same phenomenon, the learning curve. Some of these other terms are as follows: progress functions, experience curves, cost improvement curves. For the most part these terms are assumed to be interchangeable, although the term *learning curve* is used more frequently. This designation includes some items that are not considered normally as learning elements, for instance, improvements in methods or in tooling, or such capital improvements as facilities and machinery. All of these can result in reduced costs and a steeper slope for the learning curve.

The wide range of applicability would suggest there are few constraints in the application of the principles that are stated here, but in practice one must remember that information presented herein on learning curves is based on approximate information. Learning curve data should be treated as estimates rather than discrete values.

5.2.3 Approaches

There are two approaches to learning curves: The *Wright* (cumulative average) system and the *Crawford* (unit) system. When comparing the systems, it may be observed that, for the same curve slope and unit number, the numerical values for cumulative average cost for the Wright system and unit cost for the Crawford system are one and the same. Hence if one plots a curve using these values, it will result in a common line (see Figure 5.3). It may be observed from this plot that the Wright system unit value curve falls below the cumulative average line, and the plot for the unit cost value is the *common* line as shown in Figure 5.3. The cumulative average curve for the Crawford system can be seen to fall above the common line.

The only problem with the common plot in the foregoing approach lies in the observation that the *units* on the y axis or ordinate for the Wright system are *cumulative average cost per unit*, whereas the units on the Crawford system y axis are simply *cost per unit*. Since the two systems are constructed using a different data base, conversion from one to the other cannot be made directly. However, as one can observe from reference to Table 5.2, the Wright system cumulative average value is exactly equal to the Crawford system unit value.

5.2.3.1 Wright System.
The Wright system was developed first, dating from the 1930s. It assumes that a plot of observed coordinate data points on logarithmic paper will approximate a straight line. The coordinate axes consist of the ordinate based on cumulative average cost in man-hours or dollars per unit, and

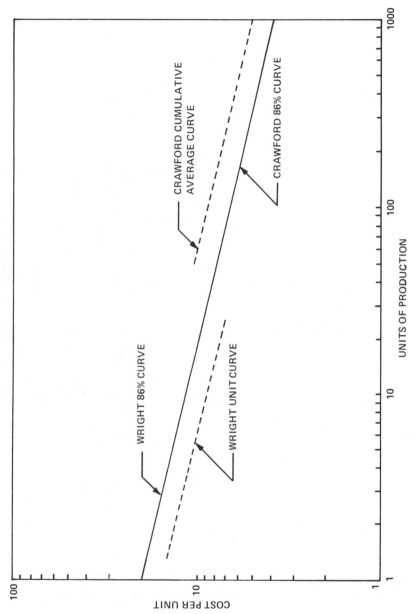

Figure 5.3. Graphical comparison of Wright versus Crawford curves.

TABLE 5.2. Summaries of Wright and Crawford Data

Item	Slope	2	3	4	5	7	10	25	50	100
					Quantity					
A. Crawford										
System	95	0.950	0.922	0.903	0.888	0.866	0.843	0.788	0.749	0.711
Log-linear	90	0.900	0.846	0.810	0.783	0.744	0.705	0.613	0.552	0.497
unit curve	85	0.850	0.773	0.723	0.686	0.634	0.583	0.470	0.400	0.340
	80	0.800	0.702	0.640	0.596	0.535	0.477	0.355	0.284	0.227
	75	0.750	0.634	0.563	0.513	0.446	0.385	0.263	0.197	0.148
	70	0.700	0.568	0.490	0.437	0.367	0.306	0.191	0.134	0.093
	65	0.650	0.505	0.423	0.368	0.298	0.239	0.135	0.087	0.057
Cumulative	95	0.975	0.957	0.944	0.932	0.915	0.895	0.844	0.804	0.766
average	90	0.950	0.915	0.889	0.868	0.835	0.799	0.708	0.643	0.581
	85	0.925	0.874	0.836	0.806	0.762	0.712	0.692	0.510	0.438
	80	0.900	0.834	0.786	0.747	0.690	0.632	0.492	0.402	0.327
	75	0.875	0.794	0.737	0.692	0.626	0.559	0.408	0.315	0.242
	70	0.850	0.756	0.690	0.639	0.566	0.493	0.336	0.246	0.178
	65	0.825	0.718	0.644	0.589	0.510	0.434	0.276	0.191	0.130
B. Wright										
System	95	0.900	0.866	0.844	0.829	0.806	0.784	0.731	0.694	0.659
Unit curve	90	0.800	0.739	0.701	0.675	0.638	0.602	0.521	0.469	0.421
	85	0.700	0.619	0.571	0.538	0.494	0.452	0.362	0.307	0.260
	80	0.600	0.506	0.454	0.418	0.371	0.329	0.242	0.193	0.154
	75	0.500	0.402	0.348	0.314	0.269	0.230	0.155	0.116	0.086
	70	0.400	0.305	0.255	0.224	0.185	0.152	0.093	0.065	0.045
	65	0.300	0.216	0.174	0.149	0.118	0.093	0.051	0.033	0.021
Log-linear	95	0.950	0.922	0.903	0.888	0.866	0.843	0.788	0.749	0.711
cumulative	90	0.900	0.846	0.810	0.783	0.744	0.705	0.613	0.552	0.497
average	85	0.850	0.773	0.723	0.686	0.634	0.583	0.470	0.400	0.340
curve	80	0.800	0.702	0.640	0.596	0.535	0.477	0.355	0.284	0.227
	75	0.750	0.634	0.563	0.513	0.446	0.385	0.263	0.197	0.148
	70	0.700	0.568	0.490	0.437	0.367	0.306	0.191	0.184	0.093
	65	0.650	0.505	0.423	0.368	0.298	0.239	0.135	0.087	0.057

the abscissa, which is the number of units produced or completed. Tables have been computed and are available for each percentage value of learning curve slope beginning with 60% up to a value of 99%. Each entry in the table gives values for the cumulative total, cumulative average, and unit values for each percentage point of the learning curve and for each unit of production up to 1000 units. In general, the Wright system of plotting learning curve values will yield a smooth curve, since cumulative average values are used in plotting data. This is especially true when working with actual data as opposed to projected values [2].

5.2.3.2 Crawford System.
The Crawford system for learning curve analysis assumes ordinate values based on the unit values, as opposed to a cumulative

average of these values. The coordinate points for the Crawford system, or unit cost system, are formulated such that the cost or value for each unit is plotted directly at the particular unit in question, that is, the time or cost for the tenth unit, or the 30th unit, forms the basis for the plot point. A plot of several observed points for a Crawford curve on logarithmic paper approximates a straight line (see Figure 5.2). The ordinate displays the unit values in man-hours or cost in dollars per unit; the abscissa values are based on the number of units produced or completed. Tables have been produced for each value of learning curve slope from 60% up to a value of 99%. Each entry in the table gives values for the cumulative total, cumulative average, and unit value for each percentage point of the curve and for each unit of production up to 1000 units [2].

Although most companies originally used the Wright system, in recent years many companies have adopted the Crawford system, and at present approximately 92% of all firms utilize the Crawford or unit cost system [3].

5.3 PRELIMINARY CONSIDERATIONS

Prior to the application of learning curve analytical techniques, the cost estimator must be aware of some preliminary considerations and concepts relative to the use of learning curves. The principal preliminary considerations that must be understood at the outset are described in the following sections.

5.3.1 Theoretical First Unit (TFU) Cost

If improvement curves are plotted from actual cost data, the slope and TFU may be determined from any two points on the curve. An estimate of an improvement curve may be developed also, provided one has an estimate of the TFU and a projected curve slope. Since both the TFU and the rate of improvement (i.e., 80%) are estimates, this type of application must be used with great care. An error in judgement of ±5% (curve slope) will affect the cumulative total cost of 1000 units by as much as 68%, depending on the slope of the particular curve.

The TFU cost is defined as the cost or resources required, whether in man-hours or dollars, of producing the first unit. It is called "theoretical" since rarely will the cost of producing the number one, or first unit, equate to the actual number of man-hours or dollars required to produce unit number one in a production sequence. In a phased sequence the development or test units are produced first and serve two purposes: to work out any design or development problems and to work out any production or manufacturing problems. Since in many cases these development units do not represent complete assemblies, they cannot be assumed to represent a production sequence. They do, however, provide experience and can be utilized in the process to develop cost data for the TFU in a production sequence.

In such a process, the estimate for the number one unit's cost is used to determine the starting point for the improvement curve, and the curve is drawn from this point. This approach is complicated by working with an estimate of the TFU and also from using an assumed slope value for the improvement curve. Errors in one are compounded by the effects of the other.

In the more popular approach, the estimator begins by estimating the costs or man-hours required to produce a particular unit in the production sequence, say unit 30 or 100, constructing an improvement curve through this point and then backing up the curve to find the cost of the TFU (Figure 5.4). The decision as to what unit to use should be based on the type and complexity of the item and experience with the particular manufacturing facility. This is the preferred methodology.

Another technique for estimating the TFU is based on a company's previous experience. The typical vendor has had previous experience with production of a particular type of hardware. Usually there is ample historical data that can be used to compute the cost elements to produce a new item. This "estimate by comparison" usually involves the estimator and representatives of the various departments. Comparable hardware items, processes, and the like for which costs are known are selected as a guide. Elements of time and materials are deleted from, or added to, the cost estimate as required. Thus the individual cost elements are priced for a subject configuration, and a TFU cost is computed. This method requires a detailed step-by-step analysis of the differences in design and manufacturing process for a new item versus previous experience.

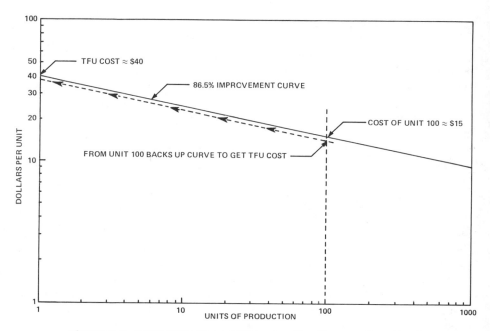

Figure 5.4. Determination of TFU using the "back-up" method.

5.3.2 Learning Curve Slope Ranges

The slope values displayed herein are approximate and could vary as much as $\pm 10\%$, depending on the particular application, and depend on the unique design in question (if one is considering a hardware application). The improvement curve will tend to be higher in slope value (90–95%) for those cases that are automated to a great extent, for tooling that has been termed ''hard'' tooling, or where an automatic machine process is involved. Also, the job content, when examined in detail, will have an effect on learning curve slope. If the job requirements contain principal elements that are repetitive in nature, the learning curve slope will be steeper, signifying a high degree of learning. When a production rate is increased, the tendency will be for the slope of the improvement curve to flatten.

If a study is made of a situation involving an improvement curve analysis for a lower-level package, some information must be available explaining the type of work or process being performed, for example, machining, sheet metal work, or automatic electronics assembly. If the job contains partly handwork and partly machining, a rule of thumb must be applied to indicate a flatter improvement curve value as the percentage of machine time goes up. Hands-on labor versus machine time effect on the learning curve slope is quantified as follows:

1. 75% hand assembly / 25% machining = 80% (slope)
2. 50% hand assembly / 50% machining = 85% (slope)
3. 25% hand assembly / 75% machining = 90% (slope)

An individual operator doing recurring work on a new product using standard manufacturing techniques will yield a learning curve of approximately 85% slope.

Crawford system (unit cost) versus Wright system (cumulative average) assumptions will yield results as follows:

1. Unit cost (Crawford) assumptions will always result in a *higher* total cost estimate.
2. If an estimator assumes the Wright, or cumulative average cost method, and the opposite, or unit cost (Crawford) method is true, the resulting estimate will be *understated*.

There is an influence on the slope value for improvement curves based on the particular type of industry or industrial process involved, for example, aerospace, shipbuilding, chemical process, and construction. It is realized that curve values for these industries may not be directly related, but the slope values are listed nevertheless for comparison purposes.

Learning curve slope overall values for industry in general are as follows:

1. Aerospace, 85%
2. Shipbuilding, 80–85%

3. Complex machine tools for new models, 75–85%
4. Repetitive electronics manufacturing, 90–95%
5. Repetitive machining or punch-press operations, 90–95%
6. Repetitive clerical operations, 75–85%
7. Repetitive welding operations, 90%
8. Construction operations, 70–90%
9. Raw materials, 93–96%
10. Purchased parts, 85–88%

Factors that will in general contribute a higher learning curve slope are as follows:

1. Improved methods, or method innovations
2. Process improvement or time reduction
3. Improvements in design for improved manufacturability
4. Debugging of engineering data
5. Increased rate of production
6. Introduction of a machine to replace a hand operation

Machine-paced operations for production of machined parts such as screws, engine blocks, gears, and carefully engineered manual processes are used in the assembly of small electronic parts on a printed circuit. These operations show little or no learning after the initial setup, and therefore have a "flatter" learning curve with higher percentage value.

5.4 ANALYTICAL TECHNIQUES

The solutions of learning or progress function problems fall roughly into the following categories or methods: (1) graphical, with the use of a learning curve template; (2) manual, also a graphical technique that involves plotting two or three points on logarithmic graph paper; (3) the use of established equations; (4) use of values from tables; (5) *composite* learning curve problems, (6) use of a microcomputer. Solution methods involving either Wright or Crawford system data are generally made by the same methodology, as is illustrated in the following example problems. Any solution will require one of the following combinations: (1) the slope of the learning curve and first unit cost; (2) the cost of a specific unit and slope of the curve; (3) a series of two or more points for graphical solutions; and (4) the slope of the curve and one other point. Whether solution of a problem is by the tabular solution or use of established equations, it is advisable to check answers by the graphical method (solution method (1)).

5.4.1 Mathematical Relations

$$Y = AX^b \quad \text{(basic equation)} \tag{5.1}$$
$$\log Y = \log A + b \log X \quad \text{(computing form)}$$

where Y = dollars or man-hours per unit
A = first unit cost or first unit time
X = number of units, or unit number
b = exponent of the geometric progression equation, or a measure of rate of reduction (the negative exponent indicates the function is decreasing from left to right)
m = slope given in positive hundredths (i.e., 0.8 for an 80% learning curve) for a log-linear learning curve.

$$b = \frac{\log(m)}{\log(2)} \quad \text{(see Table 5.1)} \tag{5.2}$$

$$A = \frac{Y}{X^b} \tag{5.3}$$

where A = cost of first unit or time
Y = cost of particular unit
X = number of units, or unit number
b = exponent of the geometric progression formula, or a measure of rate of reduction

$$Y = FA \tag{5.4}$$

where A = cost of first unit or time
F = factor from table
Y = dollars or man-hours per unit (tabular solution)

$$A = \frac{Y}{F} \tag{5.5}$$

where A = cost of first unit or time
F = factor from table
Y = cost of particular unit (for tabular solution)

The methodology for computation of a composite learning or progress function is a procedure whereby each subtask or subsystem is weighted in proportion to its dollar or time value for each individual subelement. The approach is as follows:

$$M_c = \sum \frac{V_{ss}}{T} M_{ss} \tag{5.6}$$

and

$$M_p = \frac{V_{ss}}{T} M_{ss} \tag{5.7}$$

where M_c = composite learning curve slope
  M_p = proportionate part of slope
  V_{ss} = value of subsystem or subtask
  T = total time or dollars for system
  M_{ss} = slope of curve for subtask or subsystem

The relationships for the microcomputer are written in the BASIC language.

```
10   REM L.C. EXPONENT
20   LET M = ?
30   B = LOG(M)/LOG(2)
40   PRINT B
```
(5.8)

where M = slope of learning curve

```
10   REM COST OF PARTICULAR UNIT
20   LET A = ?
30   LET X = ?
40   LET B = ?
50   Y = A*X∧(B)
60   PRINT Y
```
(5.9)

where A = cost of first unit or time
  X = number of units or unit number
  Y = cost of particular unit
  B = exponent of the geometric progression equation, or a measure of the rate of reduction

```
10   REM FIRST UNIT COST
20   LET X = ?
30   LET Y = ?
40   LET B = ?
50   A = Y/X∧(B)
60   PRINT A
```
(5.10)

5.4.2 Solution Procedures

Several different solution methods used to solve learning curve problems, along with sample solutions for each method, are outlined in the sections that follow.

5.4.2.1 Graphical Solutions

1. *Given:*   A = $30; slope of Wright learning curve = 80%
   Find: Cumulative average value of 80 units
   Answer: $7 per unit (see Figure 5.5).

   To solve this problem graphically, a transparent preinscribed learning curve template or protractor can be used to lay out a straight line representing the learning curve slope. Starting at the given theoretical first unit cost of $30 (as shown in Figure 5.5), the learning curve line is constructed with the template slope guide. The cumulative average value of 80 units is read from the curve as shown by the dotted line on Figure 5.5. Reading vertically to the curve from the 80-unit point and then horizontally to the cumulative cost per unit axis results in a cumulative cost per unit of the first 80 units of $7.

2. *Given:*   Although the slope is unknown, four points on a production learning curve are known: unit number 1 = $40, unit number 4 = $25.60, unit number 8 = $20.48, and unit number 20 = $15.25.
   Find: Slope of production learning curve. Actually two points would be the minimum number required to define a learning curve. The four points are plotted on logarithmic paper, and a straight edge is used to connect them. Although rarely will the curve connect all of the points, approximate or ''best fit'' results are usually acceptable.
   Answer: 80% (see Figure 5.6).

5.4.2.2 Algebraic Solutions Using Established Equations

1. *Wright* system problem as follows:
   Given: Slope = 85%; A, first unit cost = $50
   Find: Y, or cost of sixtieth unit
   Solution:

$$b = \frac{\log(m)}{\log(2)} \tag{5.2}$$

$$= \frac{\log(0.85)}{\log(2)} = -0.234$$

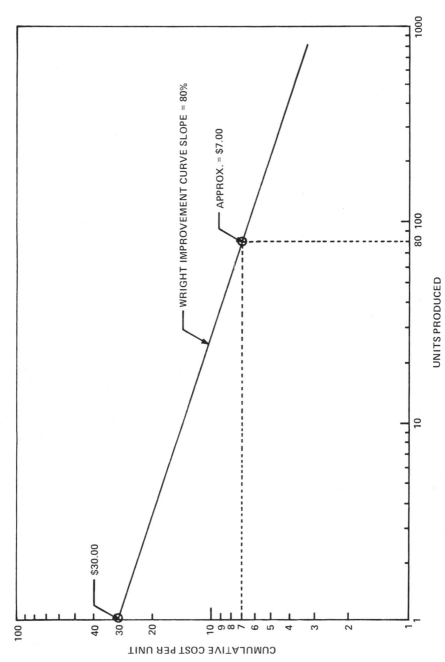

Figure 5.5. Solution of improvement curve problem using graphical technique.

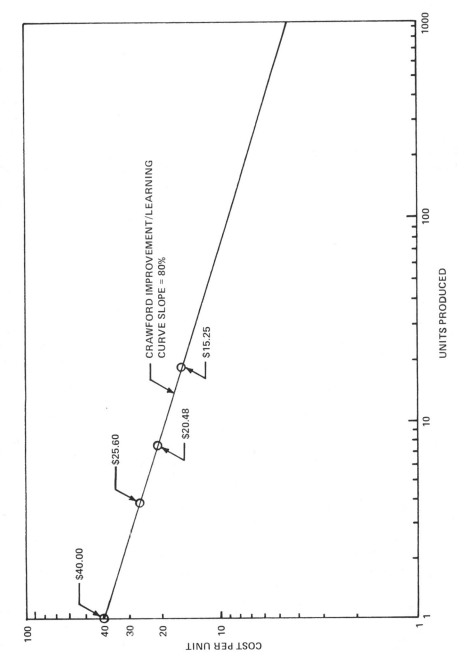

Figure 5.6. Solution of improvement curve when given four points.

$$Y = AX^b \tag{5.1}$$

$$\log Y = \log A + b \log X$$

$$\log Y = \log(50) - (0.234) \log(60)$$

$$\log Y = 1.282$$

$$Y = 19.145 \quad \text{or} \quad \$19.15 \text{ per unit}$$

2. *Crawford* system problem as follows:

   Given: Slope = 90%, $X = 200$ units, $Y = \$65$ per unit

   Find: A, first unit cost

   Solution:

$$b = \frac{\log(m)}{\log(2)} \tag{5.2}$$

$$= \frac{\log(0.90)}{\log(2)}$$

$$= -0.152$$

$$A = \frac{Y}{X^b} \tag{5.3}$$

$$\log A = \log Y - b \log X$$

$$\log A = \log(65) + (0.152) \log(200)$$

$$\log A = 2.163$$

$$A = 145.435 \quad \text{or} \quad \$145.44.$$

5.4.2.3 Tabular Solutions.   This methodology requires a set of tables constructed from either Wright or Crawford data.

1. *Given:*   Slope = 83%; value of A, or unit one = \$250, *Wright* system

   Find: Cost of unit number 100 (Y); obtain the factor from a table for unit one.

   Solution:

$$Y = FA \tag{5.4}$$

$$= (0.290)(250)$$

$$Y = 72.495 \quad \text{or} \quad \$72.50 \text{ per unit}$$

2. *Given:*   Slope = 90%; value of Y = \$800 at X = 100, using *Crawford* System

    Find: Value of A, unit number one. Obtaining the factor for unit 100 from a table (see Table 5.2), F = 0.497 (for slope = 90%, X = 100).

    Solution:

$$A = \frac{Y}{F} \tag{5.5}$$

$$A = \frac{800}{0.497}$$

$$A = 1609.658 \quad \text{or} \quad \$1609.66$$

5.4.2.4 Composite Learning Curve. The use of the term ''composite learning curve'' results from the necessity to integrate results from two or more learning systems into a common learning system. A sample problem is illustrated in Figure 5.7.

Given: Final assembly cost = \$100,000, with learning curve slope of 80%; electronics cost = \$300,000, with a learning curve slope of 93%; structures cost = \$200,000, with a learning curve slope of 85%; total manufacturing cost = \$600,000.

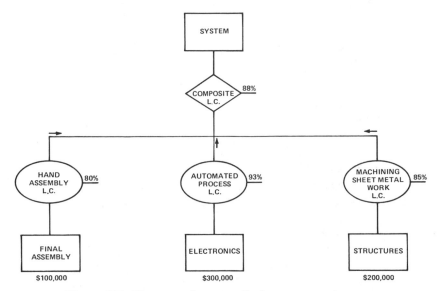

Figure 5.7. Diagram of composite improvement curve.

Find:　Slope for composite learning curve

$$M_c = \Sigma \left(\frac{V_{ss}}{T} \right) M_{ss}$$

$$M_c = \left[\left(\frac{100,000}{600,000} \right) 80 + \left(\frac{300,000}{600,000} \right) 93 + \left(\frac{200,000}{600,000} \right) 85 \right]$$

$$M_c = \tfrac{1}{6}(80) + \tfrac{1}{2}(93) + \tfrac{1}{3}(85)$$

$$M = 88.167 \quad \text{or} \quad 88.2\%$$

5.4.2.5 Solution of Learning Curve Problems by Use of Microcomputer

Given:　First unit cost $A = 50$, $X = 60$, slope of learning curve = 85%
Find:　Y, cost of sixtieth unit

1. Program to calculate B is as follows:

```
10   REM L.C. EXPONENT
20   LET M = 0.85
30   B = LOG(M)/LOG(2)                              (5.8)
40   PRINT B
RUN  . . . . . . . .   B = −0.234
```

```
10   REM COST OF UNIT 60
20   LET A = 50
30   LET X = 60
40   LET B = −0.234
50   Y = A∗X∧(B)                                    (5.9)
60   PRINT Y
RUN  . . . . . . . .   Y = $19.15 PER UNIT
```

2. Program to calculate first unit cost A
Given:　Slope = 90%, $X = 200$, $Y = 65$
To Find:　First unit cost A. To calculate B, program as follows:

```
10   REM L.C. EXPONENT
20   LET M = 0.90
30   B = LOG(M)/LOG(2)                              (5.8)
40   PRINT B
RUN  . . . . . . . .   B = −0.152
```

```
10  REM FIRST UNIT COST A
20  LET X = 200
30  LET Y = 65
40  LET B = -0.152
50  A = Y/X (B)
60  PRINT A
RUN  . . . . . . .  A = $145.44
```

(5.10)

5.5 EFFECTS OF DESIGN CHANGES ON THE LEARNING CURVE

Minor design changes will for the most part not have a significant effect on the slope of the learning curve. However, if the change affects the proportion of hands-on labor to machine time, the effect on the learning curve could be substantial. If there is an increase in the hands-on labor, then one could expect the slope of the learning curve to increase. Conversely, if the proportion of hands-on labor decreases and the proportion of machine or automatic time increases, expectations would be for the slope of the learning curve to flatten.

If the change is really a major change in design of the product or in the manufacturing techniques, one would expect the learning curve to be influenced by this activity. The change may be so significant in terms of production hours that the process will indicate movement back up the learning curve (see Figure 5.4) to a position that will approximate the hours required for the new unit. This activity has been commonly referred to as a ''production break.'' There was a programmed break of 18 months in the production schedule of NASA's space shuttle that was planned to allow the results of a research and development program to be factored into the design configuration. An analysis was made during this break as to whether the costs of the changes were *recurring* or *nonrecurring* for each of the separate contracts. This determination will have a substantial impact on the total program cost of the space shuttle.

The calculation of the learning losses from a production break in the space shuttle program was the subject of a report published by the National Aeronautics and Space Administration [4].

5.6 FACTORS AFFECTING LEARNING CURVE SLOPE

The improvement rate in the manufacturing of a product is not entirely due to the performance of an individual worker and the amount of time he consumes in the manipulation of tools and equipment. The improvement rate and the slope of the learning curve are, in fact, due to the combined effects of learning by individuals, improvements in manufacturing methods, and overall efficiency brought about by the management. The value of unit number one and the slope of the learning curve are related as much to the effectiveness of the initial planning and efficiency of tooling as they are to efforts by individual production workers.

The production worker level of experience has a definite relationship to the slope of the learning curve. If a particular worker is experienced in the particular type of task, he will likely have a *lower* first unit time and a lower rate of improvement, or flatter, slope curve.

On the other hand, a novice or inexperienced worker will post a higher initial time but a steeper rate of improvement (steeper slope). This hypothesis was substantiated in a test in which an inexperienced worker was assigned to do a task that was previously done by an experienced worker. The novice posted a higher first unit time, and a steeper slope on his learning curve for the particular task.

5.7 OTHER INFORMATION ON LEARNING CURVES

There is a wealth of information available in the open literature, as well as in privately published reports, on learning curves and their use and applicability to various industries. The bibliography to this reference manual includes 14 books, articles, and papers that contain more detailed information on learning curves and their application. A few notable publications on specific areas of interest to the cost estimator, and their contents, are described in brief below.

5.7.1 Learning Losses Due to Production Interruptions

The losses experienced after a break or stoppage in sequence of a production cycle portend an extremely complex situation and involve numerous variables, some of uncertain quantity and quality. There are no discrete equations to define the losses during a gap in production. The techniques employed are therefore related to a prediction or forecast of the losses that take place, based on the conditions that exist in the production environment. Such parameters as (1) learning curve slope, (2) number of predecessor units, and (3) length of time the production sequence is halted are utilized in formulating a prediction model.

The pertinent current publications related to this subject are few in number but are reviewed in reference [4] to provide an understanding of the problem. Example problems are illustrated along with appropriate trend curves to show the approach. Solved problems are also given to show the application of the models to actual cases or production breaks in the real world.

5.7.2 Learning in Small Lots

John G. Carlson [5] offers a method of establishing a small-lot work measurement program where none exists, or validating an existing small-lot allowance structure. The consequences of using time study and synthetic time data for short-run standards are discussed. Also, the determination of appropriate measures of improvement for learning plus the prediction of improvement factors as necessary ingredients of small-lot production standards are studied in some detail.

5.7.3 Learning Curve / Complexity Relationships

The principle of complexity analysis and its special relationship with learning/cost improvement curve theory is explored in reference [6]. A bottoms-up approach for the analysis of the complexity of a typical system is presented. Starting with the subsystems of a particular system, the step-by-step procedure for analysis of the complexity of an overall system is given. The learning curves for the various subsystems are determined, as well as the concurrent members of relevant design parameters. Trend curves are then plotted for the learning curve slopes versus the various design-oriented parameters, for example, number of parts versus slope of learning curve, or number of fasteners versus slope of learning curve.

Representative cuts are taken from each trend curve and a figure-of-merit analysis is made for each of the subsystems. Based on these values, a characteristic curve is plotted that is indicative of the complexity of the particular subsystem. The figure-of-merit versus learning curve slope is plotted. Each characteristic curve is based on a universe of trend curve data taken from data points observed for the subsystem in question. Thus a characteristic curve is developed for each of the subsystems in the overall system.

A composite complexity analysis is performed to determine the manufacturing complexity for the overall system. A procedure is outlined to define the steps in computation for this value (along with an illustrative example). A narrative description is given for the limitations in scope of the manufacturing complexity analysis.

5.7.4 Incentives During Learning

The progress of industry today is characterized by rapid development of products and production facilities. It involves a continuous process of breaking in and changing of methods, products, facilities, and, most important of all, personnel. This process entails technological, social, organizational, psychological, and even political problems. The material in reference [7] concerns one such problem, *productivity*, during learning periods, when personnel are learning new skills or developing new methods or new products. The learning curve is suggested as a basis for setting time standards during the learning period, mainly for the purpose of increasing productivity.

5.7.5 Misapplications of the Learning Curve Concept

In high technology industries there are many factors that obscure the true significance of the learning curve. Instead of portraying the increased productivity resulting from skill acquired in repetitive operations, the curve (cumulative actual hours per unit of production) actually reflects budgetary and other management directed influences. The disturbing factors are identified in reference [8] and remedial measures suggested.

5.7.6 Learning in Manual Operations

Hancock and Sathe [9] presented the results of industrial studies concerning the number of cycles required by an operator to attain a predetermined time value for a manual operation. Also proved are the effects of short breaks (coffee breaks), medium breaks (overnight), and longer breaks (10–11 days) for their effects on the net cycle time.

5.7.7 Learning Curves from Standard Time Data

The learning curve is a powerful estimating tool according to Hartmeyer [10]. It makes possible the use of standard time data for estimating, regardless of the production quantity involved. Standard times apply to well-established and well-planned work carried out by experienced workers. In practice, it takes many production units to achieve this situation; standard hours are normally well below what is actually required to do the work. The proper way to use standard data is to determine how many units would have to be produced to achieve standard performance, and then use the learning curve techniques to account for the additional time that will inevitably be required for low-volume runs, or for the first portion of high-volume runs.

5.7.8 Learning in Mechanical Assembly Tasks

A series of exploratory learning tests were made to determine the feasibility of relating the learning progress for mechanical assembly tasks to design parameters or features [11]. If design features exhibit sufficient sensitivity or learnability to programmed changes in the design configuration, then it should be possible to forecast the potential learning progress of any mechanical assembly task. A comparison of the predicted learning curve slope as determined by the model with an actual learning curve plotted from experimental data, indicated an apparent error of less than 1%. Results from the experimental runs and the successful trial application of the prediction model satisfied the objectives of this research.

REFERENCES

1. Wright, T. P. "Factors Affecting the Cost of Airplanes," *Journal of Aeronautical Science*, Vol. 3, No. 2, (1936).
2. Defense Documentation Center. Experience Curve Tables. U.S. Army Missile Command, Redstone Arsenal, Ala., September 1962, AD #612803 and #612804.

3. Hartung, W. G. *Cost Estimate Errors Resulting from the Use of Learning Curve Methods.* ESD-TR-69-295. Cost Analysis Division, Air Force Systems Command, USAF, L. G. Hanscom Field, Bedford, Mass., 1972.

4. Delionback, L. M. *A Prediction Model to Forecast the Cost Impact from a Break in the Production Schedule.* NASA TM-78131, George C. Marshall Space Flight Center, Redstone Arsenal, Ala., 1977.

5. Carlson, J. G. *Production Standards for Small-Lot Manufacturing.* AIIE Monograph Series, No. 6, 1977.

6. Delionback, L. M. *Manufacturing Complexity Analysis.* NASA Technical Memorandum No. X73373; February, 1977.

7. Turban, E. *Incentives During Learning—An Application of the Learning Curve Theory and a Survey of Other Methods.* AIIE Monograph Series, No. 6, 1977.

8. Young, S. L. *Misapplications of the Learning Curve Concept.* AIIE Monograph Series, No. 6, 1977.

9. Hancock, W. M. and P. Sathe. *Learning Curve Research on Manual Operations.* Research Report 113A, MTM Association for Standards and Research, Undated.

10. Hartmeyer, F. C. *Learning Curves—From Electronics Industry Cost Estimating Data.* Ronald Press, New York, 1964.

11. Delionback, L. M. A Design-Oriented Prediction Model for Learning Rates of Individual Mechanical Assembly Tasks. Unpublished Ph.D. dissertation, Oklahoma State University, School of Engineering, 1972.

6

DETAILED COST ESTIMATING*

RODNEY D. STEWART, PE, CCA, CPE

6.1 THE ANATOMY OF A DETAILED ESTIMATE

The detailed cost estimating process, like the manufacture of a product, is comprised of parallel and sequential steps that flow together and interact to culminate in a completed estimate. Figure 6.1 shows the anatomy of a detailed estimate. This figure depicts graphically how the various cost estimate ingredients are synthesized from the basic man-hour estimates and material quantity estimates. Man-hour esimates of each basic skill required to accomplish the job are combined with the labor rates for these basic skills to derive labor dollar estimates. In the meantime, material quantities are estimated in terms of the units by which they are measured or purchased, and these material quantities are combined with their costs per unit to develop detailed direct material dollar estimates. Labor overhead or burden is applied to direct material costs. Then travel costs and other direct costs are added to produce total costs; general and administrative expenses and fee or profit are added to derive the "price" of the final esimate.

The labor rates are applied to the basic man-hour estimates are usually "composite" labor rates; that is, they represent an average of the rates within a given skill category. For example, the engineering skill may include draftsmen, designers, engineering assistants, junior engineers, engineers, and senior engineers. The number and titles of engineering skills vary widely from company to company, but the use of a composite labor rate for the engineering skill category is common practice. The composite labor rate is derived by multiplying the labor rate for each skill by the percentage of man-hours of that skill required to do a given task and adding the results. For example, if each of the six skills have the following labor rates and percentages, the composite labor rate is computed as follows:

*Adapted from Rodney D. Stewart, *Cost Estimating*, Wiley, 1982, by permission of the publisher.

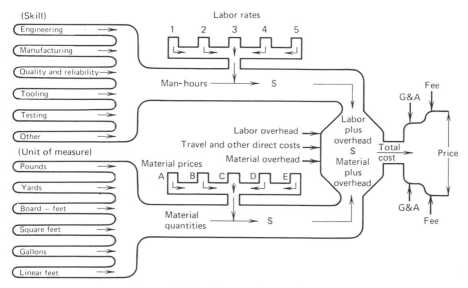

Figure 6.1. Anatomy of an estimate.

Skill	Labor Rate ($/h)	Percentage in the Task
Draftsman	$ 6.00	7
Designer	$ 8.00	3
Engineering assistant	$10.00	10
Junior engineer	$13.00	20
Engineer	$15.00	50
Senior engineer	$18.00	10
Total		100

Composite labor rate = $(0.07 \times \$6.00) + (0.03 \times \$8.00) + (0.10 \times \$10.00) + (0.20 \times \$13.00) + (0.50 \times \$15.00) + (0.10 \times \$18.00) = \$13.56$. Similar computations can be made to obtain the composite labor rate for skills within any of the other categories.

Another common practice is to establish separate overhead or burden pools for each skill category. These burden pools carry the peripheral costs that are related to and are a function of the man-hours expended in that particular skill category. Assuming that the burden pool is established for each of the labor skills shown on Figure 6.1, we can write an equation to depict the entire process. This equation is shown on Figure 6.2. Although the equation appears to be complex because of the number of factors included, the mathematics consist only of multiplication and addition. So far we have only considered a one-element cost estimate. The addition of multielement work activities or work outputs will greatly increase the number of mathematical computations, and it becomes readily evident that the anatomy of

$$T = \{[(E_H \times E_R) \times (1 + E_O)] + [(M_H \times M_R) \times (1 + M_O)] + [(TO_H \times TO_R)$$

$$\times (1 + TO_O)] + [(Q_H \times Q_R) \times (1 + Q_O)] + [(TE_H + TE_R) \times (1 + TE_O)]$$

$$+ [(O_H \times O_R) \times (1 + O_O)] + S_D + S_O + [M_D \times (1 + M_{OH})]$$

$$+ T_D + C_D + OD_D\} \times \{GA + 1.00\} \times \{F + 1.00\}$$

(a)

$$T = \{(L1_H \times L1_R) \times (1 + L1_O)] + [(L2_H \times L2_R) \times (1 + L2_O) \cdots$$

$$+ [(LN_H \times LN_R \times (1 + LN_O)] + S_D + S_O + [M_D \times (1 + M_{OH})]$$

$$+ T_D + CD + OD_D\} \times \{1 + GA\} \times \{1 \times F\}$$

Where: $L1, L2, \ldots LN$ are various labor rate cateogires

(b)

Symbols:

T = total cost
E_H = engineering labor hours
E_R = engineering composite labor rate in dollars per hour
E_O = engineering overhead rate in decimal form (i.e., $1.15 = 115\%$)
M_H = manufacturing labor hours
M_R = manufacturing composite labor rate in dollars per hour
M_O = manufacturing overhead rate in decimal form
TO_H = tooling labor hours
TO_R = tooling composite labor rate in dollars per hour
TO_O = tooling overhead in decimal form
Q_H = quality, reliability, and safety labor hours
Q_R = quality, reliability, and safety composite labor rate in dollars per hour
Q_O = quality, reliability, and safety overhead rate in decimal form
TE_H = testing labor hours
TE_R = testing composite labor rate in dollars per hour
TE_O = testing overhead rate in decimal form
O_H = other labor hours
O_R = labor rate for other hours category in dollars per hour
O_O = overhead rate for ther hours category in decimal form
S_D = major subcontract dollar
S_O = other subcontract dollars
M_D = material dollars
M_{OH} = material overhead in decimal form ($10\% = 0.10$)
T_D = travel dollars
C_D = computer dollars
OD_D = other direct dollars
GA = general and administrative expense in decimal form ($25\% = 0.25$)
F = fee in decimal form ($0.10 = 10\%$)

Figure 6.2. Generalized equation for cost estimating (a) Specific labor rate categories; (b) general labor rate categories.

TABLE 6.1. Estimating Time as a Percentage of Total Job Time

	Existing Technology (%)	High Technology (%)
Defining the output	4.6	14.6
Formulating the schedule and ground rules	1.2	1.2
Estimating materials and labor-hours	1.2	1.2
Estimating overhead, burden, and G&A	0.3	0.3
Estimating fee, profit, and earnings	0.3	0.3
Publishing the estimate	0.4	0.4
Total	8.0	18.0

an estimate is so complex that computer techniques for computation are highly desirable if not essential.

6.1.1 Time, Skills, and Labor-Hours Required to Prepare an Estimate

The resources (skills, calendar time, and man-hours) required to prepare a cost estimate depend on a number of factors. One factor is the estimating method used. Another is the level of technology or state of the art involved in the job or task being estimated. A rule of thumb can be used to develop a rough idea of the estimating time required. The calendar time required to develop an accurate and credible estimate is usually about 8% of the calendar time required to accomplish a task involving existing technology and 18% for a task involving a high technology (i.e., nuclear plant construction, aerospace projects). These percentages are divided approximately as shown in Table 6.1.

Note that the largest percentage of the estimating time required is for defining the output. This area is most important because it establishes a good basis for estimate credibility and accuracy as well as making it easier for the estimator to develop supportable man-hour and material estimates. These percentages also assume that the individuals who are going to perform the task or who have intimate working knowledge of the task are going to assist in estimate preparation. Hence the skill mix for estimating is very similar to the skill mix required for actually performing the task.

Man-hours required for preparation of a cost estimate can be derived from these percentages by multiplying the task's calendar period in years by 2000 man-hours per man-year, multiplying the result by the percentage in Table 6.1, and then multiplying the result by 0.1 and by the number of personnel on the estimating team. Estimating team size is a matter of judgment and depends on the complexity of the task, but it is generally proportional to the skills required to perform the task (as mentioned).

Examples of the application of these rules of thumb for determining the resources required to prepare a cost estimate follow:

1. A 3-year, high-technology project involving 10 basic skills or disciplines would require the following number of man-hours to estimate:

$$3 \times 2000 \times 0.18 \times 100 = 1080 \text{ man-hours}$$

2. A 6-month "existing-technology" project requiring five skills or disciplines would require $0.6 \times 2000 \times 0.08 \times 0.1 \times 5 = 48$ man-hours to develop an estimate

These relationships are drawn from the author's experience in preparing and participating in a large number of cost estimates and can be relied on to give you a guideline in preparing for the estimating process. But remember that these are "rules of thumb," and exercise caution and discretion in their application.

6.2 DISCUSSION OF TYPES OF COSTS

Detailed estimating requires the understanding of and the distinction between initial acquisition costs, fixed and variable costs, recurring and nonrecurring costs and direct and indirect costs. These distinctions are described in the material that follows.

6.2.1 Initial Acquisition Costs

Businessmen, consumers, and government officials are becoming increasingly aware of the need to estimate accurately and to justify the initial acquisition cost of an item to be purchased, manufactured, or built. When we speak of initial acquisition costs, we are usually referring to the total costs to procure, install, and put into operation a piece of equipment, a product, or a structure. Initial acquisition costs do not consider costs associated with the use and possession of the item. Individuals or businesses who purchase products are beginning to give more serious consideration to maintenance, operation, depreciation, energy, insurance, storage, and disposal costs before purchasing an item, whether it be an automobile, home appliance, suit of clothes, or industrial equipment. Because of continuing inflation and the constant fluctuation in the rate of inflation, it is as important to estimate accurately the most probable initial acquisition cost as it is to consider the cost savings brought about by the use of the item being acquired. Initial acquisition costs include planning, estimating, designing, and/or purchasing the components of the item; manufacturing, assembly, and inspection of the item; and installing and testing the item. Initial acquisition costs also include marketing, advertising, and markup of the price of the item as it flows through the distribution chain.

6.2.2 Fixed and Variable Costs

The costs of all four categories of productive outputs (processes, products, projects, and services) involve both fixed and variable costs. The relationship between fixed and variable costs depends on a number of factors, but it is principally related to the kind of output being estimated and the rate of output. Fixed cost is that group of costs involved in an on-going activity whose total will remain relatively constant regardless of the quantity of output or the phase of the output cycle being estimated. Variable cost is the group of costs that vary in relationship to the rate of output. Therefore, where it is desirable to know the effect of output rate on costs, it is important to know the relationship between the two forms of cost as well as the magnitude of these costs. Fixed costs are meaningful only if they are considered at a given point in time, since inflation and escalation will provide a variable element to "fixed" costs. Fixed costs may only be truly fixed over a given range of outputs. Rental of floor space for a production machine is an example of a fixed cost, and its use of electrical power will be a variable cost.

6.2.3 Recurring and Nonrecurring Costs

Recurring costs are repetitive in nature and depend on continued output of a like kind. They are similar to variable costs because they depend on the quantity or magnitude of output. Nonrecurring costs are incurred to generate the very first item of output. It is important to separate recurring and nonrecurring costs if it is anticipated that the costs of continued or repeated production will be required at some future date.

6.2.4 Direct and Indirect Costs

As discussed earlier, direct costs are those that are attributable directly to the specific work actrivity or work output being estimated. Indirect costs are those that are spread across several projects and allocable on a percentage basis to each project.

Table 6.2 is a matrix giving examples of these costs for various work outputs.

6.3 COLLECTING THE INGREDIENTS OF THE ESTIMATE

Before discussing the finer points of estimating, it is important to define the ingredients and to give you a preview of the techniques and methods used to collect these estimate ingredients.

6.3.1 Labor-Hours

Since the expenditure of labor-hours is the basic reason for the incurrence of costs, the estimating of labor-hours is the most important aspect of cost estimating. La-

TABLE 6.2. Examples of Costs for Various Outputs

	Process	Product	Project	Service
Initial acquisition costs	Plant construction costs	Manufacturing costs, marketing costs, and profit	Planning costs, design costs, manufacturing costs, test and checkout costs, and delivery costs	
Fixed costs	Plant maintenance costs	Plant maintenance costs	Planning costs and design costs	Building rental
Variable costs	Raw material costs	Labor costs	Manufacturing costs, test and checkout costs, and delivery costs	Labor costs
Recurring costs	Raw materials costs	Labor and material costs	Manufacturing costs, test and checkout costs, and delivery costs	Labor costs
Nonrecurring costs	Plant construction costs	Plant construction costs	Planning costs and design costs	Initial capital equipment investment
Direct costs	Raw materials	Manufacturing costs	Planning, design manufacturing, test and checkout and delivery costs	Labor and materials costs
Indirect costs	Energy costs	Marketing costs and profit	Energy costs	Energy costs

bor-hours and manpower requirements are estimated by four basic techniques: (1) use of methods, time, and motion (MTM) techniques; (2) the man-loading or staffing technique; (3) direct judgment of man-hours required; (4) and the use of man-hour/manpower estimating handbooks.

MTM methods are perhaps the most widespread methods of deriving man-hour and skill estimates for industrial processes. These methods are available from and taught by the MTM Association for Standards and Research, located in Fair Lawn, New Jersey. The association is international in scope and has developed five generations of MTM systems for estimating all aspects of industrial, manufacturing, or machining operations. The MTM method subdivides operator motions into small increments that can be measured and provides a means for combining the proper manual operations in a sequence to develop man-hour requirements for accomplishing a job.

The man-loading or staffing technique is perhaps the simplest and most widely used method for estimating the man-hours required to accomplish a given job. In this method, the estimator envisions the job, the work location, and the equipment or machines required, and estimates the number of people and skills that would be needed to staff a particular operation. The estimate is usually in terms of a number of people for a given number of days, weeks, or months. From this staffing level, the estimated on-the-job man-hours required to accomplish a given task can be computed.

Another method that is closely related to this second method is the use of direct judgment of the number of man-hours required. This judgment is usually made by an individual who has had direct hands-on experience in either performing or supervising a like task.

Finally, the use of handbooks is a widely used and accepted method of developing man-hour estimates. Handbooks usually provide larger time increments than the MTM method and require a specific knowledge of the work content and operation being performed.

6.3.2 Materials and Subcontracts

Materials and subcontract dollars are estimated in three ways: (1) drawing "take-offs" and handbooks; (2) dollar-per-pound relationships; and (3) direct quotations or bids. The most accurate way to estimate material costs is to calculate material quantities directly from a drawing or specification of the completed product. Using the quantities required for the number of items to be produced, the appropriate materials manufacturer's handbook, and an allowance for scrap or waste, one can accurately compute the material quantities and prices. Where detailed drawings of the item to be produced are not available, a dollar-per-pound relationship can be used to determine a rough order of magnitude cost. Firm quotations or bids for the materials or for the item to be subcontracted are better than any of the previously mentioned ways of developing a materials estimate because the supplier can be held to his or her bid.

6.3.3 Labor Rates and Factors

The labor rate, or number of dollars required per man-hour, is the quantity that turns a man-hour estimate into a cost estimate; therefore the labor rate and any direct cost factors that are added to it are key elements of the cost estimate. Labor rates vary by skill, geographical location, calendar date, and the time of day or week they are applied. Labor rates vary from more than $3 per hour (the minimum wage in 1980) for hourly paid personnel to more than $30 per hour for salaried personnel. Labor rates vary graphically by a factor of 2.6:1 in the continental United States and 3.61:1 if Alaska is included. The calendar date affects the labor rate because inflation must be added each year to adjust wages to the cost of living increases encountered during that year. For hourly paid personnel, overtime premiums of 150% are common for hours worked over 40 hours per week, and 250% for work accomplished on Sundays or holidays. Shift premiums and hazardous duty pay are also added to hourly wages to develop the actual labor rate to be used in developing a cost estimate. Wage rate structures vary considerably depending on union contract agreements. Once the labor rate is applied to the man-hour estimate to develop a labor cost figure, other factors are commonly used to develop other direct cost allowances such as travel costs and direct material costs.

6.3.4 Indirect Costs, Burden, and Overhead

Burden or overhead costs for engineering activities very often are as high as 100% of direct engineering labor costs, and manufacturing overheads go to 150% and beyond. A company that can keeps its overhead from growing excessively, or a company that can successfully trim its overhead, can place itself in an advantageously competitive position. Since overhead more than doubles the cost of a work activity or work output, trimming the overhead has a significant effect on reducing overall costs.

6.3.5 Administrative Costs

Administrative costs range up to 20% of total direct and indirect costs for large companies. General and administrative costs are added to direct and overhead costs and are recognized as a legitimate business expense.

6.3.6 Fee, Profit, or Earnings

The fee, profit, or earnings will depend on the amount of risk the company is taking in marketing the product, the market demand for the item, and the required return on the company's investment. This subject is one that deserves considerable attention by the cost estimator. Basically, the amount of profit depends on the astute business sense of the company's management. Few companies will settle for less than 10% profit, and many will not make an investment or enter into a venture unless they can see a 20–30% return on their investment.

6.3.7 Assembly of the Ingredients

Once resource estimates have been accumulated, the process of reviewing, compiling, organizing, and computing the estimate begins. This process is divided into two general subdivisions of work: (1) reviewing, compiling, and organizing the input resource data, and (2) computation of the costs based on desired or approved labor rates and factors. A common mistake made in developing cost estimates is the failure to perform properly the first of these work subdivisions. In the process of reviewing, compiling, and organizing the data, duplications in resource estimates are discovered and eliminated; omissions are located and remedied; overlapping or redundant effort is recognized and adjusted; and missing or improper rationale, backup data, or supporting data are identified, corrected, or supplied. A thorough review of the cost estimate input data by the estimator or estimating team, along with an adjustment and reconcilation process, will accomplish these objectives.

Computation of a cost estimate is mathematically simple since it involves only multiplication and addition. The number of computations can escalate rapidly, however, as the number of labor skills, fiscal years, and work breakdown structure elements are increased. One who works frequently in ground-up, industrial engineering man-hour and material cost estimating will quickly come to the conclusion that some form of computer assistance is required. Computer programs capable of performing the basic computations required to develop a cost estimate are available at a nominal cost from the federal government or from a number of computer software firms. Some programs can be obtained from the Computer Operations Services and Management Information Center (COSMIC) at the University of Georgia, Athens, Georgia. In addition, there are companies that specialize in automatic data processing equipment and services for accounting, economics, and estimating applications.

With the basic ingredients and basic tools available, we are now ready to follow the steps required to develop a good detailed cost estimate. All steps are needed for any good cost estimate. The manner of accomplishing each step, and the depth of information needed and time expended on each step, will vary considerably depending on what work activity or work output is being estimated. These steps are as follows:

1. Develop the work element structure.
2. Schedule the work elements.
3. Retrieve and organize historical cost data.
4. Develop and use cost estimating relationships.
5. Develop and use production learning curves.
6. Identify skill categories, levels, and rates.
7. Develop labor hour and material estimates.
8. Develop overhead and administrative costs.
9. Apply inflation and escalation factors.
10. Price (compute) the estimated costs.
11. Analyze, adjust, and support the estimate
12. Publish, present, and use the estimate.

6.4 THE FIRST QUESTIONS TO ASK (AND WHY)

Whether you are estimating the cost of a process, product, or service, there are some basic questions you must ask to get started on a detailed cost estimate. These questions relate principally to the requirements, descriptions, location, and timing of the work.

6.4.1 What Is It?

A surprising number of detailed cost estimates fail to be accurate or credible because of a lack of specificity in describing the work that is being estimated. The objectives, ground rules, constraints, and requirements of the work must be spelled out in detail to form the basis for a good cost estimate. First, it is necessary to determine which of the four generic work outputs (process, product, project, or service) or combination of work outputs best describe the work being estimated. Then it is necessary to describe the work in as much detail as possible.

6.4.2 What Does It Look Like?

Work descriptions usually take the form of detailed specifications, sketches, drawings, materials lists, and parts lists. Weight, size, shape, material type, power, accuracy, resistance to environmental hazards, and quality are typical factors that are described in detail in a specification. Processes and services are usually defined by the required quality, accuracy, speed, consistency, or responsiveness of the work. Products and projects, on the other hand, usually require a preliminary or detailed design of the item or group of items being estimated. In general, more detailed designs will produce more accurate cost estimates. The principal reason for this is that as a design proceeds, better definitions and descriptions of all facets of this design unfold. The design process is an interactive one in which component or subsystem designs proceed in parallel; component or subsystem characteristics reflect on and affect one another to alter the configuration and perhaps even the performance of the end item. Another reason that a more detailed design results in a more accurate and credible cost estimate is that the amount of detail itself produces a greater awareness and visibility of potential inconsistencies, omissions, duplications, and overlaps.

6.4.3 When Is It to Be Available?

Production rate, production quantity, and timing of production initiation and completion are important ground rules to establish before starting a cost estimate. Factors such as a raw material availability, labor skills required, and equipment utilization often force a work activity to conform to a specific time period. It is important to establish the optimum time schedule early in the estimating process, to establish key milestone dates, and to subdivide the overall work schedule into identifiable increments that can be placed on a calendar time scale. A work output schedule placed on a calendar time scale will provide the basic inputs needed to compute start-up costs, fiscal-year funding, and inflationary effects.

6.4.4 Who Will Do It?

The organization or organizations that are to perform an activity, as well as the skill and salary levels within these organizations, must be known or assumed to formulate a credible cost estimate. Given a competent organization with competent employees, another important aspect of developing a competitive cost estimate is the determination of the make or buy structure and the skill mix needs throughout the time period of a work activity. Judicious selection of the performers and wise time phasing of skill categories and skill levels can rapidly produce prosperity for any organization with a knowledge of its employees, its product, and its customer.

6.4.5 Where Will It Be Done?

Geographical factors have a strong influence on the credibility and competitive stature of a cost estimate. In addition to the wide variation in labor costs for various locations, material costs vary substantially from location to location, and transportation costs are entering even more heavily into the cost picture than in the past. The cost estimator must develop detailed ground rules and assumptions concerning location of the work and then estimate costs accurately in keeping with all location-oriented factors.

6.5 THE ESTIMATE SKELETON: THE WORK ELEMENT STRUCTURE

The first step in developing a cost estimate of any type of work output is the development of a work element structure (sometimes called a work breakdown structure). The work element structure serves as a framework for collecting, accumulating, organizing, and computing the direct and directly related costs of a work activity or work output. It also can be and usually is used for managing and reporting resources and related costs throughout the lifetime of the work. There is considerable advantage in using the work element structure and its accompanying task descriptions as the basis for scheduling, reporting, tracking, and organizing as well as for initial costing. Hence it is important to devote considerable attention to this phase of the overall estimating process. A work element structure is developed by subdividing a process, product, project, or service into its major work elements, then breaking the major work elements into subelements, and subelements into subsubelements, and so on. There are usually 5–10 subelements under each major work element.

The purpose of developing the work element structure is fivefold:

1. To provide a lower-level breakout of small tasks that are easy to identify, man-load, schedule, and estimate
2. To provide assurance that all required work elements are included in the work output

3. To reduce the possibility of overlap, duplication, or redundancy of tasks

4. To furnish a convenient hierarchical structure for the accumulation of resources estimates

5. To give greater overall visibility as well as depth of penetration into the makeup of any work activity

6.6 THE HIERARCHICAL RELATIONSHIP OF A DETAILED WORK ELEMENT STRUCTURE

A typical work element structure is shown in Figure 6.3. Note that the relationship resembles a hierarchy where each activity has a higher activity, parallel activities, and lower activities. A basic principle of work element structures is that the resources or content of each work element are made up of the sum of the resources or content of elements below it. No work element that has lower elements exceeds the sum of those lower elements in resource requirements. The bottommost elements are estimated at their own level and sum to higher levels. Many numbering systems are feasible and workable. The numbering system shown is one that has proven workable in a wide variety of situations.

One common mistake in using work element structures is to try to input or allocate effort to every block, even those at a higher level. Keep in mind that this should not be done because each block or work element contains only that effort included in those elements below it. If there are no blocks below it, then it can contain resources. If there is need to add work activities or resources not included in a higher level block, add an additional block below it to include the desired effort. Level 1 of a work element structure is usually the top level, with lower levels numbered sequentially as shown. The "level" is usually equal to the number of digits in the work element block. For example, the block numbered 1.1.3.2 is in Level 4 because it contains four digits.

6.7 FUNCTIONAL ELEMENTS DESCRIBED

When subdividing a work activity or work output into its elements, the major subdivisions can be either functional or physical elements. The second level in a work element structure usually consists of a combination of functional and physical elements if a product or project is being estimated. For a process or service, all second-level activities could be functional. Functional elements of a production or project activity can include activities such as planning, project management, systems engineering and integration, testing, logistics, and operations. A process or service can include any of hundreds of functional elements. Typical examples of the widely dispersed functional elements that can be found in a work element structure for a service are advising, assembling, binding, cleaning, fabricating, inspecting, packaging, painting, programming, projecting, receiving, testing, and welding.

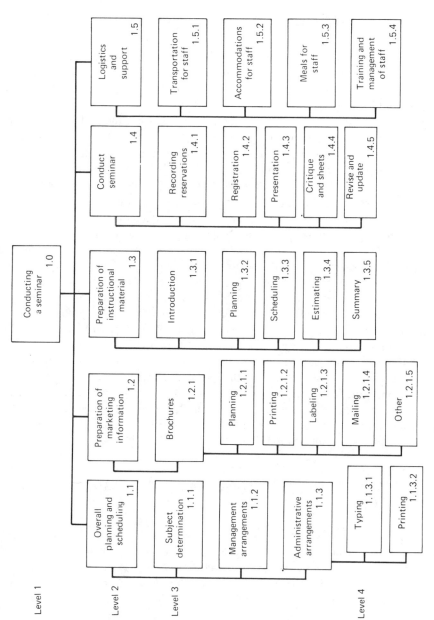

Figure 6.3. Typical work element structure.

195

6.8 PHYSICAL ELEMENTS DESCRIBED

The physical elements of a work output are the physical structures, hardware, products, or end items that are supplied to the consumer. These physical elements represent resources because they take labor and materials to produce. Hence they can and should be a basis for the work element structure.

Figure 6.4 shows a typical work element structure of just the physical elements of a well-known consumer product, the automobile. The figure shows how just one automobile company chose to subdivide the components of an automobile. For any given product or project, the number of ways that a work element structure can be constructed are virtually unlimited. For example, the company could have included the carburetor and engine cooling system as part of the engine assembly (this might have been a more logical and workable arrangement since it is used in costing a mass production operation). Note that the structure shows a Level 3 breakout of the body and sheet metal element, and the door (a Level 3 element) is subdivided into its Level 4 components.

This physical element breakout demonstrates several important characteristics of a work element structure. First, note that Level 5 would be the individual component parts of each assembly or subassembly. It only took three subdivisions of the physical hardware to get down to a point where the next level breakout would be the individual parts. One can see rapidly that breaking down every Level 2 element three more levels (down to Level 5) would result in a very large work element structure. Second, to convert this physical hardware breakout into a true work element structure would require the addition of some functional activities. To provide the manpower as well as the materials required to procure, manufacture, assemble, test, and install the components of each block, it is necessary to add an "assembly," "fabrication," or "installation" activity block.

6.9 TREATMENT OF RECURRING AND NONRECURRING ACTIVITIES

Most work consists of both nonrecurring activities, or "one-of-a-kind" activities needed to produce an item or to provide a service, and recurring or repetitive activities that must be performed to provide more than one output unit. The resources requirements (man-hours and materials) necessary to perform these nonrecurring and recurring activities reflect themselves in nonrecurring and recurring costs.

Although not all estimates require the separation of nonrecurring and recurring costs, it is often both convenient and necessary to separate costs because one may need to know what the costs are for an increased work output rate. Since work output rate principally affects the recurring costs, it is desirable to have these costs readily accessible and identifiable.

Separation of nonrecurring and recurring costs can be done in two ways through the use of the work element structure concept. First, the two costs can be identi-

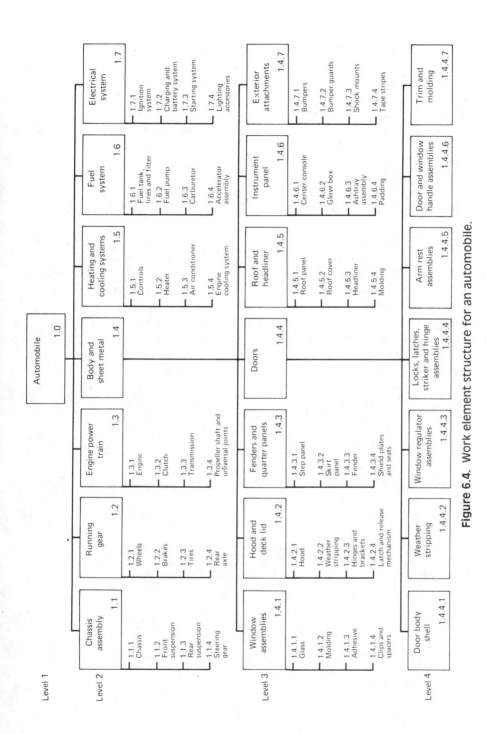

Figure 6.4. Work element structure for an automobile.

197

fied, separated, and accounted for within each work element. Resources for each task block would, then, include three sets of resource estimates: (1) nonrecurring costs, (2) recurring costs, and (3) total costs for that block. The second convenient method of cost separation is to start with identical work element structures for both costs and develop two separate cost estimates. A third estimate, which sums the two cost estimates into a total, can also use the same basic work element structure. If there are elements unique to each cost category, they can be added to the appropriate work element structure.

6.10 WORK ELEMENT STRUCTURE INTERRELATIONSHIPS

As shown in the automobile example, considerable flexibility exists concerning the placement of physical elements (the same is true with functional elements) in the work element structure. Because of this, and because it is necessary to define clearly where one element leaves off and the other takes over, it is necessary to provide a detailed definition of what is included in each work activity block. For example, in the automotive example, the rear axle unit could have been located and defined as part of the power train or as part of the chassis assembly rather than as part of the running gear. Where does the rear axle leave off and the power train begin? Is the differential or part of the differential included in the power train? These kinds of questions must be answered—and they usually are answered—before a detailed cost estimate is generated, in the form of a work element structure dictionary. The dictionary describes exactly what is included in each work element and what is excluded; it defines where the interface is located between two work elements; and it defines where the assembly effort is located to assemble or install two interfacing units.

A good work element structure dictionary will prevent many problems brought about by overlaps, duplications, and omissions because detailed thought has been given to the interfaces and content of each work activity.

6.10.1 Skill Matrix in a Work Element Structure

When constructing a work element structure, keep in mind that each work element will be performed by a person or group of people using one or more skills. There are two important facets of the labor or work activity for each work element: skill mix and skill level. The skill mix is the proportion of each of several skill categories that will be used in performing the work. Skill *categories* vary widely and depend on the type of work being estimated. For a residential construction project, for example, typical skills would be bricklayer, building laborer, carpenter, electrician, painter, plasterer, or plumber. Other typical construction skills are structural steelworker, cement finisher, glazier, roofer, sheet metal worker, pipefitter, excavation equipment operator, and general construction laborer. Professional skills such as lawyers, doctors, financial officers, administrators, project managers, engineers, printers, writers, and so forth are called on to do a wide variety of direct-labor activities. Occasionally, skills will be assembled into several broad categories (such as engineering, manufacturing, tooling, testing, and quality assurance) that correspond to overhead or burden pools.

Skill *level*, on the other hand, depicts the experience or salary level of an individual working within a given skill category. For example, engineers are often subdivided into various categories such as principal engineers, senior engineers, engineers, associate engineers, junior engineers, and engineering technicians. The skilled trades are often subdivided into skill level categories and given names that depict their skill level; for example, carpenters could be broken down into master carpenters, journeymen, apprentices, and helpers. Because skill categories and skill levels are designated for performing work within each work element, it is not necessary to establish separate work elements for performance of each skill. A work element structure for home construction would not have an element designated carpentry because carpentry is a skill needed to perform one or more of the work elements (i.e., roof construction, wall construction).

6.10.2 Organizational Relationships to a Work Element Structure

Frequently all or part of a work element structure will have a direct counterpart in the performing organization. Although it is not necessary for the work element structure to be directly correlatable to the organizational structure, it is often convenient to assign the responsibility for estimating and for performing a specific work element to a specific organizational segment. This practice helps to motivate the performer, since it gives him or her responsibility for an identifiable task, and it provides the manager greater assurance that each part of the work will be accomplished. In the planning and estimating process, early assignment of work elements to those who are going to be responsible for performing the work will motivate them to do a better job of estimating and will provide greater assurance of completion of the work within performance, schedule, and cost constraints because the functional organizations have set their own goals. Job performance and accounting for work accomplished versus funds spent can also be accomplished more easily if an organizational element is held responsible for a specific work element in the work element structure.

6.11 METHODS USED WITHIN THE DETAILED ESTIMATING PROCESS

The principal methods used *within* the detailed estimating process are detailed resource estimating, direct estimating, estimating by analogy, firm quotes, handbook estimating, and the parametric estimating technique mentioned earlier. These methods are described briefly in the following sections.

6.11.1 Detailed Resource Estimating

Detailed resource estimating involves the synthesis of a cost estimate from resource estimates made at the lowest possible level in the work element structure. Detailed estimating presumes that a detailed design of the product or project is available and that a detailed manufacturing, assembly, testing, and delivery schedule is available for the work. This type of estimating assumes that skills, man-hours, and materials can be identified for each work element through one or more of the methods that follow. A detailed estimate is usually developed through a synthesis of work element estimates developed by various methods.

6.11.2 Direct Estimating

A direct estimate is a judgmental estimate made in a "direct" method by an estimator or performer who is familiar with the task being estimated. The estimator will observe and study the task to be performed and then quote his or her estimate in terms of man-hours, materials, and/or dollars. For example, a direct estimate could be quoted as "so many dollars." Many expert estimators can size up and estmate a job with just a little familarization. One estimator I know can take a fairly complex drawing and, within just a few hours, develop a rough order-of-magnitude estimate of the resources required to build the item. Direct estimating is a skill borne of experience in both estimating and in actually performing the "hands-on" work.

6.11.3 Estimating by Analogy (Rules of Thumb)

This method is similar to the direct estimating method in that considerable judgment is required, but an additional feature is the comparison with some existing or past task of similar description. The estimator collects resources information on a similar or analogous task and compares the task to be estimated with the similar or analogous one. The estimator would say that "this task should take about twice the time (man-hours, dollars, materials, etc.) as the one used as a reference." This judgmental factor (a factor of 2), would then be multiplied by the resources used for the reference task to develop the estimate for the new task. A significant pitfall in this method of estimating is the potential inability of the estimator to identify subtle differences in the two work activities and, hence, to be estimating the cost of a system based on one that is really not similar or analogous.

6.11.4 Firm Quotes

One of the best methods of estimating the resources required to complete a work element or to perform a work activity is the development of a firm quotation by the supplier or vendor. The two keys to the development of a realistic quotation are (1) the solicitation of bids from at least three sources and (2) the development of a detailed and well-planned request for quotation. Years of experience by many organizations in the field of procurement have indicated that three bids are the optimum from a standpoint of achieving the most realistic and reasonable price at a reasonable expenditure of effort. The acquisition of at least three bids provides sufficient check and balance and furnishes bid prices and conditions for comparison, evaluation, and selection. A good request for quotation (RFQ) is essential, however, to evaluate the bids effectively. The RFQ should contain ground rules, schedules, delivery locations and conditions, evaluation criteria, and specifications for the work. The RFQ should also state and specify the format required for cost information. A well-prepared RFQ will result in a quotation or proposal that will be easily evaluated, verified, and compared with independent estimates.

6.11.5 Handbook Estimating

Handbooks, catalogs, and reference books containing information on virtually every conceivable type of product, part, supplies, equipment, raw material, and finished material are available in libraries and bookstores, and directly from publishers. Many of these handbooks provide labor estimates for installation or operation as well as the purchase costs of the item. Some catalogs either do not provide price lists or provide price lists as a separate insert to permit periodic updates of prices without changing the basic catalog description. Information services provide microfilmed cassettes and on-line data bases for access to the descriptions and costs of thousands and even tens of thousands of items.

If you produce a large number of estimates, it may pay to subscribe to a microfilm catalog and handbook data access system, or, at least, to develop your own library of data bases, handbooks and catalogs.

6.11.6 The Learning Curve

As discussed in Chapter 5, the learning curve is a graphical representation of the reduction in time, resources, or costs either actually or theoretically encountered in the conduct of a repetitive production-motivated human activity. The theory behind the learning curve (and there are data available to confirm this theory for some specific applications) is that successive identical operations after the first one will take less time, use fewer resources, or cost less than preceding operations. The term "learning" is used because it relates primarily to the improvement of mental or manual skills observed when an operation is repeated, but "learning" can also be achieved by a shop or organization through the use of improved equipment, purchasing, production, or management techniques. When the "learning curve" is used in applications other than those involving the feedback loop and that brings improvement of an individual's work activities, it is more properly named by one or more of the following terms:

Productivity improvement curve
Manufacturing progress function

Experience curve

Progress curve

Improvement curve

Production improvement curve

Production acceleration curve

Time reduction curve

Cost improvement curve

Learning curve theory is based on the concept that as the total quantity of units produced doubles, the hours required to produce the last unit of this doubled quantity will be reduced by a constant percentage. This means that the hours required to produce unit 2 will be a certain percent less than the hours required to produce unit 1; the hours required to produce unit 4 will be the same percent less than the hours required to produce unit 2; the hours required to produce unit 8 will be the same percent less than unit 4; and this constant percentage of reduction will continue for doubled quantities as long as uninterrupted production of the same item continues. The complement of this constant percentage of reduction is commonly referred to as the "slope." This means that if the constant percentage of reduction is 10%, the slope would be 90%. Table 6.3 gives an example of a learning curve with 90% slope when the number of hours reequired to produce the first unit are 100.

The reason for using the term "slope" in naming this reduction will be readily seen when the learning curve is plotted on coordinates with logarithmic scales on both the x and y axes (in this instance, the learning "curve" actually becomes a straight line). But first, let us plot the learning curve on conventional coordinates. You can see by the plot in Figure 6.5 that it is truly a curve when plotted on conventional coordinates, and that the greater the production quantity, the smaller the incremental reduction in man-hours required from unit to unit.

When the learning curve is plotted on log-log coordinates, as shown in Figure 6.6, it becomes a straight line. The higher the slope, the flatter the line; the lower the slope, the steeper the line.

The effects of plotting curves on different slopes can be seen on the chart shown

TABLE 6.3. Learning Curve Values

Cumulative Units	Hours per Unit	Percent Reduction
1	100.00	
2	90.00	10
4	81.00	10
8	72.90	10
16	65.61	10
32	59.05	10

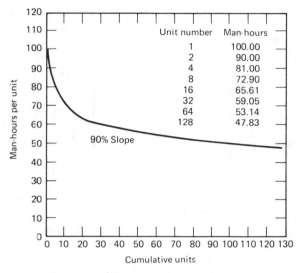

Figure 6.5. Learning curve on a linear plot.

in Figure 6.7. This chart shows the effects on man-hour reductions of doubling the quantities produced 12 times.

Formulas for the unit curve and the cumulative average curve are shown on Table 6.4.

Care should be taken in the use of the learning curve to avoid an overly optimistic (low) learning curve slope and to avoid using the curve for too few units in

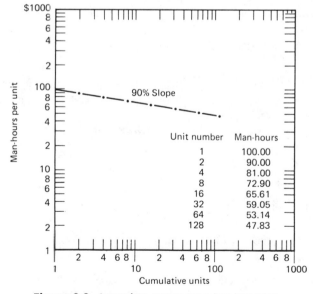

Figure 6.6. Learning curve on a log-log plot.

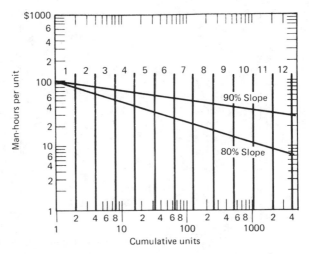

Figure 6.7. Comparison between two learning curves.

production. Most learning curve textbooks point out that this technique is credibly applicable only to operations that are done by hand (employ manual or physical operations) and that are highly repetitive.

6.11.7 Man-Loading Methods

One of the most straightforward methods of estimating resources or man-hours required to accomplish a task is the man-loading, or shop-loading, method. This estimating technique is based on the fact that an experienced participant or man-

TABLE 6.4. Learning Curve Formulas

Unit curve $Y_X = KX^N$
where Y_X = number of direct labor man-hours required to produce the Xth unit
$\quad\quad K$ = number of direct labor man-hours required to produce the first unit
$\quad\quad x$ = number of units produced
$\quad\quad n$ = slope of curve expressed in positive hundredths (e.g., $n = 0.80$ for an 80% curve)

$$N = \frac{\log_{10}n}{\log_{10}2}$$

Cumulative average curve

$$V_X \approx \frac{K}{X(1 + N)} [(x + 0.5)^{(1 + N)} - (0.5)^{(1 - N)}]$$

where V_X = the cumulative average number of direct labor man-hours required to produce x units ager of any activity can usually perceive, through judgment and knowledge of the activity being estimated, the number of individuals of various skills needed to accomplish a task. The shop-loading method is similar in that the estimator can usually predict what portion of an office or shop's capacity will be occupied by a given job. This percentage shop-loading factor can be used to compute man-hours or resources if the total shop manpower or total shop operation costs are known. Examples of the man-loading and shop-loading methods based on 1896 man-hours per man year are shown in Table 6.5.

6.11.8 Statistical and Parametric Estimating as Inputs to Detailed Estimating

Statistical and parametric estimating as discussed in chapters 3 and 7 involves collecting and organizing historical information through mathematical techniques and relating this information to the work output that is being estimated. There are a number of methods that can be used to correlate historical cost and manpower information; the choice depends principally on mathematical skills, imagination, and access to data. These mathematical and statistical techniques provide some analytical relationship between the product, project or service being estimated and its physical characteristics. The format most commonly used for statistical and parametric estimating is the *estimating relationship*, which relates some physical characteristic of the work output (weight, power requirements, size, or volume) with the cost or man-hours required to produce it. The most widely used estimating relationship is linear. That is, the mathematical equation representing the relationship is a linear equation, and the relationship can be depicted by a straight line when plotting on a graph with conventional linear coordinates for the x (horizontal) and y (vertical) axes. Other forms of estimating relationships can be derived based

TABLE 6.5. Man-Loading and Shop-Loading Methods

	Time Increment (Year)						
	1	2	3	4	5	6	7
Man-Loading Method							
Engineers	1	1	1	2	1	0	0
Hours	1,896	1,896	1,896	3,792	1,896	0	0
Technicians	3	4	4	6	2	1	0
Hours	5,688	7,584	7,584	11,376	3,792	1,896	0
Draftsmen	0	0	1	3	6	4	2
Hours	0	0	1,896	5,688	11,376	7,584	3,792
Shop-Loading Method							
Electrical shop (5 workers)	10%	15%	50%	50%	5%	0%	0%
Hours	948	1,422	4,740	4,740	474	0	0
Mechanical shop (10 workers)	5%	5%	10%	80%	60%	10%	5%
Hours	948	948	1,896	15,168	11,376	1,896	948

on the curve-fitting techniques presented in any standard textbook on statistics. For the purpose of simplicity, and to illustrate the technique of developing an estimating relationship, the following example is provided.

Suppose that 10 historical data points exist pertaining to the number of man-hours required to produce various quantities (pounds) of a product. To develop Figure 6.8 (a graphical representation of an estimating relationship that best represents the aggregate of these data points), the method of least squares is used. The least squares method defines a straight line through the data points such that the sum of the squared deviations or distances from the line is smaller than it would be for any other straight line. The resulting straight line goes through the overall ''mean'' of the data. When the data points represent a random sample from a larger population of data, the least squares line is a best estimate of the relationship for the total population. The equation of the straight line to be defined is

$$y = mx + b$$

where m is the slope of the line, and b is the point where the line intercepts the y axis.

If n is the number of data points, and x_1 and y_1 are the coordinates of specific data points, the two equations shown on Table 6.6 can be solved simultaneously to define the line that best fits the data.

The data points in Figure 6.8 are shown in Table 6.7 along with derived values of the expressions contained in the equations of Table 6.6

Substituting the appropriate values from Table 6.7 into the equations shown on Table 6.6 we get the following two equations:

$$165.2 = 10b + 860m$$

$$18,469 = 860b + 98,800m$$

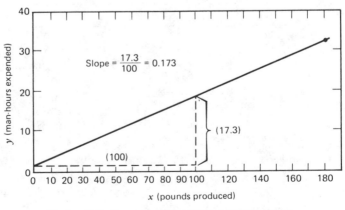

Figure 6.8. Sample estimating relationships.

TABLE 6.6 Sample Estimating Formulas

1. $\sum\limits_{i=1}^{u} y_i = nb + m \sum\limits_{i=1}^{n} x_i$

2. $\sum\limits_{i=1}^{n} y_i x_i = b \sum\limits_{i=1}^{n} x_i + m \sum\limits_{i=1}^{n} (x_i)^2$

By multiplying the first equation by -1, and dividing the second equation by 86, we can add the two equations as follows:

$$-165.2 = -10b - 860m$$

$$214.76 = 10b + 1148.84m$$

$$49.56 = 288.84m$$

and

$$m = \frac{49.56}{288.84} = 0.172$$

Therefore $b = 1.728$.

The equation for the "best-fit line," then, can be expressed as $y = mx + b$ or man-hours $= (0.172x$ pounds$) + 1.728$.

Estimating relationships, whether based on a linear best-fit curve such as the one shown or on some other statistical averaging technique have certain advantages but certain distinct limitations. They have the advantage of providing a quick estimate even though very little is known about the work output except its physical characteristics. They correlate the present estimate with past history of resource utilization on similar items, and their use simplifies the estimating process. They

TABLE 6.7. Sample Estimating Chart

x_i (pounds)	y_i (man-hours)	$(x_i)^2$	$(x_i y_i)$
20	3.5	400	70
30	7.4	900	222
40	7.1	1,600	284
60	15.6	3,600	936
70	11.1	4,900	777
90	14.9	8,100	1,341
100	23.5	10,000	2,350
120	27.1	14,400	3,252
150	22.1	22,500	3,315
180	32.9	32,400	5,922
$\sum x_i = 860$	$\sum x_i = 165.2$	$\sum (x_i)^2 = 98,800$	$\sum (x_i y_i) = 18,469$

require the use of statistical or mathematical skills rather than detailed estimating skills, which may be an advantage if detailed estimating skills are not available to the estimating organization.

On the other hand, because of their dependence on past (historical) data, they may erroneously indicate cost trends. Some products, such as mass-produced electronics, are providing more capability per pound, and lower costs per pound, volume, or component count every year. Basing electronics costs on past history may, therefore, result in noncompetitively high estimates. History should not be repeated if that history contains detrimental inefficiencies, duplications, unnecessary redundancies, rework, and overestimates. Often it is difficult to determine what part of historical data should be used to reflect future resource requirements accurately.

Finally, the parametric or statistical estimate, unless used at a very low level in the estimating process, does not provide in-depth visibility, and it does not permit determination of cost effects from subtle changes in schedule, performance, or design requirements. The way to use the statistical or parametric estimate most effectively is to subdivide the work into the smallest possible elements and then to use statistical or parametric methods to derive the resources required for these small elements.

One widely used "cost model" that uses statistical and parametric estimating techniques is the RCA "PRICE" (Programmed Review of Information for Costing and Evaluation) model. This system, designed primarily for high-technology aerospace or electronic products but adaptable to some commercial products, is marketed by RCA Corporation's Government and Commercial Systems Division in Moorestown, New Jersey and uses a centralized computer that can be accessed through commercial telephone lines. All that is required to become an expert user of PRICE is to attend a 2-week training course provided by RCA, to purchase an inexpensive computer terminal, and to pay a nominal users fee for each access to the computer. The principal benefits of this system are quick access and the ability to make comparative cost assessments of alternative approaches quickly.

It would not be advisable to use this system for competitive cost estimates where no other method of cross-checking the estimate is available. The system uses a number of "complexity" factors that are subjective in nature, and that strongly affect the magnitude of the cost output. This fact, coupled with the previously mentioned limitations of statistical and parametric cost estimating, make the model useful only for rough order-of-magnitude estimates or for cost sensitivity studies. In summary, however, parametric and statistical estimating, discussed in more detail in chapters 3 and 7 for this reference mannual, can provide viable inputs to detailed cost estimates.

6.12 DEVELOPING A SCHEDULE

Schedule elements are time-related groupings of work activities that are placed in sequence to accomplish an overall desired objective. Schedule elements for a process can be represented by very small (minutes, hours, or days) time period. The scheduling of a process is represented by the time the raw material or raw materials take during each step to travel through the process. The schedule for manufacturing a product or delivery of a service is, likewise, a time flow of the various components or actions into a completed item or activity.

A project (the construction or development of a fairly large, complex, or multidiciplinary tangible work output) contains distinct schedule elements called milestones. These milestones are encountered in one form or another in almost all projects: (1) study and analysis; (2) design; (3) procurement of raw materials and purchased parts; (4) fabrication or manufacturing of components and subsystems; (5) assembly of the components and subsystems; (6) testing of the combined system to qualify the unit for operation in its intended environment; (7) acceptance testing, preparation, packaging, shipping, and delivery of the item; (8) and operation of the item.

6.13 TECHNIQUES USED IN SCHEDULE PLANNING

There are a number of analytical techniques used in developing an overall schedule of a work activity that help to ensure the correct allocation and sequencing of schedule elements: precedence and dependency networks, arrow diagrams, critical path bar charts, and program evaluation and review techniques (PERT). These techniques use graphical and mathematical methods to develop the best schedule based on sequencing in such a way that each activity is performed only when the required predecessor activities are accomplished. A simple example of how these techniques work is shown in Figure 6.9. Eight schedule elements have been chosen, the length of each schedule activity has been designated, and a relationship has been established between each activity and its predecessor activity as in Table 6.8.

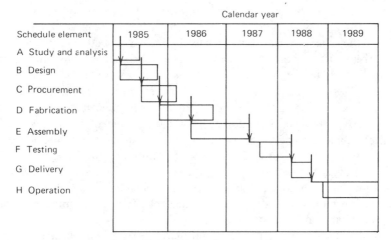

Figure 6.9. Scheduling a project.

TABLE 6.8. Schedule Relationships

Schedule Element	Title of Schedule Element	Time Required for Completion	Percent Completion Required[a]
A	Study and analysis	6 months	$33\frac{1}{3}$
B	Design	8 months	50
C	Procurement	8 months	50
D	Fabrication	12 months	$66\frac{2}{3}$
E	Assembly	12 months	100 plus 2 months
F	Testing	8 months	100
G	Delivery	4 months	100 plus 4 months
H	Operation	36 months	100

[a] Percent completion required before subsequent activity can be accomplished.

Note several things about the precedence relationships: (1) some activities can be started before their predecessor activities are completed, (2) some activities must be fully completed before their follow-on activities can be started, and (3) some activities cannot be started until a given number of months after the 100% completion date of a predecessor activity. Once these schedule interrelationships are established, a total program schedule can be laid out by starting either from a selected beginning point and working forward in time until the completion date is reached, or by starting from a desired completion date and working backward in time to derive the required schedule starting date. In many instances you will find that both the start date and completion date are given. In that instance, the length of schedule elements and their interrelationships must be established through an interactive process to develop a schedule that accomplishes a job in the required time. If all schedule activities are started as soon as their prerequisites are met, the result is the stortest possible time schedule to perform the work.

Most complex work activities have multiple paths of activity that must be accomplished parallel with each other. The longest of these paths is called a "critical path," and the schedule critical path is developed by connecting all of the schedule activity critical paths. Construction of a schedule such as that shown in Figure 6.9 brings to light a number of other questions. The first of these is, "How do I establish the length of each activity?" This question strikes at the heart of the overall estimating process itself, since many costs are incurred by the passage of time. Costs of an existing work force, overhead (insurance, rental, and utilities), and material handling and storage continue to pile up in an organization whether there is a productive output or not. Hence it is important to develop the shortest possible overall schedule to accomplish a job and each schedule element in the shortest time and in the most efficient method possible. The length of each schedule activity is established by an analysis of that activity and the human and material resources available and required to accomplish it.

A second question is, "What do I do if there are other influences on the schedule such as availability of facilities, equipment, and manpower?" This is a factor that arises in most estimating situations. There are definite schedule interactions in any multiple-output organization that must be considered in planning a single work activity. Overall corporate planning must take into account these schedule interactions in its own critical path chart to ensure that facilities, manpower, and funds are available to accomplish all work activities in an effective and efficient manner. A final question is, "How do I establish a credible 'percent complete' figure for each predecessor work activity?" This is accomplished by breaking each activity into subactivities. For instance, "design" can be subdivided into conceptual design, preliminary design, and final design. If the start of the procurement activity is to be keyed to the completion of preliminary design, then the time that the preliminary design is complete determines the percentage of time and corresponding design activity that must be completed prior to the initiation of procurement.

6.14 ESTIMATING ENGINEERING ACTIVITIES

Engineering activities include the design, drafting, analysis, and redesign activities required to produce an end item. Costing of engineering activities is usually based on man-loading and staffing resource estimates.

6.14.1 Engineering Skill Levels

The National Society of Professional Engineers has developed position descriptions and recommended annual salaries for nine levels of engineers. These skills levels are broad enough in description to cover a wide variety of engineering activities. The principal activities performed by engineers are described in the following paragraphs.

6.14.2 Design

The design activity for any enterprise includes conceptual design, preliminary design, final design, and design changes. The design engineer must design prototypes, components for development or preproduction testing, special test equipment used in development or preproduction testing, support equipment, and production hardware. Since design effort is highly dependent on the specific work output description, design hours must be estimated by a design professional experienced in the area being estimated.

6.14.3 Analysis

Analysis goes hand-in-hand with design and employs the same general skill level as design engineering. Categories of analysis that support, augment, or precede design are thermal, stress, failure, dynamics, manufacturing, safety, and main-

TABLE 6.9. Engineering Drafting Times

Drawing Letter Designation	Size	Approximate Board-Time Hours for Drafting of Class A Drawings (hr)
A	$8\frac{1}{2} \times 11$	1–4
B	11×17	2–8
C	17×22	4–12
D	22×34	8–16
E and F	34×44 and 28×40	16–40
J	34×48 and larger	40–80

tainability. Analysis is estimated by professionals skilled in analytical techniques. Analysis usually includes computer time as well as labor hours.

6.14.4 Drafting

Drafting, or engineering drawing, is one area in the engineering discipline where labor hours can be correlated to a product: the completed engineering drawing. Labor-hour estimates must still be quoted in ranges, however, becuase the labor hours required for an engineering drawing will vary considerably depending on the complexity of the item being drawn. The drafting times given in Table 6.9 are approximations for Class A drawings of nonelectronic (mechanical) parts where all the design information is available and where the numbers represent ''board time,'' that is, actual time that the draftsman is working on the drawing. A Class A drawing is one that is fully dimensioned and has full supporting documentation. An additional 8 hours per drawing is usually required to obtain approval and sign-offs of stress, thermal, supervisors, and drawing release system personnel. If a ''shop drawing'' is all that is required (only sufficient information for manufacture of the part with some informal assistance from the designer and/or draftsman), the board time man-hours required would be approximately 50% of that listed in Table 6.9.

6.15 MANUFACTURING/PRODUCTION ENGINEERING

The manufacturing/production engineering activity required to support a work activity is preproduction planning and operations analysis. This differs from the general type of production engineering wherein overall manufacturing techniques, facilities, and processes are developed. Excluded from this categorization is the design time of production engineers who redesign a prototype unit to conform to manufacturing or consumer requirements, as well as time for designing special tooling and special test equipment. A listing of some typical functions of manufacturing engineering follows:

1. Fabrication planning.

   Prepare operations sheets for each part
   List operational sequence for materials, machines, and functions
   Recommend standard and special tooling
   Make up tool order for design and construction of special tooling
   Develop standard time data for operations sheets
   Conduct liaison with production and design engineers

2. Assembly Planning

   Develop operations sheets for each part
   Build first sample unit
   Itemize assembly sequence and location of parts
   Order design and construction of special jigs and fixtures
   Develop exact component dimensions
   Build any special manufacturing aids, such as wiring harness jig boards
   Apply standard time data to operations sheet
   Balance time cycles of final assembly line work stations
   Effect liaison with production and design engineers
   Set up material and layout of each work station in accordance with operations sheet
   Instruct mechanics in construction of the first unit

3. Test planning

   Determine overall test method to meet performance and acceptance specifications
   Break total test effort into positions by function and desired time cycle
   Prepare test equipment list and schematic for each position
   Prepare test equipment design order for design and construction of special-purpose test fixtures
   Prepare a step-by-step procedure for each position
   Effect liaison with production and design engineers
   Set up test positions and check out
   Instruct test operator on first unit

4. Sustaining manufacturing engineering

   Debug, as required, engineering design data
   Debug, as required, manufacturing methods and processes
   Recommend more efficient manufacturing methods throughout the life of production

The following statements may be helpful in deriving manufacturing engineering man-hour estimates for high production rates:

1. Total fabrication and assembly man-hours, divided by the number of units to be produced, multiplied by 20 gives manufacturing engineering start-up costs.

2. For sustaining manufacturing engineering, take the unit fabrication and assembly man-hours, multiply by 0.07. (These factors are suggested for quantities up to 100 units.)

6.15.1 Engineering Documentation

A large part of an engineer's time is spent in writing specifications, reports, manuals, handbooks, and engineering orders. The complexity of the engineering activity and the specific document requirements are important determining factors in estimating the engineering labor hours required to prepare engineering documentation.

The hours required for engineering documentation (technical reports, specifications, and technical manuals) will vary considerably depending on the complexity of the work output; however, average labor hours for origination and revision of engineering documentation have been derived based on experience and these figures can be used as average labor hours per page of documentation. (See Tables 6.10 and 6.11.)

6.16 ESTIMATING MANUFACTURING/PRODUCTION AND ASSEMBLY

6.16.1 The Process Plan

A key to successful estimating of manufacturing activities is the process plan. A process plan is a listing of all operations that must be performed to manufacture a product or to complete a project, along with the labor hours required to perform each operation. The process plan is usually prepared by an experienced foreman, engineer, or technician who knows the company's equipment, personnel, and capabilities, or by a process planning department chartered to do all of the process planning. The process planner envisions the equipment, work station, and envi-

TABLE 6.10. New Documentation

Function	Man-Hours per Page
Research, liaison, technical writing, editing, and supervision	5.7
Typing and proofreading	0.6
Illustrations	4.3
Engineering	0.7
Coordination	0.2
Total[a]	11.5

[a] A range of 8–12 man-hours per page can be used.

TABLE 6.11. Revised Documentation

Function	Man-Hours per Page
Research, liaison, technical writing, editing, and supervision	4.00
Typing and proofreading	0.60
Illustrations	0.75
Engineering	0.60
Coordination	0.20
Total[a]	6.15

[a] A range of 4–8 man-hours per page can be used.

ronment; estimates the number of persons required, and estimates how long it will take to perform each step. From this information he or she derives the labor hours required. Process steps are numbered, and space is left between operations listed to allow easy insertion or omission of operations or activites as the process is modified.

A typical process plan for a welded cylinder assembly is given in Table 6.12.

The process plan is used not only to plan and estimate a manufacturing or construction process, but also it often is used as part of the manufacturing or construction work order itself. As such, it shows the shop or construction personnel each step to take in the completion of the work activity. Fabrication of items from metals, plastics, or other materials in a shop is usually called "manufacturing," whereas fabrication of buildings, structures, bridges, dams, and public facilities on site is usually called construction. Different types of standards and estimating factors are used for each of these categories of work. Here, we cover manufacturing activities.

Detailed time standards developed through job analysis usually involve the subdivision of a task down into each human body movement that is required to perform a job. These movements, such as "pick-up, place, or position," are accomplished in very small increments, usually 0.0001–0.001 minute. Because it is impractical for the estimator to break work activities into increments this small, aggregate time standards rather than detailed standards are used. These aggregate standards are developed through a synthesis of a number of small body movements into an overall body motion or work increment that ranges in time from 0.05 to 0.50 minute. The use of aggregate standards takes more estimating time to accomplish than the man-loading or shop-loading method, but there are certain advantages to using time standards. Some of these are (1) they can be used by persons that do not have an intimate familiarity with the job being estimated; (2) they promote consistency between estimates; and (3) resulting estimates are less likely to vary with the estimator because they are based on work content rather than judgment or opinion. Time standards are used extensively in estimating labor hours required for manufacturing activities.

TABLE 6.12. Process Plan

Operation Number	Labor Hours	Description
010	—	Receive and inspect material (skins and forgings)
020	24	Roll form skin segments
030	60	Mask and chem-mill recessed pattern in skins
040	—	Inspect
050	36	Trim to design dimension and prepare in welding skin segments into cylinders (two)
060	16	Locate segments on automatic seam welder tooling fixture and weld per specification (longitudinal weld)
070	2	Remove from automatic welding fixture
080	18	Shave welds on inside diameter
090	16	Establish trim lines (surface plate)
100	18	Install in special fixture and trim to length
110	8	Remove from special fixture
120	56	Install center mandrel—center ring, forward and aft sections (cylinders)—forward and aft mandrel—forward and aft rings—and complete special feature set up
130	—	Inspect
140	24	Butt weld (four places)
150	8	Remove from special fixture and remove mandrels
160	59	Radiograph and dye penetrant inspect
170	—	Inspect dimensionally
180	6	Reinstall mandrels in preparation for final machining
190	14	Finish OD—aft
	10	Finish OD—center
	224	Finish OD—forward
200	40	Program for forward ring
220	30	Handwork (three rings)
230	2	Reinstall cylinder assembly with mandrels still in place or on the special fixture
240	16	Clock and drill index holes
250	—	Inspect
260	8	Remove cylinder from special fixture—remove mandrel
270	1	Install in holding cradle
280	70	Locate drill jig on forward end and hand drill leak check vein (drill and tap), and hand drill hole pattern
290	64	Locate drill jig on aft ring and hand drill hole pattern
300	—	Inspect forward and aft rings
310	8	Install protective covers on each end of cylinder
320	—	Transfer to surface treat
340	24	Remove covers and alodine
350	—	Inspect
360	8	Reinstall protective covers and return to assembly area

6.17 MANUFACTURING ACTIVITIES

Manufacturing activities are broken into various categories of effort such as metal working and forming; welding, brazing, and soldering; application of fasteners; plating, printing, surface treating, and heat treating; and manufacturing of electronic components (a special category). The most common method of estimating the time and cost required for manufacturing activities is the industrial engineering approach whereby standards or target values are established for various operations. The term standards is used to indicate standard time data. All possible elements of work are measured, assigned a standard time for performance, and documented. When a particular job is to be estimated, all of the applicable standards for all related operations are added together to determine the total time.

The use of standards produces more accurate and more easily justifiable estimates. Standards also promote consistency between estimates as well as among estimators. Where standards are used, personal experience is desirable or beneficial but not mandatory. Standards have been developed over a number of years through the use of time studies and synthesis of methods analysis. They are based on the level of efficiency that could be attained by a job shop producing up to 1000 units of any specific work output. Standards are actually synoptical values of more detailed times. They are adaptations, extracts, or benchmark time values for each type of operation. The loss of accuracy occasioned by summarization and/or averaging is acceptable when the total time for a system is being developed. If standard values are used with judgment and interpolations for varying stock sizes, reasonably accurate results can be obtained.

Machining operations make up a large part of the manufacturing costs of many products and projects. Machining operations are usually divided into setup times and run times. Setup time is the time required to establish and adjust the tooling, to set speeds and feeds on the metal-removal machine, and to program for the manufacture of one or more identical or similar parts. Run time is the time required to complete each part. It consists of certain fixed positioning times for each item being machined as well as the actual metal-removal and cleanup time for each item. Values are listed for "soft" and "hard" materials. Soft values are for aluminum, magnesium, and plastics. Hard values are for stainless steel, tool steel, and beryllium. Between these two times would be standard values for brass, bronze, and medium steel.

6.18 IN-PROCESS INSPECTION

The amount of in-process inspection performed on any process, product, project, or service will depend on the cost of possible scrappage of the item as well as the degree of reliability required for the final work output. In high-rate production of relatively inexpensive items, it is often economically desirable to forgo in-process inspection entirely in favor of scrapping any parts that fail a simple go, no-go inspection at the end of the production line. On the other hand, expensive and sophisticated precision-manufactured parts may require nearly 100% inspection. A good rule of thumb is to add 10% of the manufacturing and assembly hours for in-process inspection. This in-process inspection does not include the in-process testing covered in the following paragraphs.

6.19 TESTING

Testing usually falls into three categories: (1) development testing, (2) qualification testing, and (3) production acceptance testing.

Rules of thumb are difficult to come by for estimating development testing because testing varies with the complexity, uncertainty, and technological content of the work activity. The best way to estimate the cost of development testing is to produce a detailed test plan for the specific project and to cost each element of this test plan separately, being careful to consider all skills, facilities, equipment, and material needed in the development test program.

Qualification testing is required in most commercial products and on all military or space projects to demonstrate adequately that the article will operate or serve its intended purpose in environments far more severe than those intended for its actual use. Automobile crash tests are an example. Military products must often undergo severe and prolonged tests under high shock, thermal, and vibration loads as well as heat, humidity, cold, and salt spray environmnets. These tests must be meticulously planned and scheduled before a reasonable estimate of their costs can be generated.

Receiving inspection, production testing, and acceptance testing can be estimated using experience factors and ratios available from previous like work activities. Receiving tests are tests performed on purchased components, parts, and/or subassemblies prior to acceptance by the receiving department. Production tests are tests of subassemblies, units, subsystems, and systems during and after assembly. Experience has shown, generally, that test labor varies directly with the amount of fabrication and assembly labor. The ratio of test labor to other production labor will depend on the complexity of the item being tested. Table 6.13 gives the test labor percent of direct fabrication and assembly labor for simple, average, and complex items.

6.19.1 Special Tooling and Test Equipment

Special-purpose tooling and special-purpose test equipment are important items of cost because they are used only for a particular job; therefore, that job must bear the full cost of the tool or test fixture. In contrast to the special items, general-purpose tooling or test equipment is purchased as capital equipment and costs are spread over many jobs. Estimates for tooling and test equipment are included in overall manufacturing startup ratios shown in Table 6.14. Under "degree of precision and complexity," "high," means high-precision multidisciplinary systems,

TABLE 6.13. Test Estimating Ratios

	Percent of Direct Labor		
	Simple	Average	Complex
Fabrication and Assembly Labor Base			
Receiving test	1	2	4
Production test	9	18	36
Total	10	20	40
Assembly Labor Base			
Receiving test	2	3	7
Production test	15	32	63
Total	17	35	70

products, or subsystems; "medium" means moderately complex subsystems or components; and "low" means simple, straightforward designs of components or individual parts. Design hours required for test equipment are shown in Table 6.15.

6.20 COMPUTER SOFTWARE COST ESTIMATING

Detailed cost estimates must include the cost of computer software development and testing where necessary to provide deliverable source code or to run the analysis or testing programs needed to develop products or services. Chapter 12 of this reference manual covers computer software estimating in detail.

Because of the increasing number and types of computers and computer lan-

TABLE 6.14. Manufacturing Startup Ratios

Cost Element	Degree of Precision and Complexity	Percent of Recurring Manufacturing Costs Lot Quantity			
		10	100	1000	10,000
Production planning	High	20	6	1.7	0.5
	Medium	10	3	0.8	0.25
	Low	5	1.5	0.4	0.12
Special tooling	High	10	6	3.5	2
	Medium	5	3	2	1
	Low	3	1.5	1	—
Special test equipment	High	10	6	3.5	2
	Medium	6	3	2	1
	Low	3	1.5	1	0.5
Composite total	High	40	18	8.7	4.5
	Medium	21	9	4.8	2.25
	Low	11	4.5	2.4	1.12

TABLE 6.15 Design Hours for Test Equipment

Type Design	Hours/ Square Foot	Standard Drawing Size	Square Feet/ Drawing	Hours/ Drawing
Original concept	15	C	2.5	38
		D	5.0	75
		H	9.0	135
		J	11.0	165
Layout	10	B	1.0	10
		C	2.5	25
		D	5.0	50
		H	9.0	90
		J	11.0	110
Detail or copy	3	A	0.7	2.1
		B	1.0	3.0
		C	2.5	7.5
		D	5.0	15.0
		H	9.0	27.0
		J	11.0	33.0

guages, it is difficult to generate overall ground rules or rules of thumb for computer software cost estimating. Productivity in computer programming is greatly affected by the skill and competence of the computer analyst or programmer. A general rule of thumb, however, is that it will take about 3 hours per program statement or line of code to perform the requirements analysis, program design, coding, and software verification for a program written in machine language or assembly language. For a program written in a higher-order language (BASIC, FORTRAN, COBOL, or PASCAL), this figure is approximately 1.87 hours per program statement. In addition to these direct man-hours, approximately 10% of the direct hours should be added for program documentation and software program management. Complicated flight software for aircraft and space systems is subjected to design review and testing in simulations and on the actual flight computer hardware. A software critical design review is usually conducted about 43% the way through the program; an integrated systems test is performed at the 67% completion mark; prototype testing is done at 80% completion; installation with the hardware is started with about 7% of the time remaining (at the 93% completion point).

6.21 LABOR ALLOWANCES

"Standard times" assume that the workers are well trained and experienced in their jobs, that they apply themselves to the job 100% of the time, that they never make a mistake, take a break, lose efficiency, or deviate from the task for any reason. This, of course, is an unreasonable assumption because there are legitimate and numerous unplanned work interruptions that occur with regularity in any work activity. Therefore, labor allowances must be added to any estimate that is made up of an accumulation of standard times. These labor allowances can accumulate to a factor of 1.5–2.5. The total standard time for a given work activity, depending on the overall inherent efficiency of the shop, equipment, and personnel, will depend on the nature of the task. Labor allowances are made up of a number of factors that are described in the following sections.

6.21.1 Variance from Measured Labor Hours

Standard hours vary from actual measured labor hours because workers often deviate from the standard method or technique used or planned for a given operation. This deviation can be caused by a number of factors ranging from the training, motivation, or disposition of the operator to the use of faulty tools, fixtures, or machines. Sometimes shortages of materials or lack of adequate supervision are causes of deviations from standard values. These variances can add 5–20% to standard time values.

6.21.2 Personal, Fatigue, and Delay (PFD) Time

Personal times are for personal activities such as coffee breaks, trips to the restroom or water fountain, unforeseen interruptions, or emergency telephone calls. Fatigue time is allocated because of the inability of a worker to produce at the same pace all day. Operator efficiency decreases as the job time increases. Delays include unavoidable delays caused by the need for obtaining supervisory instructions, equipment breakdown, power outages, or operator illness. PFD time can add 10–20% to standard time values.

6.21.3 Tooling and Equipment Maintenance

Although normal or routine equipment maintenance can be done during other than operating shifts, there is usually some operator-performed machine maintenance activity that must be performed during the machine duty cycle. These activities include adjusting tools, sharpening tools, and periodically cleaning and oiling machines. In electroplating and processing operations, the operator maintains solutions and compounds, and handles and maintains racks and fixutres. Tooling and equipment maintenance can account for 5–12% of standard time values.

6.21.4 Normal Rework and Repair

The overall direct labor hours derived from the application of the preceding three allowance factors to standard times must be increased by additional amounts to account for normal rework and repair. Labor values must be allocated for rework of defective purchased materials, rework of in-process rejects, final test rejects, and addition of minor engineering changes. Units damaged on receipt or during handling must also be repaired. This factor can add 10–20% direct labor hours to those previously estimated.

6.21.5 Engineering Change Allowance

For projects where design stability is poor, where production is initiated prior to final design release, and where field testing is being performed concurrently with production, an engineering change allowance should be added of up to 10% of direct labor hours. Change allowances vary widely for different types of work activities. Even fairly well-defined projects, however, should contain a change allowance.

6.21.6 Engineering Prototype Allowance

The labor hours required to produce an engineering prototype are greater than those required to produce the first production model. Reworks are more frequent, and work is performed from sketches or unreleased drawings rather than production drawings. An increase over first production unit labor of 15–25% should be included for each engineering prototype.

6.21.7 Design Growth Allowance

Where estimates are based on incomplete drawings, or where concepts only or early breadboards only are available prior to the development of a cost estimate, a design growth allowance is added to all other direct labor costs. This design growth allowance is calculated by subtracting the percentage of design completion from 100% as shown in the following tabulation:

Desirable Design Completion Percentage	Percentage of Design Completed	Design Growth Allowance (%)
100	50	50
100	75	25
100	80	20
100	90	10
100	100	0

6.21.8 Cost Growth Allowances

Occasionally a cost estimate will warrant the addition of allowances for cost growth. Cost growth allowances are best added at the lowest level of a cost estimate rather than at the top levels. These allowances include reserves for possible misfortunes, natural disasters, strikes, and other unforeseen circumstances. Reserves should not be used to account for normal design growth. Care should be taken in using reserves in a cost estimate because they are usually the first cost elements that come under attack for removal from the cost estimate or budget. Remember, cost growth with an incomplete design is a certainty, not a reserve or contingency! Defend your cost growth allowance, but be prepared to relinquish your reserve if necessary.

6.22 ESTIMATING SUPERVISION, DIRECT MANAGEMENT, AND OTHER DIRECT CHARGES

Direct supervision costs will vary with the task and company organization. Management studies have shown that the span of control of a supervisor over a complex activity should not exceed 12 workers. For simple activities, the ratio of supervisors to employees can go down. But the 1 : 12 ratio (8.3%) will usually yield best results. Project management for a complex project can add an additional 10–14%. Other direct charges are those attributable to the project being accomplished but not included in direct labor or direct materials. Transportation, training, and reproduction costs, as well as special service or support contracts and consultants, are included in the category of "other direct costs."

Two cost elements of "other direct costs" that are becoming increasingly prominent are travel and transportation costs. Air, bus, and rail fares as well as private conveyance costs are increasing at a rate higher than the general inflation rate because rapidly fluctuating fuel costs comprise a large part of the cost per passenger mile. For this reason a frequent check on public and private conveyance rates and costs is mandatory. Most companies provide a private vehicle mileage allowance for employees who use their own vehicles in the conduct of company business. Rates differ and depend on whether the private conveyance is being utilized principally for the benefit of the company or principally for the convenience of the traveler. Regardless of which rate is used, the mileage allowance must be periodically updated to keep pace with actual costs. Many companies purchase or lease vehicles to be used by their employees on official business, and sometimes personal travel.

Per diem travel allowances or reimbursement for lodging, meals, and miscellaneous expenses must also be included in overall travel budgets. These reimbursable expenses include costs of a motel or hotel room; food, tips, and taxes; local transportation and communication; and other costs such as laundry, mailing costs, and on-site clerical services. Transportation costs include the transport of equipment, supplies, and products, as well as personnel, and can include packaging, handling, shipping, postage, and insurance charges.

6.23 THE USE OF "FACTORS" IN DETAILED ESTIMATING

Although the use of "factors" in estimating is not recommended, the practice is becoming increasingly common, particularly in high-technology work activities and work outputs. One company uses an "allocation factor," which allocates miscellaneous labor-oriented functions to specific functions such as fabrication or assembly. This company adds 14.4% to fabrication hours and 4.1% to assembly hours to cover miscellaneous labor-hour expenditures associated with these two functions. It is also common to estimate hours for planning, tooling, quality and inspection, production support, and sustaining engineering based on percentages of manufacturing and/or assembly hours. Tooling materials and computer supplies are sometimes estimated based on so much cost per tooling hour, and miscellaneous shop hardware (units, bolts, fasteners, cleaning supplies, etc.), otherwise known as "panstock," is estimated at a cost per manufacturing hour.

The disadvantage of the use of such factors is that inefficiencies can become embedded in the factored allowances and eventually cause cost growth. A much better method of estimating the man-hours and materials required to accomplish these other direct activities is to determine the specific tasks and materials required to perform the job by man-loading, shop-loading, or process-planning methods. When the materials, labor hours, and other direct costs have been estimated, the basic direct resources required to do the job have been identified. The estimator can now move into the final steps of the detailed estimating process with the full assurance that all work elements and all cost elements have been included in the detailed estimate.

6.24 SUMMARY

In summary, detailed cost estimating involves meticulous penetration into the smallest feasible portions of a work output or work activity, and the systematic and methodical assembly of the resources in all cost, work, and schedule elements. Detailed estimating requires detailed design, manufacturing, and test descriptions, and involves great time, effort, and penetration into the resources required to do the job. Wherever possible, detailed estimates should be used to establish a firm and credible cost estimate and to verify and substantiate higher-level parametric estimates.

7

PARAMETRIC ESTIMATING

JOSEPH HAMAKER, CCA

Predictions are very difficult to make, especially when they are about the future.

ATTRIBUTED TO MARK TWAIN

7.1 INTRODUCTION

This chapter introduces the concept of parametric cost estimating. The major concepts, origins and applicability of the technique are examined. The development and normalization of the data base and the derivation of cost estimating relationships are covered. Techniques and concepts useful in the application of parametric estimating to various types of estimating situations are discussed. Finally, the major trends and directions in the field of parametric estimating are presented.

7.1.1 An Overview Of Parametric Estimating

Parametric estimating is the process of estimating cost by using mathematical equations that relate cost to one or more physical or performance variables associated with the item being estimated. Estimating the cost of a new building by multiplying the number of square feet by the anticipated dollars per square foot is a simple example of parametric estimating.

Broadly speaking, parametric estimating is usually distinguished from other approaches to cost estimating, such as detailed estimating as discussed in Chapter 6. Parametric estimating is used in a wide and increasing variety of applications including aeronautics and space, the military and commercial aircraft industries, the chemical industry, shipbuilding, construction, mining, power plants, computers, computer software, electronics and many other settings. Although more often used in the earlier phases of definition, parametric models are sometimes used up to and even throughout the detailed design, production, and operational phases of projects. Sometimes, especially before detailed designs are available, the parametric approach is the only estimating technique used in a project. As the design matures, parametrics might be used in conjunction with detailed engineering estimating, either as a method of independent check or as the primary estimating method for selected elements of cost.

Because parametric estimating relies upon statistical equations that relate cost to some other variable or variables, parametric estimating is sometimes called statistical estimating. Although terminology varies from industry to industry, parametric estimating equations are often called cost estimating relationships, or CERs, the terminology adopted in this chapter. Cost is the dependent variable in CERs while the physical or performance inputs are the independent variables. CERs can relate cost to many different types of independent variables (e.g., dollars per square feet for buildings, dollars per cubic feet for chemical process pressure vessels, dollars per pound for spacecraft, dollars per kilowatt for electrical power plants, dollars per horsepower for motors, dollars per kilobyte for computers, dollars per line of code for software, dollars per page for documentation, dollars per pound of thrust for jet engines).

The equations that define the relationship between the independent variables and cost are usually based on historical information. For example, a builder might estimate the cost of a new house at so many dollars per square foot based on the costs of the last several similar homes he has built. Likewise, the cost of a new electrical power plant might be based on the cost per kilowatt of recent plants with similar characteristics. Although not always the case, most CERs are derived using some kind of statistical regression analysis (such as the method of least squares) that fits a line or curve through a graph of historical data points (Figure 7.1).

Usually, CERs are derived to estimate specific basic categories of cost such as design and development cost, initial capital cost, the cost of an initial production unit, annual operating cost, operating cost per use, or some other distinct element of cost. Once such basic elements are established using CERs, any number of other analytical cost techniques may be employed to further process the cost. For instance, learning curve theory might be used to determine the unit cost of subsequent production units (see Chapter 5, "Learning Curves"). Alternately, the parametrically estimated cost elements might be entered into equations that aggregate basic cost elements into life cycle cost. The term CER is sometimes used to describe almost any mathematical equation having to do with cost. In this chapter, however, parametric estimating is more strictly defined as the process of estimating basic elements of cost using relationships that relate cost to some physical or performance variable.

Some of the basic aspects of parametric estimating were introduced in Chapter 1, "Fundamentals of Cost Estimating". The basis for the statistical methods used to derive the estimating equations was discussed in Chapter 3, "Statistical Techniques in Cost Estimation". The method was contrasted with the detailed cost estimating methods in Chapter 6. This chapter extends the discussion of the parametric approach and examines the application of the method to common problems in cost estimating.

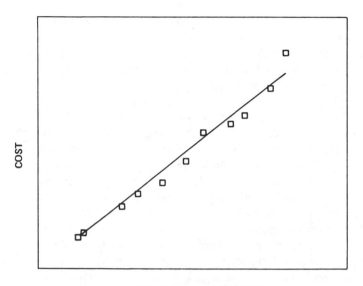

Figure 7.1. Typical cost estimating relationships.

7.1.2 Origins of Parametric Estimating

The parametric method of cost estimating is a specialized use of forecasting techniques that have come to be quite common in business, macroeconomics, social sciences, and other applications. For example, a business firm might use parametric equations or models to predict future sales for a certain product. The model might attempt to relate past sales to a time variable and thus give the business a tool for analyzing such trends as seasonal variations in sales. Economists build and use complicated econometric forecasting models that attempt to relate the variables of an industry or even the entire national economy. Such models are used to predict demand, production, employment, gross national product, and the like, based on sets of equations that fit past economic performance to predictor variables such as money supply, interest rates, and inflation rates. In the social sciences, parametric techniques are used to forecast election results, population growth, education trends, and many other phenomena.

The theoretical and mathematical roots of parametric estimating are thus found in the attempts of observers of various institutional and societal experiences to predict the future course of events. The application of statistical modeling techniques to the problem of estimating cost was first methodically pursued and documented by the Rand Corporation in the late 1950s in attempts to predict military hardware cost at very early phases of the design. The approach offered a way to obtain credible estimates of cost early in the design process for hardware such as airframes. The technique was quickly married with that of learning curve theory to estimate entire design and production run costs for hardware that was still in very conceptual design stages on the drawing board. Both government analysts and the military contractor community discovered the utility of having early estimates that did not rely upon the labor, time, and input-intensive detailed method that had heretofore been employed. Because of these relatively low resource requirements, the parametric technique was found useful for budget planning, systems analysis, and trade study purposes.

Initially, the use of parametric estimating was a rather tentative departure from the classical approach of the more detailed methods, usually involving isolated individuals or small groups within organizations. Steadily, however, the inherent utility of the method combined with continued refinements and improvements has led to its institutionalization and an impressive growth in the number of settings in which it is used. Today it is common for many organizations to use the parametric technique routinely, and many even have dedicated engineering cost groups of professional parametric estimators. Communication and cross-fertilization of ideas and techniques is spurred by a number of professional societies (see Section 7.5.5), and there are a number of commercially successful parametric cost models serving the community of parametricians (see Section 7.5.4).

With the advent of computers, especially personal microcomputers, leading to improved data base, statistical and analytical software, the adoption of parametric estimating has been further spurred. Having penetrated at least to some degree almost all cost estimating applications, the parametric technique is currently in a state of continued refinement and use.

7.1.3 Applicability of the Parametric Method

Can the total cost of a piece of hardware or even the life cycle cost of an entire project be accurately related to some limited number of physical or performance variables when there are so many other variables that are known to affect cost? The answer is yes—but of course, only when properly applied. It is the level of detail at which the method operates that perhaps most clearly sets the parametric method apart from detailed engineering estimating. Detailed engineering estimating requires large amounts of information concerning labor and material requirements and in turn provides very detailed cost information on every aspect of the project. Parametric estimating, on the other hand, does not rely on detailed information nearly as much, but instead attempts to relate cost to only the cost drivers or cost-descriptive variables of a project. Thus the premise of parametric estimating is that cost can be estimated based on predictive variables that are only analogous, and not wholly causative, to final cost.

The parametric technique is most commonly used in the definition and early design stages of projects when there is insufficient information to perform a detailed engineering estimate. Cost estimating relationships usually relate cost to relatively high-level measurements of capacity or performance—just the type of information that is available early. Parametric cost estimating is usually faster in execution than detailed methods, requires less labor resources to execute, and is usually more adaptible to computerization. The parametric approach requires good statistical relationships between cost and the cost-predictive variables, and attention is usually focused and concentrated on only the true cost drivers in a project while the less important details are ignored. This attention to the cost drivers, coupled with speed, low labor requirements, and computerization, frequently leads to the performance of cost analyses that are not practical or even possible using a detailed method. In addition, cost sensitivity studies, cost optimizations, and trade studies are a natural application of the parametric technique, both stimulated by it and made possible by it. Though impossible to quantify, parametrics can probably be credited with important cost savings over the life cycle of many projects owing to the inherent ability to deal directly with the variables that drive project cost and provide insight into ways to improve cost-effectiveness.

Given that the parametric estimating relationship has been properly derived and used, the resulting algebraic exercising of the relationship captures the entire cost of the item being estimated. A detailed estimate of the cost of a house requires detailed house plans, a bill of materials, labor skill mixes and rates, and so on. Estimating the cost of the same house parametrically using dollars per square feet only requires knowledge of the area of the structure. Thus the actual estimate is much quicker and easier to perform. The real work in parametric estimating is the methodology. The use of a dollars per area relationship based on a frame house with no basements and conventional heating and cooling to estimate the cost of a brick house with a full basement and solar heating and cooling is obviously inappropriate. Thus the most critical areas in parametric estimating are data base development and the building and application of the cost estimating model.

7.2 DATA BASE DEVELOPMENT

Some general aspects concerning the collection of historical cost data, its organization into work element structures, the mechanics of its normalization to constant price levels, and statistical analysis were covered in Chapter 2, "Cost Allocation," and Chapter 3, "Statistical Techniques in Cost Estimation." This section concentrates on the peculiar aspects of these activities as they relate to the parametric method.

7.2.1 Data Collection, Organization, and Normalization

The data necessary for a parametric data base can come from a number of sources both within and outside the organization. Although the focus of the data collection effort is cost, the data base must also include information on the corresponding cost-explanatory variables such as physical and performance characteristics, quantities produced, use of existing hardware or designs, schedule information, and other technical and programmatic influences upon cost. A common complication in parametric cost data base development is that the published sources of the cost data may not necessarily include the required technical and programmatic data, and when such data are obtained, the work element structure may differ from the cost format.

Ultimately, data to be used for parametric modeling are organized into a structure corresponding to that of the intended cost model. This may take many work element structure forms but is often more of a hardware oriented structure and at a higher level of detail than structures meant for detailed engineering estimating. It is usually, though not always, the case that the work element structure distinguishes between nonrecurring costs such as design and engineering costs, facilities, software, and support equipment, and recurring cost such as production and operations. Figure 7.2 depicts a typical work element structure that might be the basis for a parametric cost model.

Once the basic work element structure has been decided and the necessary cost data collected against the structure, the costs are then normalized to a consistent set of ground rules and assumptions. Usually the normalizations are made to make the data base homogeneous and consistent with the desired characteristics of the model.

Most organizations maintain data bases for parametric modeling in some constant year price level (with periodic updates). Each new data point that is added to the data base is converted to the baseline price level, as covered in Chapter 1, "Fundamentals of Cost Estimating." Each CER that is then developed from this data will be in the familiar price level, and costs from these CERs can be adjusted internal to the models in which they are used. Such a rule makes the data base internally consistent and keeps all CERs more comparable.

7.2.2 Bookkeeping Normalizations

There are a number of bookkeeping considerations to be taken into account when building a parametric data base. Some of these considerations will be confronted when a work element structure is decided upon. But there are other, more subtle, issues to be resolved when organizing the historical cost data of an organization. Principally these revolve around certain inclusions and exclusions of cost. In principle, decisions about what cost should and should not be collected against historical projects should be guided by considerations for maintaining a data base system for parametric modeling that is as consistent as possible with in-house accounting conventions and at the same time will provide estimated cost that includes the appropriate categories of costs for use within the organization. The following discussion cannot be a complete listing of issues because such a list is highly dependent on organization. It is, however, a minimum list, and one that should spur deliberations on additional bookkeeping considerations within each organization.

A basic issue to consider is the differentiation between in-house and out-of-house (contracted) costs. Many organizations have completed projects that, depending upon the particular make-buy plan in effect, have included both types of effort. In such cases, the data base should give careful attention to collecting both contractor and in-house cost histories of completed projects.

In-house costs are often documented less well than subcontract costs in terms of being segregated into a work element structure that is readily adaptable to parametric modeling. This is mainly because substantial insight into subcontract costs

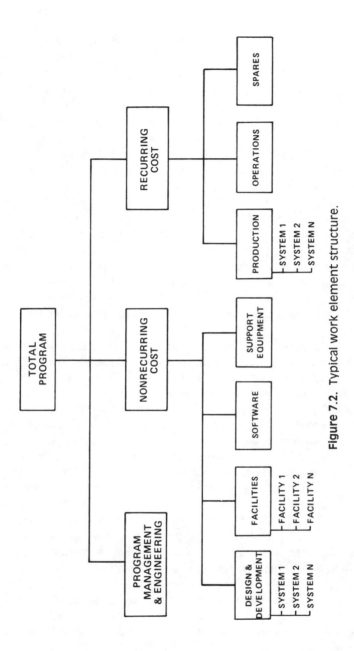

Figure 7.2. Typical work element structure.

is required for the management of the subcontractor and also because subcontracts usually provide a clearly defined hardware item or service. In-house costs, on the other hand, tend to be bookkept for accounting purposes and not necessarily against specific hardware items or services. The collection and normalization of in-house costs into a form suitable for parametric modeling can involve substantial effort.

In the area of nonrecurring costs there may be historical projects that had in-house design activities (either with or without contractor design work) in combination with contracted fabrication. It is common for such in-house design activities to have consumed not only labor but materials as well (materials consumed during design activities for breadboarding, testing, etc.).

In-house supporting research and development activities should be quantified if possible against specific historical projects. This may turn out to be difficult, depending on the thoroughness and accessability of organization records. It may be more practical to quantify the level of in-house supporting research and development activities as a percentage function of ongoing projects. In either case, to maximize future modeling flexibility, it is preferable to account for supporting R&D separately within the nonrecurring cost data base.

Similarly, there are costs associated with supporting the institutional operations of the oganization (e.g. maintenance, facilities operations, computer resources, groundskeeping, etc.). Many organizations have specific rates or factors for such costs that might be used directly in the parametric data base. In some instances an analysis of these costs might have to be undertaken by the cost analyst to arrive at appropriate factors. Ultimately, the developer of the parametric cost model will want to include these costs as a separable cost in the output of the model and probably to make allowance either for inclusion or suppression depending on the nature of the cost study being undertaken with the model. For purely internal cost studies involving only the comparison of alternatives it is not necessary to include institutional support costs unless options are being studied that might somehow differentially effect these costs. For cost estimating activities that involve a bid to other organizations or budget inputs to parent organizations that do not provide a distinct budget line item for these types of costs, it may be appropriate to include such expenses to insure full cost recovery on potential work.

Some historical projects may have supplied in-house materials, equipment, facilities, supporting labor, in-house managed subcontract effort, or parallel development efforts (especially in high-risk projects) to contractors during the course of the contract performance that were not captured by the accounting data as part of the prime effort. Unless such practices are relatively stable and predictable as a percentage, a separate accounting of the associated costs should be undertaken and charged against the appropriate historical projects.

Within the contractor costs for historical projects there are certain considerations that require decisions prior to building the parametric data base. Standard ground rules should be developed and applied regarding certain inclusions and exclusions such as contractor fee and overhead costs. Obviously such costs should either be clearly included or excluded from the parametric data. Exclusion requires that some mechanism be made within the parametric model for the reintroduction of these costs using rates appropriate for the study at hand.

7.3 MODEL BUILDING

The development of a cost model is heavily dependent on the basic CERs that describe the situation being modeled. This section considers the essentials of model building from the point of view of CER development.

7.3.1 Common CER Equation Forms

Limiting the discussion for the moment to CERs with one independent variable, there are a large number of mathematical equation forms that can be used for cost estimating relationships. In practice however, much cost data can be fit empirically using one of the equation forms shown in Figure 7.3.

- ☐ Linear curves
- ☐ Power curves
- ☐ Exponential curves
- ☐ Logarithmic curves

As can be seen, all of these forms give either straight lines or well-behaved curves when graphed. It is rare in parametric cost estimating to use CERs that have inflection points (i.e., a change from concave to convex or vice versa). The use of such a model would suggest that there are multiple values of the independent variable that correspond to the same cost or, in the case of an S-curve, that cost "accelerates and deaccelerates" with respect to the independent variable. Data that seem to indicate such relationships are suspect and should usually be subjected to additional analysis. Although CERS are smooth curves, aggregate cost functions composed of two or more cost components may have inflection points. Consider the cost study of Figure 7.4 to determine the optimum concentration ratio (CR) for a photovoltaic power supply for a spacecraft. The expense of solar cells can be minimized by increasing the area of mirrors reflecting sunlight on the cells, although this increases the cost of the mirrors. At each CR on the abscissa, CERs were used to estimate the cost of solar cells and the cost of mirrors as defined by point design studies. Total cost, solar cells plus mirrors, shows a "cost bucket" at a CR of about 1.25.

As discussed in the introduction to this chapter, the simplest CERs are no more complicated than the dollars per square foot relationship used to estimate roughly the cost of a new building. Such CERs are of the form $y = ax$, a linear relationship where y is cost, x is the input variable, and a is the parameter based on historical data that relates the dependent variable (cost) to the independent variable. For our

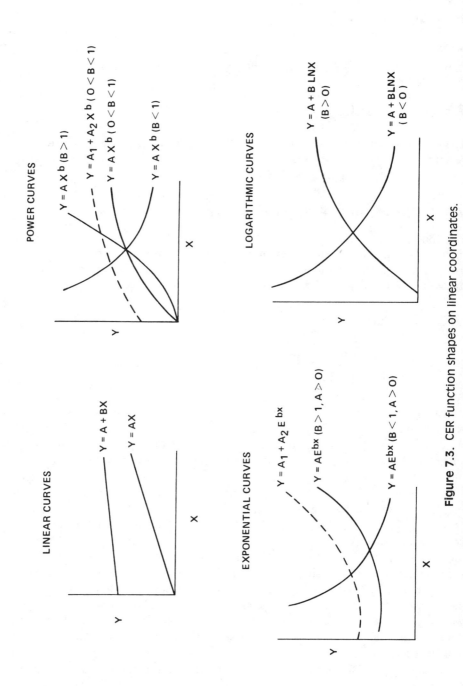

Figure 7.3. CER function shapes on linear coordinates.

234

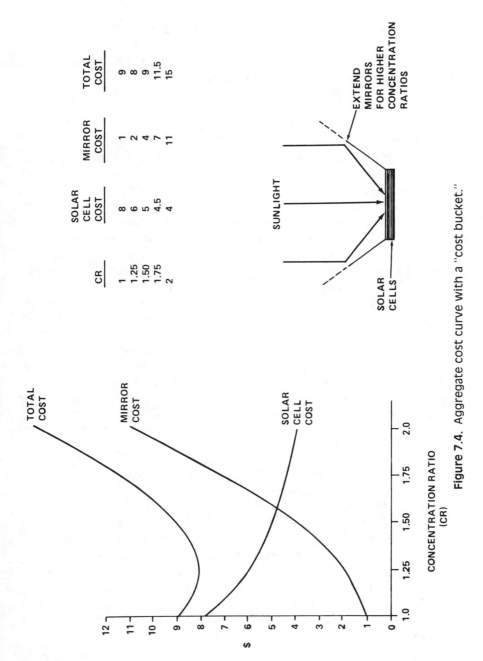

CR	SOLAR CELL COST	MIRROR COST	TOTAL COST
1	8	1	9
1.25	6	2	8
1.50	5	4	9
1.75	4.5	7	11.5
2	4	11	15

Figure 7.4. Aggregate cost curve with a "cost bucket."

235

example of estimating building cost as a function of area, x would be area in square feet and y would be dollars per square feet. Therefore if historical records indicated that several buildings of 10,000 square feet had costs of, say $60 per square foot, then the corresponding CER could be expressed as

$$y = 60(x)$$

where y is cost and x is area in square feet.

In fact, most parametric models contain more than a few such rule of thumb or factored relationships. In many applications there are usually a number of work element structure entries that are estimated quite satisfactorily in this way. Depending on the project, examples include personnel compensation (labor rate multiplied by person-hours), facilities cost (area multiplied by the cost per unit area), the facilities maintenance costs (a fraction multiplied by initial facility investment cost), "wraparound" costs such as contractor fee (bid multiplied by fee percentage), and the like. Normally, costs estimated with such simple relationships tend to be subsidiary elements.

A common sophistication to the preceding simple example is the use of other equation forms. For example, the linear equation form $y = a + bx$ is used to model cases in which there are both fixed and variable cost, the fixed cost component being given by the CER coefficient a and the variable cost component being given by the bx term. If the 10,000-square-foot building involved some fixed cost component, say land, that was invariable as far as the area of the building was concerned, this linear equation form might be an apt candidate for modeling such a circumstance. Figure 7.5 graphs a $y = a + bx$ CER with $a = \$200,000$ and $b = \$60$ per x. For comparison, the earlier $y = ax$ CER with $a = \$80$ per x is also graphed.

The use of either of these linear CERs assumes that there is a relationship between the independent variable and cost such that a change of one unit in the independent variable causes a change of some relatively constant number of dollars. The inset in Figure 7.5 demonstrates this relationship by showing that for a $y = a + bx$ CER with, for example, $a = 200,000$ and $b = 60$, successive unit changes in x from the baseline of $x = 10,000$ cause successive $60 changes in cost. Notice that as building size increased, a CER of this form would yield fewer dollars per square foot because the fixed component a is being spread over a larger number of square feet. But the variable cost component ax, is contributing a strictly linearly growing amount to cost.

One knows from everyday experience, however, that variable costs do not often scale in such a linear manner. Some items exhibit economies of scale such that as the size increases the variable cost per unit of size decreases. Large buildings generally cost less per square foot than smaller buildings, all other factors being equal. Sometimes there are diseconomies associated with scale—large diamond rings generally cost more per carat than smaller diamond rings (again, other factors being equal). The nonlinear CERs in Figure 7.3 are used to model just such situations.

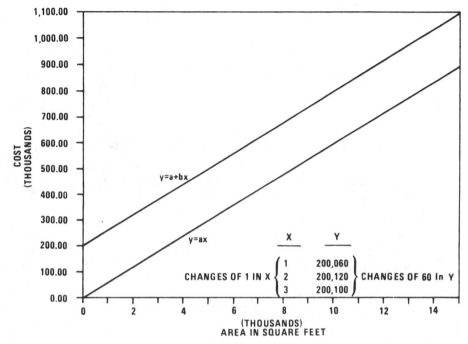

Figure 7.5. Linear CERs.

Let us examine how one of the power curves can be used to model a situation in which the cost per square foot of our 10,000-square-foot building changes as the building size increases or decreases. Imagine that we have one additional data point—a building with an area of 15,000 square feet and a total cost of, say, $1 million. We can readily see that there are economies of scale associated with this second building exceeding that which can be explained by our $y = a + bx$ CER. Why? Because our CER would predict that a 15,000-square-foot building would cost $1,100,000 ($y = 200,000 + 60$ (15,000) $= 1,100,000$) but our new data point is $100,000 less than this cost. Therefore we would like a CER that would pass through this latest data point at 15,000 square feet and $1 million, our other data point of 10,000 square feet and $800,000, and finally the zero square feet and $200,000 fixed cost data point. Without concerning ourselves yet how we suspect that a power curve is the appropriate equation form to model this circumstance, we can see that because of the fixed cost involved, the particular form of the power curve that we need is equation form 4, the $y = a_1 + a_2x^b$. We can employ some simple algebra, called the "method of two points," to solve for the terms of the equation that will pass through these three data points.

First, rearranging the equation to

$$y - a_1 = a_2x^b$$

Then taking logarithms to place the equation in linear form gives

$$\ln(y - a_1) = \ln a_2 + b \ln x$$

Substituting the values of our two data points gives two equations:

$$\ln(800,000 - 200,000) = \ln a_2 + b \ln 10,000 \tag{7.1}$$

and

$$\ln(1,000,000 - 200,000) = \ln a_1 + b \ln 15,000 \tag{7.2}$$

The two equations can be solved simultaneously by solving for $\ln a_2$ in Equation 7.1:

$$\ln a_2 = 13.305 - 9.210b$$

and substituting in Equation 7.2:

$$b = \frac{13.592 - (13.305 - 9.210b)}{9.616}$$

$$b = 0.711$$

and substituting b back into Equation 7.1 gives

$$a_2 = 860$$

Thus the CER is $y = 200,000 + 860\,x^{0.711}$. Its accuracy can be checked by solving at the three known points:

Total Area (ft^2)	Calculated Cost ($)
0	200,000
10,000	800,480
15,000	1,001,123

Figure 7.6 compares the power curve CER with the previous linear CERs. Notice that neither linear CER "fits" the 15,000-square-foot and $1 million data point. The power curve, on the other hand, because it can model economies of scale in the variable cost, does fit all three data points.

Although the use of the preceding form of the power curve is appropriate in cases involving fixed cost (i.e., the CER intersects the ordinate at some positive value), the other form of the power curve in Figure 7.3 is also very common in

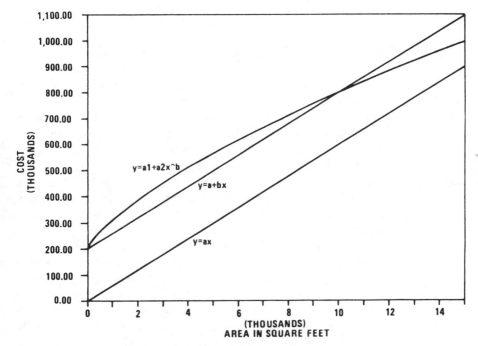

Figure 7.6. Power and linear CERs.

parametric estimating. This CER form, $y = ax^b$, because it has no additive term, intersects the axes at the origin. It is appropriate for modeling the cost of items that logically have zero cost at a zero value for the independent variable (e.g., building cost excluding land value would logically have zero cost at zero square feet). It is possible to derive such a power curve CER for our two building data points of the previous example, this time excluding the data point corresponding to the $200,000 fixed cost. The method of two points can again be used to derive the equation by first taking the logarithm of the power curve equation to convert it to a linear form:

$$\ln y = b \ln x$$

Substituting in the values of our two data points gives two equations:

$$\ln 800,000 = b \ln 10,000 \qquad (7.3)$$

and

$$\ln 1,000,000 = b \ln 15,000 \qquad (7.4)$$

The two equations can be solved simultaneously as before, obtaining

$$b = 0.551 \quad \text{and} \quad a = 5000$$

Thus our CER is $y = 5000 \, x^{0.551}$. The graph of this equation is plotted in Figure 7.7. Notice that this CER fits our two data points and also intersects the origin.

The use of the power curve assumes a relationship between the independent variable and cost such that a percentage change in the independent variable causes a relatively constant percentage change in cost. The inset in Figure 7.7 demonstrates this by showing that these particular power curve coefficients, successive 50% changes in the independent variable, cause successive 25% changes in cost. For a pure power curve of the form $y = ax^b$ the percent change in the dependent variable is a constant percentage, whereas for a power curve with a fixed cost component $y = a_1 + a_2 x^b$ the change in the dependent variable will depart from a constant percentage depending on the relative magnitude of the a_1 term.

Just as with the power curve, the exponential CER may or may not have an additive term. Let us examine the derivation of an exponential CER of form 5 by assuming that we have two points, our familiar 10,000-square-foot, $800,000 building and a new data point of 15,000 square feet and $1,700,000. (At this point in the examination of CER equation forms, the question of which equation form is most appropriate for a given set of data has not yet been addressed—indeed, with only two or three data points, several equations can be derived that fit equally well. For the current data points, 10,000 square feet at $800,000 and 15,000 at $1,700,000, another power curve could be derived to fit just as well as an expo-

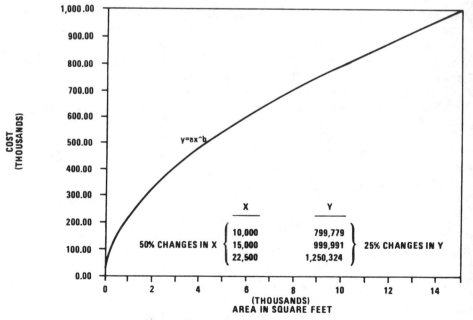

Figure 7.7. Power function CER.

nential. Its equation would be $y = 0.030x^{1.857}$. Can you use the method of two points to verify this?)

Once again, using the method of two points, we take the logarithm of the exponential equation to put it in a linear form:

$$y = ae^{bx}$$

$$\ln y = \ln a + bx \ln e$$

Substituting in our two points yields

$$\ln 800,000 = \ln a + 10,000b$$

and

$$\ln 1,700,000 = \ln a + 15,000b$$

Solving the two equations simultaneously gives

$$a = 177,111 \quad \text{and} \quad b = 0.000151$$

Thus the CER is $y = 177,111e^{0.000151x}$. The calculated costs at the two data points are:

Total Area (ft^2)	Calculated Cost ($)
10,000	801,734
15,000	1,680,382

Use of the exponential equation form for a CER assumes a relationship between the independent variable and cost such that a unit change in the independent variable causes a relatively constant percentage change in cost. This is depicted in Figure 7.8 where, for the particular $y = ae^x$ CER, successive 1000-unit changes in x cause successive 116% changes in cost.

Derivation of the exponential CER with an additive term can be performed using the same technique as before. Assuming the same two data points as before plus adding in the assumption of a fixed cost of $200,000 would yield the following CER:

$$y = 200,000 + 96,086e^{0.000183x}$$

Because the logarithmic equation is already in linear form, the method of two points is easily used to derive CERs of the form $y = a + b \ln x$. Can you verify that for the two data points of 10,000 square feet and $800,000, and 15,000 square

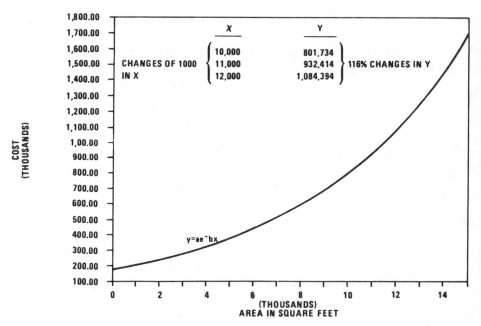

Figure 7.8. Exponential function CER.

feet and \$1,000,000, the logarithmic CER would be $y = -3,738,839 + 492,808$ ln x? The negative a term in this CER indicates that for values of x less than about 1973, the calculated cost will be negative—not a very likely situation in cost estimating. Use of this CER would require the cost analyst to define carefully the meaningful limits of independent variables so that values of x less than 1973 were excluded. In fact, all CERs should have the meaningful range of the independent variables defined and documented. There are limits associated with x-axis intercepts, as is the case here, and there are limits associated with the range of data points from which the CER was derived. In general, extrapolating much beyond the range of x values that made up the data sample is to be avoided.

7.3.2 Choosing the Right Equation Form for the CER

To this point we have been exploring the fitting of various equation types to two or three data points without regard to how one determines which equation type would best fit a larger data sample. Generally, best fit is thought of as that curve that can be drawn through the data points in such a way that the vertical distances from the CER line to the data points above the line are about equal to the sum of the vertical distances from the CER to the points below the line. Said another way, whichever equation form minimizes the absolute value of total cost deviation between the CER and the data points is mathematically the best fit.

Graphically, the most apt equation form can be determined by discovering what kind of graph paper (linear-linear, linear-logarithmic, or logarithmic-logarithmic) best permits a straight line to be drawn through the scatter plot of data. If plotting the data on linear-scaled graph paper produces a data pattern that can be fitted well with a straight line, then a best fit CER will be of a linear form (either equation form $y = ax$, if the line intersects the origin, or equation form $y = a + bx$ if the line intersects the ordinate at some positive value). If the best fit line drawn on linear paper is a curve, then replot the data on semilogarithmic paper and redraw the best fit line. A straight line here indicates that the best CER form will be one of those equation forms that has a linear form with either x or y being a logarithm (i.e., either the exponential equations or the logarithmic form. Although both exponential and logarithmic CERs fit data on semilog paper, the exponential fits logarithmic cost to a linear independent variable, whereas the logarithmic fits linear cost to a logarithmic independent variable.) If the best fit line on semilog paper is a curve, replot the data on full log paper. A straight line here indicates that a power curve is the appropriate CER equation form. In the last two instances, a slight curve on either semilog paper or log-log paper may be correctable by the addition of a constant to the CER equation (i.e., use the power curve or exponential curve which include a constant term, a_1).

After determining which equation form produces a straight line fit through the data, the next step is to derive the mathematical equation for the CER. A graphical technique, the method of two points, has been presented. In addition, there are other quite interesting graphical techniques available capable of deriving each of our CER forms. For a discussion of these graphical approaches to curve fitting see references [1 and 2].

Such graphical techniques have been largely replaced by the use of computer programs that use various statistical methods to derive CER equations. The most common curve fitting technique used by cost analysts is the method of least squares. Like the graphical methods, a least squares fit line seeks to minimize the total deviations between the y actuals y_a and the y calculated values y_c. Because some of the deviations $y_a - y_c$ are positive and some are negative, the method of least squares actually minimizes the sum of squared deviations. Least squares fit is a linear regression technique that yields a $y = a + bx$ line fitted to a scatter of data points.

The method of least squares and the use of data transformations was presented in Chapter 3, "Statistical Techniques." Only the essential formulas and procedures for deriving CERs are repeated here. For a CER with a single independent variable, the method involves solving for the two unknown CER coefficients a and b in the following two equations:

$$y_a = na + bx_a \tag{7.5}$$

$$x_a y_a = ax_a + bx_a^2 \tag{7.6}$$

where the CER is given by $y = a + bx$, and x_a and y_a are the actual data points through which the CER is to be fit. Table 7.1 demonstrates the collection of the

TABLE 7.1. Derivation of a Linear CER by Least Squares

Spacecraft Weight (lb) x	Spacecraft Cost (millions) y	x^2	xy
390	258	152,100	100,620
430	339	184,900	145,770
495	349	245,025	172,755
570	489	324,900	278,730
650	428	422,500	278,200
820	647	672,400	530,540
870	698	756,900	607,260
1,020	654	1,040,400	667,080
1,200	848	1,440,000	1,017,600
1,300	930	1,690,000	1,209,000
Totals 7,745	5,640	6,929,125	5,007,555

Equation 7.5: $5,640 = 10a + 7,745b$
Equation 7.6: $5,007,555 = 7745a + 6,929,125b$

Solving Equations 7.5 and 7.6 simultaneously gives: $a = 31.92$
$$b = 0.687$$

Which gives a least squares CER of $y = 31.92 + 0.687x$

necessary values for the solution of the least squares equation for a data set of cost versus dry weight for a particular type of spacecraft.

Because all of the CER equation forms discussed can be transformed into linear forms, the method of least squares can be applied to appropriately transformed data to obtain any of these equations. Table 7.2 shows the required data transformation required before solving the foregoing equations for b and a.

For example, Table 7.3 illustrates the use of least squares to fit a $y = ax^b$ CER to a data set of chemical process plant capital costs versus millions of cubic feet

TABLE 7.2. CER Equation Forms (One Independent Variable)

	Linear	Power	Exponential	Logarithmic
Equation form desired	$y = a + bx$	$y = ax^b$	$y = ae^{bx}$	$y = a + b \ln x$
Linear Equation form	$y = a + bx$	$\ln y = \ln a + b \ln x$	$\ln y = \ln a + bx$	$y = a + b \ln x$
Req'd. data transform	x, y	$\ln x, \ln y$	$x, \ln y$	$\ln x, y$
Regression coefficients obtained	a, b	$\ln a, b$	$\ln a, b$	a, b
Coefficient reverse transform req'd.	None	antiln $(\ln a), b$	antiln $(\ln a), b$	None
Final coefficients	a, b	a, b	a, b	a, b

TABLE 7.3 Derivation of a Power CER by Least Squares

Product Gas Output in (MBTU/hr)	Plant Cost in (millions)	Ln x	Ln y	x^2	xy
x	y				
4,300	1,080	8.37	6.98	70.00	58.44
4,600	1,170	8.43	7.06	71.13	59.58
5,000	1,190	8.52	7.08	72.54	60.32
5,200	1,250	8.56	7.13	73.21	61.01
6,000	1,340	8.70	7.20	75.68	62.64
6,500	1,480	8.78	7.30	77.08	64.09
7,800	1,650	8.96	7.41	80.32	66.39
7,900	1,640	8.97	7.40	80.54	66.43
8,400	1,710	9.04	7.44	81.65	67.27
9,000	1,890	9.10	7.54	82.90	68.69
Totals 64,700	14,400	87.43	72.56	765.05	634.87

Equation 7.5: $72.56 = 10a + 87.43b$
Equation 7.6: $634.87 = 87.43a + 765.05b$

Solving Equations 7.5 and 7.6 simultaneously gives: $a = a \ln (0.8212) = 2.273$
$$b = 0.736$$

Which gives a least squares CER of $y = 31.92 + 0.687x$

per hour of product gas output. All that is required is to first convert the x and y data pairs into logarithms before solving for the regression coefficients a and b. Notice that Table 7.2 indicates the form of the a and b that are obtained. In the case of a power curve, the regression coefficients solved for are $\ln a$ and b. Therefore, as shown in Table 7.3, a reverse transformation (i.e., antilog) of the coefficient $\ln a$ is required before the final coefficients are used to write the $y = ax^b$ CER.

The least squares method is relatively easy to program on a computer and is also readily available in commercial software packages for most computers. Another advantage of the least squares method is that the same type of statistical data used in the solution of the least squares equations can be used to calculate several measures of the goodness of fit of our regression line. Two of the more common measures of fit used by parametric cost analysts are the standard error and the correlation coefficient.

7.3.3 Measures of Goodness of Fit

The standard error measures the average amount by which y_a and y_c vary:

$$\text{S.E.} = \sqrt{\frac{\Sigma (y_a - y_c)^2}{n - 1}}$$

where n is the number of data points. Because it is desirable to have a CER that produces y calculated values that are very close to the y actuals, the smaller the standard error the better. Notice that the standard error is in the same units as y_a and y_c. In the case of a linear CER these units will be dollars, but in the case of CERs derived by transforming the data pairs to logarithms, the standard error is in log dollars.

The correlation coefficient measures the closeness of fit of the regression line to the data points by determining ratios between explained deviation and total deviation. Figure 7.9 illustrates these concepts of deviation. Total deviation is the cumulative variance between the mean or average y value (denoted by "y bar") and each of the y actuals. Total deviation breaks down into two components: (1) explained deviation which is the summed differences between the y calculated values and y bar, and (2) unexplained deviation which is the summation of the differences between the y actuals and the y calculated values.

The correlation coefficient, often symbolically denoted as r, is the unitless ratio of explained deviation to total deviation

$$r = \frac{\text{explained deviation}}{\text{total deviation}}$$

and thus is calculated by

$$r = \sqrt{\frac{\Sigma \, (y_c - y)^2}{\Sigma \, (y_a - y)^2}}$$

Some cost analysts use the value for r without taking the square root, in which case it is called the coefficient of determination and is frequently abbreviated r^2. One ordinarily wants a CER that explains as much of total deviation as possible, thereby desiring a coefficient as close to one as possible. Note that CERs with

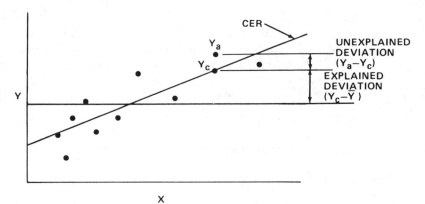

Figure 7.9. CER deviation.

relatively low slopes will have lower correlation coefficients because as the regression line flattens out, the explained deviation approaches zero. This is as it should be because a flat CER (i.e., one with a slope of $b = 0$) indicates that there is no relationship between the independent and dependent variables.

Both of the preceding statistics indicate how well the regresson line fits the historical data. In practice, the cost analyst uses this information to infer how well the CER might be expected to predict, given the assumption that the item being estimated is expected to have a similiar relationship between cost and the chosen independent variable. Other things being equal, a CER with relatively good statistics should be preferred to one with relatively poorer measures of fit.

7.3.4 Multiple Regression

Some CERs use multiple independent variables. For example, the cost of certain petrochemical plant equipment hypothetically might be related to three variables such as gas throughput (cubic feet per hour), operating temperature (in degrees), and operating pressure (in pounds per square inch). Similarly, the annual maintenance cost of an aircraft might be accurately predicted as a function of system dry weight, number of engines, and number of hours of operation per year. Such circumstances might best be modeled by a linear CER of three independent variables:

$$y = a + b_1x_1 + b_2x_2 + b_3x_3$$

or a power curve CER of three independent variables:

$$y = ax_1^{b_1}x_2^{b_2}x_3^{b_3}$$

Theoretically, the number of independent variables used in a CER can be quite high. Practically, however, it is rare in parametric estimating to see CERs with more than a very few independent variables.

The method of deriving CERs with multiple independent variables is a extension of the least squares method applied to one independent variable. Table 7.4 illustrates the transforms required to obtain the various equation forms. The regression coefficient equations and the method of solution are presented in Chapter 3.

7.4 MODEL APPLICATION

Parametric estimating is based on the cost experience of the data base from which the CERs were derived. A CER normally assumes that future business will be conducted like past business and usually offers no recognition of possibilities for basic improvements (or degradations) in processes, management, or other cost driving characteristics. It is often the case however, that the item being estimated is expected to depart from historical experience in some respect. Common solutions to this problem are the use of CER stratifications and cost adjustment factors

TABLE 7.4 CER Equation Forms (Two Independent Variables^a)

	Linear	Power	Exponential	Logarithmic
Equation form desired	$y = a + b_1 x_1 + b_2 x_2$	$y = a x_1^{b_1} x_2^{b_2}$	$y = a e^{b_1 x_1} e^{b_2 x_2}$	$y = a + b_1 \ln x_1 + b_2 \ln x_2$
Linear equation form	$y = a + b_1 x_1 + b_2 x_2$	$\ln y = \ln a + b_1 \ln x_1 + b_2 \ln x_2$	$\ln y = \ln a + b_1 x_1 + b_2 x_2$	$y = a + b_1 \ln x_1 + b_2 \ln x_2$
Req'd. input data transform	x_1, x_2, y	$\ln x_1, \ln x_2, \ln y$	$x_1, x_2, \ln y$	$\ln x_1, \ln x_2, y$
Regression coefficients obtained	a, b_1, b_2	$\ln a, b_1, b_2$	$\ln a, b_1, b_2$	a, b_1, b_2
Coefficient reverse transform req'd.	None	antiln $(\ln a), b_1, b_2$	antiln $(\ln a), b_1, b_2$	None
Final coefficients	a, b_1, b_2	a, b_1, b_2	a, b_1, b_2	a, b_1, b_2

^{a}More than two independent variables are simple extensions of two variable equations.

(the later being frequently referred to generically as complexity factors). There may be an entire excursion study performed as part of the cost analysis to derive and document such adjustments to the CERs.

In addition, some parametric cost models bring more independent variables into the regression analyses to attempt to account for programmatic differences between programs. If the differences have some quantifiable value, and if the cost estimator is armed with a good regression analysis computer program, the programmatic differences can sometimes be included in a multiple regression to derive CERs with two or more independent variables. As an example consider a production process that has, over the years, been continually improved with computer aided design techniques such that first unit production costs for new products has steadily, but not dramatically, declined. A regression analysis could include an independent variable associated with the date of the initial production unit of each of the data points in the historical data base. There are statistical testing techniques that can be used to determine if the introduced variable really does contribute to cost (discussed in Chapter 3). Theoretically, parametric cost models can make use of CERs with as many independent variables as can be found to influence cost. Practically, the cost analyst restricts the number of independent variables to those statistically significant and to those for which he can confidently develop quantifiable historical data.

7.4.1 CER Stratification

Stratification is the process of fitting a number of curves through the data base, each curve being based on a "family" of data points similiar to each other in some regard. For example, returning to our analogy of estimating the cost of new buildings, a parametric cost model might stratify the CERs into families based on the type of construction (e.g., frame, brick, or metal), number of stories (single story versus multistory), intended use (residential, commercial, industrial, etc.) and so on. A software cost model might stratify machine language code versus high-order language code. A set of CERs for aircraft frames might logically stratify into families according to the type of material (e.g., aluminum, graphite composite, or titanium). A spacecraft cost model might have stratifications corresponding to manned versus unmanned spacecraft, scientific versus communications satellites, earth orbital versus planetary, and so on. In practice, stratifications are usually made by first plotting all the data points of a data base and inspecting the result for logical stratifications.

For example, Figure 7.10 represents the cost versus dry weight data for 15 historical unmanned spacecraft. Five of the data points appear to have higher costs than the other 10. Further investigation reveals that the five high-cost satellites were planetary missions with complicated guidance and navigation systems, sophisticated scientific instruments, and strenuous reliability and design life requirements, whereas the 10 remaining data points were earth orbiting spacecraft with much simpler and less expensive missions. It would therefore be logical to stratify

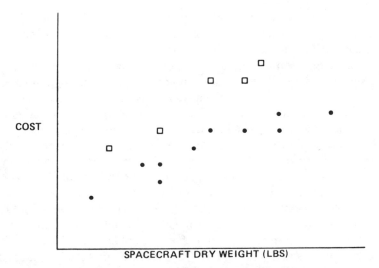

Figure 7.10. Data for 15 historical spacecraft programs.

this data base into the two families and fit curves through each of the two subsets of the data base, resulting in the CERs depicted in Figure 7.11.

Notice the CERs in this example are not parallel. Strictly fitting curves to each subset of data in a stratified data base usually results in non-parallel CERs. Sometimes this is a perfectly logical and valid result. For instance, in the given example, it may well be that for some technical reasons earth orbital spacecraft exhibit more economies of scale than do planetary spacecraft (the electrical power and propul-

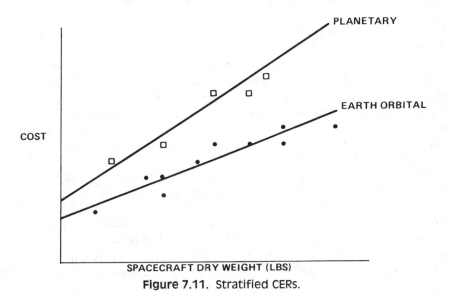

Figure 7.11. Stratified CERs.

sion demands of deep space satellites might drive up the cost of such spacecraft as they get larger, whereas increasing the size of earth orbital spacecraft is perhaps only a matter of adding a few more square feet of solar array and relatively simple reaction control components). In some instances, however, there may be no good reason for stratified CERs to have different slopes, and the cost analyst might feel that it was just statistical noise in the data points that caused the slopes to be nonparallel. In such cases, it is not unusual to fit a curve through the subset of data with the most data points (or otherwise the subset that the analyst feels best represents the true slope relationship between the independent and dependent variables) and simply assume the same slope for the other stratified data. For the spacecraft example, the cost analyst might wish to reject the argument of any valid technical reasons for the two families of spacecraft to have different slopes and assume that the planetary CER has the same slope as the earth orbital CER, as shown in Figure 7.12. The *b* value of the planetary CER is now known, and the *a* intercept can be graphically read from the plot. Alternately, there are statistical techniques that allow the slopes of stratified CERs to be based on all the data points in the sample, thus retaining the advantage of a larger sample size for each of the subsets of data. One such method, based on the introduction of "dummy variables" into the regression analysis, is discussed in reference [3].

7.4.2 Cost Adjustments and Complexity Factors

In addition to data base stratification, cost adjustment or complexity factors are often used in parametric estimating. Typically the intent is to adjust the CER calculated cost to reflect some known difference in the item being estimated and the data base from which the CER was derived. Although the following sections do

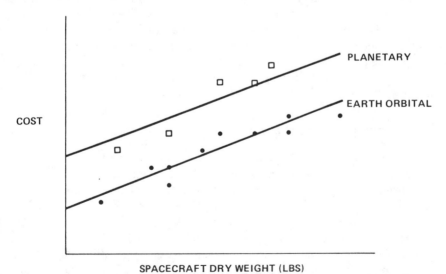

SPACECRAFT DRY WEIGHT (LBS)

Figure 7.12. Stratified CERs with assumed slope for planetary CER.

not exhaust the theoretical reasons for using cost adjustment factors, they do perhaps cover the most common adjustments.

7.4.3 Number of Developmental Units

In the design of most subsystems, there are frequently some numbers of engineering units built and utilized as brassboards, pathfinders, test units, and the like. It is desirable that an indication of the quantity of such developmental subsytems, both total units and partial units, be obtained and documented when the organization's data base is compiled. When making estimates using CERs derived from the data, the analyst may want to adjust the calculated cost if the number of anticipated developmental units differs from the average number contained in the data base. Some parametric models deal with this problem by stratification (building separate CERs corresponding to different numbers of developmental units) or by separately calculating the cost of the developmental units based on the user's definition of the number anticipated by the project being estimated.

7.4.4 Design Inheritance

Because all organizations build on their past experiences, the historical cost data base often reflects projects with some degree of design inheritance from predecessor projects. In an environment in which this practice is relatively constant and expected to continue indefinitely, the parametric method will implicitly reflect the trend because it is a part of the data base of the CERs. In applications where the degree of design inheritance is less smooth and more dependent on the particulars of the individual subsystems being designed, this factor should be explicitly accounted for. Ideally, the historical data base should be searched for some indication of the degree of new design that is inherent in each of the historical subsystem data points. However, this factor is usually more difficult to come by than, for example, the number of test units. It tends to be more subjective, and it may be that the only way to capture such data is to interview the participants of previous projects and document their judgements concerning the degree of inheritance in each of the subsystems.

7.4.5 Design Complexity

Design complexity due to a large parts count, complicated movements or mechanisms, exotic materials, critical adjustments or alignments, extremely large or extremely small-sized assemblies, critical operating temperatures or pressures, and other complexities affecting cost are also important to note in the historical data base. Some parametric cost models account for selected complexities with stratified CERs or through additional CER independent variables. The cost impact of other complexities may not be so quantifiable. Even unquantified however, the knowledge of such characteristics in the historical data base is extremely valuable because it at least serves as a basis for the user of the model to attempt to judge what cost adjustment factors should be employed to compensate for complexities in the item being estimated.

7.4.6 Production Rate Effects

The average recurring unit production cost of an item is usually inversely proportional to the number of units produced. This is generally and loosely attributed to the effects of learning or economies of scale, although technically there are two distinct and separate effects that are responsible for the cost reductions.

The first of the two production rate effects is that of direct labor learning. The more times a worker performs a repetitive operation, the more efficient that operation becomes (to a point). Different types of production operations have different learning rates. Forecasting the learning rate for a future production operation requires fairly extensive analysis of past experiences on similar production projects. This is covered in detail in Chapter 5, "Learning Curves." Parametric cost models generally employ a CER to estimate the first unit cost (also called "theoretical first unit" cost or TFU) of an item, and then apply the effects of learning as a separate calculation. This is usually the preferred method because it maintains the generality of the parametric model's CERs and allows for the effect of learning to be situation dependent as a function of the number of units to be produced.

Items produced in quantity also potentially enjoy the economies associated with automation, the second of the two production rate effects. If a large number of an item are to be produced, the manufacturing operation can be automated to a greater degree than if relatively fewer items are being produced. In parametric modeling, the tooling required for automated production ("hard tooling") is usually a nonrecurring cost, whereas the "soft tooling" required for low-production runs is more often accumulated as a recurring cost. Because of this, the first unit cost (excluding tooling) off an automated line usually costs less than the first unit cost of an item being produced in a less automated manner. Beyond the first unit cost, the unit costs with an automated production environment will generally show relatively little decrease because labor is a relatively lower percentage of total cost. Figure 7.13 shows this effect for two items, item A produced in low quantity (10 units), and item B produced in quantity (100 units).

The term "economies of scale" has a third shade of meaning associated with the observed fact that physically large items cost less per pound or cubic foot than smaller items. To some degree this is attributable to production rate effects at the next lower level of the work element structure, and to some degree it is relatable to pure size or scale.

Once the CER of a parametric cost model has been exercised to obtain the first unit cost, the choice of the proper learning curve rate should consider the anticipated production run. A relatively low production rate probably indicates use of a labor intensive manufacturing operation and will warrant use of a steeper learning curve (i.e., more learning—a learning rate perhaps in the 70–90% range). A large

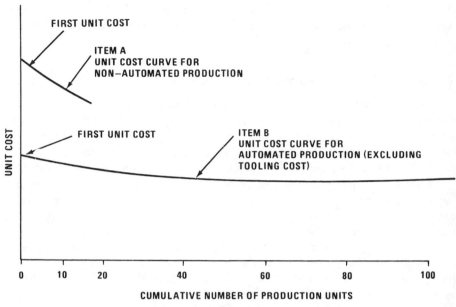

Figure 7.13. Unit cost comparisons.

production run will probably justify the assumption of a more capital intensive, automated production capability and call for the use of a flatter learning curve (i.e., less learning—perhaps in the 95 to near 100% range).

In practice, some cost estimators prefer to blur the distinction between production rate economies due to learning and production rate economies due to automation and simply account for both through the application of learning curve theory. This is not invalid because there is some learning curve rate that can be fitted to any cost reduction history whether the cost reductions are due to learning or automation. It is often the case that a given organization tends to do work that is of the same approximate production rate. Using the techniques described in Chapter 5, the cost analyst can determine his organization's typical history of cost reductions as production quantities increase and use that as a basis for predicting the appropriate rate to use in a given situation.

7.5 TRENDS AND DIRECTIONS

The parametric cost estimating approach is being used in new applications and in conjunction with complementary analytical techniques such as risk analysis, microcomputer program development, and commercial cost models. One of the more recent examinations of the field is given in reference [4].

7.5.1 New Applications and Broader Scopes

Parametric estimating is continually being expanded into new applications and applied to estimating problems of broader scope. It was relatively recently that parametrics were first successfully applied to problems in the architectural, construction, and mining industries. Evident as well, is a trend toward broadening the scope of parametric cost estimating to consider all phases of the life cycle, including operations cost. The sometimes poor record of more detailed cost estimating methods in predicting the project costs for major defense acquisition, research and development, and high technology has led to a growth in the use of the parametric technique in these areas in an attempt to take advantage of the natural tendency of the parametric technique to allow realistically for unforseen problems that lead to cost growth.

7.5.2 Parametrics and Risk Analysis

There are increasing trends in parametric cost estimating to combine the statistical techniques of parametrics with statistical risk analysis methods. All cost estimates have some degree of uncertainty associated with them. Parametric estimating, because of its statistical approach, offers the cost analyst the advantage of being able to quantify this risk. The standard error, discussed earlier as a measure of the goodness of fit, can be used to quantify this uncertainty.

The same statistical information that is tabulated and used in regression analysis to derive the CER equation and the measures of goodness of fit can be used to establish confidence intervals about the regression line as shown in Figure 7.14. Confidence intervals are discussed in reference [5]. Assuming that Figure 7.14 shows the plus or minus one and two standard deviation confidence intervals about a CER, we find that the resulting bands correspond to a probability range of about 68 and 95% respectively. The confidence intervals are curves because, as generally calculated, confidence limits take into account both the standard deviation associated with the statistical noise in a CER data base and the distance from the mean of the independent variable. For example, at x pounds the estimated cost is y. From the point of view of uncertainty associated with the historical scatter in the CER data base, the estimated cost of y has a 50% chance of being exceeded (and it also has a 50% chance of being underrun). Or, one can say there is a 68% confidence associated with a cost range of y_1 to y_2. Or the cost analyst could quote the upper bound of the 68% confidence interval, in this case y_2, and say that there is 68% confidence that the estimate would not be exceeded due to CER uncertainty. Doubling the standard deviation and the associated confidence interval would give the plus or minus 2 "sigma" cost range (y_3 to y_4). The upper limit, y_3 dollars, has a confidence level of 95%, theoretically good enough even for the most cautious manager.

Careful definition of uncertainty is in order here. The levels of confidence are restricted to only risks associated with the scatter in the CER data base as reflected by the standard error. That is, statements made about confidence based on the

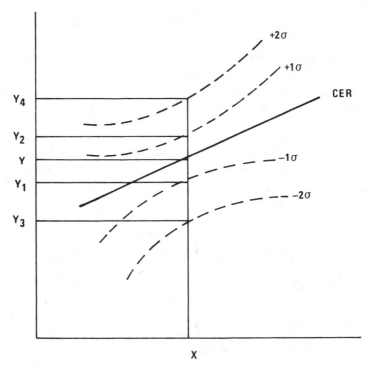

Figure 7.14. CER confidence intervals.

standard error of the CER include only those risk factors that caused the dispersion in the original data. This is true of any statistical statement. A confidence statement made about the probability of a machined part being within tolerance presumes no additional perturbation factors beyond the historical randomness of the machine's workings. If, of course, the machine is perturbed between the time the statistics were collected and the time the confidence statement was made, then the confidence statement may be mistaken.

Because probability distribution data are readily available from CERs, parametric costing is sometimes combined with cost risk analysis techniques involving Monte Carlo simulation, network analysis, and other risk assessment techniques. Typically, these approaches allow the cost analyst to deal with additional uncertainties beyond those associated with CER statistics. These risks may include CER input uncertainties, complexity factor risks, and other risks that impact cost. Chapter 8 of this reference manual, "Cost/Schedule/Technical Performance Risk Analysis," discusses these techniques in detail.

7.5.3 Computers and Parametric Cost Estimating

The wider availability of computers, and especially microcomputers, is a factor in the increased popularity of the parametric technique. Computers offer efficient means to assemble, store and retrieve the large quantities of data usually associated with parametric estimating. The laborious statistical calculations associated with the development of CERs would be impractical in many instances without computers. They provide a means to automate the large number of interdependent calculations connected with the typical parametric model. Microcomputers, especially, with the wide range of excellent data base, spreadsheet, and graphics software, have become indispensable to the parametric cost analyst. See Chapter 9, "The Use of Microcomputers for Cost Estimating," for a full discussion of the use of microcomputers in cost estimating.

7.5.4 Commercial Cost Models

An increasing number of parametric cost models are commercially available for use in a wide range of applications. One of the earliest entries in this field, and still the most popular, is the RCA PRICE family of parametric cost models (RCA PRICE Systems, Moorestown, N.J.). The PRICE models are capable of estimating various types of structural and electronic components, software, and life cycle costs for aerospace, military, and commercial applications. Other similar models include the Fast cost estimating models, which include modeling capability for equipment and electronic components, software, construction, and mining (developed by Freiman Parametric Systems, Inc., Cherry Hill, N.J. and marketed by United Information Services). There are models devoted to more narrow disciplines such as the Jensen software models (Computer Economics, Inc., Marina del Rey, Cal.). Some commercial models are resident on host computer systems and are accessed with computer terminals equipped with modems over telephone lines for either annual subscription fees or time-related use charges. Other parametric cost models are available in either document form or preprogrammed media, such as the the COCOMO software cost model [6] and numerous specialized models in the construction industry and other applications. These models are routinely advertised in the discipline and microcomputer periodicals.

7.5.5 Professional Societies

Chapter 14, "Cost Estimating as a Profession," discusses the trend toward increased professionalism in the cost estimating discipline. An increase in the level of education and training encourages the growth of the parametric method because the technique both requires and is stimulated by practitioners with a good grounding in mathematics, statistics, engineering, science, and computers.

Professional organizations whose members are involved in parametric estimating include the American Association of Cost Engineers, the American Society of Professional Estimators, the International Society of Parametric Analysts, the National Estimating Society, and the Institute of Cost Analysis.

7.6 SUMMARY

Parametric estimating offers a method for predicting cost based on historical relationships between cost and one or more predictor variables. The method is more statistical and mathematical in approach and is commonly used at a point earlier in the design process than more detailed cost estimating techniques. The structure of a parametric cost analysis is more often oriented toward hardware and other end items of cost than toward the labor and material orientation of detailed approaches. The variables against which cost is modeled are chosen for their cost predictive abilities, as opposed to their quantitative contribution to cost. Most parametric models allow the estimator to address factors such as number of test units, degree of new design, complexity, production rate effects, and other cost drivers. Because the method is rigorously attentive to modeling total historical cost against carefully selected physical and performance variables, there is an inherent tendency for parametric estimating to yield results that include the historical experience regarding various types of technical problems, design changes, test failures, schedule slips, overlooked requirements, and other difficult-to-predict contributors to ultimate project cost. Other advantages are the method's speed, adaptability to computerization, and compatibility with trade studies, sensitivity analyses, optimizations, and other analytical studies. The method is compatible with statistical quantifications of the risk or confidence associated with the resulting estimates of cost. The parametric method is being used in an increasingly wide range of industries and applications.

REFERENCES

1. Hoelscher, R. P., J. N. Arnold, and S. H. Pierce. *Graphic Aids in Engineering Computation*. Balt Publishing, Lafayette, Ind., 1952.
2. Hoelscher, R. P. "Curves and Nomographs." *Industrial Engineering Handbook*, 3rd ed., H. B. Maynard, Ed. McGraw-Hill, New York, 1971.
3. Draper, N. and H. Smith. *Applied Regression Analysis*, 2nd ed. Wiley, New York, 1980.
4. Gallagher, P. F. *Parametric Estimating for Executives and Estimators*. Van Nostrand Reinhold, New York, 1982.
5. Daniel, W. W. and J. C. Terrell. *Business Statistics*. Houghton Mifflin, Boston, Mass., 1975.
6. Boehm, B. W. *Software Engineering Economics*. Prentice-Hall, Englewood, N.J., 1981.

8

COST / SCHEDULE / TECHNICAL PERFORMANCE RISK ANALYSIS

NONA M. WHATLEY

8.1 RISK ANALYSIS

Risk analysis is a logically structured approach to quantifying uncertainty. There are three primary areas of uncertainty associated with most projects: cost, schedule, and technical performance. As project phases become more complex and costly, the requirement to quantify these uncertainties has grown. As the requirement to perform risk analysis has grown, so has the availability of computerized risk analysis techniques. Today there are a wide variety of techniques available for risk analysis. The degree to which a risk analyst applies these techniques determines the range of the risk analysis performed. An extensive risk analysis of a project would include the following areas:

1. A risk assessment of the decision to undertake the project.
2. A risk assessment of the project alternatives.
3. A risk assessment of the project cost, schedule, and technical performance.
4. An assessment of alternatives for risk reduction.
5. An assessment of project performance against the original risk assessment.
6. A revised risk assessment based on project performance.

A more limited risk analysis of a project may be performed on either the cost or schedule risk associated with a project. The extent of the risk analysis performed is usually dependent on the complexity of the project and the amount of capital investment. More than one risk analysis technique may be used to develop a particular risk assessment of a project's cost and schedule. A risk analyst may use a deterministic network analysis technique like PERT (see Section 8.3.1.3) for determining project schedule risk and a cost estimating risk analysis technique like SAM (see Section 8.3.3) for determining the cost estimating risk. Thus risk analysis is a description in which various risk analysis techniques are used to develop risk assessments. The extent of these risk assessments determines the scope of risk analysis performed.

8.2. ASPECTS OF RISK ANALYSIS

As stated by Immanuel Kant in *Critique of Pure Reason*:

> The hypothetical employment of reason has, therefore, as its aim the systematic unity of the knowledge of understanding, and this unity is the criterion of the truth of its rules. The systematic unity (as a mere idea) is, however, only a projected unity, to be regarded not as given in itself, but as a problem only. This unity aids us in discovering a principle for the understanding in its manifold and special modes of employment, directing its attention to cases which are not given, and thus rendering it more coherent.

> But the only conclusion which we are justified in drawing from these considerations is that the systematic unity of the manifold knowledge of understanding, as prescribed by reason, is a logical principle. Its function is to assist the understanding by means of ideas, in those cases in which the understanding cannot by itself establish rules, and at the same time to give to the numerous and diverse rules of the understanding, unity or system under a single principle, and thus to secure coherence in every possible way.

Logical structured approach to risk analysis is used to quantify uncertainty and to assist in the understanding of the problem. It gives unity to the collective uncertainties associated with the problem and presents them in a coherent manner. The in-depth problem immersion necessary to perform a risk assessment increases program insight, which allows for better identification of areas of agreement and disagreement, thus resulting in better communication about the problem. A structured risk assessment quantifies the interrelationships of various uncertainties, giving management a better understanding of the consequences of a decision. By identifying critical project elements, it provides management the insight and the ability to track closely and manage those areas that increase the chance for the successful completion of a project. An in-depth risk assessment brings out the inherent assumptions of the project, allowing critical review and determination of the validity of these assumptions, thus improving project definition.

The more complex a project becomes, the more the human mind is limited in understanding and identifying the interrelationship of uncertainties and the consequences of a decision. A structured logical approach increases the capability of the human mind to understand the complexities of the project and the alternative approaches to a problem. The use of computerized risk analysis techniques increases a manager's ability to quantify a large number of complex interrelated project uncertainties and defines these uncertainties in terms of project risk. The transfer of these uncertainties from the realm of the unknown to the world of identified risk increases the managability of these uncertainties. Many of the more advanced risk analysis techniques can be used as project tracking systems to continually track and forecast the success or failure of a project. Thus the use of a logical structured risk analysis provides the manager with an understanding of the risk associated with a project as well as a vehicle for determining the consequences of critical decisions.

8.2.1 Probability Theory and Expert Opinion

All risk analysis techniques require a knowledge of statistics and are based on expert opinion. The degree of statistical knowledge required depends on the particular risk analysis technique utilized; however, most require a basic practical knowledge of statistics and probability theory. It is suggested that the reader review Chapter 3 on statistical techniques or any basic statistical or probability textbook [1] before using any of the risk analysis techniques mentioned in this section.

Expert opinion is a very sensitive area in using any of the risk analysis techniques. In using expert opinions it is often necessary that the risk analysis quantify the uncertainty of expert opinion. To quantify expert opinion a risk analyst must be familiar with two basic definitions and four basic assumptions of probability theory:

Definitions:

1. **Probability** p: If an event E can occur in m cases out of a total of n possible cases, the probability of the event E occurring is:

$$p = \frac{m}{n} = \frac{\Sigma \text{ favorable cases}}{\text{total cases}} \qquad (8.1)$$

2. **Conditional Probability:** The probability that event E occurs on the condition that event F has already occurred is:

$$p \ (E/F)$$

Assumptions:

1. Each event has one and only one probability associated with it.
2. A probability of zero indicates a failure or nonoccurrence of an event. A nonzero probability indicates that the event may occur.
3. The sum of the individual probabilities for a given set is 1.
4. Given a universal set, one of the random outcomes must occur.

In dealing with expert opinion, it is very important that none of these assumptions be violated. Therefore a risk analyst should be very familiar with the techniques of gathering and quantifying expert opinion.

8.2.2 Methods for Quantifying Expert Opinion

There are several different methods of quantifying expert opinion. One is the direct method in which an analyst can request that the expert assign a probability to each value in a range of values. For example, an analyst can present a range of cost values for a particular cost element, such as 20, 40, 60, 100, or 125 million, and then request the expert to assess the probability of occurrence of each cost value.

Analyst Provided Range of Cost Value (millions)	Expert Opinion of Probability of Occurrence (%)
20	5
40	10
60	70
100	10
125	5

The analyst can also request that the expert provide or change the range of cost values as well as providing the probability of occurrence. This is the easiest and quickest way of quantifying the uncertainty associated with the expert's opinion. However, this method can often cause an expert to assign probabilities that, when summed, are greater than one.

Another direct approach is to request that the expert provide a lowest, most likely, and highest value. The analyst can then do one of the following:

1. Request the expert to provide the density function form.
2. Provide a number of density function forms from which the expert is requested to select the one that best represents the probability of occurrence.
3. Make an assumption as to the form of the density function.

One problem in using the direct approach is getting the expert to submit a range of numbers. Another problem is that the expert's opinion may vary over time. If the analyst requests the same information at a different point in time, the expert's opinion may be quite different. However, the latter method is most frequently used in quantifying the uncertainty associated with expert opinion. More rigorous and exacting techniques are defined later, together with references on the implementation of these techniques.

8.2.2.1 The Modified Churchman-Ackoff Method [2].   In this method the expert is asked to (Figure 8.1):

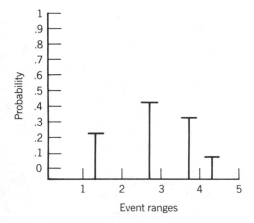

Event ranges   **Figure 8.1.** Likelihood of occurrence.

1. Define a set of event ranges that do not overlap each other and that cover all outcomes. For example, 1.01 to 2 million, 2.01 to 3 million, 3.01 to 4 million, 4.01 to 5 million.
2. Next the expert orders these event ranges by the likelihood of their occurrence. For example, 2.01 to 3 million, 3.01 to 4 million, 1.01 to 2 million, 4.01 to 5 million. Those with equal likelihood should be noted.
3. The expert is then requested to select the most likely event.
4. Next the expert is requested to rank by frequency the most likely occurrences in each range of events.
5. The results of step 3 and 4 are then compared. If differences exist, the expert should select which representation is preferred.
6. The expert is then requested to assign a ratio of occurrence to each range of events. For example, the expert may say that event one is two-thirds as likely as event three.
7. The analyst can then assign a value to any one of the event ranges. The sum of the set of event ranges will be equal to one, thereby obtaining a subjective probability for each event range.

This method reduces the likelihood of inconsistencies that occur in requesting an expert to assign probabilities to individual events [3].

8.2.2.2 The Normalized Geometric Mean Vector Method.   In this method the ratio of event occurrence is utilized to develop a judgment matrix, then the normalized geometric mean of each row is determined [4]. The normalized geometric means can then be utilized to form a probability distribution. This distribution can then be reviewed by the expert to see if it effectively represents the expert's opinion.

8.2.2.3 Gamble Method.   In this method the questions utilized to obtain the probability information are presented as a gamble [3, 5]. One of the major problems in quantifying expert opinion is the inconsistency in expert responses. This can result from not presenting the questions in an understandable manner or from variance in answers from one time to another. There are basically two approaches in quantifying expert opinion. In one the event is fixed and the probabilities vary, from which a probability distribution function is derived. In the other, the probabilities are fixed and the event varies, from which a cumulative distribution is derived [6].

8.2.2.4 Diagrammatic Method.   In this method the analyst provides a number of probability distribution functions (PDF) from which is selected the one that represents the expert's degree of uncertainty about the event. The expert is then asked to give the lowest value, the most likely value, and the highest value. This is one of the easiest and the least time-consuming approaches; however, it does require a familiarity with probability concepts [6–9].

8.2.2.5 The Delphi Technique.   The Delphi technique of quantifying expert opinion was developed by the RAND Corporation [10] to handle group assessments. This technique attempts to counteract the bias that results from the interaction between group members in developing a group estimate. In this technique each group member's opinion and reason for a particular opinion is obtained separately, thus reducing the chance that one member's opinion will be biased by another member. Their opinions and supporting reasons are then interpreted and aggregated using one of the methods previously stated. The results are presented to each member for further evaluation and substantiation. This process continues until all major inconsistencies are eliminated. The analyst then calculates a set of median values from which the group estimate is determined.

Expert opinion is the basis of any risk analysis technique. The validity of these objective opinions has a direct effect on the validity of the risk assessment performed. Therefore, the method used to quantify expert opinion is as crucial as the risk analysis technique utilized to evaluate project risk.

8.3 RISK ANALYSIS TECHNIQUES

In this discussion risk analysis techniques have been divided into three general categories:

1. Network analysis
2. Decision risk analysis
3. Cost risk analysis

Network analysis techniques review a project from an activity perspective, looking at the activities and events necessary to complete the project. These techniques attempt to represent the actual project realistically by logically and sequentially representing each activity and event in the project. The degree to which a network analysis technique realistically represents a project depends on the capabilities and limitations of the network analysis technique used. Therefore the background knowledge necessary to understand network analysis is given along with a review of some of the computerized network analysis techniques available.

Decision risk analysis techniques are presented as a separate category since a project is viewed from a decision risk perspective as opposed to the activity structure of network analysis. However, network analysis techniques may be used to perform a decision risk analysis by using the network to represent a decision tree rather than a project structure.

Cost risk analysis techniques fall in a separate category since they are primarily designed to evaluate the risk associated with a project cost estimate. Cost risk analysis techniques do not address risk from a project structure, but from a cost estimating structure, and consider the risk associated with the development of the individual cost elements.

8.3.1 Network Analysis

Over the last few years network analysis has begun to play an increasingly important role in evaluating the risk associated with many large and complex research and development projects. One of the primary reasons for this increase is the ease with which a network can realistically model a research and development project. The use of network analysis provides several benefits to the risk analyst. In developing a logic network, the analyst becomes more aware of the project structures and of potential problem areas. Once the structure of the network is developed, the analyst has an organized logical approach to the collection of cost, schedule, and performance data required for a risk assessment, as well as a way of representing and discussing the significant aspects of the project [11].

Before discussing the specific network techniques, it is necessary to explain some general concepts associated with all networks. A graphic representation of a project requires the identification of arcs, nodes, and paths. An example of a graphic representation of a project is shown in Figure 8.2. The graph begins and ends with a node represented by a rectangular box. A node represents an event that characterizes a milestone or a decision point in the project structure. The arcs represent activities or tasks to be performed and usually consume resources such as labor, time, and material. A graphic representation of a project with arcs and nodes constitutes a network. The way in which the network's arcs and nodes are connected represents the project flow, which is usually determined by the project schedule. The arcs represent the activities and resources required to accomplish the schedule. The node logic controls the flow of the activities in the network. For example, node 1 in Figure 8.2 initiates all the activities emanating from that node (arcs 1, 2, 9, 13, 14, 18, 22). The degree of control a node has over an activity

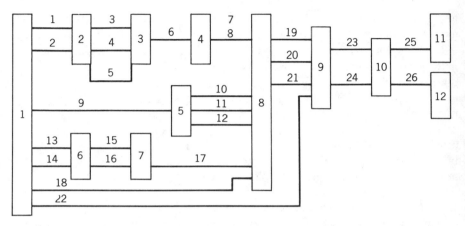

Figure 8.2. Graphic representation of a project.

depends on the node logic available in the network model used. Once a network is exercised, the flow from initiation through connecting arcs to termination is called the path.

A project network may be structured in several different ways depending on the degree of sophistication required to represent the project and the computer program used to model the project. There are three basic approaches in structuring network models: high-level network structuring; low-level network structuring; and subnetting. In a high-level network structure, several activities are grouped under one activity or arc. For example, in Figure 8.3 the activity defined as "develop airframe" incorporates such activities as design of wing structure, test wing structure, and integration of wing structure.

Nodes or events are also viewed at a high level such as complete airframe development, complete warhead development, or start engine procurement. The node "complete airframe design" and "start engine procurement" includes decisions or events such as complete wing structure design, or start wing structure design. This type of network structuring defines the project at a very high level and is usually deficient in representing a complex research and development project realistically since it disregards a large degree of uncertainty associated with each activity. However, the high-level structuring approach is usually well suited to small projects in which the tasks are repetitive and their cost and schedule outcomes are fairly predictable (known to a high degree of certainty).

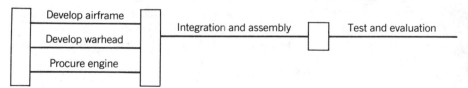

Figure 8.3. High-level network structure.

A low-level network structuring is usually considered a more acceptable approach in defining a highly complex research and development project or any project with a high degree of technical uncertainty. In a low-level network structuring approach, activities that have a high degree of uncertainty or technical complexity are reduced to the lowest level of activity. For example, the activity labeled ''develop airframe'' in Figure 8.3 would be broken out as shown in Figure 8.4. Based on the high degree of technical uncertainty in the wing design, there are two alternative designs, wing design A and wing design B, with a fallback to wing design C which has already been developed. For more advanced network models, a probability of success can be assigned to both wing designs A and B, depending on the degree of technical uncertainty associated with each design.

In the aircraft hull design there is only one design with no fallback design; therefore if the design does not succeed, the hull must be redesigned. The probability that the hull will have to be redesigned can be assigned to the accepted or rejected arcs. This low-level network could be broken down even further. For example, wing design A could be broken into the development of different wing materials. The level at which the network is designed depends on the degree of technical uncertainty associated with the arc. For instance, if the wing design had a high degree of uncertainty because of the material used, then the development of the material would be broken out and represented in the network.

An analyst may decide to utilize both a high-level and a low-level approach when computer memory limits the network size. This can be accomplished by partitioning the high-level network into ''subnetworks'' as shown in Figure 8.5. These subnetworks can be treated as a complete network, and their results can then be assigned to the high-level network. This approach allows the analyst to produce a simplified high-level network that incorporates the uncertainties of low-level activities.

Another element the risk analyst should consider in structuring the network is

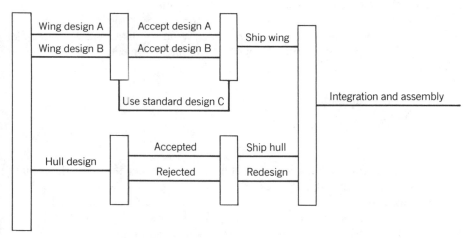

Figure 8.4. Low-level network structure.

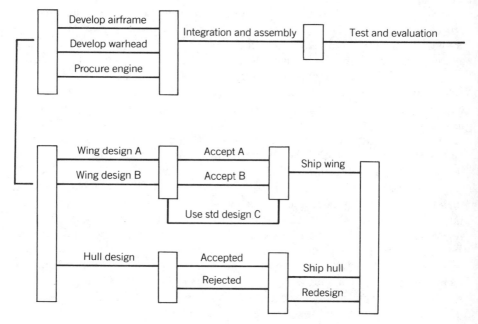

Figure 8.5. Subnetwork example.

how the output from the network is going to be utilized. If the analyst intends to use the output for a baseline cost estimate as well as a risk assessment, then the activities need to be represented in a work breakdown structure (WBS). Most advanced risk models take this into account and provide for this type of coding. The structuring of a project network using WBS codes is frequently utilized by government agencies where the cost, schedule, and technical risk must be integrated into their estimating and budget reporting requirements.

The two important concepts a risk analyst should be familiar with when using the network analysis method of risk assessment are probabilistic and deterministic modeling. These two concepts are associated with three segments of network modeling:

1. Network simulation
2. Node logic
3. Arcs

In general, a deterministic network simulation is one in which the network is structured in such a way that all activities must be completed successfully, and there is no uncertainty associated with cost, schedule, or technical performance. In a deterministic network simulation, only one pass or iteration is made through the network. In a probabilistic or stochastic network simulation, uncertainties are randomly determined sequential events that are treated as a sample of one element from a probability distribution. The two primary areas of uncertainty associated with a probabilistic network simulation are:

1. Cost, schedule, or technical performance uncertainty
2. Network path uncertainty

In cost and schedule uncertainty, each arc is assigned a probability distribution function associated with cost or schedule uncertainty. Then each element (point) in the sample is determined randomly for each successive pass or iteration of the simulation. Technical performance is usually handled by probabilistic node logic. In network path uncertainty, the path the network takes through each successive iteration of the simulation is also determined probabilistically.

In general, node logic consists of input logic and output logic. Deterministic node input logic requires an "AND" logic statement specifying that all arcs must be completed successfully for the input logic requirement to be met and thus initiate the output logic. Deterministic node output logic requires an "ALL" logic statement specifying that all arcs emanating from the node be started when the output node logic is initiated, as shown in Figure 8.6. Probabilistic node input logic varies from one network model to another; however, the general requirement is that no matter how many arcs enter the input node, only one arc has to be successfully completed to initiate the node output logic. An "OR" logic statement is a general example of probabilistic node input logic. Probabilistic output logic requires that the initiation of arcs leaving the node be determined by a specified probability. The general logic statement used to represent probabilistic output logic is "PROB," which represents a conditional logic statement "If P then Q." An example of probabilistic node logic is shown in Figure 8.7. Deterministic and probabilistic node logic can also be combined giving the following logic:

1. Deterministic input logic/probabilistic output logic
2. Probabilistic input logic/deterministic output logic

Figure 8.8 shows examples of combining deterministic and probabilistic node logic.

Caution should be taken when using the deterministic input node logic statement "AND." Remember that this input logic requires the successful completion of all arcs entering the node. If one arc fails to complete successfully, the node input logic will not be satisfied, and the node output logic will not be initiated. Therefore

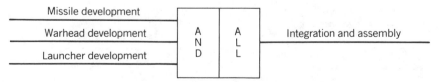

Figure 8.6. Deterministic AND/ALL node logic.

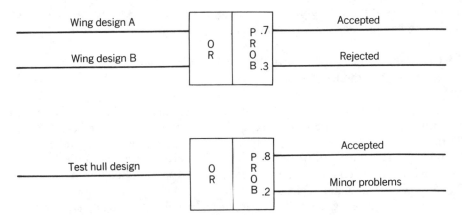

Figure 8.7. Probabilistic OR/PROB node logic.

arcs emanating from probabilistic output node logic should not be directed to deterministic node input logic, as shown in Figure 8.9.

In many network models, arcs can be either deterministic or probabilistic. Deterministic arcs have a probability of success equal to 0 or 1. If an arc's probability of success is equal to 0, then the arc will always fail to complete successfully. If it is equal to 1, then it will always succeed, given that it is not emanating from probabilistic node output logic. Probabilistic arcs have a probability of success, in practice, greater than 0 and less than 1. In developing a network logic structure, caution should also be used when assigning probabilities to arcs. For example, if a probability of zero is assigned to an arc entering a deterministic ''AND'' input node logic, the arc will fail and the ''AND'' input logic will not be satisfied; therefore the node output logic will not be initiated. Also, if a probabilistic arc is assigned a probability greater than zero or less than one, there will be a given number of times (depending on the probability assigned) in which the arc will fail

Probabilistic/deterministic node logic

Figure 8.8. Deterministic/probabilistic node logic.

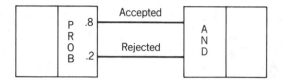

The "AND" input node will *never be satisfied*

Figure 8.9. Improper logic statement.

to complete successfully. Assignment of arc probability becomes more complex when probabilistic arcs emanate from probabilistic node logic as shown in Figure 8.10. Arc A has an 80% probability of being initiated and a 50% chance of completing successfully. Therefore 50% of the times the arc is initiated it will fail to complete successfully. Thus the probability input node logic requirement will not be met, and the output node logic "ALL" will not be initiated, and Arc C will not be started.

8.3.1.1 Network Analysis Technique.
One of the most important decisions an analyst makes, after deciding what type of risk assessment to use, is the selection of a computer model to perform the analysis. There are a number of computer models available for network analysis, and, with the increase in software development, this number is growing rapidly. A risk analyst not only needs to know what computer models are currently available, but also how to evaluate new models. This section provides a review of selected computer models currently available, as well as a general approach for evaluating new computer models. The basic approach for evaluating the computer models is as follows:

1. The basic assumptions inherent in the model
   a. Types of node logic (deterministic/probabilistic)
   b. Types of uncertainty variables assessed (time, cost performance)
   c. Type of methodology used to determine uncertainty (statistical or stochastic)
   d. Type of output generated by the model
2. Degree of computer sophistication required to operate the model
3. Computer hardware requirements

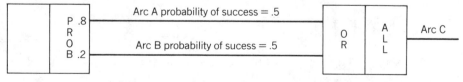

Figure 8.10. Probabilistic arc's emanating from probabilistic node logic.

8.3.1.2 Critical Path Method (CPM).

The critical path method (CPM), one of the older networking methods, was developed by Du Pont [12] in the 1950s for planning and scheduling the construction of a new facility. This method of network analysis is based on the determination of a network critical path—the path that consumes the most time and therefore determines the length of the project. Most critical path methods determine the critical path by making a forward and a backward pass as shown in Figure 8.11. Each box in the example contains two numbers. The numbers in the left half of the box are the result of the forward pass through the network. The forward pass calculates the earliest start date and the earliest end date for an activity (arc), and the earliest completion date for an event (node). For example, the earliest start date for arc e is 3 and the earliest end date is 8. However, the earliest date for event (node) D is 11 because the network has two arcs that enter node D, namely, arc e and arc d. Thus the earliest occurrence date of this event (node) must be equal to the latest possible end date of the entering activities. The number in the right half is the result of the backward pass through the network.

The backward pass calculates the latest start date and end date for each activity (arc), and the latest completion date for each event (node). This calculation is the reverse of the forward calculation, in that the times of the different activities are subtracted from the end activity. In the backward pass, when two arcs are leaving one node, diverge, and go to two different nodes, the smallest result is taken, and the calculation continues along the network. For example, arcs d and c enters node C. Arc d comes from node D; arc c comes from node E. Arc d has a time of 6,

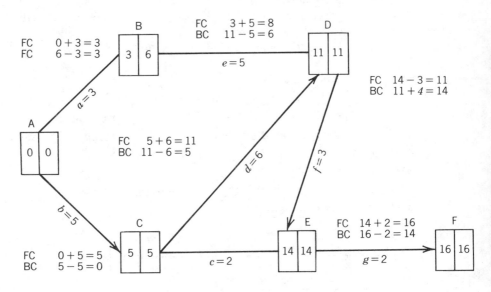

$5 + 2 = \ 7$ Forward calculation (FC)
$14 - 2 = 12$ Backward calculation (BC)

Figure 8.11. Critical path.

and node D has the latest date of 11, therefore, $11 - 6 = 5$. Arc c has a time of 2, and node E has the latest date of 14, therefore $14 - 2 = 12$. Since the smallest result is taken, the result of calculating the latest date for arc d, which is 5, is used as the latest date for event or node C.

After the forward and backward calculations are completed and the earliest and latest dates for each node are determined, then the two numbers are subtracted from one another to obtain the slack time. For example, in node B, if the two numbers are subtracted, a time of 3 is obtained. In events or nodes C, D, E, the two numbers in each box are the same and the result of the subtraction is zero. For these events there is no slack time, and these are known as critical events in the project. A chain is formed (arc with arrows) through the network from beginning to end, connecting those nodes that have no slack time. This chain is known as the critical path. To determine the basic assumptions inherent in the CPM computer model, it is necessary to evaluate the logic structure of the model and what kind of flexibility and constraints result from the logic structure. If the CPM model allows only AND ALL node logic (see Section 8.3.1), then all the project activities must to be completed successfully for the project to be completed successfully. This is a very restrictive assumption and is basically valid for projects that have well-defined tasks or activities, such as building construction, manufacturing, and assembly projects. This assumption does not allow for the failure of an activity.

All activities are required to complete successfully or the entire project will fail. This assumption is valid for a construction project where, for example, the activity of constructing the foundation must be completed successfully or the project will fail. However, this assumption does not allow for a realistic representation of a research and development project when there is a degree of uncertainty associated with activities. For example, in the R&D project shown in Figure 8.4, there are two wing designs. If wing design A fails to complete successfully, it would be unrealistic for the entire project to fail. Another characteristic of the CPM deterministic logic is that it allows for only one point estimate, a single value input. This value is usually a time value. If only one time value per activity (arc) is permitted, then CPM possesses the inherent assumption that activity completion times are known with certainty. Therefore computer models that use only CPM network analysis make two basic assumptions:

1. All activities have a 100% likelihood of accuracy and completing successfully.
2. All activity completion times are known with certainty.

These two assumptions tend to produce results that are optimistically biased and, therefore, of questionable accuracy for most projects that have any degree of uncertainty. However, these assumptions are basically valid for projects that are highly repetitive and whose activities and activities completion times are known with certainty, such as Du Pont's construction project.

The primary objective of CPM is to manage schedule risk by establishing the shortest program schedule possible and determining the critical path. Once the program schedule and critical path is determined, the schedule risk is managed by monitoring project activity times and applying necessary funds or resources to maintain the schedule. Obviously this kind of risk assessment and management is effective when the primary management goal is to bring the project in on schedule. However, CPM does not address cost or performance risk associated with a project and may have the adverse result of cost overruns and failure to meet technical performance criteria.

Most CPM computer networks do not require a high degree of computer sophistication to operate because of the deterministic characteristics of the model. Inputs are usually activity names and times and are usually entered in sequential order based on activity flow throughout the network. Most CPM network models are user-friendly and produce GANTT charts with the critical path defined, as well as activity names, times, and slack times. More sophisticated programs will also give a network drawing option. Almost every computer made either comes with a CPM program or has a CPM program that can be purchased separately. For information about CPM program availability for a particular computer, it is best to consult the computer hardware vendor.

8.3.1.3 Program Evaluation and Review Technique (PERT). The

program evaluation and review technique (PERT) was developed by the Navy [13] for the Polaris ballistic missile program in 1958 and was utilized in planning, scheduling, and controlling the project. The PERT network model is based on the CPM network model. It has the same deterministic logic structure (AND ALL logic). Therefore the same basic assumption that all activities must complete successfully for the project to complete is also true for the PERT model. However, PERT does not require that all activity completion times be known with certainty. In PERT, activity times can be entered as a triangular distribution using a minimum, a most likely, and a maximum time for each activity. This gives a probabilistic nature to the activity completion time. However, the probability associated with the completion time is statistically determined using a beta distribution. Although PERT allows a more realistic representation of a project then does CPM, it is still limited by its deterministic node logic which requires the successful completion of every activity. Therefore, PERT, like CPM, is unable to represent realistically any project in which there is a degree of uncertainty associated with an activity's successful completion.

A successor to PERT is PERT/COST, in which the minimum cost path through the network is established. Like PERT, PERT/COST still assumes the successful completion of every activity, but it does allow a cost risk assessment to be determined. Although PERT and PERT/COST do allow variation in schedule and/or cost risk associated with an activity, this variation is usually based on average, and sometimes extreme, values, which may bias the results and reduce the credibility of the risk assessment. Like CPM, the use of PERT or PERT/COST as a management tool has a narrow perspective; PERT and PERT/COST do not take into account technical performance risk or identify the risk associated with the failure of an activity. Furthermore, CPM, PERT, and PERT/COST identify only one single longest path (critical path) through the network. In reality, a project may have a number of near-critical paths which, depending on the variability associated with the time and cost estimate, may have a large probability of becoming a critical path element. The probability that an activity may be on the critical path is known as activity criticality. Thus, depending on the complexity of the project, the use of these models as risk assessment techniques may result in a significant error in the assessment of project risk.

Like the CPM computer programs, most PERT programs do not require a high degree of computer sophistication to operate. Most programs are user-friendly, offering easy data base construction and editing. PERT programs require more data elements to be entered than the CPM model because of the probabilistic nature of the activity cost and/or times. Most PERT programs produce GANTT charts with the critical path defined, in addition to activity times and/or costs, slack values, and in some cases a network drawing. PERT programs are available for almost every type of computer. For information about the PERT programs available for a particular computer hardware, it is best to consult the computer hardware vendor.

8.3.1.4 ARTEMIS Probabilistic Analysis of Network (PAN). The ARTEMIS system's probabilistic analysis of networks (PAN) is available through METIER Management Systems, Inc. [14]. PAN is similar to PERT in that it uses deterministic node logic (see Section 8.3.1). However, unlike PERT, PAN uses a Monte Carlo simulator to determine the uncertainty of time and/or cost to arrive at program risk. PAN is primarily a schedule-oriented risk model whereby cost uncertainty can be established either by using network resource aggregation or generated independent of the network. Because PAN utilizes the ARTEMIS relational data base concept, an interrelationship between time and cost can be established by mathematical options available in the ARTEMIS system. Unlike PERT, PAN gives an activity "criticality" index (see Section 8.3.1.3) which is important in identifying the near critical path of a project.

The ARTEMIS PAN model has certain advantages over the PERT models. It offers the representation of time and/or cost uncertainty using Monte Carlo simulation and three different distributions, which gives a more realistic view of program risk. PAN also has a relational data base that can be used to integrate input and output data into other ARTEMIS programs and offers easy network restructuring and development of mathematical relationships. In addition, PAN offers the development of aggregated resources per activity which can be used to cost and track these resources. However, the flexibility and effective utilization of the ARTEMIS system and PAN requires a higher degree of computer sophistication than most PERT models. To utilize the power and capability of the system effectively, the user should have some programming knowledge and/or experience. However, the system does offer "help" internal to the operation of the system, and, because of the programming type of command language, it offers a great deal of user flexibility in structuring and retrieving information produced from a PAN simulation [14, 15].

Using the NETWORK portion of ARTEMIS, one designs the model of the system or project under study and enters information such as nodes, activities, and durations. The system then uses CPM to determine the critical path through the network by calculating the early start, late start, early finish, and late finish for each node and the total and free float for each activity. Any activity that has no total float associated with it is situated on the critical path or paths (since there may be more than one critical path). A network plot can be generated from the input and computed data, which is a very good tool to use in visualizing how the various activities and nodes are interrelated and to see the critical path(s).

To be able to perform the risk analysis of the program, a little more information is required. Instead of the single time estimate used in the network portion of ARTEMIS, PAN (probabilistic analysis of networks) requires a time distribution to reflect the uncertainty of an activity duration. The time duration may take one of four forms: point, uniform, normal, or triangular. Figure 8.12 illustrates these distributions. In the case of the normal and triangular distributions, a variation from the standard definitions is used. Instead of the normal and triangular distributions being symmetric about the mean, they can be skewed to the left or the right by definition. This may yield a beta or other type distribution in form, but they will still be categorized as normal and triangular distributions. As can be seen from Figure 8.12 the point distribution is defined by a single estimate, in other words, the analyst is certain that an activity will be of a certain duration. In the case of the uniform distribution, two estimates are required. An optimistic estimate is defined as the time it will take to perform the activity if everything goes right. A pessimistic estimate is defined as the time required to perform the activity if tasks were to take the longest time (not including some catastrophic event such as an earthquake, but including rain and other such delays). Three estimates are required for the normal and triangular distributions. In addition to the optimistic and pessimistic times, a most likely time is necessary and is defined as the time the activity "probably" will take to complete its task.

As stated previously, a Monte Carlo procedure is used to determine the probability of a program finishing on time. The procedure for this is as follows:

1. Cumulative distribution functions (CDF) are generated for each activity based on the probability density function specified previously.
2. Random numbers are generated and applied to the CDF to arrive at a single time estimate for each activity.
3. The network procedure described earlier is applied to the network with the randomly generated durations, and data are retained on the early and late starts, and late finishes, and whether an activity fell on the critical path.
4. This sequence is repeated for a specified number of repetitions and data are collected on the number of times that an activity fell on the critical path (critically index), and cumulative data on the information collected in step 3.
5. Reports are generated using the collected data to help managers determine risk associated with a program [16].

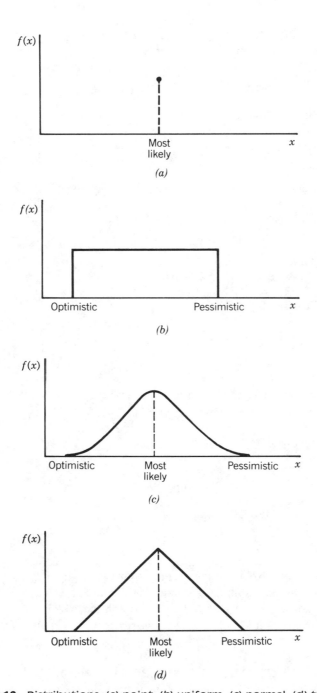

Figure 8.12. Distributions; (*a*) point, (*b*) uniform, (*c*) normal, (*d*) triangular.

The PAN model offers both prompted data entry and unprompted data entry as shown in the example from reference [14]. If prompted data entry is used, the user must use the FORMAT subcommand and must also define which fields will be entered on which line on the computer screen.

```
*ENTER NETWORK
 >FORMAT
   :PE SE DU
   :AD
   :F1 F2 F4
   :D1 D2 D3 TY
   :END
 >SWITCH PROMPT ON
 >DATA

 PE=Z1032 SE=Z1045 DU=36
 AD=REVIEW TRANSFER DESIGN
 F1=SITEA F2=RR21 F4=CNST
 D1=34 D2=37 D3=42 TY=2

 PE=
   :
   :
```

If unprompted data entry is used, data can be entered on a S line or on a B line as follows:

```
*ENTER NETWORK
 >DATA
   :A ZY942 ZX304 142
   :D CONNECT PART 2 SUBSYSTEM
   :F RDES
   :S TY=1 D1=135 D2=145
     :
     :
```

Examples of the PAN input data list are shown in Figure 8.13. An example of the PAN time-phased output data is shown in Figure 8.14.

The PAN software is available only for use on the ARTEMIS system, which utilizes Hewlett Packard hardware sold and serviced through METIER Management Systems, Inc.

8.3.1.5 Risk Information System and Network Evaluation Technique (RISNET).

The Risk Information System and Network Evaluation Technique (RISNET) is a proprietary model developed by John M. Cockerham and Associates, Inc. [17]. The RISNET model is a stochastic and deterministic network analysis program in two versions, RISNET I and RISNET II.

Unlike CPM and PERT models, RISNET integrates cost and schedule by al-

SE*	DESCRIPTION	TYPE NODE	DURATION	OPTIMISTIC	MOST LIKELY	PESSIMISTIC	TYP DIST
	RQMTS STUDY GO AHEAD	STA	-	-	-	-	-
1010	RQMTS STUDY		252	245	252	270	2
	RQMTS STUDY COMPLETE		-	-	-	-	-
1020	GVMT PROPOSAL EVAL		252	245	252	262	2
	CONTRACT GO AHEAD		-	-	-	-	-
1030	STUDIES/SIM		86	80	86	100	3
1050	SYS ENG SUPPORT		310	300	310	330	2
2010	LAUNCHER RQMTS		64	55	64	70	2
3010	DEFINE BOOSTER RQMTS		64	55	64	70	2
4010	DEFINE ELECT RQMTS		64	60	64	75	2
5010	DEFINE SENSOR RQMTS		86	80	86	100	2
6010	DEFINE DP RQMTS		86	80	86	100	2
7010	DEFINE SP RQMTS		86	80	86	95	2
8010	S/W ANALYSIS		126	120	126	150	2
10000	PROJECT MGMT		1260	1250	1260	1270	2
1021	DUMMY	DUM	-	-	-	-	-
10000	GVMT PROJ SUPPORT		1260	1250	1260	1270	2
	SDR		-	-	-	-	-
1040	STUDIES/SIM		86	80	86	100	2
1050	INTERFACE ID&DEF		214	200	214	230	2
	PDR		-	-	-	-	-
1050	STUDIES/SIM		126	120	126	135	2
	CDR		-	-	-	-	-
1060	PREP REPORT		86	70	86	90	2
2020	DUMMY	DUM	-	-	-	-	-
	IT&E PLANS & RQMTS		-	-	-	-	-
2040	DUMMY	DUM	-	-	-	-	-
1070	DUMMY	DUM	-	-	-	-	-
1080	DUMMY	DUM	-	-	-	-	-
1090	TAC DEV PLAN		42	35	42	45	2
1090	TECH DEV PLAN		42	35	45	-	1
1090	FLT TEST PLAN		42	35	45	-	1
	PLANS COMPLETE		-	-	-	-	-
1100	SUPPORT MFG		338	330	338	360	3
	BEGIN FLT SUPPORT		-	-	-	-	-
1110	FLT SUPPORT		504	500	504	515	2
			-	-	-	-	-

*Selected Event Code Number

Figure 8.13. PAN input data list.

lowing each activity to carry a fixed cost, a variable cost coefficient, and time information. The fixed cost of an activity is usually a one-time expenditure, such as a material or equipment cost. The variable cost coefficient is usually a recurring cost, such as for labor or rent which is related to the activity's duration. Time is the length of time it takes to complete the activity. The cost of an activity is a function of time where

$$c = a + b^t \tag{8.2}$$

$$\text{total cost} = \text{fixed cost} + \begin{bmatrix} \text{variable} \\ \text{cost} \\ \text{coefficient} \end{bmatrix} \times \text{time} \tag{8.3}$$

SE*	DESCRIPTION	TYPE NODE	DURATION	OPTIMISTIC	MOST LIKELY	PESSIMISTIC	TYP DIST
10000	PREP FINAL RPT		64	55	65	–	1
	LAUNCHER SDR		–	–	–	–	–
2020	LAUNCHER DESIGN		86	70	86	90	2
	DESIGN CMPLT		–	–	–	–	–
2030	DUMMY	DUM	–	–	–	–	–
2040	DUMMY	DUM	–	–	–	–	–
2060	FAB LAUNCH EQPMT		252	240	252	260	2
2060	MFG SUPPORT		252	240	252	260	2
2050	DUMMY	DUM	–	–	–	–	–
2060	FAB NTSE		200	180	200	210	2
2060	FAB C3 INTERFACE		200	190	200	220	2
	FAB COMPLETE		–	–	–	–	–
9020	SHIP TO KMR		10	–	–	–	–
	BOOSTER SDR		–	–	–	–	–
3020	ADAPTOR DESIGN		86	65	90	–	1
3030	PROCURE BOOSTER1		176	170	176	180	2
	DESIGN CMPLT		–	–	–	–	–
3030	FAB ADAPTOR1		42	40	42	50	2
3070	ENG SUPPORT		326	315	326	330	2
	TEST H/W CMPLT		–	–	–	–	–
3040	TEST		42	40	42	50	2
	TEST CMPLT		–	–	–	–	–
3050	DUMMY	DUM	–	–	–	–	–
3060	FAB ADAPTORS		200	190	200	220	2
3060	PROCURE BOOSTERS		200	190	200	210	2
	HDWR CMPLT		–	–	–	–	–
3070	IA&CO		42	40	42	55	2
	BOOSTER S/S COMPLETE		–	–	–	–	–

*Selected Event Code Number

Figure 8.13. (*Continued*)

In RISNET I, the fixed cost, the variable cost coefficient, and the activity time can be determined by the following distributions:

1. Triangular
2. Normal
3. Uniform
4. Constant
5. Exponential
6. Weibull
7. Quadratic
8. Cumulative
9. Discrete
10. Triangular—exponential
11. Exponential—triangular

When RISNET is operated as a probabilistic network model, it uses a Monte Carlo simulation technique which samples each input distribution (fixed cost, variable cost coefficient and time) and calculates $c = a + b^t$ for each activity. When

PAN PROBABILISTIC ANALYSIS

2 APRIL 1985

RESULT OF   100 SIMULATIONS

PREC. EVENT	SUCC. EVENT	DESCRIPTION	CRIT. INDEX	EARLIEST EARLY FINISH	LATEST EARLY FINISH	RANGE OF EARLY FINISH DATES
1000		RQMTS STUDY GO AHEAD	1.00	28.JUN.85	28.JUN.85	I* (JAN 85)
1000	1010	RQMTS STUDY	1.00	23.JUN.86	24.JUL.86	I** (JAN 86)
1010	1020	RQMTS STUDY COMPLETE	1.00	23.JUN.86	24.JUL.86	I** (JAN 86)
1010	1020	GVMT PROPOSAL EVAL CONTRACT	1.00	22.JUN.87	21.JUL.87	I** (JAN 87)
1020		GO AHEAD	1.00	22.JUN.87	21.JUL.87	I** (JAN 87)
1020	2010	LAUNCHER RQMTS	--	14.SEP.87	20.OCT.87	**I (JAN 87)
2010	3010	LAUNCHER SDR	--	14.SEP.87	20.OCT.87	**I (JAN 87)
1020	3010	DEFINE BOOSTER RQMTS	--	16.SEP.87	22.OCT.87	**I (JAN 87)
3010	4010	BOOSTER SDR	--	16.SEP.87	26.OCT.87	**I (JAN 87)
1020	4010	DEFINE ELECT RQMTS	--	23.SEP.87	26.OCT.87	**I (JAN 87)
4010	5010	ELECT SDR	0.61	23.SEP.87	1.DEC.87	*I (JAN 87)
1020	5010	DEFINE SENSOR RQMTS	0.61	20.OCT.87	1.DEC.87	*I (JAN 87)
5010	7010	SENSOR SDR	0.10	20.OCT.87	23.NOV.87	*I (JAN 87)
1020	7010	DEFINE SP RQMTS	0.10	22.OCT.87	23.NOV.87	*I (JAN 87)
7010		SP SDR	--	22.OCT.87	8.DEC.87	*I (JAN 87)
1020	1030	STUDIES/SIM	--	22.OCT.87	30.NOV.87	*I (JAN 87)
1030		SDR	--	22.OCT.87	30.NOV.87	*I (JAN 87)
1020	6010	DEFINE DP RQMTS	0.36	26.OCT.87	5.FEB.88	*I (JAN 87)
6010		DP SDR	0.36	26.OCT.87	28.JAN.88	*I (JAN 87)
1020	8010	S/W ANALYSIS	1.00	24.DEC.87	28.JAN.88	**I (JAN 88)
4010	4020	PRELIM DESIGN	--	28.DEC.87	29.FEB.88	**I (JAN 88)
4020		ELECT PDR	--	28.DEC.87	29.FEB.88	**I (JAN 88)
3010	3020	ADAPTOR DESIGN	--	5.JAN.88	23.FEB.88	* (JAN 88)
3020		DESIGN CMPLT	--	5.JAN.88	1.APR.88	* (JAN 88)
2010	2020	LAUNCHER DESIGN	0.61	8.JAN.88	1.APR.88	* (JAN 88)
5010	5020	PRELIM DESIGN	0.61	23.FEB.88	1.APR.88	** (JAN 88)
5020		SENSOR PDR	0.36	24.FEB.88	1.APR.88	** (JAN 88)
6010	6020	PRELIM DESIGN	0.36	25.FEB.88	1.APR.88	** (JAN 88)
6020		DP PDR	0.10	25.FEB.88	4.APR.88	** (JAN 88)
7010	7020	PRELIM DESIGN	0.10	25.FEB.88	4.APR.88	** (JAN 88)
7020		SP PDR	--	25.FEB.88	18.APR.88	** (JAN 88)
1030	1040	STUDIES/SIM	--	2.MAR.88	18.APR.88	** (JAN 88)

Range of early finish dates chart axis: JAN 84, JAN 85, JAN 86, JAN 87, JAN 88, JAN 89, JAN 90, JAN 91, JAN 92, JAN 93, JAN 94, JAN 95.

Figure 8.14. Network criticality index and spread of early finishes.

281

RISNET is operated as a deterministic network model, the most likely value is used in the total cost calculation.

RISNET II, unlike RISNET I, limits the distribution for fixed and variable costs to triangular, normal, uniform, and constant. However, in RISNET II each activity can have as many as 20 different funding categories or resource allocations, each of which having its own linear cost relationship, as shown in Figure 8.15. The activities total cost is the sum of all funding category costs (Activity 1 total cost $= C_N$). The activity has its own time distribution t_1, the same time distributions as in RISNET I, and the risk analyst also has the option of using the activity time distribution in calculating each funding category's total cost. This gives the risk analyst the option of accounting for time uncertainties associated with particular funding categories or resources. For example, one activity may have two or more types of labor associated with it, such as two senior analysts, whose time on the particular activity may vary, and thus the cost of the two funding categories will vary. However, the use of a time distribution for calculating funding category cost that is different from the time distribution used to calculate the activity time can destroy the linear relation between the time and cost for that activity. Thus the time used to calculate the funding categories may have little relationship to the actual activity time. Therefore these funding categories can best be used to account for cost estimating uncertainty and not time uncertainty. Thus, even though the option is available to use a time distribution different from the activity time, it is not recommended and could cause errors in the interrelationship between activity time and cost.

Unlike CPM and PERT models, both RISNET models have deterministic and probabilistic node logic (see Section 8.3.1) which is useful in approximating real-world decision situations that occur in complex projects. For information on RIS-NET node logic see reference [17]. The probabilistic node logic is used to represent the uncertainty that occurs in the decision process associated with complex project events, such as a particular wing design being accepted or rejected. As with event uncertainty, there are also activity uncertainties. For example, whether an activity will complete successfully or be logically eliminated, fail to be initi-

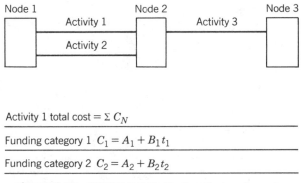

Figure 8.15. RISNET II activity funding categories.

ated, or fail to complete. These are all uncertainties related to an activity. CPM and PERT allow only for successful completion of an activity, whereas RISNET and other probabilistic models account for the uncertainty of activity completion. By combining probabilistic and deterministic node logic, arc probability, and cost and time uncertainty with a Monte Carlo simulation, RISNET network models effectively represent the cost and schedule risk associated with most complex projects. Both RISNET models also output each arc's criticality, which provides an analyst with the information needed to determine which arcs or activities have a significant probability of being on the critical path. This ability to identify near-critical paths through the network gives a better perspective of all activities, which may be critical to the project completion and therefore a more flexible risk management tool.

Neither RISNET I nor RISNET II addresses the problem of technical performance uncertainty. In most complex research and development projects there are two types of technical performance uncertainties: One is actually activity and/or event uncertainty. For example, two wing designs may be developed. One wing design may not be accepted because of its technical performance. This type of technical performance uncertainty is really an activity and/or event uncertainty. Whether it meets technical performance requirements is determined either by a probability placed on the activity (see Figure 8.10) or the probability placed on a node (see Figure 8.7). This type of probability is similar to a coin toss, with two alternatives, heads or tails. Another type of technical performance uncertainty is the probability that an activity will fall within a particular range of technical performance. For example, the wing design may have a technical performance criterion that it carry enough fuel to travel 100–150 miles. In the activity/node uncertainty example, the probability that it will fall within the range is 70%, and the probability it will not is 30%, as shown in Figure 8.16. This quantifies the uncertainty that it will or will not fall within the acceptable range, but does not quantify the probability of where within the range it will fall. However, some computer models (see Section 8.3.1.6) do evaluate the technical performance uncertainty associated with a particular activity by giving technical performance a distribution. This type of technical performance risk assessment gives management a three-dimensional view of the risk associated with the project, and the option of managing the time, cost, and technical performance risk associated with the project.

The RISNET models are more sophisticated network models than the CPM and PERT computer models and therefore require more analytical skill and time to develop the network. However, RISNET has a interactive question and answer input program that makes data entry easy, but since the data editing routine is slightly awkward and time-consuming, analysts commonly use the computer system editor to make changes to their data base. The RISNET II version is an interactive user-friendly RISNET model that utilizes a series of screens, prompts, and menus for building the data files, editing data files, simulating the network, and selecting output desired. It also provides the user with data entry help screens if necessary. The RISNET II output module gives the user a large variety of output

Event or node uncertainty

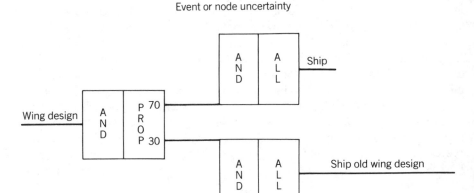

Arc or activity uncertainty

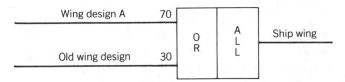

Figure 8.16. Activity/node uncertainty.

options; however, the tree structure of the output menus is difficult to understand and does require time to learn.

The RISNET output module produces graphics terminal output, printer output, and plotter output for deterministic and probabilistic simulations. In RISNET II output is also given for funding categories. Both RISNET models provide cumulative frequency distributions and frequency distributions, for time and cost by total program and for selected network intervals; critical path and arc criticality information; node and arc input information; total risk assessment cost estimate (TRACE) information [18]; fiscal year cost information; node simulation information, and terminal node information. The RISNET II program is well documented and provides an analyst guide and a user's manual.

The RISNET computer model hardware requirements are the following:

1. Hewlett-Packard 1000/A900 computer
2. 3.84 megabyte (mb) memory
3. 400 lines per minute printer (model 2608S)
4. 1600 bpi magnetic tape drive (model 7970E)
5. 65 megabyte (mb) fixed disk drive (model 7912)

6. 404 megabyte (mb) removable disk (model 7935)

7. Color graphics terminal (model 2627A)

8. Plotter (model 9782T).

Software requirements are the following:

1. RTE-A with VC & REV 2326

2. Graphics/1000-11 REV 2326 with both device independent graphics and advanced graphics.

8.3.1.6 Venture Evaluation and Review Technique (VERT). The

venture evaluation and review technique (VERT) network analyses model was developed by Moeller [19]. Like the RISNET models, VERT is a stochastic simulation network model with probabilistic node logic. The VERT model is more mathematically oriented than the RISNET models. VERT has 37 mathematical transformations which can be used to express the relationship between key variables, whereas the RISNET models have one linear relationship between time and cost (see Section 8.3.1.5).

VERT also has the added advantage of incorporating performance values as a risk factor in network evaluation, as shown in Figure 8.17. With VERT an analyst can model time, cost, and performance values and uncertainties for each activity independently of each other using one of the following 16 different statistical distributions available in VERT:

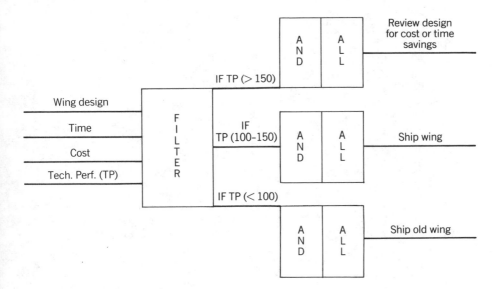

Beta

Binomial

Chi Square

Constant

Erlang

Exponential

Gamma

Geometric

Hypergeometric

Lognormal

Normal

Pascal

Poisson

Triangular

Uniform

Weibull

Activity time, cost, or performance values can be modeled as a function of any other arc's or node's time, cost, or performance parameter in the network using any of the following 37 mathematical transformations or a combination of these transformations:

Code Numbers	Transformation	Restrictions	Notes
1 or 51	$X*Y*Z$	= R	(* Means multiply)
2 or 52	$(X*Y)/Z$	= R Z NE 0.0	(NE means not equal)
3 or 53	$X/(Y*Z)$	= R Y*Z NE 0.0	
4 or 54	$1/(X*Y*Z)$	= R X*Y*Z NE 0.0	
5 or 55	$X+Y+Z$	= R	
6 or 56	$X+Y-Z$	= R	
7 or 57	$X-Y-Z$	= R	
8 or 58	$-X-Y-Z$	= R	
9 or 59	$X*(Y+Z)$	= R	
10 or 60	$X*(Y-Z)$	= R	
11 or 61	$X/(Y+Z)$	= R Y+Z NE 0.0	
12 or 62	$X/(Y-Z)$	= R Y-Z NE 0.0	
13 or 63	$X*(Y)^Z$	= R Y GT 0.0	(GT means greater than)
14 or 64	$X*(LOG_e(Y*Z))$	= R Y*Z GT 0.0	(e = natural log base)
15 or 65	$X*(LOG_{10}(Y*Z))$	= R Y*Z GT 0.0	
16 or 66	$X*(SIN(Y*Z))$	= R	
17 or 67	$X*(COS(Y*Z))$	= R	
18 or 68	$X*(ARCTAN(Y*Z))$	= R	

Code Numbers	Transformation	Restrictions	Notes
19 or 69	X GE Y ------ Z	= R	(GE means greater than or equal to)
	X LT Y ------ Y	= R	(LT means less than)
20 or 70	X GE Y ------ Y	= R	
	X LT Y ------ Z	= R	
21 or 71	X GE Y ------ Z	= R	
	X LT Y ------ X	= R	
22 or 72	X GE Y ------ X	= R	
	X LT Y ------ Z	= R	
23 or 73	(X*Y)+Z	= R	
24 or 74	(X*Y)−Z	= R	
25 or 75	(X/Y)+Z	= R Y NE 0.0	
26 or 76	(X/Y)−Z	= R Y NE 0.0	
27 or 77	(X+Y)*Z	= R	
28 or 78	(X+Y)/Z	= R Z NE 0.0	
29 or 79	(X−Y)*Z	= R	
30 or 80	(X−Y)/Z	= R Z NE 0.0	
31 or 81	X+(Y*Z)	= R	
32 or 82	X−(Y*Z)	= R	
33 or 83	X+(Y/Z)	= R Z NE 0.0	
34 or 84	X−(Y/Z)	= R Z NE 0.0	
35 or 85	−X−Y+Z	= R	
36 or 86	−X+Y+Z	= R	
37 or 87	X/Y/Z	= R Y NE 0.0 Z NE 0.0	

Transformation numbers 1–37 and 51–87 use floating point computations initially to derive a value for R. However, transformations 51–87 truncate R to an integer value whereas transformations 1–37 retain R in its floating point form.

Structuring a mathematical relationship within a VERT network consists of essentially the following three phases:

1. Long or complicated mathematical relationships need to be broken down into a series of three-variable unit transformations shown previously.

2. Values for each of the three variables X, Y, and Z in each single unit transformation must be defined. These values can be retrieved from (1) previously processed arcs or nodes, (2) constants entered on these satellite arc records, or (3) one of the previously processed transformations computed in the current series of transformations used to generate a time value for the current arc under consideration. Values calculated for each time transformation are consecutively, temporarily stored in a one-dimensional array. This enables retrieving the value calculated for a prior transformation for use in the current unit transformation. On completion of all the unit time transformations for a given arc, this temporary storage array is cleared. Thus only the values calculated for previously derived unit time transformations

developed for the current arc under consideration can be referenced. When retrieving numerical values from a previously processed arc or node, the time, cost, or performance value calculated for the referenced node or the primary (not cumulative) time, cost, or performance value generated for the referenced arc is retrieved.

3. Results of each of the unit transformations needed to develop a value for an arc's time can be either summed into the overall time value generated for the arc under consideration or it can be omitted. When the resulting value of a unit transformation is omitted, this transformation is generally an intermediate step for calculating the value of a long or complicated mathematical relationship.

TRANSFORMATION EXAMPLE. Suppose the value for the performance of a given arc is related to the time, cost, and performance values generated on this arc and other previously processed arcs and nodes as follows:

$$PA10 = \frac{(PA1 + PA2 + PA3)^*}{(PA4 * PA5 * PA6)} (TA1)^*(LOG_e(CA1 * CA2))$$

$$+ (188.6^* \frac{(TA10)}{(CA10)} + (15.8)^*(TN1) \qquad (8.4)$$

where TN1 = the time value for the node N1
    TA1 = the time value for the arc A1
   TA10 = the time value for the arc A10
    CA1 = the cost value for the arc A1
    CA2 = the cost value for the arc A2
   CA10 = the cost value for the arc A10
    PA1 = the performance value for the arc A1
    PA2 = the performance value for the arc A2
    PA3 = the performance value for the arc A3
    PA4 = the performance value for the arc A4
    PA5 = the performance value for the arc A5
    PA6 = the performance value for the arc A6
   PA10 = the performance value for the arc A10

The following dimensioned record layouts illustrate how the preceding equation is put into record form.

A10	RPERF 1 50 PA1	PA2	PA3	Trans. No. 1
A10	RPERF 2 40PA4	PA5	PA6	Trans. No. 2
A10	RPERF 3140TA1	CA1	CA2	Trans. No. 3
A10	RPERF 4 1S 1.0	2.0	3.0	Trans. No. 4
A10	RPERF 5 2SK188.6	TA10	CA10	Trans. No. 5
A10	RPERF 6 1SK15.8	TN1	K1.0	Trans. No. 6

The preceding layout illustrates that the foregoing equation can be modeled by using six sequential transformations. The first three transformations compute the values for (PA1 + PA2 + PA3), (1/(PA4 * PA5 * PA6)) and ((TA1)* (LOG$_e$(CA1 * CA2)), respectively. The letter "O" in these transformations indicates that the resultant value of each of these transformations is not summed in the performance value for arc A10. However, transformation number 4 is summed into the resulting performance value of arc A10. It pulls these three previously derived values together to derive a composite value for the first major term of the equation. Transformations 5 and 6 compute the values for the second and third terms of the equation. These values are summed directly into the resulting performance value calculated for arc A10. For more information on VERT capabilities see reference [19].

VERT allows the user to tie together mathematically any two points within the network, as well as to establish a variety of mathematical relationships between time, cost, or performance values for any given arc. Since these features are not found in the other network analysis models discussed here, VERT is an extremely powerful and flexible network-modeling risk-assessment tool for representing realistically the complex management decision problems and uncertainty associated with today's research and development projects. In general, the VERT model provides the same probabilistic printer output as the RISNET model, as well as the beta 2 measure of kurtosis and the pearsonian measure of skewness. The VERT model has been expanded by reference [20] to give fiscal year cost information, as shown in Figure 8.18, and cost by month, as shown in Figure 8.19. This cost information can be sorted according to budgetary coding structure as defined in a Department of Army pamphlet (DA PAM 11-2, 3, 4) and by WBS elements, or in the reverse order, thus establishing a crosswalk between budgetary requirements and program tracking. Another advantage of VERT is its ability to produce a total life cycle cost estimate by which various project alternatives' cost, schedule, and performance can be compared. Figures 8.20, and 8.21 show the comparison of three various helicopter programs varying in the rotor and transmission utilized. Thus each helicopter case had varying cost, schedule, and technical performance A_0. As shown in Figure 8.20, schedule and performance variance between programs were small; however, the cost variance was quite large. This cost variance was primarily due to the relationship between performance A_0 and operating and support cost (O&S). As A_0 or availability decreased, O&S increased as shown in Figure 8.21. If performance had not been integrated into the cost and schedule relationship, this cost variance might have been overlooked in evaluating the helicopter alternatives. As shown in Figure 8.22, VERT provides all the necessary information required for a three-dimensional risk assessment of a project cost, schedule, and technical performance. VERT also offers the project manager a tool by which one integrated data base can be used to plan the program; estimate the cost, schedule, and technical performance of the program; estimate the risk of the program; and track the program, as shown in Figure 8.23.

The VERT model does not require a high degree of computer sophistication to operate; however, the VERT input is in 80-column record format, which usually requires more time to create and edit to the data file. The VERT model is written

PROGRAM COSTS   (IN MILLIONS)

		1984	1985	1986	1987	1988	1989	1990	1991	1992	1993
TOTAL SYSTEM	1.0000000	5.4946	64.5578	144.3939	74.1650	135.2251	56.7522	33.9817	23.0245	23.0245	23.0245
RDT&E	1.0100000	5.4946	55.6737	0.0000	0.0000	0.0000	0.0000	0.0000	0.0000	0.0000	0.0000
DEV ENG	1.0110000	1.9475	49.5587	0.0000	0.0000	0.0000	0.0000	0.0000	0.0000	0.0000	0.0000
CONTRACTS	1.0110000	1.9475	49.5587	0.0000	0.0000	0.0000	0.0000	0.0000	0.0000	0.0000	0.0000
ROTOR	1.0110100	0.1721	0.0000	0.0000	0.0000	0.0000	0.0000	0.0000	0.0000	0.0000	0.0000
ROTOR A	10- 2- 2- 1	0.1721	0.0000	0.0000	0.0000	0.0000	0.0000	0.0000	0.0000	0.0000	0.0000
TRANS	1.0110200	0.1240	49.3704	0.0000	0.0000	0.0000	0.0000	0.0000	0.0000	0.0000	0.0000
TRANS A	10- 2- 3- 1	0.1240	0.0054	0.0000	0.0000	0.0000	0.0000	0.0000	0.0000	0.0000	0.0000
	10- 2- 3- 2	0.0000	49.3650	0.0000	0.0000	0.0000	0.0000	0.0000	0.0000	0.0000	0.0000
ENGIN PROC	1.0110300	0.2250	0.0000	0.0000	0.0000	0.0000	0.0000	0.0000	0.0000	0.0000	0.0000
ENGINE PROCURE	10- 2- 1- 1	0.2250	0.0000	0.0000	0.0000	0.0000	0.0000	0.0000	0.0000	0.0000	0.0000
AIRFRAME	1.0110400	0.8760	0.0840	0.0000	0.0000	0.0000	0.0000	0.0000	0.0000	0.0000	0.0000
AIRFRAME PROC	10- 1- 1- 0	0.8760	0.0840	0.0000	0.0000	0.0000	0.0000	0.0000	0.0000	0.0000	0.0000
AVIONICS	1.0110500	0.1800	0.0000	0.0000	0.0000	0.0000	0.0000	0.0000	0.0000	0.0000	0.0000
AVIONICS A	10- 5- 1- 1	0.1800	0.0000	0.0000	0.0000	0.0000	0.0000	0.0000	0.0000	0.0000	0.0000
ADAPTER	1.0110600	0.0828	0.0972	0.0000	0.0000	0.0000	0.0000	0.0000	0.0000	0.0000	0.0000
ADAPTOR A	10- 5- 2- 1	0.0828	0.0972	0.0000	0.0000	0.0000	0.0000	0.0000	0.0000	0.0000	0.0000
WARHEAD&FUSE	1.0110700	0.2875	0.0071	0.0000	0.0000	0.0000	0.0000	0.0000	0.0000	0.0000	0.0000
WARHEAD	10-13- 1- 1	0.2114	0.0000	0.0000	0.0000	0.0000	0.0000	0.0000	0.0000	0.0000	0.0000
FUSE	10-13- 2- 1	0.0761	0.0000	0.0000	0.0000	0.0000	0.0000	0.0000	0.0000	0.0000	0.0000
ARM INTEG/TEST	10-13- 3- 2	0.0000	0.0071	0.0000	0.0000	0.0000	0.0000	0.0000	0.0000	0.0000	0.0000
PEP	1.0200000	0.0575	0.0000	0.0000	0.0000	0.0000	0.0000	0.0000	0.0000	0.0000	0.0000
CONTRACTS	1.0210000	0.0575	0.0000	0.0000	0.0000	0.0000	0.0000	0.0000	0.0000	0.0000	0.0000
MOD SYS	1.0210100	0.0000	0.0000	0.0000	0.0000	0.0000	0.0000	0.0000	0.0000	0.0000	0.0000
MOD ARMS	1.0210200	0.0575	0.0000	0.0000	0.0000	0.0000	0.0000	0.0000	0.0000	0.0000	0.0000
ARM MODIFIC	10-13- 4- 0	0.0575	0.0000	0.0000	0.0000	0.0000	0.0000	0.0000	0.0000	0.0000	0.0000
TOOLING	1.0300000	0.8418	0.3575	0.0000	0.0000	0.0000	0.0000	0.0000	0.0000	0.0000	0.0000
CONTRACT	1.0310000	0.8418	0.3575	0.0000	0.0000	0.0000	0.0000	0.0000	0.0000	0.0000	0.0000
CONTRACT	1.0311000	0.8418	0.3575	0.0000	0.0000	0.0000	0.0000	0.0000	0.0000	0.0000	0.0000
TOOLING	18- 1- 1- 0	0.8418	0.3575	0.0000	0.0000	0.0000	0.0000	0.0000	0.0000	0.0000	0.0000
PROTO MFG	1.0400000	2.6311	5.6924	0.0000	0.0000	0.0000	0.0000	0.0000	0.0000	0.0000	0.0000

Figure 8.18. Typical program costs.

COST ACCOUNT TITLE YEAR 1986

Title	Code	OCT	NOV	DEC	JAN	FEB	MAR	APR	MAY	JUN	JUL	AUG	SEP	TOTAL
RDT&E	1.0000000	648.90	624.44	538.62	519.77	429.05	321.32	310.95	321.32	284.12	285.15	285.15	275.95	4844.733
DEV ENG	1.0100000	355.75	340.75	244.84	217.08	167.30	140.38	135.86	140.38	111.71	107.83	107.83	104.36	2174.073
CONTRACTS	1.0110000	355.75	340.75	244.84	217.08	167.30	140.38	135.86	140.38	111.71	107.83	107.83	104.36	2174.073
ROTOR	1.0110100	54.78	53.01	54.78	51.54	19.28	21.34	20.66	21.34	4.82	0.00	0.00	0.00	301.545
ROTOR A	10- 2- 2- 1	21.34	20.66	21.34	21.34	19.28	21.34	20.66	21.34	4.82	0.00	0.00	0.00	172.125
ROTOR B	10- 2- 2- 2	33.43	32.35	33.43	30.20	0.00	0.00	0.00	0.00	0.00	0.00	0.00	0.00	129.420
TRANS	1.0110200	0.00	0.00	0.00	0.00	0.00	0.00	0.00	0.00	0.00	38.43	33.43	32.35	124.027
TRANS A	10- 2- 3- 1	0.00	0.00	0.00	0.00	0.00	0.00	0.00	0.00	0.00	33.43	33.43	32.35	124.027
ENGIN PROC	1.0110300	46.50	45.00	46.50	46.50	40.50	0.00	0.00	0.00	24.81	0.00	0.00	0.00	225.000
ENGINE PROCURE	10- 2- 1- 1	46.50	45.00	46.50	46.50	40.50	0.00	0.00	0.00	24.81	0.00	0.00	0.00	225.000
AIRFRAME	1.0110400	74.40	72.00	74.40	74.40	67.20	74.40	72.00	74.40	72.00	74.40	74.40	72.00	876.000
AIRFRAME PROC	10- 1- 1- 0	74.40	72.00	74.40	74.40	67.20	74.40	72.00	74.40	72.00	74.40	74.40	72.00	876.000
AVIONICS	1.0110500	44.64	43.20	44.64	44.64	40.32	44.64	43.20	44.64	10.08	0.00	0.00	0.00	360.000
AVIONICS A	10- 5- 1- 1	22.32	21.60	22.32	22.32	20.16	22.32	21.60	22.32	5.04	0.00	0.00	0.00	180.000
AVIONICS B	10- 5- 1- 2	22.32	21.60	22.32	22.32	20.16	22.32	21.60	22.32	5.04	0.00	0.00	0.00	180.000
ADAPTER	1.0110600	0.00	0.00	0.00	0.00	0.00	0.00	0.00	0.00	0.00	0.00	0.00	0.00	0.000
WARHEAD&FUSE	1.0110700	135.44	127.54	24.52	0.00	0.00	0.00	0.00	0.00	0.00	0.00	0.00	0.00	287.500
WARHEAD	10-13- 1- 1	109.22	102.18	0.00	0.00	0.00	0.00	0.00	0.00	0.00	0.00	0.00	0.00	211.400
FUSE	10-13- 2- 1	26.21	25.37	24.52	0.00	0.00	0.00	0.00	0.00	0.00	0.00	0.00	0.00	76.100
PEP	1.0200000	0.00	0.00	0.00	0.00	0.00	0.00	0.00	0.00	0.00	0.00	0.00	0.00	0.000
CONTRACTS	1.0210000	0.00	0.00	0.00	0.00	0.00	0.00	0.00	0.00	0.00	0.00	0.00	0.00	0.000
MOD SYS	1.0210100	0.00	0.00	0.00	0.00	0.00	0.00	0.00	0.00	0.00	0.00	0.00	0.00	0.000
MOD ARMS	1.0210200	0.00	0.00	0.00	0.00	0.00	0.00	0.00	0.00	0.00	0.00	0.00	0.00	0.000
TOOLING	1.0300000	0.00	0.00	0.00	0.00	0.00	0.00	0.00	0.00	0.00	0.00	0.00	0.00	0.000
CONTRACT	1.0310000	0.00	0.00	0.00	0.00	0.00	0.00	0.00	0.00	0.00	0.00	0.00	0.00	0.000
CONTRACT	1.0311000	0.00	0.00	0.00	0.00	0.00	0.00	0.00	0.00	0.00	0.00	0.00	0.00	0.000
PROTO MFG	1.0400000	293.15	283.69	293.15	292.79	257.92	180.93	175.10	180.93	172.41	177.31	177.31	171.59	2656.286
CONTRACTS	1.0410000	293.15	283.69	293.15	292.79	257.92	180.93	175.10	180.93	172.41	177.31	177.31	171.59	2656.286
ROTORS	1.0410100	6.09	5.89	6.09	5.73	2.14	2.37	2.29	2.37	0.54	0.00	0.00	0.00	33.505
ROTOR A	10- 2- 2- 1	2.37	2.29	2.37	2.37	2.14	2.37	2.29	2.37	0.54	0.00	0.00	0.00	19.125
ROTOR B	10- 2- 2- 2	3.71	3.60	3.71	3.36	0.00	0.00	0.00	0.00	0.00	0.00	0.00	0.00	14.380
TRANS	1.0410200	0.00	0.00	0.00	0.00	0.00	0.00	0.00	0.00	2.76	3.71	3.71	3.59	13.781
TRANS A	10- 2- 3- 1	0.00	0.00	0.00	0.00	0.00	0.00	0.00	0.00	2.76	3.71	3.71	3.59	13.781
ENGIN PROC	1.0410300	108.50	105.00	108.50	108.50	94.50	0.00	0.00	0.00	0.00	0.00	0.00	0.00	525.000
ENGINE PROCURE	10- 2- 1- 1	108.50	105.00	108.50	108.50	94.50	0.00	0.00	0.00	0.00	0.00	0.00	0.00	525.000

Figure 8.19. Typical cost breakdown.

291

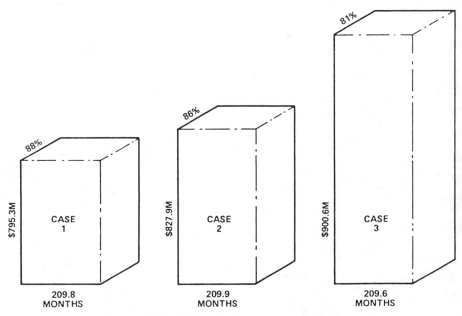

Figure 8.20. Helicopter program alternatives.

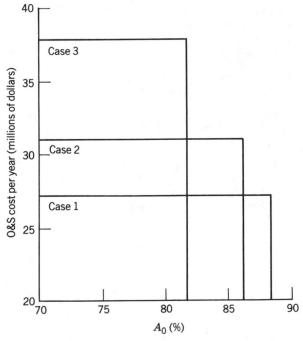

Figure 8.21. O&S cost per year versus A_0 (80% probability).

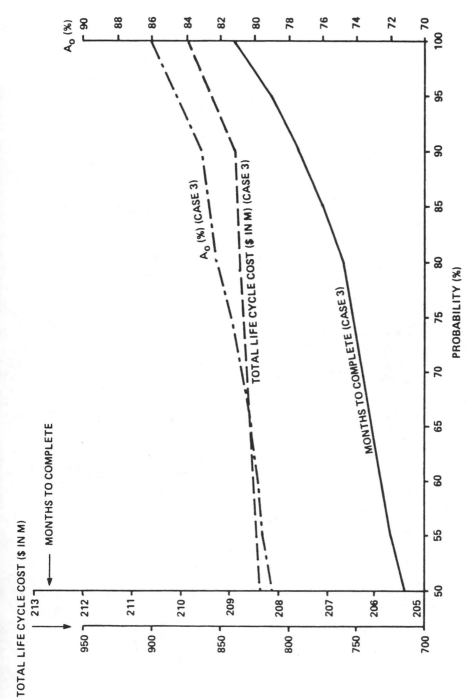

Figure 8.22. Cost/time A versus probability case 3 (standard rotor/standard transmission).

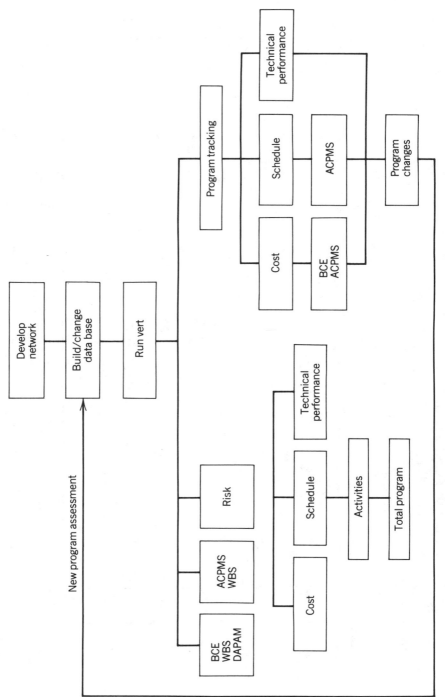

Figure 8.23. Program management using VERT.

in FORTRAN IV and is transportable to most computers, and it is currently operational on IBM, VAX 11/780, CDC, and PRIME computers.

8.3.2 Decision Risk Analysis Method

In the network analysis method of risk assessment, a project is viewed from an activity/event perspective. The uncertainties of time, cost, and technical performance are quantified probabilistically, giving a manager information on the risk associated with a project. The decision risk analysis method, on the other hand, quantifies the risk involved in the decision making process, taking into account a decision manager's pattern of performances. In network analysis, only those activities/events directly related to the project are considered. In decision risk analysis, the interrelationship of events both within and external to the project are considered.

One method of examining this interrelationship is the development of a decision tree consisting of decisions and chance events, as shown in Figure 8.24. The

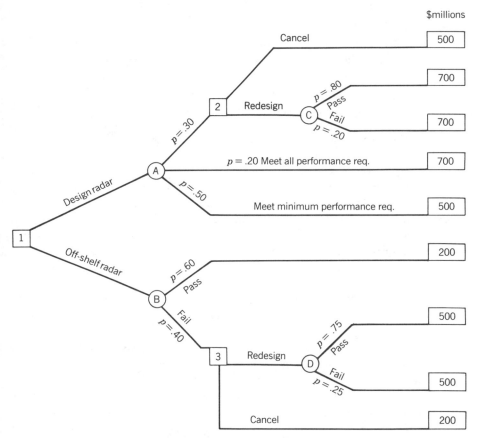

Figure 8.24. Decision tree.

squares on the decision tree represent decisions; the circles represent chance events [11, 21, 22]. In this example, the left-hand square 1 represents the decision between designing a new radar system for air defense or adapting an already available radar system (off-the shelf system). Circles A and B represent test programs followed by chance events or possible outcomes. Square 2 is another decision point which follows the chance event that the newly designed radar system fails to meet performance requirements.

Each chance event that follows a decision has a probability of occurrence. The boxes to the far right-hand side of the decision tree express the consequence in dollars of each branch of the decision tree. A decision tree is an effective way of representing critical decisions and the consequences that may result from these decisions. In developing a decision tree, an analyst must:

1. Identify the project objectives
2. Define the major decision points
3. Define the consequences of each major decision
4. Identify the probability of each consequence occurring
5. Define resolution of the consequences
6. Define the probability that the resolution will be successful
7. Define the cost or schedule impact of each problem resolution

The decision tree is developed from the previous information. The analyst has two options; using a Monte Carlo simulation (VERT or RISNET) or using a probabilistic event analysis (PEA) model. If the analyst uses the Monte Carlo simulation model approach, the probability of occurrence can be defined through successive iterations of the model using arc criticality. Variables such as cost, time, and technical performance can be obtained by requesting internal and terminal node statistics. This information can then be plotted as shown in Figure 8.25. If the analyst decides to use a probabilistic event analysis model, the actual decision tree does not have to be drawn; however, all the information needed to draw the decision tree will still have to be collected and listed. Since the model will not provide probabilistic information, expert opinion will need to be consulted. The probabilistic event analysis (PEA) model, developed by Hagood [23] requires the input information displayed in Figure 8.26.

In using the PEA model, the analyst uses program elements as areas in which a problem may occur, and milestones as major decision points. Figures 8.27 and 8.28 provide example output for the PEA model.

There are distinct advantages to both PEA models and Monte Carlo simulation models for decision risk analysis. PEA models produce results that are cost oriented and identified by fiscal year, thereby permitting the establishment of a cost reserve for budget purposes. Monte Carlo simulation of the decision tree produces information about each path of the decision tree, which in turn produces a more in-depth evaluation of each path's criticality and probability of occurrence. It also provides sufficient information to plot a project probability of success chart.

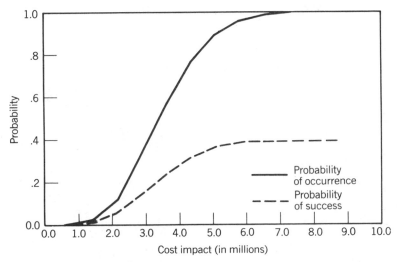

Figure 8.25. Cost impact distribution. Solid line, probability of occurrence, dashed line, probability of success.

8.3.3 Cost Estimating Risk Analysis Technique

In network risk analysis and decision risk analysis techniques, cost uncertainty is a variable associated with an activity or decision structure. In the cost estimating risk analysis technique, cost uncertainty is addressed from a cost estimating perspective. Therefore cost estimating risk analysis techniques require that the cost

Program Element	P(A)	Cost Impact Type A	P(B/A)	Cost Impact Type B	Calender Date

Figure 8.26. Input chart for PEA.

PROGRAM ELEMENTS	DATE OF IMPACT CALENDAR DATE	EXPECTED SLIPPAGE (MONTHS)	EXPECTED SLIPPAGE P.G.E.	PROB DOI	FY	AEL (IN MILLIONS)		TRACE DEFERRAL (IN MILLIONS)
MISSILE X								
PROPULSION	6/78	0.0	0.0	4/78	78	0.8	FY 78	2.19
WARHEAD	6/78	1.2	0.0	4/78	78	1.12		
FUZE	6/78	0.0	1.2	7/78	78	0.27		
AIRFRAME	9/78	0.9	1.2	10/78	79	3.6		
RADAR	9/78	0.0	2.1	11/78	79	0.27		
INTEGRATION	11/78	1.5	2.1	1/79	79	2.2	FY 79	11.67
MILESTONE								
ACCEPT TESTING	2/79	2.1	3.6	5/79	79	5.6		
OSD REVIEW	7/79	0.6	5.7	12/79	80	2.0		
DSARC	10/79	0.6	6.3	4/80	80	1.6	FY 80	3.6

Figure 8.27. PEA model output trace deferral by budget year.

PROGRAM ELEMENTS	PROB P(A)	COST IMPACT TYPE A	PROB		COST/SCHED IMPACT TYPE B	DATE OF IMPACT		EXPECTED LOSS	ADJ. EXP. LOSS
			B/A	B		CAL DATE	FY		
MISSILE X									
PROPULSION	0.20	3.0	0	0	0.0	4/78	78	0.6	0.8
WARHEAD	0.60	0.4	1.0	.6	1.0, 2.0	6/78	78	0.84	1.12
FUZE	0.25	0.8	0	0	0.0	6/78	78	0.2	0.27
AIRFRAME	0.60	1.5	.75	.45	4.0, 2.0	9/78	78	2.7	3.6
RADAR	0.20	0.5	1.0	.20	.5, 1	9/78	79	0.2	0.27
INTEGRATION	0.75	0.2	1.0	.75	2.0, 2.0	11/78	79	1.65	2.2
MILESTONES									
ACCEPTANCE	0.70	0.0	1.0	.70	6.0, 3.0	2/79	79	4.2	5.6
OSD REVIEW	0.60	0.0	1.0	.60	2.5, 1.0	7/79	79	1.5	2.0
DSARC	0.30	0.0	1.0	.30	4.0, 2.0	10/79	80	1.2	1.6
						TOTALS		13.09	17.46

Figure 8.28. PEA model output expected loss by program element.

estimating structure of the project be established. Once a project cost estimate has been developed, then the uncertainty associated with the estimate can be assessed.

One very effective computer model for cost estimating risk analysis is the Stochastic Aggregation Model (SAM) developed by Hamaker [24]. The Stochastic Aggregation Model (SAM) is currently available for the IBM Personal Computer using LOTUS 1-2-3.

8.3.3.1 Stochastic Aggregation Model (SAM).

SAM is a Monte Carlo simulation program designed to help the cost analyst quantify the uncertainty associated with a parametric cost estimate. The areas of cost risk that SAM evaluates are (1) cost estimating relationship (CER) independent variable uncertainty, (2) complexity factor uncertainty, and (3) CER statistical uncertainty.

The input required by SAM is statistical data on three areas of cost risk; output is a cost versus probability S-curve table which gives project cost as a function of the probability that the project can be completed for the estimated cost or less. The output can be plotted as an S-curve with cost on the x-axis and probability on the y-axis, as shown in Figure 8.29:

☐ The project cost risk analysis accounts for the following uncertainties in the cost estimating process:
Weight
Complexity factor
CER statistics

☐ The risk analysis allows these factors to vary over reasonable ranges (as probability distributions).

☐ The resulting simulation determined that the baseline project estimate with reserve has a 74% probability of not being exceeded.

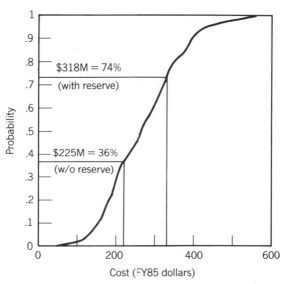

Figure 8.29. Project cost risk (cost versus probability of no overrun).

SAM works by randomly sampling probability distributions provided by the user concerning the three areas of cost risk and using the resulting values to "cost the project out" several hundred times. By so doing, SAM builds up the necessary statistical frequency data base to output the S-curve on project cost expectations. The following are required for each cost line item on the SAM:

Input Form: Independent variable X1 (e.g., weight, power). SAM requires a ±1 sigma (≈68%) confidence range on what the value of the independent variable might be. The most likely value (ML) should generally be the baseline value used in the CER estimate (but see the additional discussion on this point to follow). The low (LO) and high (HI) values should represent the lowest reasonable value and the highest reasonable value to expect, respectively, where "reasonable" means "with 68% confidence." SAM also requires distribution type T. For the independent variable, the distribution type can be any of the five distribution types now operational (Weibull, triangular, deterministic, functional, or thruput).

Complexity Factor: SAM requires the same kind of information about the complexity factor (i.e., ±1 sigma range and distribution type). The most likely value should correspond to the baseline complexity factor used for this line item in the parametric estimate. The distribution type can be Weibull, triangular, or deterministic (but *not* functional or thruput).

Other Multiplicative Factor: This is an opportunity for the user to enter any other peculiar factors (such as an inflation factor) that were used in the parametric estimate for each cost line item. SAM simply takes these as given and multiplies all random samples of cost for the line item in question by the values given. This way, SAM is "calibrated" to the parametric estimate (e.g., to the same year dollars).

CER Coefficients: Tell SAM the CER constant (A) and CER slope (B1) from the $Y = A(X1)^{B1}$ CER used for each cost line item. SAM will use this to estimate the most likely cost once SAM has randomly sampled the independent variable and complexity factor ranges.

CER Statistics: Here is where SAM accounts for the fact that CERs have statistical uncertainty associated with them. Although SAM likes to know quite a bit about the CERs, it can get by knowing just the standard error (S.E.) and number of data points (N). However, SAM can do a better job of evaluating the statistical risk of a CER if the user can also provide the other three statistical facts called "optional" on the SAM input sheet:

The mean of the independent variable data points $(\overline{X})$

The sum of the squared independent variable data points (ΣX^2)

The squared sum of the independent variable data points $(\Sigma X)^2$

When the CER was originally derived (assuming a linear regression technique such as least squares was used), these three values were calculated. However, if they were not recorded, a companion computer program to SAM called "CER Statistics" can be used to generate these values (if the user is willing to input the independent variable data points into CER Statistics).

Multivariable CER Input: SAM will accommodate CERs with up to four independent variables of the form:

$$Y = A(X1)^{B1}(X2)^{B2}(X3)^{B3}(X4)^{B4} \tag{8.5}$$

If such CERs were used in the parametric estimate, this is where SAM wants to know the other independent variable values (X2 through X4) and the other slopes (B2 through B4).

Distribution Types:

$0 < T < 1$ Weibull: The Weibull distribution has a high side tail extending beyond the given HI value that can be specified to hold some probability. Use the Weibull where there is some risk that the high value (HI) of the triangular distribution might be exceeded. Enter this high tail probability as a decimal fraction for T. Typically, Weibull tails are 5–20% probability (T = .05 to T = .2). Anytime SAM encounters such a decimal entry for T, it assumes a Weibull distribution, and the value of T is used as the probability in the high tail.

T = 1 Triangular: Use the triangular distribution for most situations where the low, most likely, and high values of either the independent variable or complexity factor are known (70% confidence band).

T = 5 Deterministic: Enter T = 5 to signal SAM that a deterministic input is desired, and enter the deterministic value desired as the most likely (ML) value. SAM will use the deterministic value as given and will not perform any type of random sampling for this input. Use the deterministic for independent variables or complexity factors that have no uncertainty.

T = 7 Functional: In most cost estimates there are "wraparound" cost line items that are functions of other cost line items (e.g., project management). These CERs need the sum of certain "above" line items as the independent variable. The T = 7 functional input can be used to make SAM sum the cost of certain above-line items (the cost as they have probabilistically been calculated) and use this as the independent variable for a wraparound CER. To signal a functional line item, enter T = 7 and specify a range of line items to be summed by entering the starting item number (M) in LO and the ending line item in HI. For example, if it is desired to sum the cost of line items five through eight and use the result as the input for a CER for line item 12, tell SAM this by entering for line item 12 the following: LO = 5, HI = 8, T = 7.

T = 8 "Thruput" Cost: Often it is desirable to "thruput" a cost number without exercising a CER and without the cost being affected by any random simulation process. Use T = 8 for any cost line item for which it is desired to thruput a cost and enter the thruput value as the independent variable ML. SAM will take the value entered in the ML position and use it as the final cost for this line item without any altering effects. The T = 8 thruput input is only valid for the independent variable T input. A T = 8 thruput for complexity factor is invalid.

Summary of Valid Distribution Type (T) Inputs:

Independent Variable		Complexity Factor	
Weibull	0 < T < 1	Weibull	0 < T < 1
Triangular	T = 1	Triangular	T = 1
Deterministic	T = 5	Deterministic	T = 5
Functional	T = 7		
Thruput	T = 8		

8.3.3.2 Example Case: Project X. An example case for Project X has been developed to aid the user. A discussion of the "SAM Input Form for Project X" and the "SAM Output for Project X" which resulted from the run follows. The example has been designed to use all the features of SAM that are currently operational.

8.3.3.2.1 SAM INPUT FORM FOR PROJECT X

1. *Structures.* Costed with a weight (pounds) versus cost CER. A probability distribution on weight was used of LO = 300 lb, ML = 500 lb, and HI =

900 lb, to be sampled as a triangular distribution. A complexity factor triangular probability distribution was also specified with LO = 0.9, ML = 1.0, and HI = 1.2. An inflation factor of 1.338 was specified to bring the CER costs from old year dollars to today's dollars. No other calibration factor was required so Other = 1.0. The structure CER used was $Y = AX^B$ or $Y = 0.58(500)^{0.654}$ with an S.E. = 0.629, and N = 9. CER statistics were available for X1 and so on as shown on the SAM Input Form. Since structure was costed with a single independent variable CER, the multivariable CER inputs are all zero.

2. *Attitude Controls.* Similar to the preceding except a Weibull distribution was specified for the complexity factor with a 15% probability of exceeding the HI value of 1.4.

3. *Communications.* Similar to the preceding except that a bivariate CER was used in which $Y = A(X1)^{B1} (X2)^{B2} = 0.011(250)^{1.269} (60)^{0.065}$.

4. *Systems Test Hardware.* The T = 8 signals a "thruput," and SAM will use the 10 entered as ML as thruput cost value (in this case, cost in millions) and will not perform any simulation around $10 million. Also T = 5 and ML = 1.0 for complexity factor signals that a deterministic complexity factor value of 1.0 is desired (again, without simulation). Since a thruput is being used, SAM will ignore all CER entries (but zeros are entered as a convenient way to cause the menu to progress during data file entry).

5. *Systems Test Operations.* The T = 7, LO = 4, and HI = 4 signals SAM that this is a Functional cost line item (specifically that Systems Test Operations is a function of line item 4-Systems Test Hardware). SAM will calculate the Systems Test Ops cost by using the simulated cost result of line item 4 as the independent variable input to the CER. Note that another feature of SAM is also illustrated where the independent variable, instead of being input into a "regular" CER, is instead input into a CER of the form $Y = 0.10(X1)^{1.0}$ which is simply a way of modeling the case where Systems Test Operations is calculated as 10% of Systems Test Hardware.

6. *Management.* Again T = 7 signals a functional line item. However, this time, since LO = 1 and HI = 5, SAM will sum the simulated costs of line item 1 through 5 and use the results as the independent variable input to the CER.

8.3.3.2.2 SAM OUTPUT FOR PROJECT X. The output run for Project X consists of (1) listing of the input data; (2) the project cost simulation results (in this case 100 samples of total project cost); (3) a summary by cost line item of both the average simulated cost and the CER cost or "no risk" cost; and, finally, (4) a confidence-cost table.

This last item, the confidence-cost table, is the "bottom line" of the risk analysis. It gives the percent confidence associated with the given cost. For Project X, the CER estimate of $62 million is only about 32% confident (68% chance that an overrun will occur). To get to a more reasonable level of confidence, say 70%, would require \$132 million (or about 113% contingency). This example is not typical of actual projects. Most of the "real" analyses performed by SAM will typically show that something like 20–40% contingency is usually sufficient to reach 60–80% confidence.

8.3.3.3 SAM Technical Notes.

For CER independent variable inputs, the correct value to input to SAM is the value used for the CER independent variable in the original baseline cost estimate, less any contingency applied for risk. For example, if electrical power was estimated as a function of a watts requirement, say 1150 watts, and this includes a 15% contingency, then the SAM most likely (ML) input should be 1000 watts since the power requirements grew due to unforeseen circumstances. The risk analysis itself is designed to evaluate the risk of a power growth and should be centered around a most likely that is risk free. However, care should be taken to try to distinguish between a contingency allowance for risk and a contingency allowance simply included to take care of miscellaneous small requirements. That is, if the extra 150 watts were added to take care of requirements in the power budget that were not itemized but are known to be present, then the 15% is not a risk allowance and should be included in the most likely SAM input.

8.3.3.3.1 HOW SAM HANDLES CER RISK. The risk of the CER is calculated by SAM as a confidence interval around the CER using the equation

$$Y \pm \text{(S.E.) (TDIST) (XTRAP)} \qquad (8.6)$$

where $Y = $ CER cost without risk, the confidence limit is a plus/minus band around the CER defined by the product of (1) the CER standard error (S.E.) and (2) a student's distribution factor (TDIST) for $N - 2$ degrees of freedom and any given percent confidence. The value TDIST is generated internally by SAM as a function of N. XTRAP is generated internally as a function of the optional CER statistics on the SAM input form X1, $\Sigma(X1)^2$, and $(\Sigma X1)^2$.

If S.E. does not apply (e.g., if a CER was not used to estimate a cost line item or if the S.E. is not available) a zero entry may be made for S.E. In such a case, SAM automatically ignores all other CER statistics entries and will not sample a CER distribution. However, for data synchronization purposes, zero entries must be made for N, X1, $\Sigma(X1)^2$ and $(\Sigma X1)^2$, X2, X3, X4, B2, B3, B4.

If multivariable CERs were used, enter the independent variables (X2, X3, X4) and slopes (B2, B3, B4). For any unneeded entries (which will be all six values if a single independent variable CER was used) enter zeros.

8.3.3.3.2 INTERPRETATION OF SAM OUTPUT. The cost risk data output by SAM should be interpreted as quantifying the cost uncertainty due to the following:

1. Uncertainty in the CER inputs (weight, power, etc.)
2. Uncertainty in the complexity factor

3. CER statistical uncertainty due to:

   a. Scatter in the CER data points (S.E.)

   b. CER sample size. The TDIST adjustment to S.E. allows for this risk by using a student's distribution for small N values. At high N values (>30 data points) the T distribution approaches the normal—all of which SAM automatically accounts for when given a value for N from the SAM Input Form.

   c. Degree of extrapolation beyond the mean of the CER data base (how well the "size" of the item being estimated matches the average of the CER data points). The XTRAP adjustment to the CER S.E. allows for this risk by causing the CER confidence intervals to spread as a function of the distance from the mean of the data.

   d. Bias of least squares log transforms. Using the linear regression technique of least squares to derive a nonlinear $Y = AX^B$ CER requires a log transform of the data. The curve fit is then made based on log values. The degree to which the CER is biased low is proportional to the S.E. but usually is on the order of 5–10% or so. SAM recognizes this bias by sampling the skewed log normal distribution for CER cost. Thus the mean cost from the CER sampling will usually be higher than the CER estimate.

Obviously there are other risks that can impact cost other than those discussed. Thus SAM does not quantify all risks associated with a cost estimate. SAM does not account for risks such as the following:

Design changes beyond those reflected by the ranges used for the CER independent variables.

Additional requirements beyond those represented by the line items costed

Risk associated with inappropriate design specifications, CERs, or complexity factors

8.3.4 Risk Factor Method

Another cost estimating risk analysis technique is the risk factor method (RFM). This method requires a project baseline cost estimate be built from an engineering work breakdown structure (WBS). Once the cost estimate has been developed, then each WBS cost element is evaluated and a risk factor is determined. The determination of a risk factor is based on the assumption that cost increases will come from two primary areas:

1. Cost uncertainties internal to the individual WBS element such as the technical complexity of this item

2. Cost uncertainties external to the individual WBS element such as design changes, funding problems, and work delays

WBS Element	Risk Factor	BCE Year 1	BCE Year 2	BCE Year 3	BCE Year 4	BCE Year 4

Figure 8.30. Input chart for RFM.

Hagood [23] developed a computer program in which each WBS element fiscal year cost is multiplied by the risk factor, giving the total risk assessment cost estimate (TRACE) value for each WBS element by fiscal year. Figure 8.30 identifies the input requirements for RFM while Figure 8.31 provides a sample program output.

The risk factor method of cost estimating risk analysis is a highly subjective approach based primarily on judgment and the assumption that cost uncertainty will increase cost. The output from this method gives a project manager budgeting information only. It does not provide any insight into the confidence of the baseline cost estimate.

8.4 APPLICATION OF RISK ANALYSIS TECHNIQUE

The degree to which a risk analysis will be performed usually depends on the size and complexity of the project being analyzed and management's decision as to the amount of time and money to be expended on the risk analysis. The three primary areas of project associated risk are cost, schedule, and technical performance. These areas are usually interdependent. Project cost depends to some extent (depending on the project) on how long the project will last. The degree of technical performance a project is aiming for can affect the project cost and schedule. An in-depth risk analysis will provide risk assessment of all three areas, resulting in an identification of the interrelationship of these variables and the associated uncertainties. It will provide extensive information about project uncertainty and provide a tracking system for project managers to use in evaluating project performance.

WBS ELEMENT	YEAR 85		YFAR 86		YEAR 87		YEAR 88		YEAR 88	
	BCE	TRACE	BCE	TRACE	BCE	TRACE	BCE	TRACE	BCE	TRACE
PROPULSION	10	1.0	10	1.5	20	3	40	6	30	4.5
WARHEAD	50	55	40	44	20	22	20	22	10	11
FUZE	1	1	2	2	3	3	2	2	1	1
AIRFRAME	10	12.5	20	25	3	37.5	20	25	20	25
RADAR	60	72	60	72	50	60	50	60	40	48
INTEGRATION & ASSEMBLY	0	0	10	12	15	18	20	24	25	30
TOTAL	140	142	142	156.5	138	146.5	152	134	106	119.5

Figure 8.31. Missile X project.

Projects that are primarily concerned with schedule risk, such as construction projects, will find CPM and PERT network analysis techniques useful. The more extensive network model can be used however, when there is a great deal of uncertainty as to how the construction project is structured.

Most complex research and development projects benefit from advanced network analysis or decision risk analysis techniques. Often, a combination of both of these techniques is the most effective approach. One primary advantage of network analysis techniques such as RISNET and VERT is their ability to be used as project tracking tools. There are two different ways this can be accomplished. One way is by using the RISNET II capability of breaking out 20 different funding categories. This feature can be used for project planning by assessing these categories as skill levels by individual names or by contracts. VERT does not break out funding categories; however, it has the capability to build a baseline cost estimate using skill levels and contract identification codes that provide the capability of tracking a project by comparing actual time, cost, and technical performance to those estimated. The network can then be revised to reflect the remaining project risk. VERT can also be used to perform "What if" exercises. For example, a project can be subnetted by contracts. When the contractor changes the schedule or technical performance criteria, a representation of this logic change can be networked.

The data between the initial contractor logic structures cost, schedule, and technical performance risk can then be compared to the results of the new network logic. This gives the project manager a better idea of the risk associated with the contractor's proposed new logic. Because VERT includes technical performance, "What if" exercises can also be performed to define the best approach (or project structure) to provide the shortest schedule, the least cost, and the highest technical performance. Both VERT and RISNET are very powerful network analysis tools; however, they both require a high level of skill to develop, analyze, and revise the network. Therefore they are most efficiently utilized by very costly complex research and development projects which have a great deal of project uncertainty and a necessity for close project tracking.

ARTEMIS system PAN models have an advantage of providing a data base management system that can integrate risk information with project planning and budgeting information. However, unless the data currently reside on the data base, a great deal of time must be expended to create the total project data base. PAN also requires the same skill level as RISNET and VERT to construct and evaluate the network. Thus PAN would be an effective networking technique to use if a project office has already established their project data base on ARTEMIS.

Decision risk analysis techniques are most effectively used when management feels that the uncertainty of a program is primarily affected by critical decisions. This type of risk analysis has its orientation toward the goals and objectives of the project and addresses the problems that may occur given a particular decision. The output from this approach to risk analysis is not as much in-depth as the advanced network analysis techniques, neither does it provide a means of project tracking. The skill level required for this type of analysis is equivalent to the PAN, RISNET, and VERT networking techniques and also requires a high degree of management input relative to the goals and objectives of the problem and the critical decision. The management participation is a distinct advantage in this method when considering in-depth project immersion and problem insight. Decision risk analysis and advanced network analysis techniques can be used together to produce the most effective risk analysis of a project by providing an integration of management performance and project structure. This requires, however, that the network analysis technique be used for more than just simulating the decision tree. It requires that decision risk analysis be used to define management decision preference (such as goals and objectives, system performance requirements, generalized project approach) and that network construction represent activities and events that lead to this defined preference. This does however, greatly increase the resources required to perform a risk analysis.

Cost estimating risk analysis has a much more limited perspective of project risk. It assesses only cost estimating risk, providing no information as to the project schedule or technical performance. The SAM cost estimating technique provides the manager with a confidence level for the cost estimate. However, in developing the confidence level, only cost estimating uncertainty is evaluated. In the risk factor method, the uncertainty associated with the design complexity, project funding, and schedule impact are considered when assessing cost risk. The advantage of the SAM technique is that it does provide a logical structural approach to evaluating cost estimating uncertainty, which requires the identification of individual cost element interdependence and probabilities. The risk factor method, on the other hand, develops a risk factor, which even though it may take into account other project uncertainty, does seem to lend itself to less rigorous quantification of risk.

REFERENCES

1. Parzen, E. *Modern Probability Theory and Its Applications*. Wiley, New York, 1960.
2. *Risk Assessment Techniques*. Defense Systems Management College, Fort Belvoir, Va., July 1983.
3. Atzinger, E. et al. *Compendium on Risk Analysis Techniques*. DARCOM Material Systems Analysis Activity, Aberdeen Proving Ground, Md., 1972.
4. Williams, C. and G. Crawford. *Analysis of Subjective Judgement Matrices*. The RAND Corporation, Santa Monica, Ca., 1980.
5. Brown, R. V., A. S. Kahr, and C. Peterson. *Decision Analysis for the Manager*. Holt, Rinehart & Winston, New York, 1974.
6. McNichols, G. R. *On the Treatment of Uncertainty in Parametric Costing*. The School of Engineering and Applied Science, The George Washington University, Washington, D.C., February 1976.
7. *Cost Uncertainty/Management Reserve Analysis*. Cost Management and Technology Division, Directorate of Cost Analysis, Deputy for Comptroller, Arament Division, Eglin AFB, Fl., January 1982.
8. *Cost Uncertainty/Risk Analysis*. Headquarters, Air Force Systems Command, Andrews AFB, Md., June 1981.

9. Jordan, H. R. and M. R. Klien. *An Application of Subjective Probabilities to the Problem of Uncertainty in Cost Analysis.* Office of the Chief of Naval Operation, Resource Analysis Group (OP-96D), Pentagon, Washington, D.C., November 1975.

10. Dalkey, N. *The Delphi Method: An Experimental Study of Group Opinion.* Rm 5888-PR, The RAND Corporation, Santa Monica, Ca., 1968.

11. *Risk Assessment Techniques.* Defense Systems Management College, Fort Belvoir, Va., July 1983.

12. Walker, M. R. and J. S. Sayer. *Project Planning and Scheduling*, Report 6959, E.I. duPont De Nemours and Co.. Wilmington, Dl. March 1959.

13. *PERT, Program Evaluation Research Task, Phase 1 Summary Report.* Special Projects Office, Bureau of Ordnance, Department of the Navy, Washington, July 1958.

14. *PAN User Guide.* Metier Management Systems Ltd., London, January 1981.

15. *Network Planning System (Arrow) User Guide (Version 5.5).* Metier Management Systems Ltd., London, July 1983.

16. Godsy, B. "Risk Analysis: A Case Study." School of Engineering, University of Alabama in Huntsville, 1985.

17. *RISNET Analyst's Guide*, John M. Cockerham & Associates, Inc., Huntsville, Al., 1972.

18. *Total Risk Assessing Cost Estimate (TRACE) Guide.* John M. Cockerham & Associates, Huntsville, Al., September 1979.

19. Moeller, G. L. *Venture Evaluation and Review Technique.* Decision Models Directorate, U.S. Army Armament Material Readiness Command, Rock Island, Il., November 1979.

20. Whatley, N. M., S. Burnett and M. W. Hagood. *TRIAD VERT Documentation.* TRIAD Microsystems, Inc. Huntsville, Al., 1985.

21. Hertz, D. B. and H. Thomas. *Risk Analysis and its Applications.* Wiley, New York, 1983.

22. Hertz, D. B. and H. Thomas. *Practical Risk Analysis*, Wiley, New York, 1984.

23. Hagood, M. W. *Baseline Cost Estimating Risk Assessment Model Users Manual.* Huntsville, Al., 1985.

24. Hamaker, J. W. *SAM User Manual.* Huntsville, Al., 1980.

9

THE USE OF MICROCOMPUTERS FOR COST ESTIMATING

ANN L. STEWART

9.1 APPROACHES TO COST ESTIMATING WITH MICROCOMPUTERS

Microcomputers—what wonderful tools they are! They are small, lightweight, accurate, and inexpensive. Computers in general, and microcomputers in specific, are becoming indispensable tools for cost estimators. Just a few years ago only the most prestigious companies could afford the mammoth room-size "high technology" machines. Now the microcomputer has become a tool that the estimator can have on his desk or in his briefcase. Even though the methodology for cost estimating is already established, there are innumerable ways in which the microcomputer can be put to use in the cost estimating profession. As pointed out in reference [1], there is no comprehensive, universal cost estimating software package that can be used in all cost estimating situations, but there are a variety of packages, each having unique features that enable them to be used for different situations. In this chapter we explore some of these packages and some of the ways the microcomputer can be used to help the estimator produce accurate estimates in an efficient and rapid manner.

9.1.1 Combining Word Processing with Number Processing—Rationale

Perhaps one of the first uses of the microcomputer by the cost estimator is to describe the assumptions and ground rules for making the cost estimate. Experienced estimators have found that no matter how good or accurate the numbers are, the estimate is not useful unless it is accompanied by detailed specifications, schedules, assumptions, ground rules, and a rationale. The word processing feature contained in word processing software programs or as part of cost estimating programs is an essential part of the estimating process. Spreadsheet programs or outline development programs can help in the development of a work element structure and work element structure dictionary before the actual estimating begins.

Several word processing programs have the capability of constructing an indented outline using the traditional work structure numbering convention (1.1, 1.2, 1.3, 1.3.1, etc.). Figure 9.1 shows such a work structure developed on Word-Perfect™, a word processor applications software package developed and marketed by Word Perfect Corporation, of Orem, Utah. This structured format is doubly useful, when combined with the mathematics capability that is built into the word processing program, for developing top level estimate summary sheets or bids. The same indented and numbered work structure outline can be used for work structure dictionaries, statements of work, or estimate report or proposal outlines and tables of contents by transferring the outline to other documents or files.

WBS FOR CLAMS1 PROJECT

1. Project Management

   1.1. Project Direction
   1.2. Procurement
   1.3. Documentation

2. Systems Engineering

   2.1. Study and Analysis
   2.2. Design

      2.2.1.   Test Fixture Design
      2.2.2.   Prototype
      2.2.3.   Flight Hardware Design

3. Prototype Fabrication and Assembly

   3.1. Rings/Proto
   3.2. Latches/Proto
   3.3. Fasteners/Proto
   3.4. Assembly/Proto

4. Flight Unit Fabrication and Assembly

   4.1. Rings/Flight
   4.2. Latches/Flight
   4.3. Fasteners/Flight
   4.4. Assembly/Flight

5. Testing

   5.1. Test Fixture Fabrication
   5.2. Instrumentation
   5.3. Prototype Testing
   5.4. Acceptance Testing

6. Delivery

Figure 9.1. Work element structure developed on WordPerfect™ software.

9.1.2 BASIC Programs

Exceedingly simple software programs in the BASIC language can be prepared with only a few program statements that can solve some of the recurring everyday equations used by cost estimators for developing cost estimating relationships and for solving learning curve problems. The smallest microcomputer can solve these problems which, in the premicrocomputer days, involved extensive manual look-up and interpolation of data from voluminous handbooks and charts. BASIC graphics programs can quickly plot unit and cumulative average costs or labor hours required for various sizes of production runs.

9.1.3 Spreadsheets

The electronic spreadsheet is perhaps the most useful generic tool made available to cost estimators. As shown later in this chapter, the electronic spreadsheet can be used for a wide variety of functions that fall into virtually every step of the cost estimating process. This versatility makes the electronic spreadsheet an essential tool for the microestimator.

Some spreadsheet programs will operate on microcomputers with as little as 64K of memory, making them economical and effective for the user who wants to make a minimal investment in capital equipment and software. Most spreadsheet programs permit the transfer of completed calculations into other programs or documents so that numerical calculation results can be integrated with text or graphics in a completed proposal or estimate report. Some spreadsheet programs permit the linking together of spreadsheets to accommodate larger cost estimates and to provide in-depth detail throughout a multilevel estimate. Examples are given in the sections that follow on how to use spreadsheets effectively for a number of estimating functions.

9.1.4 Integrated Software Packages

Integrated software packages combine the features of word processing, electronic spreadsheets, data base programs, and often communications and other microcomputer functions. For users who have microcomputers with larger memory capacities, these integrated software packages are versatile, flexible, and time-saving tools that can be configured to perform virtually all of the functions of cost estimating. Although they do not have the built-in features of specialized vertical market estimating software applications programs, their versatility and flexibility make them useful in customized applications. Some computer skills and programming knowledge are required or must be learned to establish applications templates on these integrated software packages.

9.1.5 Vertical Market Systems

Vertical market systems are those that have been designed specifically to perform the cost estimating function. They are, in general, more user friendly and require fewer computer skills than do BASIC programming, spreadsheets, or integrated software applications; but they are far more powerful in creating large or complex cost estimates. Some require the purchase of hardware and software as a package, or use special peripheral devices such as digitizers, plotters, color monitors, or special wide or high-speed printers. Usually the vertical market cost estimating system is more expensive than any of the microcomputer tools discussed, sometimes involves special user training, often requires cost estimating data-base updating of labor and material prices, and always requires greater microcomputer hardware memory and electronic data storage capacity.

As demonstrated in the several vertical market systems discussed later in this chapter, each has its own unique features and is usually more nearly suited to a specific industry, product, or cost estimating methodology. In a vertical market system, ease of use and capacity are usually gained at the sacrifice of some flexibility.

9.1.6 Estimating Interfaces with Accounting and Design

Since cost estimating is derived from the plan or design of a work activity or work output, a natural interface exists with the design function. As the engineering and business communities turn more toward computer-aided planning and computer-aided design, the interface of these disciplines with microestimating will become more compatible. Already, systems have been developed for automated takeoff of quantities, distances, areas, and volumes (by inference) from microcomputer-generated plans and drawings. Hence the electronic link between the design of the product or service and the resources required to produce that product or service is becoming stronger, more well defined, and easier to use. In addition to the electronic linkage of estimating with design at the beginning of the process, estimating is being electronically linked with job costing, cost tracking, and accounting at the end of the process. Sophisticated job cost systems are available for microcomputers that will use and update estimating information in calculating earned value, work completed, work remaining, payment schedules, and costs to complete. The cost estimating function, then, is developing stronger interfaces and links with other integrally related functions within the engineering and business disciplines.

9.2 MICROCOMPUTER USE THROUGHOUT THE ESTIMATING PROCESS

Microcomputers can be used effectively to help perform each of the 12 steps of estimating discussed in Chapter 1 of this manual. The following discussion shows *how* microcomputers can be used in each step by describing how several typical software packages are used in developing cost estimates. The software packages used are as follows:

DATACOST™, Mobile Data Services

Multiplan™, Microsoft Corporation

Lotus 1-2-3™, Lotus Development Corporation

Project Scheduler 5000™, Scitor Corporation

EasyEst™, CMS Corporation

WBS TREE™, J.M. Cockerham Associates

microPICES™, Microestimating, Inc.

Primavera Project Planner™, Primavera Systems, Incorporated

pfs File™ and pfs Report™, Software Publishing Company

AutoCAD2™, Autodesk, Incorporated

AcaDATUM™, Charles Hill Associates

EasyWriter II™, IUS Company

WordPerfect™, Word Perfect Corporation

The 12 steps of cost estimating, as described in Chapter 1, are listed as follows:

1. Develop the work element structure
2. Schedule the work elements
3. Retrieve historical cost data
4. Develop estimating relationships
5. Develop production learning curves
6. Establish skill categories, levels, and rates
7. Make labor hour and material estimates
8. Add and analyze overhead and administrative costs
9. Apply inflation and cost growth allowances
10. Compute estimate costs
11. Analyze and adjust the estimate
12. Publish/present the estimate

Each of these steps is discussed in the following sections in the light of existing and potential microcomputer capabilities.

9.3 DEVELOPING THE WORK ELEMENT STRUCTURE

Since the work element structure or work breakdown structure is the framework for the entire estimate, it is important to see how the microcomputer can help further automate its development beyond the simple outlining capability mentioned earlier.

9.3.1 Multiplan™ Template

As an example of how a work breakdown structure can be used in a simple and inexpensive spreadsheet program, a scheme was developed for estimating the costs of construction of a typical single-family residence, and the applications package used was Multiplan™ (Microsoft Corporation). The work structure that was developed is shown in Figure 9.2. Note that the typical home construction was divided into 10 major work subdivisions:

HOME BUILDING ESTIMATING TEMPLATE
PEEWEE.001

Legal & General (A-1.001)	Site Preparation (A-2.001)	Framing (A-3.001)	Plumbing (A-4.001)	HVAC (A-5.001)	Electrical (A-6.001)	Masonry (A-7.001)	Appliances & Fixtures (A-8.001)	Interior Finishing (A-9.001)	Exterior Finishing (A-10.001)
-Bldg Permit	-Purchase Lot	-Framing	-Kitchen	-HVAC	-Electrical	-Veneer	-Hot Water Heaters	-Flooring	-Cleanup
-Insurance	-Excavation	-Roofing	-Bathrm(s)	-Other #1	-Other #1	-Chimneys	-Washer/ Dryers	-Insulation	-Grading
-Util Dep	-Footings	-Gutters & Sheetmetal	-Laundry	-Other #2	-Other #2	-Fireplaces	-Refrig	-Sheetrock Walls	-Driveways
-Legal & Recording	-Foundations	-Stairs	-Septic Tank			-Other #1	-Range	-Sheetrock Ceilings	-Garage
-Eng Work	-Termite Treatment	-Porch Columns	-Other #1			-Other #2	-Dishwasher	-Paneling	-Walkways
-Plans & Spec.	-Aggragate Base	-Other #1	-Other #2				-Garbg Dis.	-Trim	-Decks
-Appraisal Fees	-Water Proofing	-Other #2					-Lighting	-Cabinets	-Fences
-Interest Expense	-Slab Floor						-Fans	-Vanity Tops	-Other #1
-Realtor Fees	-Other #1						-Other #1	-Painting	-Other #2
-Other #1	-Other #2						-Other #2	-Wallpaper	
-Other #2								-Carpet	
								-Other #1	
								-Other #2	
-Tot/Input	-Tot/Input	-Tot/Input	-Tot/Input	-Tot/Input	-Tot/Input	-Tot/Input	-Tot/Input	-Tot/Input	-Tot/Input
-Thruput	-Thruput	-Thruput	-Thruput	-Thruput	-Thruput	-Thruput	-Thruput	-Thruput	-Thruput

Copyrighted in 1984 by MOBILE DATA SERVICES, Huntsville, AL 35805 Phone: 205-536-2628

Figure 9.2. Home building estimate template developed on EasyWriter II.

1. Legal and general
2. Site preparation
3. Framing
4. Plumbing
5. HVAC
6. Electrical
7. Masonry
8. Appliances and fixtures
9. Interior finishing
10. Exterior finishing

For each work subdivision, a spreadsheet was developed to estimate labor, material, and other costs for that subdivision; then the results of these spreadsheets were summed into a total or top-level spreadsheet. Notice that the numbering sequence suggested in Chapter 1 is used to identify each work element. File names of each work item are A-1, A-2, A-3, and so on. The file extender (.001) is used to number the estimate as estimate number 1. Each of these level 2 work elements is further subdivided into level 3 work elements, two "other" categories to allow space to insert items unique to a special house design, and "total/input" and "thruput" cost elements to permit insertion of subcontractor bids and/or prime contractor cost growth allowances. This work breakdown structure was developed using the EasyWriter II™ program and was printed in 17 character per inch compressed print. It was then manually transferred to Multiplan™ for use in the construction estimating template discussed later.

9.3.2 Lotus 1-2-3™ Templates

Several templates were developed on Lotus 1-2-3™ to show how a handy spreadsheet template can be used for easy construction and microcomputer display of a work breakdown structure. Figure 9.3 shows a "blank form" work breakdown structure input template that has prenumbered blocks and spaces to insert titles or names of each work element. Coding with multiple documents must be input in alphabetical rather than numerical form because the numerical format does not permit the use of multiple decimals. This type of format is easier to understand and the work interrelationships are easier to visualize than in the word processor format shown in Figure 9.1. It is also easier to fill in and print than the word processor format shown in Figure 9.2.

Figure 9.4 uses a different numbering system that can be used when a numerical coding is required in preference to an alphabetical coding. The initial numerical codes for each work element were computed to level 3 using internal spreadsheet formulas to generate level 2 elements in increments of 1000 and level 3 elements

LVL   LOTUS WORK BREAKDOWN ENTRY FORMAT

LVL									
I				1.0					
II	1.1	1.2	1.3	1.4	1.5	1.6	1.7	1.8	1.9
III	1.1.1	1.2.1	1.3.1	1.4.1	1.5.1	1.6.1	1.7.1	1.8.1	1.9.1
	1.1.2	1.2.2	1.3.2	1.4.2	1.5.2	1.6.2	1.7.2	1.8.2	1.9.2
	1.1.3	1.2.3	1.3.3	1.4.3	1.5.3	1.6.3	1.7.3	1.8.3	1.9.3
	1.1.4	1.2.4	1.3.4	1.4.4	1.5.4	1.6.4	1.7.4	1.8.4	1.9.4
	1.1.5	1.2.5	1.3.5	1.4.5	1.5.5	1.6.5	1.7.5	1.8.5	1.9.5
	1.1.6	1.2.6	1.3.6	1.4.6	1.5.6	1.6.6	1.7.6	1.8.6	1.9.6
	1.1.7	1.2.7	1.3.7	1.4.7	1.5.7	1.6.7	1.7.7	1.8.7	1.9.7
	1.1.8	1.2.8	1.3.8	1.4.8	1.5.8	1.6.8	1.7.8	1.8.8	1.9.8

Figure 9.3. Lotus work breakdown entry format standard numbering.

in increments of 100. Four digits can be used to depict five levels of an estimate as follows:

Level	Example
Level 1	(no code)
Level 2	1000, 2000
Level 3	1100, 2100
Level 4	1110, 2110
Level 5	1111, 2111

Figure 9.5 gives the Lotus 1-2-3™ cell entries required to produce this template.

Figure 9.6 shows a typical work breakdown structure (the CLAMS1 project) that was developed using the Lotus 1-2-3™ template format. Although it is easier to visualize the box structure using this format than in the indented outline format, an even more greatly improved picture of the work breakdown structure can be

LVL   LOTUS WORK BREAKDOWN ENTRY FORMAT

I

LVL	1000	2000	3000	4000	5000	6000	7000	8000	9000
II	1000	2000	3000	4000	5000	6000	7000	8000	9000
III	1100	2100	3100	4100	5100	6100	7100	8100	9100
	1200	2200	3200	4200	5200	6200	7200	8200	9200
	1300	2300	3300	4300	5300	6300	7300	8300	9300
	1400	2400	3400	4400	5400	6400	7400	8400	9400
	1500	2500	3500	4500	5500	6500	7500	8500	9500
	1600	2600	3600	4600	5600	6600	7600	8600	9600
	1700	2700	3700	4700	5700	6700	7700	8700	9700
	1800	2800	3800	4800	5800	6800	7800	8800	9800

Figure 9.4. Lotus work breakdown entry format alternate numbering.

obtained on a graphics or computer-aided design program that permits plotting of a work structure drawing. Such a more clearly readable and understandable picture (also of the CLAMS1 project) created on AutoCAD™, is shown in Figure 9.7.

Another method of inputting and coding work elements is shown in Figures 9.8 through 9.10. This system, used in Cockerham's WBS TREE™ program, employs a single-decimal numerical WBS code with every two digits following the decimal allocated to work element designations within a given level. Numbering starts at level 2 in this four-level system as shown in Figure 9.8. The level 3 elements are shown in Figure 9.9, and the level 4 elements are shown in Figure 9.10.

9.3.3 The Sixteen Construction Divisions

Work element structures for construction usually take the form shown in Figures 9.11 through 9.26, which are screen representations of a typical division and subdivision structure used in the EasyEst™ program marketed by CMS, Incorporated.

LOTUS WORK BREAKDOWN ENTRY FORMAT

A1: 'LVL
B1: '
B2: \=
C2: \=
D2: \=
E2: \=
F2: \=
G2: \=
H2: \=
I2: \=
J2: \=
K2: \=
L2: \=
M2: \=
N2: \=
O2: \=
P2: \=
Q2: \=
R2: \=
J3: U _
A4: ^I
J4: U _
B7: U _
D7: U _
F7: U _
H7: U _
J7: U _
L7: U _
N7: U _
P7: U _
R7: U _
A8: ^II
B8: U _
D8: U _
F8: U _
H8: U _
J8: U _
L8: U _
N8: U _
P8: U _
R8: U _
B9: U 1000
D9: U +B9+1000
F9: U +D9+1000
H9: U +F9+1000
J9: U +H9+1000
L9: U +J9+1000
N9: U +L9+1000
P9: U +N9+1000
R9: U +P9+1000
B12: U \=
D12: U \=
F12: U \=
H12: U \=
J12: U \=
L12: U \=

M12: U \-
P12: U \=
R12: U \=
A13: ^III
B13: U \=
D13: U \=
F13: U \=
H13: U \=
J13: U \=
L13: U \=
N13: U \=
P13: U \=
R13: U \=
B14: U +B9+100
D14: U +D9+100
F14: U +F9+100
H14: U +F14+1000
J14: U +H14+1000
L14: U +J14+1000
N14: U +L14+1000
P14: U +N14+1000
R14: U +P14+1000
B16: U \=
D16: U \=
F16: U \=
H16: U \=
J16: U \=
L16: U \=
N16: U \=
P16: U \=
R16: U \=
B17: U \=
D17: U \=
F17: U \=
H17: U \=
J17: U \=
L17: U \=
N17: U \=
P17: U \=
R17: U \=
B18: U +B14+100
D18: U +D14+100
F18: U +F14+100
H18: U +H14+100
J18: U +J14+100
L18: U +L14+100
N18: U +N14+100
P18: U +P14+100
R18: U +R14+100
B20: U \=
D20: U \=
F20: U \=
H20: U \=
J20: U \=
L20: U \=
N20: U \=

P20: U \=
R20: U \=
B21: U \=
D21: U \=
F21: U \=
H21: U \=
J21: U \=
L21: U \=
N21: U \=
P21: U \=
R21: U \=
B22: U +B18+100
D22: U +D18+100
F22: U +F18+100
H22: U +H18+100
J22: U +J18+100
L22: U +L18+100
N22: U +N18+100
P22: U +P18+100
R22: U +R18+100
B24: U \=
D24: U \=
F24: U \=
H24: U \=
J24: U \=
L24: U \=
N24: U \=
P24: U \=
R24: U \=
B25: U \=
D25: U \=
F25: U \=
H25: U \=
J25: U \=
L25: U \=
N25: U \=
P25: U \=
R25: U \=
B26: U +B22+100
D26: U +D22+100
F26: U +F22+100
H26: U +H22+100
J26: U +J22+100
L26: U +L22+100
N26: U +N22+100
P26: U +P22+100
R26: U +R22+100
B28: U \=
D28: U \=
F28: U \=
H28: U \=
J28: U \=
L28: U \=
N28: U \=
P28: U \=
R28: U \=

B29: U \=
D29: U \=
F29: U \=
H29: U \=
J29: U \=
L29: U \=
N29: U \=
P29: U \=
R29: U \=
B30: U +B26+100
D30: U +D26+100
F30: U +F26+100
H30: U +H26+100
J30: U +J26+100
L30: U +L26+100
N30: U +N26+100
P30: U +P26+100
R30: U +R26+100
B32: U \=
D32: U \=
F32: U \=
H32: U \=
J32: U \=
L32: U \=
N32: U \=
P32: U \=
R32: U \=
B33: U \=
D33: U \=
F33: U \=
H33: U \=
J33: U \=
L33: U \=
N33: U \=
P33: U \=
R33: U \=
B34: U +B30+100
D34: U +D30+100
F34: U +F30+100
H34: U +H30+100
J34: U +J30+100
L34: U +L30+100
N34: U +N30+100
P34: U +P30+100
R34: U +R30+100
B36: U \=
D36: U \=
F36: U \=
H36: U \=
J36: U \=
L36: U \=
N36: U \=
P36: U \=
R36: U \=
B37: U \=
D37: U \=

F37: U \=
H37: U \=
J37: U \=
L37: U \=
N37: U \=
P37: U \=
R37: U \=
B38: U +B34+100
D38: U +D34+100
F38: U +F34+100
H38: U +H34+100
J38: U +J34+100
L38: U +L34+100
N38: U +N34+100
P38: U +P34+100
R38: U +R34+100
B40: U \=
D40: U \=
F40: U \=
H40: U \=
J40: U \=
L40: U \=
N40: U \=
P40: U \=
R40: U \=
B41: U \=
D41: U \=
F41: U \=
H41: U \=
J41: U \=
L41: U \=
N41: U \=
P41: U \=
R41: U \=
B42: U +B38+100
D42: U +D38+100
F42: U +F38+100
H42: U +H38+100
J42: U +J38+100
L42: U +L38+100
M42: U +M38+100
P42: U +P38+100
R42: U +R38+100

Figure 9.5. Lotus 1-2-3™ cell entries for Figure 9.4.

LVL   LOTUS WORK BREAKDOWN ENTRY FORMAT

LVL									
I				CLAMS1 PROJECT					
II	PROJECT MANAGEMENT 1000	———— 2000	———— 3000	SYSTEMS ENGINEERING 4000	———— 5000	PROTOTYPE FAB/ASSEMBLY 6000	FLIGHT UNIT/ FAB/ASSEMBLY 7000	TESTING 8000	FLIGHT HDW DELIVERY 9000
III	Project Direction 1100	Study & Analysis 2100	3100	Study & Analysis 4100	5100	Rings/ Prototype 6100	Rings/ Flight 7100	Test/Fixture Fabrication 8100	9100
	1200	Procurement 2200	3200	Design 4200	5200	Latches/ Prototype 6200	Latches/ Flight 7200	Instrument'n 8200	9200
	1300	Documentation 2300	3300	Test/Fix Design 4210	5300	Fasteners/ Prototype 6300	Fasteners/ Flight 7300	Prototype Test 8300	9300
	1400	2400	3400	Proto Design 4220	5400	Assembly/ Prototype 6400	Assembly/ Flight 7400	Acceptance Test 8400	9400
	1500	2500	3500	Flt Hdw Design 4230	5500	6500	7500	8500	9500
	1600	2600	3600		5600	6600	7600	8600	9600
	1700	2700	3700		5700	6700	7700	8700	9700
	1800	2800	3800		5800	6800	7800	8800	9800

Figure 9.6. WBS for CLAMS1 project using Figure 9.4.

This program permits the use of up to 10 subdivisions for each division and up to 100 items for each subdivision. Hence the system permits the input of a three-level estimate with up to 16,000 items. The EasyEst™ program is not limited to use on construction projects because divisions and subdivisions can be given any name the user desires.

9.3.4 Work Structure Correlation with Scheduling

As mentioned in Chapter 1 of this manual, it is often convenient and always easier to have work elements in a project coincide with schedule elements. Using the numerical coding of Figures 9.4 and 9.5, schedule elements can be given "job" numbers and titles in the Project Scheduler 5000™ program as shown in Figure 9.27.

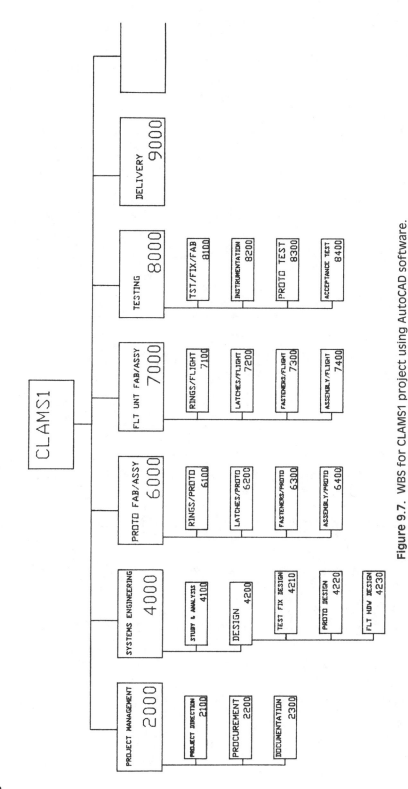

Figure 9.7. WBS for CLAMS1 project using AutoCAD software.

```
                    THE "ESTIMATOR" TEST CASE
                      WBS Level II Code Edit

        1.              NON-RECURRING PRODUCTION
        2.              RECURRING PRODUCTION
        3.              ENGINEERING CHANGES
        4.              DATA
        5.              SYSTEM TEST & EVALUATION

        6.              TRAINING SERVICE & EQUIPMENT

        7.              INITIAL SPARES
        8.              OPERATIONAL SITE ACTIVATION
        9.              OTHER PROC FUNDED PROD


F1 - scroll up one line.      F5 - delete current line.     F10 - exit.
F2 - scroll down one line.

F3 - display next page.       F6 - add WBS codes.
F4 - display previous page.

TAB - position cursor over WBS descriptor.
```

Figure 9.8. Inputting and coding work elements using WBS TREE level 2.

```
                    THE "ESTIMATOR" TEST CASE
                      WBS Level III Code Edit

        1.01            PROVISION INDUST FACILITIES
        1.02            PRODUCTION BASE SUPPORT
        1.03            DEPOT MAINT PROD EQUIP
        2.01            WIDGIT SUB-ASSEMBLY
        2.02            RECURRING ENGINEERING

        2.03            SUSTAINING TOOLING

        2.04            QUALITY CONTROL
        3.01            ECO'S-HARDWARE
        3.02            ECO'S-SUPPORT EQUIP
        4.01            DATA-TECH REPORTS
        4.02            DATA-OTHER

F1 - scroll up one line.      F5 - delete current line.     F10 - exit.
F2 - scroll down one line.

F3 - display next page.       F6 - add WBS codes.
F4 - display previous page.

TAB - position cursor over WBS descriptor.
```

```
                    THE "ESTIMATOR" TEST CASE
                      WBS Level III Code Edit

        5.01            SYSTEM TEST & EVALUATION
        6.01            TRAINING SERVICES
        6.02            TRAINING EQUIPMENT
        7.01            INITIAL SPARES
        8.01            OPERATIONAL SITE ACTIVATION

        9.01            OTHER PROC FUND PROD


F1 - scroll up one line.      F5 - delete current line.     F10 - exit.
F2 - scroll down one line.

F3 - display next page.       F6 - add WBS codes.
F4 - display previous page.

TAB - position cursor over WBS descriptor.
```

Figure 9.9. Inputting and coding work elements using WBS TREE level 3.

```
                         THE "ESTIMATOR" TEST CASE
                            WBS Level IV Code Edit

          1.0101      PROVISIONING INDUST FACIL
          1.0201      PRODUCTION BASE SUPPORT
          1.0301      DEPOT MAINT PLANT EQUIP
          2.0101      WIDGIT COMPONENT A
          2.0102      WIDGIT COMPONENT B

          2.0103      WIDGIT COMPONENT C

          2.0104      INTEGRATION & ASSEMBLY
          2.0105      SOFTWARE
          2.0106      MANUFACTURING TEST
          2.0107      SHIPPING
          2.0201      ENGINEERING SERVICES

  F1 - scroll up one line.      F5 - delete current line.      F10 - exit.
  F2 - scroll down one line.

  F3 - display next page.       F6 - add WBS codes.
  F4 - display previous page.

  TAB - position cursor over WBS descriptor.
```

```
                         THE "ESTIMATOR" TEST CASE
                            WBS Level IV Code Edit

          2.0202      PRODUCT ENGINEERING
          2.0203      PRODUCTION ENGINEERING
          2.0204      INDUSTRIAL ENGINEERING
          2.0301      RECURRING TOOL FAB
          2.0302      RECURRING TOOL MAINT

          2.0303      RECURRING TOOL CALIBRATION

          2.0401      PRODUCT ASSURANCE
          2.0402      MANUFACTURING INSPECTION
          2.0403      RECEIVING INSPECTION
          3.0101      ECO-CONTRACTOR CONTROL
          3.0102      ECO-GOVT CONTROL

  F1 - scroll up one line.      F5 - delete current line.      F10 - exit.
  F2 - scroll down one line.

  F3 - display next page.       F6 - add WBS codes.
  F4 - display previous page.

  TAB - position cursor over WBS descriptor.
```

```
                         THE "ESTIMATOR" TEST CASE
                            WBS Level IV Code Edit

          3.0201      ECO'S-SUPPORT EQUIP
          4.0101      DATA-TECH REPORTS
          4.0102      DATA-ENGINEER DRWGS
          4.0201      DATA-OTHER
          5.0101      SYSTEM TEST & EVALUATION

          6.0101      TRAINING SERVICES

          6.0201      TRAINING EQUIP-WIDGITS
          7.0101      INITIAL SPARES
          8.0101      OPERATIONAL SITE ACTIVATION
          9.0101      PROGRAM MANAGEMENT
          9.0102      WARRANTY

  F1 - scroll up one line.      F5 - delete current line.      F10 - exit.
  F2 - scroll down one line.

  F3 - display next page.       F6 - add WBS codes.
  F4 - display previous page.

  TAB - position cursor over WBS descriptor.
```

Figure 9.10. Inputting and coding work elements using WBS TREE level 4.

```
INNNNNNNNNNNNNNNNNNNNNNNNNNNNNNNNNNNNNNNNNNNNNNNNNNNNNNNNNNNNNNNNNNNNNNNNNNNN;
: You may change these descriptions to fit your needs.                       :
: Enter a D followed by the division number you want changed, e.g., D4       :
: Enter an S with the subdivision # but not the division #, e.g., S6         :
LNNNNNNNNNNNNNNNNNNNNNNNNNNNKNN Manual page # 4-23  NNNNNNNNNNNNNNNNNNNNNNNNN9
:    DIVISIONS            :      SUBDIVISIONS                                 :
: 1  GENERAL DISCIPLINES  :  1.0 BUILDINGS                                    :
: 2  SITEWORK             :  1.1 PERMITS                                      :
: 3  CONCRETE             :  1.2 TRANSPORTATION                               :
: 4  MASONRY              :  1.3 INDUSTRIAL                                   :
: 5  METAL/STRUCTURAL     :  1.4 HEAVY UTILITIES                              :
: 6  WOOD AND PLASTIC     :  1.5 POWER                                        :
: 7  THERMAL/MOISTURE CTL :  1.6 TRAFFIC CONTROL                              :
: 8  DOORS AND WINDOWS    :  1.7                                             :
: 9  FINISHES             :  1.8                                             :
: 10 SPECIALTIES          :  1.9                                             :
: 11 EQUIPMENT            :                                                  :
: 12 FURNISHINGS          :                                                  :
: 13 SPECIAL CONSTRUCTION :                                                  :
: 14 CONVEYING SYSTEMS    :                                                  :
: 15 MECHANICAL           :                                                  :
: 16 ELECTRICAL           :                                                  :
: Selection: D1!  M=Main menu, I=Item Screen, D#=change Div, S#=change Subdiv:
INNNNNNNNNNNNNNNNNNNNNNNNNNNNNNNNNNNNNNNNNNNNNNNNNNNNNNNNNNNNNNNNNNNNNNNNNNNN(
```

Figure 9.11. Divisions and subdivision 1 of EasyEst WBS.

```
INNNNNNNNNNNNNNNNNNNNNNNNNNNNNNNNNNNNNNNNNNNNNNNNNNNNNNNNNNNNNNNNNNNNNNNNNNNN;
:                                                                            :
: You can change division descriptions to your needs.                       :
:                                                                            :
LNNNNNNNNNNNNNNNNNNNNNNNNNNNNKNN Manual page # 3-3   NNNNNNNNNNNNNNNNNNNNNNNNN9
:    DIVISIONS            :      SUBDIVISIONS                                 :
: 1  GENERAL DISCIPLINES  :  2.0 ELECTRICAL UTILITIES                         :
: 2  SITEWORK!!!!!!!!!!!!! :  2.1 DEMOLITION                                  :
: 3  CONCRETE             :  2.2 EARTHWORK                                    :
: 4  MASONRY              :  2.3 PILES/CAISSONS/SHRNG                          :
: 5  METAL/STRUCTURAL     :  2.4 WATER SYSTEMS                                :
: 6  WOOD AND PLASTIC     :  2.5 PAVING/LANDSCAPING                           :
: 7  THERMAL/MOISTURE CTL :  2.6 RAILROAD WORK                                :
: 8  DOORS AND WINDOWS    :  2.7 MARINE WORK                                  :
: 9  FINISHES             :  2.8 TUNNELING                                    :
: 10 SPECIALTIES          :  2.9 SEWER SYSTEMS                                :
: 11 EQUIPMENT            :                                                  :
: 12 FURNISHINGS          :                                                  :
: 13 SPECIAL CONSTRUCTION :                                                  :
: 14 CONVEYING SYSTEMS    :                                                  :
: 15 MECHANICAL           :                                                  :
: 16 ELECTRICAL           :                                                  :
: Selection: D2                                                              :
INNNNNNNNNNNNNNNNNNNNNNNNNNNNNNNNNNNNNNNNNNNNNNNNNNNNNNNNNNNNNNNNNNNNNNNNNNNN(
```

Figure 9.12. Divisions and subdivision 2 of EasyEst WBS.

```
INNNNNNNNNNNNNNNNNNNNNNNNNNNNNNNNNNNNNNNNNNNNNNNNNNNNNNNNNNNNNNNNNNNNNNNNNNNN;
:                                                                            :
: You can change division descriptions to your needs.                       :
:                                                                            :
LNNNNNNNNNNNNNNNNNNNNNNNNNNNNKNN Manual page # 3-3   NNNNNNNNNNNNNNNNNNNNNNNNN9
:    DIVISIONS            :      SUBDIVISIONS                                 :
: 1  GENERAL DISCIPLINES  :  3.0 FORMWORK                                     :
: 2  SITEWORK             :  3.1 CAST IN PLACE                                :
: 3  CONCRETE!!!!!!!!!!!!! :  3.2 REINFORCING STEEL                           :
: 4  MASONRY              :  3.3 PRECAST CONCRETE                             :
: 5  METAL/STRUCTURAL     :  3.4 DECKS AND FINISHES                           :
: 6  WOOD AND PLASTIC     :  3.5                                             :
: 7  THERMAL/MOISTURE CTL :  3.6                                             :
: 8  DOORS AND WINDOWS    :  3.7                                             :
: 9  FINISHES             :  3.8                                             :
: 10 SPECIALTIES          :  3.9                                             :
: 11 EQUIPMENT            :                                                  :
: 12 FURNISHINGS          :                                                  :
: 13 SPECIAL CONSTRUCTION :                                                  :
: 14 CONVEYING SYSTEMS    :                                                  :
: 15 MECHANICAL           :                                                  :
: 16 ELECTRICAL           :                                                  :
: Selection: D3                                                              :
INNNNNNNNNNNNNNNNNNNNNNNNNNNNNNNNNNNNNNNNNNNNNNNNNNNNNNNNNNNNNNNNNNNNNNNNNNNN(
```

Figure 9.13. Divisions and subdivision 3 of EasyEst WBS.

```
I###########################################################################;
:                                                                           :
: You can change division descriptions to your needs.                       :
:                                                                           :
L#######################KM Manual page # 3-3    #########################9
:    DIVISIONS            :     SUBDIVISIONS                                 :
: 1  GENERAL DISCIPLINES  :  4.0 BRICK MASONRY                               :
: 2  SITEWORK             :  4.1 BLOCK MASONRY                               :
: 3  CONCRETE             :  4.2 STONE MASONRY                               :
: 4  MASONRY!!!!!!!!!!!!!! :  4.3                                            :
: 5  METAL/STRUCTURAL     :  4.4                                             :
: 6  WOOD AND PLASTIC     :  4.5                                             :
: 7  THERMAL/MOISTURE CTL :  4.6                                             :
: 8  DOORS AND WINDOWS    :  4.7                                             :
: 9  FINISHES             :  4.8                                             :
: 10 SPECIALTIES          :  4.9                                             :
: 11 EQUIPMENT            :                                                  :
: 12 FURNISHINGS          :                                                  :
: 13 SPECIAL CONSTRUCTION :                                                  :
: 14 CONVEYING SYSTEMS    :                                                  :
: 15 MECHANICAL           :                                                  :
: 16 ELECTRICAL           :                                                  :
: Selection: D4                                                             :
I###########################################################################(
```

Figure 9.14. Divisions and subdivision 4 of EasyEst WBS.

```
I###########################################################################;
:                                                                           :
: You can change division descriptions to your needs.                       :
:                                                                           :
L#######################KM Manual page # 3-3    #########################9
:    DIVISIONS            :     SUBDIVISIONS                                 :
: 1  GENERAL DISCIPLINES  :  5.0                                             :
: 2  SITEWORK             :  5.1 STRUCTURAL                                  :
: 3  CONCRETE             :  5.2 MISCELLANEOUS                               :
: 4  MASONRY              :  5.3 ORNAMENTAL                                  :
: 5  METAL/STRUCTURAL!!!! :  5.4 DECKING AND SIDING                          :
: 6  WOOD AND PLASTIC     :  5.5 PREFAB BUILDINGS                            :
: 7  THERMAL/MOISTURE CTL :  5.6                                             :
: 8  DOORS AND WINDOWS    :  5.7                                             :
: 9  FINISHES             :  5.8                                             :
: 10 SPECIALTIES          :  5.9                                             :
: 11 EQUIPMENT            :                                                  :
: 12 FURNISHINGS          :                                                  :
: 13 SPECIAL CONSTRUCTION :                                                  :
: 14 CONVEYING SYSTEMS    :                                                  :
: 15 MECHANICAL           :                                                  :
: 16 ELECTRICAL           :                                                  :
: Selection: D5                                                             :
I###########################################################################(
```

Figure 9.15. Divisions and subdivision 5 of EasyEst WBS.

```
I###########################################################################;
:                                                                           :
: You can change division descriptions to your needs.                       :
:                                                                           :
L#######################KM Manual page # 3-3    #########################9
:    DIVISIONS            :     SUBDIVISIONS                                 :
: 1  GENERAL DISCIPLINES  :  6.0 LIGHT FRAMING                               :
: 2  SITEWORK             :  6.1 HEAVY TIMBER FRAMING                        :
: 3  CONCRETE             :  6.2 TRESTLE FRAMING                             :
: 4  MASONRY              :  6.3 LAMINATED FRAMING                           :
: 5  METAL/STRUCTURAL     :  6.4 FINISH MILLWORK                             :
: 6  WOOD AND PLASTIC!!!! :  6.5 FINISH CASEWORK                             :
: 7  THERMAL/MOISTURE CTL :  6.6                                             :
: 8  DOORS AND WINDOWS    :  6.7                                             :
: 9  FINISHES             :  6.8                                             :
: 10 SPECIALTIES          :  6.9                                             :
: 11 EQUIPMENT            :                                                  :
: 12 FURNISHINGS          :                                                  :
: 13 SPECIAL CONSTRUCTION :                                                  :
: 14 CONVEYING SYSTEMS    :                                                  :
: 15 MECHANICAL           :                                                  :
: 16 ELECTRICAL           :                                                  :
: Selection: D6                                                             :
I###########################################################################(
```

Figure 9.16. Divisions and subdivision 6 of EasyEst WBS.

```
IMMMMMMMMMMMMMMMMMMMMMMMMMMMMMMMMMMMMMMMMMMMMMMMMMMMMMMMMMMMMMMMMMMMMMMMMMMMMM;
:                                                                            :
: You can change division descriptions to your needs.                       :
:                                                                            :
LMMMMMMMMMMMMMMMMMMMMMMMMMMMMKMM Manual page # 3-3    MMMMMMMMMMMMMMMMMMMMMMMMMM9
:    DIVISIONS           :       SUBDIVISIONS                                :
: 1  GENERAL DISCIPLINES :   7.0                                             :
: 2  SITEWORK            :   7.1 WATERPROOFING                               :
: 3  CONCRETE            :   7.2 INSULATION                                  :
: 4  MASONRY             :   7.3 ROOFING                                     :
: 5  METAL/STRUCTURAL    :   7.4 ARCH. SHEET METAL                           :
: 6  WOOD AND PLASTIC    :   7.5 SKYLIGHTS                                   :
: 7  THERMAL/MOISTURE CTL:   7.6 CAULKING & SEALANTS                         :
: 8  DOORS AND WINDOWS   :   7.7                                             :
: 9  FINISHES            :   7.8                                             :
: 10 SPECIALTIES         :   7.9                                             :
: 11 EQUIPMENT           :                                                   :
: 12 FURNISHINGS         :                                                   :
: 13 SPECIAL CONSTRUCTION:                                                   :
: 14 CONVEYING SYSTEMS   :                                                   :
: 15 MECHANICAL          :                                                   :
: 16 ELECTRICAL          :                                                   :
: Selection: D7                                                              :
HMMMMMMMMMMMMMMMMMMMMMMMMMMMMMMMMMMMMMMMMMMMMMMMMMMMMMMMMMMMMMMMMMMMMMMMMMMMMM(
```

Figure 9.17. Divisions and subdivision 7 of EasyEst WBS.

```
IMMMMMMMMMMMMMMMMMMMMMMMMMMMMMMMMMMMMMMMMMMMMMMMMMMMMMMMMMMMMMMMMMMMMMMMMMMMMM;
:                                                                            :
: You can change division descriptions to your needs.                       :
:                                                                            :
LMMMMMMMMMMMMMMMMMMMMMMMMMMMMKMM Manual page # 3-3    MMMMMMMMMMMMMMMMMMMMMMMMMM9
:    DIVISIONS           :       SUBDIVISIONS                                :
: 1  GENERAL DISCIPLINES :   8.0                                             :
: 2  SITEWORK            :   8.1 HOLLOW METAL                                :
: 3  CONCRETE            :   8.2 WOOD/PLASTIC DOORS                          :
: 4  MASONRY             :   8.3 SPECIAL DOORS                               :
: 5  METAL/STRUCTURAL    :   8.4 STOREFRONT & GLASS                          :
: 6  WOOD AND PLASTIC    :   8.5 FINISH HARDWARE                             :
: 7  THERMAL/MOISTURE CTL:   8.6                                             :
: 8  DOORS AND WINDOWS!!!:   8.7                                             :
: 9  FINISHES            :   8.8                                             :
: 10 SPECIALTIES         :   8.9                                             :
: 11 EQUIPMENT           :                                                   :
: 12 FURNISHINGS         :                                                   :
: 13 SPECIAL CONSTRUCTION:                                                   :
: 14 CONVEYING SYSTEMS   :                                                   :
: 15 MECHANICAL          :                                                   :
: 16 ELECTRICAL          :                                                   :
: Selection: D8                                                              :
HMMMMMMMMMMMMMMMMMMMMMMMMMMMMMMMMMMMMMMMMMMMMMMMMMMMMMMMMMMMMMMMMMMMMMMMMMMMMM(
```

Figure 9.18. Divisions and subdivision 8 of EasyEst WBS.

```
IMMMMMMMMMMMMMMMMMMMMMMMMMMMMMMMMMMMMMMMMMMMMMMMMMMMMMMMMMMMMMMMMMMMMMMMMMMMMM;
:                                                                            :
: You can change division descriptions to your needs.                       :
:                                                                            :
LMMMMMMMMMMMMMMMMMMMMMMMMMMMMKMM Manual page # 3-3    MMMMMMMMMMMMMMMMMMMMMMMMMM9
:    DIVISIONS           :       SUBDIVISIONS                                :
: 1  GENERAL DISCIPLINES :   9.0 LATH AND PLASTER                            :
: 2  SITEWORK            :   9.1 METAL STUD FRAMING                          :
: 3  CONCRETE            :   9.2 DRYWALL                                     :
: 4  MASONRY             :   9.3 ACOUSTICAL SYSTEMS                          :
: 5  METAL/STRUCTURAL    :   9.4 SPECIAL COATINGS                            :
: 6  WOOD AND PLASTIC    :   9.5 PAINTING/WALLCOVRING                        :
: 7  THERMAL/MOISTURE CTL:   9.6 CERAMIC/QUARRY TILE                         :
: 8  DOORS AND WINDOWS   :   9.7 TERRAZZO                                    :
: 9  FINISHES!!!!!!!!!!!!:   9.8 RESILIENT FLOORING                          :
: 10 SPECIALTIES         :   9.9 CARPETING                                   :
: 11 EQUIPMENT           :                                                   :
: 12 FURNISHINGS         :                                                   :
: 13 SPECIAL CONSTRUCTION:                                                   :
: 14 CONVEYING SYSTEMS   :                                                   :
: 15 MECHANICAL          :                                                   :
: 16 ELECTRICAL          :                                                   :
: Selection: D9                                                              :
HMMMMMMMMMMMMMMMMMMMMMMMMMMMMMMMMMMMMMMMMMMMMMMMMMMMMMMMMMMMMMMMMMMMMMMMMMMMMM(
```

Figure 9.19. Divisions and subdivision 9 of EasyEst WBS.

```
IMMMMMMMMMMMMMMMMMMMMMMMMMMMMMMMMMMMMMMMMMMMMMMMMMMMMMMMMMMMMMMMMMMMMMMMMMMMMMMMMM;
:                                                                               :
: You can change division descriptions to your needs.                          :
:                                                                               :
LMMMMMMMMMMMMMMMMMMMMMMMMMMKMM Manual page # 3-3   MMMMMMMMMMMMMMMMMMMMMMMMMMM9
:     DIVISIONS            :        SUBDIVISIONS                                :
: 1  GENERAL DISCIPLINES   : 10.0                                              :
: 2  SITEWORK              : 10.1 BLDG SPECIALTIES                             :
: 3  CONCRETE              : 10.2 PARTITION SYSTEMS                            :
: 4  MASONRY               : 10.3                                             :
: 5  METAL/STRUCTURAL      : 10.4                                             :
: 6  WOOD AND PLASTIC      : 10.5                                             :
: 7  THERMAL/MOISTURE CTL  : 10.6                                             :
: 8  DOORS AND WINDOWS     : 10.7                                             :
: 9  FINISHES              : 10.8                                             :
: 10 SPECIALTIES!!!!!!!!!! : 10.9                                             :
: 11 EQUIPMENT             :                                                  :
: 12 FURNISHINGS           :                                                  :
: 13 SPECIAL CONSTRUCTION  :                                                  :
: 14 CONVEYING SYSTEMS     :                                                  :
: 15 MECHANICAL            :                                                  :
: 16 ELECTRICAL            :                                                  :
: Selection: D10                                                               :
HMMMMMMMMMMMMMMMMMMMMMMMMMMMMMMMMMMMMMMMMMMMMMMMMMMMMMMMMMMMMMMMMMMMMMMMMMMMMMMM(
```

Figure 9.20. Divisions and subdivision 10 of EasyEst WBS.

```
IMMMMMMMMMMMMMMMMMMMMMMMMMMMMMMMMMMMMMMMMMMMMMMMMMMMMMMMMMMMMMMMMMMMMMMMMMMMMMMMMM;
:                                                                               :
: You can change division descriptions to your needs.                          :
:                                                                               :
LMMMMMMMMMMMMMMMMMMMMMMMMMMKMM Manual page # 3-3   MMMMMMMMMMMMMMMMMMMMMMMMMMM9
:     DIVISIONS            :        SUBDIVISIONS                                :
: 1  GENERAL DISCIPLINES   : 11.0 PARKING EQUIPMENT                            :
: 2  SITEWORK              : 11.1 DOCK LEVELERS                                :
: 3  CONCRETE              : 11.2 SEALS AND SHELTERS                           :
: 4  MASONRY               : 11.3 DOCK BUMPERS                                 :
: 5  METAL/STRUCTURAL      : 11.4 WASTE COMPACTORS                             :
: 6  WOOD AND PLASTIC      : 11.5 FOOD SVCS EQUIPMENT                          :
: 7  THERMAL/MOISTURE CTL  : 11.6 LABORATORY EQUIPMENT                         :
: 8  DOORS AND WINDOWS     : 11.7                                              :
: 9  FINISHES              : 11.8                                              :
: 10 SPECIALTIES           : 11.9                                             :
: 11 EQUIPMENT!!!!!!!!!!!! :                                                  :
: 12 FURNISHINGS           :                                                  :
: 13 SPECIAL CONSTRUCTION  :                                                  :
: 14 CONVEYING SYSTEMS     :                                                  :
: 15 MECHANICAL            :                                                  :
: 16 ELECTRICAL            :                                                  :
: Selection: D11                                                               :
HMMMMMMMMMMMMMMMMMMMMMMMMMMMMMMMMMMMMMMMMMMMMMMMMMMMMMMMMMMMMMMMMMMMMMMMMMMMMMMM(
```

Figure 9.21. Divisions and subdivision 11 of EasyEst WBS.

```
IMMMMMMMMMMMMMMMMMMMMMMMMMMMMMMMMMMMMMMMMMMMMMMMMMMMMMMMMMMMMMMMMMMMMMMMMMMMMMMMMM;
:                                                                               :
: You can change division descriptions to your needs.                          :
:                                                                               :
LMMMMMMMMMMMMMMMMMMMMMMMMMMKMM Manual page # 3-3   MMMMMMMMMMMMMMMMMMMMMMMMMMM9
:     DIVISIONS            :        SUBDIVISIONS                                :
: 1  GENERAL DISCIPLINES   : 12.0 METAL CASEWORK                               :
: 2  SITEWORK              : 12.1 RESIDENTIAL CASEWORK                         :
: 3  CONCRETE              : 12.2 HORIZ. LOUVER BLINDS                         :
: 4  MASONRY               : 12.3 DRAPERY TRACK                                :
: 5  METAL/STRUCTURAL      : 12.4 FLOOR MATS                                   :
: 6  WOOD AND PLASTIC      : 12.5                                              :
: 7  THERMAL/MOISTURE CTL  : 12.6                                              :
: 8  DOORS AND WINDOWS     : 12.7                                              :
: 9  FINISHES              : 12.8                                              :
: 10 SPECIALTIES           : 12.9                                             :
: 11 EQUIPMENT             :                                                  :
: 12 FURNISHINGS!!!!!!!!!! :                                                  :
: 13 SPECIAL CONSTRUCTION  :                                                  :
: 14 CONVEYING SYSTEMS     :                                                  :
: 15 MECHANICAL            :                                                  :
: 16 ELECTRICAL            :                                                  :
: Selection: D12                                                               :
HMMMMMMMMMMMMMMMMMMMMMMMMMMMMMMMMMMMMMMMMMMMMMMMMMMMMMMMMMMMMMMMMMMMMMMMMMMMMMMM(
```

Figure 9.22. Divisions and subdivision 12 of EasyEst WBS.

```
IMMMMMMMMMMMMMMMMMMMMMMMMMMMMMMMMMMMMMMMMMMMMMMMMMMMMMMMMMMMMMMMMMMMMMMMMMMMM;
:                                                                          :
: You can change division descriptions to your needs.                     :
:                                                                          :
IMMMMMMMMMMMMMMMMMMMMMMMMMMKMM Manual page # 3-3   MMMMMMMMMMMMMMMMMMMMMMMMM9
:     DIVISIONS         :        SUBDIVISIONS                              :
: 1  GENERAL DISCIPLINES : 13.0 INTEGRATED CEILINGS                        :
: 2  SITEWORK           : 13.1 COLD STORAGE ROOMS                          :
: 3  CONCRETE           : 13.2 PRE-ENGINEERED BLDGS                        :
: 4  MASONRY            : 13.3 ELEC. DUMB WAITER                           :
: 5  METAL/STRUCTURAL   : 13.4 ELECTRIC ELEVATORS                          :
: 6  WOOD AND PLASTIC   : 13.5 HYDRAULIC ELEVATORS                         :
: 7  THERMAL/MOISTURE CTL : 13.6 ESCALATORS                                :
: 8  DOORS AND WINDOWS  : 13.7 WATER CONNECTIONS                           :
: 9  FINISHES           : 13.8                                            :
: 10 SPECIALTIES        : 13.9                                            :
: 11 EQUIPMENT          :                                                  :
: 12 FURNISHINGS        :                                                  :
: 13 SPECIAL CONSTRUCTION :                                                :
: 14 CONVEYING SYSTEMS  :                                                  :
: 15 MECHANICAL         :                                                  :
: 16 ELECTRICAL         :                                                  :
: Selection: D13                                                           :
HMMMMMMMMMMMMMMMMMMMMMMMMMMMMMMMMMMMMMMMMMMMMMMMMMMMMMMMMMMMMMMMMMMMMMMMMMMMM(
```

Figure 9.23. Divisions and subdivision 13 of EasyEst WBS.

```
IMMMMMMMMMMMMMMMMMMMMMMMMMMMMMMMMMMMMMMMMMMHMMMMMMMMMMMMMMMMMMMMMMMMMMMMMMMMMM;
:                                                                          :
: You can change division descriptions to your needs.                     :
:                                                                          :
IMMMMMMMMMMMMMMMMMMMMMMMMMKMM Manual page # 3-3   MMMMMMMMMMMMMMMMMMMMMMMMMM9
:     DIVISIONS         :        SUBDIVISIONS                              :
: 1  GENERAL DISCIPLINES : 14.0 COMMERCIAL ELEVATORS                       :
: 2  SITEWORK           : 14.1 COMMERCIAL ESCALATOR                        :
: 3  CONCRETE           : 14.2 HOISTS AND CRANES                           :
: 4  MASONRY            : 14.3 MTL CONVEYING SYSTEM                        :
: 5  METAL/STRUCTURAL   : 14.4                                            :
: 6  WOOD AND PLASTIC   : 14.5                                            :
: 7  THERMAL/MOISTURE CTL : 14.6                                          :
: 8  DOORS AND WINDOWS  : 14.7                                            :
: 9  FINISHES           : 14.8                                            :
: 10 SPECIALTIES        : 14.9                                            :
: 11 EQUIPMENT          :                                                  :
: 12 FURNISHINGS        :                                                  :
: 13 SPECIAL CONSTRUCTION :                                                :
: 14 CONVEYING SYSTEMS!!! :                                                :
: 15 MECHANICAL         :                                                  :
: 16 ELECTRICAL         :                                                  :
: Selection: D14                                                           :
HMMMMMMMMMMMMMMMMMMMMMMMMMMMMMMMMMMMMMMMMMMMMMMMMMMMMMMMMMMMMMMMMMMMMMMMMMMMM(
```

Figure 9.24. Divisions and subdivision 14 of EasyEst WBS.

```
IMMMMMMMMMMMMMMMMMMMMMMMMMMMMMMMMMMMMMMMMMMMMMMMMMMMMMMMMMMMMMMMMMMMMMMMMMMMM;
:                                                                          :
: You can change division descriptions to your needs.                     :
:                                                                          :
IMMMMMMMMMMMMMMMMMMMMMMMMMKMM Manual page # 3-3   MMMMMMMMMMMMMMMMMMMMMMMMMM9
:     DIVISIONS         :        SUBDIVISIONS                              :
: 1  GENERAL DISCIPLINES : 15.0                                           :
: 2  SITEWORK           : 15.1 PLUMBING                                    :
: 3  CONCRETE           : 15.2 PIPING,VALVE,FITTING                        :
: 4  MASONRY            : 15.3 HVAC                                        :
: 5  METAL/STRUCTURAL   : 15.4 FIRE PROT.(HYDRANTS)                        :
: 6  WOOD AND PLASTIC   : 15.5 CNTLS/INSTRUMENTATON                        :
: 7  THERMAL/MOISTURE CTL : 15.6 SPECIAL SYSTEMS                           :
: 8  DOORS AND WINDOWS  : 15.7 BRIDGE CROSSINGS                            :
: 9  FINISHES           : 15.8                                            :
: 10 SPECIALTIES        : 15.9                                            :
: 11 EQUIPMENT          :                                                  :
: 12 FURNISHINGS        :                                                  :
: 13 SPECIAL CONSTRUCTION :                                                :
: 14 CONVEYING SYSTEMS  :                                                  :
: 15 MECHANICAL!!!!!!!!!!! :                                               :
: 16 ELECTRICAL         :                                                  :
: Selection: D15                                                           :
HMMMMMMMMMMMMMMMMMMMMMMMMMMMMMMMMMMMMMMMMMMMMMMMMMMMMMMMMMMMMMMMMMMMMMMMMMMMM(
```

Figure 9.25. Divisions and subdivision 15 of EasyEst WBS.

```
INNNNNNNNNNNNNNNNNNNNNNNNNNNNNNNNNNNNNNNNNNNNNNNNNNNNNNNNNNNNNNNNNNNNNNNNNNNNNN;
:                                                                            :
: You can change division descriptions to your needs.                       :
:                                                                            :
INNNNNNNNNNNNNNNNNNNNNNNNNKNN Manual page # 3-3  NNNNNNNNNNNNNNNNNNNNNNNNNNNN9
:   DIVISIONS          :         SUBDIVISIONS                                :
: 1  GENERAL DISCIPLINES : 16.0 CABINETS/ENCLOSURES                          :
: 2  SITEWORK          : 16.1 RESIDENTIAL                                    :
: 3  CONCRETE          : 16.2 COMMERCIAL/INDUSTRIAL                          :
: 4  MASONRY           : 16.3 POWER TRANSMISSION                             :
: 5  METAL/STRUCTURAL  : 16.4 COMMUNICATIONS                                 :
: 6  WOOD AND PLASTIC  : 16.5 CONDUIT                                        :
: 7  THERMAL/MOISTURE CTL : 16.6 CABLE TRAYS                                 :
: 8  DOORS AND WINDOWS : 16.7 WIRE AND CABLE                                 :
: 9  FINISHES          : 16.8 BOXES                                          :
: 10 SPECIALTIES       : 16.9 WIRING DEVICES                                 :
: 11 EQUIPMENT         :                                                     :
: 12 FURNISHINGS       :                                                     :
: 13 SPECIAL CONSTRUCTION :                                                  :
: 14 CONVEYING SYSTEMS :                                                     :
: 15 MECHANICAL        :                                                     :
: 16 ELECTRICAL:::::::::: :                                                  :
: Selection: D16                                                             :
HNNNNNNNNNNNNNNNNNNNNNNNNNNNNNNNNNNNNNNNNNNNNNNNNNNNNNNNNNNNNNNNNNNNNNNNNNNNNNN(
```

Figure 9.26. Divisions and subdivision 16 of EasyEst WBS.

Primavera Project Planner™, developed by Primavera Systems, Incorporated, uses cost account numbers that indicate each work element. A sample Primavera cost account code numbering and title sheet is shown in Figure 9.28.

9.4 SCHEDULING THE WORK ELEMENTS

From a scheduling standpoint, microcomputer cost estimating software packages fall into two general categories: (1) those that produce "point" estimates and (2)

```
                        WORK BREAKDOWN STRUCTURE FOR CLAMS1
CLAMS1                                                    Current Date: 06-11-85

    JOB                 NAME

    2000       PROJECT MANAGEMENT
    2100       PROJ DIRECTION
    2200       PROCUREMENT
    2300       DOCUMENTATION
    4000       SYS ENG
    4100       STUDY & ANALYSIS
    4200       DESIGN
    4210       TST/FIX DESIGN
    4220       PROTO DESIGN
    4230       FLT HDW DESIGN
    6000       PROTO FAB/ASS
    6100       RINGS/PROTO
    6200       LATCHES/PROTO
    6300       FASTENERS/PROTO
    6400       ASSEMBLY/PROTO
    7000       FL UNIT/FAB/ASS
    7100       RINGS/FLIGHT
    7200       LATCHES/FLIGHT
    7300       FASTENERS/FLIGHT
    7400       ASSEMBLY/FLIGHT
    8000       TESTING
    8100       TEST FIX/FAB
    8200       INSTRUMENTATION
    8300       PROTO TEST
    8400       ACCEPTANCE TEST
    9000       FLIGHT HDW DELIVERY
```

Figure 9.27. Work breakdown structure for CLAMS1 (PS5000).

```
-------------------------------------------------------------------------------
                          PRIMAVERA PROJECT PLANNER                          ACD3
                          Summary of Cost Account Codes              Page    1
-------------------------------------------------------------------------------

Cost Categories:

     Code     Category Title      Code     Category Title
     ----     --------------      ----     --------------
      L           LABOR            M          MATERIAL
      E           EQUIP.           S          SUBCONT.


Cost Account Titles:

     Cost Account Number                  Account Title
     -------------------      ---------------------------------------------
                  101         EXCAVATION
                  102         SOIL STABILIZATION
                  105         CONCRETE WORK
                  106         TERMITE PROTECTION
                  107         PRECAST CONCRETE
                  108         MISCELLANEOUS METAL
                  109         STRUCTURAL METAL
                  110         EXTERIOR ARCHITECTURAL TREATMENT
                  111         GLASS AND GLAZING
                  112         SHEETROCK
                  115         LUMBER
                  116         INSULATION
                  120         PAINTING
                  121         FLOORING
                  122         WALL COVERING
                  125         HARDWARE
                  130         CABINETWORK
                  131         FINISH LUMBER
                  132         BATHROOM ACCESSORIES
                  133         CARPETING
                  134         DRAPES
                  301         EXTERIOR PLUMBING
                  302         ROUGH PLUMBING
                  303         PLUMBING APPLIAMCES
                  401         EXTERIOR HVAC
                  402         ROUGH HVAC
                  403         FINISH HVAC
                  501         EXTERIOR ELECTRICAL
                  502         ROUGH ELECTRICAL
                  503         FINISH ELECTRICAL
                    1         GENERAL CONSTRUCTION
                    3         PLUMBING
                    4         HEATING,VENTILLATING & AIR CONDITIONING
                    5         ELECTRICAL
```

Figure 9.28. Primavera summary of cost account codes.

those that produce time-phased estimates. Point estimates are used for many short-term construction projects and projects of other types that are expected to occur within a single calendar year or fiscal year. Point estimates usually do not account for the fact that rates or prices will escalate over the time period during which the project is performed but assume that payment will be made at some agreed-upon time or times during the project that are keyed to percent completion rather than time passage or resource expenditure. If sequencing of tasks is done within a job that is subjected to a point estimate, this job sequencing is usually not reflected in a corresponding time phasing of resource estimates.

On the other hand, many jobs that are expected to last for a year or more are time scheduled using one of the many available critical path or "PERT"-based microcomputer software applications programs and are estimated against a derived

```
GANTT CHART REPORT  -  Current Date: 05-22-85


CLAMS1                              1987                                      1988
------------------------------------ JAN FEB MAR APR MAY JUN JUL AUG SEP OCT NOV DEC JAN FEB MAR APR MAY JUN JUL
CODE            JOB NAME             0   1   2   3   4   5   6   7   8   9   10  11  12  13  14  15  16  17  18

2000 PROJECT MANAGEMENT             0==================================================================================
2100 PROJ DIRECTION                 0==================================================================================
2200 PROCUREMENT                    0==================================================================================
2300 DOCUMENTATION                  0==================================================================================
4000 SYS ENG                        0=========================X.    .   .   .   .   .   .   .   .   .   .   .
4100 STUDY & ANALYSIS               0=============).   .   .   .   .   .   .   .   .   .   .   .   .   .   .
4200 DESIGN                         .   .   .   )====================================================================
4210 TST/FIX DESIGN                 .   .   .   )-------------).........).  .   .   .   .   .   .   .   .   .
4220 PROTO DESIGN                   .   .   .   )=============).  .   .   .   .   .   .   .   .   .   .   .
4230 FLT HDW DESIGN                 .   .   .   .   .   .   .   .   .   .   .   .   .   .   .   .   .   )=========
6000 PROTO FAB/ASS                  .   .   .   .   .   )=================).   .   .   .   .   .   .   .
6100 RINGS/PROTO                    .   .   .   .   .   )=================X.   .   .   .   .   .   .   .
6200 LATCHES/PROTO                  .   .   .   .   .   )=================X.   .   .   .   .   .   .   .
6300 FASTENERS/PROTO                .   .   .   .   .   )=================X.   .   .   .   .   .   .   .
6400 ASSEMBLY/PROTO                 .   .   .   .   .   )================X.   .   .   .   .   .   .   .
7000 FL UNIT/FAB/ASS                .   .   .   .   .   .   .   .   .   .   .   .   .   .   .   .   .
7100 RINGS/FLIGHT                   .   .   .   .   .   .   .   .   .   .   .   .   .   .   .   .   .
7200 LATCHES/FLIGHT                 .   .   .   .   .   .   .   .   .   .   .   .   .   .   .   .   .
7300 FASTENERS/FLIGHT               .   .   .   .   .   .   .   .   .   .   .   .   .   .   .   .   .
7400 ASSEMBLY/FLIGHT                .   .   .   .   .   .   .   .   .   .   .   .   .   .   .   .   .
8000 TESTING                        .   .   .   .   .   .   .   .   .   .   .   .   .   .   .   .   .
8100 TEST FIX/FAB                   .   .   .   .   .   )--------).........).   .   .   .   .   .   .
8200 INSTRUMENTATION                .   .   .   .   .   .   .   .   .   .   .   .   .   .   .   .   .
8300 PROTO TEST                     .   .   .   .   .   .   .   )===============================X.
8400 ACCEPTANCE TEST                .   .   .   .   .   .   .   .   .   .   .   .   .   .   .   .   .
9000 FLIGHT HDW DELIVERY            .   .   .   .   .   .   .   .   .   .   .   .   .   .   .   .   .


SYMBOL DEFINITIONS:

    0 PROJECT START     )===) CRITICAL
    S DATE DEPENDENCY   )---) NON-CRITICAL
    X TERMINATOR        ....) SLACK
    * MILESTONE         ):::) FINISHED
```

Figure 9.29. CLAMS1 project bar chart schedule (PS5000).

time base to develop time-based resource estimate profiles. Project Scheduler 5000™, by Scitor Corporation, an excellent microcomputer-based scheduling/estimating program based on the use of the critical path bar chart method of scheduling, is used here for illustration. Each schedule element has a job code number and title and is entered in sequence in the program with its predecessor/successor relationships and duration. The software package then calculates the critical path or critical paths and plots the resulting critical path bar chart on a time-based schedule that shows critical schedule elements, noncritical schedule elements, and slack times. Figure 9.29 shows a typical bar chart schedule output for the CLAMS1 Project. Notice that symbols are available for project start, milestones, schedule element terminators, and date dependencies. When used on a microcomputer with a color monitor, this bar chart shows up in a colorful format that depicts the critical path, noncritical elements, slack times, and completed work in different colors. A variety of time schedules are available to allow scheduling on a daily, weekly, or monthly basis. Resources can then be estimated for each schedule element to derive a completed cost estimate. Any changes in schedule, then, are automatically reflected in the time-based resource estimates once the estimate is calculated.

GANTT CHART REPORT - Current Date: 05-22-85

```
CLAMS1                              1988                1989
-----------------------------------  AUG SEP OCT NOV DEC JAN FEB MAR APR MAY JUN JUL
CODE            JOB NAME             19  20  21  22  23  24  25  26  27  28  29  30

2000 PROJECT MANAGEMENT      ========================================================X.
2100 PROJ DIRECTION          ========================================================X.
2200 PROCUREMENT             ========================================================X.
2300 DOCUMENTATION           ========================================================X.
4000 SYS ENG                 .    .    .    .    .    .    .    .    .    .    .    .
4100 STUDY & ANALYSIS        .    .    .    .    .    .    .    .    .    .    .    .
4200 DESIGN                  =========X.   .    .    .    .    .    .    .    .    .
4210 TST/FIX DESIGN          .    .    .    .    .    .    .    .    .    .    .    .
4220 PROTO DESIGN            .    .    .    .    .    .    .    .    .    .    .    .
4230 FLT HDW DESIGN          ===============).  .    .    .    .    .    .    .    .
6000 PROTO FAB/ASS           .    .    .    .    .    .    .    .    .    .    .    .
6100 RINGS/PROTO             .    .    .    .    .    .    .    .    .    .    .    .
6200 LATCHES/PROTO           .    .    .    .    .    .    .    .    .    .    .    .
6300 FASTENERS/PROTO         .    .    .    .    .    .    .    .    .    .    .    .
6400 ASSEMBLY/PROTO          .    .    .    .    .    .    .    .    .    .    .    .
7000 FL UNIT/FAB/ASS         .    .    .  )===================).   .    .    .    .
7100 RINGS/FLIGHT            .    .    .  )===================X.   .    .    .    .
7200 LATCHES/FLIGHT          .    .    .  )===================X.   .    .    .    .
7300 FASTENERS/FLIGHT        .    .    .  )===================X.   .    .    .    .
7400 ASSEMBLY/FLIGHT         .    .    .  )===================X.   .    .    .    .
8000 TESTING                 .    .    .  )=============================X.
8100 TEST FIX/FAB            .    .    .    .    .    .    .    .    .    .    .    .
8200 INSTRUMENTATION         .    .    .  )===================X.   .    .    .    .
8300 PROTO TEST              .    .    .    .    .    .    .    .    .    .    .    .
8400 ACCEPTANCE TEST         .    .    .    .    .    .  )==================X.
9000 FLIGHT HDW DELIVERY     .    .    .    .    .    .  )==================X.

SYMBOL DEFINITIONS:

    0 PROJECT START      )===) CRITICAL
    S DATE DEPENDENCY    )---) NON-CRITICAL
    X TERMINATOR         ....) SLACK
    * MILESTONE          ):::) FINISHED
```

Figure 9.29. (*Continued*)

    Both Project Scheduler 5000™ and Primavera™ account for holidays and weekends in the work schedule so that (1) only work days are counted as resource bearing, and (2) job durations can be stated in working days, but, when scheduled, the milestones and activities fit themselves to a specific yearly calendar. A typical calendar for Primavera™, for example, is shown in Figure 9.30. Notice that only working days are counted for scheduling purposes.

    Primavera Project Planner™ prints out a network path analysis. A sample is shown in Figure 9.31. Each box represents a schedule number and contains the account number, schedule element title, original duration, remaining duration, percent complete, early start date, and early finish date. This type of printout gives a visual representation of a PERT-type block diagram of the total project. (The figures shown depict only the first 21 activities of a typical project.)

9.5 RETRIEVAL OF HISTORICAL COST DATA

Once a work element structure, work element dictionary, and project schedule have been developed, the major work content of the job has been established on a

```
------------------------------------------------------------------------
                        PRIMAVERA PROJECT PLANNER
REPORT DATE 30APR85          PROJECT CALENDAR            START DATE 13DEC82

American Community Developers              Duplicate of Project HOME
------------------------------------------------------------------------
```

SUNDAY	MONDAY	TUESDAY	WEDNESDAY	THURSDAY	FRIDAY	SATURDAY
	13DEC82 0	14DEC82 1	15DEC82 2	16DEC82 3	17DEC82 4	18DEC82 WEEKEND
19DEC82 WEEKEND	20DEC82 5	21DEC82 6	22DEC82 7	23DEC82 8	24DEC82 HOLIDAY	25DEC82 WEEKEND
26DEC82 WEEKEND	27DEC82 9	28DEC82 10	29DEC82 11	30DEC82 12	31DEC82 HOLIDAY	
						1JAN83 WEEKEND
2JAN83 WEEKEND	3JAN83 13	4JAN83 14	5JAN83 15	6JAN83 16	7JAN83 17	8JAN83 WEEKEND
9JAN83 WEEKEND	10JAN83 18	11JAN83 19	12JAN83 20	13JAN83 21	14JAN83 22	15JAN83 WEEKEND
16JAN83 WEEKEND	17JAN83 23	18JAN83 24	19JAN83 25	20JAN83 26	21JAN83 27	22JAN83 WEEKEND
23JAN83 WEEKEND	24JAN83 28	25JAN83 29	26JAN83 30	27JAN83 31	28JAN83 32	29JAN83 WEEKEND
30JAN83 WEEKEND	31JAN83 33					

Figure 9.30. Project calendar (Primavera).

qualitative basis. This qualitative data can then be used to search historical records of past jobs to determine what resources were expended on similar or identical tasks within previous jobs. The microcomputer is an ideal tool for collecting, recording, organizing, and retrieving historical cost data. A data base applications package such as DBaseIII™ (Ashton-Tate) or a file manager such as pfs File™ (and pfs Report™) is appropriate for collecting historical cost data which can later be retrieved or selected based on anticipated characteristics of the new job. Integrated software packages that contain data base features are also suitable tools for cost data collection and retrieval.

To possess the capability to retrieve pertinent historical cost data rapidly, it is necessary to embark upon a long-term systematic data collection and organization effort. Before a cost data retrieval capability can exist, months and even years of data collection effort must be expended to record, segregate, organize, and enter cost data from past and ongoing work activities. The cost data must be subdivided into cost elements; the jobs must be broken down into the same size increments that are expected to be needed in new cost estimates; and adequate descriptive, supplier, delivery, and schedule information must be recorded and organized. Typical information that should be collected on each work element or schedule element of each previous or ongoing job are the following:

1. Short title
2. Description of the work

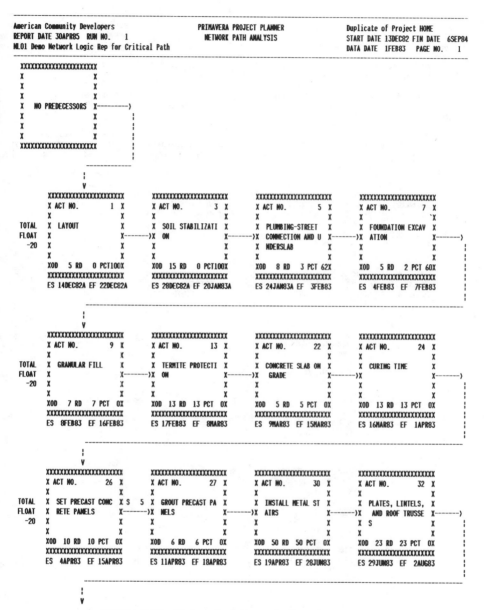

Figure 9.31. Network path analysis (Primavera).

335

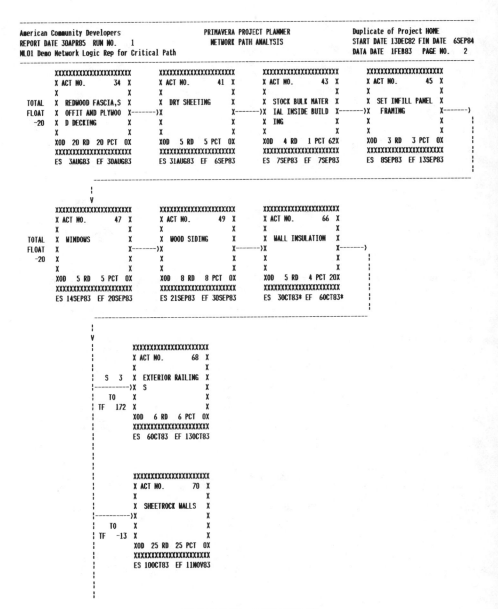

Figure 9.31. (*Continued*)

3. Supplier's name and address
4. Date work was initiated
5. Duration of the work
6. Geographical location of the work
7. Quantity or units purchased
8. Labor hour expenditures by skill
9. Material costs
10. Equipment costs
11. Other costs
12. Special terms and conditions (i.e., type of contract, special reliability or quality requirements, and accompanying documentation)
13. Weight, volume, power, or capacity

Once a large data base containing this type of information is collected, organized, and entered into a microcomputer applications data base program, the estimator can search on one or more fields to collect all of the tasks that are similar or identical to the one being estimated to determine the resources expended or estimated for previous or ongoing jobs. Typical fields that might be specified on a typical search might be the short title, supplier's name, and quantity of units purchased. For example, the estimator might search for the costs of 200-ohm potentiometers purchased from Delta Electronics in quantities of 100; or for the costs of $\frac{1}{2}$-inch copper elbows purchased from Wyck's Plumbing in quantities of 500. The other fields, then are used as qualifiers to scan the applicability of the data to the job at hand. The retrieved data base can then be narrowed down even further if desired by limiting the retrieved records to those parts or services purchased after a given date, or work performed in a specific location.

There are a large number of data base programs suitable for cost data storage and retrieval. Two examples, a database on pfs File™ and one on Lotus 1-2-3™, are shown on Figures 9.32 and 9.33. Some larger vertical market estimating soft-

```
Item #:              Date:

Description:


Supplier:                              Location:

Lbr Hrs:

Acq $:          Opn $:          Trans $:          Salvage $:

Lead Time:

Weight:          Volume:

Length:          Width:          Height:
```

Figure 9.32. Typical data base form for historical data (pfs File).

HISTORICAL DATABASE OF DIRECT COST ELEMENTS

ITEM#	DATE	DESCRIPTION	SUPPLIER	LOCATION	LBR HRS	ACQ $	OPN $	TRANS	SALVAGE$	LEAD TIME	VOLUME	WEIGHT	LENGTH	WIDTH	HEIGHT
1	15-Jun-85	Aerospace Latches	Ryan Aeronautical	Culver City, CA		$1,500			$200	3 mos					
2															
3															
4															
5															
6															
7															
8															
9															
10															
11															
12															
13															
14															
15															
16															
17															
18															
19															
20															
21															
22															
23															
24															
25															
26															
27															
28															
29															
30															
31															
32															
33															
34															
35															
36															
37															
38															
39															
40															

Figure 9.33. Typical data base for historical data (Lotus 1-2-3).

ware packages such as EasyEst™ and its big brother, ESPRI™, are marketed with ready-made data bases of information suitable for general contractors, electrical contractors, homebuilders, and the like.

The generic cost estimating program, microPICES™, by Microestimating, Inc., uses a form of data base for its "cost accounts," which are really a combination of cost and work elements arranged by cost account reference numbers. Each record in the data base contains reference number, account name, work element code number, level of the account in the work element structure, cost estimating relationship that is used, and other codes used in computations in this flexible system. A listing of cost accounts used for a sample estimate is shown in Figure 9.34.

```
Listing of current Cost Accounts in file E:PROP.MPC
Listing contains reference numbers in the range of 1  to178
File contains reference numbers in the range of 1  to178
```

Refnce Num	Account Name	WBS Code	Acct Levl	Prcs Code	Matx Code	CER Code
1	TYPE I CONFIG CONT	1.2.24.14.0	1	0	0	1
2	FAT ENGR	1.2.24.14.1.0	2	0	0	0
4	ENGINEERING		3	F1	0	0
6	TECH A		4	F1	1	2
8	HOURS		5	F1	1	2
10	RATE		5	F1	1	1
12	MANUFACTURING		3	F2	0	0
26	PROD TEST ENGR	1.2.24.14.2.0	2	0	0	0
28	ENGINEERING		3	F1	0	0
30	TECH A		4	F1	1	2
32	HOURS		5	F1	1	2
34	RATE		5	F1	1	1
36	MANUFACTURING		3	F2	0	0
50	OPTION TEST ENGR	1.2.24.14.3.0	2	0	0	0
52	ENGINEERING		3	F1	0	0
54	TECH A		4	F1	1	2
56	HOURS		5	F1	1	2
58	RATE		5	F1	1	1
60	MANUFACTURING		3	F2	0	0
74	TOTAL ENGR		2	0	4	3
76	ENGR O/H (165%)		3	0	4	3
78	TOTAL MFR		2	0	4	3
80	MFG O/H (100%)		3	0	4	3
82	SUB-TOTAL		2	0	4	3
84	GEN & ADMIN (15%)		2	0	4	3
86	TOTAL COST		3	0	4	3
88	FEE/PROFIT (10%)		2	0	4	3
90	TOTAL PRICE		3	0	4	3
92	TOTAL HOURS		2	0	4	2
94	CUM HOURS		3	0	4	3
96	TYPE II MAINT PAN	1.2.24.15.0	1	0	0	1
98	12 CHANNEL FAT ENG	1.2.24.15.1.0	2	0	0	0
100	ENGINEERING		3	F1	1	0
102	TECH A		4	F1	1	2
104	HOURS		5	F1	1	2
106	RATE		5	F1	1	1
108	MANUFACTURING		3	F2	0	0
110	24 CHANNEL PROD		2	0	0	0
112	ENGINEERING		3	F1	0	0
114	TECH A		4	0	1	2
116	HOURS		5	F1	1	2
118	RATE		5	F1	1	1
120	MANUFACTURING		3	F2	0	0
122	24 CH OPTION TEST	1.2.24.15.3.0	2	0	0	0
124	ENGINEERING		3	F1	0	0
126	TECH A		4	F1	1	2

Figure 9.34. Listing of cost accounts for sample estimate (microPICES).

```
Listing of current Cost Accounts in file E:PROP.MPC
Listing contains reference numbers in the range of1 to178
File contains reference numbers in the range of1 to178
```

Refnce Num	Account Name	WBS Code	Acct Levl	Prcs Code	Matx Code	CFR Code
128	HOURS		5	F1	1	2
130	RATE		5	F1	1	1
132	MANUFACTURING		3	F2	0	0
134	TOTAL ENGINEERING		2	0	4	3
136	ENGR O/H (165%)		3	0	4	3
138	TOTAL MFR		2	0	4	3
140	MFR O/H (100%)		3	0	4	3
142	SUB-TOTAL		2	0	4	3
144	GEN & ADMIN (15%)		2	0	4	3
146	TOTAL COST		3	0	4	3
148	FEE/PROFIT (10%)		2	0	4	3
150	TOTAL PRICE		3	0	4	3
152	TOTAL HOURS		2	0	4	2
154	CUM HOURS		3	0	4	3
156	ACCT BOTTOM LINE	1.2.24.0	1	0	0	0
158	TOTAL ENGINEERING	1.2.24.0	2	0	4	3
160	ENGR O/H (165%)		3	0	4	3
162	TOTAL MFR		2	0	4	3
164	MFR O/H (100%)		3	0	4	3
166	SUB-TOTAL		2	0	4	3
168	GEN & ADMIN (15%)		2	0	4	3
170	TOTAL COST		3	0	4	3
172	FEE/PROFIT (10%)		2	0	4	3
174	TOTAL PRICE		3	0	4	3
176	TOTAL HOURS		2	0	4	3
178	CUMLATIVE HOURS		3	0	4	3

Figure 9.34. (Continued)

9.6 DEVELOPMENT AND USE OF COST ESTIMATING RELATIONSHIPS

Often, when the product or service being estimated does not exactly fit those that have been previously manufactured or procured, it is necessary to develop a cost estimating relationship that relates the weight, volume, power, or capacity of the item to be produced to its cost or to the labor hours required for its production. This can be best accomplished by correlating the data by a means known as linear regression (used when one independent variable is used) or multiple regression (used when more than one independent variable is used). Data retrieved from the historical data base in the step discussed previously can be correlated in these CERs through the use of simple microcomputer programs written in the BASIC language. Figure 9.35 is a printout of the coding of a program called CER that can be entered with little or no modification into any microcomputer that runs with the BASIC language. Figures 9.36 and 9.37 show the input and output screens for a typical run of this CER program. Figure 9.38 is a test case run of the derived CER using an input of 3.75 pounds to determine the cost of items with that weight. In a multiple regression estimating relationship program two or more independent performance variables can be correlated with cost or hours for production. For example, cost or hours can be based on weight and power output of a transformer or motor. Sufficient historical data must be available to make a correlation, however, or the program will show an "indeterminate" solution.

```
10 CLS
20 COLOR 7
30 REM THIS PROGRAM IS NAMED "CER"
40 PRINT
50 PRINT TAB(15)"COST ESTIMATING RELATIONSHIP CALCULATIONS"
60 REM    X IS THE WEIGHT OR INDEPENDENT VARIABLE
70 REM    Y IS THE COST OR DEPENDENT VARIABLE
80 REM    X1 IS THE CUMULATIVE VALUES OF WEIGHT OF ALL POINTS
90 REM    Y1 IS THE CUMULATIVE VALUE OF THE COST OF ALL POINTS
100 REM   X2 IS THE WEIGHT SQUARED
110 REM   X3 IS THE CUMULATIVE VALUE OF THE WEIGHT SQUARED
120 REM   Y2 IS THE PRODUCT OF WEIGHT AND COST
130 REM   Y3 IS THE CUMULATIVE PRODUCT OF WEIGHT AND COST
140 REM   B IS THE INTERCEPT ON THE Y (COST) AXIS OF THE BEST FIT LINE
150 REM   M IS THE SLOPE OF THE BEST-FIT LINE
160 PRINT
170 PRINT "DATE:",DATE$
180 PRINT "TIME:",TIME$
190 PRINT
200 INPUT "ENTER THE NUMBER OF PAIRS OF POINTS TO BE EVALUATED ";N
210 PRINT
220 X1=0:Y1=0:X3=0:Y3=0
230 FOR I=1 TO N
240 INPUT "ENTER THE NEXT PAIR OF X AND Y VALUES ";X(I),Y(I)
250 NEXT I
260 PRINT "    WT";"     COST";"    CUM.WT ";"CUM CST   ";"WT.SQ
    ";"CUM.SQ    ";"CUM.PRD  "
270 FOR I = 1 TO N
280 X1=X1+X(I):Y1=Y1+Y(I):X2=X(I)^2:X3=X3+X2:Y2=X(I)*Y(I)
290 Y3=Y3+Y2
300 PRINT USING "########.##"; X(I);Y(I);X1;Y1;X2;X3;Y3
310 NEXT I
320 M=(((Y3*N)/(X1))-Y1)/(((X3*N)/(X1))-X1)
330 PRINT "THE SLOPE (M) OF THE ESTIMATING RELATIONSHIP IS: ";M
340 B=(Y1-(M*X1))/N
350 PRINT "THE INTERCEPT (B) ON THE COST AXIS IS:";B
351 PRINT "THE EQUATION FOR THE CER IS COST OR HOURS = M*X   +B"
352 PRINT "THE EQUATION FOR THE CER IS: COST (OR HOURS)=";M;"TIMES WEIGHT PLUS";
B
353 INPUT "WHAT IS A VALUE OF A TEST WEIGHT OR INDEPENDENT VARIABLE";XT
354 YT=M*XT+B
355 PRINT "THE RESULTING VALUE OF THE COST FOR THE TEST WEIGHT OR INDEPENDENT VA
RIABLE IS:";YT
360 INPUT "DO YOU WANT THIS TO BE PRINTED ON THE PRINTER?(YES/NO)";P$
370 IF P$ = "NO" THEN GOTO 550
380 IF P$ = "N" THEN GOTO 550
390 LPRINT
400 LPRINT TAB(15)"COST ESTIMATING RELATIONSHIP CALCULATIONS"
410 LPRINT
420 LPRINT DATE$,TIME$
430 LPRINT
440 X1=0:Y1=0:X3=0:Y3=0
450 LPRINT "    WT";"     COST";"    CUM.WT ";"CUM CST   ";"WT.SQ
    ";"CUM.SQ    ";"CUM.PRD  "
460 FOR I = 1 TO N
470 X1=X1+X(I):Y1=Y1+Y(I):X2=X(I)^2:X3=X3+X2:Y2=X(I)*Y(I)
480 Y3=Y3+Y2
490 LPRINT USING "########.##"; X(I);Y(I);X1;Y1;X2;X3;Y3
500 NEXT I
510 M=(((Y3*N)/(X1))-Y1)/(((X3*N)/(X1))-X1)
520 LPRINT "THE SLOPE OF THE ESTIMATING RELATIONSHIP IS: ";M
530 B=(Y1-(M*X1))/N
540 LPRINT "THE INTERCEPT ON THE COST AXIS IS:$";B
541 LPRINT
542 LPRINT "THE EQUATION FOR THE CER IS: COST(OR HOURS)=";M;"TIMES WEIGHT PLUS";
B
550 INPUT "PROCESS ANOTHER CER (YES/NO) ";A$
560 IF A$="YES" THEN GOTO 10
570 IF A$="Y" THEN GOTO 10
580 COLOR 7
590 CLS
600 LOCATE 12,35:PRINT "THANK YOU"
610 RUN "DATACOST.BAS"
620 END
```

Figure 9.35. Coding for CER BASIC program (DATACOST).

```
                    COST ESTIMATING RELATIONSHIP CALCULATIONS

        DATE:        06-15-1985
        TIME:        15:26:45

        ENTER THE NUMBER OF PAIRS OF POINTS TO BE EVALUATED  ? 4

        ENTER THE NEXT PAIR OF X AND Y VALUES ? 2,3.5
        ENTER THE NEXT PAIR OF X AND Y VALUES ? 3,7.4
        ENTER THE NEXT PAIR OF X AND Y VALUES ? 4,7.1
        ENTER THE NEXT PAIR OF X AND Y VALUES ? 6,9




        1LIST   2RUN    3LOAD" 4SAVE" 5FILES 6CONT   7,"LPT1 8LOCATE 9COLOR  10PALET
```

Figure 9.36. Input of CER BASIC program (DATACOST).

```
                    COST ESTIMATING RELATIONSHIP CALCULATIONS

        DATE:        06-15-1985
        TIME:        15:26:45

        ENTER THE NUMBER OF PAIRS OF POINTS TO BE EVALUATED  ? 4

        ENTER THE NEXT PAIR OF X AND Y VALUES ? 2,3.5
        ENTER THE NEXT PAIR OF X AND Y VALUES ? 3,7.4
        ENTER THE NEXT PAIR OF X AND Y VALUES ? 4,7.1
        ENTER THE NEXT PAIR OF X AND Y VALUES ? 6,9
            WT       COST      CUM.WT   CUM CST   WT.SQ    CUM.SQ    CUM.PRD
            2.00     3.50      2.00      3.50     4.00      4.00      7.00
            3.00     7.40      5.00     10.90     9.00     13.00     29.20
            4.00     7.10      9.00     18.00    16.00     29.00     57.60
            6.00     9.00     15.00     27.00    36.00     65.00    111.60
        THE SLOPE (M) OF THE ESTIMATING RELATIONSHIP IS:  1.182857
        THE INTERCEPT (B) ON THE COST AXIS IS: 2.314287
        THE EQUATION FOR THE CER IS COST OR HOURS = M*X   +B
        THE EQUATION FOR THE CER IS: COST (OR HOURS)= 1.182857 TIMES WEIGHT PLUS
        2.314287
        WHAT IS A VALUE OF A TEST WEIGHT OR INDEPENDENT VARIABLE?

        1LIST   2RUN    3LOAD" 4SAVE" 5FILES 6CONT   7,"LPT1 8LOCATE 9COLOR  10PALET
```

Figure 9.37. Output of CER BASIC program (DATACOST).

```
        DATE:        06-15-1985
        TIME:        15:26:45

        ENTER THE NUMBER OF PAIRS OF POINTS TO BE EVALUATED  ? 4

        ENTER THE NEXT PAIR OF X AND Y VALUES ? 2,3.5
        ENTER THE NEXT PAIR OF X AND Y VALUES ? 3,7.4
        ENTER THE NEXT PAIR OF X AND Y VALUES ? 4,7.1
        ENTER THE NEXT PAIR OF X AND Y VALUES ? 6,9
            WT       COST      CUM.WT   CUM CST   WT.SQ    CUM.SQ    CUM.PRD
            2.00     3.50      2.00      3.50     4.00      4.00      7.00
            3.00     7.40      5.00     10.90     9.00     13.00     29.20
            4.00     7.10      9.00     18.00    16.00     29.00     57.60
            6.00     9.00     15.00     27.00    36.00     65.00    111.60
        THE SLOPE (M) OF THE ESTIMATING RELATIONSHIP IS:  1.182857
        THE INTERCEPT (B) ON THE COST AXIS IS: 2.314287
        THE EQUATION FOR THE CER IS COST OR HOURS = M*X   +B
        THE EQUATION FOR THE CER IS: COST (OR HOURS)= 1.182857 TIMES WEIGHT PLUS
        2.314287
        WHAT IS A VALUE OF A TEST WEIGHT OR INDEPENDENT VARIABLE? 3.75
        THE RESULTING VALUE OF THE COST FOR THE TEST WEIGHT OR INDEPENDENT VARIABLE IS:
        6.75
        DO YOU WANT THIS TO BE PRINTED ON THE PRINTER?(YES/NO)?
        1LIST   2RUN    3LOAD" 4SAVE" 5FILES 6CONT   7,"LPT1 8LOCATE 9COLOR  10PALET
```

Figure 9.38. Output of CER BASIC program (DATACOST) showing test case.

```
EDITING OLD COST ACCOUNT FILE E:T10.MPC              microPICES V0.9R9 SN 105

     Reference Number:    11000

 (1)   Account Name:   EXAMPLE (CER 11)    (2)   WBS Code:      1.12
 (3)   Account Level:            2         (4)   Process Code:          F3
 (5)   Matrix Code:              2         (6)   CER Num:               11
 (7)   Inflation Code:           0         (8)   Escalation Code:        2
 (9)   Account Summing:         On        (10)   Account Printing:      On
(11)   Distribution Code:        0        (13)   Milestone Number:       0
(17)   Lead/Lag Months:          0

(20)   Edit and Display user defined equation

( 0)   Accept account as is              (-1)   Abort editing of this account
(-2)   Initialize account from other     (-3)   Delete this account from file

       Choice ?
```

Figure 9.39. Sample screen of microPICES showing CER.

Some cost estimating programs incorporate built-in and/or user-defined cost estimating relationships that correlate labor hours, labor dollars, or material dollars with product performance or with cost values of other portions of the estimate. One program that does this is microPICES™, by Microestimating, Inc., of Huntsville, Alabama. Two sample screens from this program are shown in Figures 9.39 and 9.40. The user-defined equation can be edited as shown on the latter of these two screens.

9.7 DEVELOPMENT OF PRODUCTION LEARNING CURVES

The development of the learning curve is another area where the microcomputer can be used to great advantage. As pointed out earlier in this reference manual, the learning curve is a powerful tool for computing expected costs or production labor hours for products or services that are produced in quantity. Again, as in the case of the cost estimating relationship, historical cost data from the cost data base can be used to develop a learning curve slope for a given product line or activity. If given quantities and unit or cumulative average costs or hours for those quantities are known, a learning curve slope for that product line can be developed using a best fit learning curve microcomputer program written in the BASIC language. A BASIC program that does this is shown in Figure 9.41. As is the case with all predictions from past data, care must be taken to assure that the data correlated are truly compatible and that past inefficiencies have not been inadvertently included.

As an example problem, assume that the tenth unit in a production run took 20

```
CER 11 EQUATION EDITWINDOW                          microPICES V0.9R9 SN 105
Type "?" for help
```

```
( ( 0.03 + ( F 1 / SUMD 1 ) ) * ( SUMA 6000 * 1.18 ) )
```

Figure 9.40. Sample screen of microPICES showing CER equation used.

```
10 CLS
20 COLOR 6
30 PRINT TAB(20) "BEST FIT LEARNING CURVE PROGRAM"
40 PRINT:PRINT:PRINT
50 PRINT "DATE:",DATE$
60 PRINT "TIME:",TIME$
70 PRINT
80 REM PROGRAM FITS "BEST" LEARNING CURVE TO DATA POINTS
90 REM USES LINEAR LEAST SQUARES ON TRANSFORMED (LOGARITHM) DATA VALUES
100 INPUT "HOW MANY PAIRS OF DATA POINTS ARE YOU GOING TO ENTER";N
110 PRINT "*****************************************************************
*
120 PRINT " 'X' is the NUMBER of the unit for which the cost or hours are known.
130 PRINT " 'Y' is the COST or HOURS for that 'X'th unit.
140 PRINT "*****************************************************************
*
150 PRINT "INPUT DATA IN THE FORM X,Y"
160 FOR I=1 TO N
170 PRINT "INPUT DATA PAIR # ";I
180 INPUT X(I),Y(I)
190 NEXT I
200 PRINT "THIS IS DATA YOU INPUT :"
210 PRINT "PAIR","X","Y"
220 FOR I=1 TO N
230 PRINT I,X(I),Y(I)
240 NEXT I
250 FOR I=1 TO N
260 LNX(I)=LOG(X(I))
270 LNY(I)=LOG(Y(I))
280 NEXT I
290 PRINT "HERE ARE TRANSFORMED DATA POINTS TO BE FIT :"
300 PRINT "PAIR","LN X","LN Y"
310 FOR I=1 TO N
320 PRINT I,LNX(I),LNY(I)
330 NEXT I
340 SX=0
350 FOR I=1 TO N
360 SX=SX+LNX(I)
370 NEXT I
380 PRINT "SUMMATION OF X VALUES IS ",SX
390 SY=0
400 FOR I=1 TO N
410 SY=SY+LNY(I)
420 NEXT I
430 PRINT "SUMMATION OF Y VALUES IS ",SY
440 SXY=0:SXSQ=0
450 FOR I=1 TO N
460 SXY=SXY+(LNX(I)*LNY(I))
470 SXSQ=SXSQ+(LNX(I)*LNX(I))
480 NEXT I
490 PRINT "SUMMATION OF X*Y VALUES IS ",SXY
500 PRINT "SUMMATION OF X^2 VALUES IS ",SXSQ
510 S=(N*SXY-(SX*SY))/(N*SXSQ-(SX*SX))
520 B=(SY/N)-(S*SX/N)
530 PRINT "S=",S
540 PRINT "B=",B
550 LC=100*2^S
560 K=EXP(B)
570 PRINT "THE THEORETICAL FIRST UNIT COST OR HOURS ARE:";K
580 PRINT "THE LEARNING CURVE PERCENTAGE IS: %";LC
590 INPUT "DO YOU WANT THIS TO BE PRINTED ON THE PRINTER?(YES/NO)";P$
600 IF P$ = "NO" THEN GOTO 690
610 IF P$ = "N" THEN GOTO 690
620 LPRINT "DATA POINTS ARE"
630 LPRINT:LPRINT "X","Y"
640 FOR I=1 TO N
650 LPRINT X(I),Y(I)
660 NEXT I
670 LPRINT:LPRINT "THE THEORETICAL FIRST UNIT COST OR HOURS ARE:";K
680 LPRINT:LPRINT "THE LEARNING CURVE PERCENTAGE IS: %";LC
690 INPUT "DO YOU WANT TO RUN ANOTHER BEST FIT LEARNING CURVE?(YES/NO)";R$
700 IF R$ = "YES" THEN GOTO 10
710 IF R$ = "Y" THEN GOTO 10
720 COLOR 7
730 CLS
740 LOCATE 12,35:PRINT "THANK YOU"
750 RUN "DATACOST.BAS"
```

Figure 9.41. Coding for best fit learning curve program (DATACOST).

BEST FIT LEARNING CURVE PROGRAM

DATE: 06-16-1985
TIME: 12:53:31

HOW MANY PAIRS OF DATA POINTS ARE YOU GOING TO ENTER? 4
###
'X' is the NUMBER of the unit for which the cost or hours are known
'Y' is the COST or HOURS for that 'X'th unit.
###
INPUT DATA IN THE FORM X,Y
INPUT DATA PAIR # 1
? 10,20
INPUT DATA PAIR # 2
? 100,19
INPUT DATA PAIR # 3
? 400,17
INPUT DATA PAIR # 4
? 550,16

Figure 9.42. Input of best fit learning curve program (DATACOST).

hours to produce, unit 100 took 19 hours to produce, unit 400 took 17 hours to produce, and unit 550 took 16 hours to produce. The user inputs the number of data pairs (4) and the values for each data pair as shown in Figure 9.42. The program transforms these numbers to logarithmic form to solve the learning curve equations presented in Chapter 5; solves for the theoretical first unit (TFU) hours; and solves for the learning curve percentage. In the sample problem, the first unit theoretically took 23.03 hours to produce and the best-fit learning "slope" curve is 96.45% (see Figure 9.43).

9.8 IDENTIFICATION OF SKILL CATEGORIES, LEVELS, AND RATES

Every cost estimating software program should have the capability of allowing the entry of "rates and factors" that will be used throughout the cost estimate. The

INPUT DATA PAIR # 4
? 550,16
THIS IS DATA YOU INPUT :

PAIR	X	Y
1	10	20
2	100	19
3	400	17
4	550	16

HERE ARE TRANSFORMED DATA POINTS TO BE FIT :

PAIR	LN X	LN Y
1	2.302585	2.995732
2	4.60517	2.944439
3	5.991465	2.833213
4	6.309919	2.772589

SUMMATION OF X VALUES IS   19.20914
SUMMATION OF Y VALUES IS   11.54597
SUMMATION OF X*Y VALUES IS 54.92748
SUMMATION OF X^2 VALUES IS 102.2222
S=   -.0520895
B=   3.136642
THE THEORETICAL FIRST UNIT COST OR HOURS ARE: 23.02641
THE LEARNING CURVE PERCENTAGE IS: % 96.45384
DO YOU WANT THIS TO BE PRINTED ON THE PRINTER?(YES/NO)? N
DO YOU WANT TO RUN ANOTHER BEST FIT LEARNING CURVE?(YES/NO)?

Figure 9.43. Output of best fit learning curve program (DATACOST).

largest job is to input the labor rates for all skill categories and skill levels and for all fiscal periods. For very detailed cost estimates the exact "forward pricing" labor rates for each skill and for each calendar month should be used. However, in many cost estimating situations, sufficient accuracy can be achieved through the use of "composite" labor rates. The composite labor rate depends on the individual labor rate for each skill and on the skill level "mix" within each skill category. The microcomputer can be used to advantage in developing composite labor rates through the use of simple spreadsheet templates such as that shown in Figure 9.44.

ESTABLISHING COMPOSITE RATES FROM AN OVERALL SKILL STRUCTURE

SKILL CATEGORY	SKILL LEVEL	LBR RATE	PCT/SKILL	INCRMNT	CATZ
ENGINEERING	SENIOR ENGINEER	$32.50	8.00%	$2.60	
	ENGINEER	$25.50	18.00%	$4.59	
	ASSOCIATE ENGINEER	$20.75	8.00%	$1.66	
	JUNIOR ENGINEER	$18.50	20.00%	$3.70	
	ENGINEERING AIDE	$12.50	12.00%	$1.50	
	DESIGNER	$15.75	10.00%	$1.58	
	DRAFTSMAN	$9.25	13.00%	$1.20	
	TECHNICIAN	$7.50	11.00%	$0.83	
COMPOSITE			100.00%	$17.65	25.00%
MANUFACTURING	MFG ENGINEER	$22.00	5.00%	$1.10	
	SHOP FOREMAN	$19.00	2.00%	$0.38	
	PROCESS PLANNER	$16.50	12.00%	$1.98	
	MASTER MACHINIST	$20.55	15.00%	$3.08	
	MACHINIST	$17.80	35.00%	$6.23	
	JOURNEYMAN	$12.50	6.00%	$0.75	
	APPRENTICE	$9.75	15.00%	$1.46	
	HELPER	$6.50	10.00%	$0.65	
COMPOSITE			100.00%	$15.64	45.00%
TOOLING	TOOLING ENGINEER	$21.50	10.00%	$2.15	
	MASTER TOOLMAKER	$18.75	20.00%	$3.75	
	TOOLMAKER	$16.50	40.00%	$6.60	
	JOURNEYMAN	$12.50	15.00%	$1.88	
	APPRENTICE	$9.50	10.00%	$0.95	
	HELPER	$6.50	5.00%	$0.33	
COMPOSITE			100.00%	$15.65	9.00%
TESTING	TEST ENGINEER	$20.50	10.00%	$2.05	
	TEST TECHNICIAN	$14.50	30.00%	$4.35	
	INSTRUMENT TECHN	$13.75	25.00%	$3.44	
	TEST OPERATOR	$10.88	35.00%	$3.81	
COMPOSITE			100.00%	$13.65	6.00%
QUAL/REL&SAFETY	RELIABILITY ENGR	$21.50	14.00%	$3.01	
	QUALITY ENGR	$21.00	10.00%	$2.10	
	SAFETY ENGR	$20.50	6.00%	$1.23	
	SENIOR INSPECTOR	$16.85	15.00%	$2.53	
	INSPECTOR	$14.50	55.00%	$7.98	
COMPOSITE			100.00%	$16.84	8.00%
OTHER	PROGRAM PLANNER	$19.50	15.00%	$2.93	
	COST ESTIMATOR	$18.25	25.00%	$4.56	
	SYSTEMS ANALYST	$16.50	6.00%	$0.99	
	PROGRAMMER	$14.75	4.00%	$0.59	
	TECH WRITER	$15.80	20.00%	$3.16	
	ADM ASSISTANT	$9.75	8.00%	$0.78	
	SECRETARY	$8.50	22.00%	$1.87	
COMPOSITE			100.00%	$14.88	7.00%
COMPOSITE RATE FOR ALL CATEGORIES		$16.06			100.00%

Figure 9.44. Composite rates for an overall skill structure (Lotus 1-2-3).

Notice that an incremental labor rate contribution for each skill level is computed based on the percent of that level in each skill category. These increments are summed to derive the composite rate for that category (engineering, manufacturing, tooling, etc.). If the skill mix changes with time throughout the duration of the project, new composite rates must be derived every time the skill *level* mix changes. The skill *category* mix, also assumed to be fixed in this example but capable of changing with time, is also used to develop a composite rate, but this time the composite rate covers *all* skill categories and can be considered a composite rate for the overall project. Use of composite labor rates will permit approximate labor dollar estimation when labor hours are estimated per skill category (engineering, manufacturing, etc.) or when an overall job manloading including all labor categories is estimated.

In Project Scheduler 5000™ by Scitor, labor rates and other unit cost values such as material costs are inserted in a resource classifications and rates table. Figure 9.45 shows how these project constants are entered on the screen. Figure 9.46 shows the resource classifications and rates table. Note that labor is tagged with an ''L,'' and other costs with an ''O.'' Project Scheduler uses resource code numbers for convenience in displaying and keeping track of up to 96 codes.

EasyEst™ permits the insertion of global rates principally through the screen shown in Figure 9.47. The unit costs for items are inserted into the on-screen form shown in Figure 9.48. Item number 7 on this screen, the cost per ordering unit, is one of the principal contents of its cost data base. Notice also that a conversion factor (item number 6) is permitted in the event that the takeoff unit is not the same as the ordering unit. For example, trenching for 12-inch pipe may require the removal of 0.556 cubic yards per linear foot of trench. If labor and material are paid for based on the number of cubic yards of subsoil removed rather than on the length of ditch excavated, this conversion factor will convert from linear feet of trench to cubic yards of excavation. This screen (in Figure 9.48) can be used for

OVERALL CONSTANTS
<hr>

```
        Starting date         =1-5-87    {These fields are initialized}
        Day of the week       =MON       {by the Project Constants menu}

        (T)ime scale          =MONTH     {day/week/month}

   Special Display Options:

        (C)ompressed display  =NO        {yes/no}

        (N)umber of shifts    =1         {day time scale only}


   Option:

        (E)nd changes to overall constants
```

Press a letter to select an option or to change a field)

Figure 9.45. Project constants table (PS5000).

RESOURCE CLASSIFICATIONS AND RATES TABLE

CODE	NAME	UNIT COST	LABOR/ OTHER	CODE	NAME	UNIT COST	LABOR/ OTHER
1	ENGINEERING'87	3460.00	L	13	LATCHES/FLIGHT	5.53	0
2	ENGINEERING'88	3757.00	L	14	RING/PROTO	1232.00	0
3	ENGINEERING'89	4036.00	L	15	RING/FLIGHT	786.00	0
4	MFG '87	3201.00	L	16	FASTENERS/PROTO	1.75	0
5	MFG '88	3457.00	L	17	FASTENERS/FLITE	1.25	0
6	MFG '89	3733.00	L				
7	TST,QUAL,REL'87	3027.00	L				
8	TST,QUAL,REL'88	3270.00	L				
9	TST,QUAL,REL'89	3531.00	L				
10	PROD TEST	0.09	L				
11	TRAVEL ENG	500.00	0				
12	LATCHES/PROTO	10.50	0				

(R)esource code, name, cost and L/0 :

(E)nd changes to resources

Press a letter to select an option >

Press PgUp or PgDn to review resources

Figure 9.46. Resource classifications and rates table (PS5000).

any unit price for any item in the data base. Only when the "quantity" is calculated and inserted (see line number 8) does this item become an estimate input. Items in the data base all have quantity values of zero; therefore, they are only a representation of the inputs required to calculate unit prices. Notice that EasyEst automatically calculates a total unit cost for the designated item based on a specific input (takeoff) quantity.

Cockerham's WBS TREE™ program permits the input of up to 16 labor titles and rates for up to three labor categories and allows input of material and subcontract costs as dollar values. Figure 9.49 shows a typical screen for a 6-month

```
: Enter a selection number  -  or an F if you are finished           :
:                                                                     :
:                                                                     :
                       Manual page # 4-7
: 0   WORK      On job # 2  - INDIAN CREEK#2        :Job# Job Name    :
: 1   CHANGE    Data base information               :                 :
: 2   TAKEOFF   Job                                 :                 :
: 3   PRINT     Report                              :                 :
: 4   ERASE     Takeoffs in job #                   :                 :
: 5   COPY      Takeoffs in job #        to job #   :                 :
: 6   CREATE    A new data base      # of jobs = 20 :                 :
:              # of divisions needed = 16           :                 :
:              # of items = 8000  ( 50 per subdivision) :             :
: 7   Today's date: 06/16/85    Phone #: (205) 536-2628 :             :
: 8   Printer: FX80            Paper size: Standard  :                 :
: Selection: 0#                                                       :
: F=Finished estimating                                               :
```

Figure 9.47. Main menu of EasyEst.

Figure 9.48. Item screen of EasyEst.

project (this program will compute an estimate for projects up to 24 months long). Notice that a discrete value can be given for each time period and each skill. The same capability is achieved in Project Scheduler 5000™ only by creating a new resource category each time the labor rate changes.

9.9 ESTIMATING LABOR HOURS AND MATERIAL QUANTITIES

Labor hours and material quantities can be estimated by a "direct" means that involves the expert judgment of the estimator; by staffing or shoploading estimat-

```
THE "ESTIMATOR" TEST CASE

ENGINEERING Labor Title and Rates

        Title        JAN85  FEB85  MAR85  APR85  MAY85  JUN85
A) PROGRAM MANAGER   28.25  28.25  28.25  29.70  29.70  29.70  0.00  0.00
B) ENGR SUPERVISOR   23.95  23.95  23.95  25.63  25.63  25.63  0.00  0.00
C) SR SYSTEM ENGR    20.11  20.11  20.11  21.52  21.52  21.52  0.00  0.00
D) SYSTEM ENGR       17.24  17.24  17.24  18.28  18.28  18.28  0.00  0.00
E) DESIGN ENGR       19.00  19.00  19.00  20.33  20.33  20.33  0.00  0.00
F) SOFTWARE ENGR     18.88  18.88  18.88  20.20  20.20  20.20  0.00  0.00
G) MECHANICAL ENGR   17.05  17.05  17.05  18.24  18.24  18.24  0.00  0.00
H) ELECTRICAL ENGR   18.40  18.40  18.40  19.66  19.66  19.66  0.00  0.00
I) ANALOG/DIGITAL    18.10  18.10  18.10  19.36  19.36  19.36  0.00  0.00
J) LOGISTICS         17.50  17.50  17.50  18.69  18.69  18.69  0.00  0.00
K) RELIABILITY ENG   16.75  16.75  16.75  17.69  17.69  17.69  0.00  0.00
L) MAINTAINABILITY   16.25  16.25  16.25  17.19  17.19  17.19  0.00  0.00
M) TECH PUBS         13.45  13.45  13.45  14.23  14.23  14.23  0.00  0.00
N) PROGRAM PLANNER   12.75  12.75  12.75  13.36  13.36  13.36  0.00  0.00
O) ENGR TECHNICIAN   10.80  10.80  10.80  11.34  11.34  11.34  0.00  0.00
P) DRAFTING           9.75   9.75   9.75  10.25  10.25  10.25  0.00  0.00
```

Enter the letter of the line you want to change or a scrolling option.
(+) next eight periods, (-) previous eight periods, (X) exit.

Figure 9.49. Labor title and rates for engineering (WBS TREE).

THE "ESTIMATOR" TEST CASE
ENGINEERING Labor Hours Edit
WBS: 1.0101 PROVISIONING INDUST

	JAN85	FEB85	MAR85	APR85	MAY85	JUN85
A) PROGRAM MANAGER	0	0	0	0	0	0
B) ENGR SUPERVISOR	160	80	0	0	0	0
C) SR SYSTEM ENGR	40	20	0	0	0	0
D) SYSTEM ENGR	0	0	0	0	0	0
E) DESIGN ENGR	80	40	0	0	0	0
F) SOFTWARE ENGR	0	0	0	0	0	0
G) MECHANICAL ENGR	40	0	0	0	0	0
H) ELECTRICAL ENGR	40	0	0	0	0	0
I) ANALOG/DIGITAL	0	0	0	0	0	0
J) LOGISTICS	0	0	0	0	0	0
K) RELIABILITY ENG	0	0	0	0	0	0
L) MAINTAINABILITY	0	0	0	0	0	0
M) TECH PUBS	0	0	0	0	0	0
N) PROGRAM PLANNER	0	0	0	0	0	0
O) ENGR TECHNICIAN	0	0	0	0	0	0
P) DRAFTING	0	0	0	0	0	0

Enter the letter of the line you want to change or a scrolling option.
(+) next eight periods, (-) previous eight periods, (X) exit.

Figure 9.50. Labor hours for engineering (WBS TREE).

ing; by manual, semiautomated, or automated takeoff of material quantities; or by reference to handbooks or data bases. In the direct estimate, the labor hours are based strictly on a judgment call by the estimator. A typical labor hour input screen for WBS TREE™ (Figure 9.50) shows the recording of direct labor hours from a direct estimate. It is often convenient, however, to use staffing and shoploading techniques to derive labor hours versus time in a time-oriented or scheduled estimate. Both staffing and shoploading techniques can be easily and conveniently performed using electronic spreadsheet formats such as those shown in Figures 9.51 and 9.52. These Lotus 1-2-3™ spreadsheet templates automatically compute

MANLOADING OR STAFFING METHOD OF ESTIMATING

MANHOURS PER MANYEAR: 1896   STARTING YEAR: 1985

PERSONNEL LOADING/HOURS:		1985	1986	1987	1988	1989	1990	1991	1992	1993	1994	1995
TOTALS	79632	7584	9480	11376	20856	17064	9480	3792	0	0	0	0
Engineers		1	1	1	2	1	0	0				
Hours		1896	1896	1896	3792	1896	0	0	0	0	0	0
Technicians		3	4	4	6	2	1	0				
Hours		5688	7584	7584	11376	3792	1896	0	0	0	0	0
Draftsmen		0	0	1	3	6	4	2				
Hours		0	0	1896	5688	11376	7584	3792	0	0	0	0
Category 4												
Hours		0	0	0	0	0	0	0	0	0	0	0
Category 5												
Hours		0	0	0	0	0	0	0	0	0	0	0
Category 6												
Hours		0	0	0	0	0	0	0	0	0	0	0

Figure 9.51. Manloading or staffing method of estimating (Lotus 1-2-3).

```
SHOPLOADING OR OFFICE LOADING METHOD OF ESTIMATING
*****************************************************************************************************
MANHOURS PER MANYEAR      1896         STARTING YEAR      1986
```

NAME OF SHOP	STAFFING	1986	1987	1988	1989	1990	1991	1992	1993	1994	1995
TOTALS	45504	1896	2370	6636	19908	11850	1896	948	0	0	0
Electrical	5	10.00%	15.00%	50.00%	50.00%	5.00%	0.00%	0.00%			
Hours		948	1422	4740	4740	474	0	0	0	0	0
Mechanical	10	5.00%	5.00%	10.00%	80.00%	60.00%	10.00%	5.00%			
Hours		948	948	1896	15168	11376	1896	948	0	0	0
Welding	0										
Hours		0	0	0	0	0	0	0	0	0	0
Shop #4											
Hours		0	0	0	0	0	0	0	0	0	0
Shop #5											
Hours		0	0	0	0	0	0	0	0	0	0
Shop #6											
Hours		0	0	0	0	0	0	0	0	0	0

Figure 9.52. Shoploading or office loading method of estimating (Lotus 1-2-3).

labor hours when certain other key variables are input. In the staffing or manloading technique shown in Figure 9.51, the numbers of engineers, technicians, draftsmen, and so on that will be "on board" the project during each calendar period (in this case each calendar year) are estimated. The estimator inserts a man-hour per man-year figure in the spreadsheet's upper left corner, inserts a "start year," and the spreadsheet does the rest. Total labor hours per year are shown under each yearly heading, and the grand total labor hours are shown at the top of the spreadsheet in the third active row.

A similar technique is used in the shoploading method shown as a printout of an electronic spreadsheet form in Figure 9.52. Again the estimator inserts the labor hours per man-year and the start year. Shop name and total staffing level of each shop are inserted in the first two columns, and the estimator determines what percentage of that shop will be occupied by the project during each calendar period. The spreadsheet does the rest, computing total labor hours for each calendar year as well as total estimated labor hours.

In Project Scheduler 5000™, the estimator inserts the start time, duration, and number of units of each resource to be expended each period during the "duration." The program uses previously stored unit prices to compute labor, materials, and total costs for this resource/schedule element. The resource screen, accompanied by overall scheduling information for the "job" or work element, appears to the operator as shown in Figure 9.53. Note that scheduling information such as predecessors, start time, and duration of this job are also shown on this screen. Notice that Project Scheduler 5000™ refers to only one element of work as a "job," whereas EasyEst refers to an entire project as a job. Reference [2] contains tabular material that will assist the estimator in developing labor hour and material estimates.

```
JOB: 7100    JOB NAME: RINGS/FLIGHT
SEQ   RESOURCE CLASS    START  DURATION   END      UNITS        COST
  1    2 ENGINEERING '88    2      2        4       4.00      29896.00
  1    5 MFG '88            0      2        2       2.00      13828.00
  1    6 MFG '89            2      2        4       2.00      14932.00

  1   15 RING/FLIGHT        0      4        4      20.00      62880.00



LABOR TOTALS                                       16.00      58656.00
OTHER TOTALS                                       80.00      62880.00
TOTAL COSTS $                                      96.00     121536.00

(J)ob Code:=7100   (N)ame:=RINGS/FLIGHT                  (S)tart time:=0
(P)redecessors:=4230 0 0 0 0 0 0 0 0                     (D)uration:=4
Select a CHANGE option )               (R)esources   (U)se   (E)xit
```

Figure 9.53. Resource loading into bar chart (PS5000).

9.10 ESTIMATING OVERHEAD, ADMINISTRATIVE COSTS, AND FEE

Most cost estimating computer programs have provisions for adding overhead or burden to one or more categories or classes of costs and provide a place to compute costs of money, administrative costs, and fee or profit. Cockerham's WBS TREE™, for example, accommodates an overhead "pool" for each of its three skill categories; computes fringe benefits on all labor; calculates material overhead costs based on a given input percentage; figures general and administrative costs from the subtotal of labor, overhead, burden, and other direct charges; computes cost of money; and calculates a fee based on an input fee percentage requirement. The program does this at each level of the work element structure, which is not required as a printout in most proposals but which could come in handy if the customer wanted to purchase only a portion of the project, say one or two work elements. A typical output sheet for WBS TREE™ is shown in Figure 9.54.

EasyEst™ permits an input tax percentage and "burden" percentage for each of its possible nine cost "classes" or cost elements. Since the cost classes can be named by the estimator, several labor burdens, representing various labor burden pools could be used. Figure 9.55 is a sample "Class Totals Report" that shows the cost breakout by cost classes (major division and subdivision reports, equivalent to a work element breakout, are shown later). Bond costs and profit are added to the subtotal costs as shown in Figure 9.56. (Note: This figure shows profit included on top of the bond costs, which is not allowed in some organizations).

Certain scheduling/estimating programs, such as Project Scheduler 5000™, do not have a provision for adding overhead, burden, administrative costs, and profit at the top levels to the estimate. This can be done *within* the program by using "loaded" labor rates; that is, by multiplying the direct labor rates by the required

```
PROJECT: THE "ESTIMATOR" TEST CASE              JMCA WBS TREE v1.0                    PAGE:    8
WBS:    2.01    WIDGIT SUB-ASSEMBLY             COST BREAKDOWN SUMMARY: DOLLARS       DATE: 06-11-85
```

	JAN85	FEB85	MAR85	APR85	MAY85	JUN85	TOTAL
ENGINEERING:							
ENGR SUPERVISOR	96	0	0	0	0	0	96
SR SYSTEM ENGR	804	563	402	430	430	430	3061
SYSTEM ENGR	3448	2896	2758	2925	2925	2925	17877
SOFTWARE ENGR	3021	3021	3021	3232	3232	3232	18758
ANALOG/DIGITAL	724	724	724	774	774	774	4495
RELIABILITY ENG	670	134	0	0	0	0	804
MAINTAINABILITY	130	130	130	138	138	138	803
TOTAL ENGINEERING	8893	7468	7035	7499	7499	7499	45894
ENGINEERING OVERHEAD	2878	2410	2270	2270	2270	2270	14368
MANUFACTURING:							
MANUFACT SUPVSR	5612	5417	5353	5673	5673	5673	33400
SHIFT SUPVSR	12441	12441	12298	13038	13038	13038	76293
MANUFACTURE OPS	3478	3276	3276	3440	3440	3440	20349
PRODUCTION PLNG	4113	2910	1358	0	0	0	8381
PRODUCTION TEST	2912	1456	0	0	0	0	4368
MACHINE SHOP	13687	13687	13687	14102	14102	14102	83367
ASSEMBLY-DEPT A	354075	346675	339275	346314	340218	340218	2066775
ASSEMBLY-DEPT B	78648	75386	66468	68336	68186	68186	425209
TOTAL MANUFACTURING	474965	461248	441714	450902	444656	444656	2718142
MANUFACTURING OVERHEAD	752880	731736	700968	694240	684400	684400	4248648
SUPPORT LABOR:							
CLERICAL	2379	2091	2091	2155	2155	2155	13025
GRAPHICS	1442	1442	1442	1486	1486	1486	8784
SHIPPING	3418	3418	3418	3518	3518	3518	20808
TOTAL SUPPORT LABOR	7239	6950	6950	7159	7159	7159	42617
SUPPORT LABOR OVERHEAD	4040	3880	3880	3880	3880	3880	23440
FRINGE	206261	199780	191394	195535	192912	192912	1178794
MATERIALS:							
RAW MATERIAL	5050000	5120000	5120000	5120000	5120000	5120000	30650000
PURCHASED PARTS	2253000	1738000	1025000	620000	619000	619000	6874000
SUB-CONTRACTS	51500	51500	51500	51500	51500	51500	309000
STD. COMMERCIAL	15000	15000	15000	15000	15000	15000	90000
OTHER MATERIALS	38600	38600	38600	38600	38600	38600	231600
SHOP SUPPLIES	2600	2600	2600	2600	2600	2600	15600
SCRAP & REWORK ($)	2900	2600	2400	2200	1800	1800	13700
TOTAL MATERIALS	7413600	6968300	6255100	5849900	5848500	5848500	38183900
MATERIAL OVERHEAD	889632	836196	750612	701988	701820	701820	4582068

Figure 9.54. Cost breakdown summary (WBS TREE).

percentages and adding these costs to the direct labor rates. Since labor alone or even a single category of labor may vary in burden or overhead content from other categories or cost estimates, it is better to add these costs at a higher level in the estimate. It is for this reason that programs like Project Scheduler 5000™ permit transfer of cost outputs to other spreadsheet or data base programs for further manipulation and/or enhancement. A sample Project Scheduler 5000™ data file on the "CLAMS1" Project was imported into Lotus 1-2-3™ for massaging and enhancement as shown in Figure 9.57. Although this transfer and enhancement requires

```
PROJECT: THE "ESTIMATOR" TEST CASE              JMCA WBS TREE v1.0                            PAGE:      9
WBS:    2.01    WIDGIT SUB-ASSEMBLY         COST BREAKDOWN SUMMARY: DOLLARS                   DATE: 06-11-85
```

	JAN85	FEB85	MAR85	APR85	MAY85	JUN85	TOTAL
OTHER DIRECT COST:							
TRAVEL	1000	1000	1000	1000	1000	1000	6000
TOTAL ODC	1000	1000	1000	1000	1000	1000	6000
SUB TOTAL, G & A BASE	9761388	9218969	8360924	7914381	7894105	7894105	51043871
GENERAL & ADMINISTRATION	1757050	1659414	1504966	1424589	1420939	1420939	9187897
SUB-TOTAL COST	11518438	10878383	9865891	9338970	9315043	9315043	60231768
COST OF MONEY:							
ENGINEERING	123	103	97	97	97	97	614
MANUFACTURING	77484	75308	72141	71450	70437	70437	437257
SUPPORT	152	146	146	146	146	146	879
MATERIAL	14827	13937	12510	11700	11697	11697	76368
GENERAL & ADMIN.	12202	11524	10451	9893	9868	9868	63805
TOTAL COST OF MONEY	104787	101017	95345	93285	92244	92244	578922
TOTAL COST	11623225	10979400	9961236	9432255	9407288	9407288	60810690
PROFIT/FEE	1094252	1033446	937260	887202	884929	884929	5722018
TOTAL PRICE	12717477	12012846	10898495	10319457	10292217	10292217	66532708

Figure 9.54. (Continued)

some microcomputer systems analysis skills, it is often cost-effective as compared to the acquisition of more costly programs that perform this function automatically.

9.11 INFLATION, ESCALATION, AND COST GROWTH

The microcomputer is an ideal tool for applying inflation, escalation, and other cost growth allowances because these allowances change frequently and apply throughout the cost estimate.

9.11.1 Inflation

Statistical inflation studies in various industries have shown that the inflation rate varies with product or service definition. For example, the inflation rate of energy costs has differed from that of electronic products. The microcomputer offers the possibility of segmenting the work into smaller work elements to which inflation rates are applied on a selective basis. Hence the overall inflation rate of a product or service depends upon the *mix* of inflation rates for work elements within that product or service. Applying different inflation rates for various elements of a job through conventional manual or semiautomated means has been a sophistication

```
Job # 1                       MOBILE DATA SERVICES                    Page 5
INDIAN CREEK#1               3502 Pan.Dr;P.O.Box 5042                06/11/85
                              Huntsville, AL  35805
```

CLASS TOTALS REPORT

# Class	Cost	Tax%	Tax	Cost Total	Burden%	Burden$	Total
1 MATERIAL	164893	5%	8245	173138	10.00%	17314	190452
2 LABOR	160727	13%	20894	181621	20.00%	36324	217946
3 EQUIPMNT	11153	0%	0	11153	12.00%	1338	12491
4 SUBCONT	17500	0%	0	17500	8.00%	1400	18900
9 OTHER	500	0%	0	500	0.00%	0	500
TOTALS =	354773		29139	383912		56376	440289

EasyEst Estimating System (c) 1984 CMS
For use by MOBILE DATA SERVICES only

Figure 9.55. Class totals report (EasyEst).

not often adopted because of the sheer magnitude of the computation job. The microcomputer's speed and ease of use now makes this sophistication attractive for smaller estimates. Tables of inflation rates for various products and services are available from the U.S. Department of Commerce and from the various trade, professional, and manufacturing associations.

9.11.2 Escalation

Cost escalation allowances or cost growth allowances can be easily handled by the microcomputer through the use of simple formulas in spreadsheets. Figure 9.58 is

```
Job # 1                        MOBILE DATA SERVICES                      Page 6
INDIAN CREEK#1                3502 Pan.Dr;P.O.Box 5042                   06/11/85
                               Huntsville, AL  35805
--------------------------------------------------------------------------------

       ------------------------------------------------------------------
       JOB COST BEFORE PROFIT, BOND, $ BURDENS                $440,289
       BOND    =         2.00%                                  $8,806
       PROFIT =         10.00%                                 $44,909
       JOB  TOTAL   =                              $494,004
       ------------------------------------------------------------------
```

```
--------------------------------------------------------------------------------
                  EasyEst Estimating System (c) 1984 CMS
                    For use by MOBILE DATA SERVICES only
```

Figure 9.56. Cost report showing bond and profit added (EasyEst).

a printout of a sample spreadsheet that computes adjusted estimates based on in-complete design. The theory behind this spreadsheet is that if an item that is es-timated to cost $75 is only 75% designed, then the effort to bring the design to 100% completion brings the total cost to 100% or $100. Although this is an as-sumption and does not *always* hold true, the theory does give some quantitative input to the estimation of incompletely designed products or services. In product costing, the manufacturing cost may exceed this rule because the remaining 25% of design may, in reality, double or triple the product cost. In a complex project, percentages of design completion can be divided into the estimated cost of each subsystem as shown in Figure 9.30 to derive an approximation of the cost esca-

CLAMS PROJECT COSTS BY TIME PERIOD WITH OH, G&A, AND FEE ADDED
****

	JAN 87	FEB 87	MAR 87	APR 87	MAY 87	JUN 87	JUL 87	AUG 87	SEP 87	OCT 87
ENGINEERING'87	7.0	7.0	7.0	12.0	12.0	12.0	3.0	3.0	3.0	3.0
ENGINEERING'88	0.0	0.0	0.0	0.0	0.0	0.0	0.0	0.0	0.0	0.0
ENGINEERING'89	0.0	0.0	0.0	0.0	0.0	0.0	0.0	0.0	0.0	0.0
MFG '87	0.0	0.0	0.0	0.0	0.0	0.0	4.6	4.6	2.6	2.6
MFG '88	0.0	0.0	0.0	0.0	0.0	0.0	0.0	0.0	0.0	0.0
MFG '89	0.0	0.0	0.0	0.0	0.0	0.0	0.0	0.0	0.0	0.0
TST,QUAL,REL'87	0.0	0.0	0.0	0.0	0.0	0.0	0.0	0.0	0.0	0.0
TST,QUAL,REL'88	0.0	0.0	0.0	0.0	0.0	0.0	0.0	0.0	0.0	0.0
TST,QUAL,REL'89	0.0	0.0	0.0	0.0	0.0	0.0	0.0	0.0	0.0	0.0
UNITS	7.0	7.0	7.0	12.0	12.0	12.0	7.6	7.6	5.6	5.6
COSTS	$24,220.00	$24,220.00	$24,220.00	$41,520.00	$41,520.00	$41,520.00	$25,104.60	$25,104.60	$18,702.60	$18,702.60
OVERHEAD (45%)	$10,899.00	$10,899.00	$10,899.00	$18,684.00	$18,684.00	$18,684.00	$11,297.07	$11,297.07	$8,416.17	$8,416.17
SUBTOTAL (L+OH)	$35,119.00	$35,119.00	$35,119.00	$60,204.00	$60,204.00	$60,204.00	$36,401.67	$36,401.67	$27,118.77	$27,118.77
TRAVEL ENG	$500.00	$500.00	$500.00	$1,000.00	$1,000.00	$1,000.00	$0.00	$0.00	$0.00	$0.00
LATCHES/PROTO	$0.00	$0.00	$0.00	$0.00	$0.00	$0.00	$336.00	$0.00	$0.00	$0.00
LATCHES/FLIGHT	$0.00	$0.00	$0.00	$0.00	$0.00	$0.00	$0.00	$0.00	$0.00	$0.00
RING/PROTO	$0.00	$0.00	$0.00	$0.00	$0.00	$0.00	$2,464.00	$0.00	$0.00	$0.00
RING/FLIGHT	$0.00	$0.00	$0.00	$0.00	$0.00	$0.00	$0.00	$0.00	$0.00	$0.00
FASTENERS/PROTO	$0.00	$0.00	$0.00	$0.00	$0.00	$0.00	$56.00	$0.00	$0.00	$0.00
FASTENERS/FLITE	$0.00	$0.00	$0.00	$0.00	$0.00	$0.00	$0.00	$0.00	$0.00	$0.00
OTHER	$500.00	$500.00	$500.00	$1,000.00	$1,000.00	$1,000.00	$2,856.00	$0.00	$0.00	$0.00
(DC) TOTALS	$24,720.00	$24,720.00	$24,720.00	$42,520.00	$42,520.00	$42,520.00	$27,960.60	$25,104.60	$18,702.60	$18,702.60
LBR,OH,&ODC	$35,619.00	$35,619.00	$35,619.00	$61,204.00	$61,204.00	$61,204.00	$39,257.67	$36,401.67	$27,118.77	$27,118.77
G&A (2.5%)	$890.48	$890.48	$890.48	$1,530.10	$1,530.10	$1,530.10	$981.44	$910.04	$677.97	$677.97
LBR,OH,ODC,G&A	$36,509.48	$36,509.48	$36,509.48	$62,734.10	$62,734.10	$62,734.10	$40,239.11	$37,311.71	$27,796.74	$27,796.74
FEE (10%)	$3,650.95	$3,650.95	$3,650.95	$6,273.41	$6,273.41	$6,273.41	$4,023.91	$3,731.17	$2,779.67	$2,779.67
TOTAL EST/PD	$40,160.42	$40,160.42	$40,160.42	$69,007.51	$69,007.51	$69,007.51	$44,263.02	$41,042.88	$30,576.41	$30,576.41
GRAND TOTAL	$1,514,042.04									

Figure 9.57. CLAMS Project costs with overhead, G&A, and fee added (PS5000 figures sent to Lotus 1-2-3 for manipulation).

lation that can be expected in a project owing to incomplete design at its outset. Cost escalation due to other escalation drivers, also very subjective in nature, can be accounted for by using multipliers or factors that modify the cost elements within an estimate to reflect past experience or projected cost growth due to changing geographical, political, competitive, or demographic conditions.

9.11.3 Other Allowances

A microcomputer-generated table and figure (Figures 9.59 and 9.60, respectively) show the results of a 1982 study by the Business Round Table (see reference [3]). This study indicated that productivity of construction workers in direct "hands-on" work was only 32.4% of the total job hours available. Personal time (trips to the restroom, drinking fountain, telephone calls, etc.), authorized breaks, and late starts and early quits totaled about 6.9% of the total job time in the study. Acquisition, maintenance, servicing, and repair of tools and equipment used about 5.4%

```
*********************************************************************************************************************
  NOV 87    DEC 87    JAN 88    FEB 88    MAR 88    APR 88    MAY 88    JUN 88    JUL 88    AUG 88    SEP 88    OCT 88

     4.0       4.0       0.0       0.0       0.0       0.0       0.0       0.0       0.0       0.0       0.0       0.0
     0.0       0.0       4.0       4.0       4.0       4.0       4.0       4.0       4.0       4.0       4.0       4.0
     0.0       0.0       0.0       0.0       0.0       0.0       0.0       0.0       0.0       0.0       0.0       0.0
     0.0       0.0       0.0       0.0       0.0       0.0       0.0       0.0       0.0       0.0       0.0       0.0
     0.0       0.0       0.0       0.0       0.0       0.0       0.0       0.0       0.0       0.0       0.0       0.0
     0.0       0.0       0.0       0.0       0.0       0.0       0.0       0.0       0.0       0.0       0.0       0.0
     5.0       5.0       0.0       0.0       0.0       0.0       0.0       0.0       0.0       0.0       0.0       0.0
     0.0       0.0       5.0       5.0       5.0       5.0       5.0       0.0       0.0       0.0       0.0       0.0
     0.0       0.0       0.0       0.0       0.0       0.0       0.0       0.0       0.0       0.0       0.0       0.0
     9.0       9.0       9.0       9.0       9.0       9.0       9.0       4.0       4.0       4.0       4.0       4.0
$28,975.00 $28,975.00 $31,298.00 $31,298.00 $31,298.00 $31,298.00 $31,298.00 $14,948.00 $14,948.00 $14,948.00 $14,948.00 $14,948.00

$13,038.75 $13,038.75 $14,084.10 $14,084.10 $14,084.10 $14,084.10 $14,084.10 $6,726.60 $6,726.60 $6,726.60 $6,726.60 $6,726.60
$42,013.75 $42,013.75 $45,382.10 $45,382.10 $45,382.10 $45,382.10 $45,382.10 $21,674.60 $21,674.60 $21,674.60 $21,674.60 $21,674.60

    $0.00     $0.00     $0.00     $0.00     $0.00     $0.00   $500.00     $0.00     $0.00     $0.00     $0.00   $500.00
    $0.00     $0.00     $0.00     $0.00     $0.00     $0.00     $0.00     $0.00     $0.00     $0.00     $0.00     $0.00
    $0.00     $0.00     $0.00     $0.00     $0.00     $0.00     $0.00     $0.00     $0.00     $0.00     $0.00     $0.00
    $0.00     $0.00     $0.00     $0.00     $0.00     $0.00     $0.00     $0.00     $0.00     $0.00     $0.00     $0.00
    $0.00     $0.00     $0.00     $0.00     $0.00     $0.00     $0.00     $0.00     $0.00     $0.00     $0.00     $0.00
    $0.00     $0.00     $0.00     $0.00     $0.00     $0.00     $0.00     $0.00     $0.00     $0.00     $0.00     $0.00
    $0.00     $0.00     $0.00     $0.00     $0.00     $0.00     $0.00     $0.00     $0.00     $0.00     $0.00     $0.00
    $0.00     $0.00     $0.00     $0.00     $0.00     $0.00   $500.00     $0.00     $0.00     $0.00     $0.00   $500.00
$28,975.00 $28,975.00 $31,298.00 $31,298.00 $31,298.00 $31,298.00 $31,798.00 $14,948.00 $14,948.00 $14,948.00 $14,948.00 $15,448.00

$42,013.75 $42,013.75 $45,382.10 $45,382.10 $45,382.10 $45,382.10 $45,882.10 $21,674.60 $21,674.60 $21,674.60 $21,674.60 $22,174.60

$1,050.34 $1,050.34 $1,134.55 $1,134.55 $1,134.55 $1,134.55 $1,147.05 $541.87 $541.87 $541.87 $541.87 $554.37

$43,064.09 $43,064.09 $46,516.65 $46,516.65 $46,516.65 $46,516.65 $47,029.15 $22,216.47 $22,216.47 $22,216.47 $22,216.47 $22,728.97

$4,306.41 $4,306.41 $4,651.67 $4,651.67 $4,651.67 $4,651.67 $4,702.92 $2,221.65 $2,221.65 $2,221.65 $2,221.65 $2,272.90

$47,370.50 $47,370.50 $51,168.32 $51,168.32 $51,168.32 $51,168.32 $51,732.07 $24,438.11 $24,438.11 $24,438.11 $24,438.11 $25,001.86


                    ***********************************************************************************
                      NOV 88    DEC 88    JAN 89    FEB 89    MAR 89    APR 89    MAY 89    JUN 89

                         0.0       0.0       0.0       0.0       0.0       0.0       0.0       0.0
                         2.0       2.0       4.0       4.0       0.0       0.0       0.0       0.0
                         0.0       0.0       2.0       2.0       2.0       2.0       2.0       2.0
                         3.0       3.0       0.0       0.0       0.0       0.0       0.0       0.0
                         4.9       4.9       3.0       3.0       3.0       0.0       0.0       0.0
                         2.3       2.3       7.2       7.2       1.5       1.5       1.5       1.5
                         0.0       0.0       0.0       0.0       0.0       0.0       0.0       0.0
                         0.0       0.0       0.0       0.0       0.0       0.0       0.0       0.0
                         0.0       0.0       0.0       0.0       2.0       2.0       2.0       2.0
                        12.2      12.2      16.2      16.2       8.5       5.5       5.5       5.5
                   $42,415.55 $42,415.55 $60,081.95 $60,081.95 $31,104.50 $20,733.50 $20,733.50 $20,733.50

                   $19,087.00 $19,087.00 $27,036.88 $27,036.88 $13,997.03 $9,330.08 $9,330.08 $9,330.08
                   $61,502.55 $61,502.55 $87,118.83 $87,118.83 $45,101.53 $30,063.58 $30,063.58 $30,063.58

                        $0.00     $0.00     $0.00     $0.00     $0.00     $0.00     $0.00     $0.00
                        $0.00     $0.00     $0.00     $0.00     $0.00     $0.00     $0.00     $0.00
                      $884.80   $884.80   $884.80   $884.80     $0.00     $0.00     $0.00     $0.00
                        $0.00     $0.00     $0.00     $0.00     $0.00     $0.00     $0.00     $0.00
                   $15,720.00 $15,720.00 $15,720.00 $15,720.00     $0.00     $0.00     $0.00     $0.00
                        $0.00     $0.00     $0.00     $0.00     $0.00     $0.00     $0.00     $0.00
                      $800.00   $800.00   $800.00   $800.00     $0.00     $0.00     $0.00     $0.00
                   $17,404.80 $17,404.80 $17,404.80 $17,404.80     $0.00     $0.00     $0.00     $0.00
                   $59,820.35 $59,820.35 $77,486.75 $77,486.75 $31,104.50 $20,733.50 $20,733.50 $20,733.50

                   $78,907.35 $78,907.35 $104,523.63 $104,523.63 $45,101.53 $30,063.58 $30,063.58 $30,063.58

                   $1,972.68 $1,972.68 $2,613.09 $2,613.09 $1,127.54 $751.59 $751.59 $751.59

                   $80,880.03 $80,880.03 $107,136.72 $107,136.72 $46,229.06 $30,815.16 $30,815.16 $30,815.16

                   $8,088.00 $8,088.00 $10,713.67 $10,713.67 $4,622.91 $3,081.52 $3,081.52 $3,081.52

                   $88,968.03 $88,968.03 $117,850.39 $117,850.39 $50,851.97 $33,896.68 $33,896.68 $33,896.68
```

Figure 9.57. (*Continued*)

```
COMPUTATION OF ADJUSTED ESTIMATES BASED ON INCOMPLETE DESIGN
*************************************************************
SUBSYSTEM      % DESIGN    ORIGINAL    ADJUSTED
               COMPLETED   ESTIMATE    ESTIMATE
*************************************************************
STRUCTURAL      80.00%      $65,286     $81,608
ELECTRICAL POWER 65.00%     $21,824     $33,575
CONTROL         75.00%      $52,689     $70,252
COMMUNICATIONS  85.00%     $148,222    $174,379
ENVIRONMENTAL   70.00%      $38,964     $55,663
THERMAL         95.00%      $69,981     $73,664
FLUIDS          45.00%      $15,824     $35,164

TOTAL COSTS                $412,790    $524,305

COST GROWTH ALLOWANCE                  $111,515
COST GROWTH PERCENTAGE                   27.02%
```

NOTE:Original estimate is divided by the percentage of design completion to compute adjusted estimate.

Figure 9.58. Adjusted estimates based on incomplete design (Lotus 1-2-3).

of the time, while transporting of the tools, equipment, and supplies used 4.6% of the job hours for a total of 10%. Workers spent 6.3% of their time requesting and receiving instructions from their supervisors, a full 32% of their time waiting for other operations to be completed or idle due to improper job scheduling, and 12.4% of their time traveling to and from the job. This left only 32.4% for direct, hands-on work!

Microcomputer-based project scheduling programs will help reduce these allowances through more effective and efficient scheduling of resources, and data collection, storage, and analysis programs will help estimate and apply the required allowances for more realistic cost estimates and bids.

9.12 SYNTHESIZING AND PUBLISHING THE COST ESTIMATE

The final steps of computing, analyzing, adjusting, and publishing the cost estimate will bring the capability of the microcomputer into full play. High computation speeds, coupled with the ability to view estimate outputs before they are printed, enable the estimator to make quick last-minute adjustments, additions, and corrections. And the increasingly high-quality printing of relatively inexpensive letter quality printers, dot matrix printers, and plotters will help produce a final microcomputer-generated estimate report that is professional looking as well

```
CONSTRUCTION CONTRACTOR SITE ACTIVITY ANALYSIS
      (From 1982 Business Round Table Study)
*************************************************
DIRECT WORK                              32.40%
INSTRUCTIONS                              6.30%
PERSONAL, BREAKS, LATE STARTS,EARLY QUITS 6.90%
TOOLS & MATERIALS, TRANSPORTING          10.00%
TRAVELING                                12.40%
WAITING & IDLE                           32.00%

              SUM                        100.00%
```

Figure 9.59. Construction contractor site activity analysis (Lotus 1-2-3).

CONSTRUCTION CONTRACTOR SITE ANALYSIS
(from 1982 Business Round Table Study)

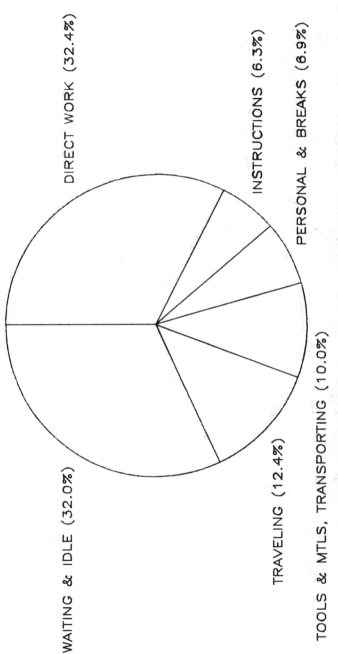

DIRECT WORK (32.4%)

INSTRUCTIONS (6.3%)

PERSONAL & BREAKS (6.9%)

WAITING & IDLE (32.0%)

TRAVELING (12.4%)

TOOLS & MTLS, TRANSPORTING (10.0%)

Figure 9.60. Pie chart of construction contractor site activity (Lotus 1-2-3).

as accurate. Cost estimating programs that have been downloaded to microcomputers often do not have the desired on-screen viewing of results and quick turnaround capabilities but usually have a larger capacity and occasionally more features. An interactive program specifically prepared with the microcomputer user in mind and with on-screen editing and viewing of inputs and outputs will take the fullest advantage of the microcomputer.

Figures 9.61 and 9.62 show the Multiplan™ template for the work breakdown structure shown earlier in this chapter for home construction estimating. The top-level sheet (Figure 9.62) is automatically generated each time it is loaded by importing lower-level sheets (represented here by a level 2 sheet, "Site Preparation," as Figure 9.61) into the top-level spreadsheet. This spreadsheet program represents the simplest form of estimate computations.

9.12.1 Microcomputer Graphics Outputs

A microcomputer feature that will significantly enhance the cost estimator's ability to analyze and adjust the estimate to obtain the most effective spread of resources,

HOME BUILDING ESTIMATING TEMPLATE JOB TITLE:SAMPLE ESTIMATE

Copyright 1984 by MOBILE DATA SERVICES, P.O. Box 5042, Huntsville, AL 35805, Phone: 205-536-2628

SHEET #:A-2.001 NAME: —— SUBCON TOT $1771.00 MTL SUBTOT $1328.30 OTHER:$15500.00

DATE: CATEGORY: SITE PREPARATION CATEGORY SUBTOTAL: $18599.30

DESCRIPT	SUBCONTRACT/LABOR			MATERIALS			OTHER	MATERIAL QUANTITIES			TOTAL
	PRICE/UNITS	QUANTITY	DOLLARS	PRICE/UNITS	QUANTITY	DOLLARS	DOLLARS	DEPTH	WIDTH	VOLUME	DOLLARS
Purchase Lot			$0.00			$0.00	$15500.00				$15500.00
Excavation	$250.00	1	$250.00			$0.00					$250.00
Footings	$0.80 /lin ft	120	$96.00	$39.00 /cu yd	4.44	$173.33		8	18	4.44	$269.33
Ft								0.67	1.5		
Foundations	$0.60 /block	400	$240.00	$0.48 /block	400	$192.00					$432.00
Termite Treatment	$35.00 /house	1	$35.00			$0.00					$35.00
Aggragate Base	$250.00	1	$250.00			$0.00					$250.00
Water-Proofing			$0.00			$0.00					$0.00
Slab Floor	$0.45 /sq ft	2000	$900.00	$39.00 /cu yd	24.69	$962.96		4		24.69	$1862.96
ft								0.33			
Other #1			$0.00			$0.00					$0.00
Other #2			$0.00			$0.00					$0.00
TOT/INPUT											$0.00
THRUPUT											

Figure 9.61. Home construction template PEEWEE A-2.001 (Multiplan).

```
HOME BUILDING ESTIMATING TEMPLATE  JOB TITLE:SAMPLE ESTIMATE
########################################################################################
Copyright 1984 by MOBILE DATA SERVICES, P.O. Box 5042, Huntsville, AL  35805, Phone:  205-536-2628
_____
     MULTIPLAN FILE #: PEEWEE.001              NAME:
_____
DATE:01/06/84                    TOP COST SUMMARY                   GND TOTAL: $109059.30
########################################################################################
ELEMT        DESCRIPTION        SUBCON  MATERIALS  OTHER    THRUPUT    COST    PERCENT        BARCHART
########################################################################################
A-1  Legal and General Costs    $0.00     $0.00 $17550.00           $17550.00  16.09%  ###########################

A-2  Site/Foundation Preparation $1771.00 $1328.30 $15500.00        $18599.30  17.05%  ############################

A-3  Framing and Related Costs   $3000.00 $2700.00  $175.00 $5000.00 $10875.00  9.97%  ################

A-4  Plumbing and Related Costs  $1500.00 $2100.00  $500.00 $4000.00  $8100.00  7.43%  ###########

A-5  HVAC and Related Costs      $2500.00  $400.00   $75.00  $200.00  $3175.00  2.91%  ####

A-6  Electrical and Related Costs $400.00  $300.00   $50.00 $6000.00  $6750.00  6.19%  #########

A-7  Masonry and Related Costs   $4000.00 $1250.00   $50.00 $7000.00 $12300.00 11.28%  ##################

A-8  Appliances and Fixtures      $150.00  $750.00   $50.00 $8000.00  $8950.00  8.21%  ############

A-9  Interior Finishing           $750.00 $3000.00   $10.00 $9000.00 $12760.00 11.70%  #################

A-10 Exterior Finishing            $0.00    $0.00    $0.00 $10000.00 $10000.00  9.17%  #############

          SUBTOTALS $14071.00 $11828.30 $33960.00 $49200.00 $109059.30
```

Figure 9.62. Home construction template PEEWEE.001 (Multiplan) (top sheet).

and to publish an attractive and useful estimate report, is the display and plotting of graphs or charts showing the estimate results. Figures 9.63 through 9.66 (plotted using Project Scheduler 5000™ graphics) show typical resource plots that are useful for analyzing and displaying estimate results. Plots of resources versus time; comparative plots of resource quantities; plots of labor costs, other direct costs, and total costs versus time, and cumulative costs versus time are desirable displays for the total estimate results as well as for selected work elements.

9.12.2 Cost Summaries by Work Element

Cost estimators should have a detailed cost summary available as backup material or for submittal with the proposal or bid. Two types of cost summaries are shown in Figures 9.67 and 9.68. Figure 9.67 is a typical construction estimate cost summary report by subdivision. This is a point estimate; that is, the resources are not spread by time. Note that each "item," or level 4 element, is listed in its proper place along with the takeoff quantity, unit cost, and total cost for the item. Subdivisions (level 3 elements) and divisions (level 2 elements) are subtotaled, and a grand total (level 1) is shown at the end of the estimate summary.

Figure 9.68 is a typical top-level cost summary sheet for a time-oriented work breakdown structure based cost estimate. Backing up the two sheets of printout for

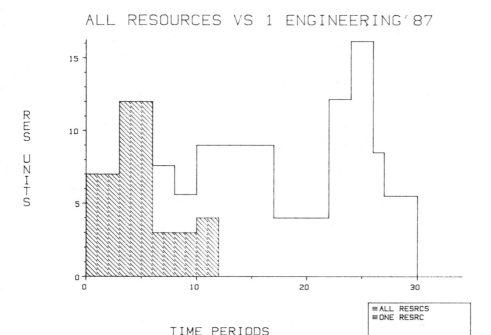

Figure 9.63. Plot showing all resources versus engineering 87 (PS5000).

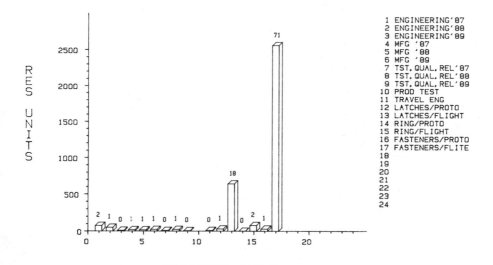

Figure 9.64. Plot showing use of all resource codes (PS5000).

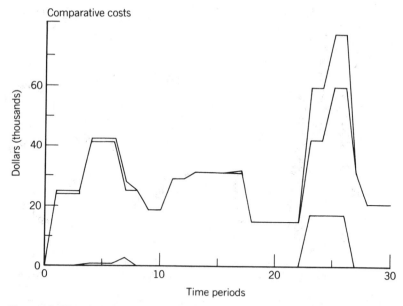

Figure 9.65. Plot showing comparative costs per time period (PS5000).

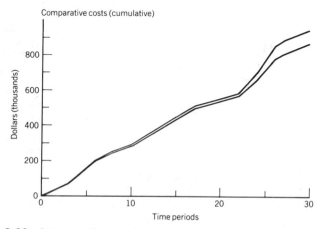

Figure 9.66. Comparative costs (cumulative) per time period (PS5000).

Job # 1
INDIAN CREEK#1

MOBILE DATA SERVICES
3502 Pan.Dr;P.O.Box 5042
Huntsville, AL 35805

Page 1
06/11/85

ITEM REPORT, SORTED BY SUBDIVISION

Item # Description	Take-Off	Class	Conversion	Order Qty	Unit Cost	Cost	Total
DIVISION 1 -- GENERAL DISCIPLINES							
SUBDIVISION 1.1 -- PERMITS							
1.110 WATERWAY WORK PERMIT	1 EA	9 OTHER	x1.00	1.00 EA	500.000	500.00 =	500
**** SUBDIVISION TOTAL =							500
SUBDIVISION 1.4 -- HEAVY UTILITIES							
1.410 INITIAL CONNECTION	1 LS	4 SUBCONT	x1.00	1.00 LS	10000.000	10800.00 =	10800
**** SUBDIVISION TOTAL =							10800
DIVISION TOTAL =							11300
DIVISION 2 -- SITEWORK							
SUBDIVISION 2.2 -- EARTHWORK							
2.231 EXTRA EXCAVATION	50 CY	3 EQUIPMNT	x1.00	50.00 CY	1.140	64 +	
		2 LABOR	x1.00	50.00 CY	7.280	494 =	557
2.232 MISC EXCAVATION	50 CY	3 EQUIPMNT	x1.00	50.00 CY	1.140	64 +	
		2 LABOR	x1.00	50.00 CY	7.280	494 =	557
2.233 TRENCH FOR 16" PIPE	4510 LF	3 EQUIPMNT	x0.5560	2508.00 CY	1.140	3202 +	
		2 LABOR	x0.5560	2508.00 CY	7.280	24758 =	27960
2.234 TRENCH FOR 12" PIPE	180 LF	3 EQUIPMNT	x0.5560	101.00 CY	1.140	129 +	
		2 LABOR	x0.5560	101.00 CY	7.280	997 =	1126
2.235 TRENCH FOR 8" PIPE	4640 LF	3 EQUIPMNT	x0.5560	2580.00 CY	1.140	3294 +	
		2 LABOR	x0.5560	2580.00 CY	7.280	25469 =	28763
2.236 TRENCH FOR 6" PIPE	80 LF	3 EQUIPMNT	x0.5560	45.00 CY	1.140	57 +	
		2 LABOR	x0.5560	45.00 CY	7.280	444 =	502
2.240 BACKFILL FOR 16" PIPE	4510 LF	3 EQUIPMNT	x1.2740	5746.00 CY	0.350	2252 +	
		2 LABOR	x1.2130	5471.00 CY	1.240	9199 =	11452
2.241 BACKFILL FOR 12" PIPE	180 LF	3 EQUIPMNT	x1.4420	260.00 CY	0.350	102 +	
		2 LABOR	x1.3760	248.00 CY	1.240	417 =	519
2.242 BACKFILL FOR 8" PIPE	4640 LF	3 EQUIPMNT	x1.5870	7364.00 CY	0.350	2887 +	
		2 LABOR	x1.5150	7030.00 CY	1.240	11821 =	14707
2.243 BACKFILL FOR 6" PIPE	80 LF	3 EQUIPMNT	x1.8030	145.00 CY	0.350	57 +	
		2 LABOR	x1.72	138.00 CY	1.240	232 =	289
**** SUBDIVISION TOTAL =							86433

EasyEst Estimating System (c) 1984 CMS
For use by MOBILE DATA SERVICES only

Figure 9.67. Subdivision cost summary (EasyEst).

the total or top level are detailed cost sheets of similar format for every work element in the work element structure (levels 2, 3, and 4). Although this printout forms a voluminous output, it is required by many government procurement offices and prime contractors and is useful as backup material for the estimating organization.

9.12.3 The Estimate Report

Most microcomputer word processing programs permit the insertion of cost numbers derived from spreadsheet, scheduling, or data base programs into a word processor document. This allows the cost estimator to construct an excellent cost estimate report consisting of both numerical and written material that describes the

ITEM REPORT , SORTED BY SUBDIVISION

Item # Description	Take-Off	Class	Conversion	Order Qty	Unit Cost	Cost	Total
SUBDIVISION 2.4 -- WATER SYSTEMS							
2.410 CONNECT TO EXIST 8" MAIN	6 EA	2 LABOR	x0.8920	6.00 HR	20.000	162.72 =	163
2.411 16" DUCTILE IRON PIPE	4510 LF	1 MATERIAL	x0.9350	4217.00 LF	19.200	93516 +	
		2 LABOR	x0.8920	4023.00 LF	14.450	78827 =	172344
2.412 12" DUCTILE IRON PIPE	180 LF	1 MATERIAL	x0.9350	169.00 LF	12.750	2489 +	
		2 LABOR	x0.8920	161.00 LF	9.250	2019 =	4508
2.413 8" DUCTILE IRON PIPE	4640 LF	1 MATERIAL	x0.9350	4339.00 LF	7.500	37587 +	
		2 LABOR	x0.8920	4139.00 LF	6.150	34517 =	72103
2.414 6" DUCTILE IRON PIPE	80 LF	1 MATERIAL	x0.9350	75.00 LF	5.500	476 +	
		2 LABOR	x0.8920	72.00 LF	3.930	384 =	860
2.421 16" BUTTERFLY VALVES	5 EA	1 MATERIAL	x0.9350	5.00 EA	1400.000	8085 +	
		2 LABOR	x0.8920	5.00 EA	335.000	2271 =	10356
2.422 12" GATE VALVES	6 EA	1 MATERIAL	x0.9350	6.00 EA	900.000	6237 +	
		2 LABOR	x0.8920	6.00 EA	220.000	1790 =	8027
2.423 8" GATE VALVES	8 EA	1 MATERIAL	x0.9350	8.00 EA	485.000	4481 +	
		2 LABOR	x0.8920	8.00 EA	165.000	1790 =	6271
2.424 16X16X16" TEES	4 EA	1 MATERIAL	x0.9350	4.00 EA	665.000	3072 +	
		2 LABOR	x0.8920	4.00 EA	83.000	450 =	3522
2.425 16X16X8" TEES	1 EA	1 MATERIAL	x0.9350	1.00 EA	600.000	693 +	
		2 LABOR	x0.8920	1.00 EA	75.000	102 =	795
2.426 12X12X12" TEES	3 EA	1 MATERIAL	x0.9350	3.00 EA	350.000	1213 +	
		2 LABOR	x0.8920	3.00 EA	55.000	224 =	1436
2.427 8X8X8" TEES	6 EA	1 MATERIAL	x0.9350	6.00 EA	170.000	1178 +	
		2 LABOR	x0.8920	6.00 EA	35.000	285 =	1463
2.428 16X8" REDUCERS	2 EA	1 MATERIAL	x0.9350	2.00 EA	220.000	508 +	
		2 LABOR	x0.8920	2.00 EA	37.000	100 =	609
2.429 8X16" REDUCERS	2 EA	1 MATERIAL	x0.9350	2.00 EA	80.000	185 +	
		2 LABOR	x0.8920	2.00 EA	19.800	54 =	238
2.431 12" CUTTING-IN SLEEVES	3 EA	1 MATERIAL	x0.9350	3.00 EA	600.000	2079 +	
		2 LABOR	x0.8920	3.00 EA	220.000	895 =	2974
2.432 8" CUTTING-IN SLEEVES	3 EA	1 MATERIAL	x0.9350	3.00 EA	400.000	1386 +	
		2 LABOR	x0.8920	3.00 EA	165.000	671 =	2057
2.433 16" BENDS	3 EA	1 MATERIAL	x0.9350	3.00 EA	425.000	1473 +	
		2 LABOR	x0.8920	3.00 EA	48.000	195 =	1668
2.434 12" BENDS	3 EA	1 MATERIAL	x0.9350	3.00 EA	220.000	762 +	
		2 LABOR	x0.8920	3.00 EA	37.000	151 =	913
2.435 8" BENDS	2 EA	1 MATERIAL	x0.9350	2.00 EA	115.000	266 +	
		2 LABOR	x0.8920	2.00 EA	24.000	65 =	331

Figure 9.67. (*Continued*)

product or service being estimated, the ground rules and conditions for the estimate, and the estimate rationale, along with the numerical estimate results, in one document.

An estimate is only as good as the accompanying description of what is estimated and how the estimate was performed. It is necessary to place all of the facts concerning the estimate into one well-organized document, whether it be for internal use or for transmittal to the customer. A high-quality microcomputer with a letter quality or near letter quality printer and a good word processing software package will help produce the type of integrated cost estimate document that is required as good estimating practice.

```
Job # 1                        MOBILE DATA SERVICES                      Page 3
INDIAN CREEK#1              3502 Pan.Dr;P.O.Box 5042                    06/11/85
                             Huntsville, AL  35805
--------------------------------------------------------------------------------

         I T E M   R E P O R T ,   S O R T E D   B Y   S U B D I V I S I O N

      Item #  Description      Take-Off    Class    Conversion  Order Qty  Unit Cost    Cost      Total
      -----------------------------------------------------------------------------------------------------
      2.436 6" BENDS             2 EA    1 MATERIAL  x0.9350    2.00 EA    80.000     185 +
                                         2 LABOR     x0.8920    2.00 EA    19.800      54 =          238
      2.437 FIRE HYDRANTS        8 EA    1 MATERIAL  x0.9350    8.00 EA   780.000    7207 +
                                         2 LABOR     x0.8920    8.00 EA   210.000    2278 =         9485
****  SUBDIVISION  TOTAL  =                                                                       300363

      SUBDIVISION  2.5 -- PAVING/LANDSCAPING
      2.510 CURB/GUTTER REMOVAL 40 LF    3 EQUIPMNT  x0.9350   38.00 LF     0.690      29 +
                                         2 LABOR     x0.8920   36.00 LF     1.820      89 =          118
      2.511 REPLACE CURB & GUTTER 40 LF  1 MATERIAL  x0.9350   38.00 LF     4.450     195 +
                                         2 LABOR     x0.8920   36.00 LF     8.050     393 =          588
      2.530 PATCH 6'WIDE PAVING 390 LF   1 MATERIAL  x1.41    550.00 SY     4.500    2859 +
                                         2 LABOR     x1.34    523.00 SY     3.350    2376 =         5234
      2.535 RESTORE 6' STRIP OF SOD 9410 LF 1 MATERIAL x0.6240 5872.00 SY   1.500   10173 +
                                         2 LABOR     x0.5950 5599.00 SY     1.180    8959 =        19132
****  SUBDIVISION  TOTAL  =                                                                        25073

DIVISION TOTAL  =                                                                                 411868


DIVISION 3 -- CONCRETE

      SUBDIVISION  3.1 -- CAST IN PLACE
      3.110 ADDITIONAL CLASS B CONCR 10 CY 1 MATERIAL x0.8890   9.00 CY    42.950   446.47 =         446
      3.120 ADDITIONAL CRUSHED STONE 50 CY 1 MATERIAL x0.8890  45.00 CY     9.700   504.16 =         504
      3.130 CALCIUM CHLORIDE    500 LB   1 MATERIAL  x0.8890  445.00 LB     1.500   770.96 =         771
****  SUBDIVISION  TOTAL  =                                                                          1722

DIVISION TOTAL  =                                                                                    1722


DIVISION 13 -- SPECIAL CONSTRUCTION

      SUBDIVISION 13.7 -- WATER CONNECTIONS
      13.710 CONNECT AT VILLAGE HALL 1 LS 4 SUBCONT  x1.00     1.00 LS  5000.000  5400.00 =         5400
****  SUBDIVISION  TOTAL  =                                                                          5400

DIVISION TOTAL  =                                                                                    5400
--------------------------------------------------------------------------------
```

EasyEst Estimating System (c) 1984 CMS
For use by MOBILE DATA SERVICES only

Figure 9.67. (*Continued*)

9.13 MICROCOMPUTER HARDWARE FOR THE ESTIMATOR

Although most microcomputers will perform the estimating and analysis functions described in this chapter, some characteristics that are desirable to meet the requirements of cost estimating are described in the following sections.

9.13.1 The Microcomputer

A microcomputer using the MS-DOS™ (Microsoft Corporation) operating system will provide the widest selection of cost estimating and related software. Since the

```
Job # 1                          MOBILE DATA SERVICES                        Page 4
INDIAN CREEK#1                   3502 Pan.Dr;P.O.Box 5042                     06/11/85
                                 Huntsville, AL  35805
----------------------------------------------------------------------------------------
```

ITEM REPORT, SORTED BY SUBDIVISION

Item # Description	Take-Off	Class	Conversion	Order Qty	Unit Cost	Cost	Total
DIVISION 15 -- MECHANICAL							
SUBDIVISION 15.7 -- BRIDGE CROSSINGS							
15.700 PIPE SUPT BRACKETS	26 EA	1 MATERIAL	x0.9780	26.00 EA	80.000	2402 +	
		2 LABOR	x1.8420	48.00 HR	24.000	1562 =	3965
15.710 INSTALL PIPE ON BRIDGE	400 LF	3 EQUIPMNT	x0.1470	59.00 HR	5.350	354 +	
		2 LABOR	x0.1380	56.00 HR	24.000	1822 =	2176
15.715 REPAIR PIPE UNDER BRIDGE	1 LS	4 SUBCONT	x1.00	1.00 LS	2500.000	2700.00 =	2700
15.720 TRAFFIC CONTROL DUR CONS	16 HR	2 LABOR	x0.9210	15.00 HR	14.000	284.76 =	285
15.730 PREP/PIPE INSTALLATION	400 LF	2 LABOR	x0.0370	15.00 HR	24.000	488.16 =	488
15.740 RELOCATE ELEC ON BRIDGE	10 HR	2 LABOR	x0.9210	10.00 HR	24.000	325.44 =	325
15.745 PATCH PAINT ON BRIDGE	200 SF	1 MATERIAL	x0.9780	196.00 SF	0.100	23 +	
		2 LABOR	x0.9210	185.00 SF	0.150	38 =	60
**** SUBDIVISION TOTAL =							9999
DIVISION TOTAL =							9999
JOB SUBTOTAL =							440289

```
------------------------------------------------------------------------------------------
                     EasyEst Estimating System (c) 1984 CMS
                     For use by MOBILE DATA SERVICES only
```

Figure 9.67. *(Continued)*

MS-DOS™ operating system has been around for several years, there are numerous microcomputers that offer it. A machine with at least 512 kilobytes of memory and a hard disk for information storage will be desirable and will run most cost estimating and scheduling software packages. A color monitor and color graphics screen capability, although not mandatory, would be highly desirable for the cost estimating computer because many of the finest cost estimating packages use color displays for both character highlighting and for graphics. A color monitor will make it easier to discern and distinguish information types and graphics displays. Look for a user-friendly keyboard capable of holding keyboard templates for the

```
Job # 1                        MOBILE DATA SERVICES                    Page  5
INDIAN CREEK#1               3502 Pan.Dr;P.O.Box 5042                   06/11/85
                               Huntsville, AL   35805
---------------------------------------------------------------------------

       -----------------------------------------------------------------
       JOB COST BEFORE PROFIT, BOND, $ BURDENS             $440,289
       BOND    =          2.00%                              $8,806
       PROFIT =          10.00%                             $44,909
       JOB   TOTAL   =                         $494,004
       -----------------------------------------------------------------
```

```
---------------------------------------------------------------------------
                   EasyEst Estimating System (c) 1984 CMS
                   For use by MOBILE DATA SERVICES only
```

Figure 9.67. (*Continued*)

various software packages you will use. A separate numeric keypad and separate arrow keys are desirable since you will be entering lots of numbers and will need to move your cursor all around spreadsheets with ease.

9.13.2 The Printer and Plotter

A wide-carriage printer capable of emphasized printing in compressed print is a must for the cost estimator. This type of printer will produce the many columns

```
PROJECT: THE "ESTIMATOR" TEST CASE          JMCA WBS TREE v1.0                    PAGE:     2
WBS:    * TOTAL *                         COST BREAKDOWN SUMMARY: DOLLARS         DATE: 06-11-85
```

	JAN85	FEB85	MAR85	APR85	MAY85	JUN85	TOTAL
ENGINEERING:							
PROGRAM MANAGER	7119	7119	7119	7484	7484	7484	43810
ENGR SUPERVISOR	10394	8335	6419	6920	6869	6869	45805
SR SYSTEM ENGR	14922	10216	7240	6026	6026	6026	50454
SYSTEM ENGR	15240	14964	10689	9432	9140	9140	68606
DESIGN ENGR	22116	19000	17480	18378	17484	17484	111942
SOFTWARE ENGR	12461	5853	5664	6060	6060	6060	42158
MECHANICAL ENGR	4842	2728	2046	2262	2189	2189	16256
ELECTRICAL ENGR	5226	3312	2576	2752	2752	2752	19371
ANALOG/DIGITAL	3620	2172	2172	2323	2323	2323	14934
LOGISTICS	9275	7525	5775	6168	4673	4673	38088
RELIABILITY ENG	6767	5829	5360	4953	4953	4953	32816
MAINTAINABILITY	1885	1755	1755	1857	1857	1857	10965
TECH PUBS	6725	6725	6725	7115	7115	7115	41520
PROGRAM PLANNER	4590	4590	3570	3206	3206	3206	22369
ENGR TECHNICIAN	2938	2678	2678	2812	2812	2812	16731
DRAFTING	6084	3588	2418	1189	1189	1189	15657
TOTAL ENGINEERING	134203	106389	89685	88938	86132	86132	591480
ENGINEERING OVERHEAD	45103	35752	30034	27659	26805	26805	192137
MANUFACTURING:							
MANUFACT SUPVSR	10089	8370	6780	7048	7014	7014	46313
SHIFT SUPVSR	14243	13556	13070	13917	13856	13856	82499
INDUSTRIAL ENGR	4426	4373	4373	4590	4590	4590	26941
MANUFACTURE OPS	5267	4158	3755	3943	3943	3943	25007
QUALITY ASSUR	5107	5016	4332	4309	4309	4309	27383
PRODUCTION PLNG	5296	3201	1533	182	182	182	10575
PRODUCTION TEST	5132	3640	1456	758	758	758	12501
INSPECTION	3203	3168	3168	3294	3294	3294	19421
RECEIVING	1372	1372	1372	1413	1413	1413	8354
MACHINE SHOP	15973	14898	14595	15163	15038	15038	90705
ASSEMBLY DEPT A	358856	349043	341051	348264	342047	342047	2081308
ASSEMBLY DEPT B	79924	76256	67338	69232	69083	69083	430915
TOTAL MANUFACTURING	508887	487049	462822	472113	465526	465526	2861922
MANUFACTURING OVERHEAD	793200	761856	726024	718440	708144	708144	4415808
SUPPORT LABOR:							
CLERICAL	6965	6633	6056	6093	6093	6093	37932
GRAPHICS	1932	1932	1788	1843	1843	1843	11181
FACILITIES	9792	3672	0	0	0	0	13464
SHIPPING	3617	3560	3560	3665	3665	3665	21732
TOTAL SUPPORT LABOR	22306	15797	11404	11600	11600	11600	84309
SUPPORT LABOR OVERHEAD	10808	8192	6352	6272	6272	6272	44168
FRINGE	279466	255879	236843	240514	236568	236568	1485838

Figure 9.68. Top-level cost summary sheet (WBS TREE).

of numerical and cost information that are common to cost estimates. A small plotter ($8\frac{1}{2}$ × 11-inch sheets is acceptable) is highly desirable to plot resource histograms, bar charts, pie charts, simple engineering sketches, and scheduling charts that will accompany the estimate. Multicolor printers and plotters are nice but not absolutely necessary.

```
PROJECT: THE "ESTIMATOR" TEST CASE              JMCA WBS TREE v1.0                          PAGE:    3
WBS:    * TOTAL *                        COST BREAKDOWN SUMMARY: DOLLARS                     DATE: 06-11-85
```

	JAN85	FEB85	MAR85	APR85	MAY85	JUN85	TOTAL
MATERIALS:							
RAW MATERIAL	5210000	5220000	5220000	5220000	5220000	5220000	31310000
PURCHASED PARTS	2283000	1738000	1025000	620000	619000	619000	6904000
SUB-CONTRACTS	81500	66500	51500	51500	51500	51500	354000
STD. COMMERCIAL	15000	15000	15000	15000	15000	15000	90000
OTHER MATERIALS	65900	50600	44900	44300	44300	44800	294800
SHOP SUPPLIES	3000	2950	2850	2850	2850	2850	17350
SCRAP & REWORK ($)	3500	2600	2400	2200	1800	1800	14300
TOTAL MATERIALS	7661900	7095650	6361650	5955850	5954450	5954950	38984450
MATERIAL OVERHEAD	919428	851478	763398	714702	714534	714594	4678134
TOOLING	301200	55000	0	400	0	0	356600
OTHER DIRECT COST:							
TRAVEL	28700	14100	10200	4600	6200	9200	73000
COMPUTING	12500	500	500	500	500	500	15000
FACILITIES	1065000	500000	0	0	0	0	1565000
TOTAL ODC	1106200	514600	10700	5100	6700	9700	1653000
SUB TOTAL, G & A BASE	11782702	10187623	8698912	8241588	8216731	8220291	55347846
GENERAL & ADMINISTRATION	2120886	1833772	1565804	1483486	1479012	1479652	9962613
SUB-TOTAL COST	13903589	12021395	10264717	9725073	9695742	9699943	65310459
COST OF MONEY:							
ENGINEERING	1928	1527	1284	1182	1146	1146	8211
MANUFACTURING	81634	78408	74720	73939	72880	72880	454460
SUPPORT	405	307	238	235	235	235	1656
MATERIAL	15324	14191	12723	11912	11909	11910	77969
GENERAL & ADMIN.	14728	12735	10874	10302	10271	10275	69185
TOTAL COST OF MONEY	114018	107168	99839	97570	96440	96446	611481
TOTAL COST	14017607	12128563	10364555	9822644	9792183	9796389	65921940
PROFIT/FEE	1320841	1142033	975148	923882	921096	921495	6204494
TOTAL PRICE	15338448	13270595	11339704	10746526	10713278	10717883	72126434

Figure 9.68. (*Continued*)

9.13.3 Software

The minimum software requirement for a cost estimator should be:

- ☐ A spreadsheet program
- ☐ A data base program
- ☐ A word processing program
- ☐ At least one ''vertical market'' cost estimating software applications program
- ☐ BASIC language for programming simple in-house programs

In addition to these minimum software requirements, the cost estimator may wish to acquire the following eventually:

- [ ] A graphics or microcomputer-aided design program
- [ ] A scheduling/costing program
- [ ] An in-house "customized" cost estimating software package
- [ ] A communications or integrated software applications package

9.13.4 Peripheral Devices

Other peripheral devices that are desirable for a cost estimating microcomputer installation are as follows:

- [ ] An uninterruptible power supply
- [ ] A digitizer (for drawing takeoffs)
- [ ] A surge protector (if not incorporated in the uninterruptible power supply)

9.14 SUMMARY AND FINAL ADVICE

As can be seen by the foregoing, there are a number of ways cost estimates can be produced and cost analysis and estimating functions can be performed using the microcomputer. You should customize your specific hardware and software complement to fit your specific needs. Contact a Certified Professional Estimator, Certified Cost Analyst, or Certified Cost Engineer for advice concerning estimating techniques and methods to use in microestimating and consult with your computer hardware dealer for sound advice on the equipment to purchase. Start out with a machine that is expandable to at least the capacities stated and gradually acquire software as you need it and as your microestimating skills improve. Above all, keep abreast of the expanding capabilities of microcomputers, and you will reap many rewards as you proceed into the world of cost estimating with microcomputers.

REFERENCES

1. Stewart, R. D. and A. L. Stewart. *Cost Estimating with Microcomputers.* McGraw-Hill, New York, 1986.
2. Stewart, R. D. *Cost Estimating.* Wiley, New York, 1982.
3. "Cost Estimating in Construction: A Study," Business Round Table, New York, 1982.

10

CONSTRUCTION COST ESTIMATING

JAMES D. STEVENS, PHD, PE

10.1 INTRODUCTION

Construction cost estimating is the process whereby a party interested in the construction of a facility attempts to determine the expenditure of resources (money, machines, manpower, materials, and time) necessary to realize his goal (to produce a competitive bid, to realize a profit, to insure timely completion, etc.). The two parties primarily interested in construction cost estimating are the owner, who will have to pay for the construction of the facility, and the contractor, who must determine a price to charge the owner that represents the anticipated construction costs plus markup (profit and contingencies). Others with an interest in construction cost estimating are the architect/engineer (A/E) who must design a facility within the owner's budget, regulatory agencies, and financial institutions needing a basis for construction loans. Contractual arrangements among these parties may be either traditional, where the owner contracts with the A/E for drawings and specifications and then contracts with the contractor for construction, or nontraditional, such as design-build or professional construction management, where the A/E and contractor work together in the design phase. The method used by the cost estimator depends on (1) the type of project for which the cost estimate is to be prepared, (2) the type of contract form to be used for the project, (3) the most cost-effective degree of estimate, and (4) any contractual requirement imposed by the owner.

10.1.1 Overview

Many elements of construction cost estimating are similar to those mentioned in other sections of this work. The goal of this chapter is to familiarize the reader with concepts, procedures, and considerations that may be different from those in other fields, without unnecessarily repeating basics. In construction cost estimating, practitioners use a variety of forms, formats, and procedures. Also, each practitioner adds to the *science* of cost estimating some *art*, based on his experience and the requirements of his company. However, regardless of format or procedures, the goal of all construction cost estimators is, first, to predict accurately the cost of a project, and second, to quote a price that will secure the project, at a profit, for his company. In this chapter, figures, tables, and examples typical of those used in construction cost estimating, have been kept very simple to convey the concepts discussed. The reader should refer to other publications, such as those published by Robert Snow Means Company, Inc., for more detailed information in various aspects of construction cost estimating. Also, in this chapter, the contractual arrangement is assumed to be traditional unless otherwise noted (i.e., the cost estimator is provided detailed drawings and specifications by the owner upon which to base his estimate).

10.1.2 Consideration of Construction Type

Construction cost estimating methodology varies with types of construction projects. Construction of residential housing, commercial buildings, institutional buildings, and the like is often called building construction, or vertical construction. Projects of this type are usually estimated by a method generally known as *time and materials*. Construction of highways, dams, tunnels, airports, and the like is called heavy construction, horizontal construction, or engineered construction. Cost estimating for these projects is usually based on approximate quantities with the estimate yielding a cost per unit. A third category, industrial construction, which deals with manufacturing plants, refineries, and the like, is basically a combination of heavy and building construction. In general, cost estimating for building construction is more accurate than for heavy construction for a variety of reasons: (1) greater use of standard designs, materials, and practices in building construction; (2) building contractors usually work closer to home where a working relationship already exists with the local work force, subcontractors, and material suppliers; (3) building construction often involves repetition of construction operations from floor to floor, site to site, and so on; and (4) equipment used in building construction is usually smaller and easier to replace or repair than that used in heavy construction. Heavy construction is often carried on away from material suppliers and labor pools; therefore, the cost estimator must consider transportation, labor turnover, equipment repair, and other problems that might arise in a remote area. Additionally, heavy construction often deals with one-of-a-kind construction operations and/or specifically engineered facilities quite unlike any the contractor has previously encountered. Consequently, the cost estimator for heavy construction must judiciously apply contingency costs to reduce the risk of losing money.

Whatever the approach to construction cost estimating, the practitioner must be experienced in the type of construction planned and have the ability to work fast and accurately. Computers can be used to perform most of the necessary calculations, extensions, and so on, but only experience can identify hidden costs and/or savings.

10.1.2.1 Building Construction. Construction cost estimating for the contractor in building construction is primarily identifying the materials to be erected by performing a quantity takeoff from detailed drawings and specifications furnished by the owner, pricing the materials to be used, estimating the time it will take crews of labor and equipment for construction, then determining the cost of the crews. To this result the contractor will add the cost of subcontracted work, various overhead items, and his expected profit and contingencies, to obtain the price he will quote to the owner.

10.1.2.2 Heavy Construction. In heavy construction, identifying the materials is not as straightforward as in building construction. The primary reason for this is that the existing condition of the earth's surface must usually be disturbed by removing or adding soil, then the quantities of various materials used in construction will depend on the condition of the prepared surface. For example, the plans for a new road will contain drawings showing profiles of the terrain on which the road is to be built and soil boring logs, which will show the types of soil in selected locations. However, exact quantities cannot be determined until the earthwork is actually performed. Therefore the contractor must base his cost estimate on predicted quantities instead of actual quantities. These predicted quantities are provided by the owner in the form of a list of pay items to which the contractor quotes a price per unit for the various materials and construction operations involved in the project. These prices per unit must contain the cost of material, material handling, labor, equipment, subcontracts, and a portion of the total overhead and profit.

10.1.3 Consideration of Contract Form

Construction cost estimating is approached differently for different types of contracts, at least by the contractor. In a cost-plus type contract, where the contractor is reimbursed for his costs and his profit equation is predetermined (i.e., percent of cost, fixed fee, incentive fee, etc.), a high degree of accuracy is not as critical as in a fixed-price contract, where there is a high risk of losing money if the estimate is low or not getting the job if the estimate is high.

10.1.3.1 Cost-Plus Contracts. Cost-plus contracts are often used in construction for privately financed projects. Two advantages of a cost-plus contract to the owner are that the project can commence prior to availability of a complete set of plans and drawings, and changes are easy to incorporate as the project progresses. An advantage to the contractor is that the project represents very low financial risk. The cost estimate by a contractor for a cost-plus contract usually possesses a fairly low degree of accuracy. In a cost-plus-percent contract, where the contractor receives reimbursement for his cost plus a negotiated percent of that cost as profit, and a cost-plus-fixed-fee, where the contractor receives reimbursement for his cost plus a negotiated fixed profit, the contractor's cost estimate is usually less detailed. In a cost-plus-incentive-fee contract the contractor must develop a cost estimate to obtain a target cost. A negotiated set of percentages or fees is then tied to actual cost by the contract. If the actual cost of the project is at the target cost, a certain fee is paid to the contractor. If the actual cost is higher than the target cost, the contractor gets a lower fee, and if the actual cost is lower, a higher fee.

The contract documents provided to the contractor for a cost-plus contract vary. Since the contractor gets reimbursed his total costs, the owner need not provide a detailed set of plans and specifications. It may be to the owner's benefit to negotiate with a sketchy set of documents, then have the contractor collaborate with the designer during preparation of the detailed plans and specifications.

10.1.3.2 Lump-Sum Contracts.

Lump-sum is a fixed-price contract where the contractor must provide the owner with a single price for the total project. Lump-sum contracts are almost always used for construction of structures for public works and are often used for privately financed projects. The advantages of a lump-sum contract to the owner are in knowing what the project will cost prior to commencement, and the expectation that, because of competition among potential contractors, the project will be completed for a minimum cost. The advantage to the contractor is that he knows exactly what must be done, and he has a strong incentive to work efficiently, thereby cutting his construction costs and increasing his profit. For the contractor, a lump-sum contract represents high financial risk. The contractor must perform a detailed cost estimate to reduce the risk.

Lump-sum contracts are usually awarded as a result of competitive bids. To insure fairness, all contractors preparing a cost estimate for a bid must be estimating the same work. Therefore the owner must provide a complete and detailed set of plans and specifications and insure that all potential bidders are made aware of any changes, additions, or deletions entered during the period of cost estimate preparation.

10.1.3.3 Unit-Price Contracts.

Most heavy or engineered construction is done with unit-price contracts. A unit price contract is primarily a fixed-price contract containing a series of pay items with quantities of units of various material and labor items assigned to each. The contractor must do a detailed cost estimate for each pay item, based on the quantities given in the contractual documents, but need not do an exhaustive quantity survey of either the site or the plans and specifications. However, a prudent contractor will usually, time permitting, survey some quantities, comparing the plans and specifications to the job site, because knowledge of erroneous quantities in the contract can be used to increase his profit.

Unit-price contracts are awarded on the basis of low bids, actually the lowest summation of the fixed-price bids that must be stipulated for each item. Owing to the uncertainty of quantities on a large project to be constructed at a site unprepared at time of award, assumed quantities based on a survey by the owner are used for cost estimating. The owner must provide the contractor with a complete set of plans and specifications, but not necessarily to a scale that would permit an accurate quantity takeoff of earthwork. The plans and specifications contain detailed sections of various items to be constructed and the assumed quantities of each item to be considered in the cost estimate.

10.1.4 Degrees of Cost Estimating

A construction cost estimate is prepared to predict, with as much certainty as is cost-effective, the actual cost that will be incurred in constructing a facility. The owner is usually interested in a budget estimate that yields a "ballpark" figure of perhaps $\pm 5\%$ for use in determining the economic feasibility of constructing the facility. The contractor is interested in a very accurate, detailed estimate on which to base the price he quotes the owner.

The methods used by the two parties are somewhat different and represent the risk of a poor estimate. The owner, with a $\pm 5\%$ estimate, can often determine the economic feasibility of the project and make the decision of whether to proceed with construction. A cost estimating error of a few percent will affect the owner's rate of return on investment, but will most likely not turn a profitable venture into a losing one. On the contrary, a cost estimating error of a few percent can easily change the contractor's profit situation. If the cost estimate is high, the contractor probably will not get the job, and if the estimate if low, the contractor may lose money on the project.

It is impossible to know what costs will be incurred until after the fact, so the problem facing the estimator is how best to predict the actual cost with the information he has available at the time. Therefore the proper approach to preparing a cost estimate for a particular project is basically a function of the availability of usable data and the cost-effectiveness of the effort involved.

For instance, an owner may have completed a project in the recent past for which all the returns are in, allowing exact knowledge of the project costs. If the owner wants to undertake another project that is similar, he may use the past project cost as a cost estimate of the new project. This approach is certainly inexpensive but may also be ineffective. For a small cost the owner can obtain data that compare present costs of projects to those of like projects constructed in the past, thus allowing him to consider factors such as inflation. For further costs, data can be obtained that index not only the complete project but items such as labor, equipment, and material by geographical location. The services of consultants can allow problems associated with the prior venture to be compared to problems anticipated on the current venture to modify the cost estimate. The services of an architect/ engineer to prepare plans and specifications for the proposed project further raise the cost but also produce a much better cost estimate. Finally, plans and specifications can be used to prepare a detailed estimate that has both high cost and high effectiveness.

10.1.5 Bidding Strategy

Bidding strategy is the art, or science, of acquiring profitable contracts in the face of competition. Bidding strategy must address which fixed-price contracts to bid on and how best to propose cost-plus work. Circumstances that may warrant passing up a project are: (1) when timing conflicts with other projects; (2) when time allotted in the contract to complete the project is insufficient; (3) when special equipment or experience is needed which gives a competitor a large advantage; (4) when the project is located in a remote area of strong unions where local contractors are competing; (5) when the owner's engineer is less than responsive; (6) when there are one or more desperate bidders looking for a project just to hang on; and (7) when the necessary financial resources of the contractor are needed elsewhere.

Bidding strategy also involves adjusting the markup on bids to compete with known and unknown competitors. This strategy can be based on statistical data from several previous bids, but must be tempered with current data, such as the amount of work available and financial condition of competitors. A special case, the unbalanced bid, is a strategy utilized by the contractor against the owner in an effort to increase profit.

Another aspect of bidding strategy concerns bidding on a project at break-even or a loss to establish a reputation or a position for follow-on work.

10.2 PRELIMINARY COST ESTIMATING

Preliminary cost estimating is the process whereby the owner determines the expected cost of a project to a degree that permits him to decide whether to proceed with construction. Preliminary cost estimating is also used by the contractor for cost-plus contracts and as a first step in detailed estimating for lump-sum or unit-price contracts.

10.2.1 Overview

Past experience and historical data personally accumulated is the best information to use for cost estimating, but owners often do not have reliable recent, personally obtained data. Therefore owners must rely on data supplied by other sources and tailor it to fit the situation.

10.2.2 Preliminary Cost Estimating for Building Construction

Cost estimating for building construction by the owner often involves trying to determine an approximate cost for the construction of a facility, or a subsystem of a facility, that can be characterized as having a certain design capacity, volume, or area.

10.2.2.1 Area and Capacity Estimates.

The simplest form of a preliminary estimate results from assuming a constant unit cost per unit of area or capacity. A school building may cost $50 per square foot or $4000 per desk; a parking garage may cost $20 per square foot or $6000 per parking space; and a hospital may cost $50,000 per bed. A great amount of cost data pertaining to various types of facilities has been compiled and published in estimating manuals. Two of the more frequently used manuals are *Dodge Construction Systems Costs*, published by McGraw-Hill Information Systems Co., and *Means Building Construction Cost Data*, published by the Robert Snow Means Co. Table 10.1 shows an example of average building costs for a vocational technical adult school; Table 10.2 shows locality adjustments that have been compiled and published in *Dodge Construction Systems Costs*.

The format used in the *Means Building Construction Cost Data* manual for unit cost data and locality adjustments is illustrated in Tables 10.3 and 10.4. To account for the fact that unit costs do in fact vary as a function of project size, the *Means*

TABLE 10.1. Average Building Costs: Vocational Technical Adult Schools (20,000–80,000 Square Feet)

Building System	Low Average $/SF	Low Average % TOT	Average $/SF	Average % TOT	High Average $/SF	High Average % TOT
Foundations	$2.64	5.0%	$3.12	5.0%	$4.53	6.0%
Floors on grade	3.75	7.1	4.29	6.9	5.29	7.0
Superstructure	10.08	19.1	11.08	17.8	12.84	17.0
Roofing	2.64	5.0	3.12	5.0	3.78	5.0
Exterior walls	6.92	13.1	8.67	13.9	10.57	14.0
Partitions	4.28	8.1	5.54	8.9	6.80	9.0
Wall finishes	1.26	2.4	1.56	2.5	1.51	2.0
Floor finishes	2.11	4.0	2.43	3.9	3.02	4.0
Ceiling finishes	0.53	1.0	0.62	1.0	0.76	1.0
Conveying systems	0.00	0.0	0.00	0.0	0.00	0.0
Specialties	3.17	6.0	3.36	5.4	3.78	5.0
Fixed equipment	2.64	5.0	3.67	5.9	4.53	6.0
HVAC	3.75	7.1	4.29	6.9	5.29	7.0
Plumbing	2.11	4.0	2.49	4.0	3.02	4.0
Electrical	6.92	13.1	8.03	12.9	9.82	13.0
Gross building costs	$52.80	100%	$62.25	100%	$75.54	100%

Source: *Dodge Construction Systems Costs*. Cost Information Systems, McGraw-Hill, Princeton, N.J., 1985.

TABLE 10.2. Locality Adjustments

Location		Labor	Material	General
Birmingham	AL	0.73	0.84	0.78
Tuscaloosa	AL	0.68	0.83	0.75
Jasper	AL	0.73	0.84	0.78
Florence	AL	0.67	0.93	0.80
Huntsville	AL	0.71	0.80	0.75
Los Angeles	CA	1.26	1.05	1.15
Santa Monica	CA	1.22	1.03	1.12
Honolulu	HI	1.08	1.27	1.17

Source: *Dodge Construction Systems Costs*. Cost Information Systems, McGraw-Hill, Princeton, N.J., 1985.

manual uses the project size modifier curve shown in Figure 10.1 and explained in Table 10.5.

10.2.2.2 Systems Estimates.

Published reference manuals can also be used to estimate the cost of individual components of a constructed facility. This type of estimate usually requires some preliminary design information or design assumptions. The procedure for estimating the cost of precast concrete wall panels, taken from the 1985 *Dodge Construction Systems Costs* manual, is illustrated in Table 10.6.

10.2.2.3 Comparable Facility Estimates.

For many types of facilities, or subsystems of facilities, published unit cost data may be either unavailable or unsuited for the intended application. In this case, simple equations derived from past experience of the designer may be used. One type of equation used for this purpose has the form:

$$C_p = C_e \frac{S_p}{S_e} \qquad (10.1)$$

where C_p = total cost of proposed facility
C_e = total cost of a similar existing facility
S_p = area or capacity of the proposed facility
S_e = area or capacity of the existing facility
n = an exponent appropriate for the type of facility, usually in the range 0.60 to 0.95
C_n = cost per square foot of total facility

TABLE 10.3. Building Square Foot Unit Costs

S.F., C.F., and Percent of Total Costs	Unit	Unit Costs			Percent of Total		
		0.25	Median	0.75	0.25	Median	0.75
Schools Vocational	S.F.	40.75	54.45	72.60			
Total project costs	C.F.	2.55	3.47	4.81			
Masonry	S.F.	1.54	6.34	9.07	4.60	8.00	13.70
Roofing	S.F.	.69	1.18	2.26	.80	1.80	2.20
Equipment	S.F.	1.01	1.75	3.44	1.90	3.20	4.60
Plumbing	S.F.	2.71	4.00	5.75	5.40	7.00	8.50
HVAC	S.F.	5.75	7.15	11.80	9.30	12.50	17.00
Electrical	S.F.	4.42	5.95	8.91	9.50	11.80	13.90
Total: mechanical and electrical	S.F.	10.20	14.65	22.45	21.10	29.70	36.00
Per pupil, total cost	Pupil	2,480	14,930	22,100			
Total: mechanical and electrical	Pupil	840	2,020	5,200			

Source: Means Building Construction Costs. Robert Snow Means, Kingston, Mass., 1985.

TABLE 10.4. City Cost Indexes

| | | Alabama | | | | | |
| | | Mobile | | | Montgomery | | |
Division		Mat.	Inst.	Total	Mat.	Inst.	Total
2	Site Work	118.6	89.3	105.2	87.4	90.5	88.9
3.1	Formwork	97.0	85.6	88.2	102.2	76.5	82.3
3.2	Reinforcing	83.0	77.6	80.8	83.0	76.4	80.3
3.3	Cast in place conc.	100.1	94.5	96.6	101.4	93.4	96.4
3	Concrete	95.6	89.6	91.7	97.4	85.3	89.6
4	Masonry	91.6	83.8	85.6	86.0	76.2	78.4
5	Metals	93.9	83.9	90.3	94.8	82.0	90.2
6	Wood and plastics	91.9	89.3	90.4	101.3	77.0	87.9
7	Moisture protection	87.2	83.3	86.0	88.4	75.4	84.3
8	Doors, windows, glass	98.8	81.5	89.6	98.6	76.2	86.8
9.1	Lath and plaster	92.3	86.3	87.7	108.6	77.3	84.7
9.2	Dry wall	91.5	87.4	89.6	99.8	76.0	88.6
9.5	Acoustical work	94.3	89.2	91.5	94.3	76.2	84.5
9.6	Flooring	113.7	89.0	107.2	99.1	76.2	93.1
9.8	Painting	121.7	78.1	87.4	119.9	76.1	85.5
9	Finishes	100.0	84.4	91.6	101.6	76.1	88.0
10–14	Total div. 10–14	100.0	82.7	94.8	100.0	80.2	94.1
15	Mechanical	97.5	80.9	89.0	99.1	73.8	86.1
16	Electrical	89.2	92.3	91.4	90.4	76.2	80.3
1–16	Weighted average	97.1	85.8	90.9	96.1	78.8	86.6

Source: Means Building Construction Costs. Robert Snow Means, Kingston, Mass., 1985.

Equation 10.1 reflects the fact that as facilities become larger in area, or of greater capacity, the construction cost increases, but not in linear proportion.

Example 10.1: A circular concrete tank of 6000-ft^3 capacity was constructed at a cost of \$40,000. What will a similar tank cost if the capacity will be 10,000 ft^3?

Solution: For many structural components that have a given volume or capacity, the exponent n in the equation can be assumed to be 0.75. Therefore

$$C_p = C_e \left(\frac{S_p}{S_e}\right)^n$$

$$C_p = \$58,674$$

(10.1)

Example 10.2: An 80,000-ft^2 office building was constructed for \$48/ft^2. What will a comparable 120,000-ft^2 complex cost per square foot?

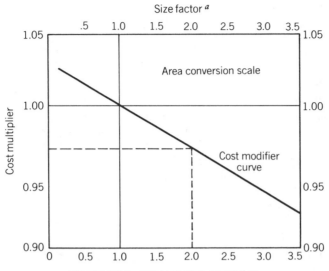

Figure 10.1. Project size modifier.

Solution: For estimating the cost of buildings on a square foot basis, the exponent in the foregoing equation is often assumed to be 0.85. Note, however, that C_p in the equation is total facility cost, not cost per square foot. Therefore

$$C_p = C_e \left(\frac{S_p}{S_e}\right)^n \tag{10.1}$$

$$= \$5,420,118$$

TABLE 10.5. Square Foot Project Size Modifier

Building Type	Square Foot Base Size		
	Median Cost per Square Foot	Typical Size Gross Square Feet	Typical Range Gross Square Feet
Schools, Jr. High	57.35	92,000	52,000–119,000
Schools, Sr. High	56.20	101,000	50,500–175,000
Schools, vocational	54.45	37,000	20,500– 82,000
Sports Arenas	44.70	15,000	5,000– 40,000
Supermarkets	37.40	20,000	12,000– 30,000
Swimming pools	64.50	13,000	7,800– 22,000

Source: Means Building Construction Costs. Robert Snow Means, Kingston, Mass., 1985.
[a]The size factor for the project is determined by dividing the project area in square feet by the typical project size for the particular building type. With this factor, enter the area conversion scale at the appropriate size factor and determine the appropriate cost multiplier for your building size.

TABLE 10.6 Average Systems Costs

Exterior Walls Masonry			
	Labor	Material	Total
Precast Concrete			
Precast Wall Panel			
Flat with plain finish	2.60	8.12	10.72
Metal ties	0.12	0.14	0.26
Caulking	0.37	0.22	0.59
Total per square foot	3.09	8.48	11.57
Precast Wall Panel			
Flat with sandblast finish	2.60	8.75	11.35
Metal ties	0.12	0.14	0.26
Caulking	0.37	0.22	0.59
Total per square foot	3.09	9.11	12.21
Precast Wall Panel			
Flat with exposed aggregate	3.20	10.40	13.60
Metal ties	0.12	0.14	0.26
Caulking	0.37	0.22	0.59
Total per square foot	3.69	10.76	14.45
Precast Wall Panel			
Shaped with plain finish	3.50	10.50	14.00
Metal ties	0.12	0.14	0.26
Caulking	0.37	0.22	0.59
Total per square foot	3.99	10.86	14.85
Special Panel			
Facespan 3/4″ flat	3.50	6.10	9.60
Total per square foot	3.50	6.10	9.60

Source: *Dodge Construction Systems Costs*. Cost Information Systems, Mcgraw-Hill, Princeton, N.J., 1985

or

$$= \frac{\$5,420,118}{120,000}$$

$$C_p = \$45.17/\text{ft}^2$$

If the estimator has historical data pertaining to a particular type of facility, he can derive the appropriate value of n for use in the equation.

10.2.2.4 Time Estimates.
The owner often requests a preliminary estimate for the time of construction along with a preliminary estimate for the cost of construction. Just as the cost of the facility increases nonlinearly with size, the time of construction increases nonlinearly with size, also. Actually, the time of construction is probably more closely related to the cost of the facility than it is to the size of the facility. Therefore an approach similar to that used before can be employed with a comparable estimating equation of the form:

$$T_p = T_e \left(\frac{C_p}{C_e} \right)^n \qquad (10.2)$$

where T_p = time to construct the proposed facility
$\quad\quad T_e$ = time to construct an existing facility
$\quad\quad C_p$ = cost of proposed facility
$\quad\quad C_e$ = cost of existing facility
$\quad\quad n$ = exponent in the range of 0.25 to 0.40

Example 10.3: An existing facility was constructed in 180 days at a cost of $2 million. If a value of $n = 0.33$ applies, how long will it take to construct a comparable facility that will cost $4 million?
Solution:

$$T_p = 180 \left(\frac{\$4,000,000}{\$2,000,000} \right)^{0.33}$$

$$T_p = 180(1.26)$$

$$T_p = 226 \text{ days}$$

As with the examples in the previous section, the estimator can derive values of n that pertain to a particular type of facility for which he has historical data.

10.2.3 Preliminary Cost Estimating for Heavy Construction

Owners and contractors typically take very different approaches to estimating the costs associated with engineered construction projects. The contractor will formulate labor crew compositions, compute crew costs, estimate crew productivity, evaluate contingencies, and so on. However, it is not practical for the owner or design engineer to expend this degree of cost estimating effort. As long as the owner recognizes that his estimate contains some acceptable level of uncertainty, then time saving methods for estimating costs are justified. Recent court decisions have held owners and design engineers liable for reasonable accuracy of their cost estimates. Although the preliminary estimates do not have to be absolutely accurate, they should be based on some type of rational analysis.

10.2.3.1 Estimating Highway Construction.

For highway-related construction projects, the owner is represented by a state or local highway department. State highway departments typically estimate construction costs using historical bid data associated with previous construction projects. For example, if contractors have consistently bid $26 per linear foot for 30-inch reinforced pipe culverts, then it is not unreasonable to expect similar bids on future work. However, the cost estimating process is not always that straightforward. Highway projects are bid on a unit price basis. The overall project is organized into a number of discrete work items, and unit prices are solicited for each work item. The highway department would, therefore, have access to cost data similar to the hypothetical cost data shown in Table 10.7. Assume we wish to make use of the data shown in Table 10.7 to estimate the cost of a similar project that will be bid in the near future. The following factors may affect the way in which the Table 10.7 data are used to construct the engineer's estimate:

1. Costs will vary as a function of time. The cost of asphaltic materials is especially sensitive to supply and demand and other unpredictable economic factors.
2. Costs will vary as a function of the project location and local conditions. Local soil and geographic conditions will affect excavation costs. The cost of base, aggregate, and paving materials will vary as a function of the haul distance from natural sources, stockpiles, and batch plants.
3. Costs will also vary as a function of project type and project specifications.

TABLE 10.7 Hypothetical Unit Cost Data

	Proj A	Proj B	Proj C
Project location	Dist 2/Div 3	Dist 3/Div 2	Dist 2/Div 5
Project date	6/83	9/82	8/83
Project type	GBD, 4 miles	GBD, 4.2 miles	GBD, 3.1 miles
Contract award	$3.2 million	$3.6 million	$2.1 million

			Unit Price Bids—Project A		
Bid Items	Unit	Quantity	Contractor 1	Contractor 2	Contractor 3
Mobilization	ls	1	$100,000	$120,000	$111,000
Excav., uncl.	cy	200,000	0.90	1.20	1.40
Excav., borrow	cy	400,000	2.00	1.80	2.30
Aggr base	ton	12,000	8.00	8.10	8.10
Bit surf	ton	2,000	16.80	17.40	19.20
15″ culvert	lf	2,000	11.10	11.20	11.20
Wire fence	lf	50,000	0.60	0.70	0.80
Seeding	lb	6,000	1.10	1.20	0.60
⋮	⋮	⋮	⋮	⋮	⋮

For example, a grade, base, and drain project may include a small amount of paving for secondary crossroads. The cost per ton of bituminous surfacing of the crossroads will not necessarily be the same as the cost per ton for a major paving project.

4. Costs for lump-sum bid items will vary considerably from project to project. Costs for mobilization, clearing, and other lump-sum items can not always be predicted from previous project costs.

5. Unit costs submitted by the contractor may not reflect the cost of performing the work activity. Contractors unbalance unit price bids for a number of reasons.

Most public works organizations maintain historical records of contractor bid data by cost code. An analysis of these data can provide a very valuable preliminary estimating tool. The analysis begins by first determining just what factors or dependent variables affect the magnitude of the bids that are likely to be submitted under a given cost code. An important variable for most cost codes is the anticipated material quantity. Other factors include the type of project (interstate, rural, etc.), and the geographical location.

The preliminary estimating tool, or equation, must therefore include these three variables. A predictive equation involving the three dependent variables can be developed using multiple regression analysis. The first step in the regression analysis is to generate a number of plots to obtain a general idea of variable relation-

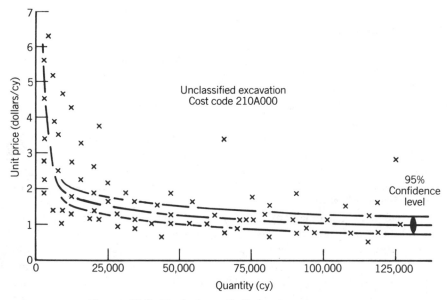

Figure 10.2. Typical predictive regression curve.

ships. An attempt to fit curves of various types (straight line, parabola, log transformation, etc.) to representative data will, it is hoped, produce curves that can be
used uniformly on all cost codes.

A standard regression analysis is then performed for each cost code to produce
an equation that will predict unit cost as a function of quantity, geographical location, and project type. If we wish to predict low bids for each cost code, then
the data set must be low bids from previous contract awards.

A predictive regression equation for one cost code is shown in Figure 10.2.
The figure shows the original data points that were used to develop the equation
and the 95% confidence interval for the mean. Since cost is plotted as a function
of quantity in the figure, the variations due to geographical location and project
type are not indicated. If the regression analysis is determined by statistical tests
to be significant, then we can conclude that the mean of submitted low bids will
fall between the dashed lines 95% of the time.

10.3 DETAILED COST ESTIMATING

Detailed cost estimating is the process whereby the contractor arrives at a timely
expenditure of resources necessary to complete a construction project in accordance with the plans and specifications provided by the owner. The estimate must
be very accurate to insure both getting the job and making a profit. Unlike cost
estimating by the owner, a contractor cannot tolerate a $\pm 5\%$ estimate, at least not
as a normal business practice. Therefore, the contractor must be meticulous in his
estimating procedures.

10.3.1 Overview

The first step in considering a potential construction project is determining whether
to proceed with cost estimating. Cost estimating is expensive (approximately 0.25–
1.0% of total bid price) and time-consuming, so a prudent contractor must determine if the project fits into the future plans of the company, if the company will
be in a competitive position to bid on the project, and if the potential profit makes
the preparation of a cost estimate worthwhile. Typically, a contractor does not get
reimbursed for the expense of preparing a cost estimate except as a part of the
markup if he gets the job. Therefore a cost estimate should get high-level management attention and should be prepared with utmost care. During the preparation
of the detailed cost estimate the cost estimator should stay in close contact with
the superintendent and other key construction personnel to insure that there is
agreement on methods and procedures to be estimated and later followed.

In preparing his estimate, the contractor must consider both the direct and indirect costs of construction. Although the allocation of costs to these two categories is not uniform throughout the construction industry, direct costs are generally those costs that are incurred only for a particular project, such as labor,

materials, equipment, and consumables, and indirect costs are generally those that are incurred as a normal cost of doing business but not wholly attributable to a particular project, such as office overhead, interest on money borrowed, and salaried supervision. Indirect costs are highly dependent on the project time schedule and the cash flow produced by progress payments.

Basic direct costs are estimated by determining the quantities and costs of the various resources needed to construct the project, such as material, labor, and equipment, under standard conditions. These costs must then be adjusted for expected productivity depending on less objective factors such as crew skill levels, learning from previous jobs, availability of materials when needed, location of project site, construction methods, environmental or weather conditions, and expected inflation.

10.3.2 Building Construction

Cost estimating for direct costs in building construction involves identifying and pricing the materials to be used and determining the labor/equipment expenditure necessary to construct the project. Plans and specifications supplied by the owner are used by the contractor for cost estimating. These plans and specifications contain drawings, verbal descriptions, and references to other documents, which are all used in the estimating procedure.

10.3.2.1 Quantity Takeoffs.
The first step in preparing the detailed cost estimate is the quantity takeoff, whereby the material items are identified, separated by division and section (as found in the specifications), then priced. For example, Table 10.8 shows a quantity takeoff of the items on Figure 10.3. Non-material items such as finishing concrete must also be identified and priced.

In this simple example the estimator has identified the various items shown on the drawing, counted the number of standard units that will be needed, established the price and source of the material, and arrived at a total price for like units. Finally, a page total is calculated for all materials identified on the drawing. By following this process on all the drawings, a project total material estimate can be calculated. This process is not as simple as it first seems because drawings often

TABLE 10.8 Quantity Takeoff

Quantity Takeoff Item	Takeoff	Waste %	Quantity	Unit	Price/unit	Source	Total
4 × 4 S4S	0.064	0.10	0.070	MBF	360.00	Todd	25.20
4 × 8 S2E DougFir	0.340	0.10	0.374	MBF	395.50	Todd	147.92
4 × 8 Rough Treated	0.075	0.10	0.083	MBF	575.00	Todd	47.73
					Drawing	Total	220.84

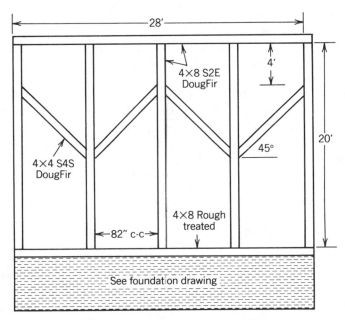

Figure 10.3. Typical cross section.

show the same material in different views, or show some part of the project as a typical section and do not show all such sections. Also, the estimator needs to know what drawing has the necessary information for the quantity takeoff. Figure 10.3 shows a foundation with no detail, so the estimator must go to another drawing to get the information he needs for the quantity takeoff.

Quantities identified on the quantity takeoff should be expressed in the unit of pricing and should be increased for waste caused by trimming, overlapping, or shrinking. Historical factors for breakage and loss must also be added.

10.3.2.2 Labor Rates. When the quantity takeoff is completed, the estimator must determine the number of man-hours and trades necessary to perform the erection of the materials. This is accomplished by using experience and/or standards. Table 10.9 shows a standard that might be used to construct the structure in Figure 10.3.

Most workers included in direct costs are hourly paid employees. Hourly cost per worker is based on the base wage rate taken from the appropriate union agreement or employee contract. To this is added mandatory employer contributions such as FICA, union contributions, or fringe benefits such as retirement, and other costs such as travel. Table 10.10 shows a typical hourly labor cost calculation. Salaried workers included in direct costs require the same mandatory contributions, plus some optional contributions according to their contracts and other costs. Table 10.11 shows a typical salary labor cost calculation.

TABLE 10.9 Standard Crew Output: Heavy Framing

	Crew	Daily Output	Unit
4″ × 4″	C1	0.72	MBF
4″ × 6″	C1	0.68	MBF
4″ × 8″	C1	0.64	MBF
4″ × 10″	C1	0.59	MBF
⋮ ⋮ ⋮	⋮	⋮	⋮

When federal funding is involved in a project, the labor rates must be adjusted to reflect the prevailing wage in accordance with the Davis-Bacon Act. State funded projects also require paying the prevailing wage in many locations.

10.3.2.3 Equipment Rates.
Equipment costs assigned to a project's direct costs should represent an amount necessary to own and operate the pieces of equipment plus an amount for eventual replacement. The cost for a particular piece of equipment would consist of a portion of owning costs made up of initial cost, insurance, interest, taxes and storage, plus operating costs made up of fuel, oil, grease, maintenance, repairs, and operator's wages.

Exact costing of a piece of equipment is very difficult because it requires ac-

TABLE 10.10 Hourly Labor Cost Calculation

Hourly Cost—Carpenter	Journeyman	9/01/85
	Comments	Dollars/hour
Base wage rate (BWR)		13.12
Mandatory contributions		
FICA	7.05% of BWR	0.92
Workman's compensation	7.11% of BWR	0.93
Unemployment insurance	1.90% of BWR	0.25
Union contributions		
Retirement		0.40
Health and security		0.90
Vacation	0.17 in BWR	0.0
Apprenticeship fund		0.13
Industry fund		0.05
Administration dues		0.05
Other contributions		
Travel	6.00/Day	0.75
Miscellaneous	Tolls 1.60/day	0.20
Total hourly cost		17.71

TABLE 10.11 Salary Labor Cost Calculation

Hourly Cost—Stevens, Victor F.	401	12 2295	Qual. Cont.
	Comments	Dollars/Year	Dollars/Hour
Annual salary (AS)	230 days/year	35,000.00	19.02
Mandatory contributions			
FICA	7.05% of AS	2,467.50	1.34
Workman's compensation	7.11% of AS	2,488.50	1.35
Unemployment insurance	1.90% of AS	665.00	0.36
Optional contributions			
Retirement	7.00% of AS	2,450.00	1.33
Insurance	$123/Month	1,476.00	0.80
Profit sharing	$100/Month est.	1,200.00	0.65
Bonus	Estimated	5,000.00	2.72
Other contributions			
Travel	$6/Day on job		0.75
Miscellaneous	0.0		0.00
Total annual cost		50,747.00	
Annual workdays	230		
Total hourly cost			28.33

curately predicting such variables as inflation, tax rates, and equipment utilization during the ownership period. Table 10.12 shows one method of calculating an hourly cost for a piece of equipment based on expected utilization and tax rates, but no inflation. The hourly cost should be adjusted in following years based on changes in these variables.

Equipment is sometimes used for several projects during a period, making cost accounting per project difficult. Companies faced with this situation may wish to carry equipment as indirect costs. Another scheme often used is to cost the equipment at prevailing rental rates, thus eliminating concern about fluctuating owning and operating costs caused by changes in insurance, taxes, interest rates, and repair rates as the equipment ages.

From the labor and equipment rates, the cost estimator can develop a crew estimate for a standard crew. Table 10.13 shows a typical standard crew calculation.

In the next section the process for cost estimating for direct costs of building construction on fixed-price jobs are broken down, analyzed, and discussed further.

10.3.2.4 Subcontracts.

Most construction projects undertaken by general contractors cannot be completed entirely by the contractor's own workforce; therefore subcontractors must be engaged. The cost estimator must clearly delineate the

TABLE 10.12 Hourly Cost for Owned Equipment

Machine Ownership Analysis				Model: 6390		Purchased: 1/1/85	

A. Ownership analysis:

B. Delivered price — 650,000

   Cash down — 0

   Trade-in — 200,000

   Total down — 200,000 −

   = 200,000

C. Unpaid balance — = 450,000

D. Adjusted tax basis — 450,000

   Unpaid balance — 450,000

   Cash down payment — 0

   Book value of trade — 93,636

   Total — 543,636

E. Planned ownership period — 7

F. Estimated value at sell — 166,000

G. Finance charge — 162,000

H. Finance period (years) — 4

I. Invest. tax credit (%) — 6.67

J. Depreciation factor (%) — 100

K. Residual factor (%) — 0

L. Corporate tax rate (%) — 46

I.

1 Total cash payment / Cash down/trade-in — 200,000

2 Unpaid balance — + 450,000

3 Finance charge — + 162,000

   Total — 812,000

Hourly operation cost

a. Fuel — 28.50

b. Lube, oil, filters — 1.32

c. Tires — 4.67

d. Repairs — 19.87

e. Special items — 0.50

f. Insurance — 2.06

g. Operator's wages — 22.50

h. Total — 79.42

Total operating costs

a. Annual scheduled hours — 1800

b. Availability — × 0.95

c. Annual operating hours — = 1710

d. Hourly operating cost — × 79.42

e. Annual operating cost — = 135,808

f. Ownership period — × 7

g. Total — = 950,657

Revenue potential

a. Hourly charge — 157.00

b. Annual Operating Hours — × 1710

c. Annual Revenue — = 268,470

d. Ownership Period — × 7

e. Total — = 1,879,290

TABLE 10.12 (Continued)

Machine Ownership Analysis		Model:	6390		Purchased: 1/1/85	
II.	Total tax deductions				Net profit over life	
4	Investment tax credit		6,261	a.	Total revenue potential	1,879,290
5	Depreciation deduction	+	250,073	b.	Total operating cost −	950,657
6	Interest deduction	+	74,520	c.	Total income before taxes =	928,633
	Total		360,853	d.	Tax owed −	427,171
				e.	Net income after taxes =	501,462
III.	Net resale after taxes			f.	Total owning cost −	361,507
7	Market value at sell		166,000	g.	Net profit =	139,955
8	Book value at sell	−	0			
9	Additional income	=	166,000			
10	Tax on add. income	−	76,360			
	Total	=	89,640			
	TOTAL OWNING COST SUMMARY					
I.	Total cash payment					
II.	Total tax deductions					
III.	Net resale after taxes		89,640			
IV.	Total owning cost		361,507			

Source: Handbook of Earthmoving. Caterpillar Tractor Company, Peoria, Ill., 1981.

TABLE 10.13 Standard Crew Cost

Number	Daily Cost: Crew: Crew Member	CE 15 Dollars/hour EA	Dollars/hour	Dollars/WD
1	Foreman	19.48	19.48	155.84
4	Carpenters	17.71	70.84	566.72
2	Laborers	14.60	29.20	233.60
1	Equip. operator	16.85	16.85	134.80
1	Small crane	30.00	30.00	240.00
1	Pickup truck	12.75	12.75	102.00
	Hourly crew cost		179.12	
*	Workday @ 8 hr			
	Field overhead @ 5%			71.65
	Daily crew cost			1504.61

work items to be handled by subcontractors, obtain price quotes from various subcontractors, then factor selected prices into the cost estimate. The cost estimator must also determine any administrative responsibilities and interference or scheduling problems involved in subcontracted work that would increase the cost of the general contractor's work items.

10.3.2.5 Indirect Costs. Cost estimating of indirect costs in building construction involves calculating the proportion of office overhead items, such as management salaries, secretarial services, and utilities, which are attributable to the particular project. Since this is a time-consuming and inexact task, and since indirect costs are generally less than 15% of total project costs, contractors often use a percentage of direct costs, based on historical data, as an estimate of indirect costs. For instance, if total indirect costs for the company last year were $5 million and direct costs of all projects were $100 million, then applying an indirect cost of 5% to the calculated direct cost of a particular project would be acceptable.

Another very important cost, which may be either considered direct or indirect, is the cost of financing. The contractor must either borrow or use his own money to pay for the resources expended during construction. Factors such as the schedule for progress payments, retainage, and interest rates are of great importance. In times of high interest rates, neglecting to consider cash flow can give a contractor a false sense of security and can turn what looked like a successful bid with a satisfactory profit into a financial disaster.

10.3.3 Heavy Construction

Heavy construction is usually performed using unit-price contracts and competitive bids. Cost estimating for direct costs in heavy construction involves identifying and pricing material, labor, and equipment for specific parts of the total job, called pay items. Plans, specifications, and a pay item list are supplied by the owner to potential bidders.

10.3.3.1 List of Pay Items.

On a heavy construction project using a unit-price contract, such as a road building project, the owner furnishes the bidding contractor a list of pay items. Each pay item is an item of work or material and has a quantity assigned to it by the owner's engineer. Table 10.14 shows a portion of a typical list of pay items. The contractor must estimate and submit a bid on each of these pay items. Since the list of pay items does not include all of the normal direct cost items of the project (i.e., temporary structures, services, etc.) the contractor must apportion these costs among the pay items.

10.3.3.2 Unit Prices.

The bid for each pay item must be expressed as a price for one unit of the pay item, that is, a unit price. To do this, the cost estimator usually estimates the total direct cost for the pay item, then divides by the number of units. Utmost care must be exercised in the calculations because the amount the contractor will be paid during the project will be the unit price bid multiplied by the actual number of units accomplished. For items such as excavation, a few cents difference on the unit price becomes a significant amount when multiplied by a large number of units.

TABLE 10.14 Unit-Price Pay Item List

Pay Item	Description	Quantity	Unit	Unit-Price	Extension
1	Mobilization	1	LS		
2	Clear and Grub	1	LS		
3	Unclass excavation	1,100	CY		
4	Borrow excavation	12,500			
⋮	⋮	⋮	⋮		
17	Remove exist pavement	20,000	SY		
⋮	⋮	⋮	⋮		
74	Right-of-way marker	15	EA		
⋮	⋮	⋮	⋮		
123	Steel beam guardrail	450	LF		
124	Bituminous course type HB	927	TN		
⋮	⋮	⋮	⋮		
231	Rebar (bridge)	213,460	LB		
232	Bridge stress monitor	2	EST	2500.00	5000.00
⋮	⋮	⋮	⋮		
345	Seed for landscaping	765	LB		
346	Fertilizer for seed	2.5	TN		
⋮	⋮	⋮	⋮		
431	Demobilization	1	LS		

10.3.3.3 Distribution of Indirect Costs.

Theoretically, the cost estimator, after determining the total direct cost of all the pay items, could apply a percentage of that cost as indirect cost. This indirect cost could then be spread evenly among the pay items. Markup (i.e., profit, contingencies, etc.) could likewise be spread evenly, creating a balanced bid. However, experience shows that the accuracy of the quantities given on the list of pay items varies and that some items are often eliminated by the owner's representative on the job site. To protect against losing overhead costs, the cost estimator usually apportions more of the overhead to pay items that are felt to represent mandatory job requirements and realistic quantities. Table 10.15 shows a partial unit-price bid that is balanced.

10.3.3.4 Unbalanced Bids.

The legal, binding bid on a unit-price contract is a number of bids, one for each pay item. The successful bidder, called the lowest apparent bidder, is determined by the lowest sum of the extensions of the unit price bids. Table 10.16 shows an example of a bidding summary. Since the bids are based on assumed quantities, albeit reasonable, the lowest apparent bidder may not in fact have offered the lowest price for the project, but this cannot be ascertained until the work is done. Therefore the goal of the cost estimator on a unit-price contract is to be the lowest apparent bidder. In Table 10.16, Contractor B has obviously inflated his unit prices for mobilization and clear and grub, while deflating his unit prices for landscaping and demobilization in an effort to earn more money early in the project, thus improving his cash flow. This type of unbalancing can lead to the bid being thrown out by the owner if the unbalancing is blatant. Also, in Table 10.16, Contractor C has inflated his unit price for unclassified excavation while deflating his unit price for borrow excavation. This type of unbalancing is used when the cost estimator believes the estimated quantities provided to be in error. In this case, the provided estimated quantity is low for unclassified excavation and high for borrow excavation. This type of unbalancing can lead to increased profits if the cost estimator's predictions are correct.

10.3.4 Cash Flow Analysis

When preparing a construction cost estimate, the estimator needs to know the cost of the money he must borrow to meet his financial obligations. Also of concern is the maximum amount he must borrow, or the credit limit he must establish with his lending institution. Most construction contracts contain provisions for progress payments to the contractor. These payments are made either on some regular basis, such as monthly, or when certain project milestones have been reached. A monthly progress payment theoretically compensates the contractor for the value of work put in place during the month. But, because some time is usually required for the owner to approve the contractor's payment request, and because some retainage is withheld from each progress payment, the contractor is forced to borrow money or to use money he could otherwise invest to meet his financial obligations. When

TABLE 10.15 Balanced Unit-Price Bid

Pay Item	Description	Quantity	Unit	Unit-Price	Extension
1	Mobilization	1	LS	35,000.00	35,000.00
2	Clear and grub	1	LS	45,600.00	45,600.00
3	Unclass excavation	1,100	CY	11.65	12,815.00
4	Borrow excavation	12,500		9.85	123,125.00
		...	...		...
17	Remove exist pavement	20,000	SY	5.00	100,000.00
		...	...		...
74	Right-of-way marker	15	EA	495.00	7,425.00
		...	...		...
123	Steel beam guardrail	450	LF	22.35	10,057.50
124	Bituminous course type HB	927	TN	25.00	23,175.00
		...	...		...
231	Rebar (bridge)	213,460	LB	.48	102,460.80
232	Bridge stress monitor	2	EST	2,500.00	5,000.00
		...	...		...
345	Seed for landscaping	765	LB	1.95	1,491.75
346	Fertilizer for seed	2.5	TN	375.00	937.50
		...	...		...
431	Demobilization	1	LS	35,000.00	35,000.00
					1,813,475.00

398

TABLE 10.16. Bidding Summary

No.	Bidding Summary Description	Project: Quantity	13A85 Unit	Contractor A		Contractor B		Contractor C	
				Unit-Price	Extension	Unit-Price	Extension	Unit-Price	Extension
1	Mobilization	1	LS	35,000.00	35,000.00	60,000.00	60,000.00	36,500.00	36,500.00
2	Clear and Grub	1	LS	45,600.00	45,600.00	65,780.00	65,780.00	44,000.00	44,000.00
3	Unclass excav.	1,100	CY	11.65	12,815.00	10.98	12,078.00	20.00	22,000.00
4	Borrow excav.	12,500	...	9.85	123,125.00	9.25	115,625.00	6.25	78,125.00
	...			...	...	...	...	...	...
17	Remv. exist pvmt.	20,000	SY	5.00	100,000.00	4.90	98,000.00	5.10	102,000.00
	...	...	...			...		...	
74	R-O-W Marker	15	EA	495.00	7,425.00	510.00	7,650.00	450.00	6,750.00
123	Steel beam gdrl.	450	LF	22.35	10,057.50	21.75	9,787.50	22.50	10,125.00
124	Bit. Crs. Ty. HB	927	TN	25.00	23,175.00	25.50	23,638.50	25.00	23,175.00
		...			...		...		...
231	Rebar (bridge)	213,460	LB	.48	102,460.80	.43	91,787.80	.47	100,326.20
232	Bridge str. mon.	2	EST	2,500.00	5,000.00	2,500.00	5,000.00	2,500.00	5,000.00
		...				...		...	
345	Seed for Lndscpg.	765	LB	1.95	1,491.75	.50	382.50	2.00	1,530.00
346	Fertil. for seed	2.5	TN	375.00	937.50	100.00	250.00	385.00	962.50
		...	...		...	...	...		...
431	Demobilization	1	LS	35,000.00	35,000.00	10,000.00	10,000.00	33,550.00	33,550.00
					1,813,475.00		1,956,734.50		1,865,932.00

financing the project for the contractor, a bank typically opens an account for the contractor and extends him a line of credit to cover the overdrafts that occur as he pays for the project labor, materials, and consumables. The interest charged on the overdraft amount is usually some number of percentage points above the prime interest rate. The first step in determining the finance charges associated with a particular project is to estimate how the value of the work put in place will vary throughout the project. The rate of the monthly value of the work put in place usually increases in the early stages of the project, then remains relatively constant at some rate for a period of time, and then decreases in the later stages of the project. A Critical Path Method (CPM) schedule, as discussed in Section 10.4, is very valuable for cash flow analysis, but if the contractor has not yet developed a project schedule, he can estimate the value of work that will be put in place each month using the following equation:

$$\frac{R_{max}}{R_{av}} = \frac{200}{(100 + t_f - t_i)} \qquad (10.3)$$

where R_{max} = maximum monthly value of work put in place
R_{av} = project total cost/months duration
t_i = % complete when the value of work put in place is no longer increasing
t_f = % complete when the value of work put in place starts decreasing.

The relationship between these variables is illustrated in Figure 10.4.

Example 10-4: The total estimated value of the work to be put in place on a given project is $500,000. The duration of the project is 10 months. If the maximum rate of work put in place is sustained from the end of the second month (t_i

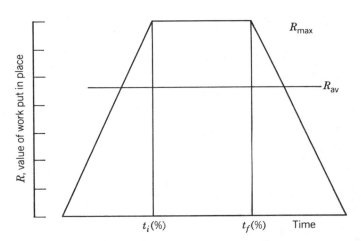

Figure 10.4. Value of work in place diagram.

= 20%) to the end of the seventh month (t_f = 70%), then what is the expected value of the work put in place for each of the 10 months?

Solution: The magnitude of R, the value of work put in place, varies with time as shown in Figure 10.4.

$$R_{av} = \frac{\$500,000}{10 \text{ months}} = \$50,000 \text{ per month}$$

$$\frac{R_{max}}{R_{av}} = \frac{200}{100 + t_f - t_i} = \frac{200}{100 + 70 - 20} = 1.333$$

$$R_{max} = 1.33(\$50,000) = \$66,667 \text{ per month}$$

$$R3 = R4 = R5 = R6 = R7 = \$66,667 \text{ per month}$$

The remaining values of R can be computed using interpolation and referring to Figure 10.4. For example, the rate of the value of work put in place during the first month ranges from $0 per month at the beginning of the month to a rate of $66,667/2 = $33,333 at the end of the month. The average rate during the first month, $R1$ = ($33,333 + 0)/2 = $16,667. The average rate for the other months are shown in Figure 10.5.

Example 10-5: For the preceding $500,000 project, what finance charges will result if the contractor must borrow money at an interest rate of 1.5% per month? Assume the owner holds back 10% as retainage, and assume a one-month delay between completing the work and receiving the progress payment. The contractor anticipates making a profit of 5%. How much money must he borrow each month?

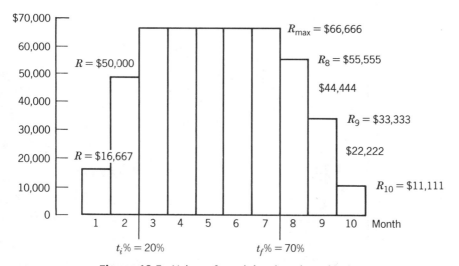

Figure 10.5. Value of work in place bar chart.

TABLE 10.17. Preliminary Cash Flow Analysis

A Month	B R Val WK IN PLC	C Cum Val WK IN PLC	D Cum Prf C × 0.05	E Spent ($) C − D	F Rcd ($) C × 0.90	G Deficit E − F	H Fin Chg. G × .015
1	16,667	16,667	833	15,834	[a]	15,834	238
2	50,000	66,667	3,333	63,334	15,000	48,333	725
3	66,667	133,334	6,667	126,667	60,000	66,667	1,000
4	66,666	200,000	10,000	190,000	120,001	69,999	1,050
5	66,667	266,667	13,333	253,334	180,000	73,334	1,100
6	66,667	333,334	16,667	316,667	240,000	76,667	1,150
7	66,667	400,001	20,000	380,001	300,001	80,000	1,200
8	55,555	455,556	22,778	432,778	360,001	72,777	1,092
9	33,333	488,889	24,444	464,445	410,000	54,444	817
10	11,111	500,000	25,000	475,000	440,000	35,000	525
11	0	500,000	25,000	475,000	450,000	25,000	375
12			retainage	released	500,000	0	0

Total finance chg		9,271
Pct of contract		1.85
Max amt financed		80,000

Solution: The cash flow analysis is performed in Table 10.17. The values of R computed in the previous example are listed for each month in Column B. The cumulative value of the work put in place is computed in Column C, and the contractor's monthly profit is computed in Column D. Subtracting profit from the cumulative value of work put in place results in the expenditures shown in Column E. The progress payments received by the contractor are listed in Column F, and his deficits (expenditures less receipts) are shown in Column G. The monthly finance charges are therefore computed as 0.015 times the monthly deficit as shown in Column H. The contractor's total finance charges will be $9271, or 1.85% of the contract amount.

The preceding example is typical of a financial analysis that can be very easily performed using a microcomputer spreadsheet program.

10.4 TIME SCHEDULES IN COST ESTIMATING

The old adage "time is money" is very important to developing an accurate cost estimate for a construction project. A time schedule, prepared by the contractor, showing when major parts of the construction project start and end is usually required by the contract. For small projects a simple time schedule such as a bar chart may suffice; for larger projects more elaborate network schedules may be required.

10.4.1 Overview

Network scheduling requires the project to be broken down into *activities*, with the set of all activities making up the entire project, and each activity's relationship with every other activity to be defined. These relationships may represent those dictated by technology, such as building the foundation before the walls, those suggested by economics, such as excavating for the septic tank and drain field while the equipment is on location for foundation work, and those based on common sense, policy, prejudice, or the whimsy of the cost estimator. The basic assumptions for creating a network schedule are (1) the project can be broken down into a group of activities, (2) each activity can be assigned a duration, and (3) the logical relationship among activities is known and fixed in the network.

For government work the time schedule is often required to be a critical path method, CPM. The CPM is a network schedule developed in the 1950s for use by the Du Pont Chemical Company [4]. Its use requires discipline and a commitment by the contractor to update it continually. In return for this commitment the CPM becomes a powerful tool for construction management and, when used with a computer, can assist the construction cost estimator in a variety of ways. One of the primary values of the CPM/computer combination is the ability to perform *what if* calculations by changing various estimating variables and observing what happens to the project time schedule.

A CPM network reflecting the most efficient utilization of resources represents an optimum time based on direct costs. To do this work in a shorter period is usually possible but at a somewhat greater direct cost because of decreased efficiency caused by the need to work overtime, hire and train more labor, obtain additional equipment, or to increase subcontractor contribution. However, this increased direct cost may actually lead to an overall cost savings on the project by decreasing the construction time. Elements affected positively by a decrease in project time include job overhead, cash flow, new job opportunity, and potential delay damages. When indirect costs are considered, a technique called *least-cost scheduling* can be employed to balance these two cost categories and indicate a schedule that will produce the least total project cost.

A CPM network can be treated by a technique called *resource leveling*, in an attempt to level out the manpower utilization per day. This situation promotes a more stable work force and reduces time lost to training new workers.

A CPM schedule can also be used for calculating progress payments by assigning value of work in place to the various activities.

Many construction cost estimators are reluctant to use CPM unless it is a contract requirement, and then prefer to leave much of the work to consultants. One reason for this reluctance is that CPM requires changes in existing estimating methods. But like any new and different tool, CPM must be worked with and integrated into the estimating procedures before it becomes valuable. Also, because CPM schedules often become involved in legal conflicts when trying to decide interference and/or delay by parties to a construction contract, construction cost estimators/schedulers hesitate to expose their estimated schedule lest it be viewed as a basis for litigation.

In addition to CPM, which is a deterministic model (i.e., the output is determined to be a fixed value), there are stochastic models (i.e., the output is a probability distribution) that are used by some of the larger, more progressive construction firms. The most common of these is PERT (Program Evaluation and Review Technique) which was developed by the U.S. Navy for use in the Polaris Missile Program. PERT, which was developed at about the same time as was CPM, is very similar to CPM and provides the cost estimator with essentially the same information.

Another stochastic model uses a technique called Monte Carlo simulation to simulate the project timing. This method of producing time schedules is different from CPM and PERT and is quite limited in current usage.

10.4.2 CPM Schedules

CPM is a network technique where every activity is placed in a network in accordance with its logical relationship to other activities and is assigned a fixed duration. There is at least one path through the network, from start to finish, that controls the project length—the critical path. By adding the durations of the activities on a critical path the project duration is found. There is only one answer, thus the process is termed deterministic. Also, for those activities not on a critical path, the amount of flexibility they have in starting and completing (called float or slack) can be calculated.

10.4.2.1 Arrow Diagramming.
The first step in creating a schedule is to identify the activities that will make up the project and specify their logic relationships by creating a list of immediate preceding activities (IPA) for each activity in the project. Table 10.18 shows the activities and the IPA list for a simple remodeling project.

The most common way to display a CPM schedule is with an arrow diagram which is drawn using the IPA list. A generic activity is shown in Figure 10.6. The nodes at the ends of the activity are called events. To facilitate the computerization of CPM calculations, all activities are identified by numbered pairs. The tail of the arrow is the "i" node, the head is the "j" node, and the activity is identified by the numbered pair (i, j) as shown in Figure 10.7. It is a requirement that each activity have a unique i, j pair and that $i < j$, thereby permitting the computer algorithm to identify an activity, plus determine its direction and logic relationship with other activities.

TABLE 10.18. IPA List—Remodeling Project

IPA	Activity	Description
	T	Get permit
	A	Order new windows
	Q	Order appliances
	R	Order plasterboard
	E	Order counters
	U	Order flooring
	P	Strip room
P	S	Remove plasterboard
S	O	Remove old windows
S	B	Rough-in plumbing
S	C	Rough-in electrical
B, C	F	Insulate walls
O, A	D	Install new windows
D, F, R, T	G	Install plasterboard
E, M	H	Install counters
H, Q	W	Install sink
W	J	Install dishwasher
W	K	Install disposal
H, Q	L	Install range
G, U	M	Install flooring
G, U	N	Install doors
N, L, J, K	V	Paint
V	I	Trim

Figure 10.6. Generalized CPM arrow diagram.

Some relationships among activities cannot be expressed by normal activity arrows alone. This difficulty is overcome by using logic "dummies." Figure 10.8 shows an application of the use of a logic dummy. Figure 10.9 shows a numbered dummy utilized to insure a unique i, j pair for each activity.

10.4.2.2 Precedence Diagramming. Another common method of displaying the CPM is with a precedence diagram. A generic activity is shown in Figure 10.10. The node is the activity, and "C" is the activity's name. The links connect two activities.

Figure 10.11 shows a precedence diagram drawn utilizing the IPA list from Figure 10.8. Logic dummies are not needed in precedence diagrams, but starting and ending dummies are often used to insure a single starting and a single ending activity, again to facilitate computerization.

There is an easy way of determining where to place activities in a precedence diagram, called *sequence steps*. If activity R follows B, and B is on step 2, then R is on step 3. Therefore any activity must be on a step higher than any of its immediate predecessors. Example 10.6 shows the usefulness of sequence steps.

Example 10.6: To determine the sequence steps for the schedule in Figure 10.12, first see if either a starting or ending dummy is needed. Since A is the only activity with no predecessor, no starting dummy is needed. Activities D and E have no successors, thus there is more than one ending activity, so an ending dummy, labeled "End," is listed with its predecessors.

The procedure for determining sequence steps is as follows: A has no predecessors so it will be on step 1. B and C follow A so can be on step 2. D follows B and C on step 3, and E follows B also on step 3. End follows D and E on step 4.

With the sequence steps determined, the activities can be drawn in the proper horizontal position, above their sequence step, and then connected with lines showing logic relationships.

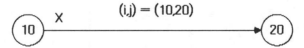

Figure 10.7. Typical CPM arrow diagram.

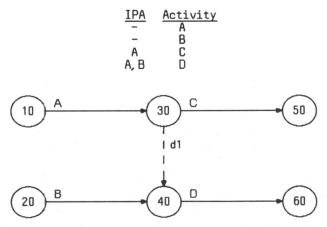

Figure 10.8. CPM logical dummy activity.

10.4.2.3 CPM Calculations. Before the CPM calculations can begin, the cost estimator must assign time durations to each activity in the project. In construction the durations are usually expressed in workdays required to complete an activity. A cost estimator may determine these durations by checking past records or standards, by asking the superintendent or workers who will perform the activity, or by making an educated guess. He may also want to add or subtract some days based on expected weather, or expectation of some particular interruption or contingencies. Table 10.19 introduces CPM terminology, Figure 10.13 shows a common method of labeling the activities, and Table 10.20 explains the labeling methodology.

To begin the CPM calculations, all activities that have no predecessors will be assigned an ES = 0. This means the project starts at the end of Day 0. The convenient convention of starting and stopping each activity at the end of a workday

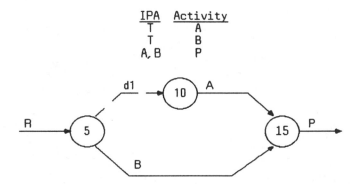

Figure 10.9. CPM unique path dummy utilization.

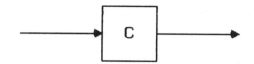

Figure 10.10. Precedence diagram generic activity.

simplifies the CPM calculations and allows easy determination of the number of days worked. Example 10.7 shows how the calculations for the CPM network in Figure 10.14 are carried out.

Example 10.7: To begin the calculations, a forward pass must be performed to establish the earliest that activities can start and finish.

Forward Pass:

1. A starts at 0; therefore ES = 0
2. EF(A) = ES(A) + Duration (A) = 0 + 2 = 2
3. B can start when A finishes; therefore ES(B) = 2
4. C can start when A finishes; therefore ES(C) = 2
5. EF(B) = 2 + 4 = 6; EF(C) = 2 + 3 = 5
6. ES(D) = 6; EF(D) = 6 + 3 = 9
7. E depends on both C and d1. C finishes at 5, but d1 finishes at 6 (follows B); therefore ES(E) = 6; EF(E) = 6 + 4 = 10
8. ES(F) = 10; EF(F) = 10 + 2 = 12

IPA	Activity
–	A
–	B
A	C
A, B	D

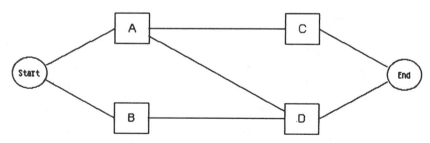

Figure 10.11. Typical precedence diagram.

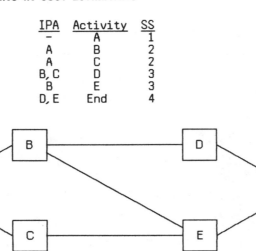

IPA	Activity	SS
–	A	1
A	B	2
A	C	2
B, C	D	3
B	E	3
D, E	End	4

Figure 10.12. Sequence steps in a precedence diagram.

Backward Pass:

1. F must finish at 12; therefore LF(F) = 12; LS(F) = 12 − 2 = 10
2. D and E must not delay F so they must finish by 10; therefore LF(D) = LF(E) = 10; LS(D) = 10 − 3 = 7; LS(E) = 10 − 4 = 6

TABLE 10.19. CPM Terminology

Expression	Description
Early start	The earliest an activity can start
Early finish	The earliest an activity can finish
Late start	The latest an activity can start
Late finish	The latest an activity can finish
Total float	Maximum time that an activity can be delayed without delaying completion of the project
Free float	Maximum time that an activity can be delayed without delaying the start of any succeeding activity
Forward pass	To find earliest start times and earliest finish times for all activities
Backward pass	To find latest start times and latest finish times for all activities
Critical path	A path from start to finish made up of activities that have no float

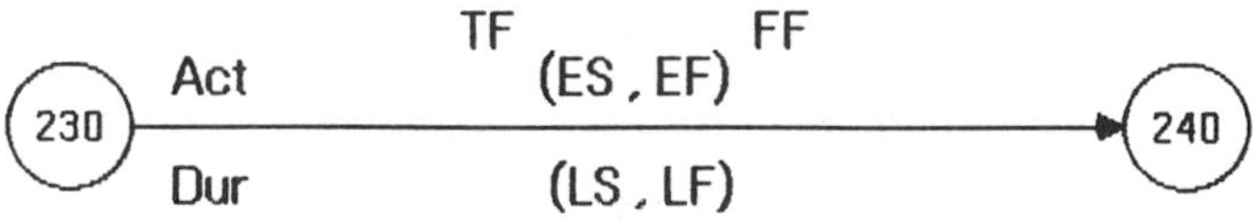

Figure 10.13. CPM activity labeling.

3. C must finish by LS(E) therefore LF(C) = 6; LS(E) = 6 − 3 = 3
4. B must finish by LS(D) and LS(E); therefore LF(B) = 6; LS(B) = 6 − 4 = 2
5. A must finish by LS(B) and LS(C); therefore LF(A) = 2; LS(A) = 2 − 2 = 0

Total Float: subtract ES from EF for each activity.
Free Float: subtract each EF from the earliest ES that follows it.

Those activities that have TF = FF = 0 are on the critical path. The critical path is made up of all activities that must start and stop on a certain day. Activities not on the critical path have float, which means they can be delayed by one or more days without delaying project completion. Some hints for checking the CPM network calculations are as follows:

1. At least one starting and one ending activity must be on a critical path.
2. All critical paths must be continuous from start to finish.
3. Total Float must be greater than or equal to the Free Float for every activity.
4. Any activity with a Total Float = 0 must be on a critical path.

In summary, when the time estimates for the various activities are placed on the activities, the CPM can be calculated and the time to milestones and project completion can be determined. In addition to the times, the sequence of activities called the *critical path*, which control the times, can be identified. The CPM arrow

TABLE 10.20. Activity Labels—Arrow Diagram

Act (activity): unit of work or a step in the project
Dur (duration): number of workdays the Act should require
EF (early finish): ES + Dur
ES (early start): latest of the EFs of all preceding Acts
LS (late start): LF − Dur
LF (late finish): earliest of the LSs of all succeeding Acts
TF (total float): LS − ES
FF (free float): earliest ES of any succeeding Act − EF of the Act

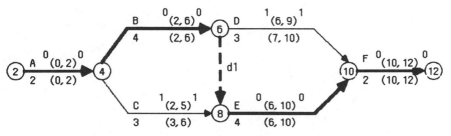

Figure 10.14. A CPM network.

diagram for the sample remodeling project of Table 10.18 is shown in Figure 10.15, with the CPM calculations on the activities and the critical path identified by darker print. The CPM precedence diagram of the same project is shown in Figure 10.16. This identification shows the cost estimator where additional resources can be applied to decrease the project duration. Also, the network schedule allows the estimator to see quickly what effect varying the time of any activity will have on milestone times. The calculations for this project are shown in tabular format in Table 10.21.

10.4.2.4 Least-Cost Scheduling. One of the operations that can be performed on the CPM schedule is called least-cost scheduling, or schedule compression. Least-cost scheduling is an optimization process whereby project activities are shortened to reduce the overall project length. When activities are shortened

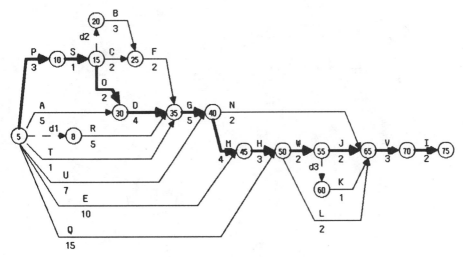

Figure 10.15. CPM arrow diagram for sample remodeling projects.

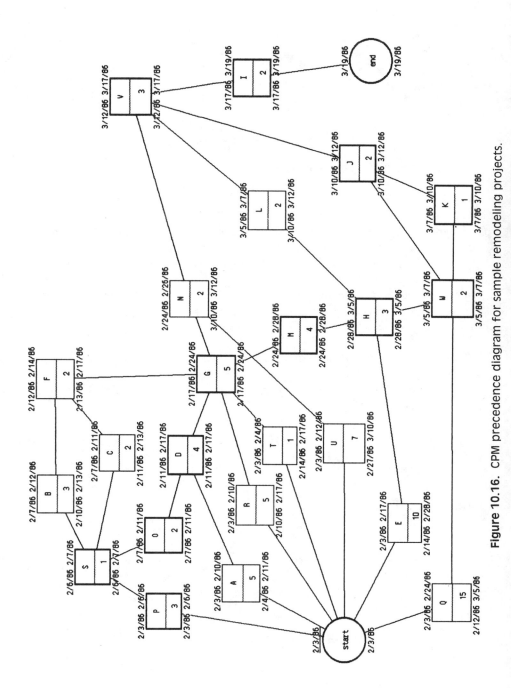

Figure 10.16. CPM precedence diagram for sample remodeling projects.

412

TABLE 10.21. CPM Calculations—Remodeling Project

Act	i	j	Dur	ES	EF	LS	LF	TF	FF	Crit
d1	5	8	0	—	—	—	—	—	—	
P	5	10	3	0	3	0	3	0	0	C
A	5	30	5	0	5	1	6	1	1	
T	5	35	1	0	1	9	10	9	9	
U	5	40	7	0	7	8	15	8	8	
E	5	45	10	0	10	9	19	9	9	
Q	5	50	15	0	15	2	22	7	7	
R	8	35	5	0	5	5	10	5	5	
S	10	15	1	3	4	3	4	0	0	C
d2	15	20	0	—	—	—	—	—	—	
C	15	25	2	4	6	6	8	2	1	
O	15	30	2	4	6	4	6	0	0	C
B	20	25	3	4	7	5	8	1	0	
F	25	35	2	7	9	8	10	1	1	
D	30	35	4	6	10	6	10	0	0	C
G	35	40	5	10	15	10	15	0	0	C
M	40	45	4	15	19	15	19	0	0	C
N	40	65	2	15	17	24	26	9	9	
H	45	50	3	19	22	19	22	0	0	C
W	50	55	2	22	24	22	24	0	0	C
L	50	65	2	22	24	24	26	2	2	
d3	55	60	0	—	—	—	—	—	—	
J	55	65	2	24	26	24	26	0	0	C
K	60	65	1	24	25	25	26	1	1	
V	65	70	3	26	29	26	29	0	0	C
I	70	75	2	29	31	29	31	0	0	C

their direct costs increase. When the overall project is shortened its indirect cost decreases. Therefore a cost estimator may be able to effect a savings if the schedule can be shortened and the indirect cost savings is greater than the increased direct cost.

To take advantage of least-cost scheduling, the cost estimator must do certain things not required by normal CPM time schedules:

1. Assign a minimum duration, less than or equal to the normal duration, for every activity, called *crash duration.*
2. Assign to each activity a direct cost, greater than the normal cost, to complete the activity at the minimum duration, called *crash cost.*

An assumption must be made as to the relationship between direct cost and duration as the activity is shortened. The simplest assumption, often called *simple compression*, is that the relationship is linear. For example, if an activity can be shortened by three days for an additional $300, then it can be shortened by two days for $200 more, or one day for $100 more. Other assumptions, often called *complex compression*, assume a nonlinear relationship. For example, an activity may cost an additional $50 to shorten one day, $75 to shorten a second day, and $130 to shorten a third day.

When all of the activities in the CPM schedule have direct costs assigned, the estimator must then calculate the indirect costs savings, on a daily basis, that would be realized by an earlier than anticipated project completion. The procedure for finding the least-cost schedule involves searching the critical path for activities that can be shortened by adding resources at a cost less than that saved by the corresponding shortening of the project duration. The procedure is complicated by the fact that there are generally multiple critical paths, each a sequence of activities that force the project to a specific duration. To shorten the project duration by one day, a day must be saved in each critical path, or nothing will be gained. Also, as the least-cost process continues more and more critical paths are developed. When the direct cost to shorten every critical path, thus the project duration, by one more day exceeds the savings realized by the day saved, then the least-cost schedule is found. Example 10.8 illustrates the least-cost scheduling process with a simple CPM schedule modified for least cost.

Example 10.8: Figure 10.17 shows a normal CPM schedule with successive iterations of shortening (only the forward pass is shown). Table 10.22 shows a worksheet containing the required calculations.

Step 1: It can be seen from Figure 10.17 that there is one critical path, B–E. From Table 10.22, B costs $60 per day to shorten and E costs $75 per day. B can

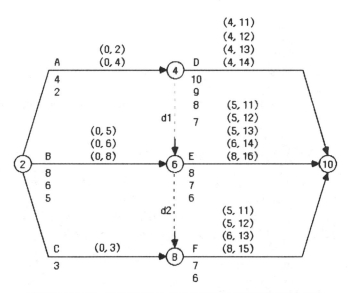

Figure 10.17. Successive shortening of CPM schedule.

be shortened two days, shortening the project duration from 16 to 14 days, increasing the direct costs from $3800 to $3920, decreasing the indirect costs from $1600 to $1400, and decreasing the total cost from $5400 to $5320.

Step 2: There are now two critical paths, A–D and B–E, both of which must be shortened to realize any savings. The least-cost way to shorten is to shorten B and D by one day each, at an additional direct cost of $85, which reduces the project duration to 13 days.

Step 3: There are still two critical paths, A–D and B–E, but B is at its crash duration so D and E are shortened by one day, at an additional direct cost of $100, resulting in a project duration of 12 days.

Step 4: There are now three critical paths, A–D, B–E, and C–F, that must be shortened. Shortening D, E, and F is the least-cost way but leads to a $200 increase in direct costs, a $100 decrease in indirect cost, and a total project cost increase of $100. At this point there is no further reduction in total cost possible. Also, the least-cost calculations must stop because both B and E, which make up a complete critical path, are at their crash durations. Even though other activities in other critical paths can be shortened, once any critical path is at its crash duration no further shortening can be effected. Figure 10.18 shows a plot of project direct costs, indirect costs, and total cost versus workdays required to complete project.

10.4.2.5 Payment Progressing.
The CPM with associated costs can be an enormous aid in determining value in place for progress payments. If the contractor and the owner agree on monetary or percent values for each activity prior to project commencement, then at payment time the contractor receives credit for all completed activities, and only the activities in progress must be evaluated. Also, by using such an arrangement, the contractor can determine his expected cash flow very accurately. Figure 10.19 illustrates this concept. The value in place for each activity, expressed as a percent of the total contract price, is shown in the activity boxes. The date in the upper right is the scheduled completion date for each activity. The progress line for 1/31/85 shows that the value of work in place is the percentage represented on activities A, B, C, F, G plus the value of activities D and I as determined by observation.

10.4.2.6 Resource Leveling.
Often resources stand idle waiting to be utilized. CPM can assist the cost estimator in acquiring better utilization of resources, thereby reducing costs. The critical paths in the CPM identify those activities that must be completed in the time assigned or the project will be delayed. Those activities not on a critical path have some float or time that they could be delayed without delaying the project completion. If a part of the resource allocation of a noncritical activity can be eliminated without causing an increase in duration to create a new critical path, a savings may be realized by reduced standby time, reduced total number of workers to be trained, or reduced amount of equipment to be mobilized. Example 10.9 shows a simple illustration of this concept. Example 10.9 assumes that all workers are interchangeable and that the man-days

TABLE 10.22. Least-Cost Schedule Worksheet

	Cost ($)		DUR Days								
Act	Crash	Normal	Crash	Normal	Dif ($)	Dif Dur	Dollars/Day	Days	Cut		
A	500	400	4	2	100	2	50				
B	980	800	8	5	180	3	60	2			
C	700	600	3	2	100	1	100		1		
D	600	500	10	6	100	4	25				
E	950	800	8	6	150	2	75		1	1	1
F	1000	700	7	4	300	3	100		1	1	1

Project duration						16	14	13	12	11
Days reduced							2	1	1	1
Dollars/day							60	85	100	200
Dollars increase							120	85	100	200
Direct cost						3800	3920	4005	4105	4305
Indirect cost						1600	1400	1300	1200	1100
Total cost						5400	5320	5305	5305	5405

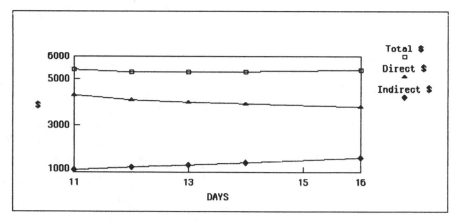

Figure 10.18. Project costs versus workdays.

required for each activity remain the same as long as the crew size is within range. Although these may be poor assumptions for an entire project, the technique can be used for leveling the workload of a particular trade or a particular type of equipment.

Example 10.9: Figure 10.20 shows a simple CPM schedule with the critical path indicated by darker lines. Table 10.23 first shows the schedule as an early start schedule with all activities starting on their early start times and taking their

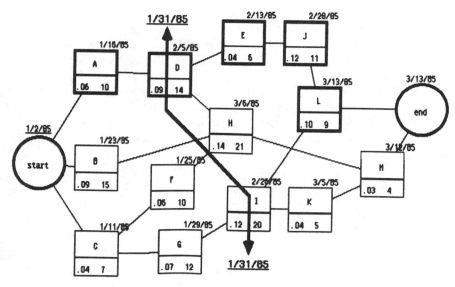

Figure 10.19. Payment progressing example.

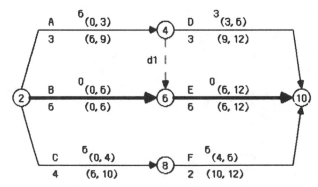

Figure 10.20. CPM critical path.

normal durations. Table 10.23 also shows a schedule with the manning per day leveled by redistribution of workers on activities with float. Note that critical activities must always be manned at normal if the project completion date is to be maintained.

14.4.3 PERT Schedules

PERT (Program Evaluation and Review Technique) was developed in the 1950s by the U.S. Navy [5] for the Polaris missile program. Although it is similar to CPM, and most of the rules of network manipulation are the same, the techniques were developed independently. Basically, the only difference between the two methods is that activity durations are described by a probability distribution in PERT instead of as a fixed number of days as in CPM. The PERT model has the constraint that each activity's duration must be represented by a continuous probability distribution whose mean t_e, standard deviation σ, and variance σ^2 can be calculated.

Using PERT, the cost estimator must assign three estimates to each activity: a pessimistic estimate, a most likely estimate, and an optimistic estimate. The most likely estimate closely resembles the CPM fixed duration, whereas the pessimistic and optimistic estimates show the variability or uncertainty of the expected duration. Given the three estimates and the constraint of continuity, the cost estimator can calculate the mean t_e, standard deviation σ, and variance σ^2 for each activity using the following equations:

$$t_e = \frac{o + 4m + p}{6} \tag{10.4}$$

$$\sigma = \frac{p - o}{6} \tag{10.5}$$

$$\sigma^2 = \left(\frac{p - o}{6}\right)^2 \tag{10.6}$$

TABLE 10.23. Resource Leveling Calculations

Activity	Normal Duration	Man-Days	Crew Normal	Size Minimum	1	2	3	4	5	6	7	8	9	10	11	12	Total
A	3	15	5	3	5	5	5										15
B	6	24	4	4	4	4	4	4	4	4							24
C	4	16	4	1	4	4	4	4									16
D	3	9	3	1				3	3	3							9
E	6	24	4	4							4	4	4	4	4	4	24
F	2	12	6	4					6	6							12
Total	Man-days	100			13	13	13	11	13	13	4	4	4	4	4	4	= 100

Activity	Normal Duration	Man-Days	Crew Normal	Size Minimum	1	2	3	4	5	6	7	8	9	10	11	12	Total
A	3	15	5	3		3	3	3	3	3							15
B	6	24	4	4	4	4	4	4	4	4							24
C	4	16	4	1	2	2	2	2	2	2	2	2					16
D	3	9	3	1							3	3	1	1	1		9
E	6	24	4	4							4	4	4	4	4	4	24
F	2	12	6	4									4	4	4		12
Total	Man-days	100			6	9	9	9	9	9	9	9	9	9	9	4	= 100

where o = optimistic estimate
       m = most likely estimate
       p = pessimistic estimate

Using the mean or expected time for each activity, the network calculations can be carried out as in CPM, identifying the critical path and expected project length. However, unlike CPM, the expected project length thus determined is the expected time or the mean duration of the project.

The central limit theorem, a mathematical tool from statistics, says that the sum of a group of continuous distributions, such as the activities on a critical path, would tend toward a continuous, normal distribution with a mean equal to the sum of the means of the activities in the critical path and a variance equal to the sum of the variances. From this knowledge, the cost estimator can determine not only the expected duration of the project but also the probability of finishing early, late,

TABLE 10.24. *Z* **Table**

Z	Probability of Completing by T_S	Z	Probability of Completing by T_S
−3.0	0.00	0.0	0.50
−2.5	0.01	0.1	0.54
−2.0	0.03	0.2	0.58
−1.5	0.07	0.3	0.62
−1.4	0.09	0.4	0.66
−1.3	0.11	0.5	0.69
−1.2	0.12	0.6	0.73
−1.1	0.14	0.7	0.76
−1.0	0.16	0.8	0.79
−0.9	0.18	0.9	0.82
−0.8	0.21	1.0	0.84
−0.7	0.24	1.1	0.86
−0.6	0.27	1.2	0.88
−0.5	0.31	1.3	0.90
−0.4	0.35	1.4	0.92
−0.3	0.38	1.5	0.93
−0.2	0.42	2.0	0.98
−0.1	0.46	2.5	0.99
0.0	0.50	3.0	1.00

$$Z = \frac{T_S - T_E}{\sigma}$$

where Z = table value
       T_S = number of workdays
       T_E = expected project duration
       σ = project standard deviation

or on time. The advantage of using a normal distribution is that standard tables such as the Z table, shown in Table 10.24, are readily available to assist in the calculations. Example 10.10 shows how PERT would be used on the remodeling project from Table 10.18.

Example 10.10: Table 10.25 shows the activities (critical activities are marked with *) along with their means, standard deviations, and variances. The critical path activities' means and variances are summed to produce a project mean (T_E and project variance σ^2), then a project standard deviation σ, can be determined. Using the equation

$$Z = \frac{(T_S - T_E)}{\sigma} \tag{10.7}$$

questions about the project distribution can be answered, such as the probability of being finished by a certain day T_S.

TABLE 10.25. PERT Calculations—Remodeling Project

CRIT	ACT	O	M	P	t_e	σ	v
	A	5	5	5			
	B	2	3	4			
	C	2	2	3			
*	D	2	4	4	3.7	0.33	0.11
	E	10	10	10			
	F	2	2	3			
*	G	4	5	6	5.0	0.33	0.11
*	H	3	3	4	3.2	0.17	0.03
*	I	1	2	4	2.2	0.50	0.25
*	J	1	2	3	2.0	0.33	0.11
	K	1	1	2			
	L	2	3	3			
*	M	3	4	5	4.0	0.33	0.11
	N	1	2	2	1.8	0.17	0.03
*	O	2	2	3	2.2	0.17	0.03
*	P	3	3	5	3.3	0.33	0.11
	Q	15	15	15			
	R	5	5	5			
*	S	1	1	2	1.2	0.17	0.03
	T	1	1	1	1.0		
	U	7	7	7	7.0		
*	V	2	3	4	3.0	0.33	0.11
*	W	1	2	3	2.0	0.33	0.11
					$T_E =$	42	$V =$	1.14
					$=$	1.07		

$$Z = \frac{42 - 42}{1.1} = 0 \qquad P(Z = 0) = 0.50$$

says that there is a 50/50 chance for the project to finish by the expected time of 42 days. What is the probability of being finished by day 41?

$$Z = \frac{41 - 42}{1.1} = -0.9 \qquad P(Z = -0.9) = 0.18$$

Although the PERT model works well with one critical path, when several paths are critical, or when several paths with different variances are near critical, the project distribution calculations become unwieldy. This is because each calculation is for only one path, so to find the probability of finishing by a certain time, joint probabilities of all paths that could potentially control the project length must be calculated. Simulation techniques can simplify determining the project distribution without the constraint that all activity distributions be continuous.

10.4.4 Monte Carlo Simulation Schedules

Simulation using Monte Carlo techniques is a stochastic process that can resolve some of the shortcomings of the PERT model, such as handling noncontinuous activity distributions and multiple critical, or near-critical, paths. This is done by associating a random number to a probability distribution to simulate a probable value. Example 10.11 shows how this process works with three common distributions, two continuous and one noncontinuous.

Example 10.11: An activity M (framing building) is expected to take 20 days. The cost estimator considers the probability of being a certain number of days late to be about the same as being the same number of days early, and that the distribution is normal with a mean of 20 days and a standard deviation of 2 days. This normal distribution to be used for the simulation is shown in Figure 10.21. From PERT:

$$Z = \frac{T_S - T_E}{\sigma} = \frac{T_S - 20}{2} \qquad (10.8)$$

Therefore,

$$T_S = 2Z + 20 \text{ and } Z = f(\#) \qquad 0 \le \# < 1$$

Then any random number between 0 and 1 can be equated to Z (using the Z table), and a value of T_S can be calculated. T_S will then be used as the duration for activity M in the CPM algorithm.

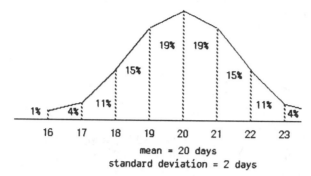

Figure 10.21. Example 10-11, normal distribution.

Another activity P (material delivery) is expected to take 7 weeks. Since deliveries are only once a week, it is possible that the material will arrive in 6 weeks. (30 workdays), 7 weeks (35 workdays), and so on, but not 32 workdays, for instance. The probability that the delivery will be on time (7 weeks) is assessed as 50%, 1 week early (6 weeks) as 20%, 1 week late (8 weeks) as 30%, and less than 6 or more than 8 weeks essentially zero. Figure 10.22 shows this noncontinuous distribution. A random number is selected such that $0 \leq \# < 1$; then $0 \leq \# < 0.20 = 6$ weeks, $0.20 \leq \# < 0.70 = 7$ weeks, and $0.70 \leq \# < 1 = 8$ weeks. This leads to a 20% chance the duration is 6 weeks, 50% chance the duration is 7 weeks, and a 30% chance the duration is 8 weeks.

Another activity R (place driveway) takes one day, no more, no less. Therefore any random number means a 100% chance the activity's duration will equal one day. Figure 10.23 shows this continuous, nonvariable distribution.

The three distributions of Example 10.11 illustrate the method of using Monte Carlo simulation to assign durations to the activities. These assignments correspond to the activities' probability distributions. After the activities in a network are assigned durations by Monte Carlo simulation, the CPM algorithm is used for network calculations and the project length determined. This length represents a

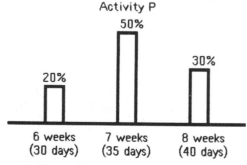

Figure 10.22. Activity P noncontinuous distribution.

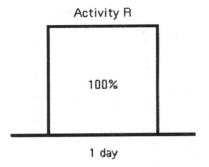

Activity R

100%

1 day

Figure 10.23. Activity R continuous nonvariable distribution.

possible project length. If this process of assigning durations, then solving the CPM calculations is repeated many times, the density of resultant project lengths will describe the probability distribution for the project. Figure 10.24 shows a typical set of simulation distributions.

This method eliminates the need for activities to be described by continuous distributions and the need to keep track of changing critical paths. Therefore this model, made possible by high-speed computers, may be better (mathematically) than either the CPM or PERT models.

Although simulation overcomes some major problems of PERT, it has shortcomings of its own. To get good results from simulation, the determination of activity durations using random numbers and the subsequent CPM calculations must be repeated many times, which requires a high-speed, large-memory computer. Also, this simulation technique assumes that all activities are independent and that the probability distribution of all activities can be described. Another major problem with simulation techniques is that the critical path is not identified—and possibly changes with different iterations. The critical path is important to the project management team for project control and should be identified. Therefore simulation techniques used in conjunction with PERT, or some scheme that uses

Simulated Project Duration - 1000 iterations

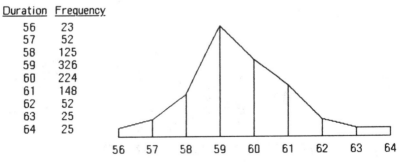

Duration	Frequency
56	23
57	52
58	125
59	326
60	224
61	148
62	52
63	25
64	25

56 57 58 59 60 61 62 63 64

Figure 10.24. Typical simulation distribution.

an expected activity time for one iteration to produce a likely critical path, may be more effective than a pure simulation.

10.5 SUMMARY OF CONSTRUCTION COST ESTIMATING

The objective of construction cost estimating is to produce an accurate, cost-effective prediction of what a project will cost to construct. The owner of a proposed project uses cost estimates to decide whether to proceed with construction and as a guideline to evaluate prices quoted by contractors. Contractors use cost estimates as a basis for pricing their services.

Although all construction cost estimates have a common goal, the methods employed by cost estimators depend very much on the type of project, type of contract, and detail of estimate required. Estimates for direct cost in building construction are usually developed by taking off quantities of materials to be erected from the plans and specifications and identifying the necessary construction operations. Crews are then assigned and costs determined for labor, equipment, material, and so on. In heavy construction, the direct cost estimate is usually developed by estimating the entire cost of operations involving a given material, and then determining a price per unit based on assumed quantities provided in the list of pay items. These unit prices must include cost of required work not covered by the pay items and may be unbalanced to earn more money from early progress payments, to capitalize on suspected errors in assumed quantities from the pay item list, and to disguise costs from competitors. In all construction cost estimating, indirect costs and markup must be added to the direct costs to arrive at a price for construction of the project.

When fixed-price contracts are used, the cost estimate must be very detailed and accurate to insure against losing money and to increase chances of obtaining the job. Fixed-price contracts are high risk for contractors. When cost-plus contracts are used, there is less emphasis on accuracy because there is considerably less risk for the contractor. Variations of contract form lead to different degrees of cost estimating, depending on the risk to the cost estimator's company. Since each cost estimate represents considerable indirect cost to a company, which is usually unrecoverable except as indirect costs charged on all company jobs, it behooves the cost estimator to produce the degree of cost estimate that is most cost-effective.

Although the dollars represented by direct and indirect costs are very important, time is of equal importance. Cash flow during the course of a project can change the profit or loss to a company by several percent. Therefore a cost estimator must consider the cash flow as carefully as any other operation. If progress payments are tied to certain milestones, then the cost estimator should consider advancing those milestones even if it increases the direct cost of the project.

Time schedules are produced for each project to assist in planning and control. Small projects may need only simple schedules such as bar charts, whereas large and/or complex projects may benefit from network schedules. CPM is a network schedule frequently used and often required for public works and other large projects. In addition to scheduling project timing, CPM is used by cost estimators to help produce least-cost schedules, where an increase in direct cost is traded for a decrease in indirect cost, caused by a decrease in project time, to give a lower total project cost. CPM is also a useful tool to the cost estimator for leveling resources used on a project and to simplify determining work in place for progress payments.

Two other network scheduling techniques used by some construction cost estimators are PERT and Monte Carlo Simulation. Although these techniques are not currently used to a great extent in construction, some of the more progressive construction companies with high-speed computers are investigating their potential. PERT is similar to CPM but accommodates variability in the duration of project activities. The rules for using PERT are much the same as for using CPM, in fact, CPM is a special case of PERT, where all activities have a variability of zero. Monte Carlo simulation uses random numbers to simulate a possible duration, based on probability, for each activity and then calculates project timing using the CPM algorithm. By repeating this process many times, a project distribution is generated that represents the probable timing of the project as determined by probable activity durations.

Many tools are currently available to the construction cost estimator, and many others are being developed. Among these are cost estimating handbooks that give up-to-date costs for most construction materials and operations, electromechanical devices to simplify quantity takeoffs from drawings, computers to assist in calculations, and sophisticated scheduling techniques. However, no tool is as important to the construction cost estimator as experience. The lessons learned from past successes and failures are his most important assets.

REFERENCES

1. *Dodge Construction Systems Costs.* Cost Information Systems, McGraw-Hill, Princeton, N.J., 1985.
2. *Means Building Construction Costs.* Robert Snow Means, Kingston, Mass., 1985.
3. *Handbook of Earthmoving.* Caterpillar Tractor Company, Peoria, IL., 1981.
4. Walker, M. R. and J. S. Sayer. *Project Planning and Scheduling.* Report 6959, E. I duPont de Nemours and Company, Inc., Wilmington, Del., March 1959.
5. *PERT, Program Evaluation Research Task, Phase I Summary Report.* Special Projects Office, Bureau of Ordnance, Department of the Navy, Washington, D.C., July 1978.

11

COST ESTIMATING IN MANUFACTURING

JOHN N. LOVETT, JR., PHD, PE

11.1 INTRODUCTION

Cost estimating is particularly important to the manufacturer to price a product competitively and realize profit. Direct costs, such as wages of a machine operator, are more easily determined than indirect costs, such as supervision. Costs associated with manufacturing may be fixed or variable. Administrative costs, for example, are usually fixed, or independent of the volume of product. Material costs are variable since they depend on volume of product. The cost estimator must, therefore, classify the costs of manufacturing accordingly.

Manufacturing expenses fall into several categories, including the following:

Engineering, design, and development costs
Manufacturing labor
Equipment and tooling costs
Material costs
Supervision
Quality control, reliability, and testing costs
Receiving and shipping costs
Packaging costs
Material handling and inventory costs
Distribution and marketing costs
Financing
Taxes and insurance
General and administrative expenses
Plant overhead (or burden)

It is desirable to choose individuals with expertise in specific categories to facilitate the collection of cost data. Otherwise, the cost estimator will be faced with single-handedly attempting to gather data from a myriad of sources within and outside the company. These sources typically include engineering drawings, bills of material, process or routing sheets, master production schedules, accounting records, vendor and catalog information, labor rate schedules, standard time data, and repair and maintenance schedules. Therefore a team approach is needed for cost estimating in manufacturing.

A team of individuals must be selected carefully by the cost estimator to ensure reliable cost data. Each should be assigned one or more of the cost categories listed and asked to return a figure in a specified format (per unit, per hour, etc.) usable by the team leader for the overall estimate. Those with engineering and technical skills would evaluate design and development costs. Those with manufacturing and assembly experience would estimate costs associated with equipment, tooling, material, production, and in-process handling. Shipping and warehouse supervisors may provide expertise in the cost areas of material handling and inventory policy, packaging, and receiving and shipping. An industrial engineer would normally examine costs associated with quality control and reliability and production volume based on standard times. An accountant would be helpful in providing overhead, administrative, and related cost figures. Finally, a representative of the marketing department could offer input on distribution and marketing costs. The principal cost estimator, or team leader, should accept responsibility for assimilating these cost inputs to arrive at a per unit manufacturing cost and ensuring that no relevant cost components have been omitted.

If considerable historical data are available in usable form within the plant, the cost estimator may be able to calculate reliable percentages for cost components (such as quality control, overhead, and packing costs) relative to other costs. To illustrate this point, consider the following simplified worksheet used to estimate the selling price of a metal shelf bracket:

MANUFACTURING COST OF SHELF BRACKET B2006 (RUN OF 1000)

Factory labor (press operator, material handler, painter, packer)	5.25 hr @ $4.08/hr	$ 21.42
Supervisory labor	10% of factory labor	2.14
Inspection and quality control	8% of factory labor	1.71
Total labor		$ 25.27
Plant overhead (utilities, repair, maintenance, insurance, etc.)	115% of total labor	29.06
Administrative expense	12% of total labor	3.03
Material		175.00
Subtotal		$232.36
Packaging	4% of subtotal	9.29
Total manufacturing cost		$241.65
Profit (15%)		36.25
Selling price for 1000 units		$277.90
Selling price per unit		$ .28

11.2 LABOR COSTING

In estimating labor costs of manufacturing, it is desirable to separate the categories of engineering and design activities from those of manufacturing and assembly. Repetitive factory tasks are much easier to cost accurately, given the modern development of work measurement techniques. Engineering activities, on the other hand, are more difficult to cost. A good deal of conceptualization and revision are involved in the design process. In addition, the amount of analysis and drafting work cannot be easily predicted in the early stages of a particular project.

11.2.1 Engineering and Design

Probably the most accurate cost estimate for an engineering design effort may be obtained by requesting an estimate of the projected number of project hours from an experienced design engineer. Such a person will rely on historical data and judgment based on similar projects. The design engineer should also specify the skill categories and skill levels required to complete the design. Labor rates for each skill category and level of participant are assigned from company salary schedules or estimated from the table of position descriptions and recommended salary ranges published by the National Society of Professional Engineers (NSPE). This table is reproduced in Figure 11.1.

To use this table, an income base rate is first chosen. This will probably be the average annual salary for entry level engineers converted to an hourly labor rate. The NSPE table then recommends income ranges for the various position levels as percentages of the base rate. Suppose, for example, that the entry level salary for an engineer hired by a company is $26,000. This gives $13 per hour for a 2000-hour work year. A senior engineer (Level V) would be expected to receive 185–255% of this base, or $24.05–$33.15 per hour.

Estimating the costs of analysis involves not only considering labor hours but also computer time. The cost of computing time depends on whether in-house micro- or mainframe computers are employed or time is purchased from a remote system. It also depends on whether software programs may be on hand, purchased, or must be developed. The cost of development of computer software is commonly underestimated and therefore represents an area where considerable caution must be exercised in cost estimating. See Chapter 12 of this reference manual for the techniques to be utilized in software cost estimating.

Procedures for estimating drafting time are changing owing to the rapid implementation of micro- and minicomputers and computer-aided design/computer-aided manufacturing (CAD/CAM) systems. CAD/CAM systems are combinations of computer hardware (terminals, screens, printers) and software providing the capabilities to generate and alter engineering drawings, produce various views (both two- and three-dimensional), and instruct automatic machining centers to fabricate the designed product. Systems are on the market for circuit board design as well as design of mechanical parts. The traditional view of the draftsman leaning over his table with T-square, compass, and pen in hand, wondering if his next arrowhead will be drawn uniformly, is rapidly disappearing. Drafting time has been

Position Descriptions and Recommended

	Engineer I/II	Engineer III	Engineer IV	Engineer V
Equivalent Federal General Schedule Grade*	GS-5 7	GS-9	GS-11	GS-12
General Characteristics	This is the entry level for professional work. Performs assignments designed to develop professional work knowledges and abilities, requiring application of standard techniques, procedures, and criteria in carrying out a sequence of related engineering tasks. Limited exercise of judgment is required on details of work and in making preliminary selections and adaptations of engineering alternatives	Independently evaluates, selects, and applies standard engineering techniques, procedures, and criteria, using judgment in making minor adaptations and modifications. Assignments have clear and specified objectives and require the investigation of a limited number of variables. Performance at this level requires developmental experience in a professional position or equivalent graduate level education	As a fully competent engineer in all conventional aspects of the subject matter of the functional area of the assignments, plans and conducts work requiring judgment in the independent evaluation, selection, and substantial adaptation and modification of standard techniques, procedures and criteria. Devises new approaches to problems encountered. Requires sufficient professional experience to assure competence as a fully trained worker, or for positions primarily of a research nature, completion of all requirements for a doctoral degree may be substituted for experience	Applies intensive and diversified knowledge of engineering principles and practices in broad areas of assignments and related fields. Makes decisions independently on engineering problems and methods, and represents the organization in conferences to resolve important questions and to plan and coordinate work. Requires the use of advanced techniques and the modification and extension of theories, precepts and practices of his field and related sciences and disciplines. The knowledge and expertise required for this level of work usually result from progressive experience
Direction Received	Supervisor screens assignments for unusual or difficult problems and selects techniques and procedures to be applied on nonroutine work. Receives close supervision on new aspects of assignments	Receives instructions on specific assignment objectives, complex features, and possible solutions. Assistance is furnished on unusual problems and work is reviewed for application of sound professional judgment	Independently performs most assignments with instructions as to the general results expected. Receives technical guidance on unusual or complex problems and supervisory approval on proposed plans for projects	Supervision and guidance relate largely to overall objectives, critical issues, new concepts, and policy matters. Consults with supervisor concerning unusual problems and developments
Typical Duties & Responsibilities	Using prescribed methods performs specific and limited portions of a broader assignment of an experienced engineer. Applies standard practices and techniques in specific situations, adjusts and correlates data, recognizes discrepancies in results and follows operations through a series of related detailed steps or processes	Performs work which involves conventional types of plans, investigations, surveys, structures, or equipment with relatively few complex features for which there are precedents. Assignments usually include one or more of the following: Equipment design and development, test of materials, preparation of specifications, process study, research investigations, report preparation and other activities of limited scope requiring knowledge of principles and techniques commonly employed in the specific narrow area of assignments	Plans, schedules, conducts or coordinates detailed phases of the engineering work in a part of a major project or in a total project of moderate scope. Performs work which involves conventional engineering practice but may include a variety of complex features such as conflicting design requirements, unsuitability of conventional materials, and difficult coordination requirements. Work requires a broad knowledge of precedents in the specialty area and a good knowledge of principles and practices of related specialties	One or more of the following: (1) In a supervisory capacity, plans, develops, coordinates and directs a large and important engineering project or a number of small projects with many complex features. A substantial portion of the work supervised is comparable to that described for engineer IV. (2) As individual researcher or worker, carries out complex or novel assignments requiring the development of new or improved techniques and procedures. Work is expected to result in the development of new or refined equipment, materials, processes, products, and/or scientific methods. (3) As staff specialist, develops and evaluates plans and criteria for a variety of projects and activities to be carried out by others. Assesses the feasibility and soundness of proposed engineering evaluation tests, products, or equipment when necessary data are insufficient or confirmation by testing is advisable. Usually performs as a staff advisor and consultant as to a technical speciality, a type of facility or equipment, or a program function
Responsibility for Direction of Others	May be assisted by a few aides or technicians	May supervise or coordinate the work of draftsmen, technicians and others who assist in specific assignments	May supervise or coordinate the work of engineers, draftsmen, technicians, and others who assist in specific assignments	Supervises, coordinates, and reviews the work of a small staff of engineers and technicians, estimates manpower needs and schedules and assigns work to meet completion date. Or, as individual researcher or staff specialist may be assisted on projects by other engineers or technicians
Typical Position Titles	Junior Engineer, Associate Detail Engineer, Engineer in Training, Ass't Research Engineer, Construction Inspector	Engineer or Assistant Engineer, Project, Plant, Office, Design, Process, Research Inspector, Engineering Instructor	Engineer or Assistant Engineer, Resident, Project, Plant, Office, Design, Process, Research, Chief Inspector, Assistant Chief	Senior or Principal Engineer, Resident, Project, Office, Design, Process, Research, Ass't Division Engineer, Associate Professor, Project Leader
Education	Bachelor's Degree in engineering from an ABET accredited curriculum, or equivalent, plus appropriate continuing education			
Registration Status	Certified Engineer-in-Training	Registered Professional Engineer		
Typical Professional Attainments	Member of Professional Society (Associate Grade)	Member of Professional Society (Member Grade)		
	Member of Technical Societies (Associate Grade or Equivalent)			Member of Technical Societies (Member Grade), Publishes engineering papers, articles, text books
Recommended Income Range (Percent of Specified Income Base Rate)	90% — 130%	120% — 170%	150% — 210%	185% — 255%

*Shown for comparison of job characteristics and responsibility levels only, not to indicate desirable salary levels

Figure 11.1. Position descriptions and recommended income ranges for engineers.

Income Ranges for Engineers

Engineer VI	Engineer VII	Engineer VIII	Engineer IX
GS-13	GS-14	GS-15	GS-16, 17, 18
Has full technical responsibility for interpreting, organizing, executing and coordinating assignments Plans and develops engineering projects concerned with unique or controversial problems which have an important effect on major organization programs This involves exploration of subject area, definition of scope and selection of problems for investigation and development of novel concepts and approaches Maintains liaison with individuals and units within or outside his organization with responsibility for acting independently on technical matters pertaining to his field. Work at this level usually requires extensive progressive experience	Makes decisions and recommendations that are recognized as authoritative and have an important impact on extensive engineering activities. Initiates and maintains extensive contacts with key engineers and officials of other organizations and companies, requiring skill in persuasion and negotiation of critical issues. At this level individuals will have demonstrated creativity, foresight, and mature engineering judgment in anticipating and solving unprecedented engineering problems, determining program objectives and requirements, organizing programs and projects, and developing standards and guides for diverse engineering activities	Makes decisions and recommendations that are recognized as authoritative and have a far-reaching impact on extensive engineering and related activities of the company. Negotiates critical and controversial issues with top level engineers and officers of other organizations and companies. Individuals at this level demonstrate a high degree of creativity, foresight, and mature judgment in planning, organizing, and guiding extensive engineering programs and activities of outstanding novelty and importance	An engineer in this level is either (1) in charge of programs so extensive and complex as to require staff and resources of sizeable magnitude (e g research and development, a department of government responsible for extensive engineering programs, or the major component of an organization responsible for the engineering required to meet the objectives of the organization), or (2) is an individual researcher or consultant who is recognized as a national and/or international authority and leader in an area of engineering or scientific interest and investigation
Supervision received is essentially administrative with assignments given in terms of broad general objectives and limits	Supervision received is essentially administrative with assignments given in terms of broad general objectives and limits	Receives general administrative direction	
One or more of the following (1) In a supervisory capacity (a) plans, develops, coordinates, and directs a number of large and important projects or a project of major scope and importance, or (b) is responsible for the entire engineering program of an organization when the program is of limited complexity and scope. The extent of his responsibilities generally require a few (3 to 5) subordinate supervisors or team leaders with at least one in a position comparable to level V. (2) As individual researcher or worker conceives, plans, and conducts research in problem areas of considerable scope and complexity. The problems must be approached through a series of complete, conceptually related studies, are difficult to define, require unconventional or novel approaches, and require sophisticated research techniques. Available guides and precedents contain critical gaps, are only partially related to the problem, or may be largely lacking due to the novel character of the project. At this level the individual researcher generally will have contributed inventions, new designs, or techniques which are of material significance in the solution of important problems. (3) As a staff specialist serves as the technical specialist for the organization (division or company) in the application of advanced theories, concepts, principles, and processes for an assigned area of responsibility (i.e., subject matter, function, type of facility or equipment, or product). Keeps abreast of new scientific methods and developments affecting his organization for the purpose of recommending changes in emphasis of programs or new programs warranted by such developments	One or both of the following (1) In a supervisory capacity is responsible for (a) an important segment of the engineering program of an organization with extensive and diversified engineering requirements, or (b) the entire engineering program of an organization when it is more limited in scope. The overall engineering program contains critical problems the solution of which requires major technological advances and opens the way for extensive related development. The extent of his responsibilities generally requires several subordinate organizational segments or teams. Recommends facilities, personnel, and funds required to carry out programs which are directly related with and directed toward fulfillment of overall organization objectives. (2) As individual researcher and consultant is a recognized leader and authority in his organization in a broad area of specialization or in a narrow but intensely specialized field. Selects research problems to further the organization's objectives. Conceives and plans investigations of broad areas of considerable novelty and importance for which engineering precedents are lacking in areas critical to the overall engineering program. Is consulted extensively by associates and others with a high degree of reliance placed on his scientific interpretations and advice. Typically, will have contributed inventions, new designs, or techniques which are regarded as major advances in the field	One or both of the following (1) In a supervisory capacity is responsible for (a) an important segment of a very extensive and highly diversified engineering program, or (b) the entire engineering program when the program is of moderate scope. The programs are of such complexity that they are of critical importance to overall objectives, include problems of extraordinary difficulty that often have resisted solution, and consist of several segments requiring subordinate supervisors. Is responsible for deciding the kind and extent of engineering and related programs needed for accomplishing the objectives of the organization, for choosing the scientific approaches, for planning and organizing facilities and programs, and for interpreting results. (2) As individual researcher and consultant, formulates and guides the attack on problems of exceptional difficulty and marked importance to the organization or industry. Problems are characterized by their lack of scientific precedents and source material, or lack of success of prior research and analysis so that their solution would represent an advance of great significance and importance. Performs advisory and consulting work for the organization as a recognized authority for broad program areas or in an intensely specialized area of considerable novelty and importance	
Plans, organizes, and supervises the work of a staff of engineers and technicians. Evaluates progress of the staff and results obtained and recommends major changes to achieve overall objectives. Or, as individual research or staff specialist may be assisted on individual projects by other engineers or technicians	Directs several subordinate supervisors or team leaders, some of whom are in positions comparable to Engineer VI, or, as individual researcher and consultant, may be assisted on individual projects by other engineers and technicians	Supervises several subordinate supervisors or team leaders, some of whose positions are comparable to Engineer VII, or, individual researchers some of whose positions are comparable to Engineer VII and sometimes Engineer VIII. As an individual researcher and consultant may be assisted on individual projects by other engineers or technicians	
Senior or Principal Engineer. Division or District Engineer. Production Engineer. Assistant Division District or Chief Engineer. Consultant. Professor. City or County Engineer	Principal Engineer. Division or District Engineer. Department Manager. Director or Assistant Director of Research. Consultant. Professor. Distinguished Professor or Department Head. Assistant Chief or Chief Engineer. City or County Engineer	Chief Engineer. Bureau Engineer. Director of Research. Department Head or Dean. County Engineer. City Engineer. Director of Public Works. Senior Fellow. Senior Staff. Senior Advisor. Senior Consultant. Engineering Manager	Director of Engineering. General Manager. Vice President. President. Partner. Dean. Director of Public Works
or makes presentations, gives lectures, provides training, etc			
220% — 300%	260% — 360%	300% — 450%	Open Negotiated

Figure 11.1 (Continued)

reportedly cut by 80% or more after drafting personnel have learned to use a CAD system.

Approximate board-time hours for hand drafting Class A drawings, depending on the sheet size, are given in reference [1]. These vary from 1 to 4 hours for 8 $\frac{1}{2}$ × 11-inch size to 40 to 80 hours for 34 × 48-inch size and larger. In a CAD system, such drawings are "drawn," dimensioned, and verified on a computer terminal before being plotted to any desired size on a plotter. Original drawings and subsequent alterations may be stored in computer memory and on printout and called back quickly, avoiding the common fumbling through drawer files to locate a drawing. Unfortunately, comparable drafting time estimates are not available at present for the newer CAD systems. Attitudes of draftsmen govern to a large extent their productivity under CAD systems. For this reason, the cost estimator will probably have to rely on the judgments of technical or drafting personnel when estimating drawing times under a computerized system.

As an example of engineering and design cost estimating, consider a senior engineer in the company mentioned previously who is directing an effort toward design of a new automobile carburetor. The design and related labor activities may be estimated as follows:

Senior design engineer	50 hr @ $30.00	$ 1,500.00
Design engineer	1,120 hr @ 19.50	21,840.00
Engineering aides (2)	350 hr @ 6.00	2,100.00
Computer programmer	120 hr @ 15.00	1,800.00
Draftsman	80 hr @ 12.50	1,000.00
Totals	1,720 hr	$28,240.00

This may be converted to a cost per hour by dividing the total labor cost by the total hours, giving $16.42 per hour.

In addition to labor costs, costs related to design may include space, utilities, printing and duplicating, supplies, fringe benefits, computing time, travel, construction of prototypes, and so forth. Report writing and documentation time may be included in the total labor time at a suggested rate of 8–12 man-hours per page for new documentation and 4–8 man-hours per page for revised documentation [2].

When a product leaves the drawing board, the industrial or manufacturing engineer takes over. Responsibilities of the manufacturing engineer include preparation of routing sheets for assembly; tool, jig, and fixture design; methods design; determination of standard times; assembly line balancing; establishment of testing, inspection, and quality control procedures; and monitoring and work simplification throughout the manufacturing activity. For batch runs up to 100 units, Stewart [1] has suggested that it takes approximately 20 man-hours of the manufacturing engineer's time to start up the process for each man-hour per unit of fabrication and assembly time; 7% of the total fabrication and assembly man-hours should provide an estimate of the manufacturing engineer's time for sustaining the manufacturing process.

As an example of cost estimating for the manufacturing engineering activity, consider two engineers who, through the use of predetermined time standard techniques (see Section 11.2.2.2), have estimated the cycle time for fabrication and assembly of one unit of a new product to be 13.24 hours. The product is to be produced in a batch of 50 units. Total time is thus $50 \times 13.24 = 662$ hours. According to the foregoing guidelines, man-hours of start-up time for the two engineers are estimated at $13.24 \times 20 = 264.8$, or 132.4 hours per engineer. Their time throughout the run would be estimated at $662 \times 0.07 = 46.34$ man-hours. Total involvement would be $264.8 + 46.34 = 311.14$ man-hours, or 155.57 hours per engineer. If the labor rate of one engineer is $20 per hour and the other is $25 per hour, the cost estimate is therefore $155.57 (\$20 + \$25) = \$7000.65$, or $22.50 per man-hour.

11.2.2 Standard Time Data

To provide an accurate cost estimate for manufacturing processes, the estimator must have detailed time estimates for all phases of plant operations. Normally these would include setup and run times for machining and related tasks, assembly cycle times, handling times among work stations, and down and repair times.

Often an attempt is made to hasten the estimating process at this point by taking the number of finished items produced over the last few weeks and dividing by the number of labor hours expended, thus giving a "parts per hour" result. In plants where little effort has been made toward improving work methods and setting time standards, the estimator is accepting a result that could be improved markedly by the application of industrial engineering principles. One goal of management in any manufacturing plant should be the betterment of work methods. This improves worker performance and productivity by providing more efficient and less fatiguing ways to perform tasks.

The traditional industrial engineering approach to methods improvement, developed originally by Frederick W. Taylor and Frank and Lillian Gilbreth, involved observation and analysis of a task by an "outsider." This resulted in recommendations to management for improving the task by redesigning the work station and/or eliminating unnecessary and fatiguing motions of the worker. Once the method was improved, direct time study was used to compute a standard cycle time for the task.

Recently, industrial engineers have more fully recognized the importance of worker input and involvement in methods design. Consequently worker participation programs, commonly called "work simplification" plans, have been established. These provide the worker with the feeling that his own ideas are relevant and eliminate the attitude that changes are forced on him. The principles of motion economy and work station design are still applied, but in a more beneficial manner.

In explaining to workers the importance of time standards to cost estimating, training, and forecasting, the industrial engineer should emphasize the fact that the purpose of a time standard is to improve efficiency, not to force the worker to produce faster. A time standard is the amount of time in which a worker, performing at an average pace, should be expected to complete a task, with allowance provided for rest and personal breaks. Such a standard must be determined only by a trained analyst. Once computed for each manufacturing task, it is invaluable to the cost estimator in assigning labor costs.

11.2.2.1 Direct Time Study.

The majority of time standards in United States plants are still established by direct time study, although predetermined systems continue to gain acceptance. The disadvantage of direct time study, from the cost estimator's viewpoint, is that a manufacturing process must of course be functioning before the study may be accomplished. This is not necessarily so for predetermined systems (see Section 11.2.2.2).

Assuming the manufacturing task to be timed has been planned efficiently, the direct time study technique proceeds through the following steps:

1. The analyst decides what type of timing device to employ and whether to observe directly, film, or videotape the workers.

2. The analyst chooses the workers to be observed and meets with them to discuss the purpose and methodology for the study.

3. The analyst observes a worker performing a repetitive task through several cycles, recording the cycle times on a worksheet (if direct observation, rather than filming, is used).

4. A statistical field check is performed after several cycle times are recorded to determine how confident the analyst may be in accepting the calculated average cycle time as representative of the true average. If the number of observations is inadequate, more cycles are observed and the check made again.

5. Based on experience, the analyst assigns a rating factor to the worker as a measure of the individual worker's pace relative to the analyst's judgment of an average pace for the task. (Average pace is commonly set at 100% rating factor.)

6. The average cycle time over all cycle times recorded is calculated and multiplied by the decimal form of the rating factor, giving the "normal" time.

7. An allowance time (usually for a day's work) is determined by the analyst. Allowance usually includes rest for overcoming fatigue, personal breaks, delays (waiting for materials, equipment failures, etc.).

8. The normal time is adjusted to reflect the allowance. The resulting cycle time is called the "standard" time for the task.

Four points should be emphasized. First, the preceding steps must be carried out by a trained, experienced time study analyst. Second, the standard time should represent a task for which the principles of work simplification and methods design have already been applied. Third, the cycle times collected by the analyst should be approximately normally distributed (see Section 3.2). Fourth, the time standard loses its validity if the method changes even slightly.

To illustrate how a direct time study might proceed, consider a cost estimator who must project the number of machined gear blank castings that can be produced per 8-hour work day in the machine shop of a foundry. At present the gear blanks are precision bored by an engine lathe operator. This machining method is considered best under current conditions, although the lathe operator has difficulty keeping up.

The cost estimator has been asked by management to determine if a numerically controlled lathe may be economically justified. Therefore a standard time is needed for the present method to compare to a projected time for the proposed method. The written standard practice for the present operation is simplified as follows:

Obtain gear blank from supply cart

Chuck blank in lathe

Bore hole

Remove blank

Repeat cycle

At the beginning of the day, the drill bit is loaded in the tailstock of the lathe, and machine adjustments are made. This typically takes 15 minutes. At the end of the day, 30 minutes are required for cleanup and replacement of cutting oil. Personal breaks amount to 25 minutes per day on average. Each of these times was determined through a work sampling study, as discussed later.

Following the previously outlined steps, a time study analyst would first decide the type of timing device to use and whether to observe directly or film the subject. Videotaping is becoming increasingly popular for recording tasks for methods design and time study, supplanting 16-millimeter movie film as the recording medium. Often a clock, called a microchronometer, is placed near the worker so that its face registers elapsed time on film. A drawback is the psychological effect filming has on the subject, frequently causing the worker to make more mistakes than normal. Remote filming or video taping is therefore more effective.

This attitude of the worker is not entirely overcome by direct observation either, since the time study analyst is usually standing very close to the worker. For this reason, it is important for the analyst to meet with the subject prior to the study.

In traditional direct observation time study, a time study board with mounted stopwatch and recording form is used for "snapback" or "continuous" cycle time readings. In the first method the hands of the watch are snapped back to zero after each cycle (or element if a long cycle is divided into shorter elements) just after the cycle time has been observed. The time is then recorded by the analyst. In the continuous method, better suited to short cycle times, the watch is allowed to run for the duration of the observation period. Continuous timing is generally more accurate.

Variations on these methods have been introduced in recent years. Some study boards have as many as four stopwatches mounted, with linkage among them and a lever that can sequentially start, reset, and stop the watches. Thus the analyst may always read a watch that is stopped at the correct cycle time. The digital electronic time study board is probably the easiest to use. It has the capabilities of "freezing" on a small screen the elapsed cycle time while continuing an internal clock. This gives the analyst, by pushing a button, time to read and record the displayed cycle time while the clock continues. When the button is released, the displayed time "catches up" with the internal clock time.

For our example, suppose the time study analyst decides to observe a lathe operator directly with a digital time study board. The next step is to solicit the confidence and cooperation of the worker by discussing the purpose and methodology for the study. The analyst should emphasize that the time standard resulting from the study is not meant to force the operator to work faster, but provides necessary information for cost estimating, operator training, and output projecting. The worker should be encouraged to avoid altering his or her usual pace during the study.

Now the analyst is ready to observe the task from a clear vantage point out of the worker's area of movement. The recording form should contain cells for recording element or cycle times, and locations for noting deviations from the normal cycle (dropping a casting, for example). Forms also include areas for sketching the workplace and recording materials and tools used, machine settings, and so forth. For our example, assume the following cycle times (in minutes) were recorded for boring gear blanks:

$$0.58 \quad 0.62 \quad 0.54 \quad 0.65 \quad 0.63 \quad 0.59 \quad 0.62 \quad 0.65$$

A statistical field check may be performed to determine if eight observations is an adequate number to provide confidence that the calculated average cycle time is close to the true average. The check assumes the cycle times are normally distributed, which is almost always the case in practice. To be certain would necessitate the collection of a large number of observations, say 100 or more, and a statistical comparison of the distribution of observed values to a theoretical normal probability distribution. See Section 3.2. A common working equation, whose derivation is given in Barnes [3] follows:

$$n' = \left(\frac{40 \sqrt{n\sum x^2 - (\sum x)^2}}{\sum x} \right)^2 \tag{11.1}$$

where n = the number of cycle times recorded
$\quad \sum x$ = the sum of all cycle times recorded
$\quad \sum x^2$ = the sum of squares of all cycle times recorded
$\quad n'$ = the required number of cycle time observations to provide 95% confidence that the calculated average cycle time does not deviate from the true average by more than 5%

A customary confidence level is 95% and a ± 5% precision level used in practice. The factor 40 in the formula is derived based on these percentages and will change if either percentage is changed. Incidentally, the precision level is not necessarily 100% minus the confidence level.

In our example,

$$n = 8$$

$$\Sigma x = 0.58 + 0.62 + 0.54 + 0.65 + 0.63 + 0.59 + 0.62 + 0.65 = 4.88$$

$$\Sigma x^2 = (0.58)^2 + (0.62)^2 + \cdots + (0.65)^2 = 2.9868$$

Thus

$$n' = \left(\frac{40 \sqrt{(8)(2.9868) - (4.88)^2}}{4.88}\right)^2 = 5.37$$

Since n' is less than n, the analyst concludes that eight cycle time observations are adequate to predict the true average cycle time within 5% with 95% statistical confidence. No more observations are necessary. Of course, this is not the case if n' exceeds n.

At this point, the analyst assigns a rating factor to the performance of the worker being observed. This factor is designed to compare the observed performance to that considered average for this type of task. For example, if the average pace is 100%, a faster-than-average worker might be assigned a rating of 110%. By multiplying the rating (in decimal form) by the calculated average time, an average cycle time considered representative of the typical worker is determined. This is called the normal time.

Performance rating is the weakest link in the chain of steps leading to the time standard. It requires, on the part of the analyst, sound judgment, considerable experience, and thorough knowledge of the task. Much effort over the years has been devoted to attempting to remove the subjectivity inherent in performance rating. Consequently several rating systems have been introduced, including the Westinghouse, synthetic, and objective systems. A discussion of these systems is beyond the scope of this chapter. The interested reader is referred to Niebel [4]. It is enough to say that predetermined time data systems, discussed in the next section, do not rely on rating at all. This is probably a major reason they are gaining wider acceptance.

For illustrative purposes, suppose the analyst in our example judges the worker observed to be performing slightly slower than average pace. A rating of 95% might be assigned.

To apply this rating and determine the normal time, the average cycle time must first be computed as follows:

$$\text{average time} = \frac{\Sigma x}{n} = \frac{4.88}{8} = 0.61 \text{ minute} \tag{11.2}$$

Then,

$$\text{normal time} = (0.61) \times (0.95) = 0.579 \text{ minute}$$

In other words, since the observed worker was considered slower than average, the normal cycle time should be quicker (less) than the observed worker average.

An allowance time for this task is another difficult value to develop. The reader is again referred to Niebel [4] for recommendations. The most reliable method for assigning allowances is work sampling. Simply stated, work sampling is a statistical technique whereby, at random intervals, a worker is observed and actions (working, idle, etc.) recorded. Over a large number of observations, an accurate percentage of the worker's time may be assigned to allowances.

Work sampling studies established, in our example, a total allowance time for the lathe work of 70 minutes per 8-hour working day, or 14.58% of the total work time (480 minutes). An allowance factor is computed as

$$\frac{\text{total work time}}{\text{total work time} - \text{total allowance time}}$$

$$= \frac{100\%}{100\% - 14.58\%} = 1.1707 \quad \text{or} \quad \left[\frac{1}{1 - (70/480)}\right] = 1.1707 \tag{11.3}$$

The normal time is then multiplied by the allowance factor to give the standard time, as follows:

$$\text{standard time} = (0.579)(1.171) = 0.678 \text{ minute}$$

Thus a worker performing the machining task on the gear blank at an average pace could be expected to produce

$$\frac{480 \text{ minutes}}{0.678 \text{ minute per piece}} = \frac{708 \text{ finished gear blanks}}{\text{per day}}$$

The cost estimator may compare this result to that projected for the numerically controlled lathe, with capital and other relevant cost components also included in the engineering economic analysis.

11.2.2.2 Predetermined Systems.

The previous section states that direct time study is limited to tasks already underway and is hampered by inherent weaknesses such as rating. Since 1938, efforts to develop standard time values for basic motions have resulted in several "predetermined motion-time data" systems. Basically, these systems divide most manual work into basic motion categories, similar to the original 17 motions of Frank Gilbreth, and assign standard times to these motions. Time data tables are thus generated and employed in calculating standard times for tasks divisible into the basic motions.

Predetermined systems are important to cost estimating in manufacturing because they provide means by which proposed tasks may be assigned standard times. In addition, systems such as the popular Methods-Time Measurement (MTM) do not require the application of a rating factor.

Cost estimating for bidding and forecasting purposes frequently requires a projection of the number of items expected to be produced per unit time in a manufacturing process. Often the item is new, and the estimator must work from designs rather than current production methods. If the manufacturing process may be subdivided into basic elements of motion, predetermined motion-time data tables can be used to project the production rate.

How were these tables devised? Through years of filming various repetitive tasks over an array of industries, fundamental motions common to all tasks were identified. These included reaching, grasping, turning, releasing, and so forth. Each general category of motion was subdivided into particular types. Grasp, for example, could involve the grasp of a tiny object, a cylindrical object, or a flat object. Slight time variations were noted among the types of general motion.

Next, each specific type of motion was accurately timed while viewing many films of varied operations, each including the relevant motion. With so much sample data available, these elemental times could be "leveled" to achieve an accurate standard time. Years of application and experience have subsequently verified the accuracy of these standards.

In 1948 H. B. Maynard, G. J. Stegemerten, and J. L. Schwab published *Methods-Time Measurement* [5]. Since that time, MTM has become one of the most popular predetermined systems in use in the world. The M.T.M. Association monitors, revises, and promotes MTM systems and offers training to become certified in application of the systems. The use of MTM should not be attempted by an untrained analyst.

MTM employs a unit of time called a time measurement unit (TMU). One TMU equals 0.00001 hour or 0.036 second. Thus very short elemental motions may be analyzed. For example, grasping an object by itself, when the object is easily grasped, typically takes only 2 TMUs (0.072 second).

In applying MTM the analyst lists all left- and right-hand motions required to perform the job properly. A left- and right-hand, or operation, chart is commonly used for this step. Working from the chart, times are assigned to each motion from the MTM tables. In the situation where two unequal motions are performed simultaneously, the longer or limiting motion only is assigned the time. The sum of TMUs for all limiting motions thus gives the task cycle time. This may be converted to seconds or minutes as desired.

To use the tables it is necessary to classify certain motions. Reach time, for example, depends on the distance the hand travels and the location of the object sought. Consequently, detailed design of the workplace and method must precede application of MTM or any other predetermined system.

The original, and most detailed, level of MTM developed is now called MTM-1. It includes the following basic motions with their more specific cases: reach, move, turn, apply pressure, grasp, position, release, disengage, eye travel and

TABLE I — REACH — R

Distance Moved Inches	Time TMU A	B	C or D	E	Hand In Motion A	B	CASE AND DESCRIPTION
3/4 or less	2.0	2.0	2.0	1.6	1.6	1.6	A — Reach to object in fixed location, or to object in other hand or on which other hand rests.
1	2.5	2.5	3.6	2.3	2.3	2.3	
2	4.0	4.0	5.9	3.5	3.5	2.7	
3	5.3	5.3	7.3	4.5	4.5	3.6	B — Reach to single object in location which may vary slightly from cycle to cycle.
4	6.1	6.4	8.4	4.9	4.9	4.3	
5	6.5	7.8	9.4	5.3	5.3	5.0	
6	7.0	8.6	10.1	5.7	5.7	5.7	
7	7.4	9.3	10.8	6.1	6.1	6.5	C — Reach to object jumbled with other objects in a group so that search and select occur.
8	7.9	10.1	11.5	6.5	6.5	7.2	
9	8.3	10.8	12.2	6.9	6.9	7.9	
10	8.7	11.5	12.9	7.3	7.3	8.6	D — Reach to a very small object or where accurate grasp is required.
12	9.6	12.9	14.2	8.1	8.1	10.1	
14	10.5	14.4	15.6	8.9	8.9	11.5	
16	11.4	15.8	17.0	9.7	9.7	12.9	E — Reach to indefinite location to get hand in position for body balance or next motion or out of way.
18	12.3	17.2	18.4	10.5	10.5	14.4	
20	13.1	18.6	19.8	11.3	11.3	15.8	
22	14.0	20.1	21.2	12.1	12.1	17.3	
24	14.9	21.5	22.5	12.9	12.9	18.8	
26	15.8	22.9	23.9	13.7	13.7	20.2	
28	16.7	24.4	25.3	14.5	14.5	21.7	
30	17.5	25.8	26.7	15.3	15.3	23.2	
Additional	0.4	0.7	0.7	0.6			TMU per inch over 30 inches

TABLE II — MOVE — M

Distance Moved Inches	Time TMU A	B	C	Hand In Motion B	Wt. (lb.) Up to	Dynamic Factor	Static Constant TMU	CASE AND DESCRIPTION
3/4 or less	2.0	2.0	2.0	1.7	2.5	1.00	0	
1	2.5	2.9	3.4	2.3				
2	3.6	4.6	5.2	2.9	7.5	1.06	2.2	
3	4.9	5.7	6.7	3.6				A — Move object to other hand or against stop.
4	6.1	6.9	8.0	4.3				
5	7.3	8.0	9.2	5.0	12.5	1.11	3.9	
6	8.1	8.9	10.3	5.7				
7	8.9	9.7	11.1	6.5	17.5	1.17	5.6	
8	9.7	10.6	11.8	7.2				B — Move object to approximate or indefinite location.
9	10.5	11.5	12.7	7.9	22.5	1.22	7.4	
10	11.3	12.2	13.5	8.6				
12	12.9	13.4	15.2	10.0	27.5	1.28	9.1	
14	14.4	14.6	16.9	11.4				
16	16.0	15.8	18.7	12.8	32.5	1.33	10.8	
18	17.6	17.0	20.4	14.2				
20	19.2	18.2	22.1	15.6	37.5	1.39	12.5	C — Move object to exact location.
22	20.8	19.4	23.8	17.0				
24	22.4	20.6	25.5	18.4	42.5	1.44	14.3	
26	24.0	21.8	27.3	19.8				
28	25.5	23.1	29.0	21.2	47.5	1.50	16.0	
30	27.1	24.3	30.7	22.7				
Additional	0.8	0.6	0.85					TMU per inch over 30 inches

TABLE III A — TURN — T

Weight	30°	45°	60°	75°	90°	105°	120°	135°	150°	165°	180°
Small — 0 to 2 Pounds	2.8	3.5	4.1	4.8	5.4	6.1	6.8	7.4	8.1	8.7	9.4
Medium — 2.1 to 10 Pounds	4.4	5.5	6.5	7.5	8.5	9.6	10.6	11.6	12.7	13.7	14.8
Large — 10.1 to 35 Pounds	8.4	10.5	12.3	14.4	16.2	18.3	20.4	22.2	24.3	26.1	28.2

(Time TMU for Degrees Turned)

TABLE III B — APPLY PRESSURE — AP

FULL CYCLE

SYMBOL	TMU	DESCRIPTION
APA	10.6	AF + DM + RLF
APB	16.2	APA + G2

COMPONENTS

SYMBOL	TMU	DESCRIPTION
AF	3.4	Apply Force
DM	4.2	Dwell, Minimum
RLF	3.0	Release Force

TABLE IV — GRASP — G

TYPE OF GRASP	Case	Time TMU	DESCRIPTION
PICK-UP	1A	2.0	Any size object by itself, easily grasped
	1B	3.5	Object very small or lying close against a flat surface
	1C1	7.3	Interference with Grasp on bottom and one side of nearly cylindrical object. Diameter larger than 1/2"
	1C2	8.7	Diameter 1/4" to 1/2"
	1C3	10.8	Diameter less than 1/4"
REGRASP	2	5.6	Change grasp without relinquishing control
TRANSFER	3	5.6	Control transferred from one hand to the other.
SELECT	4A	7.3	Larger than 1" x 1" x 1" — Object jumbled with other objects so that search and select occur.
	4B	9.1	1/4" x 1/4" x 1/8" to 1" x 1" x 1"
	4C	12.9	Smaller than 1/4" x 1/4" x 1/8"
CONTACT	5	0	Contact, Sliding, or Hook Grasp.

TABLE V — POSITION* — P

CLASS OF FIT		Symmetry	Easy To Handle	Difficult To Handle
1—Loose	No pressure required	S	5.6	11.2
		SS	9.1	14.7
		NS	10.4	16.0
2—Close	Light pressure required	S	16.2	21.8
		SS	19.7	25.3
		NS	21.0	26.6
3—Exact	Heavy pressure required.	S	43.0	48.6
		SS	46.5	52.1
		NS	47.8	53.4

SUPPLEMENTARY RULE FOR SURFACE ALIGNMENT

P1SE per alignment: >1/16 ≤1/4"	P2SE per alignment: ≤1/16"

*Distance moved to engage—1" or less.

TABLE VI — RELEASE — RL

Case	Time TMU	DESCRIPTION
1	2.0	Normal release performed by opening fingers as independent motion.
2	0	Contact Release

TABLE VII — DISENGAGE — D

CLASS OF FIT	HEIGHT OF RECOIL	EASY TO HANDLE	DIFFICULT TO HANDLE
1—LOOSE—Very slight effort, blends with subsequent move.	Up to 1"	4.0	5.7
2—CLOSE—Normal effort, slight recoil.	Over 1" to 5"	7.5	11.8
3—TIGHT—Considerable effort, hand recoils markedly.	Over 5" to 12"	22.9	34.7

SUPPLEMENTARY

CLASS OF FIT	CARE IN HANDLING	BINDING
1—LOOSE	Allow Class 3	
2—CLOSE	Allow Class 3	One G2 per Bind
3—TIGHT	Change Method	One AP8 per Bind

TABLE VIII — EYE TRAVEL AND EYE FOCUS — ET AND EF

Eye Travel Time = $15.2 \times \frac{T}{D}$ TMU, with a maximum value of 20 TMU.

where T = the distance between points from and to which the eye travels.

D = the perpendicular distance from the eye to the line of travel T.

Eye Focus Time = 7.3 TMU.

SUPPLEMENTARY INFORMATION
- Area of Normal Vision = Circle 4" in Diameter 16" from Eyes
- Reading Formula = 5.05 N Where N = The Number of Words.

EFFECTIVE NET WEIGHT

Effective Net Weight (ENW)	No. of Hands	Spatial	Sliding
	1	W	W x F_C
	2	W/2	W/2 x F_C

W = Weight in pounds
F_C = Coefficient of Friction

METHODS-TIME MEASUREMENT
MTM-1 APPLICATION DATA

1 TMU	= .00001 hour		1 hour	= 100,000.0 TMU
	= .0006 minute		1 minute	= 1,666.7 TMU
	= .036 seconds		1 second	= 27.8 TMU

Do not attempt to use this chart or apply Methods-Time Measurement in any way unless you understand the proper application of the data. This statement is included as a word of caution to prevent difficulties resulting from mis-application of the data.

MTM ASSOCIATION
FOR STANDARDS
AND RESEARCH

16-01 Broadway
Fair Lawn, N.J. 07410

© Copyright 1973

MTMA 101
PRINTED IN U.S.A.

SUPPLEMENTARY MTM DATA

TABLE 1 – POSITION – P

Class of Fit and Clearance	Case of Symmetry	Align Only	Depth of Insertion (per ¼") >0≤1/8"	>1/8≤¾	>¾≤1¼	>1¼≤1¾
21 .150"–.350"	S	3.0	3.4	6.6	7.7	8.8
	SS	3.0	10.3	13.5	14.6	15.7
	NS	4.8	15.5	18.7	19.8	20.9
22 .025"–.149"	S	7.2	7.2	11.9	13.0	14.2
	SS	8.0	14.9	19.6	20.7	21.9
	NS	9.5	20.2	24.9	26.0	27.2
23* .005"–.024"	S	0.5	0.5	16.3	10.7	21.0
	SS	10.4	17.3	24.1	26.5	28.8
	NS	12.2	22.9	29.7	32.1	34.4

*BINDING–Add observed number of Apply Pressures.
DIFFICULT HANDLING–Add observed number of G2's.
†Determine symmetry by geometric properties, except use S case when object is oriented prior to preceding Move.

TABLE 1A – SECONDARY ENGAGE – E2

CLASS OF FIT	DEPTH OF INSERTION (PER 1/4") 2	4	6
21	3.0	4	6
22	3.2	4.3	5.4
23	6.8	5.8	7.0
		9.2	11.5

TABLE 2 – CRANK (LIGHT RESISTANCE) – C

DIAMETER OF CRANKING (INCHES)	TMU (T) PER REVOLUTION	DIAMETER OF CRANKING (INCHES)	TMU (T) PER REVOLUTION
1	8.5	9	14.0
2	9.7	10	14.4
3	10.6	11	14.7
4	11.4	12	15.0
5	12.1	14	15.5
6	12.7	16	16.0
7	13.2	18	16.4
8	13.6	20	16.7

FORMULAS:

A. CONTINUOUS CRANKING (Start at beginning and stop at end of cycle only)
   TMU = [(N×T)+5.2]×F+C

B. INTERMITTENT CRANKING (Start at beginning and stop at end of each revolution
   TMU = [(T+5.2) F+C]×N

C = Static component TMU weight allowance constant from move table
F = Dynamic component TMU weight allowance factor from move table
N = Number of revolutions
T = TMU per revolution (Type III Motion)
5.2 = TMU for start and stop

TABLE IX – BODY, LEG, AND FOOT MOTIONS

TYPE		SYMBOL	TMU	DISTANCE	DESCRIPTION
LEG-FOOT MOTION		FM	8.5	To 4"	Hinged at ankle.
		FMP	19.1	To 4"	With heavy pressure.
		LM__	7.1	To 6"	Hinged at knee or hip in any direction.
			1.2	Ea. add'l inch	
SIDE STEP		SS_C1	17.0	<12"	Use Reach or Move time when less than 12". Complete when leading leg contacts floor.
			0.6	12"	
		SS_C2	34.1	Ea. add'l inch	Lagging leg must contact floor before next motion can be made.
			1.1	12"	
				Ea. add'l inch	
TURN BODY		TBC1	18.6	—	Complete when leading leg contacts floor.
		TBC2	37.2	—	Lagging leg must contact floor before next motion can be made.
WALK		W__FT	5.3	Per Foot	Unobstructed.
		W__P	15.0	Per Pace	Unobstructed.
		W__PO	17.0	Per Pace	When obstructed or with weight.
VERTICAL MOTION		SIT	34.7		From sitting position.
		STD	43.4		From standing position.
		B,S,KOK	29.0		Bend, Stoop, Kneel on One Knee.
		AB,AS,AKOK	31.9		Arise from Bend, Stoop, Kneel on One Knee
		KBK	69.4		Kneel on Both Knees.
		AKBK	76.7		Arise from Kneel on Both Knees.

(HORIZONTAL MOTION)

TABLE X – SIMULTANEOUS MOTIONS

EASY to perform simultaneously.

Can be performed simultaneously with PRACTICE.

DIFFICULT to perform simultaneously even after long practice. Allow both times.

MOTIONS NOT INCLUDED IN ABOVE TABLE

TURN–Normally EASY with all motions except when TURN is controlled or with DISENGAGE.
APPLY PRESSURE–May be EASY, PRACTICE, or DIFFICULT. Each case must be analyzed.
POSITION–Class 3–Always DIFFICULT.
DISENGAGE–Class 3–Normally DIFFICULT.
RELEASE–Always EASY.
DISENGAGE–Any class may be DIFFICULT if care must be exercised to avoid injury or damage to object.

*W – Within the area of normal vision.
O – Outside the area of normal vision.
**E = EASY to Handle.
D = DIFFICULT to Handle.

Figure 11.2. (Continued)

focus, body, leg, and foot motions, and simultaneous motions. These motions with their TMUs are presented in table form and conveniently printed on a pocket card by the M.T.M Association (See Figure 11.2).

To illustrate the use of methods design and MTM-1 to arrive at a standard time for labor costing, consider the simple assembly station of Figure 11.3. The worker accesses three small parts from boxes to assemble a valve. The valve stem is obtained from the box on the left. Then a rubber "O" ring from the center box is obtained and placed on the stem. Next a valve housing is obtained from the box on the right, and the stem is screwed into the housing. The assembly is then placed into a fourth box for disposal.

In analyzing the task for methods improvement, an operation chart detailing all left- and right-hand motions was produced. The current method was also timed according to the procedure of Section 11.2.2.1. The standard time was calculated to be 0.110 minute after the appropriate allowance was applied. Thus about 4364 valve assemblies could be expected to be completed per 8-hour working day.

The operation chart revealed that the left hand, which held the valve stem initially, was acting as a vise. This was also true when the right hand gripped the valve housing for insertion of the stem. Since these holding motions were non-productive, the analyst sought to eliminate them with a new design. This proposed design for the task is illustrated in Figure 11.4.

The proposed design called for two assemblies to be produced per cycle rather than one. This was accomplished by substituting three pairs of gravity-feed bins for the three boxes, thus eliminating the reach over into a box and fumbling for a part, and allowing both hands to perform identical motions during a cycle. A simple fixture was designed in front of the worker to hold two valve housings. The "O" ring could be slid into the housing and the valve stem screwed down. This would seat the "O" ring. A foot pedal was designed to release the assemblies from the fixture into a gravity chute, conveying them to a box below the worktable.

An operation chart was prepared for the proposed method to facilitate assigning TMU values for each motion from the MTM-1 tables. Release of the assemblies by the foot action was not a limiting motion and therefore not relevant to the cycle time. The assignment of TMUs is as follows:

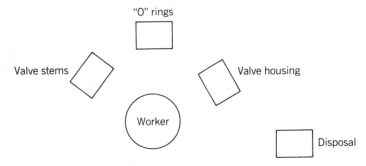

Figure 11.3. Original method for assembling valves.

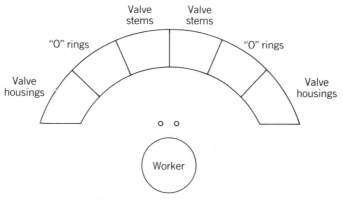

Figure 11.4. Proposed method for assembling valves.

Motion	MTM-1 Classification	TMU
Reach 10 inches to bin 1	R10B	11.5
Grasp valve housing	G1C1	7.3
Move housing 10 inches to fixture	M10C (weight less than 2.5 lb)	13.5
Release housing into fixture	RL1	2.0
Reach 10 inches to bin 2	R10B	11.5
Grasp "O" ring	G1B	3.5
Move "O" ring 10 inches to housing	M10C	13.5
Release "O" ring into housing	RL1	2.0
Reach 10 inches to bin 3	R10B	11.5
Grasp valve stem	G1C2	8.7
Move stem 10 inches to housing	M10C	13.5
Position stem over housing	P2 (symmetric object)	16.2
Turn stem 45° to start threads	T45	3.5
Release stem ⎫	RL2 0	
Grasp stem ⎬ 10 required	G2 5.6	
Turn stem 45° ⎭	T45 3.5 9.1 × 10 =	91.0
Release stem	RL1	2.0
Total TMUs		211.2

Cycle time = (211.2)(0.036) = 7.6032 seconds or 0.1267 minute
Allowance = 20 minutes per 8-hour working day
From Equation 11.3, the allowance factor

$$\frac{1}{1 - (20/480)} = 1.0435$$

Standard time per assembly = (0.1267)(1.0435)/2 = 0.066 minute

The number of assemblies per day projected for the new method would therefore be

$$\frac{480 \text{ minutes per day}}{0.066 \text{ minutes per piece}} = 7273 \text{ pieces per day}$$

This represents an increase in output equal to

$$\frac{7273 - 4364}{4364} \times 100\% = 66.7\%$$

The savings in labor cost may be determined based on the savings in time per piece between the old and new methods as

$$\frac{0.110 - 0.066}{0.11} \times 100\% = 40\% \text{ savings in labor costs}$$

In certain situations it is desirable economically to apply a less detailed MTM system than MTM-1. A second level, called MTM-2, was developed to meet this need. MTM-2 employs 10 categories of motions more applicable to longer-cycle, simple tasks where the cycle is not highly repetitive. It has been established through use that the error between MTM-2 and MTM-1 results for cycle times longer than one minute is less than 5%.

Other levels of MTM are also available for various circumstances. The M.T.M. Association supplies details on these systems and their uses.

One recent effort to simplify MTM even further resulted in a system called MOST* (Maynard Operation Sequence Technique). MOST is said to be at least five times faster to apply than MTM-1 with very little loss in accuracy. This is because MOST utilizes only 16 time values as compared to 37 for MTM-2 and identifies only three basic motion sequences—general move, controlled move, and tool use. Each basic sequence has subactivities to which time-related index numbers are assigned. It is easy to memorize the sequence of index numbers to hasten the calculation of a time standard. Owing to the general nature of the motion categories, MOST is limited as MTM-2 to longer-cycle tasks. However, many United States companies are adopting MOST and training their work measurement personnel in its use. For a detailed description of MOST by the person who first applied it, the reader is referred to K. B. Zandin [6].

An older predetermined motion-time data system still in wide use is Work-Factor†. This system was also developed from film analyses, but additionally provides time estimates for mental activity. The four procedures of the system are called ''Detailed Work-Factor,'' ''Ready Work-Factor,'' ''Brief Work-Factor,''

---

*MOST is a registered trademark of H. B. Maynard and Company, Inc.

†Work-Factor and its four procedures are registered trademarks of Science Management Corporation.

and ''Mento-Factor.'' Detailed Work-Factor is applied to daywork and includes 764 time values in its table. Ready Work-Factor is less detailed and also useful for training employees in work simplification concepts. Brief Work-Factor combines elements into work segments. It is useful in analyzing batch production, manual portions of operations involving mostly machine time, and nonrepetitive tasks with long cycle times (clerical and maintenance work, for example).

Mento-Factor is an interesting system applicable to operations including primarily inspection, proofreading, problem solving, and other mental processes. It recognizes 13 basic mental processes. Examples are See, Discriminate, Decide, Recall, and Compute. Time units may be assigned to the fundamental processes so they may be summed to obtain a standard time. Examples of the use of this and other Work-Factor systems are provided in Niebel [4].

The three preceding predetermined motion-time data systems are in common use and available on microcomputer software. The microcomputer provides faster time standard estimates by storing system table data and avoiding computational errors and rechecking. A 32K memory is adequate for using these software packages.

Predetermined systems permit engineering economic analyses to decide whether capital expenditures for plant or equipment are warranted. They may also provide valuable in cost estimating engineering design activities (see Section 11.2.1), particularly using the Mento-Factor system.

In summary, the following general guidelines might prove helpful in choosing a predetermined motion-time data system to employ:

Situation	Recommended Systems
Short-duration repetitive operations (less than one-minute cycle time)	MTM-1, Detailed Work-Factor
Longer-duration, less repetitive operations	MTM-2, MOST, Ready Work-Factor
Batch production and clerical work	Brief Work-Factor
Engineeering, inspection, mental processes	Mento-Factor

11.2.3 Labor Rate Schedules

Each manufacturing firm should have a labor rate schedule giving standard rates of pay for each grade of labor employed. This is established depending on qualifications, prevailing market rates, terms of a labor union contract, and/or geographical location. It is important to set rates that fairly represent a job classification relative to other jobs in the organization.

Frequently, separate labor rate schedules will be generated for hourly and salaried workers. The principal reason for this is to reflect the different ways in which indirect costs (fringe benefits, paid leave, etc.) are determined for each group.

The following reflects a sampling of a labor rate schedule for hourly employees in a certain manufacturing company:

Classification	Average Hourly Rate
Entry level unskilled	$3.50
Air tool operator	3.90
Spot welder	4.10
Welder	4.50
Machine tool operator	6.50

Labor rate schedules are particularly important to the cost estimator in computing manufacturing costs per unit or per job. For example, the standard time determined for each task in the production of a finished product may be multiplied by the labor rate for that task, then summed over all tasks to obtain the total contribution to direct labor. Suppose a finished assembly requires the following manufacturing steps, with standard times and labor rates assigned:

Task	Standard Time (Minutes)	Labor Rate (per Hour)
1. Produce mold from foundry pattern	3.20	3.60
2. Cast part	0.24	3.50
3. Bore and ream casting	3.88	6.50
4. Mill keyway	5.75	6.50
5. Deburr casting	0.64	4.00
6. Paint casting	0.59	3.60

Excluding material-handling personnel, the total direct labor cost per unit would be

$$[(3.20)(\$3.60) + (0.24)(\$3.50) + (3.88)(\$6.50) + (5.75)(\$6.50)$$
$$+ (0.64)(\$4.00) + (0.59)(\$3.60)]/60 = \$1.33$$

11.2.4 Indirect Labor

Indirect labor costs include the employer's contribution to employee Social Security, unemployment insurance, worker's compensation insurance, liability insurance, health insurance, pensions, vacations, holidays, sick leave, and so forth. Generally, it is not difficult to calculate a percentage for indirect costs which may be applied to direct labor costs. This percentage may be determined by summing all costs in the foregoing categories for the year, dividing by total annual wages, and multiplying by 100%.

In the example at the end of the preceding section, assuming indirect labor costs are 40% of direct labor, the total labor cost per unit would be:

$$\$1.33 + (\$1.33)(0.40) = \$1.86$$

11.3 MATERIALS COSTING

Direct materials include raw materials purchased and not manufactured by the company that become part of the final product. Indirect materials, such as lubricants, welding rods, and other supplies are consumed in the manufacturing process but are not a part of the final product.

Direct materials may be altered or remain unaltered through the steps of manufacturing. Unaltered materials are, of course, more easily costed from supplier data. The cost of materials altered in the process must be determined by adjusting the raw material cost to include losses due to scrap, finishing, shrinkage, and so forth.

To estimate direct material costs for materials altered in the process, finishing allowances are initially added to the engineering drawings to determine the unit size for the "rough" article. Other allowances, such as shrinkage, scrap from defective items, and waste must also be included to determine the quantity of material needed. The final quantity is then multiplied by the unit cost with consideration given to any quantity price breaks.

11.3.1 Bill of Material

One of the most useful in-house sources of information for materials cost estimating is a detailed listing of all components of a finished product. This listing is called a bill of material. The bill of material should show the number and name of each part and its source, either purchased or manufactured. For example, Figure 11.5 shows a bill of materials for a desk-top rolling index file.

Bills of material, especially for complex products, are commonly stored in a

```
                        Bill of Material

             Stock No. 02285     Rolling Index File

          Component
Stock No.   Description          Quantity       Source
------------------------------------------------------------------

  00214   Aluminum Base            1       Manufactured
  00220   Rubber Feet              4       Purchased
  00215   Brass Shaft              1       Purchased Precut,
                                              Drilled, & Tapped
  00216   Brass Washer             2       Purchased
  00217   Cotter Key               2       Purchased
  00230   Plastic Drum             1       Manufactured
  00231   Plastic Collar           2       Manufactured
  00232   Plastic Handle           2       Manufactured
  00218   Set Screw                2       Purchased
  00233   Plastic Index Tabs      26       Manufactured
  00235   Paper Letter Inserts    26       Purchased
  00236   Cardboard File Cards    520       Purchased Precut
```

Figure 11.5. Bill of material.

computer file for easy access. The bill of material for a finished product may include only a group of subassemblies, coded to allow access to any desired subassembly file for a more detailed breakdown.

In the example, costing for the purchased items may be accomplished from accounting or vendor information. Manufactured parts 230, 231, and 232 are manufactured in-house from molded sheet plastic. In specifying the amount of stock needed, allowances for both waste and shrinkage are necessary (scrap is negligible in this case). To illustrate, waste for the plastic collar is estimated to be 21.5%, due to molding a circular collar from a long, thin sheet of rectangular plastic. Twenty-six such collars may be produced from one sheet, allowing for shrinkage. Scrap plastic is sold back to the supplier at 50% its original cost for recycling. Direct material cost per file unit for the plastic collars is calculated as follows:

Base cost of one sheet of plastic, 4 × 8 feet	$2.60	
Cost per file unit (26 collars per sheet, 2 collars per unit)		0.20
Waste (21.5% of base cost)	0.559	
Waste per file unit ($0.559/13)		0.043
Recovery of waste (50% of waste value of $0.559)	−0.280	
Recovery of waste per file unit ($0.280/13)		−0.022
Direct material cost of collars per index file unit		$0.221

The base of the file unit is manufactured from one-half-inch (outside diameter) aluminum tubing. Tubing is purchased in 16-foot lengths, sawed to proper length, bent, end-smashed, and punched with a compound die on a blanking press. In this case, bending, waste, and scrap allowances had to be considered in costing the base component. Bending allowances are calculated from standard handbook formulas.

11.3.2 Master Production Schedule

The sum of all component costs gives the per unit cost of the direct materials used in the finished product. Sometimes, however, a total batch cost for a production run is desired. In this situation, direct material cost for the batch is calculated from the master production schedule, a forecast of the number of units of the product to be produced over a particular planning horizon. The master production schedule, in conjunction with the bill of material, produces a material requirements plan for the forecasting period. As stated earlier, these are commonly stored on computer files so that material requirements are generated in printout form.

A production engineer usually participates in the development of a master production schedule. This individual is therefore helpful to the cost estimator in supplying relevant data from the schedule for costing purposes.

11.3.3 Inventory/Order Costs and Policy

An inventory of component parts, in-process assemblies, and finished products is necessary in virtually all manufacturing activities and may contribute significantly to costs of materials. The objective of an inventory policy is to minimize cost of the policy by determining when and how much to order while meeting the requirements of the master production schedule. Relevant costs may be order, storage, and shortage costs.

The optimization of an inventory/order policy can be approached from several different standpoints. Mathematical models, either deterministic or probabilistic, may be applied under certain simplifying assumptions to generate an optimal order quantity that minimizes total cost. Dynamic programming techniques are also applicable under certain conditions to specify when and how much to order throughout several production periods. Simulation models, which seek to imitate probabilistic inventory situations, are useful when historical data are present to specify the input distributions. These models are widely available in operations research and management literature [7, 8].

To examine how the cost estimator might employ inventory models to cost materials, we present two examples. The first illustrates the application of a mathematical model to a static inventory situation. The second presents a multiperiod policy to which a dynamic programming technique is applied.

In both of the examples, two basic costs are considered. The inventory order cost, or procurement cost, is primarily a clerical cost for processing a purchase requisition for material. Inventory models usually assume that this cost is fixed, or independent of the number of units of material ordered. In other words, it costs essentially the same to process a requisition for 10,000 bolts as for 100. The order cost, which may be denoted C_o, must be determined by tracing the routing of the requisition, applying work measurement techniques to the clerical effort required in each step (see Section 11.2.2), and converting the total time to a labor cost figure. Cost of supplies is also included.

The second relevant cost in the examples to follow is the inventory holding (storage, carrying) cost. The holding cost, denoted C_H, is dependent on the number of units of material stored and the length of time in storage. It is commonly stated as a "per unit, per unit time" cost, such as $0.04 per unit per day. Storage cost is found by considering the following components and converting to the appropriate unit basis:

Cost of money tied up in inventory which could be invested elsewhere

Cost of warehouse space (rent, utilities, etc.)

Cost of material-handling equipment and labor

Cost of spoilage, theft, and obsolescence

Cost of insurance and taxes on the stored items

In the first example, a classical static inventory system, the optimal quantity of units of material to order and the timing of the order is determined by calculus methods to minimize total cost of the policy. This policy is recommended to management and, if adopted and checked, will result in an accurate cost estimate for inventory.

Three simplifying assumptions are necesary to develop this model. First, the demand or usage rate for the item of material is assumed to be linear and known with certainty. Second, the lead time (time between which an order for the item is placed and when it actually arrives or becomes available for use in the manufacturing process) is assumed fixed. Third, the model is developed without the possibility of penalty costs (such as production downtime) being incurred if the inventory is depleted before a new order can replenish it. It might be noted that models may also be developed if any or all of these assumptions are relaxed, but of course they become more complex.

For the first example, suppose the cost estimator has determined the order cost C_o to be $38 for a particular item used in manufacturing and the holding cost $0.053 per unit per week. About 8520 of these items are consumed each week in the manufacturing process. On the average, it takes 12 days to receive a shipment from the vendor after an order has been placed. Figure 11.6 presents the situation graphically.

Referring to the figure, a vertical line on the "sawtooth" curve represents a complete replenishment of inventory after an order of Q units has been received. Of course, the requisition for this order would have been placed 12 days earlier.

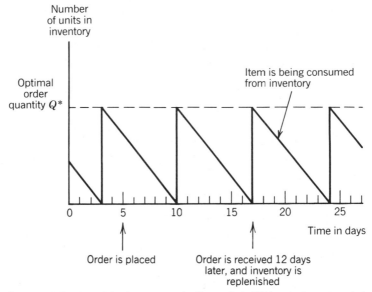

Figure 11.6. Graphical representation of static inventory model.

Items are then consumed in the manufacturing process as the curve moves diagonally downward toward a zero inventory level. By assumption, the curve can never dip below zero since this would indicate a shortage of items. As shown, an order is placed when inventory reaches a particular level to insure replenishment 12 days later before shortage occurs.

After a number of 7-day cycles, an average level of inventory may be computed in terms of the replenishment level (or order quantity Q) and the zero level. In other words,

$$\text{average inventory level} = \frac{Q + 0}{2} = \frac{Q}{2} \text{ units per week} \qquad (11.4)$$

The inventory holding cost may then be written in terms of the average inventory level as

$$\text{holding cost per week} = C_H \frac{Q}{2} \text{ dollars} \qquad (11.5)$$

The order cost per week is found as

$$C_o \frac{D}{Q} \qquad (11.6)$$

where D is the weekly demand (8520 units) and D/Q the number of units ordered per order. Total cost TC is then

$$TC = C_o \frac{D}{Q} + C_H \frac{Q}{2} \qquad (11.7)$$

To determine an optimal quantity Q^* to order each time an order is placed to minimize total cost, the total cost equation is differentiated with respect to Q, and the first derivative set equal to zero. The resulting expression is solved for Q as follows:

$$\frac{d(TC)}{dQ} = -C_o \frac{D}{Q2} + \frac{C_H}{2} = 0 \qquad (11.8)$$

and

$$Q^* = \sqrt{\frac{2C_o D}{C_H}} \qquad (11.9)$$

In the example, with C_o = \$38, C_H = \$0.053, and D = 8520,

$$Q* = \sqrt{\frac{2(38)(8520)}{0.053}} = 3495 \text{ units}$$

This value may be substituted back into the total cost equation to find the minimum cost of the policy, as follows:

$$TC* = (38)\frac{8520}{3495} + (0.053)\frac{3495}{2} = \$185.25 \text{ per week}$$

The simplest way to find the inventory level at which an order is placed is to use similar triangles and Figure 11.6. Calling the inventory level at which an order is placed y, by similar triangles

$$\frac{Y}{Q*} = \frac{5 \text{ days}}{7 \text{ days}} \quad \text{or} \quad y = \frac{5}{7}Q* = \frac{5}{7}(3495) = 2496 \text{ units}$$

To summarize, the recommendation would be to place an order for 3495 units of the item whenever the inventory level reaches 2496 units. This will insure replenishment 12 days later when inventory will be exhausted. Total cost of the policy is \$185.25 per week. This cost figure may be used by the cost estimator if management is willing to adopt the recommended policy.

In the second example, forecasts indicate a varying demand for another item used in the manufacturing process. The forecasting period is 5 weeks, with the following numbers of units projected for the planning horizon:

Week	Number of Units Demanded
1	150
2	200
3	125
4	250
5	175

To simplify the solution, instantaneous replenishment (in other words, zero lead time) is assumed. The options are to order at the beginning of week 1 only the units demanded in week 1, or those demanded in weeks 1 and 2, or those demanded in weeks 1, 2, and 3, or those demanded in weeks 1, 2, 3, and 4, or the entire demand of 900 units for all 5 weeks. Similar options present themselves at the beginning of each of the following weeks.

The minimum cost inventory policy for this situation may be found by dynamic programming using a network analysis. Researchers have shown that it is never optimal to split the demand in any period when ordering. For example, one would never order 250 units at the beginning of week 1, use 150 units in week 1 and the remaining 100 units in week 2, then have to reorder midway through week 2. In other words, orders are placed only at the beginning of the weeks. This leads to the construction of a simple table, shown in Figure 11.7, for determining only those options that are feasible. The same C_o = $38 and C_H = $0.053 are assumed as before.

To construct the table, first list the week 1 order options. These are 150 units (demand for week 1 alone), 350 units (enough to cover weeks 1 and 2), 475 units (for weeks 1, 2, and 3), and so forth. Now consider the fact that two costs influence the best option for period 1—the order cost and the holding cost. Each time an order is placed, $38 is incurred. But holding a large number of items over several weeks may also incur a substantial inventory holding cost. A balance is sought. There may be some point when it becomes more expensive to keep storing items than to reorder. The table finds this point and eliminates those options beyond this point as infeasible.

Mechanically, this may be accomplished by multiplying, for each option, the *additional* units ordered (relative to the previous option) by the number of periods they must be stored by the storage cost per unit per period. Confused? Look at the second option for week 1 in Figure 11.7.

This option represents ordering at the beginning of week 1 for weeks 1 and 2. One hundred and fifty of the units are used in week 1 and assumed not inventoried. Two hundred additional units, however, must be stored through week 1 for use in week 2. Total cost of this option would be

$$\$38 + (200)(1 \text{ inventory period})(\$0.053) = \$48.60$$

Week	Possible Order Option (No. of Units)	Order Cost C_o = $38	Inventory Holding Cost (With C_H = $0.053)	Feasible? (Holding Cost $\leq C_o$?)
1	150	38	---	Yes
	150 + 200 = 350	38	(200)(1)(0.053) = 10.60	Yes
	350 + 125 = 475	38	(125)(2)(0.053) = 13.25	Yes
	475 + 250 = 725	38	(250)(3)(0.053) = 39.75	No
2	0	---	---	Yes
	200	38	---	Yes
	200 + 125 = 325	38	(125)(1)(0.053) = 6.62	Yes
	325 + 250 = 575	38	(250)(2)(0.053) = 26.50	Yes
	575 + 175 = 750	38	(175)(3)(0.053) = 27.82	Yes
3	0	---	---	Yes
	125	38	---	Yes
	125 + 250 = 375	38	(250)(1)(0.053) = 13.25	Yes
	375 + 175 = 550	38	(175)(2)(0.053) = 18.55	Yes
4	0	---	---	Yes
	250	38	---	Yes
	250 + 175 = 425	38	(175)(1)(0.053) = 9.28	Yes
5	0	---	---	Yes
	175	38	---	Yes

Figure 11.7. Order options for a multiperiod inventory problem.

The third option would incur an additional storage cost for the 125 units needed in week 3 of

$$(125)(2 \text{ inventory periods})(\$0.053) = \$13.25$$

thus giving a total cost of this option of

$$\$48.60 + \$13.25 = \$61.85$$

The fourth option in week 1 requires ordering for weeks 1, 2, 3, and 4. This option would be infeasible, because the additional 250 units held over three periods incurs a holding cost greater than the cost of reordering, specifically,

$$(250)(3 \text{ inventory periods})(\$0.053) = \$39.75 > \$38$$

Thus it would be more economical to reorder prior to this point. No additional option need be considered in week 1 after an infeasible option is reached.

Feasible options are likewise determined for the succeeding weeks. A network of options may be constructed as illustrated in Figure 11.8.

The first level of nodes in the network represents the options of ordering only for one week. Hence a zero is placed below each node, indicating no inventory carryover. The second level represents the options of ordering for two weeks, thus holding inventory over one week. Levels 3 and 4 are interpreted similarly.

To illustrate, the node labeled A in Figure 11.8 signals the beginning of week

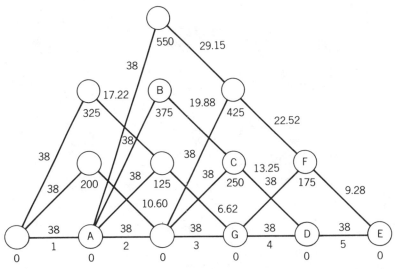

Figure 11.8. Network of feasible order quantities over five weeks.

2. The line connecting nodes A and B indicates the option of ordering 575 units for weeks 2, 3, and 4. This order costs $38, the cost placed on the line. Two hundred of these units are consumed during week 2 to meet demand. Thus 375 units remain at the beginning of week 3. This number is placed below node B. Since 375 units are held over one week, this incurs an additional cost of $(375)(\$0.053) = \$19.88$, placed on the line connecting nodes B and C. As one moves from node B to C, 125 units are being consumed during week 3, leaving 250 units at node C. Since these 250 units are held over another period, a cost of $(250)(\$0.053) = \$13.25$ is incurred, placed on the line connecting nodes C and D. The 250 units are consumed during week 4, thus bringing the inventory level back to zero at node D. At this point another order must be placed to meet the demand in week 5. Note that the sum of all costs along the path illustrated, $71.13, is the same, except for roundoff error, as the total cost of the same option listed in Figure 11.7, $38 + $6.62 + $26.50 = $71.12.

Every line emanating from a level 1 node in the network has a cost affixed equal to C_o. Lines emanating from all other nodes have costs equal to the inventory level under the node multiplied by C_H.

Generally, a unique optimal path may be found through the network, resulting in a choice of best options in each week to minimize total cost of the order policy over all weeks. This is found by determining the least-cost path into each node *from the right*, beginning with the next-to-last column of nodes. For example, in Figure 11.8 the lesser-cost path into node G from the right would be EFG ($91.28 + $38 = $47.28) rather than EDG ($38 + $38 = $76). This path is marked by a right-pointing arrow for later reference. As the least-cost options are determined

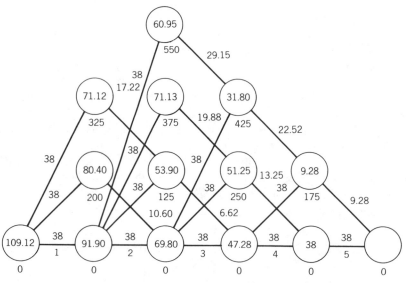

Figure 11.9. Determination of the optimal order policy.

moving to the left, the cumulative costs along those paths are written in the nodes. This results in a network such as Figure 11.9.

Now beginning with the first node on the left, the optimal path may be easily traced by following the arrows. Out of the first node, one is directed to level 3, then down to level 2 in week 2 to level 1 in week 3. This is the option of ordering 475 units at the beginning of week 1 to cover weeks 1, 2, and 3. At the beginning of week 4, the preferred option is to order 425 units for weeks 4 and 5. Total cost of this policy is \$109.12, read from the leftmost node.

The cost generated by either the mathematical model or dynamic programming approach may be viewed by the cost estimator as an additional material cost, even though there is a labor component present in the order cost. However, inventory and order costs are generally considered not as direct material costs but as material burden or overhead. If such is the case, they will be included in the overall calculation of a factory overhead percentage.

11.4 EQUIPMENT AND TOOLING COST ESTIMATING

Estimating the cost of manufacturing equipment involves allocating capital cost over the life of the equipment and considering overhead directly applicable. Equipment or machine overhead will normally include utilities, floor and space, and maintenance and repair. Tooling costs include the cost of purchased or produced machine tools and depend on tool life under various machining conditions.

11.4.1 Cost Models

A basic model for computing equipment cost includes an annualized cost of capital (investment) in the machine and an application of machine overhead. The resulting cost figure may then be converted to an hourly rate and added to the hourly labor rate for operation of the machine.

As a simple example, consider a milling machine purchased for \$125,000. Based on past experience and vendor data, the manufacturer expects to operate the machine 15 years, after which it will be sold for a projected \$18,000. An overhead rate on the machine has been estimated to be 55%. The machine is expected to operate one 8-hour shift 300 days per year.

To determine an hourly machine cost, first annualize the capital cost and salvage values using standard engineering economy principles. Employing the company's minimum attractive rate of return on investment of 10%, the annual equivalent cost of capital and salvage value is

$$\$125,000 \ (A/P, \ 10, \ 15)-\$18,000 \ (A/F, \ 10, \ 15)$$
$$= \$125,000 \ (0.131474)-\$18,000 \ (0.031474) = \$15,867.72$$

Since the total number of operating hours per year is $(300)(8) = 2400$, the hourly cost of capital will be

$$\frac{\$15,867.72}{2400} = \$6.61$$

Applying the overhead rate, the total hourly machine cost will be

$$\$6.61 + (\$6.61)(0.55) = \$6.61 + \$3.64 = \$10.25$$

Determination of the machine overhead rate depends on an estimate of the relevant overhead factors relative to the machine usage, or

$$\text{Machine overhead rate per machine hour} = \frac{\text{overhead amount}}{\text{machine hours}}$$

$$(11.10)$$

Overhead in the example included, per year,

Power consumed	$5207.25
Floor space	1250.00
Regular maintenance	820.00
Repair	1450.00
Total	$8727.25

The overhead rate per machine hour would therefore be, as before,

$$\frac{\$8727.25}{2400} = \$3.64$$

Note that $8727.25 is 55% of the annual cost of capital and salvage value, $15,867.72.

In addition to the basic equipment and overhead costs, certain manufacturing processes, particularly machining or metal cutting, incur additional costs that must be considered in an overall cost estimate. These are classified into setup costs, tooling costs, tool-changing costs, machining (run-time) costs, and handling costs. Because the latter three costs each involve a labor component, they must be estimated from time study techniques (Section 11.2.2).

Since tool life directly influences tooling costs and aggregate tool-changing time, much research has been dedicated to developing models that accurately predict tool life under various cutting conditions. The principal difficulty in finding a reliable model lies, of course, in the myriad of factors influencing tool wear. These include type of cutting tool material, type of stock, chip removal rate, cutting fluids, tool geometry, and rigidity of the setup. Nevertheless, techniques are available for estimating tooling costs.

For example, suppose a 2-inch-diameter medium carbon wrought alloy steel shaft is to be turned down 0.150 inch over a 24-inch cut on an engine lathe, using a high-speed steel cutting tool. The *Machining Data Handbook* [9] recommends under these conditions a speed of 105 feet per minute and feed of 0.015 inch per revolution. The machining (run) time T_m for the cut will be

$$T_m = \frac{L}{FN} \tag{11.11}$$

where L is the length of cut, F the feed, and N the revolutions per minute (rpm) for the lathe. For a given speed S and diameter of the workpiece D,

$$N = \frac{S}{\pi D} \tag{11.12}$$

In the example,

$$N = \frac{105 \text{ feet per minute}}{(3.14159)(\frac{2}{12} \text{ feet})} = 200 \text{ rpm}$$

$$T_m = \frac{24 \text{ inches}}{(0.015 \text{ inches per revolution})(200 \text{ rpm})} = 8.00 \text{ minutes}$$

Average tool life T_L for high-speed steel may be estimated from graphs for a known cutting speed from Lindberg [10]. In this case, assume T_L is estimated to be 27 hours. If a tool costs $C_T = \$20$ to replace, the tool cost per unit produced would be

$$C_T \frac{T_m}{T_L} = \$20 \, \frac{8.00 \text{ minutes}}{(27 \text{ hours})(60 \text{ minutes per hour})} = \$0.10 \tag{11.13}$$

Machining times and tool costs for other machining operations (milling, drilling, shaping, boring, broaching, and grinding) may be calculated in a similar manner using appropriate equations. For example, see DeGarmo, Black, and Kohser [11].

11.4.2 Standard Data Tables

Tooling cost represents only one of five components of machining costs, as previously stated. The other four involve a labor component; the operating cost; which in turn depends upon the setup, run, and handling; and tool handling times. Standard work measurement techniques may be used to determine these times. This, however, is rarely necessary for standard machining operations because tables are widely available for accurately estimating these times. McNeill and Clark [12] provide numerous tables for all types of operations.

Setup time typically includes receiving job instructions, procuring tools and gauges, studying drawings, performing computations for speed and feed, installing and adjusting tools in the machine, installing fixtures such as clamps, making a trial run, tearing down, cleaning the machine, and resharpening tools. Several items may be produced from one setup.

Run time includes the time required to machine the part, as calculated in the previous section. It may also be estimated from tables.

Handling time is the time required to load and unload the part. Tool handling, or changing time, is the time required to replace a worn or broken tool. Handling time is normally incurred per cycle (piece) whereas tool handling occurs intermittently.

In the previous example, where a portion of a shaft is turned down on an engine lathe, run time T_m was calculated as 8.00 minutes. Using standard tables, setup time T_{SU} would be estimated as 39.95 minutes and handling time T_H as 0.85 minute. Tool changing time T_c is estimated as 1.15 minutes.

Total per unit cost is the sum of setup cost, machining cost, tool cost, tool changing cost, and handling cost, each computed on a per-unit basis. Assume the labor rate for the lathe operator is $9.50 per hour and indirect labor (overhead) rate 40%. Then the operator cost C_o is

$$C_o = \$9.50 + \$9.50\,(0.40) = \$13.30 \text{ per hour} = \$0.2217 \text{ per minute}$$

Assume a production run of $R = 500$ shafts. Total per unit cost is

$$\frac{(T_{SU})(C_o)}{R} + (T_m)(C_o) + \left(\frac{T_m}{T_L}\right)(C_T) + (T_c)\left(\frac{T_m}{T_L}\right)(C_o) + (T_H)(C_o) \quad (11.14)$$

$$\frac{(39.95 \text{ minutes})(\$0.2217/\text{minute})}{500 \text{ units}} + (8.00 \text{ minutes per unit})(\$0.2217/\text{minute})$$

$$+ \frac{8.00 \text{ minutes per unit}}{(27 \text{ hours})(60 \text{ minutes per hour})} (\$20)$$

$$+ (1.15 \text{ min}) \frac{8.00 \text{ minutes per unit } (\$0.2217/\text{minute})}{(27 \text{ hours})(60 \text{ minute per hour})}$$

$$+ (0.85 \text{ minutes per unit})(\$0.2217/\text{minute})$$

$$= \$0.0177 + \$1.7733 + \$0.0988 + \$0.0013 + \$0.1884 = \$2.08$$

For the entire batch, the total cost would be estimated as

$$(500 \text{ units})(\$2.08 \text{ per unit}) = \$1040$$

11.5 QUALITY CONTROL, RELIABILITY, AND TEST ESTIMATING

Another important aspect of manufacturing is quality control. In the broad sense, quality control may encompass acceptance sampling, control charting, and testing for development, qualification, and reliability. Costs associated with such programs include those for planning and implementation, inspection, and equipment.

Acceptance sampling is a statistical procedure for determining whether a vendor's product meets the quality standards of the purchaser. It is commonly done on a lot-by-lot basis when large numbers of identical items are ordered for the manufacturing activity. A random sample of items is drawn from a submitted lot, and the percentage of defective items in the lot is inferred from the information provided by the sample.

If all manufacturers employed statistical control charting techniques, there would be little need for acceptance sampling. The control chart, introduced in 1924 by Dr. Walter Shewhart of the Bell Telephone Laboratories, is a simple statistical tool for monitoring and controlling quality of manufactured goods. It has been widely adopted in Japan but to a much lesser degree in the United States. Those companies that have successfully adopted it now often find it less costly to sustain by integrating it at the level of the production worker, thereby letting the person most influential in the control of quality plot and interpret the chart.

Many inspection procedures for acceptance sampling or control charting require only simple observation of the product. Others may require gauging, weighing, or testing by electronic, optical, ultrasonic, or other sophisticated devices. The cost estimator typically must factor in the costs of inspection personnel as well as test equipment for such programs. Other relevant costs will include those for analysis of statistical quality data and for scrap and rework.

11.5.1 Inspection

Inspection and testing costs will include wages, overhead, and training for inspection personnel as well as equipment, space, utilities, special workplaces, and supplies (forms, for example). Inspection personnel may be on-line workers who inspect as they assemble, or those trained only for inspection and testing work. In the former case, it will probably be unnecessary to allot a proportion of wages to inspection and a proportion to manufacturing for cost estimating. In the latter situation, of course, labor costs will be an integral part of a quality control program. Labor costs are estimated as per Section 11.2.

11.5.2 Analysis

The cost of analyzing data collected for quality control purposes may vary widely. Once a standard control charting program is underway, costs may involve only the time for the worker or inspector to perform simple hand calculations and plot points on a graph. In cases where many charts are maintained, computer time may be costed for periodic input of data and printouts. The most expensive situation would be the detailed analysis of an extensive qualification testing program (for a missile system, for example) when numerous parameters must be measured.

11.5.3 Scrap and Rework

The ultimate goal of any quality control program should be zero defectives. This is virtually impossible to achieve in the manufacturing environment. Consequently, one result of implementation of a quality control plan is an estimate of the percentage defective of manufactured product. The quality control chart is designed to maintain the observed quality characteristic in a random yet stable pattern about this average percent defective. Only an act of management can change the average once a process is brought under control.

Either statistical sampling or 100% inspection will catch defective items. If they cannot be repaired, they must be scrapped. In certain cases, however, rework may be possible to bring the item to acceptable standards. The amount of scrap or rework may be estimated from control chart data or other historical sources. Scrap costs may reflect a total loss or a recovery from recycling, such as in the foundry industry. Rework commonly involves machining, refitting, and further inspection, but of course will not exceed the cost of manufacturing a replacement item.

In estimating costs associated with quality control, reliability, and testing, the analyst should also consider the economic feasibility of these programs. For example, in cases where inexpensive items are produced with little or no defects, the most desirable program may be none at all. In the manufacture of critical components, however, 100% inspection with its higher costs may be required.

One final note is important. The cost estimator should be aware of the rapid development and implementation of sophisticated automatic inspection equipment, replacing human inspectors. Often an economic comparison of alternatives may favor automatic gauging and inspection. Therefore the cost estimate for planning purposes should consider this option.

11.6 OTHER COSTS

In practically all instances, an extensive manufacturing cost estimate will include the components presented in previous sections. Other costs that might be considered are as follows:

Packing costs
Receiving and shipping costs
Marketing and distribution costs
Financing costs
Taxes and insurance

Most of these have been mentioned in the preceding discussion, although they probably do not warrant separate sections. They may or may not be relevant to the cost estimator in a particular circumstance.

The myriad of manufacturing costs necessary for an estimator to price products competitively, compare alternatives, adjust wage rates, and recommend options to management requires considerable skill and patience and a team approach. This discussion has provided a method by which costs may be classified and methodically estimated.

REFERENCES

1. Stewart, R. D. *Cost Estimating*. Wiley, New York, 1982.

2. Alford, L. P. and J. R. Bangs, Eds. *Production Handbook*. Ronald, New York, 1953.

3. Barnes, Ralph M. *Motion and Time Study, Design and Measurement of Work*. 7th ed., Wiley, New York, 1980.

4. Niebel, Benjamin W. *Motion and Time Study*. 7th ed., Richard D. Irwin, Homewood, Il., 1982.

5. Maynard, H. B., G. J. Stegemerten, and J. L. Schwab. *Methods-Time-Measurement*. McGraw-Hill, New York, 1948.

6. Zandin, K. B. *MOST Work Measurement Systems*. Dekker, New York, 1980.

7. Taha, Hamdy A. *Operations Research : An Introduction*. 3rd ed., Macmillan, New York, 1982.

8. Turner, W. C., J. H. Mize, and K. E. Case. *Introduction to Industrial and Systems Engineering*. Prentice-Hall, Englewood Cliffs, N. J., 1978.

9. Metcut Research Associates. *Machining Data Handbook*. Metcut Research Associates, Inc., Cincinnati, Oh., 1966.

10. Lindberg, R. A. *Processes and Materials of Manufacture*. 3rd ed., Allyn and Bacon, Newton, Mass., 1983.

11. DeGarmo, E. P., J. T. Black, and R. A. Kohser. *Materials and Processes in Manufacturing*. 6th ed., Macmillan, New York, 1984.

12. McNeill, T. F. and D. S. Clark. *Cost Estimating and Contract Pricing*. American Elsevier, New York, 1966.

12

SOFTWARE COST ESTIMATING

RODNEY D. STEWART, PE, CPE, CCA

12.1 TYPES OF SOFTWARE

The cost of computer software depends very much on the function that the software is designed to perform. These functions are broadly subdivided into the following three levels:

1. Processing—lowest level
2. Monitoring—intermediate level
3. Control—highest level

All information processing systems function on the lowest level, some also function on the intermediate level, and some that function on the first two levels also function on the highest level. The implication of these three levels is that, other things being equal, computer program developments on the highest level will tend to be more costly than those at the intermediate level, and those at the second level will tend to be more costly than those at the lowest level. The three levels are defined in the material that follows.

12.1.1 Processing Software

Computations (i.e., logical transformations) are performed by the computer program system, but direct program-controlled feedback is limited to checks within the data manipulation (i.e., computer program) sequence, apart from console start and stop commands. This is the lowest level of the hierarchical classification; all information processing (and computer program) systems function at this level.

Typical applications in this category would include accounting, scientific computation, information retrieval, and file processing. There are exceptions to the general rule: an accounting system can be part of a management information system that performs functions at the monitoring level.

12.1.2 Monitoring Software

In addition to processing, a direct, program-controlled feedback loop exists to one or more other computer program systems and/or sensors but is used solely to initiate, terminate, and validate information flows. This is the intermediate level of the hierarchical classification; some of the information processing (and computer program) systems that do processing also function at the monitoring level.

Typical applications in this category would include "watching" systems such as surveillance, satellite tracking, communications status, inventory status, and the like.

12.1.3 Control Software

In addition to processing and monitoring, the direct, program-controlled feedback loop to one or more other computer program systems and/or sensors is used by the computer program system to attempt restraint of the external environment. This is the highest level of the hierarchical classification; some of the information processing (and computer program) systems that do processing and monitoring also function at the control level. Typical applications in this category include command and control, industrial process control, and management control.

12.2 TYPES OF SOFTWARE COST ESTIMATES

Regardless of the level of software being estimated, there are two general categories of estimates: (1) detailed estimates and (2) parametric estimates. Detailed software estimates involve the subdivision of the software development job into its components, subcomponents, tasks and subtasks; the estimation of labor hours, materials, equipment, travel, and computer time for each task and subtask; and the application of labor rates and material prices to the resource estimates to derive total direct costs. Parametric software estimates usually take into account past experience in the form of empirical equations, nomographs, ratios, or rules of thumb to derive costs at some level above the detailed tasks and subtasks.

12.3 DETAILED SOFTWARE COST ESTIMATING

Detailed software cost estimating is accomplished in much the same way as any other work activity or work output using the basic 12 steps of estimating described in Chapter 1:

1. Develop the work element structure.
2. Schedule the work elements.

3. Retrieve and organize historical cost data.

4. Develop and use cost estimating relationships.

5. Develop and use production learning curves.

6. Identify skill categories, levels, and rates.

7. Develop labor hour and material estimates.

8. Develop overhead and administrative costs.

9. Apply inflation and escalation (cost growth) factors.

10. Price (compute) the estimated costs.

11. Analyze, adjust, and support the estimate.

12. Publish/present the estimate.

Figure 12.1 is a simplified three-level work element structure for a hypothetical software product called "COSTREND." In any software development project it is first necessary to construct a work element structure of the type shown and then to define each work element in sufficient detail to permit accurate application of labor and material quantity estimates. For a more complicated software project, say a monitoring or monitoring and control software system, the work element structure will be correspondingly more complex and may proceed down to level 5 or 6 if necessary to provide sufficient granularity for accurate application of quantity estimates at the lowest task or subtask level.

Once the work element structure has been constructed and defined, the software project elements are scheduled on a time basis as shown in Figure 12.2. As the work structure and schedule development proceeds, applicable historical data must be collected, analyzed, adjusted, and applied in steps 3, 4, and 5 through the use of data bases, cost estimating relationships, and/or learning curves. Care must be taken to purge historical data of past inefficiencies and to incorporate productivity advances that have occurred in the time since the historical data was generated. The estimator must take into account new developments such as screen generators; preestablished modules and subroutines; templates; display management systems; graphics, word processing, and data base modules; simplified languages like ADA; and other programming aids. Analysis and adjustment of past data into a usable format may take the form of "rules of thumb" such as those shown for selected software functions in Figure 12.3, or may result in parametric estimating methods discussed later in this chapter.

12.3.1 Software Development Phases

Detailed software estimating includes and requires the definition and sizing of each of seven process phases as follows:

1. Information processing analysis

2. Information processing design

3. Computer program design

4. Computer program coding and checkout

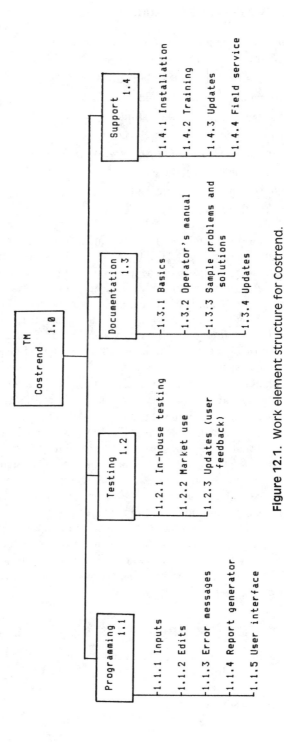

Figure 12.1. Work element structure for Costrend.

Organization: Data Systems, Incorporated	Costrend TM Development Schedule									Name: R. Roberts Date: Nov. 15 (1987)		
	1988											
	Jan	Feb	Mar	Apr	May	Jun	Jul	Aug	Sep	Oct	Nov	Dec
Programming (1.1)	▨	▨	▨	▨	▨							
Testing (1.2)				▨	▨	▨	▨	▨				
Documentation (1.3)						▨	▨	▨	▨			
Delivery									△			
Support (1.4)										▨	▨	▨
Notes:												

Figure 12.2. Schedule for costrend development.

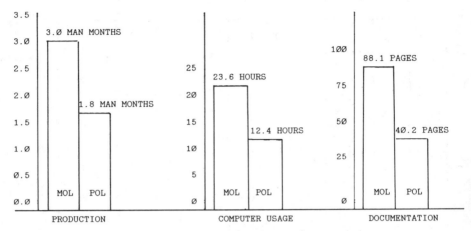

Figure 12.3. Estimating rules of thumb for software.

5. Computer program functional test

6. Information processing integration test

7. Information processing installation and implementation

These phases are described in detail in subsequent sections.

12.3.1.1 Information Processing Analysis. This phase assumes that a requirement has been established for a certain information processing application (e.g., command and control, management information) and covers the activities necessary to define and document the characteristics of the particular problem and the performance of the information processing end product. For example, included are analyses of the user's environment such as any existing interfacing information processing system, potential equipment availability and other technological constraints, economic trade-offs, and evaluation of proposed customer redirections. Information processing analysis results in concurred-upon and updated documents that define the design and performance requirements the information processing end product (such as the new or modified system) must satisfy.

12.3.1.2 Information Processing Design. Based on the design and performance requirements documented from information processing analysis, this phase includes the definition of detailed design and performance requirements for functional elements of the information processing end product, for example, translator, data retrieval, and man-computer interaction. Included are such activities as (1) definition of major functions and their interrelationships; (2) analysis of design and performance criteria for each of these functions as well as proposals for design changes; and (3) preparation of plans for production of the computer program end product, initial and revised documentation, testing computer program elements and the entire information processing system (end product) testing, and training of the user. Information processing design results in concurred-upon and updated documents that detail the functions to be performed by the computer/computer program and interfacing operators.

12.3.1.3 Computer Program Design.

This phase is based on receipt of the detailed functional design from information processing design and covers all work necessary to design and document the computer program end product as prescribed. For example, included are activities to design the computer program structure, data bases, tables, message formats, and utility programs as well as changes to the computer program.

Computer program design also includes the preparation and updating of such associated products as user manuals, operator handbooks, and training materials. Computer program design results in a concurred-upon and updated detailed design specification for the computer program end product (and the associated user manuals and handbooks). User manuals, operator handbooks, and training materials reflect the functional design produced as a part of information processing design. In time sequence, however, these associated products can be prepared later, or in *parallel with* computer program design or computer program coding and checkout. A generally acceptable way of relating the development of associated products to the main process flow of computer program development is needed.

12.3.1.4 Computer Program Coding and Checkout.

This phase is based on receipt of the detailed computer program design specification from computer program design and covers all necessary work to (1) produce and document the computer program in accordance with the current detailed design specification and (2) perform in-house tests. Included are such activities as coding, desk checking, computing test (or runs), integration of individual units into a computer program system, preparation of the data base, error detection and correction, and compiling or assembling and listing of code. Computer program coding and checkout results in a completed computer program end product, tested in-house to assure conformity with the current detailed specifications, and ready for demonstration tests for the user and/or procuring agency.

12.3.1.5 Computer Program Functional Test.

This phase covers demonstration tests of the computer program end product conducted for the use and/or procuring organization, usually in a simulated environment or at the developer's facility. For those computer program developments where the user's and the developer's facilities are the same (e.g., in case of in-house computer programming) this step is skipped. Computer program functional test includes conduct of the demonstration tests (based on test plans prepared as a part of information processing design), analysis, and documentation of the results. All necessary work to remedy errors revealed by these tests is charged to the appropriate previous steps (e.g., information processing analysis, information processing design, computer program design, or computer program coding and checkout). Computer program functional test results in a computer program end product that is ready for demonstration tests in a live operational environment.

12.3.1.6 Information Processing Integration Test.
This phase covers demonstration tests conducted at an operational facility under "live" environmental conditions and includes conduct of the tests (based on a test plan produced as a part of information processing design), analysis, and documentation of the results. All necessary work to remedy errors revealed by these tests should be charged to the appropriate previous steps (e.g., information processing analysis, information processing design, computer program design, computer program coding and checkout, or computer program functional test). Information processing integration test results in a computer program that is a proven part of the information processing system (end product) in conformance with the detailed design specifications.

12.3.1.7 Information Processing Installation and Implementation.
This phase covers all necessary work to install and check out the information processing end product at operational site(s) (other than the one selected for the information processing integration test) and will usually apply only when there is more than one operational location. This step also includes user training, as well as any phaseover activities, in the event that an information processing system (manual or automatic) already exists. Information processing installation and implementation results in an operational information processing end product at all sites.

12.3.2 Factors Affecting Detailed Software Cost Estimates

The principal factors affecting the costs of computer software programs are the computer equipment configuration and performance and the characteristics of the software product. For detailed cost estimates of computer software to be accurate, these factors must be known or assumed prior to beginning the detailed cost estimating process. The following will serve as a checklist to assist the estimator in ensuring that vital technical data about the hardware and about the program's requirements are known before the cost estimating process begins.

12.3.2.1 Computer Equipment Configuration and Performance.

1. Computer and peripheral designations (brand names and model numbers)
2. Numbers of each computer and peripheral units required
3. Computer speed (memory cycle time and add time)
4. Memory type and capacity

5. Storage type and capacity
6. Bits per memory word
7. Input devices and channels, type, and transfer rate
8. Output devices and channels, type, and transfer rate
9. Time-sharing capability (multi-user)
10. Multiprocessing capability (multitasking)
11. Compiler requirements
12. Communications equipment brand and model number
13. Communications transfer rates
14. Number of separate operational sites
15. Number and type of interfacing information processing systems

12.3.2.2 Software Product Characteristics

1. Number of decision making functions
2. Number of computation functions
3. Number of information storage and retrieval functions
4. Number of subprograms
5. Interrelation of subprograms
6. Severity of storage and/or timing problems
7. Degree of need for a common data base
8. Total number of new deliverable machine instructions
9. Number of fields in the data base (if applicable)
10. Number of characters per field
11. Number of input messages or variables
12. Number of output messages or variables
13. Degree of documentation required
    - ☐ User's manual
    - ☐ Programmer's manual
    - ☐ Written tutorial
    - ☐ Programmed tutorial
14. Testing requirements
    - ☐ Number of sites
    - ☐ Number of users per site
    - ☐ Duration of testing program
15. User support requirements
    - ☐ Customization
    - ☐ On-site support
    - ☐ Telephone support
    - ☐ Training

12.3.3 Establishing Skill Categories, Skill Levels, and Labor Rates

It is axiomatic that the degree of skill, competence, and experience of the software development personnel will have a large effect on the outcome of the detailed labor hour resource estimates as well as the final software cost estimate. Skill categories need to be carefully established as well as an appropriate mix of skill levels within these categories to accomplish the job in an efficient and effective manner. Figure 12.4 is a listing of typical skill categories and skill levels for a software development project. These personnel will have capabilities and experience in management, analysis, engineering, computer science, programming, statistics, mathematics, technical writing, and even in publishing. Selection of quality personnel to fill all positions is of vital importance to completion of the software development project on time and within the allocated resources.

TYPICAL SKILL CATEGORIES AND SKILL LEVELS

USED IN SOFTWARE DEVELOPMENT

SKILL CATEGORIES	SKILL LEVELS
Program Management	Program Manager Project Manager Project Engineer Cost Estimator
Systems Analysts	Senior Systems Analyst Systems Analyst Systems Data Analyst
Programmers	Senior Programmer Programmer Coding Specialist
Data Entry Personnel	Senior Technician Technician Junior Technician Clerical
Documentation Specialists	Documentation Manager Editor Senior Technical Writer Technical Writer Proofreader

Figure 12.4. Skills.

Labor rates that are commensurate with experience, productivity, and skill levels should be established that will attract the high-quality individuals needed, and allowance should be made for merit increases during the lifetime of the project. Higher labor rates with higher corresponding productivities usually result in lower overall costs than lower labor rates with correspondingly lower productivities because productive personnel can be rapidly moved into new projects. Once the work element structure, schedule, skill categories, and levels, and labor rates are established, the estimation of labor hours, computer time, and materials can begin.

12.3.4 Estimating, Pricing, and Publishing the Estimate

Once the first six steps of the estimating process have been completed, the key remaining job is to forecast the labor hours, computer time, travel, and materials required to acccomplish the software development job (step 7). The remaining steps are routine in nature (but important) and will flow smoothly if the proper groundwork has been laid in the first six steps.

In the detailed estimating process of computer software, this author recommends the expert-opinion approach using experienced software development professionals. Many times the people who are going to be actually doing the work, provided that they are experienced people, know better than anyone else how long it is going to take to accomplish the detailed tasks involved in software development. If the work has been broken down for them sufficiently as previously prescribed, and if the hardware and the product has been adequately defined, the one who is going to do the work, or his/her immediate supervisor, is the most qualified person to make the resource estimates. These estimates will be reviewed and compared with parametrically developed estimates prior to final budget establishment as a check and balance; but the performer or supervisor must have an input in the early stages of the estimating process.

In estimating labor hours for software development, the iterative nature of software itself must be considered. Ample time must be allocated for checking, debugging, rerunning, editing, and limits testing of each submodule, module, and program. Care must be taken to assure that labor skills are time phased and that the skill *mix* is adjusted as the development schedule progresses to allow for the application of higher skill levels during the more difficult parts of the development process (i.e., startup and reevaluation after testing), and lower skill levels to accomplish routine data entry, error checking, proofreading, and maintenance functions. Mainframe programs and microcomputer programs (see Chapter 9) are available to assist in the computerized pricing of software cost estimates. Many of these are the same programs that will perform the pricing functions for hardware projects or services.

Computerized pricing of detailed software cost estimates includes the application of inflation and escalation factors; the addition of overhead, administrative costs, and fee or profit; and the adjustment of estimates if required to meet design-to-cost or budgetary criteria.

12.4 PARAMETRIC SOFTWARE COST ESTIMATING

Since software development is itself an iterative process, it is often very difficult to quantify the many inputs required to perform a detailed estimate if the estimate is needed *before* definition is complete. Since an estimate is a forecast or prediction, it must be given before the work starts to fit its definition as well as to be of value to the organization who is bidding or planning the work. Hence the need for a faster and perhaps simpler way of developing a cost estimate for software.

There are numerous parametric software cost estimating models available at present, and several selected systems are described in this chapter. Most of these systems are based on the foreknowledge of several important software characteristics, one of which is invariably *the number of program instructions or program statements*. The persistent requirement for this information is paradoxical at best because the number of program statements is usually not known with a great degree of certainty until the programming is complete. But, by comparing programs with similar programs of like complexity and content, it is possible to achieve a "ballpark" estimate of the number of program statements that will be required for a given software development project.

One of the models that is discussed later, the RCA PRICE model, has recently added a new PRICE S-Z module that will assist the estimator in more accurately sizing the program coding job for software development projects. This model uses the functionality of the end software plus certain qualitative inputs to determine the number of designers, programmers, and coders needed to do the job. Inputs include such information as the number and type of input screens, the number and type of output reports, and the number of design reviews and Beta test sites. Selected software parametric cost estimating models are described in the following sections.

12.4.1 The COCOMO Model

The COCOMO model is described in a book entitled Software Engineering Economics by Barry W. Boohm [1]. This is not just a desirable book, but an essential reference book for anyone who is planning, scheduling, estimating, or carrying out a software project. This book is truly a classic in the area of software cost estimating. It is a scholarly work that contains detailed descriptions of the methodology for the cost estimating of software (and cost estimating in general, for that matter) as well as hard and factual numerical, quantitative data drawn from actual software projects. The in-depth discussions of all aspects of software engineering and its cost and resource requirements reflect the author's keen insight into the underlying problems in estimating the cost of computer software projects. His firsthand knowledge of the pitfalls, remedies, and the systematic procedures needed to gain some semblance of credibility in estimating the cost of software projects and products are clearly indicated.

Two of the most important parts of the book, not readily observed by merely scanning the pages, but discernable in a thorough reading and study of the volume, are the definitions of "verification" and "validation."

1. **Verification:** Answers the question, "Are we building the product right?"
2. **Validation:** Answers the question, "Are we building the right product?"

Since verification of software usually precedes the validation, one can see that an iterative process must be used in software development (since we cannot usually tell if we have exactly the right product until it is already built).

The author provides an excellent "goal structure" and a detailed work or task element breakdown structure for a typical software project. The goal structure precisely defines specific goals under each of three general goal categories:

☐ Human relations (includes user friendliness)
☐ Resource engineering (cost of the software)
☐ Program engineering (technical requirements)

A total of 28 goals are listed for successful software engineering. The implication of this exposition is that the goals of the software project must be fully defined before software design and subsequent estimating can begin. The author further subdivides these software engineering goals into product goals (to achieve a successful software development product), process goals (to carry out a successful software development process), and then into quantitative and qualitative descriptions of these goals.

Having developed a goal structure, the software cost estimator or cost analyst must then develop a work element/work breakdown structure activity hierarchy against which resources can be estimated and allocated. The book advocates the following major level 2 subdivisions in this work element structure:

☐ Software management
☐ Software systems engineering
☐ Software programming
☐ Software test and evaluation (verification and validation)
☐ Software data (documentation)
☐ Software implementation (field support)
☐ Software maintenance (updates, corrections)

These major work elements are subdivided into a total of 61 subelements.

One of the nice things about the procedures recommended in *Software Engineering Economics* is that they are applicable to a wide variety of types and sizes of software projects, and the procedures are written in a generic manner. For example, the data base covers projects requiring from 7 to 7,000 man-months to complete, and the data base of 63 projects contains:

- ☐ Seven business systems or applications
- ☐ Ten control systems or applications
- ☐ Thirteen human/machine interface applications
- ☐ Seventeen Scientific applications
- ☐ Eight support applications
- ☐ Eight systems applications

The user can select the part of the data base that is most applicable to his or her impending software project.

The cost model presented, termed COCOMO (for COnstructive COst MOdel), is presented in three levels for top-level, intermediate, and lower-level parametric estimating; the level of estimating depends on the degree of definition of the project.

Other useful features and information are as follows:

1. Typical project phases, activities, and milestones ("waterfall" scheduling model) are listed.
2. The author's seven basic steps in software cost estimation are discussed:
   a. Establish objectives.
   b. Plan for required data and resources.
   c. Pin down software requirements.
   d. Work out as much detail as possible.
   e. Use several independent techniques and sources.
   f. Compare and iterate estimates.
   g. Follow up.
3. Levels of software complexity are defined.
4. A list of factors not included in the parametric software resource data base is given.
5. Answers to the following questions are provided:
   a. Why does software development cost as much as it does?
   b. What factors make the cost of software go up or down, and how do they interact?
   c. What activities consume most of the cost?
   d. How can new software techniques reduce software cost?
6. A distinction between "material economics" and "human economics" in software development is provided.
7. A discussion of "advancemanship," which is the *premium value of early*

definition of requirements, design specifications, and validation, even for small projects, is furnished.

8. A listing, along with detailed equations, charts, and text descriptions of the estimating and use of 15 software, computer, project, and personnel attributes is furnished.

9. A detailed discussion of software project planning and control is provided.

10. Blank forms, checklists, and an extensive bibliography of software reference books are included.

The most astute statement in the book regards software estimating data bases: *The only really reliable data base for software cost estimating is that which has been developed by the organization that is going to do the work.*

For the serious parametric software cost estimator, the COCOMO model and its accompanying book bear considerable information that deserves in-depth study.

12.4.2 The PRICE S Parametric Cost Model

RCA Price Systems of Cherry Hill, New Jersey, markets two on-line parametric software pricing systems: PRICE-S and PRICE-SL. PRICE-S estimates software costs for design, implementation, test, and integration. PRICE-SL estimates the costs for support after the system is installed.

PRICE-S uses four parameters of the aggregate type whose descriptions follow: application, platform, resource, and complexity.

Application is a measure of the difficulty of the task and is determined by the programming mix of mathematics, string manipulation, real time, and commmand and control. PRICE-S provides an application value for various types of programming. The model uses an average, weighted by the portion of the code that falls into each category, to compute the application value for the total program or software system being estimated.

Platform is a description of the operating environment for the final system. It accounts for such things as reliability testing and documentation requirements. Values range from 0.6 to 0.8 for internally developed production center software to 2.5 for manned space flight software. The numerical value is, of course, not as important as the category, but the values do give an additional language for discussion, and interpolation is often used. (Interpolation by customers has led to a recognition of category distinctions that were not originally anticipated. Ground mobile systems were split into commercial and military categories, for instance.)

Resource is an aggregate measure of skill levels, experience, computer operating charges, productivity, labor rates, and overhead. The values of resource are stable across organizations in the same type of work—defense oriented organizations run 3.2–3.5; management information systems have typical resource values of 2.0–2.5 (this does depend on the cost elements that are included). Deleting some cost elements will result in lower resource values.

Complexity is a measurement of the relative difficulty of the task for the resources available. Is the project old hat and the crew top level? Is it basically new business utilizing an inexperienced crew? Is a new language or new hardware involved? Is it a multinational project? These considerations give an adjustment to a standard complexity of 1. "Calibrated" users may adjust their "standard" complexity to a value other than 1 for the fine-tuning of the models.

Many other variables are used in the PRICE-S model, such as number of instructions and utilization, but these four are the principal parametric variables. The application variable is multipled internally by the number of instructions to give a variable that is used as the size measure of the programming task. Platform determines the manner in which the task is to be done—the level of documentation, testing, and so on. The model can then estimate the time for completion assuming a "proper" work force. Complexity will mainly adjust the schedule, whereas resource primarily adjusts the costs.

It was decided to use the PRICE-S parametric variables for the software support cost estimating model when PRICE-SL was developed. PRICE-SL estimates costs for "growth," "enhancement," and "maintenance" and distributes these costs over the support life.

The growth and enhancement costs are estimated by applying PRICE-S directly to code "modules" which are then integrated into the system. The parametric variables are used in the same way that they are used in PRICE-S for these two categories. The costs are then distributed over the support life by combinations of incomplete beta functions.

Maintenance costs are estimated by charging for each error repaired. The parametric variables utilized in estimating are the following:

1. The number of errors in the new code—delivered, added, or changed
2. The detection rate of the errors
3. The repair rate for the errors

For instance, errors in the code (delivered or added) are an increasing function of application and complexity (as well as such items as schedule acceleration) and a decreasing function of platform and resource (as well as schedule stretch-out).

The model assumes that application and platform remain fixed for all work. The development complexity helps to determine the original error size but is then modified to the nominal value of 1 for other computations. Resource can have different values for development, growth, enhancement and maintenance, although the model will use the development resource as a default value.

At present, RCA PRICE is introducing PRICE S-Z, which provides the all-too-often missing factor in software cost estimating—the number of estimated program statements. Usefulness of this program is inherently very good—detailed field testing by many users is expected to confirm this, and the model should be well established by the time this reference manual is published.

12.4.3 The SLIM Parametric Software Cost and Schedule Estimating Model

The Software Lifecycle Integration Model (SLIM), marketed by Quantitative Software Management, Inc. of McLean, Virginia, is a decision support tool for effectively budgeting, planning, and managing software development. It uses the PERT algorithm, Monte Carlo simulation, sensitivity profiling, and linear programming techniques that take into account limiting constraints to provide accurate cost, time, staffing, and reliability projections. Confidence levels and risk factors are calculated to provide the manager with the hard data needed to make decisions on cost, schedule, effort, staffing, and quality.

SLIM is based on the Rayleigh/Norden model. It has been developed into a fully integrated automated software development decision support system by Quantitative Software Management, Inc. and can be uniquely tuned to any organization with a surprisingly small quantity of the organization's own data. Actual results in seven years of use have been most favorable.

SLIM's accuracy has been validated for more than 1000 systems of all types, for example, business, real time, avionics, telecommunications and message switching, scientific, command and control, operating systems, and process control. For more information about SLIM see reference [2].

12.4.4 JPL Software Simulation Model

Reference [3] describes an intriguing research program at the Jet Propulsion Laboratory in Pasadena, California, to develop a dynamic system simulation model of the software life cycle process. The model uses a flow of resources approach, including tasks, people, time, and budgets, to simulate functionally the software development life cycle process. The model is based on a total of 62 attributes relating to such characteristics as size, schedule constraints, language, and product, computer, personnel, and project characteristics as follows:

SIZE ATTRIBUTES

Number of functions (new)	PDL size (modified)
Number of modules (new)	Code size (modified)
PDL size (new)	Data base size
Code size (new)	Retest size
Number of packages	Percent code delivered
Number of functions (modified)	Number of deliverables
	Number of work tasks
Number of modules (modified)	

SCHEDULE CONSTRAINTS

Scheduled time
Test time
Number of builds

LANGUAGE ATTRIBUTES

Specification language	Programming language
Design language	User language

PRODUCT ATTRIBUTES

Degree of legacy	Application type
Product complexity	Required quality
Requirements stability	Degree of real-time adaptation involved
Design coupling	System architecture

COMPUTER ATTRIBUTES

Execution time constraint	Percent computer availability
Main storage constraint	Percent work at development site
Computer access mode	Computer turnaround time

PERSONNEL ATTRIBUTES

Overall skill and qualifications	Skill with computer
Skill with language	Ability to program
Skill with applications	Ability to work as team
Skill with methods	Ability to communicate
Skill with environment	Ability to manage

PROJECT ATTRIBUTES

Modern practices	Use of team approaches
Degree of automation	Degree of technological risk
Use of reviews and audits	Organizational complexity
Use of libraries	Classified environment
Degree of matrix management	Degree of standardization
User involvement	Customer experience
Organizational efficiency	Concurrent HW development
Quality of tools	Quality of environment

Two software life cycle models of the Jet Propulsion Laboratory/National Aeronautics and Space Administration and one from the Defense Department were analyzed by JPL, and a generic model was then synthesized from the assessed strengths and weaknesses of all three. This formed the baseline from which to develop a work breakdown structure for software development.

The principal investigators of this work are continuing to collect data and expect to publish the model at about the time this book will be available to cost estimators.

12.4.5 ESD Parametric Software Cost Estimating Model

References [4, 5, and 6] present work accomplished by the United States Air Force Electronics Systems Division at Bedford, Massachusetts, on the development of parametric equations to determine the total number of man-months required, the total number of computer hours required, the number of new machine language instructions, and the number of months elapsed for small, medium, and large software development projects. The equations were derived from actual program development data from 67 projects. The four equations for each size job compute the following:

$$Y_1 = \text{total man-months}$$

$$Y_2 = \text{total computer hours}$$

$$Y_3 = \text{number of new machine language instructions}$$

$$Y_4 = \text{months elapsed}$$

Empirical equations were developed using best-fit multiple regression statistical techniques. Equations for estimating costs of computer program production (program design, code, and test) for a small system, 1–9 man-months are as follows:

$$Y_1 = -0.92x_1 - 0.47x_2 + 1.45x_3 + 0.78x_4 + 1.13x_6 - 2.07x_{12} + 4.75$$

$$Y_2 = 6.95x_1 - 6.11x_2 + 14.02x_3 + 16.83x_4 + 41.41x_5 - 7.13x_{11} + 21.05$$

$$Y_3 = 1084x_1 - 354x_2 + 415x_3 + 17x_7 + 1219x_9$$
$$- 267x_{10} - 2586x_{12} + 1666$$

$$Y_4 = -0.88x_4 + 1.86x_5 + 1.78x_6 + 0.06x_7 - 0.86x_{11}$$
$$- 2.61x_{13} + 5.35x_{14} + 5.08$$

Equations for estimating costs of computer program production (program design, code, and test) for a medium sized system, 10–79 man-months, are as follows:

$$Y_1 = 7.22x_5 + 4.04x_6 + 2.64x_9 - 13.25x_{10} - 9.27x_{11} + 66$$

$$Y_2 = 271x_5 + 5x_7 + 0.75x_8 - 324x_{11} + 426x_{12} + 95$$

$$Y_3 = 11108x_5 + 13x_8 + 6127x_{10} - 14843x_{11} + 3892x_{12}$$
$$+ 10620x_{13} + 24760x_{14} - 4068$$

$$Y_4 = 1.5x_1 + 4.0x_5 + 0.16x_7 + 0.01x_8 - 3.17x_{11} + 5.57$$

Equations for estimating costs of computer program production (program design, code, and test) for a large system, 80–260 man-months are as follows:

$$Y_1 = 47.55x_6 + 1.84x_7 - 28.04x_{10} - 89.12x_{11} + 197.77$$

$$Y_2 = 2.48x_5 + 11.47x_7 - 161.51x_{11} + 429$$

$$Y_3 = 16467x_5 + 4924x_6 - 3124x_{10} - 14586x_{11}$$
$$- 16583x_{12} + 17944x_{14} + 33919$$

$$Y_4 = 4.8x_1 + 0.50x_3 + 0.02x_7 + 0.01x_8 + 5.08x_{11} + 4.02x_{14} + 12.60$$

The definitions of the variables used in the preceding equations are as follows:

Cost Variables

Y_1 *Total number of man-months* including first-line supervision to program, design, code, test, and document the program not including the cost of any associated executive or utility program.

Y_2 *Total number of computer hours* used by all developmental computers.

Y_3 *Number of new machine language instructions* written for this program (system) not including reused subroutines, logical blocks, and subprograms.

Y_4 *Months elapsed*—completion data for program delivery minus start data for program design. At the time of program delivery the program is ready to be installed in the operational computer to begin system test. The program design activity uses the operating system description and operational specifications as inputs to develop program design specifications and flow charts.

Predictor Variables:

x_1 *MOL versus POL* coded POL = 1; MOL = 0. POL uses procedure-oriented or compiler language for source statement—MOL uses machine-oriented assembly symbolic language source statements.

x_2 *Small versus large-scale* developmental computer systems, coded small = 0; large = 1. Machines with less than or equal to 16,000 words of core memory are small—those with more than 16,000 are large.

x_3 *Need for innovation* in the information processing system; coded yes = 1, no = 0. Innovation means either a new data processing application of a known programming technique and/or a new technique for a known application. *New* means new to the people involved.

x_4 *Stringent timing* as a constraint on programming design; coded yes $= 1$, no $= 0$.

x_5 *First programming effort on computer*; coded yes $= 1$, no $= 0$.

x_6 *Program developed at more than one location*; coded yes $= 1$, no $= 0$.

x_7 *Number of subprograms* in this program (system)—divisions in the program design for logical reasons and/or division of programming labor.

x_8 Total *number of classes* of items in the data base. *Classes* means categories or types of items such as names of people, salaries, cities, states, or any characteristics or information for which there are many items or entries.

x_9 Logarithm to the base 10 of x_8.

x_{10} *Estimate of customer* knowledge or *experience* with the development of automatic data processing systems; coded extensive $= 3$, limited $= 2$, vague $= 1$.

x_{11} *Percent programmers participating in design*

$$= \frac{\text{number programmers participating in design}}{\text{maximum number of programmers}}$$

coded in decimal. Design may include both requirements analysis conducted to specify in detail the performance requirements of this information processing system and the operational design activity to translate these requirements into operational design specifications that indicate how the needs will be satisfied.

x_{12} *Percent clerical instructions*, coded in decimal—bookkeeping, sorting, searching, and file maintenance instructions as compared with mathematical input/output, logical control, and self-checking instructions.

x_{13} *Percent transformation (or reformatting) data functions*, coded in decimal, as compared with generation, information storage and retrieval, control, data acquisition and display, and decision making functions.

x_{14} *Percent generation functions* to produce desired outputs, coded in decimal, as compared with other functions defined in x_{13} including the transformation functions.

x_{15} Logarithm to the base 10 of x_7.

x_{16} The *computer at the operational site different* from the computer used for program development; coded yes $= 1$, no $= 0$.

x_{17} *Log_{10} average turnaround time experienced by the programmers.* Turnaround time is the total elapsed time in hours between submission and return of a computer run.

x_{18} *Log_{10} number of words in the data base.* Data base is the subset of tables that describe the environment of the problem that the program is solving and/or the files to be processed. If the data base changes in size relatively often, indicate an average size.

x_{19} *Log_{10} number of output message types*, for example, number of unique displays or reports (these may be variations of data within their specific formats).

If the foregoing equations are used for software cost estimation, care should be taken to adjust the estimates for increases in programming and systems development productivity that have become available in the estimate producing organization since the equations were generated.

12.4.6 Other Software Cost Estimation Models

Other software parametric cost estimating models are the Avon, Wolverton, Boeing, Walston Felix, and Doty models, which are described in references [7, 8, 9, 10, and 11], respectively. These models are compared with the COCOMO model in reference [12].

12.5 A CASE STUDY: A SOFTWARE COST ESTIMATE FOR AN ESTIMATING SYSTEM

As a case study of a detailed estimate for a software project, a development project for a microcomputer-based cost estimating system is presented. The development job will start in October 1987, and proceed for 12 months to completion. Skills to be used are a project manager, cost estimator, cost analyst, quality control cost estimator, statistical engineer, chief programmer, programmers, systems analysts, technical writers, and clerical support. An overhead of 43% is included in the labor rates, general and administrative costs are 3%, and the projected fee or profit is 12%. The estimate will be prepared using the Project Scheduler 5000 microcomputer software package. Following are the definition of the work, resource estimate rationale, and final cost estimate.

12.5.1 Definition of the Work

The objective of the work is to develop a parametric cost estimating module that will serve as a teaching tool applicable as a "real-world" applications tool for utilization in industry and government, and which can be used interactively on microcomputers. The module will be user friendly and capable of manipulating data bases of cost information to develop program or project cost estimates rapidly.

12.5.1.1 Overview. In the production of the parametric cost estimating module, the very latest in high technology equipment, methods, and information from projects and services being used for sophisticated applications will be applied to the easy solution of problems confronting the program cost analyst and the program cost estimator. The best features of existing products, software library, and extensive data files will be coupled with the latest in microestimating techniques to develop a user-friendly module containing high technology capabilities.

12.5.1.2 The User Interface. Project management offices are confronted with the need to rapidly and credibly create and update in-depth cost estimates with very little information on hand. Estimates must be fiscal year based to fit into time-oriented budgetary plans; costs must be subdivided into categories of research and development, production, facilities, and in-house personnel to fit the appropriate budgetary authorization and appropriation categories; and sufficient depth must be provided to demonstrate compliance with budgetary ground rules and constraints. Budgetary estimates must fit fiscal year funding profiles and must be tailored to the availability of funds as well as to the product or service being estimated. To do all of these things competently, the program management estimator must have an easy to use, parametric cost estimating system that will rapidly produce in-depth estimates.

Cost estimating systems that are available at present to system, project, or program management office estimators do not possess either the capability or the user friendliness required to operate in a dynamic program office environment. Although many microcomputer cost estimating systems are available, both in the public sector and as commercially available applications packages, none has all of the features required for daily project or program office estimating usage. The special design considerations required for this package are as follows:

1. Ability to relate costs to schedule and performance requirements
2. Ability to change estimates rapidly based on changes in mission or deployment profile
3. Ability to subdivide costs into standard budget categories
4. Ability to change cost estimates rapidly based on schedule acceleration/ slippage, and stretching, compression, elimination or addition of schedule elements
5. Ability to update the estimate rapidly based on changing economic indices
6. Ability to alter estimate funding profile to conform to budget constraints
7. Ability to provide in-depth rationale and backup for resource estimates
8. Ability to subdivide costs into basic cost elements (labor, materials, equipment, travel, computer services, etc.)
9. Ability to subdivide costs into work breakdown structure elements
10. Ability to enter allowances for program cost growth either at the top level or selectively at the lower levels of the cost estimate

```
MICROSOFTWARE                    OCT             NOV             DEC                 JAN             FEB
--------------------------------- 7   14  21  28  4   11  18  25  2   9   16  23  30  6   13  20  27  3   10
CODE        JOB NAME              0   1   2   3   4   5   6   7   8   9   10  11  12  13  14  15  16  17  18

100 INITIAL MEETING               0===).   .   .   .   .   .   .   .   .   .   .   .   .   .   .   .   .
105 MILESTONE 1                   .   .   .   .   .   .   .   .   .   *   .   .   .   .   .   .   .   .
110 SYSTEM ANALYSIS               .   )=================================).  .   .   .   .   .   .   .   .
130 PROG DESIGN 1                 .   )=================================).  .   .   .   .   .   .   .   .
135 MILESTONE 2                   .   .   .   .   .   .   .   .   .   *   .   .   .   .   .   .   .   .
140 PROG DESIGN 2                 .   .   .   .   .   .   .   .   )=========================).  .   .
150 SCREEN DISPLAY 1              .   )=================================).  .   .   .   .   .   .   .   .
160 SCREEN DISPL2                 .   .   .   .   .   .   .   .   )=========================).  .   .
170 SCREEN DISP3                  .   .   .   .   .   .   .   .   .   .   .   .   .   .   )===========
180 DRAFT PLAN 1                  .   )=================================).  .   .   .   .   .   .   .   .
190 DRAFT PLAN 2                  .   .   .   .   .   .   .   .   .   .   .   .   )=================).  .
195 MILESTONE 3                   .   .   .   .   .   .   .   .   .   .   .   .   .   .   .   .   .   .
200 DRAFT PLAN 3                  .   .   .   .   .   .   .   .   .   .   .   .   .   .   )===========
210 FINAL PLAN                    .   .   .   .   .   .   .   .   .   .   .   .   .   .   .   .   .   .
220 PROTOTYPE 1                   .   )=================================).  .   .   .   .   .   .   .   .
230 PROTOTYPE 2                   .   .   .   .   .   .   .   .   )=========================).  .   .
240 PROTOTYPE 3                   .   .   .   .   .   .   .   .   .   .   .   .   .   .   )===========
250 PROTOTYPE 4                   .   .   .   .   .   .   .   .   .   .   .   .   .   .   .   .   .   .
260 OPERATIONAL MODULE            .   .   .   .   .   .   .   .   .   .   .   .   .   .   .   .   .   .
270 DRAFT USER MANUAL             .   )=================================).  .   .   .   .   .   .   .   .
280 FINAL USER MANUAL             .   .   .   .   .   .   .   .   .   .   .   .   .   .   .   .   .   .
290 PROGRAMMER'S GUIDE            .   )=================================).  .   .   .   .   .   .   .   .
300 PROG GUIDE 2                  .   .   .   .   .   .   .   .   )=========================).  .   .
310 PROG GUIDE 3                  .   .   .   .   .   .   .   .   .   .   .   .   .   .   )===========
320 PROG GUIDE 4                  .   .   .   .   .   .   .   .   .   .   .   .   .   .   .   .   .   .
330 FINAL PROG GUIDE              .   .   .   .   .   .   .   .   .   .   .   .   .   .   .   .   .   .
340 TRAINING PREPARATION          .   .   .   .   .   .   .   .   .   .   .   .   .   .   .   .   .   .
350 TRAINING USERS                .   .   .   .   .   .   .   .   .   .   .   .   .   .   .   .   .   .
360 MAINT TNG PREPARATION         .   .   .   .   .   .   .   .   .   .   .   .   .   .   .   .   .   .
370 TNG MAINT USERS               .   .   .   .   .   .   .   .   .   .   .   .   .   .   .   .   .   .
380 PROGRAM REVIEW                0===============================================================

SYMBOL DEFINITIONS:

    O PROJECT START        )===) CRITICAL
    S DATE DEPENDENCY      )---) NON-CRITICAL
    X TERMINATOR           ....) SLACK
    * MILESTONE            ):::) FINISHED
```

```
MICROSOFTWARE                    FEB     MAR             APR             MAY             JUN
--------------------------------- 17  24  2   9   16  23  30  6   13  20  27  4   11  18  25  1   8   15  22
CODE        JOB NAME              19  20  21  22  23  24  25  26  27  28  29  30  31  32  33  34  35  36  37

100 INITIAL MEETING               .   .   .   .   .   .   .   .   .   .   .   .   .   .   .   .   .   .   .
105 MILESTONE 1                   .   .   .   .   .   .   .   .   .   .   .   .   .   .   .   .   .   .   .
110 SYSTEM ANALYSIS               .   .   .   .   .   .   .   .   .   .   .   .   .   .   .   .   .   .   .
130 PROG DESIGN 1                 .   .   .   .   .   .   .   .   .   .   .   .   .   .   .   .   .   .   .
135 MILESTONE 2                   .   .   .   .   .   .   .   .   .   .   .   .   .   .   .   .   .   .   .
140 PROG DESIGN 2                 .   .   .   .   .   .   .   .   .   .   .   .   .   .   .   .   .   .   .
150 SCREEN DISPLAY 1              .   .   .   .   .   .   .   .   .   .   .   .   .   .   .   .   .   .   .
160 SCREEN DISPL2                 .   .   .   .   .   .   .   .   .   .   .   .   .   .   .   .   .   .   .
170 SCREEN DISP3                  ====X.  .   .   .   .   .   .   .   .   .   .   .   .   .   .   .   .   .
180 DRAFT PLAN 1                  .   .   .   .   .   .   .   .   .   .   .   .   .   .   .   .   .   .   .
190 DRAFT PLAN 2                  .   .   .   .   .   .   .   .   .   .   .   .   .   .   .   .   .   .   .
195 MILESTONE 3                   .   *   .   .   .   .   .   .   .   .   .   .   .   .   .   .   .   .   .
200 DRAFT PLAN 3                  =========).  .   .   .   .   .   .   .   .   .   .   .   .   .   .   .   .
210 FINAL PLAN                    .   .   )=========================================).  .   .   .   .   .
220 PROTOTYPE 1                   .   .   .   .   .   .   .   .   .   .   .   .   .   .   .   .   .   .   .
230 PROTOTYPE 2                   .   .   .   .   .   .   .   .   .   .   .   .   .   .   .   .   .   .   .
240 PROTOTYPE 3                   =========).  .   .   .   .   .   .   .   .   .   .   .   .   .   .   .   .
250 PROTOTYPE 4                   .   .   )=================================).  .   .   .   .   .   .   .
260 OPERATIONAL MODULE            .   .   .   .   .   .   .   .   .   .   )==============================
270 DRAFT USER MANUAL             ===================================).  .   .   .   .   .   .   .   .   .
280 FINAL USER MANUAL             .   .   .   .   .   .   .   .   .   .   )==============================
290 PROGRAMMER'S GUIDE            .   .   .   .   .   .   .   .   .   .   .   .   .   .   .   .   .   .   .
300 PROG GUIDE 2                  .   .   .   .   .   .   .   .   .   .   .   .   .   .   .   .   .   .   .
310 PROG GUIDE 3                  =========).  .   .   .   .   .   .   .   .   .   .   .   .   .   .   .   .
320 PROG GUIDE 4                  .   .   )==============================================================
330 FINAL PROG GUIDE              .   .   .   .   .   .   .   .   .   .   .   .   .   .   .   .   .   .   .
340 TRAINING PREPARATION          .   .   )==============================================================
350 TRAINING USERS                .   .   .   .   .   .   .   .   .   .   .   .   .   .   .   .   .   .   .
360 MAINT TNG PREPARATION         .   .   )==============================================================
370 TNG MAINT USERS               .   .   .   .   .   .   .   .   .   .   .   .   .   .   .   .   .   .   .
380 PROGRAM REVIEW                ===============================================================================
```

Figure 12.5. Software development schedule.

```
MICROSOFTWARE              JUN  JUL                 AUG                      SEP                OCT
----------------------------- 29   6   13  20  27   3   10  17  24  31   7   14  21  28   5   12
CODE         JOB NAME        38   39  40  41  42   43  44  45  46  47   48  49  50  51  52  53

100 INITIAL MEETING
105 MILESTONE 1
110 SYSTEM ANALYSIS
130 PROG DESIGN 1
135 MILESTONE 2
140 PROG DESIGN 2
150 SCREEN DISPLAY 1
160 SCREEN DISPL2
170 SCREEN DISP3
180 DRAFT PLAN 1
190 DRAFT PLAN 2
195 MILESTONE 3
200 DRAFT PLAN 3
210 FINAL PLAN
220 PROTOTYPE 1
230 PROTOTYPE 2
240 PROTOTYPE 3
250 PROTOTYPE 4
260 OPERATIONAL MODULE     ====X.
270 DRAFT USER MANUAL
280 FINAL USER MANUAL      ===============X.
290 PROGRAMMER'S GUIDE
300 PROG GUIDE 2
310 PROG GUIDE 3
320 PROG GUIDE 4           ========================).
330 FINAL PROG GUIDE                           )===============================X.
340 TRAINING PREPARATION   ====================).
350 TRAINING USERS                    )===X.
360 MAINT TNG PREPARATION  ====================).
370 TNG MAINT USERS                   )===X.
380 PROGRAM REVIEW         ======================================================X.
```

SYMBOL DEFINITIONS:

O PROJECT START	)===)	CRITICAL
S DATE DEPENDENCY	)---)	NON-CRITICAL
X TERMINATOR	....)	SLACK
* MILESTONE	):::)	FINISHED

Figure 12.5. *(Continued)*

11. Ability to view graphic output of calculated results rapidly
12. Ability to print out cost estimate results in flexible tabular report format and to plot graphic results

Each of the preceding design considerations will be implemented in an environment of easy interaction and conversational interface with the user. The software will be configured to flow with the estimating process and to relate to the user in a natural and transparent manner to permit the estimator to concentrate on doing the estimate rather than on operating the computer. The estimator will be able to proceed stepwise through the 12 basic steps of estimating as shown in Figure 12.1 or will be able to enter an existing estimate at any step to make modifications as necessary.

12.5.1.3 The Module Design.

The cost estimating module will use submodules of the existing estimating software packages and new modules developed specifically to meet the program office estimator's environmental requirements. The design will include the following:

☐ Menu-driven selection of major functions and menu director
☐ Spreadsheet-style input of data
☐ On-screen display of estimate results
☐ Color graphic viewing of estimate trends
☐ Flexible tabular cost estimate output reports
☐ Plotting of estimate trend graphs and histograms

TABLE 12.1. Microsoftware Total Cost by Work Element

Job	Name	Total Cost	Current Date: 12-20-87
100	Initial meeting	8,393.00	
105	Milestone 1	0.00	
110	System analysis	32,218.00	
130	Prog. design 1	20,619.60	
135	Milestone 2	0.00	
140	Prog. design 2	25,996.00	
150	Screen display 1	8,321.20	
160	Screen displ 2	7,671.20	
170	Screen displ 3	19,888.00	
180	Draft plan 1	8,405.20	
190	Draft plan 2	7,645.20	
195	Milestone 3	0.00	
200	Draft plan 3	11,600.00	
210	Final plan	32,894.00	
220	Prototype 1	25,312.00	
230	Prototype 2	20,122.00	
240	Prototype 3	21,585.00	
250	Prototype 4	40,429.00	
260	Operational module	72,272.00	
270	Draft user manual	14,580.00	
280	Final user manual	19,626.00	
290	Programmer's guide	7,601.60	
300	Prog. guide 2	4,781.60	
310	Prog. guide 3	4,951.60	
320	Prog. guide 4	26,491.60	
330	Final prog. guide	36,088.00	
340	Training preparation	7,503.00	
350	Training users	3,754.00	
360	Maint. tng. preparation	12,256.00	
370	Tng. maint. users	4,054.00	
380	Program review	13,631.00	
		518,689.80	

Job	Name	Labor	Units Cost	Other	Units Cost	Total Cost
100	Initial meeting	168.00	5,455.00	15.00	2,938.00	8,393.00
105	Milestone 1	0.00	0.00	0.00	0.00	0.00
110	System analysis	898.00	24,260.00	23.43	7,958.00	32,218.00
130	Prog. design 1	707.60	18,715.60	2.38	1,904.00	20,619.60
135	Milestone 2	0.00	0.00	0.00	0.00	0.00
140	Prog. design 2	869.00	21,440.00	18.38	4,556.00	25,996.00
150	Screen display 1	327.00	7,710.00	0.76	611.20	8,321.20
160	Screen displ 2	286.00	7,060.00	0.76	611.20	7,671.20
170	Screen disp 3	782.00	19,280.00	0.76	608.00	19,888.00
180	Draft plan 1	357.00	8,010.00	0.49	395.20	8,405.20
190	Draft plan 2	305.00	7,250.00	0.49	395.20	7,645.20
195	Milestone 3	0.00	0.00	0.00	0.00	0.00
200	Draft plan 3	481.00	11,208.00	0.49	392.00	11,600.00
210	Final plan	1,024.50	25,150.00	9.68	7,744.00	32,894.00
220	Prototype 1	918.00	21,820.00	4.36	3,492.00	25,312.00
230	Prototype 2	679.00	16,630.00	4.36	3,492.00	20,122.00
240	Prototype 3	733.00	18,093.00	4.36	3,492.00	21,585.00
250	Prototype 4	1,437.50	34,675.00	16.36	5,754.00	40,429.00
260	Operational module	2,770.00	66,850.00	15.95	5,422.00	72,272.00
270	Draft user manual	561.00	12,428.00	2.69	2,152.00	14,580.00
280	Final user manual	847.00	18,890.00	0.92	736.00	19,626.00
290	Programmer's guide	288.00	6,960.00	0.80	641.60	7,601.60
300	Prog. guide 2	180.00	4,140.00	0.80	641.60	4,781.60
310	Prog. guide 3	191.00	4,310.00	0.80	641.60	4,951.60
320	Prog. guide 4	1,095.50	25,850.00	0.80	641.60	26,491.60
330	Final prog. guide	1,653.50	34,760.00	1.66	1,328.00	36,088.00
340	Training preparation	326.50	6,175.00	1.66	1,328.00	7,503.00
350	Training users	35.00	680.00	20.04	3,074.00	3,754.00
360	Maint. tng. preparation	538.00	11,336.00	1.15	920.00	12,256.00
370	Tng. maint. users	45.00	980.00	20.04	3,074.00	4,054.00
380	Program review	368.00	7,935.00	24.10	5,696.00	13,631.00
		18,871.10	448,050.60	193.51	70,639.20	518,689.80

TABLE 12.3. Microsoftware Total Project Cost Summary Including G&A and Fee: Parametric Cost Estimating Module

Week Number	1	2	3	4	5	6	7	8
Man-Weeks								
Project manager	40	42.07	42.07	42.07	42.07	42.07	42.07	42.07
Cost estimator	20	23.43	23.43	23.43	23.43	27.43	27.43	29.43
Cost analyst	20	21.7	21.7	15.7	15.7	19.7	19.7	23.7
·Qual. ctrl. cost est.	20	3.14	3.14	3.14	3.14	3.14	3.14	3.14
Statistical eng.	10	21.43	5.43	5.43	5.43	5.43	5.43	5.43
Chief programmer.	40	52.43	52.43	52.43	52.43	52.43	52.43	52.43
Programmer.	0	160	160	160	160	160	160	160
Sys. analyst	20	20	20	20	20	20	20	20
Tech. writer	1	40	40	40	40	40	40	40
Clerical	5	80	80	80	80	80	80	80
Total units	176	464.2	448.2	442.2	442.2	450.2	450.2	456.2
Total labor costs	$5,590.00	$11,611.95	$11,131.95	$10,891.95	$10,891.95	$11,211.95	$11,211.95	$11,451.95
Travel	$1,872.00	$0.00	$0.00	$0.00	$0.00	$0.00	$0.00	$0.00
Computer lease	$80.00	$13,540.00	$0.00	$0.00	$0.00	$0.00	$0.00	$0.00
Car rental	$234.00	$0.00	$0.00	$0.00	$0.00	$0.00	$0.00	$0.00
Trip expense	$832.00	$0.00	$0.00	$0.00	$0.00	$0.00	$0.00	$0.00
Total other	$3,018.00	$13,540.00	$0.00	$0.00	$0.00	$0.00	$0.00	$0.00
Subtotals	$8,608.00	$25,151.95	$11,131.95	$10,891.95	$10,891.95	$11,211.95	$11,211.95	$11,451.95
G&A at 3%	$258.24	$754.56	$333.96	$326.76	$326.76	$336.36	$336.36	$343.56
Subtotal	$8,866.24	$25,906.51	$11,465.91	$11,218.71	$11,218.71	$11,548.31	$11,548.31	$11,795.5
Fee at 12%	$1,063.95	$3,108.78	$1,375.91	$1,346.25	$1,346.25	$1,385.80	$1,385.80	$1,415.4
Grand total	$9,930.19	$29,015.29	$12,841.82	$12,564.95	$12,564.95	$12,934.11	$12,934.11	$13,210.9

☐ Easy file handling for copying, erasing, or creating new estimates
☐ Transfer of data between estimates
☐ Six parametric equation forms plus a user-defined form
☐ Manipulation (creation, copying, deletion) and editing of selected data bases
☐ Computation of statistical coefficients
☐ Error checking and messages
☐ Help message screens
☐ Full mathematical function capability
☐ Learning curve analysis (lot quantities, identification of discontinuities, changes in slope, comparison)

A schedule for accomplishment of the work is shown in Figure 12.5.
Six parametric equation forms are used in the program for use in organizing

9	10	11	12	13	14	15	16
42.07	40	40	40	40	40	40	40
29.43	22	20	20	20	20	22	20
23.7	9	10	13	13	13	13	20
3.14	4	4	4	4	4	4	4
5.43	4	4	4	4	4	4	4
52.43	45	45	45	45	45	45	40
160	140	140	140	140	140	140	140
20	20	20	20	20	20	20	20
40	40	40	40	40	40	40	40
80	80	80	80	80	80	80	80
456.2	404	403	406	406	406	408	408
$11,451.95	$9,760.00	$9,720.00	$9,840.00	$9,840.00	$9,840.00	$9,920.00	$9,970.00
$2,340.00	$0.00	$0.00	$0.00	$0.00	$0.00	$1,404.00	$0.00
$0.00	$7,044.00	$0.00	$0.00	$0.00	$0.00	$0.00	$5,133.60
$234.00	$0.00	$0.00	$0.00	$0.00	$0.00	$312.00	$0.00
$1,040.00	$0.00	$0.00	$0.00	$0.00	$0.00	$936.00	$0.00
$3,614.00	$7,044.00	$0.00	$0.00	$0.00	$0.00	$2,652.00	$5,133.60
$15,065.95	$16,804.00	$9,720.00	$9,840.00	$9,840.00	$9,840.00	$12,572.00	$15,103.60
$451.98	$504.12	$291.60	$295.20	$295.20	$295.20	$377.16	$453.11
$15,517.93	$17,308.12	$10,011.60	$10,135.20	$10,135.20	$10,135.20	$12,949.16	$15,556.71
$1,862.15	$2,076.97	$1,201.39	$1,216.22	$1,216.22	$1,216.22	$1,553.90	$1,866.80
$17,380.08	$19,385.09	$11,212.99	$11,351.42	$11,351.42	$11,351.42	$14,503.06	$17,423.51

and analyzing data and estimating future performance. The six equation forms follow:

- ☐ $Y = ax^b$
- ☐ $Y = ae^{xt}$
- ☐ $Y = a + bx + cz$
- ☐ $Y = ax + x^b$
- ☐ $Y = ax^b + cz$
- ☐ A user-defined equation capability

For each of these equations, the program module will be able to derive and compare the following appropriate parameters related to goodness of fit:

TABLE 12.3. *(Continued)*

Week Number	17	18	19	20	21	22	23	24
Man-Weeks								
Project manager	40	40	40	40	20	40	40	4●
Cost estimator	15	15	15	15	15	12.5	12.5	12.5
Cost analyst	20	20	20	20	10	10	9	1●
Qual. ctrl. cost est.	4	4	4	4	4	4	4	
Statistical eng.	4	4	4	4	2	4	4	
Chief programmer.	40	40	40	40	30	40	40	4●
Programmer.	140	140	140	140	160	160	160	16●
Sys. analyst	20	20	20	20	10	10	10	1●
Tech. writer	40	40	40	40	15	40	40	4●
Clerical	80	80	80	80	80	80	80	8●
Total units	403	403	403	403	346	400.5	399.5	400.5
Total labor costs	$9,770.00	$9,770.00	$9,770.00	$9,770.00	$8,040.00	$9,500.00	$9,460.00	$9,500.0●
Travel	$0.00	$0.00	$0.00	$0.00	$0.00	$1,404.00	$0.00	$0.0●
Computer lease	$0.00	$0.00	$0.00	$0.00	$0.00	$5,101.60	$3,216.00	$968.0●
Car rental	$0.00	$0.00	$0.00	$0.00	$0.00	$156.00	$0.00	$0.0●
Trip expense	$0.00	$0.00	$0.00	$0.00	$0.00	$312.00	$0.00	$0.0●
Total other	$0.00	$0.00	$0.00	$0.00	$0.00	$6,973.60	$3,216.00	$968.0●
Subtotals	$9,770.00	$9,770.00	$9,770.00	$9,770.00	$8,040.00	$16,473.60	$12,676.00	$10,468.0●
G&A at 3%	$293.10	$293.10	$293.10	$293.10	$241.20	$494.21	$380.28	$314.0●
Subtotal	$10,063.10	$10,063.10	$10,063.10	$10,063.10	$8,281.20	$16,967.81	$13,056.28	$10,782.0
Fee at 12%	$1,207.57	$1,207.57	$1,207.57	$1,207.57	$993.74	$2,036.14	$1,566.75	$1,293.8
Grand total	$11,270.67	$11,270.67	$11,270.67	$11,270.67	$9,274.94	$19,003.94	$14,623.03	$12,075.8●

☐ Correlation matrix
☐ Coefficient of determination
☐ Coefficient of correlation
☐ F-value
☐ Degrees of freedom

12.5.2 Estimation of Resource Requirements

Job 100: Initial Meeting: Shall be preceded by 168 hours of detail work designed to present an encompassing plan for the total structure of the overall project including a rough draft of the program flow, sample screen layouts, and an analysis of the cost estimating problem.

Job 110: System/Subsystem Analysis Module: Shall be preceded by 1600 hours of detailed analysis and review resulting in critical path flow charts of the program

25	26	27	28	29	30	31	32
40	40	40	40	40	40	40	40
12.5	12.5	12.5	12.5	12.5	12.5	12.5	12.5
10	12	10	10	10	0	0	0
4	4	4	4	4	4	4	4
4	4	4	4	4	4	4	4
40	40	40	41	41	39	39	39
158	158	158	158	158	200	200	200
10	10	10	10	10	0	2	0
40	40	40	40	40	40	40	40
80	80	80	80	80	80	80	80
398.5	400.5	398.5	399.5	399.5	419.5	421.5	419.5
$9,451.00	$9,531.00	$9,451.00	$9,481.00	$9,481.00	$9,790.00	$9,842.00	$9,790.00
$0.00	$0.00	$0.00	$0.00	$1,404.00	$0.00	$0.00	$0.00
$968.00	$968.00	$968.00	$968.00	$968.00	$3,896.00	$0.00	$0.00
$0.00	$0.00	$0.00	$0.00	$234.00	$0.00	$0.00	$0.00
$0.00	$0.00	$0.00	$0.00	$624.00	$0.00	$0.00	$0.00
$968.00	$968.00	$968.00	$968.00	$3,230.00	$3,896.00	$0.00	$0.00
$10,419.00	$10,499.00	$10,419.00	$10,449.00	$12,711.00	$13,686.00	$9,842.00	$9,790.00
$312.57	$314.97	$312.57	$313.47	$381.33	$410.58	$295.26	$293.70
$10,731.57	$10,813.97	$10,731.57	$10,762.47	$13,092.33	$14,096.58	$10,137.26	$10,083.70
$1,287.79	$1,297.68	$1,287.79	$1,291.50	$1,571.08	$1,691.59	$1,216.47	$1,210.04
$12,019.36	$12,111.65	$12,019.36	$12,053.97	$14,663.41	$15,788.17	$11,353.73	$11,293.74

with all inherent design features. Additionally, at this meeting, milestones of the program design as outlined and developed by the programmers will be available for review.

Jobs 130 and 140: Program Design Analysis Report: Shall be preceded by 1550 hours of current hardware capabilities analysis and a recommendation of the language for software development. Sample coding and documentation of available languages will be available for evaluation. Compatibility problems currently existing between Microcomputers will be reviewed with the latest solutions insured to minimize cost and maximize performance of the equipment.

Jobs 150, 160, and 170: Preliminary Screen Displays: Screen displays will be based upon concurrent efforts made at Jobs 110 and 130. An additional 800 hours of detailed work has been designed to produce easy-to-use screens and helpful responses for the user. The screens demonstrated will be the final version. A detailed structure of all screens with support documentation will be reviewed. Full

TABLE 12.3. *(Continued)*

Week Number	33	34	35	36	37	38	39	40
Man-Weeks								
Project manager	40	40	40	40	40	40	40	40
Cost estimator	12.5	12.5	12.5	12.5	12.5	12.5	12.5	12.5
Cost analyst	2	0	0	0	2	0	0	0
Qual. ctrl. cost est.	4	4	4	4	4	4	4	4
Statistical eng.	4	4	4	4	4	4	8	0
Chief programmer.	39	39	39	39	39	39	39	40
Programmer.	200	200	200	200	200	200	200	80
Sys. analyst	0	0	2	0	0	0	2	0
Tech. writer	40	40	40	40	40	40	40	40
Clerical	80	80	75	75	75	80	80	80
Total units	421.5	419.5	416.5	414.5	416.5	419.5	425.5	296.5
Total labor costs	$9,870.00	$9,790.00	$9,790.00	$9,740.00	$9,820.00	$9,790.00	$9,962.00	$6,760.00
Travel	$0.00	$1,404.00	$0.00	$0.00	$0.00	$0.00	$1,404.00	$0.00
Computer lease	$0.00	$0.00	$0.00	$0.00	$0.00	$0.00	$0.00	$0.00
Car rental	$0.00	$156.00	$0.00	$0.00	$0.00	$0.00	$234.00	$0.00
Trip expense	$0.00	$312.00	$0.00	$0.00	$0.00	$0.00	$624.00	$0.00
Total other	$0.00	$1,872.00	$0.00	$0.00	$0.00	$0.00	$2,262.00	$0.00
Subtotals	$9,870.00	$11,662.00	$9,792.00	$9,740.00	$9,820.00	$9,790.00	$12,224.00	$6,760.00
G&A at 3%	$296.10	$349.86	$293.76	$292.20	$294.60	$293.70	$366.72	$202.80
Subtotal	$10,166.10	$12,011.86	$10,085.76	$10,032.20	$10,114.60	$10,083.70	$12,590.72	$6,962.80
Fee at 12%	$1,219.93	$1,441.42	$1,210.29	$1,203.86	$1,213.75	$1,210.04	$1,510.89	853.54
Grand total	$11,386.03	$13,453.28	$11,296.05	$11,236.06	$11,328.35	$11,293.74	$14,101.61	$7,798.34

utilization of existing function and special command keys available to configuration hardware will be demonstrated.

Jobs 180, 190, 200, and 210: Test Plans: For review in Jobs 110 through 170, 650 hours have already been dedicated. Also, 500 hours on reviewing and implementing customer comments will be expended prior to completion of Job 200. A walk-through of the program module will be demonstrated with a review of the rationale for data base operation and formula usage. Final form will be developed 1000 hours after this review stage is reached.

Jobs 220–260: Module Development and Demonstration: 51,222.5 hours have been estimated for prototype development and operational module completion.

Jobs 270 and 280: User Manual: The user manual will fall into two periods. The first will require 550 man-hours and fall under four customer review periods. The final version will require 850 man-hours and consist of a Quick Reference

41	42	43	44	45	46	47	48
40	40	40	40	30	30	30	30
12.5	12.5	12.5	12.5	5	5	5	5
2	0	0	0	2	0	0	0
2	2	2	2	1	1	1	1
0	0	0	0	0	0	0	0
40	20	20	20	20	20	20	20
80	80	80	80	60	60	60	60
0	0	2	0	0	0	2	0
40	40	40	40	40	40	40	40
80	80	80	80	80	80	80	80
296.5	274.5	276.5	274.5	238	236	238	236
$6,790.00	$6,110.00	$6,162.00	$6,110.00	$5,025.00	$4,945.00	$4,997.00	$4,945.00
$0.00	$0.00	$2,808.00	$0.00	$0.00	$0.00	$0.00	$0.00
$0.00	$0.00	$64.00	$1,328.00	$0.00	$0.00	$0.00	$0.00
$0.00	$0.00	$780.00	$0.00	$0.00	$0.00	$0.00	$0.00
$0.00	$0.00	$2,496.00	$0.00	$0.00	$0.00	$0.00	$0.00
$0.00	$0.00	$6,148.00	$1,328.00	$0.00	$0.00	$0.00	$0.00
$5,790.00	$6,110.00	$12,310.00	$7,438.00	$5,025.00	$4,945.00	$4,997.00	$4,945.00
$203.70	$183.30	$369.30	$223.14	$150.75	$148.35	$149.91	$148.35
$6,993.70	$6,293.30	$12,679.30	$7,661.14	$5,175.75	$5,093.35	$5,146.91	$5,093.35
$839.24	$755.20	$1,521.52	$919.34	$621.09	$611.20	$617.63	$611.20
$7,832.94	$7,048.50	$14,200.82	$8,580.48	$5,796.84	$5,704.55	$5,764.54	$5,704.55

Guide (QRG), a tutorial section for novice and advanced users, and a technical user section.

Jobs 290–330: Programmer's Guide: Allocation has been made of 3000 hours for developing a programmer's guide in hard copy and documented in the source code. Detailed instructions will be provided in every module with a structure showing the dependency and interdependency of each application.

Jobs 340–370: System Training: Training for users will take 350 man-hours and include overhead view graphs, computer simulation programs, and a tutorial disk for computer-assisted instruction. ADP personnel training will require 575 man-hours and will feature the same training material as user training with courseware geared for support of existing program.

Job 380: Status Reporting: Status reports will be periodically made to management and to the customer. Reporting requirements are estimated at 3312 hours.

TABLE 12.3. *(Continued)*

Week Number	49	50	51	52	53	Grand Total
Man-Weeks						
Project manager	30	20	0	2	2	1930.6
Cost estimator	5	5	0	0	2	765.9
Cost analyst	2	0	0	0	2	455.6
Qual. ctrl. cost est.	2	1	0	0	1	185.1
Statistical eng.	0	0	0	0	0	191.4
Chief Programmer.	20	20	1	1	2	1935.4
Programmer.	60	60	0	0	0	7010.0
Sys. analyst	0	0	0	0	0	500.0
Tech. writer	40	40	1	0	10	1947.0
Clerical	80	80	0	0	40	3950.0
Total units	239	226	2	3	59	18871.1
Total labor costs	$5,050.00	$4,595.00	$50.00	$100.00	$915.00	$448,050.60
Travel	$0.00	$0.00	$0.00	$0.00	$1,404.00	$15,444.00
Computer lease	$0.00	$0.00	$0.00	$0.00	$0.00	$45,211.20
Car rental	$0.00	$0.00	$0.00	$0.00	$156.00	$2,496.00
Trip expense	$0.00	$0.00	$0.00	$0.00	$312.00	$7,488.00
Total other	$0.00	$0.00	$0.00	$0.00	$1,872.00	$70,639.20
Subtotals	$5,050.00	$4,596.00	$50.00	$100.00	$2,787.00	$518,689.80
G&A at 3%	$151.50	$137.85	$1.50	$3.00	$83.61	$15,560.69
Subtotal	$5,201.50	$4,732.85	$51.50	$103.00	$2,870.61	$534.250.49
Fee at 12%	$624.18	$567.94	$6.18	$12.36	$344.47	$64,110.06
Grand total	$5,825.68	$5,300.79	$57.68	$115.36	$3,215.08	$598,360.55

12.5.3 Cost Estimate Outputs

Table 12.1 shows total costs by work element; Table 12.2 shows the number of units of labor and other resources as well as the total costs; and Table 12.3 shows the total cost for each week including G&A and fee or profit. Notice the estimated hours each week for each skill at the top of Table 12.3.

The foregoing description has been an example of a *detailed* software cost estimate.

12.6 SUMMARY

In summary, there are two basic methods of estimating the costs of a software project, the detail estimating method and the parametric method. The detail estimating method requires greater project definition but tends to be more accurate and credible, whereas the parametric method requires less detail but may not be as accurate. The ideal estimating situation is to use both methods and cross-check their results. If large deviations exist, the ground rules and assumptions for each estimate should be thoroughly reviewed for inconsistencies. As the state of the art of cost estimating improves, and as software estimating techniques, methods, and data become more sophisticated and readily available, software cost estimating will become more of a skill and less of an art. Look for some exciting computer-assisted estimating systems for software cost estimation in the very near future and continuation of developments in this ever-expanding field.

REFERENCES

1. Bohm, B. W. *Software Engineering Economics*. Prentice-Hall, Englewood Cliffs, N.J., 1981.

2. Putnam, L. H., and R. M. Cline. "The SLIM Software Cost and Schedule Estimating Model." Proceedings of the 1984 Summer Simulation Conference, Society for Computer Simulation, Boston, Mass., 1984.

3. Mc Kenzie, M., et al. "A Dynamic-System Simulation Model of the Software Development Process." Jet Propulsion Laboratory, Pasadena, Cal., 1984.

4. LaBolle, V. *The Development of Equations for Estimating the Costs of Computer Program Production*. USAF, ESD, 1966.

5. Weinwurm, G. F. *Data Elements for a Cost Reporting System for Computer Program Development*. USAF, ESD, 1966.

6. Fleishman, T. *Current Results from the Analysis of Cost Data for Computer Programming*. USAF, ESD, 1966.

7. Aron, J. D. "Estimating Resources for Large Programming Systems." In Report on a Conference Sponsored by NATO Science Committee, Rome, Italy, October 1969.

8. Wolverton, R. W. "The Cost of Developing Large-Scale Software." *IEEE Transactions on Computers*, Vol. C-23, No. 6, 615-636 (June 1974).

9. Black, R. K. E., R. P. Curnow, R. Katz, and M. D. Gray, "BCS Software Production Data." RADC-TR-77-116 (AD-A039852), Appendix B, March 1977.

10. Walston, C. E. and C. P. Felix, "A Method of Programming Measurement and Estimation." *IBM Systems Journal*, Vol. 16, No. 1, 54-73 (1977).

11. Herd, J. R., J. N. Postak, W. E. Russell, and K. R. Stewart, *Software Cost Estimation Study: Study Results*, Vol. 1 (of two). Final Technical Report, RADC-TR-77-220 (AD-A042264), Doty Associates, Inc., Rockville, Md., June 1977.

12. James, J. H. "Validation of Source Software Cost Estimation Models." Proceedings of the 1984 Summer Computer Simulation Conference, Society for Computer Simulation, 1984.

13

ASPECTS AFFECTING COST ESTIMATION IN GOVERNMENT PROCUREMENT

RICHARD H. SHUFORD, JR., DBA

13.1 FEDERAL GOVERNMENT PHILOSOPHIES AND POLICIES

"Direct procurement expenditures by Federal agencies continue to account for approximately one-fifth of the total Federal budget and involve over 130,000 Federal employees. In FY 1984, Federal Government contracting totaled more than $190 billion and consisted of over 21 million contracting actions, as compared with 1975 . . . when $56 billion was spent through the Federal Procurement process." [1]

13.1.1 Governmental Perspective

The federal government uses its procurement process for several purposes: (1) to acquire supplies and services for governmental purposes, (2) to enhance the enforcement of specific labor laws by requiring compliance by government contractors, (3) to reduce high-density unemployment by awarding to contractors in areas meeting specific criteria, (4) to promote small businesses through set-aside portions of total procurement buy requirements, (5) to promote research and accelerate the development of advanced technologies, (6) to maintain an industrial base capable of rapid expansion, (7) to support federal prison industries, (8) to enhance competition, (9) to support foreign military and economic assistance, and (10) to promote small and minority business subcontracting. These multiple purposes and federal sovereignty result in the process of federal procurement being different in many respects from common commercial practices. Cost estimates pertaining to contracts awarded under the federal procurement process cannot in most cases be as precisely inclusive as commercial practices may permit.

498

13.1.2 General Statutory Requirements

The modern statutes governing federal procurement came into being following disclosure of improper and fraudulent practices during World War II. Much of the current approach to contracting in the federal government was established by two acts: (1) The Armed Services Procurement Act of 1947, which governed the procurement systems of the Department of Defense, the U. S. Coast Guard, and, later, the National Aeronautics and Space Administration and (2) Title III of the Federal Property and Administrative Service Act of 1949, which governed the procurement systems of most federal civilian agencies. Numerous regulations were promulgated from these statutes, with the Armed Services Procurement Regulation (ASPR) being the most comprehensive. Subsequently, ASPR was redesignated as the Defense Acquisition Regulation (DAR) [2], which is structured now in keeping with the overall Federal Acquisition Regulation (FAR) mentioned later.

Through the years the federal procurement process has not kept pace with changing times and was strongly criticized by the Congress for its inefficiency, ineffectiveness, and resulting waste in federal spending. Under Congressional pressure, there has been established a new, single regulation for use by all federal agencies in the acquisition of supplies and services with appropriated funds. The new regulation is designated as the Federal Acquisition Regulation (FAR) and became effective April 1, 1984 [3].

The FAR was promulgated initially for the Department of Defense, General Services Administration, and the National Aeronautics and Space Administration. The purposes stated for these agencies are to ''(a) produce a clear understandable document that maximizes feasible uniformity in the acquisition process, (b) reduce the proliferation of agency acquisition regulations, (c) implement recommendations made by the Commission on Government Procurement, the Federal Paperwork Commission, various Congressional groups and others, and (d) facilitate agency, industry and public participation in the development and maintenance of the FAR and agency acquisition regulations'' [4].

Public Law 93-400 fixes responsibility with the Administrator for Federal Procurement Policy for the policy direction in the implementation of a single system of government wide procurement regulations, specifically in the procurement of (1) property, other than real property in being; (2) services, including research and development; and (3) construction, alteration, repair, and maintenance of real property.

In addition to these major statutory and regulatory requirements, the federal procurement process is also bound by several other constraints in its contracting relationships.

13.1.3 Broad Policies

Agencies of the federal government are required by Executive Order 11222 of May 8, 1965, and Title 5, Code of Federal Regulations (CFR) 735, to establish standards of conduct for their employees. Broad policies seek to prescribe conduct of employees, relationships of officials as parties to contracts, financial disclosure by selected employees, practices that eliminate competition or restrain trade, and contingent fees for obtaining government contracts.

For several decades the federal government has established as its underlying policy in the procurement process the necessity for contracting officers to obtain competition. The importance of competition lies in the general requirement for procurements to be formally advertised. When advertising is not feasible or practicable, there is authorized, by statute, a group of exception circumstances that permit the use of negotiation. These exceptions to formal advertising authorize that purchases and contracts may be negotiated as follows:

1. If determined to be necessary in the public interest during a national emergency declared by Congress or the President.
2. If the public exigency will not permit the delay incident to advertising.
3. If the aggregate amount involved is not in excess of the applicable small purchase limitation.
4. For personal or professional services.
5. For any service to be rendered by any university, college, or other educational institution.
6. If the supplies or services are to be acquired and used outside the United States, its possessions, its territories, and Puerto Rico.
7. For medicines or medical supplies.
8. For supplies purchased for authorized resale.
9. For perishable or nonperishable subsistence supplies.
10. For supplies or services for which it is impracticable to secure competition by formal advertising.
11. For supplies or services that the agency head determines to be experimental, developmental, or research work, or for making or furnishing supplies for experiment, test, development or research.
12. For supplies or services whose acquisition the agency head determines should not be publicly disclosed because of their character, ingredients, or components.
13. For equipment that the agency head determines to be technical equipment for which (1) standardization and interchangeability of parts are necessary in the public interest and (2) acquisition by negotiation is necessary to ensure that standardization and interchangeability.
14. For supplies or services for which the agency head determines that bid prices received after formal advertising are unreasonable as to all or part of the requirements, or were not independently reached in open competition.
15. If otherwise authorized by law.
16. For technical or special supplies if the agency head determines (1) that they

require a substantial initial investment or an extended period of preparation for manufacture; and (2) that formal advertising (a) would be likely to result in additional cost to the Government because of duplication of investment or (b) would result in duplication of necessary preparation that would delay the acquisition unduly.

17. If the agency head determines that (1) it is in the interest of national defense to have a plant, mine, or other facility, or a producer, manufacturer, or other supplier available for furnishing property or services in case of a national emergency; or (2) the interest of industrial mobilization in case of such an emergency, or the interest of national defense in maintaining active engineering, research, and development would otherwise be subserved [5].

The cost estimator may find these exceptions lengthy, but they tend to reflect many of the policy considerations whereby the cost estimate may be "justified" to the government contracting officers.

13.2 PROCUREMENT PLANNING REQUIREMENTS

The nature of federal governmental operations is such that the executive branch must prepare comprehensive plans for the acquisition of supplies and services. The primary reason is the system of checks and balances provided by the Constitution. The executive branch must provide Congress annually a request for funds to operate the government for the next fiscal year. However, the budget process has become complex and highly structured through the years.

The budget now contains numerous categories and classifications. The Congress has altered earlier submission requirements and now receives from the President a budget consisting of program elements. A program element, for example, is the military construction for the Department of the Army. This would include all funds needed for all construction activities during the covered fiscal year. Single-figure cost estimates for each project at each construction location are indicated in the budget narrative. Most of the cost estimates are prepared at least 18 months in advance of the budget submission, and this means that the requirements determination portion of the process preceded the cost estimate by at least six months.

Although the timetable for the President to submit a budget to Congress is fixed by law, there is no legal timetable for the Congress to complete its hearings, investigations, and enactment of a bill appropriating funds to be used in the budget year. Cost estimates based on current-year dollars are therefore misleading.

13.2.1 Agency Acquisition Plans

Procurement involving large-scale construction projects, major weapon systems, and similar activities that would spend funds over several years have resulted in the program element structure being expanded so that the Congress can see the length and magnitude of the commitment it is making when it authorizes funding.

Thus one now sees agencies preparing acquisition plans for Congressional review that show current-year budget requests and requests for the next four "outyears." An example of this program planning is the Five Year Defense Plan prepared by the Department of Defense (DOD). Within this department, the guidance for major system acquisitions is contained in DOD Directives 5000.1 and 5000.2 [6].

For the cost estimator, the government's planning, programming, and budgeting process results in the need for estimates to include indexing of costs for inflation and deflation adjustments and supporting rationale that is amenable to easy verification.

13.2.2 Annual Budget Cycle

Within the federal government, the Office of Management and Budget is fundamentally responsible for bringing the agency annual budget estimates into a single budget document [7]. Following review and approval by the President, the fiscal year budget is submitted to the Congress and is available to the public, usually each February.

The budget process requires passage by Congress of two separate pieces of legislation. One piece is the authorization bill which permits the Executive Branch to undertake the type of activity contained in the budget request. A second bill is the appropriation bill which provides the funding authority. Typically a program that will extend over several years may be authorized, but it is funded only on an annual basis.

The budget process thus can require a program cost estimate that may extend over the life of the program—sometimes called a life cycle cost estimate. Additionally, there can be a need for the fiscal year cost estimate. Congress has been reluctant to fund programs more than one year at a time since history has shown cost growth, overruns, and faulty performance.

13.2.3 Multiyear Procurements

The DOD, in particular, has been constrained unnecessarily by the annual budget. Many of its major systems involve circumstances in which the productive capacity of the contractor cannot satisfy the total requirement in a year. The contractor is reluctant to proceed into second and third year production because of the uncertainty of Congressional appropriation. Commercial businesses are willing to make these types of multiyear contracts and to gain the cost advantage when multiple start-ups are eliminated.

Multiyear contracting by DOD has gained wider acceptance by the Congress because the Congress now receives the Five Year Defense Plan and conducts hearings with considerable information about the executive branch's intentions for the current year and the four outyears. In the FY 1985 budget, DOD proposed 12 multiyear candidates for a projected savings of $1.1 billion. Of these, nine programs were approved for a projected savings of $1 billion. Since FY 1982, Congress has had 32 programs for multiyear contracts. Currently the FY 1986 budget contains six multiyear candidates for an estimated savings of $1.3 billion [8]. Savings in these examples are computed from reduction or elimination of multiple start-ups, efficiencies in continuous production, and avoidance of multiple procurement administrative costs.

These estimated savings by DOD for "big ticket" items such as the F-16 airframe, Multiple Launch Rocket System (MLRS), and B-1B bomber, represent major attempts by the Congress to cooperate in lowering the defense costs. Many other areas may qualify for multiyear procurement.

O'Brien [9] suggests that candidates for multiyear procurement must have the following attributes to be viable:

1. A significant total cost savings
2. Stable requirements and configuration
3. Stable funding
4. High degree of cost confidence which permits fixed price or fixed price incentive contracting
5. Confidence in the contractor(s) capability.

Section 17.102-3 of the FAR indicates that use of multiyear contracting is encouraged to take advantage of one or more of the following:

1. Lower cost
2. Enhancement of standardization
3. Reduction of administrative burden in the placement and administration of contracts
4. Substantial continuity of production or performance, thus avoiding annual start-up costs, preproduction testing cost, makeready expenses, and phaseout cost
5. Stabilization of contractor work forces
6. Avoidance of the need for establishing and "proving out" quality control techniques and procedures for a new contractor each year
7. Broadening the competitive base with opportunity for participation by firms not otherwise willing or able to compete for lesser quantities, particularly in cases involving high start-up costs
8. Provide incentives to contractors to improve productivity through investment in capital facilities, equipment, and advanced technology.

To qualify for multiyear procurement one of the preceding objectives must be satisfied, and the following criteria must be present:

1. The use of a multiyear contract will result in total reduced costs.
2. The minimum need for the item to be purchased is expected to remain sub-

stantially unchanged during the contemplated contract period in terms of production rate, acquisition rate, and total quantities.

3. There is a reasonable expectation that, throughout the contemplated contract period, the department or agency will request funding for the contract at the level required to avoid contract cancellation.

4. There is a stable design for the item to be acquired, and the technical risks associated with such items are not excessive.

5. The estimates of both the cost of the contract and the anticipated cost avoidance through the use of a multiyear contract are realistic [10].

While the objectives cited and the criteria established for multiyear procurement are desirable and reasonable, a reminder to all contracting officers and agency heads is also given in the FAR. The reminder states "specific statutory authority is needed for an agency to make financial commitments for amounts greater than those appropriated annually by the Congress."

The political realities of the planning, programming, and budgeting process in the federal government are such that generally only "big ticket" items will be multiyear procured. These are the only requirements where an agency head may be willing to "do battle" with the Congress to win approval.

Since the FAR does authorize multiyear procurement and "big ticket" items have been accepted by Congress, perhaps there is a challenge for the cost estimating community to develop a standardized methodology and format for cost estimates acceptable to Congress for lesser-value items. Many governmental requirements are for the same items year after year. Economical lot purchasing with quantity discount price breaks should be standard practice in both government and industry.

13.3 COST ESTIMATION IN GOVERNMENT CONTRACTS

Contracting within the federal government permits the use of a wide variety of contract types. There are two broad classifications of contract types: the fixed-price and the cost-reimbursement contract. In general, the fixed-price contract usually establishes a firm price. It may, however, leave portions of the price open and provide for later adjustment. The fixed-price contract stipulates that the contractor guarantees performance of the contract. The cost-reimbursement contract is used when the scope of work cannot be adequately described for the contractor to guarantee performance.

In former years, the cost-reimbursement contract was widely used in many circumstances where a fixed-price contract, with economic price adjustment, could have been used. The Competition in Contracting Act of 1984 (Public Law 98-369) provides new controls on noncompetitive procurement. In 1984, of all military procurement dollars, 82% were under fixed-price contracts, up from 75% in 1981

[8]. Each of the major contract types and their uses are discussed in the following sections.

13.3.1 Firm-Fixed-Price Contracts

A firm-fixed-price contract provides for a price that is not subject to any adjustment on the basis of the contractor's cost experience in performing the contract. This contract type places on the contractor maximum risk and full responsibility for all costs and resulting profit or loss. It provides maximum incentive for the contractor to control costs and perform effectively and imposes a minimum administrative burden upon the contracting parties.

A firm-fixed-price contract is suitable for acquiring commercial products or commercial-type products or for acquiring other supplies or services on the basis of reasonably definite functional or detailed specifications when the contracting officer can establish fair and reasonable prices at the outset, such as when the following conditions are met:

1. There is adequate price competition.
2. There are reasonable price comparisons with prior purchases of the same or similar supplies or services made on a competitive basis or supported by valid cost or pricing data.
3. Available cost or pricing information permits realistic estimates of the probable costs of performance.
4. Performance uncertainties can be identified and reasonable estimates of their cost impact can be made, and the contractor is willing to accept a firm fixed price representing assumption of the risks involved [11].

The reliability of the cost estimating process is fully tested in the firm-fixed-price contract. The development of the cost estimate should recognize that the contractor bears the entire risk of both cost and performance. Cost control measures are the generally accepted approach to insuring that the contractor achieves the profit estimated prior to the contract award.

13.3.2 Fixed-Price Contracts with Economic Price Adjustment

A fixed-price contract with economic price adjustment provides for upward and downward revision of the stated contract price upon the occurrence of specified contingencies. Economic price adjustments are of the following three general types:

1. Adjustments based on established prices. These price adjustments are based on increases or decreases from an agreed-upon level in published or otherwise established prices of specific items or the contract end items.
2. Adjustments based on actual costs of labor or material. These price adjust-

ments are based on increases or decreases in specified costs of labor or material that the contractor actually experiences during contract performance.

3. Adjustments based on cost indexes of labor or material. These price adjustments are based on increases or decreases in labor or material cost standards or indexes that are specifically identified in the contract.

A fixed-price contract with economic price adjustment may be used when (1) there are serious doubts concerning the stability of market or labor conditions that will exist during an extended period of contract performance, and (2) contingencies that would otherwise be included in the contract price can be identified and covered separately in the contract. Price adjustments based on established prices should normally be restricted to industrywide contingencies. Price adjustments based on labor and material costs should be limited to contingencies beyond the contractor's control. Additional requirements are the following:

1. In establishing the base level from which adjustment will be made, the contracting officer shall ensure that contingency allowances are not duplicated by inclusion in both the base price and the adjustment requested by the contractor under the economic price adjustment clause.

2. In contracts that do not require submission of cost or pricing data, the contracting officer shall obtain adequate information to establish the base level from which adjustment will be made and may require verification of data submitted [12].

When cost elements are subject to significant fluctuation in price, the fixed-price with economic price adjustment (EPA), provides the cost estimator with a viable contract method to accommodate the fluctuation. In this method, the allocation of risk is as follows: (1) the contractor has the risk of the cost of the job minus the costs that are subject to EPA, (2) EPA costs are shared between the government and the contractor, and (3) the contractor has the entire risk of those costs that exceed the EPA ceiling.

13.3.3 Fixed-Price Incentive Contracts

A fixed-price incentive contract is a fixed-price contract that provides for adjusting profit and establishing the final contract price by application of an equation based on the relationship of total final negotiated cost to total target cost. The final price is subject to a price ceiling, negotiated at the outset. A fixed-price incentive contract is appropriate under the following conditions:

1. A firm-fixed-price contract is not suitable.

2. The nature of the supplies or services being acquired and other circumstances of the acquisition are such that the contractor's assumption of a de-

gree of cost responsibility will provide a positive profit incentive for effective cost control and performance.

3. If the contract also includes incentives on technical performance and/or delivery, the performance requirements provide a reasonable opportunity for the incentives to have a meaningful impact on the contractor's management of the work [13].

Incentive contracts are designed to encourage contractors to improve their contract performance in the area of cost and at times in quality and/or delivery schedule performance. The contractor's risks are determined by the following ingredients when there is a single firm target contract: target costs, target profit, price ceiling, and the sharing equation. Initially, the target cost is negotiated as a point within a range of possible actual costs. The target cost is based on a good cost estimate at a point in time that permits both the government and the contractor an equal chance of overrunning or underrunning costs. Minimum costs are the contractor's risk. Between the minimum cost and the target cost there is a shared risk condition, and, finally, the contractor has the risks from the target cost upper limit to the contract ceiling price.

13.3.4 Fixed-Ceiling-Price Contracts with Retroactive Price Redetermination

A fixed-ceiling-price contract with retroactive price redetermination provides for (1) a fixed ceiling price and (2) retroactive price redetermination within the ceiling after completion of the contract. A fixed-ceiling-price contract with retroactive price redetermination is appropriate for research and development contracts estimated at $100,000 or less when it is established at the outset that a fair and reasonable firm-fixed price cannot be negotiated and that the amount involved and short performance period make the use of any other fixed-price contract type impracticable.

1. A ceiling price shall be negotiated for the contract at a level that reflects a reasonable sharing of risk by the contractor. The established ceiling price may be adjusted only if required by the operation of contract clauses providing for equitable adjustment or other revision of the contract price under stated circumstances.
2. The contract should be awarded only after negotiation of a billing price that is as fair and reasonable as the circumstances permit.
3. Since this contract type provides the contractor no cost control incentive except the ceiling price, the contracting officer should make clear to the contractor during discussion before award that the contractor's management effectiveness and ingenuity will be considered in retroactively redetermining the price [14].

This retroactive redetermination contract allows for the final contract price to be negotiated based on work having been completed and the cost of performance being actual, audited costs. All costs are shared risks between the government and contractor up to the ceiling price. The contractor bears complete risks for costs above the ceiling price.

13.3.5 Fixed-Price Contracts with Prospective Price Redetermination

A fixed-price contract with prospective price redetermination provides for (1) a firm fixed price for an initial period of contract deliveries or performance and (2) prospective redetermination, at a stated time or times during performance, of the price for subsequent periods of performance.

A fixed-price contract with prospective price redetermination may be used in acquisitions of quantity production or services for which it is possible to negotiate a fair and reasonable firm fixed price for an initial period, but not for subsequent periods of contract performance.

1. The initial period should be the longest period for which it is possible to negotiate a fair and reasonable firm fixed price. Each subsequent pricing period should be at least 12 months.

2. The contract may provide for a ceiling price based on evaluation of the uncertainties involved in performance and their possible cost impact. This ceiling price should provide for assumption of a reasonable proportion of the risk by the contractor and, once established, may be adjusted only by operation of contract clauses providing for equitable adjustment or other revision of the contract price under stated circumstances [15].

The fixed-price prospective contract can be described as a series of two or more firm-fixed price contracts that are negotiated at fixed times during the performance of the contract. The need for more cost data based on experience is the motivation for creating this type of contract relationship. The contractor has all of the risks for the fixed price in the initial period, but he has the opportunity to negotiate a new price based on new cost information in each period following the initial contract period.

13.3.6 Firm-Fixed-Price, Level-of-Effort Term Contracts

A firm-fixed-price, level-of-effort term contract requires (1) the contractor to provide a specified level of effort, over a stated period of time, on work that can be stated only in general terms and (2) the government to pay the contractor a fixed dollar amount.

A firm-fixed-price, level-of-effort term contract is suitable for investigation or study in a specific research and development area. The product of the contract is usually a report showing the results achieved through application of the required level of effort. However, payment is based on the effort expended rather than on the results achieved [16].

The contractor agrees in advance on the level of effort to be provided, and the government accepts that the contract result cannot be achieved for less than the agreed effort. Therefore the contractor has full allocation of risks within the level of effort provided. The cost estimate must make provision for work that cannot be clearly defined in this type of contract.

13.3.7 Cost-Sharing Contracts

A cost-sharing contract is a cost-reimbursement contract in which the contractor receives no fee and is reimbursed only for an agreed-upon portion of its allowable costs. A cost-sharing contract may be used when the contractor agrees to absorb a portion of the costs in the expectation of substantial compensating benefits [17]. The agreement on the share equation determines the risk assumed by the contractor in a cost-sharing contract. The government's cost risk is reduced only by the shared portion. Since no fee (profit) can be earned by the contractor, the usefulness of this type contract is the benefit of gaining experience that could provide a competitive edge.

13.3.8 Cost-Plus-Incentive-Fee Contracts

The cost-plus-incentive-fee contract is a cost-reimbursement contract that provides for the initially negotiated fee to be adjusted later by an equation based on the relationship of total allowable costs to total target costs. This contract type specifies a target cost, a target fee, minimum and maximum fees, and a fee adjustment equation. After contract performance, the fee payable to the contractor is determined in accordance with the equation. The equation provides, within limits, for increases in fee above target when total allowable costs are less than target costs, and decreases in fee below target fee when total allowable costs exceed target costs. This increase or decrease is intended to provide an incentive for the contractor to manage the contract effectively. When total allowable cost is greater than or less than the range of costs within which the fee-adjustment formula operates, the contractor is paid total allowable costs, plus the minimum or maximum fee.

A cost-plus-incentive-fee contract is appropriate for development and test programs when (1) a cost-reimbursement contract is necessary and (2) a target cost and a fee adjustment equation can be negotiated that are likely to motivate the contractor to manage effectively.

The contract may include technical performance incentives when it is highly probable that the required development of a major system is feasible and the government has established its performance objectives, at least in general terms. This approach may also apply to other development programs, if the use of both cost and technical performance incentives is desirable and administratively practical.

The fee adjustment equation should provide an incentive that will be effective over the full range of reasonably foreseeable variations from target cost. If a high maximum fee is negotiated, the contract shall also provide for a low minimum fee that may be a zero fee or, in rare cases, a negative fee [18].

In cost-reimbursement type contracts, since the government bears the significant share of the risk, the contractor's fee (profit) is limited by statute and, in some instances, by departmental regulation. Title 10, U. S. Code 2306(d) limits the fee to 10% for supply and service contracts and 15% for experimental, research, development, and test costs. The Department of Defense Acquisition Regulations extend the statutory limitations to apply to cost-plus-incentive-fee contracts.

The contractor is assured of a minimum fee above allowable costs but can increase the fee if final costs are less than target costs. The profit motive thus becomes the driving force to enhance the target fee set for the target cost.

13.3.9 Cost-Plus-Award-Fee Contracts

A cost-plus-award-fee contract is a cost-reimbursement contract that provides for a fee consisting of (1) a base amount fixed at inception of the contract and (2) an award amount that the contractor may earn in whole or in part during performance and is sufficient to provide motivation for excellence in such areas as quality, timeliness, technical ingenuity, and cost-effective management. The amount of the award fee to be paid is determined by the government's judgmental evaluation of the contractor's performance in terms of the criteria stated in the contract. This determination is made unilaterally by the government and is not subject to the disputes clause.

The cost-plus-award-fee contract is suitable for use under the following conditions:

1. The work to be performed is such that it is neither feasible nor effective to devise predetermined objective incentive targets applicable to cost, technical performance, or schedule.
2. The likelihood of meeting acquisition objectives will be enhanced by using a contract that effectively motivates the contractor toward exceptional performance and provides the government with the flexibility to evaluate both actual performance and the conditions under which it was achieved.
3. Any additional administrative effort and cost required to monitor and evaluate performance are justified by the expected benefits.

The number of evaluation criteria and the requirements they represent will differ widely among contracts. The criteria and rating plan should motivate the contractor to improve performance in the area rated, but not at the expense of at least minimum acceptable performance in all other areas.

Cost-plus-award-fee contracts provide for evaluation at stated intervals during performance, so that the contractor will periodically be informed of the quality of performance and the areas in which improvement is expected. Partial payment of fees generally corresponds to the evaluation periods. This makes effective the incentive that the award fee can create by inducing the contractor to improve poor performance or to continue good performance [19].

The entire risk of costs is the government's risk. There is a fixed amount plus an award amount in the fee schedule. Pre-award criteria determine the basis for the government's subjective evaluation of the award fee amount. Since cost-effective management is generally a major attribute in judging the award fee, the cost estimate and cost control reliability are significant in contractor's performance points.

13.3.10 Cost-Plus-Fixed-Fee Contracts

A cost-plus-fixed-fee contract is a cost-reimbursement contract that provides for payment to the contractor of a negotiated fee that is fixed at the inception of the contract. The fixed fee does not vary with actual cost, but may be adjusted as a result of changes in the work to be performed under the contract. This contract type permits contracting for efforts that might otherwise present too great a risk to contractors, but it provides the contractor only a minimum incentive to control costs.

A cost-plus-fixed-fee contract is suitable for use as follows:

1. The contract is for the performance of research or preliminary exploration or study, and the level of effort required is unknown.
2. The contract is for development and test, and using a cost-plus-incentive-fee contract is not practical.

A cost-plus-fixed-fee contract normally should not be used in development of major systems once preliminary exploration, studies, and risk reduction have indicated a high degree of probability that the development is achievable and the government has established reasonably firm performance objectives and schedules [20].

This contract type results in the government taking all of the cost risks and the contractor no cost risk. The contractor is, however, controlled with respect to costs by contractual requirements as to whether the costs are allocable, allowable, and reasonable. Cost-plus-fixed-fee (CPFF) contracts limit the amount of profit a contractor can earn to the fixed amount of dollars above the cost agreed to by the fee. The indefiniteness of the work specifications frequently results in changes in the scope of work, and when this occurs the fee dollars are renegotiated.

13.3.11 Indefinite-Delivery Contracts

There are three types of indefinite-delivery contracts—definite-quantity contracts, requirements contracts, and indefinite-quantity contracts. The appropriate type of indefinite-delivery contract may be used when the exact times and/or quantities of future deliveries are not known at the time of contract award.

A definite-quantity contract provides for delivery of a definite quantity of specific supplies or services for a fixed period, with deliveries to be scheduled at designated locations upon order.

A definite-quantity contract may be used when it can be determined in advance that (1) a definite quantity of supplies or services will be required during the contract period and (2) the supplies or services are regularly available or will be available after a short lead time.

A requirements contract provides for filling all actual purchase requirements of designated government activities for specific supplies or services during a specified contract period, with deliveries to be scheduled by placing orders with the contractor. Specific requirements are as follows:

1. For the information of offerors and contractors, the contracting officer states a realistic estimated total quantity in the solicitation and resulting contract. This estimate is not a representation to an offeror or contractor that the estimated quantity will be required or ordered, or that conditions affecting requirements will be stable or normal. The contracting officer may obtain the estimate from records of previous requirements and consumption, or by other means, and should base the estimate on the most current information available.

2. The contract states, if feasible, the maximum limit of the contractor's obligation to deliver and the government's obligation or order. The contract may also specify maximum or minimum quantities that the government may order under each individual order and the maximum that it may order during a specified period of time.

    A requirements contract may be used when the government anticipates recurring requirements but cannot predetermine the precise quantities of supplies or services that designated government activities will need during a definite period. Generally, a requirements contract is appropriate for items or services that are commercial products or commercial-type products. Funds are obligated by each delivery order, not by the contract itself.

3. When a requirements contract is used to acquire work (e.g., repair, modification, or overhaul) on existing items of government property, the contracting officer specifies in the schedule that failure of the government to furnish such items in the amounts or quantities described in the schedule as "estimated" or "maximum" will not entitle the contractor to any equitable adjustment in price under the Government Property clause of the contract.

    An indefinite-quantity contract provides for an indefinite quantity, within stated limits, of specific supplies or services to be furnished during a fixed period. Deliveries are scheduled by placing orders with the contractor with the following provisions:

1. The contract requires the government to order and the contractor to furnish at least a stated minimum quantity of supplies or services and, if as ordered, the contractor to furnish any additional additional quantities, not to exceed a stated maximum. The contracting officer may obtain the basis for the maximum from records of previous requirements and consumption, or by other means, but the maximum quantity should be realistic and based on the most current information available.

2. To ensure that the contract is binding, the minimum quantity must be more than a nominal quantity, but it should not exceed the amount that the government is fairly certain to order.

3. The contract may also specify maximum or minimum quantities that the government may order under each delivery order and the maximum that it may order during a specific period of time.

An indefinite-quantity contract may be used when (1) the government cannot predetermine, above a specified minimum, the precise quantities of supplies or services that will be required during the contract period and (2) it is inadvisable for the government to commit itself for more than a minimum quantity. An indefinite-quantity contract should be used only for items or services that are commercial products or commercial-type products and when a recurring need is anticipated. Funds for other than the stated minimum quantity are obligated by each delivery order, not by the contract itself [21].

Since indefinite delivery contracts are typically for commercial products or commercial-type products, the cost risk lies essentially with the contractor. The minimum quantity or definite quantity price determination should reflect all the cost elements and provide for a profit. In most cases, the indefinite delivery contracts can be treated in cost estimation in the same manner as a fixed-price contract.

13.3.12 Time-and-Materials, Labor-Hour, and Letter Contracts

A time-and-materials contract provides for acquiring supplies or services on the basis of (1) direct labor hours at specified fixed hourly rates that include wages, overhead, general and administrative expenses, and profit and (2) materials at cost, including, if appropriate, material handling costs as part of material costs.

A time-and-materials contract may be used only when it is not possible at the time of placing the contract to estimate accurately the extent or duration of the work or to anticipate costs with any reasonable degree of confidence.

A labor-hour contract is a variation of the time-and-materials contract, differing only in that materials are not supplied by the contractor.

A letter contract is a written preliminary contractual instrument that authorizes the contractor to begin immediately manufacturing supplies or performing services. A letter contract may be used when (1) the government's interests demand that the contractor be given a binding commitment so that work can start immediately and (2) negotiating a definitive contract is not possible in sufficient time to meet the requirement. However, a letter contract should be as complete and definite as feasible under the circumstances. When a letter contract award is based on price competition, the contracting officer shall include an overall price ceiling in the letter contract [22].

The government accepts the cost risk in the time-and-materials contract and labor-hour contract. The inability to estimate accurately the scope and duration of work results in a contract similar to the cost-plus-fixed-fee type.

Letter contracts typically require that a contractor's price proposal with cost and pricing data be submitted and that a defined contract will be negotiated at a future date. The letter contract is a convenience to the government to get work started immediately, such as in emergencies.

13.3.13 Federal Supply Schedule Contracting

The General Services Administration (GSA) has the responsibility for acquiring items of supply used by multiple federal agencies. Interagency agreements are established to determine requirements, procedures, and similar matters. Items qualifying under the agreements are placed on a Federal Supply Schedule with a national stock number so that individual agencies may order against contracts established by GSA.

To qualify for the Federal Supply Schedule, the annual business volume would normally exceed $20,000 if regional in scope. National scope schedules require an expected annual volume of $200,000. These agreements are typically indefinite-delivery and indefinite-quantity contracts [23].

13.3.14 Facilities Contracts

A facilities contract means a contract under which government facilities are provided to a contractor or subcontractor by the government for use in connection with performing one or more related contracts for supplies or services. It is used occasionally to provide special tooling or special test equipment.

Typically this type of contract is used in a government-owned, contractor-operated plant where the contractor also has a second contract of the cost-plus-fee type. It is also used for support of industrial preparedness programs [24].

13.3.15 Construction and Architect-Engineer Contracts

The government publicly announces all requirements for architect-engineer services and negotiates contracts for these services based on the demonstrated competence and qualifications of prospective contractors to perform the services required at fair and reasonable prices (See Pub. L.92-582,40 U.S.C. 541 et seq.). Sources for architect-engineer contracts shall be selected in accordance with the special procedures, rather than the formal advertising or source selection procedures.

Agencies evaluate each potential contractor in terms of the following:

1. Professional qualifications necessary for satisfactory performance of required services
2. Specialized experience and technical competence in the type of work required
3. Capacity to accomplish the work in the required time
4. Past performance on contracts with government agencies and private industry in terms of cost control, quality of work, and compliance with performance schedules
5. Location in the general geographical area of the project and knowledge of the locality of the project, provided that application of this criterion leaves an appropriate number of qualified firms, given the nature and size of the project
6. Acceptability under other appropriate evaluation criteria

When the use of design competition is approved by the agency head or a designee, agencies may evaluate firms on the basis of their conceptual design of the project. Design competition may be used when:

1. Unique situations exist involving prestige projects, such as the design of memorials and structures of unusual national significance
2. Sufficient time is available for the production and evaluation of conceptual designs
3. The design competition, with its costs, will substantially benefit the project [25]

13.3.16 Contracts with Educational Institutions

Educational institutions enjoy a unique relationship with the federal government since these institutions frequently are associated with work classified as research and development, training, or other special work. As such, the determination of allowable costs for indirect cost elements is an important element of the contract. The Office of Management and Budget (OMB) Circular No. A-21, "Cost Principles for Educational Institutions," revised, has been incorporated by reference in the Federal Acquisition Regulations (FAR). This circular provides the principles for determining applicable costs [26].

13.3.17 Contracts with State and Local Governments

Government contracts with state and local governments also enjoy unique contract relationships. These special relationships, in terms of allowability of costs, are set forth in Office of Management and Budget (OMB) Circular No. A-87, "Cost Principles for State and Local Governments,'' revised. The provisions of Circular No. A-87 have been incorporated into the FAR by reference [27].

13.4 COST ACCOUNTING STANDARDS AND PRINCIPLES

Public Law 91-379 established the requirement that certain national defense contractors and subcontractors must comply with Cost Accounting Standards (CAS), published by the Cost Accounting Standards Board (CASB). These contractors are required to disclose in writing and to follow consistently the CASB cost accounting practices.

13.4.1 Applicability of Government Standards

The dollar value threshold requirement states that ''any business unit that is selected to receive a CAS-covered negotiated national defense contract or subcontract of $10 million or more shall submit a Disclosure Statement before award'' [28].

Business segments of a parent company involved in a contract covered under CAS can expect to submit a separate disclosure statement if their costs included in the total contract price exceed $100,000.

Certain contracts are exempt from the CAS requirements. The exemptions include (1) formally advertised contracts, (2) negotiated contracts or subcontracts less than $100,000, (3) small business contracts, and (4) certain contracts with foreign governments.

Details of the CASB standards and regulations are available from the Superintendent of Documents, U.S. Government Printing Office, publication Y3.C82:6ST2/976. Table 13.1 lists the number and titles of the major CASB standards.

13.4.2 Special Cost Terms

In performing cost estimation for potential government contracts, the use by the government of special cost terms requires that the estimator recognize the notions and ideas contained in the government language. Proposals submitted to the government will normally undergo three types of analysis: pricing analysis, cost analysis, and technical analysis.

Price analysis involves techniques to ensure a fair and reasonable price. It would normally involve one or more of the following: (1) comparison of price quotations received in response to the solicitation to isolate the best price, (2) comparison of prior quotations and contract prices with current quotations for the same or similar end items, (3) application of rough yardsticks to highlight significant inconsistencies that warrant additional pricing inquiry, (4) comparison with competitive published price lists and indexes, and (5) comparison of the proposed prices with independent government cost estimates.

TABLE 13.1. Selected Cost Accounting Standards

Number	Title
401	Consistency in Estimating, Accumulating, and Reporting Costs
402	Consistency in Allocating Costs Incurred for the Same Purpose
403	Allocation of Home Office Expenses to Segments
404	Capitalization of Tangible Assets
405	Accounting for Unallowable Costs
406	Cost Accounting Period
407	Use of Standard Costs for Direct Material and Direct Labor
408	Accounting for Costs of Compensated Personnel Absence
409	Depreciation of Tangible Capital Assets
410	Allocation of Business Unit G&A Expense to Cost Objectives
411	Accounting for Acquisition Cost of Material
412	Composition and Measurement of Pension Costs
413	Adjustment and Allocation of Pension Costs
414	Cost of Money as an Element of the Cost of Facilities Capital
415	Accounting for the Cost of Deferred Compensation
416	Accounting for Insurance Costs
417	Cost of Money as an Element of the Cost of Capital Assets under Construction
418	Allocation of Direct and Indirect Costs
420	Accounting for Independent Research and Development Costs and Bid and Proposal Costs

Source: Cost Accounting Standards, Cost Accounting Standards Board, U.S. Government Printing Office, YS.C82:6ST2/976.

Cost analysis likewise includes a number of individual techniques. Any of the following might be used: (1) the evaluation of the necessity for and reasonableness of cost elements, including allowance for contingencies; (2) projection of the bidder's cost trends, using current and historical cost and pricing data; (3) an appraisal of estimates for labor, material, and facility requirements from the technical viewpoint; (4) reasonableness of scrap and spoilage factors; (5) separate examination of indirect cost rates, labor rates, and cost of money; (6) comparison of costs from the bidder in previous estimates; and (7) price stability of basic labor and materials.

Technical analysis includes (1) quantities and kinds of material proposed, (2) the need for the number and kinds of labor hours and mix of labor skills, (3) special tooling and facilities proposed, (4) general logistical matters, and (5) other technical requirements generating cost.

13.4.3 Standards

As used initially in this section, we discuss the term "standards" from the viewpoint of assessing whether a cost element and value can be accepted by the government. Second, the term "'standard" is reviewed in terms of cost accounting systems.

Cost elements may be allowed if they are considered reasonable, can be justified as allocable to the contract, and are in consonance with standards promulgated by CASB.

The following example illustrates the evaluation process for reasonableness. The contractor's proposal contained the cost element direct labor and stated that the basis for the estimate was a prior production run plus 10%. One hundred hours were estimated at a rate of $10 per direct labor hour. The government questioned the estimate by stating that the application of a learning curve results in an estimate that is 10% lower than the prior production run.

In a second incident, the same contractor's estimate for scrap was challenged. The contractor estimated 10% of direct material as scrap. The government questioned this cost element, citing that the industry average was 5% of direct material.

The Defense Acquisition Regulations contain, in Section 15, standards or criteria for judging the reasonableness of specific costs, such as bonding, compensation for personal services, insurance and indemnification, recruitment, rental royalties, severance pay, travel cost, and automatic data processing equipment leasing costs.

Cost can be allocated to a government contract if (1) it is incurred specifically for the contract, (2) it benefits both the contract and other work, or both government work and other work, and can be distributed to them in reasonable proportion to the benefits received, or (3) it is necessary to the overall operation of the business, although a direct relationship to any particular cost objective (contract) cannot be shown.

Some organizations have their cost accounting systems designed around the use of a standard cost for all cost elements. The government permits the use of standard cost systems with predetermined rates for government contracts so long as the system has a proper approach for adjustment of actual cost variances from the standard costs used.

13.4.4 Cost Principles

The cost estimator, preparing for government contracts, should become familiar with the cost principles that contain a significant allocability rule. Such rules distinguish either between individual cost objectives, business base groupings, or fiscal periods. Rules for allocability of costs have been established for automatic data processing leasing costs, compensation for personal services costs, economic morale, health, welfare, food service and dormitory costs, credits, losses on other contracts, maintenance and repair costs, organization costs, patent cost, reconversion costs, recruitment costs, rental costs, selling costs, service and warranty costs, special tooling and special test equipment, taxes, and termination costs.

In addition to the foregoing principles, the FAR in Part 31 established specific principles of nonallowability for bad debts, contributions and donations, fines and penalties (except those incurred to satisfy specific contract terms), research, development, and engineering costs designed to lead to new products for sale to the general public, interest on borrowed funds, federal income and excess profit taxes, and taxes in connection with financing, refinancing, refunding operations or re-organizations.

Because of the widespread number of cost elements that have special rules or principles associated with government contracts, the cost estimator can benefit by establishing a comprehensive checklist of permissible and nonpermissible cost elements that can be used in government contracts.

13.5 COST GROUPING AND STRUCTURES

The most significant government agency engaging in large and small contract efforts is the Department of Defense (DOD). The fiscal year 1986 DOD Budget contained budget authority requests by major appropriation titles in five categories (expressed in billion dollars): Military Personnel, $73.4; Operations and Maintenance, $82.5; Procurement, $106.8; RDT&E, $39.3; and Other, $11.7. DOD outlays accounted for 25.7 % of federal outlays in fiscal year 1985 [8].

13.5.1 Five-Year Defense Plan

The DOD budget is supported by the Five-Year Defense Plan. This plan formats from the current budget year through the next four budget years. These programs can frequently be identified with specific line items in the DOD budget. Initially, the major programs may be grouped according to missions such as shown in Table 13.2.

If the cost estimation effort is to be complete from a broad planning perspective, the estimator for DOD contract items will want to get copies of the federal budget. This will provide the dollar amounts requested by year for each program. For example, under the FY 85 Appropriation title for Research, Development, Test, and Evaluation, Navy, there is included line item 178—Aircraft engine component improvement program.

13.5.2 Program Management

Program management as a major structural approach for management control received its strongest endorsement with the publication of Department of Defense Directive No. 5000.1 on July 13, 1971, "Acquisition of Major Defense Systems." This directive specified as major those programs requiring special management, programs with an estimated RDT&E cost in excess of 50 million dollars, or an estimated production cost in excess of 200 million dollars. The directive further states that programs meeting these criteria shall be managed by a single individual (program manager) who shall have a charter providing sufficient authority to accomplish recognized program objectives.

Cost estimation for defense programs quickly adopted the use of the Military

TABLE 13.2. Mission Categories: Defense, Military[a]

Major Missions and Programs	1983 (Actual)	1984 (Estimate)	1985 (Estimate)	1986 (Estimate)	1987 (Estimate)
Strategic forces[b]	19.7	26.3	31.6	33.9	32.7
General purpose forces	98.8	99.7	128.2	151.0	168.7
Intelligence and communications	17.3	20.1	25.8	28.7	30.9
Airlift and sealift	4.3	5.6	7.5	9.6	9.6
Guard and reserve[c]	12.1	12.9	16.5	19.0	21.8
Research and development	18.7	21.4	27.0	30.5	32.0
Central supply and maintenance[d]	21.6	22.5	26.5	29.3	32.1
Training, medical, and other general personnel activities	42.2	44.2	35.6	40.1	43.4
Administration and associated activities	4.1	4.8	5.6	6.6	7.1
Support of other nations	0.7	0.7	0.7	0.9	0.9
Total budget authority	239.5	258.2	305.0	349.6	379.2
Prior-year funds and other financial adjustments	−0.8	0.9	0.7	0.7	0.7
Total obligational authority	238.7	259.1	305.7	350.3	379.9

[a] Functional code 051; in billions of dollars.
[b] Excludes strategic systems development included in the research and development category.
[c] Excludes research and development in other program areas on systems approved for production.
[d] Military retired pay is included in training, medical, and other general personnel activities through 1984. In 1985 and later years, military retired pay is funded on an accrual basis with costs distributed to all mission categories.
Source: Budget of the United States, Fiscal Year 1985.

Standard (MIL-STD) 881A, Summary Work Breakdown Structure (WBS) as the fundamental vehicle for preparing detailed cost estimates. MIL-STD 881B presents the Summary WBS for seven classifications of systems: aircraft, electronics, missile, ordnance, ship, space, and surface vehicle. Cost models grew from these efforts, and the need for estimation of the cost of a material system over its life cycle led to the life-cycle cost model.

Life-cycle costs are categorized as research and development (R&D), investment, and operating and support (O&S). R&D costs are all costs resulting from applied research, engineering design, analysis, development, test, evaluation, and managing development efforts related to a specific material system. Table 13.3 reflects the structure for cost elements in this category. Investment includes nonrecurring and recurring costs. Nonrecurring investment cost elements generally occur only once in the production cycle of a system and are generally not dependent on the size of the buy. They are engineering and capitalization costs incurred initially to obtain the total production capability. Recurring investment cost elements occur as a result of the size of the production buy or occur repeatedly in the production of a system or its components. They are the costs incurred to actually produce and acquire the item. Table 13.4 illustrates the investment cost elements. O&S costs are the costs necessary to operate and maintain the capability. Such costs include military pay and allowances, maintenance, training costs, and replacement of equipment and supplies. Table 13.5 identifies the O&S cost elements.

Using the cost element structures indicated in Tables 13.3 through 13.5, estimates are prepared for consideration in the DOD decision process. Three significant estimates are prepared. The baseline cost estimate is prepared by the material developer (DOD component responsible) and is the first deliberate, detailed and complete cost estimate made for the new system. The estimate is performed early in the program and serves as the base point for all subsequent tracking and auditing purposes. A WBS is established concurrently with the baseline estimate.

An independent cost estimate (ICE) or independent parametric cost estimate

TABLE 13.3. Research and Development Cost Elements

Element Number	Cost Element
1.00	Research and development cost
1.01	Development engineering
1.02	Producibility engineering and planning
1.03	Tooling
1.04	Prototype manufacturing
1.05	Data
1.06	System test and evaluation
1.07	System/project management
1.08	Training services and equipment
1.09	Facilities
1.10	Other

TABLE 13.4. Investment Cost Elements

Element Number	Cost Element
2.000	Investment cost
2.010	Nonrecurring investment
2.011	Initial production facilities (IPF)
2.012	Industrial facilities/production base support
2.013	Other nonrecurring
2.020	Production
2.021	Manufacturing
2.022	Recurring engineering
2.023	Sustaining tooling
2.024	Quality control
2.025	Other
2.030	Engineering changes
2.040	System test and evaluation
2.050	Data
2.060	System/project management
2.070	Operational/site activation
2.080	Training services and equipment
2.090	Initial spares and repair parts
2.100	Transportation
2.110	Other

TABLE 13.5. Operating and Support Cost Elements

Element Number	Cost Element
3.010	Military personnel
3.011	Crew pay and allowances
3.012	Maintenance pay and allowances
3.013	Indirect pay and allowances
3.014	Permanent change of station
3.020	Consumption
3.021	Replenishment spares
3.022	Petroleum, oil, and lubricants
3.023	Unit training, ammunition, and missiles
3.030	Depot maintenance
3.031	Labor
3.032	Matériel
3.033	Transportation
3.040	Modifications, matériel
3.050	Other direct support operations
3.051	Maintenance, civilian labor
3.052	Other direct
3.060	Indirect support operations
3.061	Personnel replacement
3.062	Transients, patients, and prisioners
3.063	Quarters, maintenance, and utilities
3.064	Medical support
3.065	Other indirect

(IPCE) is normally prepared at the headquarters level. This estimate is independent of functional, program manager, or contractor influence. The focus of the ICE is to consider cost at a higher level of the WBS and is predicated upon actual historical costs encountered in similar programs. This estimate is used to test the reasonableness of the proponent estimates at key decision points.

13.5.3 Contracting

Under the concept of life-cycle costing, an estimator preparing estimates for major systems should recognize that, although economies of scale may exist if the estimates are prepared for the total stated requirement, rarely are contracts made initially for the full requirement. On major systems, the government tends toward incremental funding in the Congressional appropriations. This results in limiting contracting officers as to how much they may obligate in contracts. In addition, the political realities of government contracting are such that the government will spread contracts among several states to stimulate support from multiple constituencies.

13.6 SEPARATE COST PRINCIPLES

As a matter of policy, the government discourages the awarding of personal services contracts since the government is required, by law, to acquire its personnel under the civil service laws. In practice, personal services contracts are awarded when the government requires performances on site, can actively supervise the contractor's personnel, and wishes to retain full responsibility for the function within the authority of an authorized federal official or employee.

13.6.1 Compensation for Personal Services

Generally, compensation for personal services must meet the test of reasonableness. This cost standard test judges that compensation is reasonable if the total compensation conforms generally to the compensation paid by other firms of similar size, similar industry, or in the same geographic area for similar services or work performed.

The allowability of components of total compensation in personal contracts is significant to the cost estimator. Cost rules applicable are contained in FAR 31.205-6.

13.6.2 Special Contracts and Grants

The Office of Management and Budget has developed special cost principles for contracts and grants with nonprofit organizations. These cost principles are contained in OMB Circular No. A-122, Cost Principles for Nonprofit Organizations.

A nonprofit organization is defined as a business entity organized and operated exclusively for charitable, scientific, or educational purposes, of which no part of the net earnings benefit any private shareholder or individual. In addition, no substantial part of the activities carried out relate to propaganda or otherwise attempting to influence legislation or participating in any political campaign on behalf of any candidate for public office. Also, a nonprofit organization is exempt from federal income taxation under Section 501 of the Internal Revenue Code.

13.7 CONSTRAINTS OUTSIDE THE COST ESTIMATE

Cost-reimbursement and cost-sharing government contracts are required to contain a limitation of cost clause. The obligation on the contractor under this clause is to project costs in the next 60-day period (or 30–90 days) and to determine if these costs, plus the costs previously incurred, will exceed 75% (or 75–85%) of the original estimated cost.

This clause is a contract mechanism to insure a review of cost in relation to work progress and to force the government contracting officer to make a decision whether to continue the contract. Estimators for such contracts should always bear in mind that the government is not obligated to continue performance of the contract or incur costs in excess of the original estimated cost.

13.7.1 Limitation of Costs Clause

The limitation of costs clause is frequently the trigger mechanism for termination of research and development contracts in which multiple contracts are awarded with competing technologies seeking solutions for a single requirement. It is also the trigger mechanism to revise the scope of work and cost estimate where progress is favorable and in the interest of the government.

13.7.2 Practices and Decision Precedents

There are provisions within the government's contract structure where errors in estimates can be corrected. Before the bid opening, a new bid can be submitted and the original bid withdrawn. After the bid opening, but before award, when the bidder can prove conclusively that a mistake has been made, the contracting officer can accept a corrected bid. Obviously, if correction of the mistake, after the bid opening, makes the bidder the lowest bidder, the highest degree of proof of the mistake is required.

The government contracting officer is charged with notice of mistakes on the face of a bid (incorrect totaling of prices, failure to insert unit prices, inconsistency of unit prices and extended prices). Frequently, the invitation to bid will specify that in evaluating bids, the unit prices will govern. The General Accounting Office, however, has held that if evidence establishes a mistake in unit price, the extended price prevails, since a bid cannot be accepted with notice of error.

If the government contracting officer suspects the low bid contains a mistake, he must request the bidder to verify his bid. If such verification has been made and the bidder confirms the price, the contracting officer is under no obligation to inquire further.

Numerous legal cases have established precedents of the allowability or non-allowability of costs in specific situations. Estimators with unusual cost situations should seek legal counsel or seek a preaward determination from area audit agencies. The Defense Contract Administration Service may provide technical specialists, and the Defense Contract Audit Agency may provide audit assistance to help determine various skills and costs.

13.8 OTHER CONSIDERATIONS IN COST ESTIMATING FOR CONTRACTS WITH THE FEDERAL GOVERNMENT

Multiyear contracts will commonly contain a special clause that states that funds are not available at present for performance under this contract beyond _____(date)_____. The government's obligation for performance on this contract beyond that date is contingent on the availability of appropriated funds from which payment for contract purposes can be made. This clause is also inserted in one-year indefinite-quantity or requirements contracts for services funded by annual appropriations that are to extend beyond the initial fiscal year. The importance of this clause for the estimator is that the contractor must assume the full risk of termination if special termination provisions have not been made elsewhere in the contract.

The question arises, in some cases, as to whether special tooling should be government furnished or contractor acquired. The government must also decide how it is to be acquired and who is to retain title to the tooling. It is the general policy of DOD to furnish special tooling, when it is available, if by doing so it does not interfere with essential production program schedules, and if the cost to the government is less than it would be if the contractor acquired such special tooling himself.

Estimates involving production of units for commercial and defense markets should consider possible deferral of some start-up costs to allow the government to take advantage of lower prices over the number of units produced. Follow-on contracts can result from such behavior in bidding.

In many cases the quality control requirements of a contract will necessitate the development of special test equipment, or the contractor may specify that special test equipment will be government supplied. The DOD policy is to offer special test equipment to contractors. Records of inventories of equipment are maintained by the Defense Industrial Plant Equipment Center, Memphis, Tennessee, 38102. Requirements for new equipment having an acquisition cost of $1000 or more must be screened by this center.

In summary, cost estimation for use in contracting with the federal government requires, in addition to recognized techniques, knowledge of the structuring of major procurements and recognition of the special rules that the Government exercises. This operating environment prompts the professional estimator to adapt normal industry methods so that estimates supporting government bids are responsive and competitive.

There is considerable evidence that the federal government will continue its policy of seeking maximum competition in its acquisition process. As the economy becomes more dominated by service industries, the estimator will be challenged to develop criteria and cost estimates that differentiate adequately to reflect differences in knowledge, quality, and experience reliability. Professionalism will need to be incorporated both in techniques employed and communication methods. Government standards for estimates will continue to influence industrial estimating processes.

REFERENCES

1. Office of Federal Procurement Policy, Report to the Congress: Activities of the Office of Federal Procurement Policy, January–December 1984, p. 3, Washington, D.C.
2. Department of Defense Directive 5000.35, March 8, 1978, Washington, D.C.
3. Federal Register, Volume 48, No. 182, Book 2, Monday, September 19, 1983, Rules and Regulations, pp. 42101–42798, U.S. Government Printing Office, Washington, D.C.
4. Title 48, Code of Federal Regulations, Chapter 1, U.S. Government Printing Office, Washington, D.C.
5. Federal Register, Volume 48, No. 182, Book 2, pp. 42187–42192, U.S. Government Printing Office, Washington, D.C.
6. Department of Defense Directive 5000-1, "Major System Acquisition," January 18, 1977 and DOD Directive 5000.2, "Major System Acquisition Process," January 18, 1977, Washington, D.C.
7. Office of Management and Budget Circular No. A-11 (Revised), "Preparation and Submission of Annual Budget Estimates," June 21, 1971, Washington, D.C.
8. Weinberger, C. W. Department of Defense, Report of the Secretary of Defense to the Congress on the FY 1986 Budget, FY 1987 Authorization Request, and FY 1986–1990 Defense Programs, February 4, 1985, Washington, D.C., p. 85.
9. O'Brien, Frank. "A Simple View of Multi-Year Funding for High Value Items," *Estimator*, 1982, pp. 6–7.
10. Federal Acquisition Regulation, Part 17, Section 103-1, U.S. Government Printing Office, Washington, D.C.
11. Federal Acquisition Regulation, Part 16.202, U.S. Government Printing Office, Washington, D.C.
12. Ibid., Part 16.203.
13. Ibid., Part 16.403.
14. Ibid., Part 16.206.
15. Ibid., Part 16.205.
16. Ibid., Part 16.207.
17. Ibid., Part 16.303.
18. Ibid., Part 16.404-1.
19. Ibid., Part 16.404-2.

20. Ibid., Part 16.306.
21. Ibid., Part 16.501.
22. Ibid., Part 16.601.
23. Ibid., Part 38.2.
24. Ibid., Part 45.301.
25. Ibid., Part 36.2.
26. Ibid., Part 31.302.
27. Ibid., Part 31.602.
28. Ibid., Part 30.201-1.

14

COST ESTIMATING AS A PROFESSION

RAYMOND H. CRONINGER, CPE

14.1 COST ESTIMATING DEFINED

"Estimating is the art of approximating a probable worth or cost, extent, quantity, quality, or character of something based on information available at the time. Cost and Price Estimating is defined as the art of predetermining the lowest realistic cost and price of an item or activity that assures a normal profit." The above are quotes from the National Estimating Society.

Hence the estimating profession includes all persons whose occupations are concerned with estimating and its many derivative functions. These functions involve the accumulation and reporting of cost, cost control, and the establishment of standards for labor hours and material costs. All persons engaged in estimating should have as their common objective the desire to promote and advance the profession of estimating for themselves and for the public good.

Since procurement philosophies and patterns are never static, estimating and pricing are now, more than ever, dominant elements in the acquisition cycle. There is a constant concern for cost, a philosophy that must be demonstrated by innovative policies equitable to buyer and seller alike, accomplished by a documented factual approach at the outset of the procurement cycle.

14.2 EVOLUTION OF COST ESTIMATING

Estimating had a rather sordid and fragmented beginning in the early life of man when food, clothing, and personal protection were obtained by the use of rocks and clubs. Transportation from one place to another was accomplished by walking or by riding beasts of the day. Thus individuals were required to determine (estimate) the size of a rock or club needed and the type of beast required to meet his needs.

Biblical records inform us that large structures, for example, pyramids, towers, buildings, walls, and bridges were built with the use of slave labor and crude tools to cut stone and wood. Huge stones were cut and used to build these structures. Some wood and animal hides were used to assist in getting rocks to high levels. Soon man learned to build wood fulcrums and to use animals to move stones to building sites and to help lift them into place. Again, man had to make estimates to determine the number of rocks, hides, wood, slaves, and animals needed to perform the necessary work.

As man progressed, he began to bargain and trade with other individuals and tribes. He soon learned that some suitable medium of exchange was needed. Pretty rocks, beads, handmade jewels, and some crudely made coins satisfied the requirements for expanded needs and wants. Thus man soon learned the terms *value* and *price*. This also established a need to keep a record of these valuable trading possessions. As man became more familiar with the value of exchange items, he began to realize his wealth and eventually demanded improved housing, transportation, clothing, and more luxuries, therefore, progressing in his crude but persistent way toward a more modern standard of living that eventually brought him into the industrial age; and now, into the information age.

14.3 MOVEMENT INTO THE INDUSTRIAL AGE

During the early years of the movement into the industrial age, man struggled to learn improved and more professional ways of competing and prospering in business. He learned that detailed and realistic cost and performance records were a must, and that expanded education was an important factor in meeting established goals. It was also learned that detailed cost records alone would not satisfy his needs to meet competition. To meet public demand for quality products, all company personnel must become more efficient to keep down production costs and achieve product quality.

Historical cost records were considered very important to support future estimating, but cost records alone would not provide all the information and data necessary to establish new item and product cost. Further, engineering estimates alone would not provide all the necessary information and data to develop realistic item and/or product price for the competitive market. Thus the title of estimator came into being for those persons assigned the responsibility for developing realistic cost and price information and data, regardless of education and assigned job title, and became known in most areas of operation. Such titles as cost estimator, materials estimator, production processes estimator, quality and test requirements estimator, and facilities estimator became common. These titles were assigned in addition to the person's educational title, for example, accountant, engineer, analyst, and statistician.

Movement into the twentieth century brought on a more sophisticated life style and industry's demand for more detailed estimating methods. This required extensive changes in management and operating procedures, accounting systems, and estimating techniques. Thus industry operating procedures and manufacturing processes became more complex. Personnel at all levels of operation had to be reoriented or retrained to coordinate and implement these changes properly. Such terms as design-to-cost, life-cycle cost, value engineering, and cost reduction soon became standard working phrases. Requests for proposals (RFP) and Requests for quotation (RFQ) became more detailed and demanding, as did the attached technical description of the scope of work.

14.4 ESTIMATORS SEEK PROFESSIONALISM

During the industrial evolutionary period, individuals selecting engineering, accounting, statistics, or management as their field of endeavor began seeking ways to expand their expertise. Professional organizations began to be formed for the purpose of exchanging ideas through workshops, seminars, and conferences. Regularly published newsletters and technical publications provided two other means for exchanging experiences and ideas. Organization members and nonmembers were encouraged to write articles for publication in technical journals. Organizational headquarters and chapters used newsletters to inform members of current activities and plans.

During this industrial evolutionary period estimators began to evidence their importance and to be recognized as part of the overall company management and contract negotiation team. Thus the National Estimating Society was formed to provide a means for the exchange of ideas and information. The Society soon realized the importance of the estimator, sought certification, and encouraged all persons engaged in the various aspects of estimating to apply, regardless of job classification. The certification program soon caught the eyes of industry management and resulted in further recognition of the estimator's importance.

14.5 EDUCATIONAL DISCIPLINES

Since the estimating profession includes those persons who work in the various functional areas of an industry, it places responsibility on each to become thoroughly knowledgeable of that particular area and to develop the skills necessary to support the overall estimating needs. Following is a list of derivative functions concerned with estimating.

Program planning	System cost analysis
Program budgeting	Price analysis
Proposal/program management	Cost analysis
Financial management	Life-cycle-cost-analysis
Business administration	Parametric cost analysis

Economic forecasting	Design-to-cost
Operation analysis	Value engineering
Financial analysis	Estimating
Systems analysis	Cost estimating
Budget analysis	Price estimating
Time and motion analysis	Pricing

Completing an estimate is a team effort that requires the use of techniques and skills of persons qualified in the specific functional area of concern. Each person must be obedient to such needs and be thoroughly knowledgeable of total estimating requirements, rules, and applicable regulations. Important skills will include planning, scheduling, charting, data comparisons from varied data sources, employment of learning curves, use of models, and the application of inflation factors.

14.6 EDUCATION/TRAINING

The support of industry's ever increasing need for sophisticated estimates in all functional areas of operation requires employees to have a well-rounded educational background and to develop full support effort capabilities in all other functional areas. A functional area cannot operate independently of another functional area and ensure the employer competition in the current marketplace. To fully support the employer's estimating, cost control, management, and competitive needs, each employee must look beyond those educational subjects of study required to earn a Bachelor's or Master's degree in a given area of concentration. He must now extend his educational capabilities through special formal studies, self-study, and through the exchange of ideas to assure that he can be totally supportive of the employer's needs.

Extensive competitive procurement has forced industry management to press for more detailed records maintenance and more realistic cost estimating. Such pressures have resulted in papers and books on certain areas of cost estimating, cost controls, management techniques, cost modeling, design-to-cost, life-cycle costing, and many other subjects.

The National Estimating Society and other professional organizations supply lists of such books and some technical publication articles for self-study to those individuals seeking certification in their chosen profession.

There are additional ways for the estimator to improve estimating capabilities and to acquire new techniques and skills. An active member in one or more professional organizations encounters first-class speakers on appropriate technical subjects. Regularly scheduled professional meetings explain a new technique, the way some company solved a given problem, how a company improved their competitive position through better cost control, the use of a computer as a labor saving device in proposal preparation, or some other area of operation. The energetic and forward looking estimator can usually find a better, and perhaps cost saving, way to attack a problem by reading published articles.

14.7 PERSONAL QUALITIES AND QUALIFICATIONS

An estimator must possess certain qualities or attributes to be considered trustworthy by an employer. He must possess an impeccable moral character, maintain a high standard of conduct, be studious, objective, cooperative, friendly, a leader, a coordinator, eager to learn and improve, and always consider himself as an important person in overall industry management.

The estimator must always be capable of displaying his job qualifications. He must become thoroughly knowledgeable of the industry organizational structure, the lines of responsibility and communication, and learn the various functional areas' responsibilities for developing estimating information and data. He must be able and willing to develop confidence in fellow workers, maintain confidentiality and integrity, and abide by the company standards of conduct. To this must be added the ability and intent to assist and support fellow employees.

14.8 FUNCTIONAL DERIVATIVES

The term ''functional derivatives'' as applied to estimating refers to the various operational departments of a business, that is, the organizational structure elements responsible for performing specific functions. It is the responsibility of employees in each functional area to determine the extent of effort required to support overall company budget needs, cost estimates for proposal preparation, plus any revisions or modifications. Cost estimates for fiscal year budgets are normally based on the balance of known work on hand plus additional new work the company anticipates. Proposal cost estimates are always developed on the basis of a definitively described scope of work.

When a company receives a request for proposal (RFP)/request for quotation (RFQ), a determination must be made relative to what portion of the scope of work must be assigned to each functional area for preparation of the cost estimate. Each functional area is usually requested to review the entire scope of work and identify those portions for which they are totally responsible and the support required from other organizational elements. From this, company management can develop a detailed scope of work breakdown and a time-phased schedule for use in developing the detailed estimates for the entire RFP/RFQ.

Since competition has become so keen, it is axiomatic that estimates of the future be accurate and based on actual cost when available. Accurate records of historical costs at all levels of operation must have been maintained for ready reference purposes. Mechanization of budgets, cost estimates, and proposal preparation have become a must to speed up the activity. The use of EDP requires standardization to preclude revision of software programs for processing variants.

A word of caution is that historical information and data should not always be taken at face (record) value. These data must be adjusted for changes in labor rates, material prices, overhead rates, general and administrative (G&A) rates, and the current rate of inflation before use. There will also be occasions when new items must be priced for which historical data are not available. In such instances item plans, descriptions, and item drawings will have to be reviewed to determine the amount of effort required and whether item comparability information and data are available. If so, comparable prices can be applied, or complexity factors may have to be used. In every event it is the estimator's responsibility to screen thoroughly all items against historical cost information and data to derive a reasonable cost. Research of current material and labor rates, plus some consultation with other experienced persons is a continuous process before an entire procurement package can be priced. The practice of screening all item descriptions against those on which historical costs are available and adjusting for variances will usually result in a priced proposal being in a highly competitive position.

Since personnel of numerous disciplines and skills are required to complete a scope of work, it is essential that involved estimators maintain a harmonious relationship with the entire company personnel staff. To become a really effective estimator, a thorough working knowledge of each labor discipline of the company should be developed. There must be no misunderstanding between the estimator and any member of the estimating team. Today's estimators must continually seek new ways to improve their capabilities to develop the lowest realistic cost and price of an item(s) to assist the employer in meeting and beating tough competition.

There are multiple historical sources in the records of an industry. Two main data sources are the summary cost records entitled ''General Book of Accounts,'' and the detail cost records entitled ''Departmental Cost Ledgers'' or ''Shop Records.'' The departmental cost ledgers are summarized and posted to the general book of accounts, normally at the end of each month or company account reporting period. Cost data recorded in the departmental cost ledger accounts are derived from individual department work orders or shop orders that bear the amount by labor type and materials utilized. It must be noted that some industries price such orders based on established standards, which requires periodic adjustment to actuals, whereas other industries price their orders based on the current effective labor rates and material prices. In either event, there is a basis for tracing costs by cost element from point of incurrence to the departmental cost ledgers, to the general book of accounts, and thence to the periodic reports prepared for operation and management personnel to compare performance to budget data for the period(s) reported.

It is axiomatic that the estimator fully understand the company's entire accounting system, particularly the various departmental cost ledgers and the detailed costs recorded therein. It is at this detail record level that estimators will look for the historic cost data needed to develop a bottoms-up historical cost estimate. From the recorded direct labor hours, direct materials, and other materials relative to a given task being estimated, the current direct labor rates and material prices must be applied to complete a detailed estimate. Other methods of developing the estimate may be performed in summary form once the historical data are deemed to have a relatively direct relationship to the task being estimated. This is referred to as comparative cost estimating or forecasting to obtain a quick result. A third method is to use what is referred to as complexity factors. This approach requires comparing the complexity of the work to be estimated to that previously performed and of record.

Some functional costs are common in all departments, for example, types of direct labor, indirect labor, overhead, and some common material items, but the costs will vary based on manpower loading requirements, the specific task being performed, and the amount of activity required on each task. Other cost items will be peculiar to the particular department functions. The estimator must be aware of such variations in departmental costs to preclude overlooking their significant value in performing an estimate. Another common practice is the establishment of separate overhead or burden pools for each functional task. These pools carry peripheral costs that are related to and are a function of the man-hours expended in a particular functional task. The structural makeup of an estimate is so complex that computer techniques for compilation are essential.

14.9 PROFESSIONAL CERTIFICATION

It is a mark of achievement and a distinct honor to obtain a certification title. Becoming a certified cost estimator can assure recognition along with the potential for upward mobility in the job market. The presence of a certificate on the office wall is impressive, but, more important, it implies the earning of the title and position of a professional. Continued application of one's estimating capabilities should increase credibility, self-esteem, and in turn help to ensure continued professionalism in the field of estimating.

Since cost estimating requires the knowledge and efforts of varied educational disciplines, the title of Certified Professional Estimator is available to all who can pass the certification requirements of the National Estimating Society. Several other organizations engaged in cost analysis and cost estimating or the expanded use of final cost information also have test certification programs for their members. The test qualification requirements are unique to each organization. Therefore to acquire certification in two or more organizations one must pass their separate test requirements. Table 14.1 provides a list of six such organizations that provide test program certifications. Each of the six professional organizations listed have specific provisions for obtaining certification and for certification retention. All perform cost analysis, cost estimating, or related support functions.

14.9.1 National Estimating Society

The National Estimating Society administers the examination for Certified Professional Estimator. The national headquarters' address is listed in Table 14.2. The society office furnishes a list of required study material and informs the local chapter of your request. A local chapter representative will assist with examination preparation and provide the date and location of the examination. All exams are conducted at the chapter level.

The society provides for certification retention by reexamination or through a

TABLE 14.1. Organization Certification Requirements

Professional Organization	Type of Certificate[a]	Certification by Exam	Recertification		
			By Credit		By Exam
National Estimating Society	CPE(1)	X	X	or	X
Institute of Management Accounting	CMA	X	X		
American Association of Cost Engineers	CCE(1)	X	X	or	X
	CCC	X	X	or	X
National Contract Management	CPCM	X	X		
Association	CACM	X	X		
Institute of Cost Analysis	CCA	X			
American Society of Professional Estimators	CPE(2)	X			
	CCE(2)	X			
Society of American Value Engineers	CVS	X	X	or	X

[a]CACM   Certified Associate Contracts Manager
CCA   Certified Cost Analyst
CCC   Certified Cost Consultant
CCE(1) Certified Cost Engineer
CCE(2) Certified Construction Estimator
CMA   Certified Management Accountant
CPCM   Certified Professional Contract Manager
CPE(1)   Certified Professional Estimator
CPE(2)   Certified Professional Estimator
CVS   Certified Value Specialist

professional credit plan every five years. The professional credit plan consists of a specified amount of continuing education, for example, attendance at regularly scheduled seminars, conferences, plus study or teaching provisions, all related to cost estimating.

14.9.2 Institute of Management Accounting

The Institute of Management Accounting administers the examination for Certified Management Accountant. The Institute's address is listed in Table 14.2. The Institute furnishes a list of required study material, site locations, and testing dates.

The recertification program consists of a specified amount of continuing education activity in each of the three years subsequent to receipt of the initial CMA certificate. Documentation of continuing education activities is required to retain certification.

TABLE 14.2. Professional Society Locations

National Estimating Society
1001 Connecticut Avenue
Suite 800
Washington, D.C. 20036

Institute of Management Accounting
10 Paragon Drive
Dept. A, P.O. Box 405
Montvale, NJ 07645

American Association of Cost Engineers
308 Monongahela Building
Morgantown, WV 26505-5468

National Contract Management Association
6728 Old McLean Village Drive
McLean, VA 22101

Institute of Cost Analysis
7111 Marlan Drive
Suite A
Alexandria, VA 22307

American Society of Professional Estimators
6911 Richmond Highway
Alexandria, VA 22306

International Society of Parametric Analysts
6803 Whittier Avenue
McLean, VA 22101

Society of American Value Engineers
221 LaSalle Street
Suite 2026
Chicago, IL 60601

14.9.3 American Association of Cost Engineers

The American Association of Cost Engineers administers the examination for a Certified Cost Engineer or a Certified Cost Consultant. The Association's address is listed in Table 14.2. The Association furnishes a list of subject material in preparation for the four-part examination, plus sample examination material, a list of locations, and examination dates.

The Association provides for certification retention through a professional credit plan or by reexamination every three years.

14.9.4 National Contract Management Association

The National Contract Management Association administers the examination for Certified Professional Contracts Manager. The Association's address is listed in Table 14.2. The Association furnishes study material necessary for the scheduled six-hour essay examination for CPCM and provides for certification retention through a professional credit plan.

14.9.5 Institute of Cost Analysis

The Institute of Cost Analysis administers the examination for Certified Cost Analyst. The Institute's address is listed in Table 14.2.

At present the Institute does not have a recertification program. It is understood that the Institute's "Board of Regents" is studying recertification requirements to assure that those certified are staying abreast of current cost analysis needs.

14.9.6 American Society of Professional Estimators

The American Society of Professional Estimators administers the examination for certification in one or more of the 17 construction estimating disciplines (CED). The Society's address is listed in Table 14.2. At present the society does not have a recertification program.

14.9.7 Society of American Value Engineers

The Society of American Value Engineers has a certification program that results in the designation of a member as a Certified Value Specialist (CVS). Its address is listed in Table 14.2.

14.9.8 International Society of Parametric Analysts

At present the International Society of Parametric Analysts (address is listed in Table 14.2) does not have a certification program.

14.10 A NEW, CHANGING ENVIRONMENT IN COST ESTIMATING

A number of activities are underway to improve, expand, and increase the importance of cost estimates, cost estimators, and the cost estimating profession. Legislation has been introduced and enacted in Congress to bring to the public attention the need for improved cost estimating in both the private and public sectors. Professional societies have been formed and are growing rapidly in membership, scope, and influence. The curriculums of colleges and universities are beginning to include more courses in economics, business, accounting, and management for technical as well as nontechnical degrees. More publications, books, and magazine articles in technical, nontechnical, and media publications are including information on cost estimating, cost control, and cost management. Cost estimating is a truly growing and expanding function in today's society. The disciplines, functions, and methodologies described in this book collectively make up this emerging field of cost estimating. Each aspect of cost estimating can and may very well grow into a profession of its own (i.e.: parametric estimating, industrial engineering type estimating, etc.). In this, the dawn of the information age, conscientious adherence to the belief that a good cost estimate is a necessary input to informed management decisions will make this growth and expansion of the estimating profession a reality and will result in cost estimates that can be relied on by managers in industry and government, and by the public, in accurately predicting and forecasting the resources required to produce work.

REFERENCES

1. Stewart R. D. *Cost Estimating*. Wiley, New York, 1982.
2. Stewart, R. D. *Proposal Preparation*. Wiley, New York, 1984.
3. Earles, M. E. *Factors, Formulas, and Structures for Life Cycle Costing*, 2nd ed. E. E. Press, Concord, Mass., 1981.
4. Boehm, B. W. *Software Engineering Economics*. Prentice-Hall, Englewood Cliffs, N.J.,1981.
5. Harrison, R. S. *How To—Cost Estimating Manual*. Lockheed Corp., Burbank, Cal., 1984.
6. Department of Defense. *Planning, Programming, and Budgeting System*. The Joint DOD/GAO Working Group on PPBS, Washington, D.C., September 1983

15

ARTIFICIAL INTELLIGENCE IN COST ESTIMATING

JAMES D. JOHANNES, PHD

15.1 INTRODUCTION

Estimating project costs involves two major problems. One problem is the high level of risk and uncertainty in the estimate. The risk and uncertainty are basically attributable to three factors: (1) requirements are subject to change; (2) innovation may be required during the project; and (3) risks are inherent in the project's life-cycle since errors, which may cause iteration over prior activities, are inevitable. Each of these factors tends to increase project costs. Good estimating involves working from firm requirements, understanding the required product, and carefully managing the development to ensure that the costs are not overrun.

The second major problem in estimating costs is the lack of accurate measures of prior costs—the lack of a quantitative historical cost data base. Without reference standards it is nearly impossible to estimate the cost of a new project accurately. The available information usually is not organized or disseminated at the proper level needed for estimation. This problem can be solved only by proper cost summaries archived and disseminated for each project effort.

Many features of artificial intelligence (AI) make it attractive for application to a cost estimation problem. Marvin Minsky [1] defined artificial intelligence as ". . . the science of making machines do things that would require intelligence if done by men." A different definition, similar in spirit but allowing for shifting standards, is given by Elaine Rich [2] ". . . the study of how to make computers do things at which, at the moment, people are better." A primary difference between artificial intelligence and more traditional data processing approaches is summarized by the maxim, "Knowledge is Power." The operative word is knowledge, rather than data or processor speed. Knowledge-intensive systems attempt to model the imperfectly understood decision processes of the domain practitioner and, like the human practitioner, make decisions with less than perfection.

An interface exists between artificial intelligence and system engineering. A system engineering process is created to translate the operational problem into a proposed engineering solution. The postulated system solution may include hardware, firmware, or only software components. The primary questions in this embryonic stage are concerned with defining the exact nature of the problem: what general solution will solve the problem, whether the operational problem can be solved by combining (or recombining) existing system components, or will a totally new system development be required. The potential costs of the solution are contrasted with the expected benefits to the customer. The emphasis in this phase should be on what the problem is, as opposed to how it is to be solved.

Two major alternatives exist for developing a project cost estimate. An estimate of total cost can first be derived by some means, such as comparison with a similar project, and the appropriate percentages can be allocated to each part of the project. The percentages can be based on experience with other projects or on rules of thumb. The result is a detailed cost breakdown such as might be required for a cost proposal.

The problem with this approach is that the entire process depends on one initial total cost estimate. Sufficient care should be taken to ensure that the allocation of costs is reasonable and supported by a large knowledge base of historical data. However, even if the allocation is perfect, the whole cost estimate could be off by an order of magnitude. It is extremely difficult, if not impossible, to use this method for project costing. It is, however, good for preproposal planning or for a quick estimate based on a productivity factor or a dollar factor for planning purposes, but not for bidding.

The second costing procedure is essentially the inverse of the first. The project definition is decomposed top-down until the functional elements are sufficiently small to be estimated; that is, until they are sufficiently small for the function to be understood well enough to size, evaluate, and cost. The project cost estimate will prove to be correct and include provision for sufficient support resources only if proper preparations are made before the cost is estimated. These include the following:

Decomposing the project into manageable tasks (detailed work breakdown structure)

Analyzing the project efforts required

Identifying the risk areas and planning for risk management

Anticipating typical problems and delays

Identifying support resources needed

On the basis of this information, detailed schedules and cost information can be prepared, and the total project cost estimate can then be developed. This forms the basis for management of the project and the nucleus of the project plan. Before addressing the specifics of AI as applied to cost estimation, it is necessary for the reader to understand certain basic concepts and terms as related to cost estimating, system engineering, strategy, tactics, plans, experience, and heuristics.

The primary *system engineering* function to be performed is the cost analysis of the operational environment and the user's problems, with the goal of redefining their problems in precise engineering terms. The basic approach is to perform an analysis of the operational requirements specified in the statement of need by thoroughly defining the system and the environment in which the system must perform. This system definition analysis should result in a clear understanding of the user's needs, including the system environment, constraints, and effectiveness measures as perceived by the customer. Once complete, this will allow management to perform planning, risk analysis, and the definition of specific criteria for the attainment of the systems milestones. One hopes that this will result in a realistic proposal that from the beginning calls for documentation, reviews, and audits, not only by name, but also by defining specifically what their content will be and the criteria of acceptance to be applied at each phase of the development to meet the needs of the current customer.

A company's *strategy* is a continuous matching of anticipated opportunities and problems in the industry with distinctive company strengths—and limitations. This strategy should be amplified and clarified into policy, which serves as a more specific guide to executives in the various functional divisions of the company.

The strategy can make or break an organization. The difference between a *plan* and a strategy is that a plan is not a strategy until it has been translated into a set of action decisions. Strategy concentrates on basic directions, major thrusts, and overriding priorities of plans, and, once selected, allocates resources to them. *Tactics* are defined as the means of executing previously defined plans to secure the objectives designated by strategy. Strategy furnishes tactics with the opportunity to strike and with the prospect of success. Many concerns in strategic planning are simply attempts to answer the question about plan payoff. The main reason a strategy does not succeed is the inability of management to bring strategic planning down to current decisions. Strategic planning can pay off if the strategy is implemented properly.

The development and communication of a cost strategy is the most important single activity of top management. The maxim, "Managing means looking ahead," is an indication of the importance of cost planning and forecasting in management. Cost planning and plans of action are perhaps the most important phase of management. Support for the statement that a plan of action is indispensable for an organization to succeed is provided by the manager. It is interesting to note that experience plays a major role in determining if a plan has value. Some of the highlights concerning plans are the following:

1. Only one plan can be put into action at a time.
2. Plans can be divided into numerous subplans.
3. Plans must be continuous.
4. New plans should immediately follow previous plans.
5. Plans should be flexible.

Plans alone cannot make an organization successful. Action by the organization is required for success to occur. Plans play a very important role in focusing attention on and guiding the action of an organization. Without plans, actions would be random activities and chaos could result. The cost estimation plan must be continuous in guiding action. When one plan terminates, another one must follow immediately. This replacement process repeats itself as required. The cost plans must "bend" to accommodate adjustments introduced from pressure or current circumstances. Plans should lay out the actions as precisely as possible. Only one plan can be put into operation at a time. More than one plan would mean duality, confusion, and disorder.

Experience is the only thing that finally determines the true value of a plan. Determining what knowledge is relevant to a given problem becomes crucial when the expert knows many different things [3]. Retrieval of the exact knowledge to solve the problem at hand is the optimum procedure to pursue. The costing expert must figure out what knowledge is needed from what is already known without being explicitly told all the information. When knowledge is improved, the expert will assimilate the current set of data and determine how it affects the area of expertise. Experts are in a constant state of obtaining new knowledge to stay abreast of the changes in the state of the experts' knowledge base.

A *heuristic* is a rule of thumb, strategy, trick, simplification, or any other kind of device that drastically limits search for solutions in large problem spaces. Heuristics do not guarantee optimal solutions; in fact, they do not guarantee any solution at all; all that can be said for a useful heuristic is that it offers solutions that are good enough most of the time. A heuristic search technique [4] uses information about a particular problem domain to help reduce the search space; the question, then, is how to search the given space efficiently for the optimal cost estimation.

15.2 KNOWLEDGE-BASED COST ESTIMATION PARADIGM

The basic cost estimation paradigm can be summarized as "machine-in-the-loop," where all project cost estimation activities are machine mediated and supported. Initially the system will automatically document the occurrence of every costing activity and ensure the proper sequencing and coordination of all the activities performed by the individuals involved in the project.

The knowledge-based cost estimation paradigm of the future will provide a set of tools and capabilities integrated into an "assistant" that directly supports the human cost estimators in the cost estimation processes. All life-cycle costing activities are machine mediated and supported by the knowledge-based assistant as directed by the manager of the project. These activities will be recorded to provide the "corporate memory" of the system evolution and will be used by the system to determine how the parts interact, what assumptions they make about each other, the rationale behind each evolutionary step, how the project satisfies its requirements, and how to explain all these to the cost estimator and to project management.

This knowledge base will be dynamically acquired as a by-product of the cost estimation and actual management of each project. It must include not only the individual manipulation steps that ultimately lead to an implementation, but also the rationale behind those estimation steps. To make the process possible, it will be necessary to formalize all life-cycle activities. For the knowledge-based cost estimation assistant to begin to participate in the activities described previously, and not merely record them, the activities must be at least partially formalized. Formalization is the most fundamental basis for automated support; it creates the opportunity for the assistant to undertake responsibility for the performance of the activity, analysis of its effects, and eventually decide which activities are appropriate. Not only will individual costing activities become increasingly formalized, but so, too, will coordinated sets of them which accomplish larger costing steps. In fact, the costing process itself will be increasingly formalized as coordinated activities among multiple projects.

A cost estimation expert system must be able to make decisions on a par with a cost estimator primarily because its structure reflects the manner in which human specialists arrange and make inferences from their knowledge of the subject. The system is driven by a data-base of inexact and judgmental knowledge. Data (knowledge) about the problem domain may be of various forms. Some data may be applicable to the knowledge base; these are generally called (inference) rules since their function is to deduce (new) facts about the domain from the existing data. Other data may take the form of heuristics for deciding when rules or project data can be usefully applied.

The type of computer program that is used to develop an expert system cannot have its flow of control and data utilization rigidly fixed because such a structure is ill-adapted for simulating a human's responses to a complex, rapidly changing, and unfamiliar environment. Instead, such a program must examine the state of the world at each step of the decision process and react appropriately because new stimuli continually arise.

The knowledge base needs change with time. The cost management support system will need to be modified to represent the knowledge efficiently as cost data changes or as the trade-offs of the present project become better understood. Compiled knowledge systems are relatively efficient and fast. The computation time of the system will be drastically reduced by the compilation of knowledge.

A way to organize knowledge is in frames, also called data structures, in which all knowledge about a particular object, event, or functionally identifiable chunk of work is stored. These frames can include more than just attribute data; they can also contain rules to express more complex facts or relationships, to specify default values for pieces of information about an object when that information is not explicitly given, and to invoke or link to other frames when applicable data conditions or patterns are met. In this method, the organization and structure of the knowledge (frames containing data and rules semantically linked to other frames dynamically, in terms of the current situation) is used to constrain and guide the cost estimator to a smaller and more tightly bounded search space of possible candidate solutions.

Frame approaches allow the implementation of "deeper-level" reasoning such as abstraction and analogy. Reasoning by analogy is an important expert activity. One can also represent the objects, part of the project, and processes of the domain of expertise at this level. What is important are the relations between objects. Deep-representation expert systems perform inference using relations represented by frames. A frame system organizes the objects and their relations into entities (recognizable collections of objects). Thus a frame system implements the semantics of some of the relations between objects. With a frame system you can represent objects of the domain of expertise as well as the process, strategies, and so on, that are also part of the domain.

An interesting and much discussed feature of frame-based processing is the ability of a frame to determine whether it is applicable in a given situation [5]. The idea is that a likely frame is selected to aid in the process of understanding the current situation (dialogue, cost estimate, problem), and this frame in turn tries to match itself to the data it discovers. If it finds that it is not applicable, it can transfer control to a more appropriate frame. Before addressing solution search techniques, some concepts from graph and game theory should be presented. Formally, a *graph* consists of a nonempty set N, whose elements are called *nodes*, and a set A whose elements are called *arcs*. Every arc in A is a pair of nodes from the set N. A tree is a special case of a graph. It is defined as an acyclic connected graph for which the path between any two nodes is unique. For people, diagrams are the most convenient way of dealing with graphs and trees; but for computers, a set of pairs is easier to represent. In AI, trees and graphs are used to represent games. A game, as used in this context, represents the steps of the process of finding solutions to the subprocesses of the cost estimating problem. It is represented by a directed graph, or tree, with a set of nodes called positions and a set of arcs called moves. Moving from one node to another by way of an arc is accomplished by following a specific rule for that move. The new position node is called the *successor* of the previous node. *Terminal nodes*, also referred to as leaves, are nodes representing possible solutions to the game.

The *minimax* procedure of two-person game theory, could be used as a technique for searching the cost estimation solution trees. The goal would be to find a good plan by generating a reasonable portion of the tree starting from the present, and then make a move on the basis of this partial knowledge. Once the partial tree exists, minimaxing requires a means for estimating the value of its cost estimation. A function assigning such a value is called a *static evaluation function*, which serves the same purpose as the heuristic function used in an ordered search. If the partial tree contains any nodes that are terminal for the entire tree, the static evaluation function conventionally returns a cost estimation plan that would be based on the estimator's best inputs.

The points at which heuristic information can be applied in a search include the following:

1. Deciding which node to expand next, instead of doing the expansions in a strictly breadth-first or depth-first order
2. In the course of expanding a node, deciding which successor or successors to generate—instead of blindly generating all possible successors at one time
3. Deciding that certain nodes should be discarded, or pruned from the search tree

Ordered state space search is one that always selects the most promising cost plan based on the estimator inputs, the company's strategy, and the current historic knowledge of projects.

15.3 FORMAL MODELS

A formal model for a problem domain is a system of definitions and rules that permits a human being to reason about the objects in the domain and their interrelations. Such models are desirable, and perhaps necessary, precursors to any techniques for mechanical reasoning and problem solving in that domain. The shallow knowledge of the models will allow the inference engine to associate the deep knowledge within the knowledge base.

The knowledge base must contain the knowledge and understanding of a subject matter and incorporate the logical aspect of human intelligence. It must be able to generate problem solutions from situations never before encountered and not anticipated by the cost system designers. It must be able to infer the true state of the system from incomplete and/or inaccurate measurements. The knowledge concerning each domain must, at least conceptually, be available in the knowledge base that is utilized by the various tools that reason about the current state of the costing system. This knowledge is represented in a fashion appropriate for external use and is also represented internally in such a way that it can be accessed, updated, and efficiently maintained. Several external representations will often be desired. For example, the form in which a costing expert presents knowledge to the knowledge base may differ drastically from the form in which the system represents this information to someone who is not a cost expert. For the nonexpert, the knowledge would be explained in lay terms, detailing some aspect of the knowledge about certain objects or situations.

15.4 A FRAME-BASED SYSTEM

The following 12 areas of cost estimating are outlined in Chapter 1:

1. Develop the work element structure
2. Schedule the work elements

   3. Retrieve and organize historical data
   4. Develop and use cost estimation relationships
   5. Develop and use production learning curves
   6. Identify skill categories, skill levels, and labor rates
   7. Develop labor-hour and material estimates
   8. Develop overhead and administrative costs
   9. Apply inflation and escalation (cost growth) factors
  10. Price or compute the estimated costs
  11. Analyze and adjust the estimate
  12. Publish and present the estimate so that is can be used effectively

Cost estimating, then, is the process of developing a sequence of actions or a plan to achieve a goal, that is, estimating the cost of a work activity. This definition is also true for most problem solving techniques.

Planning is the problem of selecting a sequence of actions that best achieves mission goals and meets both implicit and explicit mission and vehicle constraints. A plan is constructed on the basis of the current knowledge of the state of the world. The world is the current state of the vehicle and its environment. In the world of cost estimating, a detailed plan is required for the actions to be implemented in the near future. As time passes and the system's knowledge of the state of the world is updated or improved, a new plan would be constructed for a better cost estimate of the work activity. This is called replanning.

Requirements for putting this type of planning/replanning construct into effect include such mechanisms as the ability to retain the outputs from one stage of the process to be utilized as inputs to another stage, that is, a knowledge base. This type of requirement for a hierarchical planner could be resolved by using the frame concept in expert systems. Once the frames are in place and have been verified by the cost estimating expert, the next step to be performed by the knowledge engineer is to work with the expert and define the heuristics to be utilized in the different steps or stages of the cost estimating process. As with the knowledge engineer, the heuristics used would depend greatly on the expert's input and partly on the vehicle used to implement the expert system. Therefore the rest of this section concentrates on the development of the frames for the example system.

15.4.1 Building Work Element Structures

A frame for containing the information needed to help the manager or estimator develop the detailed nomenclature, coding, definitions, and interactions in a work element structure could be as follows:

```
GENERIC BWES Frame
            WES-Name:   Work element structure
            WES-Desc :  Text
            WES-Code :  Integer
```

WES-Rels :   Relationships
WES-Type :   Cost type (recurring or nonrecurring)

The user would be prompted for these inputs during this step of the process. The criteria used for the formulation of the output could be the number of levels in the work element structure, the number of subelements under any one element, recurring or nonrecurring cost, and the arrangement of the elements themselves. The output of this stage would be the list of work elements, the diagram of the work element structure, and the work element dictionary.

15.4.2 Skill Category and Skill Mix Determination

A frame for containing the information needed to help the manager or estimator develop the structure of a skill category, a skill level hierarchy, and the mix for an organization, and apply this skill mix to a specific work activity, or set of work activities could be as follows:

```
GENERIC SCSM Frame
        SCSM-Name:    Skill category and skill mix
        SCSM-Catg :   Composite labor rate (dollars)
        SCSM-LabN :   Skill level name
        SCSM-LabR :   Skill level rate
        SCSM-MRat :   Skill mix ratios over time
        SCSM-CRat :   Skill composite rates over time
```

The user would be prompted for the inputs during this step of the process. The criteria used for the formulation of the output could be the duration of the work activity, the business and technical content of the work activity, and the interaction with other work activities such as the staffing constraints. The output of this stage is the list of the skill categories and skill levels, a graphic plot of the skill mix over time, and the composite labor rates per time period.

15.4.3 Scheduling and Resource Adjustments

A frame for containing the information needed to help the estimator schedule activities and resources on a time basis, permitting acceleration, slippage, extension, and deletion of schedule elements with proportional redistribution of resources when the work activity time frame changes is as follows:

```
GENERIC SRA Frame
        SRA-WES:    Work element activity pointer
        SRA-Fund:   Funding class
        SRA-Rall :  Resource allocations
        SRA-Rdpa:   Relations to other activities/funding
```

The user would be prompted for the inputs during this step of the process. The criteria used for the formulation of the output would be the durations of the work activity and the interaction with the other work activities. The output of this stage would be the resource distribution by work activity, a histogram or bar chart of the the available funding versus the needed funding, and a plot showing the optimum for the resource profiles.

15.4.4 Cost Growth and Contingency Estimation

A frame for containing the information needed to help the estimator compute the allowance for cost growth due to incomplete design and to establish cost contingencies and escalation factors would be as follows:

```
GENERIC CGCE Frame
          CGCE-WES:   Work element structure pointer
          CGCE-Num:   Integer; identifier for this WES
          CGCE-Cost:  Cost estimate for activity (dollars)
          CGCE-Sklr:  Skill level required
          CGCE-Skla:  Skill level available
          CGCE-Time:  Time allowed for work activity
          CGCE-Desn:  Percent of design completed
          CGCE-Risk:  Risk factor
          CGCE-Next:  Pointer to next CGCE frame for next activity
                      involved
```

The user would be prompted for these inputs during this step to the process. The criteria used for the formulation of the output would be the cost growth due to (1) incomplete design, (2) degree of customer involvement in work activity, (3) amount of flexibility of the labor base, (4) sophistication of the vehicle used for estimating, and (5) the past history of estimating and scheduling activities. The output of this stage would be the program contingency and program cost growth allowances for the overall program, contingency for each work element, and the cost growth for each work element.

15.4.5 Parametric Estimating

This is the stage in which heuristics are used to predict the future based on past knowledge. Here the knowledge engineer and cost estimator will maintain close communication in defining a workable system. A frame for containing the information needed to help the estimator develop the estimate would be as follows:

```
GENERIC PEST Frame
          PEST-WES:   Work element structure pointer
          PEST-Cost:  Element cost (dollars)
          PEST-Time:  Time schedule for each element
          PEST-Ppar:  Principal parameters for each element
          PEST-Mix:   Labor and materials mix per element
```

PEST-Mcos: Cost, recurring or nonrecurring, per element
PEST-Next : Pointer to next PEST frame for next work activity

The user would be prompted for these inputs during this step of the process. The criteria used for the formulation of the output could be whether the labor or materials are based on recurring or nonrecurring costs, the total program time constraints, the structure of a new estimate, and the principal technical parameters for the new estimate. The output of this stage would be a plot of the cost versus time for the program, the labor/materials histograms, and the recurring/nonrecurring cost histograms.

15.4.6 Cost Factor Development and Use

A frame for containing the information needed to help the estimator calculate percentages and direct cost interactions, and determine the effect of total direct costs on overhead, would be as follows:

GENERIC CFD Frame
CFD-WES: Work element structure pointer
CFD-Labc: Labor cost for work element
CFD-Matc: Material cost for work element
CFD-Totc : Total cost for work element
CFD-Toto : Total overhead or indirect costs
CFD-Next: Pointer to next CFD frame for next work activity

The user would be prompted for these inputs during this step of the process. The criteria used for the formulation of the output would be the established work element structure, the level of significance target value, and the strawman job description. The output of this stage would be the list of important factors to consider and sensitivity plots. For example, overhead versus various direct cost elements, and the strawman cost estimate.

15.4.7 Make-or-Buy Criteria and Determination

A frame for containing the information needed to help the estimator determine the degree of premachining, preassembly or premanufacture of raw materials and parts would be as follows:

GENERIC MBCD Frame
MBCD-Resh: Resources versus costs for in-house work
MBCD-Resv: Resources versus cost for vendor work
MBCD-Mix : History mix of in-house versus vendor
MBCD-Sch : Schedule variations of in-house versus vendor

The user would be prompted for these inputs during this step of the process. The criteria used for the formulation of the output would be the funding profile for the proposed project, schedule for the proposed project, and the desirable make/buy ratio versus time. The output for this stage would be the make/buy structure, all-make project costs, all-buy project costs, and optimum mix project costs.

15.4.8 Determining Mix and Magnitude of Independent Research and Development

The output of this stage is heavily dependent on the heuristics chosen to process the input and output. A frame for containing the information needed to help the estimator analyze technology advancement efforts to determine their relation to the overall product line and market growth objectives would be as follows:

```
GENERIC MMIR Frame
        MMIR-Name:   MMIR effort name
        MMIR-Fund :  MMIR funding per effort
        MMIR-Key  :  Key words for effort
        MMIR-Gomx:   Company goals and objectives matrix pointer
        MMIR-Time :  Schedule for each technology effort
        MMIR-Next :  Pointer to next MMIR frame for next technology
                     effort
```

The criteria used for the formulation of the output would be the range of budget efforts permitted, funding and time limitations, and amount of duplication permitted between efforts. The output of this stage would be the plan of action for independent research and development, priority of each advancement, and estimated funding profile versus budget for additional research.

15.4.9 Profit and Profitability Determination and Planning

A frame for containing the information needed to help the estimator track profit and profitability and establish achievable objectives and goals would be as follows:

```
GENERIC PPDP Frame
        PPDP-Hist:   Profit history of element
        PPDP-Ret :   Return on investment versus time
        PPDP-Fin :   Company income parameters
```

The user would be prompted for these inputs during this step of the process. The criteria used for the formulation of the output would be the degree of reliance on cash flow, the degree of importance of future growth for the company, and the mix of short-term versus long-term profit objectives as stated by the company. The output of this stage would be the capital investment allocation, the profitability projection, and the cost reduction initiatives.

15.4.10 Purchasing Decision Making (Source Evaluation and Selection)

A frame for containing the information needed to help the estimator perform a detailed analysis of several bids against an internally produced estimate follows. This provides a recommendation of a bidder with the highest probability of performing the work activity within a given fixed goal value.

```
GENERIC PDSE Frame
        PDSE-Bnam:   Name of bidder
        PDSE-Bid   :   Pointer to the detailed cost proposal
        PDSE-Ibid  :   Pointer to the detailed independent cost proposal
        PDSE-Bhis  :   History factor for bidder
        Pdse-Next  :   Pointer to next PDSE frame for next bidder involved
                       in the analysis
```

The criteria used for the formulation of the output would be the scheduled completion date and consequences of a slippage per month (in dollars), the overall project budget profile, and the scoring factors for technical, cost, and schedule performance. The output of this stage would be an estimate of merit for each proposed bidder, a bidder ranking list, and a "probability of completion" factor for each bidder considered.

15.5 SUMMARY

All of the discussed stages would require interfacing capability with each other. Several development tools are available on the commercial market that could be used to implement the outlined system. Primary among these are KEE (Knowledge Engineering Environment) [6] and KL-ONE [7].

Cost estimating using artificial intelligence is truly in its infancy at present, but such concepts, properly and conscientiously applied, will provide the best tool yet in the quest for more accurate, credible, and realistic cost estimates. Artificial intelligence techniques are ideally suited for cost estimating, and the reader can expect to see the frequent introduction of new estimating tools using these techniques in the remainder of the 1980s and well into the 1990s.

REFERENCES

1. Minsky, M. "A Framework for Representing Knowledge," *in The Psychology of Computer Vision*. P. Winston, Ed. McGraw-Hill, New York, 1975, 211-277.

2. Rich, E. *Artificial Intelligence*. McGraw-Hill, New York, 1983.

3. Hayes-Roth, F., D. A. Waterman, and D. B. Lenat, Eds. *Building Expert Systems*. Addison-Wesley, Reading, Mass., 1983.

4. Nilsson, N. J. *Principles of Artificial Intelligence*. Tioga Publishing Co., Palo Alto, Cal., 1980.

5. Fikes, R. E. and T. P. Kehler. "The Role of Frame-Based Representation in Reasoning," *Communications ACM*, Vol. 28, No. 9, 904–920 (September 1985).

6. Kehler, T. P. and G. D. Clemson. "An Application Development System for Expert Systems," *System Software*, Vol. 3, No. 1, 212–224 (January 1984).

7. Brachman, R. J. and J. G. Smchmolze. "An Overview of the KL-ONE Knowledge Representation System," *Cognitive Science*, Vol. 9, No. 2, 171-216, (April 1985).

BIBLIOGRAPHY

Boehm, Barry W. *Software Engineering Economics*. Prentice-Hall, Englewood Cliffs, N.J., 1981.

Clark, Forrest D. and A. B. Lovenzoni. *Applied Cost Engineering*. Dekker, New York, 1985.

Del Mar, Donald. *Operations and Industrial Management*; McGraw-Hill; New York; 1985.

Draper, N. R. and N. Smith. *Applied Regression Analysis*, 2nd ed. Wiley, New York, 1981.

Earles, Mary Eddins. *Factors, Formulas, and Structures for Life Cycle Costing*, 2nd ed. Eddins-Earles Publishing, Concord, Mass., 1981.

Fisher, Gene H. *Cost Considerations in Systems Analysis*. American Elsevier, New York, 1971.

Goldman, Thomas A. *Cost Effectiveness Analysis*. Praeger, New York, 1971.

Grant, Eugene L. et al. *Principles of Engineering Economy*. Wiley, New York, 1982.

Hillier, Frederick S. and Gerald J. Lieberman. *Introduction to Operations Research*, 4th ed. Holden-Day, San Francisco, 1986.

Jelen, Frederic C. and James H. Black. *Cost and Optimization Engineering*, 2nd ed. McGraw-Hill, New York, 1983.

Jordan, Raymond B. *How to Use the Learning Curve*. Cahner Books, Boston, Mass., 1972.

Kaplan, Seymour. *Energy Economics*. McGraw-Hill, New York, 1983.

Miller, Irwin, and John E. Freund. *Probability and Statistics for Engineers*, 3rd ed. Prentice-Hall, Englewood Cliffs, N.J., 1985.

Moder, Joseph J. et al. *Project Management with CPM, PERT, and Precedence Diagramming*, 3rd ed. Van Nostrand Reinhold, New York, 1983.

Newnan, Donald G. *Engineering Economic Analysis*, 2nd ed. Engineering Press, San Jose, Cal., 1983.

Ostwald, Phillip F. *Cost Estimating*. Prentice-Hall, Englewood Cliffs, N.J., 1984.

Riggs, James L. *Production Systems: Planning, Analysis and Control*, 3rd ed. Wiley, New York, 1981.

Salvendy, Gavriel. *Handbook of Industrial Engineering*. Wiley, New York, 1982.

Shannon, Robert E. *Systems Simulation, The Art and Science*. Prentice-Hall, Englewood Cliffs, N.J., 1975.

Shelly, Gary B. and Thomas J. Cashman. *Complete Fundamentals for an Information Age*. Anahiem Publishing, Brea, Cal., 1984.

Stewart, Rodney D. and Ann L. Stewart *Microestimating for Civil Engineers, Microestimating for Mechanical Engineers*, and *Microestimating for Chemical Engineers*. McGraw-Hill, New York, 1986/1987.

Wilson, Frank C. *Industrial Cost Controls*. Prentice-Hall, Englewood Cliffs, N.J., 1971.

DICTIONARY OF ESTIMATING TERMS*

Abnormal Fluctuation in Economy (AFIE) Clause: A government contract clause that permits coverage of the costs resulting from abnormal fluctuations in the economy. See Economic Price Adjustment, Escalation Clause.

Absorption: The process of distributing indirect or overhead costs over a defined resource base such as labor hours, labor dollars, material dollars or total cost so that, at the end of an accounting period, the indirect costs will be totally "absorbed."

Accessorial Cost/Charge: Certain expenses that will be charged as an addition to the sale price of material delivered. These expenses include transportation costs, packing, crating, handling, loading, and unloading costs.

Account: A record, usually in the form required for double entry bookkeeping, of transactions relating to a person, an item of property, an asset, liability, capital, or elements of revenues, or funds for a given fiscal period. A summarized presentation of such transactions in a financial statement in ledger form.

Account Balance: The net excess of debits over credits in an account, or vice versa—described as "debit balance" or "credit balance"—or in case of equality, "zero balance."

Account Number: A number used to designate general, subsidiary ledger, or overhead accounts.

Accounting: The classifying, recording, summarizing, reporting, verifying, analyzing, and interpreting of the economic and financial data of a business.

Accounting Calendar: A calendar that sets forth the organization's fiscal year divided into 12 months, each of which contains either four or five weeks.

*Adapted, by permission, from the National Estimating Society Dictionary. National Estimating Society, 1001 Connecticut Ave. NW, Suite 800, Washington, D.C. 20036.

Accounting Document: Any form or original record that evidences a financial or property transaction. For example, voucher, invoice, bill, contract, receipt, order, requisition, or procurement directive.

Accounting Period: A definite period of time (month, quarter, year) for which financial transactions are recorded. In the public sector may be fixed by legislative or other regulatory action. In the private sector the accounting year may be fixed to coincide with the natural annual seasonal cycle of an enterprise.

Accounting Policy: A defined course of action in the accounting area adopted or prescribed to be followed by those with the responsibility for the function.

Accounting Principles: Fundamental or basic rules or laws of action, governing the policies and procedures relating to accounting and based on desirable objectives for financial or economic control and administration.

Accounting Report: A formal statement, with or without narrative or exposition, showing financial condition at a given time or the results of transactions or operations for a given period.

Accounting System: An operating plan, including methods, procedures, and forms for classifying, recording, and summarizing financial data for a given enterprise or undertaking.

Accrued Expenditures: Charges incurred for goods and services received and other assets acquired, regardless of whether payment for the charges has been made.

ACRS: Accelerated capital recovery system. A method of depreciating property and real assets.

Acquisition Cost: Total expenditures estimated or incurred for the development, manufacture, construction, and installation of an item of physical or intangible property, or the total acquisition cost of a group of such items.

Actual Cost: A cost sustained in fact, on the basis of costs incurred, as opposed to a standard, predetermined, or estimated cost. Actual costs to date include cost of direct labor, direct material, and other direct charges, specifically identified to appropriate cost accounts as incurred, and overhead costs and general administrative expenses reasonably allocated to cost accounts.

Adequate Price Competition: Exists if offers are solicited and at least two responsible offerors who can satisfy the purchaser's requirements independently contend for a contract to be awarded to the responsive and responsible offeror submitting the lowest evaluated price by submitting priced offers responsive to the expressed requirements of the solicitation.

Adjustment: An entry or entries made to correct an account or actuals. A correction supported by a prescribed voucher, such as a labor adjustment sheet.

Administrative Costs/Expense: Those costs that have to do with phases of operations not directly identifiable with the production, sale, or financing of operations. They are costs incurred in connection with policy formation and the overall direction of a business. Salaries of major executives and general services such as accounting, contracting, and industrial relations are included in this category.

Advance Payment: An advance of money in anticipation of performance under a contract or contracts. Generally required to be deposited in a special account and accounted for separately from other funds. To be distinguished from progress payments.

Advertised Contract: A contract resulting from the selection of a firm from among several who respond to formally advertised bids. Usually is a fixed-price contract.

Algorithm: A mathematical set of ordered steps that lead to the optimal solution of a problem in a finite number of operations.

Allocable Cost: A cost is allocable if it is assignable or chargeable to one or more cost objectives in accordance with the relative benefits received or other equitable relationships defined or agreed to between contractual parties.

Allocated Manufacturing Material: Direct material of a usage nature not specifically identified in a bill of material.

Allocation: (1) Financial—A method or combination of methods that will result in a reasonable distribution of indirect or overhead costs. In deciding upon appropriate allocation bases for overhead costs; benefits received, equity, and logic are decisive factors. (2) Engineering—The methodical division of a requirement, such as volume, weight, reliability, or maintainability, downward to constituent system, subsystems, and so on in such a manner that each is assigned a part of the requirement that is appropriate to its hardware level and state of the art. (3) Government—An official piece of paper issued to a major command or other operating agency. It is a funding document and represents cash that can be committed and obligated.

Allotment/Allotted Funds: In government: (1) An authorization by the head or other authorized employee of a customer agency to incur obligations within a specified amount pursuant to an appropriation or other statutory provision; (2) the amount of funds that the government has made available to cover billings from the contractor relative to a given contract.

Allowable Cost: A cost that meets the test of reasonableness, allocability, and is in consonance with standards set by the Cost Accounting Standards Board (if applicable) or otherwise conforms to generally accepted accounting principles, specific limitations, or exclusions set forth between contractual parties.

Allowance: (1) Money furnished in addition to prescribed rates of pay to cover such items as quarters, subsistence, clothing, or travel. (2) Prescribed amount of items of supply or equipment provided for an individual or organization. (3) Resources added to basic estimates to account for cost growth; contingency; personal, fatigue, and delay time; scrap; waste; engineering changes; natural disasters; and so on.

Alteration Cost: The cost of making physical changes in property, such as cutting new openings, and moving partitions, that do not add to the value of the asset.

Alternate: (1) A proposal for a different design or program solution other than the one specified in a request for proposal. (2) A proposal different from the baseline bid. (3) One of two or more bids on one item, submitted on different basis by the same bidder, as provided for in the invitation to a bid. *Note*: Not to be confused with option. See Option.

Amortization: That amount of write-off to profit and loss each year in addition to normal and true depreciation permitted by the Internal Revenue Service in computing taxes. The partial or total write-off of development costs against hardware costs.

Annual Appropriations: Also known as one-year appropriations. In government procurement, appropriations that are generally used for current administrative, maintenance, and operational programs, including the procurement of items classified as "expense." These appropriations are available for obligation for one fiscal year and for expenditures for two additional years. This additional two-year period for expenditure may be extended by Congress.

Annual Funding: In government procurement the Congressional practice of limiting authorizations and appropriations to one fiscal year at a time. The term should not be confused with two-year or three-year funds which permit the executive branch more than one year to obligate.

ANOVA: Analysis of Variance: used in the statistical evaluation of the appropriateness of estimating relationships.

Appraise: To set a value on, as goods; to estimate the amount of; hence, to judge as to quality, status, and so on.

Appraised Value: A value estimated by appraisers after physical examination of capital property (or an item thereof) or the review of all the factors that would affect its value.

Appropriation: In government procurement an annual authorization by an Act of Congress to incur obligations for specified purposes and to make payments out of the Treasury. Appropriations are subdivided into budget activities, subheads, programs, projects, and so on. Must be accompanied by an authorization to be viable.

As-of-Date: (1) A date (day, month, year) associated with a cost reporting that signifies the data contained in the report reflect the information existing as of that date. (2) A date for retroactive application in recording financial transactions occurring before or on that date, but not actually recorded on that date, particularly to permit a more accurate reporting at the end of a fiscal period.

Asset: Anything owned having monetary value. Property including notes, accounts, accrued earnings, revenues receivable, and cash or its equivalent.

Assumption: A supposition on the current situation, or a presupposition on the future course of events, either or both assumed to be true in the absence of positive proof. Necessary in the process of planning, scheduling, estimating, and budgeting.

Asymptote: A curve that continuously approaches a baseline, axis, or curve but does not meet it within a finite distance.

Attrition: The reduction in a work force caused by loss of personnel and material. The reduction of work force due to transfer, resignation, layoff, or retirement, or in the case of military, release from active duty.

Attrition Rate: A factor, normally expressed as a percentage, reflecting the degree of personnel or material losses due to various causes within a specified period of time.

Audit: The systematic examination of financial records and documents and the securing of other financial evidence by confirmation, physical inspection, or examination.

Audit Report: A report prepared as the result of an audit or examination of the accounts, records, estimate detail, or administrative operating policies, procedures, and practices of a corporate entity, contractor, agency, or individual.

Authorization: In government procurement an annual act of Congress to proceed on a government project. Must be accompanied by an appropriation to be viable. Basic substantive legislation enacted by congress that acts on or continues the legal appropriation of a federal program or agency.

Automated Takeoff: In computerized estimating, the process of electronically extracting quantity information from computer-aided design systems for the purpose of developing bills of materials, lengths, areas, volumes, and parts counts that are subsequently converted to cost information through mathematical relationships.

Average: A typical quantity or value that is representative of a group or series of quantities or values related to a common subject.

Average Lot Release Cost: The amount resulting from the division of the costs accumulated against a lot release by the number of units in that release.

Award Fee: A contractual provision by which the customer determines the fee paid to the contractor on the basis of performances during the contract.

Backlog: Generally, the value of unfilled orders at a particular time.

Back Order: The quantity of an item requisitioned by ordering activities that is not immediately available for issue, but which is recorded as a stock commitment for future issue.

Backup Data: Detailed information consisting of data supporting a cost estimate, proposal, or bid. See Support Data.

Balance-to-Complete Estimates: The labor, materials, and costs necessary to complete a program/project from a given point in time. Combined with actuals to derive the total cost. See Cost-to-Complete.

Base: As in distribution base or base for factor application. The denominator (direct labor hours/dollars, material dollars, units, weight, etc.) used in the development of a factor or rate.

Base/Basic Labor: A term referring to "hands on" or "doing" labor hours. These labor hours form the base for the application of factors for supporting labor functions.

Base Year: A term used to define a year which is: (1) the economic base for dollar amounts in a proposal estimate; (2) the base for rate calculation or projection; or (3) the starting point for the application of inflation factors.

Base Year Costs or Base Year Dollars: Dollars that are expressed in the economic condition of a specific year and do not include escalation or inflation for future years. See Constant Year Dollars.

Baseline Cost Estimate: The first deliberate, detailed estimate of acquisition and ownership costs. This estimate is normally performed in support of costing required for high-level decisions and serves as the base point for all subsequent tracking, auditing, and traceability.

Benefit Cost Analysis: An analytical approach to solving problems of choice. It requires (1) the definition of objectives; (2) identification of alternative ways of achieving each objective; and (3) the identification for each objective or alternative that yields the required level of benefits at the lowest cost. It is often referred to as cost-effectiveness analysis when the benefits of the alternatives cannot be quantified in terms of dollars. See Cost Effectiveness Analysis.

Best-Fit-Line: A line that passes through a group of data point values in a manner that best represents the trend of the data points. The "least squares method" is frequently used to compute this line-of-best-fit.

Bias: An effect that systematically distorts a statistical result. The distortion may be small enough to ignore or large enough to invalidate the results. It may be due to the sample design, the sampling process, or the estimating technique. Analysts try to use "unbiased" techniques.

Bid: Normally implies a response to a customer-initiated request for proposal or quotation: may be either competitive or of single-source nature. In past years a bid was usually simpler in documentation requirements than a proposal. However, in current usage the term bid is often synonymous with proposal.

Bid Bond: A guarantee furnished by a prospective supplier or contractor assuring that the contractor will enter into a contract on which the contractor has bid.

Bid Comparison: The technical, management, and cost evaluations and analysis conducted by a buyer to develop a ranking of bids.

Bid Price: A price offered subject to immediate acceptance for a specific amount of goods and/or services.

Bidding and Proposal Expense: Funds required to conduct the activity or effort directed toward the preparation and presentation of solicited or unsolicited proposals with the intent of obtaining a customer funded contract for a new or improved product or service, or to obtain contractual support for research and development effort.

Bill of Materials: A descriptive and quantitative listing of all the materials, supplies, parts, and components required to produce a complete end item, assembly, or subassembly; to overhaul or repair such an item; or to construct or repair a structure or facility item.

Billing: The preparation and submittal of reports indicating accrued expenses through a specific time period or milestone for payment by the customer.

Block Buy: The purchase of more than one year's requirement under a single year's contract. A total quantity is contracted for in the first contract year.

Bond: A certificate indicating a promise to repay a debt at a specified time. Security for performance of an obligation.

Booked Costs: See Cost Incurred.

Bookkeeping: The recording of financial data for the purpose of accounting, usually under the system known as double-entry bookkeeping and under an accounting system designed by an accountant.

Bottoms-up Estimate: See Detail or Grass Roots Estimate.

Breakdown (Price, Cost, etc.): An orderly subdivision of the cost elements, work elements, or schedule elements that constitute the total work activity or work output.

Breakeven Point: The unit at which the financial return from cumulative product sales equal or recover the cost of the investment required to produce the product.

Budget: (1) A statement, in financial terms, of projected or expected operations of an accounting entity for a given period. (2) The portion of the total cost allocated or assigned to a particular task or set of tasks.

Budget Authorization: An administrative action, normally within the chain of command or management, approving an operating budget for use in execution of a program or programs.

Budget Cycle: (1) General: the period of time that elapses from the initiation of the budget process to the completion thereof for a particular fiscal year. (2) Government: a 24-month cycle that covers the planning, programming, budgeting, enactment, and execution phases.

Budget Estimate or Budgetary Estimate: (1) Government: an estimated fund requirement for any element included in a budget. Collectively, all estimated fund requirements for a particular operating agency or component or consolidation thereof. (2) General: the approximate cost of performing, or completing, the effort required in fulfillment of the performer's understanding of the job. Budget estimates, when requested by a customer, are usually for fiscal planning purposes or for obtaining funding in anticipation of placing an order and do not represent a formal commitment. See Cost Estimate.

Budget Year: The fiscal year that is the subject of new budget estimates.

Budgeting: The process of translating approved or negotiated resource requirements (manpower and material) into time-phased financial targets or goals.

Burden: See Indirect and Overhead.

Calendar Year: The period from January 1 through December 31. (Distinguished from fiscal year.)

Cancellation Ceiling: On contract cancellation, the maximum amount that a customer will pay the supplier which the supplier would have recovered as a part of the unit price, had the contract been completed. (A term used in multiyear contracting.)

Capital: (1) The excess of assets over liabilities of an accounting entity. (2) The expendable or revolving funds used to finance enterprise or activity. (3) The assets of an enterprise, especially fixed property.

Capital Assets: Assets of a permanent character having continuing value.

Capital Expenditure: An expenditure made for the acquisition of, or addition and betterments to, fixed assets.

Cash: Includes coin, currency, money orders, checks, or other forms of exchange, on hand or on deposit, subject to withdrawal on demand. The most liquid form of assets.

Cash Basis of Accounting: A system of accounting whereby (1) revenues are accounted for as collected, and (2) expenditures are accounted for as payments are made.

Cash Discount: A reduction in the amount due on an account if paid within a stated period. (*Note:* The term is not to be confused with Trade Discount).

Cash Flow: The difference in cash between accounts receivable and payable with adjustments made for delinquent accounts and payment check processing.

Ceiling: (In government estimating): (1) The maximum amount on an incentive type contract, usually expressed as a percentage of the contract target cost. (2) The amount of independent research and development (IR&D) and/or bidding and proposal expense recognized by negotiation with the government as allowable during a given year for contract pricing and costing.

Certificate: In government contracting, under public law and Federal Acquisition Regulations, each contractor is required to submit cost or price data and certify to their currentness, accuracy, and completeness prior to the award of most contracts unless the price is based on adequate competition, established catalog, or market prices of commercial items sold to the general public or prices set by law or regulation.

Certified Cost Analyst (CCA): A person who has been certified by the Institute of Cost Analysis after having passed a rigorous test or after having displayed and documented extensive training, experience, and capabilities in cost analysis.

Certified Cost Engineer (CCE): A person who has been certified by the American Association of Cost Engineers after having passed a rigorous test or having displayed and documented extensive training, experience, and capabilities in cost engineering.

Certified Professional Estimator (CPE): A person who has been certified by the National Estimating Society after having passed a rigorous test or after having displayed and documented extensive training, experience, and capabilities in cost estimating.

Charge Number: The sequence or series of digital and/or alphabetical code numbers designed for controlling and sorting accounting information for cost accumulation, reporting, and management use. The charge number also provides cost information in relation to contract work breakdown structure and organization identity.

Chart of Accounts: A list of accounts systematically arranged, applicable to a specific concern, giving account names and numbers, if any. A chart of accounts, accompanied by descriptions of their use and of the general operation of the books of account, becomes a classification or manual of accounts: a leading feature of a system of accounts.

Code: A system of alphabetical, numeric, or alphanumeric characters or symbols designating work breakdown structure (WBS) elements, accounts, vouchers, reports, files, schedules, and documents or items in such a manner that the symbols used will facilitate classification, tabulation, or analysis.

Coefficient of Correlation: A measure of the relationship (correlation) between two variables. Ranges from $+1$ when a perfect positive correlation exists (as x increases, y increases linearly) to a -1 when there is a perfect negative correlation. A correlation coefficient of zero indicates no relationship between the variables. See Correlation Coefficient.

Coefficient of Determination: A measure used in regression analysis. It ranges from zero to one and is developed by dividing the variation in y (dependent variable) explained by the regression equation by the total variation in y. A coefficient of determination of 0.89 means 89% of the total variation was explained by the regression equation.

Commitment: (1) An offer or proposal to a customer or a supplier, or acceptance of an offer from the customer, leading to the execution of a contractural instrument or purchase order. (2) A firm administrative reservation of funds, based upon firm procurement directives, orders, or requisitions; or requests that authorize the creation of an obligation without further recourse to the official responsible for certifying the availability of funds. (3) A contract or other legal obligation for goods or services to be furnished.

Commitment Basis of Accounting: The method of accounting for the available balance of an appropriation, fund, or contract authorization whereby commitments are recorded in the accounts as reductions of the available balance.

Comparative Cost Estimating: Comparing the job (or portions of it) to be done to all or parts of a previously completed job for which valid and comparable cost and technical information is available. This method of cost estimating can be applied to any level of work, detailed or summary, for estimating the cost producing elements or the cost itself. Generally, a proficient cost estimator will use this method to some extent, consciously or unconsciously, because his experience and natural thought processes force this measurement or appraisal. In comparative cost estimating, complexity factors or ratios may be used and applied to the known costs or cost elements to create the estimates—if enough information is available on the completed program to make a valid comparison of the new with the old program. Other terms that apply to this kind of estimating are specific analogy, cost history, estimating by comparison, comparative analysis, "key factor estimating," delta from a previous estimate. See Cost Estimating Methods.

Competition: An environment of varying dimensions relating to buy-sell relationships in which the buyer induces, stimulates, or relies on conditions in the marketplace that cause independent sellers to contend for the award of a contract and/or the sale of the product.

Competitive Negotiation: A negotiated procurement that: (1) is initiated by a request for proposals, which states the customer's (or buyer's) requirements and the criteria for evaluation of offerors; (2) contemplates the submission of timely proposals by the maximum number of possible offerors; (3) usually provides discussion with those offerors found to be within the competitive range; and (4) concludes with the award of a contract to the one offeror whose offer, price and other factors considered, is most advantageous to the customer (or the buyer).

Complexity Factor: A judgement or experience factor to evaluate the degree of unknowns, complexity of design, or difficulty of manufacturing anticipated with a new end item as compared to a similar, previously produced item.

Component: An article that is normally a combination of detailed parts, subassemblies, and assemblies, is a self-contained element of a complete operating equipment end item, and performs a function necessary to the operation of that equipment. It is normally a work element of the second lower level below a subsystem (that is, below an equipment item).

Composite Cost Per Hour Rate: The total estimated direct hours for a given time divided into the total estimated dollars for the same period.

Composite Inflation Index: An index that combines the effects of price level changes and is used to convert constant (base) year dollar costs to current (real) year dollars.

Composite Rate: A labor, overhead, or other rate that has been weighted to account for a mix of different skill categories and skill levels.

Conceptual Estimating: The method of estimating used when little information is available other than gross overall program definition for the products and services to be supplied. Usually this entails the compiling of estimates where the basis is restricted to preliminary specifications, any related or descriptive information, gross weight statements, or complexity comparisons to previously completed products or programs. Comparative, parametric, or statistical estimating methods are used in conceptual estimating.

Confidence Level: The degree of probability that actual cost will fall within an expressed interval of the estimated cost, for example, $\pm 5\%$ of the estimated cost.

Consideration: The value that accrues to a company in return for a benefit passing from the company to another organization or individual outside of the company. It may take the form of money, material, a legal right, goodwill, or other compensation.

Constant (Base) Year Dollars: This phase is always associated with a base year and reflects the dollar "purchasing power" for that year. An estimate is in constant dollars when prior year costs are adjusted to reflect the level of prices of the base year, and future costs are estimated without inflation. A cost estimate is said to be expressed in "constant dollars" when the effect of changes in the purchasing power of the dollar (inflation) has been removed.

Consumable Material: Material that after issue from stock is consumed in use or that, while having continuing life, becomes incorporated in other property, thus losing its identity.

Consumption Rate: The actual or estimated quantity of an item consumed or expended during a given time interval, expressed in quantities by the most appropriate unit of measurement.

Consumption-Type Items: Those items that are either consumed in use or that lose their original identity during periods of use by incorporation into or attachment upon another assembly.

Contingency: An allowance or amount added to an estimate to cover a possible future event or condition arising from unknown causes, the cost outcome of which is indeterminable at a present time.

Contingent Fund: Money set aside to provide for unforeseen expenditures or for anticipated expenditures of uncertain amount.

Contingent Liability: A possible but not certain liability depending on some uncertain future event. In government procurement, represented largely by contract repricing and quantity-variance clauses. In business, includes liability under a guarantee or endorsement of a negotiable instrument.

Continuing Appropriation: In government procurement also known as no-year appropriations. These appropriations provide funds for completing long-range projects, and the funds appropriated remain available for obligation and expenditure until the projects are completed and/or the funds are expended. Normally established for long-term construction and procurement of complex investment items.

Continuous Audit: Any audit that is performed continuously or at intervals during the fiscal period to uncover and correct undesirable practices and errors before the end of the year, as well as to relieve the auditor's workload thereafter.

Contract: (1) An agreement, enforceable by law, between two or more competent parties, to do or not to do something not prohibited by law, for a legal consideration. (2) Any type of agreement or order for the procurement of supplies and services. It includes unqualified notices of award and contracts of a fixed price, cost, cost plus a fixed fee, or incentive type. It also may provide for the issuance of job orders, task orders or task letters thereunder and letter contracts and purchase orders. It includes amendments, modifications, and supplemental agreements to the basic contract.

Contract Bond: A guarantee, backed by cash or other security, of the faithful performance and fulfillment of all the undertakings, covenants, terms, conditions, and agreements contained in a contract. It may include a guarantee of the payment of all labor and material bills incident thereto. These two guarantees may be written separately; the first as a performance bond; the second as a payment bond.

Contract Cost Analysis: The review and analysis of contractor's cost or price data to determine whether it is an accurate estimate of what the contract should cost, assuming economy and efficiency.

Contract Ceiling: A value established in the contract beyond which the customer has no obligation to pay.

Contract Data Requirements List (CDRL): In government procurement a customer listing used to identify and establish the data and documentation required by a contract. Such a list is made a part of the contract.

Contract End Item: A deliverable equipment or facility that is formally accepted by the procuring agency in accordance with requirements in a detailed specification.

Contract Funds Status Report: A part of the formalized reporting system used in government contracts that deals specifically with funding and fiscal requirements.

Contract Line Item Number (CLIN): A contract instrument used to: (1) administer and control contracts; (2) authorize, time limit, or content limit portions of a contract; (3) administer funds and appropriations on a contract; (4) procure options for additional quantities or services; and (5) pay contractors for work performed in a contract.

Contract Price Analysis: (1) The examination and evaluation of a prospective price without evaluation of separate cost elements. (2) Tracking of a cost proposal from price summary to supporting data and verifying the proper application of rates and factors.

Contract Price Baseline: The final detail cost estimate accepted for the purpose of definitizing the contract and providing a price base for tracking contract changes.

Contract Pricing: A series of actions used to obtain, evaluate, assess, verify, and adjudge cost or pricing information and to record the steps taken to ascertain that prices agreed to have been determined to be fair and reasonable.

Contract Pricing Proposal: The instrument required of an offeror for the submission or identification of cost or pricing data. In government procurement the DD Form 633 (Contract Pricing Proposal) is the general purpose form that provides a standard format by which an offeror submits to the Government the proposed price with supporting information.

Contract Type: Refers to a specific pricing arrangement employed for the performance of work under contract. Specific pricing (or compensation) arrangements, expressed as contract types, including firm fixed-price (FFP), fixed-price incentive (FPI), cost-plus-fixed-fee (CPFF), cost-plus-incentive-fee (CPIF), and several others. Among special arrangements that use fixed-price or cost-reimbursement pricing provisions are indefinite delivery contracts, basic ordering agreements, letter contracts, and others.

Contract Underrun (Overrun): The amount by which the final cost is less than (or exceeds) the contract target cost.

Contractor: A term used in procurement to denote the party performing the task or service or providing the equipment, hardware, facility, or end item called out in a contract with the customer or buyer.

Contractor Acquired Property: All items of tangible property procured or otherwise furnished by a contractor in performance of a contract.

Contractor Cost Data Reporting: A reporting structure used in government procurement consisting of specific definitions, requirements, and formats.

Contractor Furnished Equipment: That portion of contractor furnished property that is included in the end item.

Contractor Furnished Property: Property, other than customer furnished and contractor acquired property, used by the contractor in the performance of a contract.

Contractor Weighted Average Share (CWAS): In government procurement a technique for determining and expressing numerically the degree of cost risk a contractor has assumed, based on the percentage of commercial and firm-fixed-price competitive government work to total work for a given calendar year.

Contribution Margin: The excess of revenues over the variable costs.

Conversion Cost: A grouping of direct labor and manufacturing overhead into a single summary cost element.

Coordinates: The two elements of reference of any point on a grid chart. One element, the abscissa (or x), is measured by horizontal distance from a vertical perpendicular axis; the other element, the ordinate (or y), is measured by vertical distance from a horizontal base line. Abscissas to the right of the vertical axis are positive; to the left, negative. Ordinates above the horizontal base line are positive; below, negative. The point of intersection of the axis, called the point of origin, has the value zero for both abscissa and ordinate. Generally, curves relating to estimating and economic statistics are confined to one quadrant, with both abscissas and ordinates positive.

Correlation: Statistical technique used to determine the degree to which variables are related or associated. It does not prove or disprove a causal relationship.

Correlation Coefficient: A mathematical measure of the degree of association between two variables in a series of observations (on the assumption that the relationship between the two variables is a straight line). Its value must lie between +1 and -1, either extreme denoting complete dependence of one variable on the other, and zero denoting no association. A plus shows that an upward movement of one is accompanied by an upward movement of the other; a minus shows that an upward movement of one is accompanied by a downward movement of the other. See Coefficient of Correlation.

Cost: The amount paid or payable for the acquisition of materials, property, or services. In contract and proposal usage denotes dollars and amounts exclusive of fee or profit (i.e., cost does not include profit or fee). Also used with a descriptive adjective such as "acquisition cost," or "product cost." Although dollars or other monetary units are normally used as the unit of measure, the broad definition of cost equates to economic resources, that is, manpower, equipment, real facilities, supplies, and all other resources necessary to accomplish work activities or to produce work outputs.

Cost Account: The focal point at which actual costs are accumulated and the lowest level at which the planned value of work accomplished is required to be compared to actual costs for progress analysis.

Cost Accounting: That branch of accounting dealing with the classification, recording, allocation, summarization, and reporting of current and prospective costs. Included in the field of cost accounting are the design and operation of cost systems and procedures; the determination of costs by departments, functions, responsibilities, activities, products, territories, periods, and other units; the comparison of costs of different periods, of actual with estimated or standard costs, and of alternative costs; and the presentation and interpretation of cost data as an aid to management in controlling current and future operations.

Cost Accounting Standards: In government procurements cost accounting principles (standards) established by the Cost Accounting Standards Board for the purpose of achieving uniformity and consistency in the treatment of costs by defense contractors and subcontractors.

Cost Accounting System: An accounting system designed to record costs by contract, project, production lot for hardware, or other cost objectives through assignment of specific work order or cost accounts for costs applicable to the cost objective.

Cost Allocation: A method, usually mathematical, of assigning direct or indirect cost equitably to one or each of several of the objectives for which the cost was jointly incurred. Also the act of assigning such costs.

Cost Analysis: The methodical organization and systematic study of actual costs, statistical data, and other information on current and completed work. Cost analysis also includes the extrapolation of these cost data to completion, comparisons and analyses of these data, and comparisons of cost extrapolations on a current contract with the cost data in the contract value for reports to customers, program and functional managers, and price estimators. In the procurement organizations of the U.S. government, cost analysis is the review and evaluation of a contractor's cost or pricing data and of the judgmental factors applied in projecting from the data to the estimated costs to form an opinion on the degree to which the contractor's proposed costs represent what the performance of the contract should cost, assuming reasonable economy and efficiency.

Cost Benefit Analysis: A technique for assessing the range of costs and benefits associated with a given option, usually to determine feasibility. Costs are generally in monetary terms. See Benefit Cost Analysis.

Cost Categories: A breakdown of costs into elements. For example, the major categories of life cycle cost are acquisition, operations, support, and disposal.

Cost Center: An administrative unit selected for the purpose of controlling costs. The unit has managerial responsibility, usually consists of a related grouping of methods and facilities, and is made up of elements having common cost characteristics. Also, it is the basic unit of control in cost accounting. It is often referred to as responsibility center.

Cost Contract: (1) A contract that provides for payment of allowable costs to the contractor, to the extent prescribed in the contract, incurred in performance of the contract. (2) A cost-reimbursement contract under which the contractor receives no fee. See Cost Reimbursement Contracts.

Cost Control: The application of procedures that result in early illumination of potential changes in resource requirements and in the timely surveillance of the usage of funds to permit action that will keep costs within a predetermined range.

Cost Data: The term given to cost statistics or records of a program and which usually have not been analyzed and organized into cost information. See Cost Information.

Cost Disallowance: Costs that are not accepted for reimbursement by a customer.

Cost Driver: The portions of a system, end item, or service that have a large or major effect on the cost of the work activity or work output.

Cost-Effectiveness: A measure of the benefits to be derived from work activities or work outputs with respect to their cost.

Cost-Effectiveness Analysis: A method for examining alternative means of accomplishing a desired task or project for the purpose of selecting the means that will provide the highest possible ratio of benefits to cost. See Benefit Cost Analysis.

Cost Element: An identifiable cost subdivision or a common group of cost subdivisions that have been established as separate entities for the purpose of estimating, collecting, and reporting contract costs.

Cost Estimates: Cost estimates are grouped into four general categories. (1) *Planning cost estimates* are often referred to as "rough order of magnitude" (ROM) or "ballpark" estimates. They are intended to grossly approximate the value of a given task or program. Planning cost estimates are of a low confidence level since they are based upon loosely defined program ground rules, plans, definitions, and data. Planning estimates are generally required early in the program definition cycle. The amount of estimating detail is minimal, often a top dollar number only is derived. Planning estimates are submitted for information purposes only and do not usually represent a formal commitment. A significant allowance is usually added to planning estimates for unknowns. (2) *Budget estimates* are normally required for funding, fiscal planning, or procurement decisions. They are based upon well-defined data and ground rules but require additional work activity or work output definition before a firm price can be quoted. A budget estimate encompasses pricing accuracies that are superior to planning estimates. Budget estimates are derived through the use of preliminary functional organization estimates and gross parameters. Budget estimates do not represent a firm commitment. An allowance for growth in undefined statement of work and for unknowns is added to budget estimates. (3) *Firm cost estimates* are used in a cost proposal or bid that is intended to result in a binding contractual obligation. The firm cost estimate is based on well-defined plans, data, and product, process, project, or service characteristics and is in response to a customer firm request for proposal. Firm cost estimates require the submission of the greatest amount of detail and preparation of an extensive backup package to support contractual fact-finding and negotiations. (4) *Not to exceed (NTE)*, *not less than (NLT)* *estimates*: are commitments from a contractor as to the maximum amount (or minimum credit) to accomplish (or delete) a specific task, item, or procurement. NTE/NTL estimates are prepared from planning, budget, or firm estimate information. The amount of contingency or NTE/NTL allowance added is an estimator/management judgement factor.

Cost Estimating: The skill of accurately approximating the probable resources required to produce a work activity or a work output based on information available or that can be collected at the time. Price estimating is defined as the art or skill of predetermining the market value of an item or activity that assures an acceptable profit. See Cost and Price.

Cost Estimating Methods: The several methods of preparing cost estimates and a variety of combinations of these methods used by individual cost estimators. The combinations depend on the character and size of the effort to be estimated, the available usable historical costs and technical data, and the experience and developed skill of the estimators. Each of the methods requires an analysis of the total job and a definition of the work to be performed. Examples of cost estimating methods are as follows: (1) detailed cost estimating; (2) comparative cost estimating; (3) parametric/statistical cost estimating; (4) standards cost estimating; (5) expert opinion/roundtable cost estimating; and (6) empirical (historical) cost estimating. Refer to these terms in this dictionary for a definition of each of the estimating methods.

Cost Estimating Relationships (CERs): Mathematical expressions relating cost as the dependent variable to one or more independent cost driving variables.

The relationship may be cost-to-cost, such as using manufacturing costs to estimate quality assurance costs or using manufacturing costs to estimate costs for expendable material such as rivets, primer, or sealant. The relationship may also be cost-to-noncost, such as estimating manufacturing costs by the use of weight or using the number of engineering drawings to estimate engineering costs. (Both weight and number of engineering drawings are noncost variables.)

Cost Estimating Steps: The 12 steps of developing a cost estimate and a price. *Step 1*: Development of the work element structure *Step 2*: Scheduling of the work elements *Step 3*: Retrieval and organization of historical cost data *Step 4*: Development and use of cost estimating relationships *Step 5*: Development and use of production learning curves *Step 6*: Identification of skill categories, levels, and rates *Step 7*: Development of labor hour, material, and other direct cost estimates *Step 8*: Development and application of overhead, administrative costs, fee, etc. *Step 9*: Application of inflation and escalation factors *Step 10*: Pricing or computing estimated costs *Step 11*: Analysis, adjustment, and reconciliation of the estimate *Step 12*: Publication, presentation, and use of the estimate

Cost Estimating Uncertainty: A condition whereby resultant actual cost varies from the cost estimates because of the inherent deficiencies in cost estimating procedures rather than from a change in configuration of the work activity or work output being estimated.

Cost Factor: A cost estimating relationship (CER) in which the cost is directly proportional to a single independent variable. A brief arithmetic expression wherein cost is determined by application of a factor such as a percent, for example, initial spares percent or general and administrative percentage, or a ratio as in pay and allowance cost per worker per year.

Cost Growth: An increase in cost experienced during performance of work above a base or estimated cost figure previously established. See Escalation, Inflation.

Cost Growth Allowance: A funding amount allocated to and included in the cost estimate to accommodate cost growth.

Cost Incurred: A cost identified through the use of the accrued method of accounting and reporting or otherwise actually paid; cost of direct labor, direct materials, and direct services identified with and necessary for the performance of a contract; and all properly allocated and allowable indirect costs as shown by the books of the performer.

Cost Information: Cost data systematically organized for ease of use in producing a cost estimate. See Cost Data.

Cost Management System: A system that places an estimated planned value on items of work to be performed. Once that work is completed, the planned value can be considered to be earned value. See Earned Value.

Cost Model: An ordered arrangement of data, ground rules, assumptions, and equations that permits translation of physical resources or characteristics into costs. Consists of a set of equations, logic, programs, and input formats to specify the problem; program information, including both system description data and estimating relationships; and an output format.

Cost Objective: (1) A function, organizational subdivision, contract, or other work unit for which cost data are desired and for which provision is made to accumulate and measure. (2) The dollar cost amount targeted to be agreed to in the process of contractual negotiations.

Cost and Operational Effectiveness Analysis: A study that has the purpose of developing recommended hierarchical ordering of candidate systems based on meaningful relationships between cost and operational effectiveness.

Cost of Money: The cost of borrowing capital committed to facilities as an element of contract cost.

Cost or Pricing Data: Data consisting of all facts existing up to the time of agreement on price that prudent buyers and sellers would reasonably expect to have a significant effect on price negotiations.

Cost-plus-Award-Fee (CPAF) Contract: A cost reimbursement contract with provisions for an incentive fee to be awarded on the basis of the subjective evaluation by the customer of supplier performance against criteria established in the contract.

Cost-plus-Fixed-Fee (CPFF) Contract: A cost reimbursement contract that provides for the payment of a fixed fee to the contractor. The fixed fee, once negotiated, does not vary with actual cost but may be adjusted as a result of any subsequent changes in the products produced or services to be performed under the contract.

Cost-plus-Incentive-Fee (CPIF) Contract: A cost reimbursement contract with provision for a fee that is adjusted by formulas in accordance with the relationship that total allowable cost bears to target cost. The provision for increase or decrease in the fee depends upon allowable cost of contract performance and is designed as an incentive to the supplier to increase the efficiency of performance. Additional incentives of a technical, performance, or schedule nature may be added to the contract.

Cost-plus-Percentage-of-Cost (CPPC) Contract: A form of contract formerly used (but now illegal for use in government procurement) that provided for a fee or profit as a specified percentage of the contractor's or supplier's actual cost of accomplishing the work to be performed. Sometimes referred to as a ''percentage-of cost'' contract.

Cost Proposal: A submission by a potential supplier for the purpose of budgetary planning, source selection, or to be used for definitive negotiation, indicating the cost to the procuring agency or buyer for the conduct of specified work. The proposal, in supporting the proposed cost, includes an amount of detail commensurate with the purpose, coverage, and other characteristics of the proposal. The cost proposal may or may not be in response to a request for proposal, and it may be accompanied by an organization and management proposal and a technical proposal.

Cost Reimbursement: A family of pricing arrangements that provide for payment of allowable, allocable and reasonable costs incurred in the performance of a contract, to the extent that such costs are prescribed or permitted by the contract.

Cost Reimbursement Contract: A type of contract that provides for payment to the contractor of allowable costs incurred in the performance of the contract, to the extent prescribed in the contract and which normally contains no fee. See Cost Contract.

Cost Related Characteristics: Any of a number of product descriptive characteristics that may have an effect on, or influence the cost of designing and/or producing the product. They are sometimes called "cost predictive parameters" or "technical characteristics."

Cost Risk: An assumption of possible monetary loss in light of the complexity or unknown nature of the job or work to be done. One of the elements to be considered in the negotiation of a fair and reasonable price, as well as in determining the type of contract under which performance will occur. See Risk Analysis.

Cost/Schedule Control System Criteria (C/SCSC): A system of planned work, schedules, budgets, and earned value of work performed with specific reporting and documentation requirements.

Cost Sensitivity: A situation in which costs vary greatly with small variation or change in program or end item characteristics.

Cost Sharing: An arrangement under which the costs for a program are shared by the seller (the supplier) and the buyer (the customer).

Cost Sharing Contract: A cost reimbursement contract under which the supplier receives no fee or a small basic fee and is reimbursed only for an agreed-to portion of the target costs based on cost performance.

Cost Substantiation: The documentation that supports a cost estimate.

Cost Track (Tracking): (1) A "step-by-step" record of the revisions and updates of proposed costs from the original submittal of a baseline estimate to the final agreement on costs. (2) A historical record of selected cost information (estimated or actual) with a written analysis that explains variance among cost entries. (3) The flow of cost data from the price summary to detail support data. (4) Permanent records of successive cost estimates made for major programs and systems together with the reasons for changes.

Cost Type Contract: A contract that provides for payment to the contractor of allowable costs in the performance of the contract to the extent prescribed in the contract; also termed "cost reimbursable contract." May include profit.

Cost Underrun/Overrun: A net change due to the supplier's actual costs being under or over target or anticipated contract costs. See Contract Underrun/Overrun.

Cost Valuation: (1) Cost estimate: test of a cost estimate to confirm that it is credible, grounded on sound cost estimating methods, and founded on fact or capable of being justified, supported, and defended. (2) Cost data: test of the accuracy, accounting, or development of the resource data used to substantiate or derive a cost element.

Cost Verification: The process of checking the cost estimate for mathematical accuracy.

Credit: (1) An estimating allowance made for deleting tasks, equipment, or items from a cost estimate. (2) Any bookkeeping entry in recording a transaction the effect of which is to decrease an asset or expense account or increase either a liability, a capital, or revenue account. (3) A memo or an invoice used in dealings with customers or suppliers. See Debit.

Critical Path: The longest path in a network of events depicting a project.

Cross-Charge: Cross-charged labor is that designated task effort performed by an employee working in his normally assigned work area but doing work authorized by another company division or another labor group.

Cumulative: Becoming greater by successive additions. The summation of current expenses to cumulative totals by time periods or the addition of succeeding unit values to the total.

Cumulative Average Cost: The cost per unit that results when the summation of the costs for the units produced is divided by the units produced.

Cumulative Average Curve: A logarithmic chart of cumulative average values plotted at the last unit of each cumulative quantity.

Cumulative to Date: The total items produced, labor hours, expenses, actuals, or costs recorded to a specific date.

Current: (1) A term used in estimating to indicate the amount of expenditures or funding for specific time periods (months, quarters, years) (versus cumulative). Individual time period values that, when added, become cumulative values. (2) Amounts expressed in terms of a "current" economic year. See Current Year Dollars.

Current Asset: Unrestricted cash, or other asset, held for conversion within a relatively short period into cash or other similar asset or useful goods or services. Usually the period is one year or less, but for some items, that is, installment receivables, the period may be much longer.

Current Liability: Term used principally to identify and designate a direct liability, the liquidation or payment of which reasonably may be expected to require the use of existing resources properly classifiable as current assets or the creation of other liabilities.

Current Year Dollars: Dollars that reflect purchasing power current to the year the work is performed. Prior costs stated in current dollars are the actual amounts paid out in these years. Future costs stated in current dollars are the projected actual amounts that will be paid. Also sometimes referred to as actual dollars, then year dollars, real year dollars, inflated dollars, or escalated dollars. See Then Year Dollars.

Debit: (1) Any bookkeeping entry in recording a transaction the effect of which is to decrease a liability, revenue, or capital account or to increase an asset or expense account. (2) A memo or invoice used in dealings with customers or suppliers. See Credit.

Debt: Money, goods, or services owing to another by virtue of an agreement, expressed or implied, giving rise to a legal duty to pay.

Declared Over/Underrun: The amount of total contract cost increase or decrease that has been reported to the customer.

Defective Cost or Pricing Data: In government procurement certified cost or pricing data subsequently found to have been inaccurate, incomplete, or non-current as of the effective date of the certificate. In this case, the government is entitled to an adjustment of the negotiated price, including profit or fee, to exclude any significant sum by which price was increased because of the defective data, provided the data were relied upon by the government.

Delivery Forecast: Periodic estimates of production deliveries, used as a measure of the effectiveness of production and supply-availability scheduling and as a guide to corrective actions to resolve procurement or production bottlenecks.

Deobligation: In government procurement downward adjustment of previously recorded obligations. Attributable to contract terminations, price revisions, cost underruns on cost reimbursement contracts, and corrections of amounts originally recorded as obligations, or for convenience of the government.

Deposit: Money or other assets placed with or by another as an evidence of good faith, custody, or safekeeping. The act of placing such money or other assets.

Depreciation: The decline in value of tangible fixed assets due to such causes as wear and tear, action of the elements, inadequacy, and obsolescence, but without loss of substance. The portion of cost of tangible fixed assets calculated to have expired for any accounting period due to such causes thereby constituting an operating cost.

Desk Analysis: The cost analysis and adjustment of subcontractor or supplier quotations to highlight weaknesses, possible negotiation reductions, correction of errors, work statement adjustments, and so on. Usually done before a complete price analysis.

Desk Audit: An examination of limited scope made at a point removed from the site of operations by reference to documents and other information available at the audit point, supplemented, in some instances, by information readily obtained by correspondence or telephone.

Design-to-Cost: A management concept wherein rigorous cost goals are established during planning and analysis phases. The control of costs (design, acquisition, operating, and support) to those goals is achieved by practical trade-offs between operational capability, performance, cost, and schedule. Cost, as a key design parameter, is addressed on a continuing basis and is an inherent part of the development and production process.

Design-to-Unit-Production-Cost: Included in development or production contracts, this design-to-cost goal is a preestablished unit production price to be paid for recurring production costs and is based on a stated production quantity, rate, and time frame. This unit cost goal is used a design parameter to control system cost. In general, the goal should only include those cost elements that are under the control, or influenced by the supplier. The goals are often the subject of contract incentives.

Detailed Cost Estimating: A method of cost estimating characterized by a thorough, in-depth analysis of all tasks, components, processes, and assemblies. Requirements for labor, tooling, equipment, and material items are produced by this type of estimating. The application of labor rates, material prices, and overhead to the calculated requirements translates the estimate into dollars. This type of estimating is further characterized by the presence of complete calculations, records and quotations to support the estimate. See Cost Estimating Methods, Empirical Cost Estimating, Comparative Cost Estimating, Standards Cost Estimating, Grass Roots (Bottoms-Up) Estimating.

Detailed Audit: An examination of the books of account, or a portion thereof, whereby substantially all entries and transactions are reviewed and verified, as contrasted with an examination of selected line items.

Development Cost: Cost of a system up to the point where decision is made to procure an initial increment of the production units or the operational system. The nonrecurring costs of a system or project.

Differential Costs: The cost increases and cost decreases between alternatives.

Direct Costs: Any item of cost (or the aggregate thereof) that may be identified specifically with an end objective, such as a product, service, program, function, or project. These costs may be charged directly to a given contract charge number or they may be charged to a redistribution work order subsequently distributed to contracts over a logical base. Direct costs are the opposite of indirect costs which are classified as overhead and are distributed to contracts over a base normally composed of direct hours or dollars. See Indirect Cost.

Direct Headcount: Includes only the headcount of those individuals or organizations whose primary mission is the performance of contracts and whose labor is charged to productive/full burden-bearing work orders. Constitutes the base for contract pricing.

Direct Labor: Labor that can be specifically and consistently identified or assigned to a particular end or deliverable work activity or output and that bears full overhead.

Direct Material: The term "direct material" includes raw materials, standards, commercial items, purchased parts, purchased equipment, outside production, and subcontracted items required to manufacture and assemble completed end or deliverable products or services. Direct material often also includes the costs associated with materials or products received from other company divisions under an interdivisional support agreement.

Disallowed Costs: In government procurement costs rejected for reimbursement by the government; may be either direct costs or overhead.

Disbursements: All payments by cash, check, or voucher deductions. (To be distinguished from expenditures.)

Discount Rate: The percentage or rate used to discount future costs and benefits to arrive at their present values when one considers the time value of money.

Discounting: Discounting is a technique for converting forecasted amounts to economically comparable amounts at a common point or points in time, considering the time value of money. Once cost estimates have been generated, they must be time phased to reflect expenditure patterns. The time value of money for two or more cash flow streams is usually taken into account by computing and comparing present value costs. Present value costs are computed by applying a discount rate to each year's cost in a cost stream. Discount rates are usually developed to approximate closely the current cost of money in the financial marketplace. The purpose of discounting is to determine if the time value of money is sufficiently great to change the ranking of alternatives—a ranking that has been established on the basis of all other considerations.

Disposal Costs: The costs of disposing of a facility, property item, equipment item, scrap, by-products, or excess materials.

Disposal Credits: (1) The agreed-upon price for any part of the termination inventory sold to a contractor in the negotiations regarding a contract termination claim. (2) The proceeds of sale of any material sold to third parties by a contractor in connection with contract termination, to the extent not otherwise paid or credited to the customer.

Distributed/Distributable Labor (Costs): Any costs or labor that cannot economically be allocated to a specific task and thus are distributed across all contract tasks as a function of labor or material costs. May also cover costs such as distributed data processing costs or material costs.

Documentation: The summary and backup data that support a cost estimate. The files maintained for historical support until a contract is closed out.

DOD Planning/Programming/Budgeting System (PPBS): An integrated system for the establishment, maintenance, and revision of the U.S. Department of Defense budget as it relates to the Congressional budget cycle.

Earned Value: The monetary value of work performed to date.

Earnings: Income produced from any economic activity. (Income may be gross or net—that is, less costs, in which case it is referred to as "net earnings.")

Econometric Model: An economic model that predicts the behavior of any given parameter or variable based on the flux of dependent or independent variables that comprise the model.

Economic Analysis: A systematic approach to a given problem designed to assist the manager in solving a problem of choice. The full problem is investigated; objectives and alternatives are searched out and compared in the light of their benefits and costs through the use of an appropriate analytical framework.

Economic Life: The period of time over which the benefits to be gained from a system reasonably may be expected to accrue to the owner.

Economic Lot Size: Size of the batch that minimizes average unit cost.

Economic-Order-Quantity: That quantity derived from a mathematical technique used to determine the optimum (lowest) total variable costs required to order and hold inventory.

Economic-Order-Quantity Principle: A supply technique used to compute replenishment order quantities of consumable material whereby the cost to order is compared with the cost of carrying the inventory to achieve the most economical procurement, storage, and inventory practices. An optimum method for computing operating levels of supply after considering the cost elements involved.

Economic Price Adjustment: A contractual alteration permitted and specified by contract provisions for the upward and/or downward revision of a stated contract price based on actual experience (future years) as compared to forecasts of selected economic indices at the time the contract was negotiated.

Economics: The study of how individuals and organizations choose, with or without the use of money, to employ productive resources to produce various commodities and distribute them for consumption.

Economy: (1) Wise expenditure of money, careful use of material, management of the resources of a community. (2) The present and projected financial posture of a nation.

Efficiency: The mathematical reciprocal of a realization factor. It is expressed as a percent derived by dividing the *standard* hours by the actual hours. See Realization.

Element of Cost: A value that can be identified to a type of effort expended in the performance of a statement of work. Examples are: labor, material, overhead, and travel. See Cost Element.

Empirical Cost Estimating: The step-by-step creation of the estimate based only on the skills, knowledge, and developed intuition and working files of a proficient cost estimator based on historical (empirical) data. The amount, extent, or level of the details of the work to be performed depends on the technical definition of the job that can be obtained or deduced and the time allotted to the estimating task. See Cost Estimating Methods, Detailed Estimating, Comparative Estimating, Standards Estimating.

Equity: An interest or share in property or capital investment. The owner's or stockholders' net investment after deducting liabilities from assets—as distinguished from bondholders.

Equivalent Labor (Personnel): The required full-time personnel needed to perform a given task on regular time with normal labor loss such as (1) vacations, (2) sick leave, (3) holidays, (4) leave with pay, (5) leave without pay. Equivalent personnel is calculated by dividing the total hours (including overtime) by an equivalent personnel factor for the same time period.

Equivalent Labor (Personnel) Factor: A factor used to convert man-hours into the number of full-time employees required to accomplish a specific task within a given time period with normal labor loss such as vacations, sick leave, and holidays, without the use of overtime. Factors differ between years, by geographical location, by company and country as a result of different holiday schedules and vacation patterns. Also referred to as labor conversion factor.

Equivalent Units of Productions: A method of measuring departmental output or production when process costing is used.

Equivalent 100% In-Plant: The equivalent amount of hours and dollars involved in the combined operations of a prime contractor, supporting divisions, and subcontractors. It is stated as if the entire job were performed in the prime contractor's plant.

Escalation: A term traditionally used to indicate an upward or downward movement of cost or price due to productivity changes (factors other than inflation). See Inflation.

Escalation Clause: A contract clause that provides for upward and downward adjustment of the total contract price on the basis of increases or decreases from a forecast of the level of escalation for future years.

Established Catalog Price: A price included in a catalog, price list, schedule, or other form that: (1) is regularly stocked by a manufacturer or supplier; (2) is published or made available for inspection by customers; and (3) states prices at which sales are currently or were last made to a significant number of buyers comprising the general public or industry.

Established Market Price: A current price, established in the usual and ordinary course of trade between buyers and sellers free to bargain, that can be substantiated from sources independent of the manufacturer or supplier, although the obtaining of such pricing data may have to come from the seller.

Estimate: A term describing the resources (labor hours, material costs), travel, computer costs, and other costs required to accomplish a contract, task, or work item. It also includes the effect of rates and factors that are applied to the labor and materials to develop estimated costs.

Estimated Actuals: The costs incurred on a contract during a contractor's accounting year consisting of: (1) the direct labor and material reported in this period as actuals and not subject to revision; and (2) the applicable overhead and G&A incurred as reported to the contract on approved billing rates.

Estimated Cost: The conversion of resource estimates (labor hours and material quantities) into dollars by the application of rates and factors. The amount stated in a contract as the estimated cost. In proposal usage includes costs with no profit or fee.

Estimated Cost at Completion: The current forecast of what the final cost will be for the task, whether it be the total contract or just a portion thereof. It consists of actual costs to date plus the estimate of the balance through contract completion.

Estimated Total Price: Total cost plus fee or profit, synonymous with the price.

Estimating: Predicting or forecasting. In cost estimating, to predict costs. Generation of detailed and realistic forecasts of labor hours, material quantities, or other requirements for a task, subtask, operation, or a part or groups thereof—generally in response to a request for proposal or specific statement of work. The skill of accurately approximating the probable worth (or cost), extent, quantity, quality, or character of something based on information that is available or can be collected at the time. It also covers the generation of forecasted costing rates and factors with which estimated resource values may be converted to costs and the application of these rates and factors to establish forecasted costs.

Estimating Instructions: Direction given to supporting organizations specifying the information and inputs required from them to develop, prepare, and document a cost estimate.

Estimating Plan: A planned approach to the development of a cost proposal or a cost estimate. It covers such items as cost proposal requirements, formats, estimate sources,computing plans, analysis and use of historical costs, documentation requirements, document outlines and plans, estimate reviews, printing, and shipping plans. A complete estimating plan includes the identification of all the internal support services and requirements before *and* after proposal submittal (i.e., audit, fact finding, reviews, negotiations, etc.).

Estimating Methodology: A definition of the estimating system and how estimates are prepared.

Estimating Methods: The approach used to develop the estimate. A description of *how* estimates were derived as differentiated from rationale (substantiation of the estimated values). See Cost Estimating Methods.

Estimating Relationship: A statement of how one or more variables affect another. Can be a simple multiplier which when used against some other number establishes an estimate of hours, material cost, or some other basic estimate. A mathematical formula used to create these basic estimates. The use of estimating relationships (ERs) or cost estimating relationships (CERs) is also called "formula estimating" or "parametric estimating." See Cost Estimating Relationships.

Estimating Technique: Refers to the processes or procedures used to develop an estimate; that is, cost model, estimating relationship, improvement curve, and so on.

Estimator: A person who possesses the skill of accurately forecasting the resources and resulting costs of a work activity or work output. Estimators may be certified by the National Estimating Society as Certified Professional Estimators (CPEs).

Eurodollars: American dollars invested in Europe; investments in Europe denominated in United States dollars; a United States dollar held (as by a bank) in Europe.

Evaluate: To ascertain the value or amount of; to appraise; specifically mathematics, to express numerically.

Excess Profit: The amount of profit over and above an established dollar or percentage limit. As specifically pertaining to renegotiation, the profit derived by contractors under government contracts that, through the process of statutory renegotiation, is administratively determined to be excessive and subject to recapture by the government.

Exhibit: A supporting document to an estimate. A financial, statistical, or other statement formally presented, such as one accompanying a contract or accounting report.

Expenditure: A charge against available funds. Evidenced by voucher, claim, or other document, approved by competent authority. Expenditures represent the actual payment of funds. In the federal government, it means disbursement. Outside of the federal government it means an accrued expense or a payment for goods or services.

Expense: Costs of operation and maintenance of activities on the accrual basis for a fiscal period, as distinguished from costs of acquisition of property. Signifies cost of all services received and consumable material used or withdrawn for use for a given fiscal period.

Experience Factor: A percentage or ratio expression indicating the results of previous actual performance to influence the output in relation to input. One statistical form presenting an experience factor is the slope of improvement, or learning curve.

Expert Opinion Cost Estimating: An estimating method which utilizes experts in engineering, manufacturing, procurement, testing, and so on to produce direct judgmental estimates. See Cost Estimating Methods, Roundtable Estimating.

Exposure: The amount of contractor or company funds risked—"exposed"—in proceeding without customer funding coverage.

Extended Workweek: See Overtime.

Fact-finding: A phase in the postsubmittal period of a proposal that allows the customer to: (1) review the support data on a proposal; (2) investigate certain areas in more depth; (3) conduct audits of rates, factors, and supplier quotations used in the proposal; and (4) conduct on-site surveys and reviews of cost information retained at contractors' plants.

Factor: A numerical expression of value, or ratio, expressed as a percentage. A factor is used as a multiplier and, when combined with or related to other factors, contributes to produce a resource or cost estimate. See Cost Factor.

Factor, Judgmental: A subjective factor that is not verifiable. Judgment factors include assumptions, estimates of future conditions, rates, factor extrapolations, direct estimates, and other data where it is impractical to establish an auditable basis for an estimate and it is necessary to rely on individual experiences to establish the projected cost.

Factored Items: Labor or material estimated by the application of a factor to a labor base of hours or dollars.

Fee: In specified cost-reimbursement pricing arrangements, fee represents an agreed-to amount beyond the initial estimate of costs. In most instances, fee reflects a variety of factors, including risk, and is subject to statutory limitations. Fee may be fixed at the outset of performance, as in a cost-plus-fixed-fee arrangement, or may vary (within a contractually specified minimum-maximum range) during performance, as in a cost-plus-incentive-fee arrangement. See Contract Profit, Profit.

Fidelity Bond: Insurance against losses arising from dishonest acts of employees and involving money, merchandise, or other property; persons or positions may be covered.

Field Pricing Support: In government procurement involves the analysis of contractor pricing proposals by any or all field technical and other specialists, including plant representatives, administrative contracting officers, contract auditors, price analysts, quality assurance personnel, engineers, and legal and small business specialists.

Final Audit Clearance: In government procurement government acceptance of appropriate documentation evidencing that the company's responsibility for an item or items of government property has ceased. Such documentation may be in the form of a delivery and acceptance document; sales order or shipping document in accordance with approved disposition instructions; approved relief of accountability; approved contract closure; and so on.

Financial Analysis: An appraisal of the dollar aspects of an operation or activity.

Financial Management: The planning, organizing, directing, and controlling of the dollars and resources of a program, project, company, or agency.

Financial Report: A formal statement, or series of statements, with or without narrative or discussion, showing financial condition at a given time or results of transactions or operations for a given period, with or without comparison with budget estimates, standards, past history limitations, and the like.

Financial Statement: A formal financial report, especially one showing financial status at a given date and the results of operations for a given time.

Finished Goods: The materials or products on which, from the standpoint of the entity involved, manufacturing or processing operations have been completed and that are being held for use, consumption, or sale.

Firm-Fixed-Price Contract: A contract that provides for a total price that normally is not subject to adjustment. It is used for contracts awarded after formal advertising and in negotiated contracts when reasonably definite specifications are available and costs can be estimated with reasonable accuracy to enable the negotiation of a fair price. The contract price may be altered under the provisions of a change clause, an economic price adjustment clause, or a defective pricing clause. See Fixed-Price Contract.

First-Destination Transportation Cost: The cost of freight, cartage, handling charges, and so on involved in item shipment from the manufacturer to the first station or depot.

Fiscal Period: An accounting period of a specified time duration.

Fiscal Policy: (1) Government: The policy pursued in connection with legislation or administrative practices relating to taxation, currency, public appropriations and expenditures, government funds, and similar matters; particularly the intended effect of such legislation and administrative practices on the economy of the nation. (2) Commercial: The overall financial operating policy of a company with regard to assets, liabilities, cash flow, expenses, indebtedness, stocks, bonds, and so on.

Fiscal Year: A 12-month period selected for accounting purposes. (1) Government: The fiscal year for most agencies of the United States Government begins on the first day of October and ends on the thirtieth day of September of the following calendar year. (The fiscal year is designated by the calendar year in which it ends, i.e., the fiscal year 19X1 is the year beginning October 19X0 and ending 30 September 19X1). (2) Contractors: The fiscal year of a company can be any time period encompassing a period of one year.

Fiscal Year Buy: The procurement of a specific amount of hardware, software, or equipment with the funds provided in a specific fiscal year funding. The actual expenditure period for the procurement may cover several fiscal years.

Fiscal Year Funding: (1) Dollar amounts by fiscal year in incremental funding. (2) Dollar amounts that cover fiscal year buys under full funding. (3) Dollar amounts provided to a contract that cover a period of one fiscal year only (annual funding). The use of this term should always be clarified with additional explanation.

Fixed Asset(s): Any natural resource, subject to depletion, and any tangible asset used in the conduct of the business and not intended for sale as a part of normal operations. Tangible fixed assets include land, buildings, machinery, tools, patterns, delivery equipment, furniture, and fixtures, and so on.

Fixed Costs: Costs that do not vary with the volume of business, such as property taxes, insurance, depreciation, security, and basic utility fees.

Fixed Overhead Cost: An item of overhead cost (or the aggregate thereof) that is not considered to vary directly as a result of changes in volume of production; as opposed to variable and semivariable overhead costs.

Fixed-Price Contract: A contract that generally provides for a firm price (or under appropriate circumstances, such as changes or economic price adjustment, may provide for an adjustable price) for the supplies or services that are being procured. Fixed-price contracts are of several types so designed to facilitate proper pricing under varying circumstances: firm-fixed-price contract, fixed-price-with-escalation contract, fixed-price contract providing for the redetermination of price, fixed-price-incentive contract, and so on. See Firm-Fixed-Price Contract and the next three definitions.

Fixed-Price Contract with Provisions for Redetermination of Price: A fixed-price contract that contains provisions for the subsequent negotiated adjustment, in whole or in part, of the initially negotiated (base) price. Depending on the contract provisions, adjustments may be upward or downward, retroactive or prospective.

Fixed-Price-Incentive Contract: A fixed-price contract with provision for the adjustment of profit and price by a formula based on the relationships between negotiated and actual cost, performance, schedule, or other agreed bases. See Incentive-Type Contract.

Fixed-Price-with-Escalation Contract: A fixed-price contract that provides for the upward and downward revision of the stated contract price on the occurrence of certain economic fluctuations (i.e., materials and labor) specifically defined in the contract.

Flexible Budget: A budget containing alternative allowances to organizational subdivisions based on varying rates of production or other measures of activity. A budget subject to change as operations proceed or work is identified and finalized.

Floor Check: A work-site identification of employees on the job with the names recorded on the payroll or labor cost charges.

Forecast: The projecting of trends, commitments, obligations, and expenditures for a period of time in the future. Predicted costs or accomplishments of a plan based on projected future conditions.

Forecast Budget: Estimates prepared early in a program/project based on a prediction of the work load or volume of work to be performed.

Forfeiture: The relinquishing of rights to cash or other property for not complying with legal provisions or as compensation for the resulting damages or losses.

Formal Advertising: One of the two major methods of procurement (formal advertising and negotiated). Covers the procurement of well-defined items or services through the submittal of sealed bids. Formal advertising generally results in a fixed-price type of contract.

Forward Estimates: Projections beyond the current budget period required for integrating planning with budgeting.

Forward Pricing Arrangement: A written understanding negotiated between a supplier and a customer to use certain rates (e.g., labor, indirect, and materials) for a specified period of time in pricing contracts or contract modifications.

Forward Pricing Rates: Rates developed especially for pricing new proposals, additions, or changes to existing contracts.

Fringe Benefits: The cost of benefits furnished to employees including sick leave, holidays, employment taxes, vacations, retirement, group insurance, union pension, state workman's compensation insurance, and so on. Also included are company contributions to employee savings or personnel benefit plans.

Full Cost Pricing: The practice of including all costs in pricing decisions (as opposed to differential cost pricing).

Full Funding: In government procurement the policy of funding the total cost of end items or program hardware at the time of authorized initiation even though the expense may cover several fiscal years. Full funding applies only to the procurement appropriation and is applicable to only production contracts.

Function: Task-oriented blocks of related effort or people necessary to produce outputs (e.g., engineering, tooling, manufacturing, quality assurance, material, and program management) Roughly equivalent to skill categories.

Functional Elements: In a work breakdown structure the elements that represent intangible work activities or organizational units (e.g., project management, systems engineering and integration, operations, training, logistics, and support)

Functional Organization (Functional Cost Category): Areas of responsibility with their own definite description (e.g., engineering, manufacturing, material, and quality control). Roughly equivalent to skill categories.

Fund: A sum of money or other resource, authorized by law or a management decision, to be set aside and to be used or expended only for specified purposes.

Fund Accounting: Reporting and record keeping of financial transactions in terms of the separate funds or kinds of funds.

Funded Requirement: A need that has been recognized and provided for by allocation of funds.

Funding: An administrative action, normally within the chain of command or management, of granting and limiting authority to incur obligations and make expenditures. Money for furthering a contract or project purpose.

Funding Limit: A specific ceiling on the amount of dollars available on a contract or project through a period of time.

Funding Profile: A chart or graph showing time-phased expenditures, termination liability, and funding requirements on an incremental basis for a program or project.

Funding Profile Limit (Constraint Analysis): The funding profile limit represents the funding required based on an optimum schedule usually associated with hardware procurements.

Gantt Chart: A time-based graphic bar chart display of work scheduled and work accomplished. The chart, which emphasizes time as the most important element of production, was developed during World War I by Henry L. Gantt.

General and Administrative (G&A): A specific category of indirect expenses including funding for a company's general and executive offices; the cost of such staff services as legal, accounting, public relations, financial, and similar expenses; and other general expenses related to the overall business. A generic term used to describe expenses not directly assignable to overhead areas for engineering, manufacturing, material, and so on.

General Ledger: A book or computerized data file or set of files containing accounts recording in detail or in summary, all the transactions of a business enterprise or other accounting unit. The prime book or account for recording costs incurred by a company including its assets, liabilities, and so on.

General Overhead Accounts or Costs: Overhead accounts or costs for labor and nonlabor *not* identifiable to specific contract tasks or specific functional areas (i.e., engineering, manufacturing, and material).

Grant: A contribution, gift, or subsidy made by an organization, the government, or a company for specified purposes.

Grass Roots Estimate: An estimate developed by requesting and collecting estimates from functional organizations within a company or agency for a specific statement of work or task. Usually developed by a combination of many estimating methods and techniques but developed by the "doing" people. See Cost Estimating Methods.

Gross Commitments: The total money value of purchase orders or authorizations issued on a contract to subcontractors and suppliers.

Gross Earnings: Total profits (sales less cost of sales).

Gross Fixed Assets: Total original acquisition cost of property, plant, and certain equipment.

Gross Income: The amount of revenues, usually expressed in monetary units, derived from capital, labor, nonlabor, or combination thereof before deducting expenses and taxes.

Gross Loss: The excess of the cost of goods sold over the amount of sales; the reverse of gross profit.

Gross Profit: Sales less cost of goods sold and inventory losses, but before considering selling and general expenses, incidental income, and income deductions.

Gross Sales: Total sales, before deducting returns and allowances, but after deducting corrections and trade discounts, sales taxes, excise taxes based on sales, and sometimes cash discounts.

Hardware Cost: Costs of the tangible physical items of the work (systems, assemblies, subassemblies, components, parts, support equipment, tooling, etc.).

Headcount: The number of individuals carried on a company's payroll records, as opposed to equivalent persons developed from monthly conversions of employee working hours. An organization's headcount is equal to the number of employees assigned by company personnel records.

High-Low Points Method: A method of analyzing semivariable costs when only limited historical data are available.

Historical Cost (Data): An estimating term used to describe a set of data reflecting actual cost or past experience of a product line.

Homogeneous Data: The term used in describing items of data that are similar or essentially alike and, therefore, comparable.

Homoscedasticity: A uniform scatter or dispersion of points about a regression line in a cost estimating relationship.

Idle Capacity: The difference between rated production capacity and actual level of operation, usually in terms of percentages.

Idle Time: Lost time of employees or machines due to work stoppage from any cause. Thus time that is not productive.

Improvement: The correction of an unfavorable condition. An increment on a learning or improvement curve. A modification or updating to a building, structure, or other attachment to land which is intended to remain so attached or annexed, such as sidewalks, trees, drives, tunnels, drains, and sewers.

Improvement Curve: The continued progressive lowering of the unit production resource requirements in a manufacturing process. The improvement may result from more efficient use of resources, employee learning, new equipment/ facilities, improved flow of materials, and so on. See Learning Curve.

Incentive Arrangement: A negotiated arrangement that structures a series of relationships designed to motivate and reward the contractor for superior performance in accordance with the contract specification. See Incentive Type Contract.

Incentive Earnings: Earnings resulting from awards made under cost, schedule, or technical performance clauses of incentive contracts.

Incentive Limits: The maximum range of incentive fee in an incentive contract (expressed as dollars or points) for the total contract or its separate clauses. Since the sum of the cost, schedule, and technical incentive maximums may be greater than the maximum for the contract, incentive limits may override or effectively reduce this maximum.

Incentive Losses: Negative earnings resulting from penalties incurred under the various types of incentive contracts.

Incentive-Type Contract: A contract that may be of either a fixed price or cost-reimbursement nature, with a special provision for adjustment of the fixed price or fee. It provides for a target price, target profit/fee, and target cost as a point of departure for various incentives. It also has a maximum price or maximum fee, with price or fee adjustment after completion of the contract for the purpose of establishing a final price or fee. The final adjustment is based on the performer's actual costs plus a sliding scale of profit or fee which varies inversely with the cost, but which in no event permits the final price or fee to exceed the maximum price or fee stated in the contract. Also may include incentives for schedule, technical performance, and so on.

Income: Money or money equivalent earned or accrued during an accounting period, arising from sales, issues, and rentals of goods and services, or from the receipt of gifts and windfalls from any outside source. Usually must be qualified by such words as gross and net.

Incremental Funding: Funds provided on a periodic basis to cover the resource requirements of a contract when funds are not made available or authorized at the time of contract award.

Independent Audit: An audit performed by persons not under the administrative jurisdiction of the major entity being audited.

Independent Cost Estimate: Any cost estimate developed in organizational channels separate and independent from program channels and having the express purpose of serving as an analytical tool to validate or cross-check program office or contractor-developed estimates.

Independent Government Cost Estimate (IGCE): In government procurement, a government-prepared estimate of the probable price of a proposed procurement.

Independent Parametric Cost Estimate (IPCE): A physical and/or performance parameter-related life cycle cost estimate accomplished outside of the functional control of program proponents. The IPCE is developed to test the reasonableness of the proponent's baseline cost estimate and to provide a second opinion as to the cost of a product or service for consideration at a key decision point in the acquisition cycle.

Index Number: A ratio of the value of a subject item to the value of a similar type item for purposes of comparison. Usually expressed as a percent. For example: A price index of an item is the ratio of its price at a given time to its price at some other time, usually previously.

Indirect Cost Pool: A grouping of incurred costs identified with two or more cost objectives but not specifically identified with any final work activity or work output.

Indirect Costs: Those costs not capable of being specifically and consistently identified to direct work orders. Indirect costs are accrued and charged to overhead accounts, the sum of which is applied as burden. The cost of labor, services, or supplies not easily or readily allocable directly to a product or service.

Industrial Engineering Estimate: (1) A cost estimate made by the summation and pricing of the labor hours and material quantities required to produce tasks, end items, and components. The estimates are usually made by the persons responsible for the task or who will be doing the task. (2) An estimate based on timed or estimated labor standards, labor efficiency measures, and labor rates.

Inflation: A rise in the general level of prices unaccompanied by a rise in output (productivity).

Insurance: The purchase of protection against losses and risks. The purchase of protection against liabilities resulting from product usage.

Intangible Allowance: A cash payment to cover incidental expenses to employees relocated to new sites.

Interdivisional Transfers: (1) Price and Cost: Materials sold or transferred between a prime contractor's divisions, subsidiaries, or affiliates that are under a common control. (2) At Price: The quoted price covers a standard catalog price item including profit. (3) At Cost: Includes support division cost less profit.

Interest: The service charge for the use of money or capital, paid at agreed-to intervals by the user, and commonly expressed as an annual percentage of principal.

Internal Cost Transfers: An accounting element covering transfers and adjustments of actual recorded costs from one cost account to another when it is impractical to identify separately each individual cost item for the transfer.

Internal Operating Cost Target: Program management's estimate/target of what the costs for a given contract, project, or program will be at completion; may be lower, the same as, or higher than the contract target cost value.

Internal Rate of Return: The discount rate that results in a present value of zero in a cash flow.

Investment: The commitment of money, capital, or effort to secure profitable returns in the form of interest, income, services, or benefits.

Job Cost: Actual costs arrived at by method of cost accounting which collects charges for material, labor, and allocated overhead in the production of a specific order, a finished unit, or units.

Job Order Costing System: A product cost accumulation system used for manufacturing and construction. See Job Cost.

Joint Product Costs: The costs accumulated before the split-off point of two or more products in a process costing environment.

Journal: A book or computer data file or files of original entry for recording miscellaneous and general transactions not provided for in other specific journals such as cashbooks and sales registers.

Judgment: (1) A term used to denote the subjective estimate of labor or material based on past experience of the estimator. This experience often is not documented or substantiated by recorded data but commonly falls into the category of intuition or direct estimating. (2) A legal court determination of an amount due as a result of a judical decision.

Judgment Factors: Subjective factors that are not verifiable. Judgment factors include assumptions, estimates of future conditions, rates, factor extrapolations, direct labor requirement, and other data where it is impractical to establish an auditable basis for an estimate and it is necessary to rely on a multiple of experiences to establish the projected cost.

Kickoff Meeting: A general meeting of the principals of a proposal or cost estimating team for the purpose of outlining ground rules, assumptions, and responsibilities as they relate to proposal preparation or cost estimating.

Labor: A generic term that covers the effort of hourly skilled or salaried personnel. Usually expressed in labor-hours, or labor-months.

Labor-Hour Contract: A variant of the time and materials contract differing only in that materials are not involved in the contract or are not supplied by the contractor. In these contracts the customer agrees to pay a fixed rate (including overhead and profit) for a negotiated number of labor-hours.

Labor Standards: A set of estimated, measured, or computed values used to forecast and evaluate performance. Examples: rates of machine cutting, assembly time, and operations per hour.

Labor Unit Prices: Labor unit prices are equal to labor unit quantities multiplied by labor rates. Hence the labor unit price is the labor cost per unit of production.

Labor Unit Quantities: The number of labor time units (hours, days, weeks, months) required to produce a unit of output (e.g., welding time per foot; paving time per mile; labor hours per block laid; drafting time per drawing; writing, editing, or typing time per page). Also called "productivity."

Labor Variance: (1) Time: The difference between the standard hours priced at the standard rate and the actual hours priced at the standard rate. (2) Rate: The difference between the actual hours priced at the standard rate and the actual hours priced at the actual rate.

Labor Yield Rate: The number of on-the-job direct labor-hours anticipated during the fiscal year, excluding paid and nonpaid absences.

Lead Time: The time allowed or required to initiate, acquire, or develop an item or system so that it will be available and ready for use at a given time.

Learning Curve: (1) The learning curve is based on the assumption that as the quantity of units produced is doubled, the hours or costs to produce the units declines by a constant percentage. The constant rate of decline is the slope of the learning curve. This curve is linear when plotted on log-log coordinates. (2) A tool of calculation used primarily to project resource requirements in terms of direct manufacturing labor-hours or the quantity of material (for this purpose, usually referred to as an improvement curve) required for a production run. Used interchangeably with the term "improvement curve." Also referred to as progress curve, progress function, or experience curve. (3) Two types of learning curves are used: *Unit curves* identify the value of resources required to produce each unit; and *Cumulative curves* show the value of resources required to produce a given amount of units. A *Cumulative average curve* is developed by dividing the cumulative value by the cumulative units.

Least Squares Method: A regression method used to develop an equation that best fits a grouping of cost data points.

Level-of-Effort: Normally refers to a constant number of personnel assigned to a given job for a specified period of time.

Liabilities: Amounts owed for goods and services received or other assets acquired, and losses incurred.

Life Cycle Cost: All costs incurred during the projected life of the system, subsystem, or component. It includes total cost of ownership over the system life cycle including all research, development, test, and evaluation; initial investment; production; operating and support maintenance costs; and disposal costs.

Limited Overhead: Limited overhead is applied in lieu of full overhead to certain activities to allocate an applicable share of employee service expenses and other general and administrative costs. The amount of overhead applied is dependent on: (1) the duration and nature of the activity; (2) the support required from in-plant organizations; (3) the location at which the work is to be accomplished; and (4) the type of personnel assigned to the task.

Line-of-Best-Fit: A line that passes through a charting of data point values in a manner that best represents the trend of the data points. The "least squares" method is most frequently used to compute this line-of-best-fit.

Linear Regression: A technique for fitting a straight line to a family of plotted points on Cartesian coordinates. Used in developing cost estimating relationships.

Long-Term Debt: Bonds, notes, or other indebtedness assumed by the company that do not mature in one year.

Long-Term Receivables: Notes, accounts, and other receivables expected to be collectible after one year or after a specific operating cycle.

Lot (Material): A specific quantity of material manufactured under identical conditions, and assigned an identifying number for estimating, technical, manufacturing, production, and supply purposes.

Lot Time: The labor-hours associated with a given lot order.

Lump-Sum Appropriation: An appropriation in a specified amount made for a complete program without prescribing limitations of expenditures within the stated purpose and amount.

Lump-Sum Reduction: A term used in negotiations to mean a cost settlement or adjustment at the bottom line, without identification or allocation to cost elements.

Machine-Hour: Operation equal to that of one machine for one hour.

Macroestimating: Estimating the total job (macro) as opposed to the detailed tasks of the job (micro). Varies by degree and level from job to job. See Microestimating.

Make or Buy: The determinations by management as to which parts, components, or equipment items will be fabricated (manufactured or made) by the company or obtained from outside sources (bought).

Man-Hour: A unit of work representing the productive effort of one person in one hour. Currently referred to as a "labor-hour," "work-hour," or "hour."

Man-Month: A unit of work representing the productive effort of one person in one month. Currently referred to as a "month of labor," "work-month," or "labor-month."

Manpower: A general term that could refer to either "equivalent people" or "equivalent headcount." When specific interpretation is necessary, use of the qualifying "equivalent people" or "headcount" definition is required.

Manufacturing Labor: Generally that direct labor performed directly on the end item or processing of parts used in the finished product, and the functional testing of the product. It normally covers fabrication, assembly, and manufacturing support activities. Sometimes also includes tooling and quality control labor.

Man-Year: A unit of work representing the productive effort of one person in one year. Currently referred to as a "labor-year" or "work-year."

Margin of Safety: In finance the difference between budgeted revenue and break-even revenue.

Market Value: The value of anything as computed on the basis of market quotations or, in the absence of quotations, the amount that would induce a willing seller to sell and a willing buyer to purchase.

Material Overhead: The overhead cost attributable to purchasing, receiving, storing, warehousing, delivering, or expediting materials. Also is termed "material burden" and "material procurement (indirect) costs."

Material Prices: The costs per unit of material quantity such as dollars per pound or ton, dollars per yard, or dollars per board foot.

Material Unit Prices: Material unit prices are equal to material unit quantities multiplied by material prices. Hence the material unit price is the material cost per unit of production.

Material Unit Quantities: The numbers of units of material required for a given amount of completed work (e.g., welding rod usage per inch or foot of weld; tons of asphalt used per each mile of highway paving; number of blocks per foot of wall; and number of pounds of sheet metal per foot of ductwork). These are also called "material usage" factors.

Mathematical Model: The general characterization of a process or concept expressed in terms of mathematical equations, which enables the manipulation of variables to be accomplished to determine how the process or concept would behave in different situations. See Cost Model, Model.

Methodology: A term used in estimating to describe the methods used to develop an estimate (i.e., detailed, empirical, comparative, statistical, parametric, standards, etc.).

Microestimating: Estimating based on the aggregation of the resources required for the smallest parts of the job. Also, cost estimating with microcomputers. See Macroestimating.

Milestone: A date or event that signifies either the start or completion of a task, work item, or activity.

Milestone Billing: A plan, schedule, or table of billing (request for payment) associated with key milestones and events.

Minimum Price: The lowest price at which a specific surplus item or lot may be sold. Normally, the minimum price should not be less than the estimated scrap value of the item or lot.

Model: A model is a representation of the reality of a situation or condition being studied. Consists of a series of equations, ground rules, assumptions, relationships, constants, and variables that describe and define the situation or condition being studied. See Cost Model, Mathematical Models.

Monetary Policy: The use of controls over bank lending power, the money supply, and interest rates.

Mortgage: A lien on land, buildings, machinery, equipment, and other property (fixed or movable) given by a borrower to the lender as security for his loan; sometimes called a deed of trust or a defeasible conveyance.

Motion Study: A study of the movements (whether of a part, a machine, or an operator) involved in performing an operation to determine those from the standpoints of maximum economy and minimum operator fatigue.

Multiyear Appropriation: An appropriation that is available for incurring obligations for a definite period in excess of one fiscal year, that is, for two or more years. An obligation of funds to cover the procurement of items normally procured in individual fiscal year buys.

Multiyear Contract: A contract covering more than one year but not in excess of five fiscal years. Total contract quantities and annual quantities are planned for a particular level and type of funding. Each program year is annually budgeted and funded, and, at the time of award, funds need only to have been appropriated for the first year. The contractor, however, is protected against loss resulting from cancellation by contract provisions allowing reimbursement of costs included in the cancellation ceiling. The cancellation ceiling includes coverage for the current fiscal year procurement and advanced funding requirements for the follow-on fiscal year procurements.

Multiyear Funding: In government procurement a Congressional authorization and appropriation covering more than one fiscal year. The term should not be confused with two-year or three-year funds which cover only one fiscal year's requirement but permit the executive branch more than one year to obligate the funds.

Multiyear Procurement: In government procurement a generic term describing situations in which the Government contracts, to some degree, for more than the current-year requirement. Examples include multiyear contracts, block buys, advance procurement. Generally, advance long-lead procurements in support of a single year's requirement would not be considered a multiyear procurement.

Negotiated Contract: One obtained by direct agreement with a contractor, without formal advertising for bids, but after soliciting price quotations from qualified sources. Most frequently is a cost-reimbursable type of contract.

Negotiation: In its more *formal context*, one of the major methods of government procurement. Employed under certain permissive circumstances prescribed by statute when formal advertising is determined to be infeasible and impracticable. In its more *general context*, a bargaining process between two or more parties, each with its own viewpoints and objectives, seeking to reach a mutually satisfactory agreement on, or settlement of, a matter of common concern. In *estimating*, the give and take process of final deliberations between a buyer and a seller and/or between the company's management and its internal divisions to finalize a statement of work, program definition, cost estimate, and contract for a program or product.

No-Cost Change: A change in which no contract price change is involved, but which may or may not include overhead costs.

Noncost Data: Information that contains no cost information but that is required to complement the cost data. The noncost data contain the significant facts and assumptions to describe what is costed. Noncost data include technical descriptions, schedules, conditions under which the estimated work is to be performed, and so on.

Nonexpendable Material: Items that are not consumed in use and that ordinarily retain their original identity and characteristics during the period of use and subsequent reparable cycles.

Nonlabor: Nonlabor is generally contrasted with labor in the overhead accounting sense. Nonlabor costs include any costs incurred by a company that are not paid for through the payroll program. May also refer to material items, utilities, or services purchased.

Nonrecurring Costs: Those elements of development and investment cost that generally occur only once in the life cycle of a work activity or work output. Examples are engineering, system test, tooling, and preproduction activities. Includes basic design and development through first release of engineering drawings and data, all system and subsystem test activities (except end item acceptance testing), configuration audits, qualification testing, technical publications through initial release, basic tool and production planning through initial release, all basic tooling, prototypes, engineering models, units built for test purposes only, units not built to production configuration, and specialized work force training.

Normalize: *Data Base*: To render constant or to adjust for known differences. *Dollars*: Previous year costs are escalated to a common year basis for comparison.

Not-to-Exceed (NTE) Not Less Than (NTL): A corporate commitment to a customer that the value of an estimate plus appropriate contingency allowances will not be exceeded or be less than the firm proposal and estimates that will be submitted at a later date. The NTE or NTL value can be adjusted by changes in the statement of work, requirements, and specifications.

Obligation: The estimate of the actual amount of the cost of an item being ordered or authorized service. This estimate is carried in official accounting records and reserves funds pending completion of the contract.

Obligation Authority: In government procurement an administrative subdivision of an allotment authorizing the incurrence of obligations within a specified amount against the allotment without further recourse to the office that granted the authority. Generally, the term applies to the various agencies of the government where a specific form has been developed to facilitate the issuance of obligation authorities.

Obligation Basis of Accounting: The basis of accounting for appropriations or contract authorizations whereby obligations are recorded in the accounts when incurred, and appropriations, allotments, or contract authorizations are reduced accordingly, regardless of whether the expenditures are to be made in the same fiscal period.

Obligations Incurred: Amounts of orders placed, contracts awarded, services received, and similar transactions during a given period requiring commitment of money.

Operating Cost: (1) The total outlay in cash or its equivalent applied in carrying out a specific program or function. (2) A life cycle cost term. See Operating and Support Costs.

Operating and Support Costs: A life cycle cost term covering the cost of operating and supporting a system from initial operating capability for a given period of years. Also called ownership costs.

Optimum: The most efficient/effective use of resources to accomplish a specified task. The best use of time and resources.

Option: (1) The procurement of additional quantities, services, or portions of a work activity or work output. (2) An added technical or performance feature to a configuration, program, or proposal. *Note*: to distinguish between (1) and (2) the term "enhancement option" is often used for (2). Also note: Option should not be confused with *alternate*. See Definition.

Other Assets: Those properties having economic value that have not been previously classified, for example, goodwill, patents, licenses.

Other Direct Costs: A cost element that covers costs not usually listed under direct material, labor, or overhead. Some of these are computing, travel, freight, consultants, remote activities, and taxes.

Output: (1) Refers to the results of the efforts of a group. (2) The printout of a computer tabulation. (3) The energy or work produced by a machine or by equipment.

Overhead: (Indirect): A cost that, because of its incurrence for common or joint objectives, is not readily subject to treatment as a direct cost. Such indirect cost is incurred to benefit the total direct cost or business base. The character of overhead cost thus requires estimating, budgeting, and control techniques that take into account the total business base. Accordingly, the overhead applicable to any one work activity or work output is applied to direct hours or costs. "Indirect" is a term that is synonymous with overhead.

Overhead Budget: Management allocation of planned indirect costs to each established overhead pool or organization.

Overhead Pool: A grouping of overhead expenses determined to be applicable to a previously determined distribution base, such as manufacturing or engineering direct labor hours.

Overhead Rates: Indirect dollars per labor hour or labor cost. Cost relationships that mathematically reflect the distribution of overhead costs over a labor or cost base.

Overrun: Actual costs in excess of the contemplated or target contract cost.

Overtime: Work in excess of 8 hours a day or 40 hours a week. Overtime is a resource available to management as a means of extending available manpower and talent, but which imposes a premium labor cost to any task to which it is applied. Consists of two types: (1) *Unscheduled*, overtime that is necessary to alleviate a temporary behind-schedule condition which can have an adverse effect on other organizations if not completed in time; (2) *Scheduled*, overtime expended on a planned basis to provide "round-the-clock" support to an activity that cannot be stopped once started or to utilize machines or technical personnel to the maximum on a task.

Ownership: In government procurement ownership cost encompasses the cost elements within the operating and support cost category exclusively. Included are those costs associated with operating, modifying, maintaining, supplying, and supporting a product or system.

Parameter: A characteristic that is considered to be essential in accurately describing a problem, population, or system. The characteristic is used to calibrate, measure, or calculate a series of results or tests. It might be a design, system, equipment, or cost parameter. In cost estimating, a parameter is often hours per pounds, dollars per horsepower, hours per wire, and so on.

Parametric Cost Estimating: Parametric cost estimating is a technique that employs one or more cost estimating relationships for measurement of costs associated with the development, manufacture, and/or modification of a specified end item based on its technical, physical, or other characteristics. See Statistical Cost Estimating and Cost Estimating Methods.

Partial Payment: A payment authorized under a contract on completion of the delivery of one or more complete units called for in the contract, or on completion of one or more distinct items of service called for in the contract. Payment of an amount less than the amount due. Also a payment made against a termination claim upon prior approval before final settlement of the total termination claim.

Payment: Discharge of an obligation, in whole or in part, by money or acceptable equivalent. In the aggregate fiscal sense, the amount of cash disbursed, expenditure checks issued, or vouchers approved and scheduled for payment, net of refunds received.

Payment Bond: A guarantee of the payment by persons supplying material or services in the execution of work provided for in a contract.

Payroll: (1) A list of persons paid or entitled to be paid, with the amount due each. In addition, may include identification number, time worked or quantity produced, gross salary or wages, and deductions. (2) The amount of money necessary for distribution to those listed. (3) The organization that performs the payroll function.

Pecuniary Liability: In government procurement the statutory obligation of an individual or entity to reimburse the government for loss or improper application of funds or property arising from his failure to exercise assigned responsibilities.

Per Diem: A daily or monthly allowance to cover personal subsistence, lodging, and local transportation costs while in travel status or temporary additional duty away from one's home location.

PERT (Program Evaluation and Review Technique): A management tool for defining and integrating what must be done to accomplish and manage multiple program objectives on time.

Petty Cash: An amount of cash on hand or on deposit that is set aside for the purpose of making immediate payments of comparatively small amounts.

PFD Time: Personal, fatigue, and delay time expended by personnel in trips to the restroom and water fountain, telephone calls, unscheduled rest periods, waiting for machine repair or tools, and unscheduled supervisory guidance or training.

Physical Elements: In a work breakdown structure, the elements that represent tangible hardware (e.g., systems, subsystems, assemblies, subassemblies, components, parts, tooling, and support equipment).

Physical Standard: A quantitative normal measure (not a dollar cost) of a requirement for raw material, labor time, machine time, and so on in a manufacturing or similar process. A basis of production planning, scheduling and control; a means for determination of material, labor, and machine requirements; a means of projecting workloads in relation to capacity; a basis for determination of standard costs for use in cost control and preparation of budget estimates.

Plan: The required actions or capabilities needed to accomplish a mission. A course of action. An organized approach to the preparation of a cost estimate. See Estimating Plan.

Planned Value: An estimated value (dollars or man-hours) placed on items of work to be accomplished within a specific time by the doing organization. These values become the baselines against which the organization must control and report performance.

Planned Value of Work Accomplished Index: A percent of accomplishment calculated from the relationship of planned value of work accomplished to date, divided by actual cost expended through a reporting period. See Earned Value.

Planning: The study and analysis of a job, defining the required work details, estimating the resources required, and scheduling the work to be accomplished.

Planning Estimates: Estimates developed on the basis of preliminary information, utilizing formulas and factors in the absence of formal definition data and a complete pricing study. Used for program conceptual planning or fiscal year budgeting study purposes only, and not considered valid for contract pricing proposals; neither do they represent a commitment of a company.

Plant and Equipment or Property: Assets that are used in the normal operations of the business, have an economic life longer than one operating cycle, and will not be sold in the normal course of business; for example, machinery, buildings.

Point Estimate: (1) An estimate that measures a single numerical value rather than a range of values. (2) An estimate that is made based on total resources required to do a job but that is not time scheduled. Expenditures are estimated as if they are to be used at a single point in time. A noncalendar-based estimate.

Points of Change and Percent Change: Measures of change in an index. The terms ''points of change'' and ''percent change'' in the index do not mean the same thing. The former is the difference between the indexes at two dates; the latter is the difference expressed as a percent of the index at the earlier of the two dates.

Postaudit: An examination made after the transactions to be audited have taken place and have been recorded or been approved for recording by designated officials.

Posting: The entering of an item in a record. The act of transferring to an account the detailed or summarized data contained in a book, computer file, or document of original entry.

Potential Termination Liability: The amount of cost including applicable profit or fee which the company would reasonably expect to recover if a contract were terminated by the customer at any point during the life of the contract. See Termination Liability.

Predecessor Activity: In a critical path bar chart, an activity that precedes the activity under investigation.

Price: The dollar value a company will sell its product for or commit to a contract. Includes profit or fee added to cost.

Price Analysis: The process of examining and evaluating a prospective price without evaluation of the separate cost elements and proposed profit of the individual offeror whose price is being evaluated. It may be accomplished by (1) a comparison of submitted quotations; (2) comparison of price quotations and contract prices with current quotations for the same or similar items; and (3) the use of parameters (dollars per pound, for instance) or a comparison of proposed prices with independently developed estimates.

Price Breakdown: The orderly listing of the functional cost categories and their cost elements that constitute a price.

Price Estimating: The art or skill of predetermining the market value of an item or activity that will assure an acceptable profit.

Price Index: A ratio indicating the relationship between prices at two time periods. Labor and materials, within designated industry areas, are the two resources usually considered in determining a price index. The cost-of-living index, is a form of price index.

Price List: A listing of sales prices of a company's products, usually catalog prices.

Price Negotiation Memorandum: In government procurement a document that relates the story of the negotiation. The document has two objectives: (1) It establishes the reasonableness of the agreement reached with the successful offeror; and (2) it is the permanent record of the decisions the negotiator made in establishing that the price was fair and reasonable.

Priced Bill of Material: A list of all material and components complete with unit and total prices for a specific subassembly, assembly, or end item.

Pricer: A person from any one of several disciplines (e.g., contracting, price analysis, auditing, and others) who contributes to the final price in negotiation. Members of a company that set the sales prices of products.

Pricing: The establishment of a sales price. The development and justification of sales price proposals including the selection and projection of rates, ratios, factors, and comparative analyses with present or past programs and market evaluations.

Pricing Agreement: In government procurement a written agreement between the contractor and the government describing how the contractor's estimating system will be employed in preparing and supporting contractor price proposals. The agreement may encompass such areas as proposal structure, requirements for cost or pricing data, use of forward pricing rate agreements, pricing formulas, and identification and use of data banks.

Pricing Arrangement: An agreed-to basis between contractual parties for the payment of amounts for specified performance. Usually expressed in terms of a specific cost-reimbursement or fixed-price arrangement.

Pricing Center: A segment of a company organizationally and functionally chartered to have separate overhead accounts and its own overhead rates for use in negotiating and pricing contracts that it will perform.

Pricing—Conceptual: This type of pricing applies to price development when little information is available other than gross overall program definition and system definition for the products and/or services to be supplied. See Planning Estimate and Budget Estimate.

Pricing Guidelines or Instructions: Memos or documents containing proposal plans, strategy, organization instructions, or request for proposal requirements. See Estimating Instructions.

Pricing Rates/Forward Pricing Rates: In government procurement these are rates negotiated with the resident administrative contracting officer for use in pricing new contract proposals and follow-on business. Pricing negotiations are conducted, normally, once each year, or whenever either party determines appropriate.

Prime Cost: Cost of direct material and direct labor.

Prior Year Costs: See Sunk Costs.

Probability of Incurring Estimated Cost (PIECOST): A computer-aided procedure employing parametric techniques to estimate and track indirect costs. In government procurement, it is used for the purpose of setting the government's negotiation objective in the forward pricing of overhead and for analyzing cost incurrence trends.

Process Costing: The costing approach used when manufacturing production occurs on a continuous, regular basis and where products are produced for immediate shipment or warehouse stock.

Process Plan: An itemized listing of each task that must be accomplished to perform a job, along with the skills, time, equipment, and material required to do the job.

Procurement: The act of obtaining raw material, purchased parts and equipment, subcontract, and outside production items. The obtaining of equipment, resources, property, or services by purchasing, renting, leasing, or other means. In the supply management sense it may include the functions of design, standards determination, specification writing, selection of suppliers, funding, contract administration, and other related functions. See Purchasing.

Product: Any item proposed for sale by a company as a part of their normal marketing or sales function.

Product Cost: The total cost associated with production of a specific quantity of an item.

Product Development Costs: Includes all task/project costs incurred in conjunction with the application of scientific or technical knowledge in the development of new products, product components, processes, or improvements. May be developed in company's own funds, funded by a customer, or combination thereof.

Product Improvement Proposal: A proposal or configuration change to increase system effectiveness or extend the useful life of a product.

Product Liability Insurance: The purchase of protection against liabilities resulting from product usage.

Production Cost: Recurring costs of system hardware and support equipment.

Production Rate: The number of end items produced in a given period, as a month or year.

Production Units: The number of pounds, yards, board feet, square feet, gallons, miles, blocks, drawings, parts, pages, and so on to be produced.

Productivity: The state of yielding results, benefits, or profits. Productivity rate is a measure of the yielding of result, benefits, or profits; for example, amount of concrete poured per labor-hour.

Profit: Generally characterized as the basic motive of business enterprise; the excess of the revenues from sales of goods or services over the related cost thereof in a given transaction or over a given time. The word "profit" is used in fixed-price contracts versus "fee" in cost contracts. See Contract Profit, Fee.

Profit Ceiling: The contractual maximum profit, usually in a cost reimbursable contract expressed as a percentage of contract target cost.

Profit Center: The smallest organizationally independent segment of a company that has been charged by management with profit and loss responsibilities and whose operations must, therefore, absorb its indirect costs.

Profit Floor: The contractual minimum profit in a cost reimbursable contract, usually expressed as a percentage of contract target cost.

Profit Objective: A major goal of a company's sales effort; the difference between sales and cost of sales. In negotiations and procurement, that part of the estimated contract price that the customer and contractor try to negotiate as being appropriate for the procurement at hand.

Profitability Accounting: An accounting system designed to report the profitability of individual product lines within a given division or group.

Program Control: Includes the management disciplines and techniques to maintain schedule, data and documentation, and cost status on a program.

Program Rates: Those actual and projected direct labor and overhead rates based on (or derived from) accumulations of charges to labor accounts for contracts in a particular program.

Progress Curve: See Learning Curve.

Progress Payments: Payments made to a contractor as work progresses on a procurement, completion of a contract, or an end item. The amounts are usually based on actual expenditures and work performed at a particular stage of completion or a predetermined value based on the completion of certain milestones.

Project Budget: An operating cost (target) amount for the elements of a project.

Project Cost Report: A recurring report of expenditures incurred and forecast by a given work order or series of work orders under a contract. Also included are direct labor, direct material, and overhead costs and comparisons to estimated or actual contract values for these same costs.

Promissory Note: A written promise to pay on demand or at a fixed or determined future time a certain sum of money to, or to the order of, a specified person or to bearer.

Proposal: A solicited or unsolicited offer to provide goods or services. Usually consists of a technical, management, and cost proposal plus a model contract. In addition, a separate executive summary document is also included in most major proposals.

Prospective Pricing: A pricing decision made in advance of performance, based on analysis of comparative prices, cost estimates, past costs, or combinations of such considerations.

Purchase Discount: Reduction in sales prices offered to buyers for certain conditions, for example, favorable payments or cash, quantity buys, items for resale, and early deliveries.

Purchased Labor Cost: The cost of labor obtained from a supplier for fabrication and/or processing of hardware when the material is furnished by the buyer. Examples are machining of castings or painting and plating of parts or materials furnished by the firm. The hiring of any type of labor from another firm where the output is not a manufactured product, such as technical services.

Purchasing: The acquisition of supplies, raw materials, goods, and services at the right time, from the right vendor, and at the right cost. See Procurement.

Quotation: An expression of price and contractual terms under which a supplier would be willing to supply items or services. See Bid and Proposal.

Rate: (1) *In estimating*: the dollar value (actual or estimated) applied to such things as one hour of labor effort, one unit of computer equipment or machine usage. (2) *In manufacturing*: The number (quantity) of items being produced in a given time as a month or year (e.g., 100 automobiles per month).

Rate Schedule—General: A set of forward pricing rates based on projected (firm and likely) business volume. These rates are applicable to overall program or company activity.

Rate Schedule—Special: A set of forward pricing rates projected for pricing a particular task, project, or program that was not considered in or is not from the business base used for the development of general rates.

Ratio (Estimating): A statistical method of comparing the values of two distinct efforts and projecting the result or quotient of this comparison into future efforts being estimated.

Rationale: A term used to explain the logical basis for an estimate. Usually to document: (1) why a particular estimating method was selected; (2) how a specific estimate was developed; (3) what specific cost history was used; (4) why a given task, job, or estimate is similar to past experience and history; (5) how historical costs were used; or (6) why the estimate is realistic and credible.

Raw Material: Includes raw stock, minor components, sheet stock, wires, and so on that require further processing into manufactured goods or tools.

Raw Time: The pure, productive time to perform each task of an operation. It is derived from time study, motion study, standard data, and historical information.

Real Property: Lands, buildings, structures, utilities systems, improvements, and appurtenances thereto. Includes equipment attached to and made part of buildings and structures (such as heating systems) but not movable equipment (such as plant equipment).

Realism: The determination that all costs have been included and that estimated costs are valid.

Realization: A ratio of the actual hours used to the standard hour value used. It reflects the productivity of workers in performing a given job. It is expressed as a realization factor (variance) and is derived by dividing the actual hours by the standard hours. See Efficiency.

Receipt: (1) Money received from any source, or property received from any source. (2) A written acknowledgment of the receiving or taking of goods or money.

Receivables: A collective term used to describe amounts due or to become due from others.

Reconciliation: A determination or statement of the detailed items required to explain: (1) the difference between any two or more estimates; (2) the reason why an actual value exceeds or is less than the forecasted value; or (3) the balances of two or more related values or accounts.

Recurring Costs: Repetitive costs that vary with the quantity being produced.

Regression Analysis: The association of one or more independent variables with a dependent variable. The relationships are associative only; causative inferences are added subjectively by the analysts.

Rehabilitation Cost: Cost to restore or improve facilities, plant, property, or equipment.

Relevant Costs: Costs that are present under one of several alternatives but are absent, either in whole or in part, under other alternatives. (Also called differential costs.)

Relevant Range: A range over which a fixed cost applies. A cost element may have more than one relevant range, and, if so, the "fixed costs" may vary in a stepwise function. See Step-Fixed Costs.

Relocation Expense: Approved expenditures related to employee transfers between company or agency business locations where the new assignment will extend beyond a specific period of time.

Removal Cost: The cost of dismantling a unit of property owing to retirement from service.

Replacement Cost: The cost of replacing an existing item or group of items of tangible property.

Replacement Factor: The estimated percentage of equipment in use that will require replacement during a given period.

Reprogramming: In government procurement the transfer of funds between programs of an appropriation; a shifting of funds from the original purpose for which they were justified by Congress.

Residual Income: An excess of net income (divisional margin) over the minimum acceptable income rate. Sometimes used to designate superior performance and to trigger added compensation for managers.

Responsibility Centers: Organizational entities charged with controlling a given classification or category of costs.

Request for Proposals (RFP): A solicitation document used in negotiated procurements. It usually contains a description of the items or services to be procured, the terms and conditions, types of contracts, schedules, work statement, specifications, listing of the items to be delivered, funding, data requirements, and instructions for the preparation of technical, management, and cost proposals.

Request for Quotation: A solicitation document used in negotiated procurements. Similar in usage as an RFP. However, usually only covers the procurement of standard off-the-shelf items built to known specifications and not requiring extensive proposal documentation.

Request for Technical Proposal: The solicitation document used in the first step of two-step formal procurement which calls for technical proposals before the solicitation of cost proposals.

Research, Development, Test, and Evaluation (RDT&E) Cost: The sum of all costs resulting from applied research, engineering design, analysis, development, test, evaluation, and managing development efforts related to a specific system. See Life Cycle Costs.

Reserve: An amount of appropriations, contract authorizations, other funds, or capital set aside for savings, contingencies, or other purposes.

Retirement Fund: The fund into which retirement and disability contributions are deposited and from which amounts are withdrawn for the payment of retirement annuities.

Retroactive Pricing: A pricing action computed after a portion or all of the work specified under contract has been completed. The pricing is usually based on a review of contractor performance and recorded cost data.

Return on Investment: Net income divided by investment or operating revenues divided by operating costs. "Investment" actually denotes three financial concepts, yielding three different ratios: return on assets, return on stockholder's equity, and return on invested capital. (1) *Return on assets* equals net income divided by total assets. It reflects the amount earned from investment of all financial resources committed, including liabilities and owner's equity (total sources of funds invested in assets). (2) *Return on owner's equity* equals net income divided by funds invested by stockholders. This reflects the amount earned on funds invested by shareholders. (c) *Return on invested capital* equals net income divided by long-term liabilities plus stockholder's equity. This ROI focuses on the amount earned from long-term liabilities and stockholder's equity, or relatively permanent capital investments.

Revenue: The amount realized from sales of goods or services or the use of capital. Income.

Revision of Standard Price: A change in the former inventory standard price of an item under current procurement owing to significant change in current market price or production cost.

Revolving Fund: A fund to finance a continuing cycle of operations with receipts derived from such operations available in their entirety for use by the fund.

Risk Analysis: The evaluation of the situation, environment, or set of conditions to determine the technical, financial, or business risks inherent in the venture or mission. Can be computed using complex models, expert opinions, or intuitive judgement.

Roundtable Estimating: An estimating method whereby representatives of interested departments such as engineering, manufacturing, contracts, purchasing, and accounting may be brought together to develop costs based on experience, knowledge of the product, and knowledge of market conditions. The estimate developed by this approach is usually completed without benefit of detailed drawings, bills of material, and with very limited information concerning specifications. This technique of estimating has the advantage of speed and is relatively inexpensive; however, it lacks detailed documentation and support. Also referred to as expert opinion estimating. See Cost Estimating Methods for the specific types of methods used to develop costs.

Run Time: The second, minute, or hour value that is repeated each time a part is produced. See Setup Time.

Sales: The amount of proceeds realized or to be realized by the seller for goods or services furnished or to be furnished to the buyer.

Sales Mix: The proportion of revenues received from two or more products or services.

Scattergraph: A manual plot of cost data points that is used to project future costs based on past historical data.

Schedule: (1) A time display of the milestone events and activities of a program or project. (2) A subsidiary detailed financial or statistical table, generally in support of summary data in an exhibit.

Schedule Element Structure: The structure used to plan and identify the schedule sequence relationship of subassemblies, subcomponents, or details within the framework of the contract work breakdown structure.

Semiautomated Takeoff: In computerized estimating, the process of manually tracing or circumscribing lines and areas or counting parts or components on a drawing through the use of electronic digitizers to develop quantity information that can subsequently be converted to cost estimates.

Semivariable Costs: Costs that vary somewhat in relation to volume but their percent of change is not the same as the percent of change in volume.

Setup Time: The one-time-only portion of the job of producing a given quantity of identical parts. The setup involves the preparation of a machine for producing parts.

Settlement Expenses (Terminations): Reasonable accounting, legal, clerical, and other expenses necessary in connection with the termination and settlement of the contract and subcontracts and purchase orders. Settlement expenses include final contract audit and closeout, storage, transportation, and other costs incurred for the protection of property acquired or produced for the contract or in connection with disposition of such property.

Should Cost: In government procurement a concept of contract pricing that employs an integrated team of government procurement cost/price analysts, contract administration, audit, and engineering representatives to conduct a coordinated, in-depth cost review and evaluation of a program at the contractor's plant. Its purpose is to identify uneconomical or inefficient practices in the contractor's management and operations, to quantify the findings in terms of their impact on cost, and to develop a realistic price objective for negotiations or for the program that reflects the results of the should-cost effort.

Simulation: A model of a set of conditions or an environment of interrelated elements exercised in a manner to gain knowledge of conditions that may develop under various circumstances.

Single Source: See Sole Source.

Sinking Fund: A fund established by periodic contributions, for example, funds for retirement of bonds, payment of mortgage, or replacement of an asset.

Skill Category: Skills covering a given discipline (e.g., manufacturing, construction, pipefitting).

Skill Level: Experience or pay grades within skill categories.

Skill Mix: The proportions of each skill category and skill level in a work activity or labor force.

Software: Nonphysical or intangible portions of the work, usually computer programs or electronic data, but can also include reports, drawings, photographs, videotapes, and other nonsystem component or nonsupport equipment items.

Sole Source: Characterized as the one and only source, regardless of the marketplace, possessing a unique and singularly available performance capability for the purpose of contract award. (Sometimes used interchangeably with the term "single source.")

Source Evaluation Board: A group of personnel representing the various functional and technical areas involved in a procurement who direct, control, and perform the evaluation of proposals and produce summary facts and findings required in the source selection process.

Source Selection: The formal procurement process used to (1) call for proposals, (2) evaluate proposals, (c) pass recommendations to higher authority, or (4) award a contract to one of several bidders.

Standard Cost: The predetermined cost of each operation or each unit of finished product. It represents the value of direct material, labor, and manufacturing burden normally required under efficient conditions at normal capacity to process a unit of product. Excepting costs attributable to precise and highly predictable operations, actual costs will almost always vary from standard costs owing to factors (usually called variances) that affect performance, like employee fatigue, unforeseen interruptions, and other delays.

Standard Cost Estimating: The application and adjusting of standard estimates for machine setup and run time to each manufacturing operation or process that is required to fabricate parts, assemble them into a whole unit, and functionally test the completed unit. The standard estimates are developed from studies of historical cost data or combinations of these costs and from time and motion studies conducted by industrial engineering organizations. Standard estimates are used to develop direct labor and other kinds of manufacturing cost elements and apply to such other work as the preparation of technical publications, manuals, or handbooks. Standard cost estimating is used on parts, assemblies, or end items when the design is complete, drawings are available, and production planning of the manufacturing operations required to build the items is complete. Adjustments can be made to the standard estimates for "variances" in worker efficiency, anticipated shop loading, and other factors that might be predicted and that would increase or decrease the estimates. See Cost Estimating Methods.

Standard Hours: The number of hours a skilled worker should use to complete a given job under ideal, or perfect conditions. A standard hour is a way of establishing a relative means of measurement. See Standard Cost.

Standard Price Reductions on Sales: Inventory price reductions for items at less than full standard prices in recognition of lesser utility due to age, condition, or model.

Standard Price Variance: The difference between actual costs incurred in connection with acquisition of material and the amount recorded in the inventory accounts at standard unit costs.

Standard Volume of Activity: The basis for a single one-time budget or static budget. The standard volume of activity typically is set below the activity level that uses the full capacity of the organization.

Statement of Financial Condition: A statement that reflects the amount of assets, liabilities, and capital present as of a given date.

Statement of Resources: A statement showing the assets of a company or organization that will be available for use to accomplish its objective or mission.

Statement of Work: A document stating the confines of the contractual work to be accomplished. The part of a request for proposal or contract that defines the work a customer wants performed.

Statistical Cost Estimating: Parametric or "top-down" estimating, statistical cost analysis, cost analysis, or formula estimating. This estimating method requires an analysis of the work to be performed, but generally can be based on a less detailed definition of work than is required for other methods. In this kind of estimating, cost is estimated for the entire job, or major portions of it, using certain major or technical or physical characteristics (weight, speed, horsepower, etc.) with their relationships to costs as developed by studies of past jobs, their technical characteristics, and their costs. See Parametric Cost Estimating and Cost Estimating Methods.

Step-Fixed Costs: Fixed costs that alter their behavior as the activity level moves from one relevant range to another. See Relevant Range.

Stockholder's Equity: A corporation's original investment by shareholders plus earnings retained in the business, for example, preferred stock, common stock, retained earnings.

Subassembly: Two or more parts that form a portion of an assembly or end item. Replaceable as a whole, but having a part or parts that are individually replaceable.

Subcontract: (1) General: Any agreement, purchase order, and/or instrument, other than a prime contract, calling for the performance of work or for the making or furnishing of material required for the performance of one or more prime contracts. (2) Estimating: Current usage usually covers the procurement of major components or subsystems that require the subcontractor to do extensive design, development, engineering, and testing to meet a prime contractor's procurement specification.

Subsistence: The allowance paid to an employee on business travel or short-term assignment to cover the cost of lodging, meals, laundry, and incidental expenses while away from main facility.

Substantiation: The information provided in support of an estimate. Usually covers the data submitted as part of the estimate rationale and supports "why the estimate is good." See Rationale.

Subsystem: A subset of devices or an individual unit of hardware that constitutes a defined part of a system.

Successor Activity: In a critical path bar chart, an activity that succeeds the activity under investigation.

Sunk Costs: The total of all past expenditures or irrevocably committed funds related to a program/project.

Surcharge: Any percentage addition to a material price to cover storage, handling, transportation, and other charges.

Surety Bond: A bond that pledges indemnification of the insured against any losses caused by the individual whose name or position appears in the bond through his failure to perform faithfully the terms of contract or other appointed duties.

System Cost Analysis: (1) General: The analysis of a system consisting of the accumulation of comparable and appropriate cost and technical data; and the estimation of the costs of all or a portion of its life cycle. (2) In government procurement this activity is called "cost analysis," and the organization performing it (called by the same name) is usually under the comptroller, whereas the price analysis organization which evaluates contractors' sales proposal costs or prices is in another organization—usually the production, control, or procurement activity.

Takeoff: The process of measuring and counting the linear feet, areas, volumes, and number of units of installed parts or subassemblies from detailed drawings to develop a detailed time and materials estimate as input to a detailed cost estimate.

Target Costs: (1) Negotiating: A cost performance objective value established as contracts are negotiated and changes are authorized. (2) Contracting: Refers to target amounts in incentive type contracts (i.e., target cost, target fee, target price). (3) Cost control: The overall performance value established based on the company's cost/profit objective; therefore, the baseline against which the responsible organization must control and report performance. (4) A value, established as a result of negotiation within incentive type contracts, used as a cost objective and as basis for agreement on the target profit and target price. Used as the base point in calculating cost sharing in incentive contracts.

Target Profit or Fee: The anticipated fee or profit that the contractor will receive for meeting target cost.

Taxes: Charges levied by federal, state, or local governments. They do not include fines, penalties, or charges for services.

Then-Year Dollars: Dollars that are escalated into the time period of performance of a contract. Sometimes referred to as escalated costs, inflated costs, or real-year dollars. See Current Dollars, Base Year (for the opposites).

Time and Materials Contract: A contract providing for the purchase of supplies or services on the basis of (1) direct labor hours at specified hourly rates (including direct labor, overhead, and profit); and (2) material at cost.

Time Study: Observing, recording, or calculating the time required to perform each detailed element of an industrial operation and "leveling" of the results into a practicable attainable work standard.

Time Variance (Labor): The difference between the standard hours priced at the standard rate and the actual hours priced at the standard rate.

Total Average Labor Cost: This includes all labor hours, productive and non-productive, averaged over the quantity of units.

Total Contract Price at Completion: Consists of actuals through a specific date plus estimated cost to complete and estimated final fee/profit.

Total Contract Target Cost: The estimated cost set forth in the contract. It is adjusted upward or downward by the negotiated target cost of authorized changes.

Total Obligational Authority (TOA): In government procurement the total amount of funds available for programming in a given year, regardless of the year the funds are appropriated, obligated, or expended. TOA includes new obligational authority, unprogrammed or reprogrammed obligational authority from prior years, and unobligated balances transferred from other appropriations.

Trade Discount: A reduction in price, usually varying in percentage with volume of transactions, made by suppliers to those engaged in certain businesses.

Transaction: Any mutual agreement, contract, understanding, or exchange or transfer of cash or property between entities, individuals, or group of individuals.

Travel Costs: Normally includes all nonlabor costs approved in conjunction with temporary travel assignments, including air and local transportation costs, mileage allowances, per diem, lodging, and certain other costs. Also can include the costs of permanent relocation of personnel to off-site areas or other facilities. Labor costs expended during travel periods are not included in the travel costs. These costs are included in the appropriate statement of work task as direct labor.

Unallowable Indirect Costs: In government procurement indirect or overhead costs deemed to be improper for purposes of computing the price and/or cost of government contracts.

Uncertainty Analysis: A systematic analysis of the range of probable costs about a point estimate based on considerations of requirements, cost estimating, and technical uncertainty. The intent of such an analysis is to provide the decision maker with additional information. Such an analysis is not expected to improve the precision of the point estimate, but rather to place it in perspective with respect to various contingencies.

Under the Limit Changes: A dollar amount or allowance added to a contract to cover the costs and profit for out of scope changes that are too small in dollar value to process on an administrative basis economically. The limit (e.g., $5000, $20,000, $50,000) for under the limit changes is set forth in the contract terms and conditions. The total amount is based on a forecast of the number of under the limit changes during the life of the contract multiplied by the under limit dollar amount for each change. Since these are out of scope changes, fee or profit is also applied.

Underrun/Overrun: The dollar variation from the contract target costs through a given period.

Unit Cost (Hours): The cost in dollars or hours for an item of work output.

Unit Curve: Logarithmic chart of unit values plotted at each respective unit.

Unit Fabrication Cost: Those elements of recurring costs directly associated with the manufacture of a specific item. The costs include fabrication, assembly, purchasing, functional and acceptance testing, inspecting (quality control), and packaging of the unit for delivery or shipment.

Unit Hours: The manufacturing hours for a specific item at a particular unit location on a learning curve.

Unit Price: The cost or price of an item based on the unit of issue.

Unit Quantity: The number of deliverable units in a contract.

Unit Time: The labor hours associated with a given unit.

Unliquidated Commitments: Those commitments that are outstanding on the "as of" date of a report.

Unliquidated Obligation: An obligation incurred for which payment has not been made. It may consist of an account payable or obligation for goods and services ordered but not yet received.

Unsolicited Proposal: An unrequested or verbally requested quotation or informal bid. Usually generated from a need perceived within a company and is not related to a formal customer request for proposal.

Usage: A term to denote the additional cost to repair/replace items damaged in handling, assembling, installing, or testing items. The cost of material that must be purchased to manufacture a part over and above that specifically dimensioned in an engineering bill of material.

Validated Cost Data: Resource data that have been objectively analyzed and documented by the originator and independently evaluated by an external cost control or audit agency.

Valuation: The establishment of the worth of anything in terms of money. The value set on a product or service.

Value: The measurement of worth in terms of money.

Value Analysis: A systematic and objective evaluation of the function of a product with respect to its related cost. Its purpose is to ensure optimum value. As a pricing tool, value analysis provides insight into the inherent worth of a product.

Value Engineering: An engineering function that examines proposed designs, methods, and processes with the object of identifying techniques or processes that can produce the item more economically without significant loss of performance.

Variable Cost: A cost that changes with the rate of production of goods or the performance of services. As distinguished from "fixed" costs, which do not change with the rate of production or performance, and "semivariable" costs, which are neither entirely fixed or variable. See Fixed Costs.

Variance: Deviation or difference between a standard or forecasted value and the actual value stated in terms of cost, rate, time, weight, height, price, usage, and so on.

WBS Dictionary: A detailed description of the work elements in a work breakdown structure identifying work that is included in each element, work that is specifically excluded from each element, and indicating the interrelationship with other work elements.

WBS Elements: The individual elements of the work breakdown structure which represent the required hardware, software, services and/or data. See Work Breakdown Structure.

Weighted Guidelines: A technique for establishing profit objectives, conducting profit negotiations, and documenting the results. Consists of an assigned profit range for each element of cost with higher profits for more skilled labor plus special recognition for risk assumption, past performance, and other selected factors.

Will Cost: A concept of contract pricing that requires the submission and evaluation of what an offeror estimates it *will cost* to do the job in a specified future period. Backup data reflect projections from past and current costs for the same or similar work, to the extent actuals are available. Such pricing data are evaluated for application to a projection of future costs, as well as for whether these data may indicate the likelihood of perpetuating past inefficiencies.

Work Activity: A type of work that results from the expenditure of labor and materials to produce a nontangible output such as a process or a service.

Work Breakdown Structure (WBS): A product- or service-oriented family tree or hierarchy, composed of hardware, software, services, and other work tasks, that completely displays the project/program. A management technique for subdividing a total job into its component elements, which then can be displayed in a manner to show the relationship of these elements to each other and to the whole. The work breakdown structure can equate to an outline of a statement of work. Also called Work Element Structure.

Work-Hour: A one-hour period of work for one employee. One employee normally produces 40 work-hours in one work-week, two employees produce 80 work-hours in one work-week, and so on. Work-week, work-month, and work-year have corresponding definitions based on their respective time periods.

Work-in-Progress Inventory Costs: Costs of raw materials and conversion costs that do not result in finished goods at the end of a financial reporting period.

Work Measurement: A technique employed independently or in conjunction with cost accounting for the collection of data on actual labor hours and production of work units so that the relationship between work performed and labor-hours expended can be calculated.

Work Order: An internal company authorization to incur costs for the design, development, manufacture, purchase, assembly, test, checkout, and/or delivery of products or services. May also cover a blanket authorization to perform certain work; usually broader in scope than a job order, although work order is occasionally used synonymously with job order.

Work Output: A tangible result of the expenditure of labor and materials such as a product or a project.

Work Package: A segment of effort that is characterized by beginning and ending points clearly defined in terms of accomplishment and which can be assigned hours and dollars required to complete. Work packages are the lowest levels of the contractor's extended work breakdown structure.

Work Request: A negotiated method used to obtain ''on-site'' authorization for additional work requirements at test sites, military installations, bases, and the like. It is not used to authorize a configuration change; however, it may authorize implementation of an approved Class I change which results in a revision to a configuration.

Work Simplification: The application of a management philosophy and practice that seeks to conduct all activities, and perform all functions of an enterprise in the least complex (and, consequently, the least expensive) manner consistent with any given purpose.

Work Standard: The number of labor time units (hours, minutes, seconds, etc.) selected to accomplish each work unit for the purpose of appraising an operation.

Work Statement: See Statement of Work.

Working Capital: Excess of current assets over current liabilities.

Worth: That quality or sum of qualities of a product or service rendering it valuable or useful; often expressed in dollars.

Wraparound Rate: A total rate per hour that covers direct labor, overhead, fringe benefits, and other costs. Also may include factored labor costs, support services, travel, and material costs. *Note*: No universal definition exists in the estimating profession to cover the specific items to be included in a wrap-around rate.

Write-off: *Estimating*: An accounting entry used to create a charge against earnings for elements of cost not recognized as allowable for contract pricing. *Financial*: Charges against earnings for losses of commercial sales, subsidiary losses, losses on development of commercial items, and so on.

INDEX

Acceptance sampling, 460
Accounting, interface with estimating, 314
Accounts, book of, 533
Adjusted skill mix, 28, 29
Administrative costs, 32, 190, 352
Allowances, labor, 220, 438
Alternative hypothesis, 87, 88
Alternatives, economic comparison of, 126
American Association of Cost Engineers
    (AACE), 536
American Society of Professional Estimators
    (ASPE), 537
ANOVA, 111
Arcs, 268
Arrow diagram, 405
Artemis, 275
Artificial intelligence, 539, 540, 551
Assets, 43

BASIC programs, 313
Beta distribution curve, 23
Bidding strategy, 378
Bill of materials, 66, 67, 447
Bookkeeping normalizations, 230
Break-even point, 73
Brief work-factor, 445
Budget process, 502
Building construction, 375, 389
Burden pools, 183

CAD/CAM systems, 429, 432
Calculated variance ratio, 115
Capacity estimates, 379

Capitalized costs, 134
Cash flow, 121, 123, 397
Cash flow comparison, 121, 151
Cash flow diagrams, 122
CER forms, 233, 244
CERs, 17, 226, 234, 299, 340
    choice of, 242
    computerized, 340
    production rate effects, 253
    quantity effect on, 252
CER stratification, 249
Certification, professional, 534
COCOMO™, 474
Comparable facility estimates, 380
Complex compression, 414
Complexity, effects on learning curves, 179
Complexity factors, 251
Composite labor rates, 183
Composite learning curve, 175
Computerized parametric estimating, 256
Computing estimated cost, 37
Confidence level, 437
Constant dollars, 150
Construction cost estimating, 373, 425
Construction estimating, sixteen divisions, 319
Construction site analysis, 360
Continuous timing, in time study, 435
Control chart, 460
Conversion cost, 50
Correlation coefficients, 246
Cost:
    direct, 397, 427
    indirect 427, 446

Cost Accounting Standards (CAS), 516
Cost adjustments, 251
Cost analysis, 1, 16
  in cost accounting standards, 517
Cost breakdown, computerized, 353
Cost classifications, 42
Cost data, historical, 15
Cost data base, typical, 16
Cost estimate, anatomy of, 182
Cost estimating, 1
  definition, 528
  equations for, 184
  evolution of, 528
  twelve steps of, 1, 3, 191, 315, 545, 571
Cost estimating education, 531
Cost estimating fundamentals, 1
Cost estimating as profession, 528
Cost estimating relationship (CER) 17, 226,
    234, 299, 340
Cost growth allowances, 223
Cost improvement curves, 162
Cost ledgers, 533
Cost models, 233, 257
Cost performance, 259
Cost-plus-award fee contract, 510
Cost-plus-fixed-fee contract, 511
Cost-plus-incentive-fee contract, 509
Cost-reimbursement contract, 504
Costs:
  differential, 76
  direct, 33, 49, 389, 397, 427
  of estimate, 185
  fixed, 46, 49
  income tax, 127
  indirect, 33, 49, 58, 59, 395, 397, 427
  overhead, 33, 55, 352
  prime, 50
  semivariable, 46
  sunk, 77, 125
  variable, 46, 49
Cost-sharing contract, 509
Cost summaries, 365, 490
Cost types, 186
Cost uncertainties, 128
Cost variance, 72
Crash cost, 413
Crash duration 413, 415
Crawford curve, 162
Crawford learning curve, 160, 164
Critical path, 14, 410
Critical path method (CPM), 272, 400
  backward pass, 277
  forward pass, 272
Current dollars, 150

Data base(s), 229
  contents, 337
Data collection, 229
Data normalization, 229
Data organization, 229
Data retrieval, 334
Data storage, 334
Decision criteria, 129
Deep-representation in AI, 544
Delphi technique, 264
Dependent variable, 101, 108
Design:
  complexity, 252
  effects on learning curves, 177
  growth allowances, 222
  inheritance, 252
Detailed estimating, 182, 388
Detailed work-factor, 445
Differential analysis, 78, 79
Differential cost pricing, 83
Differential costs, 76
Direct costs, 33, 49, 389, 397, 427
Direct estimating, 200
Direct labor, 51
Direct labor standards, 68
Direct materials, 447
Discounted cash flows, 122
Discount factors, 135
Discount rate, 154
  choice of, 136
Documentation costs, 215
DOD:
  Five Year Defense Plan, 502
  multiyear contracting, 502
  multiyear procurement, 503
Drafting costs, 212
Dynamic skill mix, 26

EasyEst, 325
Economic lifetime, 126
Economics, 120
Economic selection, 141
Education and training in cost estimating, 531
Engineered construction projects, 385
Engineering:
  changes, 222
  documentation, 214
  prototypes, 222
Equivalent annual amount, 132
Equivalent annual amount comparison, 139
Equivalent annual costs:
  constant dollars, 153
  with inflation, 152
Escalation, 34, 36, 354, 355

ESD Software estimating model, 481
Estimate:
  adjustment, 38
  analysis, 38
  assumptions, 4
  ground rules, 3
  plan, 2
  publication, 39, 359
  report format, 40
  support, 38
  synthesis, 359
Estimating:
  detailed, 182
  parametric, 225
  twelve steps of, 1, 3, 191, 315, 545, 571
Estimating disciplines, 530
Estimating engineering costs, 211
Estimating formulas, 207
Estimating information, 2
Estimating interface with accounting, 314
Estimating methods, 2
Estimating relationships, 206
Estimating skills, 3
Estimating software, 315
Estimating software costs, 463
Estimating testing costs, 218
Estimator, qualities of, 532
Expenses, 45
Experience curves, 162
Expert opinion in risk analysis, 261, 262, 264
Espert system in AI, 543
Exponential CERs, 241

Facilities contracts, 514
Factors, use in detailed estimating, 224
Federal Acquisition Regulation (FAR), 499
Fee, 190, 352
Firm-fixed-price contract, 505
Firm quotes in estimating, 200
Five Year Defense Plan, 502
Fixed-ceiling-price contract, 507
Fixed costs, 46, 49, 187
Fixed-price contract, 375, 425, 504, 508
Fixed-price incentive contract, 506
Flexible budgeting, 69
Frame approaches in AI, 544
Frame-based system, 545
Full cost pricing, 83
Functional work elements, 194

Gantt charts, 274
General Services Administration (GSA), 514
GNP deflator, 147
Goodness of fit test, 91, 92, 96, 245

Graphics, computer, 361

Handbook estimating, 201
Handling time, 459
Heavy construction, 375, 395
Heuristics, 542
High-low points, 48
Historical:
  cost data, 15, 85, 333
  inflation rates, 148
  interest rates, 148
Holding cost, in inventory, 449
Homoscedasticity, 107
Hypothesis testing, 87

Income tax costs, 127
Indefinite-delivery contracts, 511
Independent cost estimate (ICE), 521
Independent variables, 101, 108, 112, 300
Indirect costs, 33, 49, 58, 59, 395, 397, 427
Indirect labor, 51, 446
Industrial standards, 31
Infinite horizon, 133
Inflation, 17, 34, 35, 354
Inflation and interest, relationship, 145
Initial acquisition costs, 186
Inspection, 460
Instantaneous replenishment, 452
Institute of Cost Analysis (ICA), 537
Institute of Management Accounting, 535
Integrated applications software, 313
Interest and inflation, relationship, 145
Internal rate of return, 134, 142
International Society of Parametric Analysts
  (ISPA), 537

Knowledge base, 545
Knowledge-intensive systems, 539
Knowledge system in AI, 543
Kolmogorov-Smirnov statistic, 92, 117
Kruskal-Wallis H-test, 115

Labor:
  direct, 51
  indirect, 51
Labor allowances, 220
Labor costing, 429
Labor costs, geographical, 19
Labor estimates, 27
Labor factors, 189
Labor-hour contract, 513
Labor quantities, 349
Labor rates, 18, 21, 183, 189, 345
Labor rate schedule, 445

Learning curve, composite, 175
Learning curve algebraic solutions, 171
Learning curve comparisons, 204
Learning curve computer programs, 170
Learning curve graphical solutions, 171
Learning curve plots, 203
Learning curves, 21, 157, 168, 201, 389
   computerized, 343
   examples, 176
   mathematics of, 169
   misapplication of, 179
Learning curve slope, 167
Learning curve tabular solutions, 174
Learning curve theory, 161
Learning function, 158
Learning incentives, 179
Learning losses, 178
Least-cost scheduling, 404, 411, 413
Least squares method, 49, 244
Letter contract, 513
Level of significance, 89
Levels of investment, multiple, 125
Liabilities, 43
Life cycle cost estimate, 502
Lotus 1-2-3™ templates, 317
Lump-sum contracts, 376

Maintenance costs, 221
Major systems, 501
Management costs, 223
Manloading, 204
   computerized, 350
Manual operations, 180
Manufacturing, 427
   effects on learning curves, 177
   engineering, 212
   estimates, 217
   overhead, 51
Marginal efficiency, 74
Margin of safety method, 76
Master production schedule, 448
Material cost standards, 66
Material estimates, 27, 32, 189
Material quantities, 349
Materials, direct, 447
Mathematical transformations, 286
Maynard Operation Sequence Technique
   (MOST), 444
Mechanical assembly tasks, 180
Methods-Time Measurement (MTM), 439
Microchronometer, 435
Microcomputer-based estimating, 38
Microcomputer hardware, 367
Microcomputer software, 371

MicroPICES™, 339
Minimax procedure, 544
Models, cost, 17, 226, 233, 234, 299, 340
Money, time value of, 120
Monte Carlo procedure, 276
Monte Carlo simulation, 296, 299, 404, 422,
   423, 426
Motion time methods (MTM), 30, 68
Multiple regression, 247
   analysis, 101, 387
Multiyear contract, 502, 503, 504, 525

National Contract Management Association
   (NCMA), 537
National Estimating Society (NES), 534
National Society of Professional Engineers
   (NSPE), 429
Net cash flow, 124
Network:
   activities, 403
   analysis, 265, 271
   models, 270
   scheduling, 403
   simulation, 268
Node logic, 268
Nonparametric statistical methods, 86, 87, 115
Nonrecurring costs, 10, 187
Normal distribution population, 86, 88
Normal time, in time study, 437, 438
Null hypothesis, 87
Number processing, 311

Operation chart, 442
Ordered state space search, 545
Organizational relationships, 199
Other costs, 33, 223
Overhead:
   manufacturing, 51
   predetermined rate, 53, 55
   service department, 63
Overhead costs, 32, 55, 352
Overhead pools, 183
Overhead rate, 56, 59

Parametric estimating, 205, 225, 236
   history, 227
Parametric statistical methods, 86, 88
Payment progressing, 415
Payment schedules, 128
Percent complete, 14
Performance rating, in time study, 437
Perpetual worth, 134
Personal, fatigue, and delay (PFD) time, 221
PERT, 12, 209, 259, 404, 418, 426

PERT/COST, 274
Physical work elements, 196
Population variance, 106
Power curves, 237
Power and linear curves, 239
Precedence diagram, 406, 411
Precedence relationships, 12
Precision level, 437
Predetermined overhead rate, 53, 55
Predetermined system, in time study, 438, 445
Present value, 129
Present value comparison, 137
PRICE-S™, 477
PRICE S-Z™, 478
Pricing, 37
Primavera™, 331
Prime costs, 50
Prime interest rate, 147
Probabilistic event analysis (PEA) model, 296
Probability distribution, 264
Probability theory, 261
Process:
    costing, 56
    manufacturing, 65
    planning, 214
Procurement cost, 449
Procurement process, 498
Production breaks, 178
Production engineering, 212
Professional certification, 534
Professional estimating societies, 257
Profit, 190
Program evaluation and review technique
    (PERT), 12, 209, 259, 274, 404, 418, 426
Program management, 519
Progress functions, 157
Project Scheduler 5000™, 332

Quantity takeoff, 389

Random numbers in Monte Carlo procedure,
    276
Rate of return:
    internal, 134
    real, 147
Rates, labor, 18
Rates and factors, 232
RCA PRICE™, 208
Real interest rates, 149
Real rate of return, 147
Recurring costs, 10, 187
Regression, multiple, 247
Regression analysis, 101
Remote filming, in time study, 235

Residual income, 82
Resource classifications, 348
Resource leveling, 404, 415
Revenue, 45
RFP/RFQ, 532
Risk analysis, 128, 255, 259, 260, 264, 306
Risk factor method (RFM), 305
RISNET™, 278
Rules of thumb, 200

Sales mix, 75
Sample variance, 109
Scattergraph, 48
Schedule performance, 259
Schedule relationships, 13, 210
Scheduling, 11, 208, 330
    correlation with WES, 321
Selection from among alternatives, 141
Semivariable costs, 46
Service department overhead, 63
Setup time, 459
Shoploading estimating, 32
    computerized, 351
Simple compression, 413
Simulation models, 449
Skill categories, 21, 22, 345
Skill dispersions, 27
Skill levels, 21, 22, 345
Skill matrix, 198
Skill mix, 347
    dynamic, 22
    static, 23
Skill mix adjustments, 25
SLIM, 479
Small lots, 178
Society of American Value Engineers (SAVE),
    537
Software:
    control, 464
    monitoring, 464
    processing, 463
    user interface, 485
Software analysis and design, 468
Software characteristics, 471
Software checkout and testing, 469
Software cost estimating, 219, 463
Software development, 465, 486
Software documentation, 469
Software estimate publishing, 473
Software estimating:
    case study, 484
    detailed, 464, 494
    rationale, 493
Software implementation, 470

Software labor estimating, 472
Software simulation, 479
Special tooling, 218, 525
Spreadsheets, electronic, 313
Spreadsheet templates, 316
Staffing estimates, 32
Standard cost, 66
Standard data tables, 458
Standard time, in time study, 442
Standard time data, 180, 428, 433
Static skill mix, 24
Statistical:
   estimating, 205
   inference, 86
   sampling, 461
   techniques, 85
Stochastic Aggregation Model (SAM), 299
Storage cost, in inventory, 449
Strategic planning, 541
Strategy, 541
Subcontract costs, 189
Successor relationships, 12
Sunk costs, 77, 125
System engineering in AI, 540, 541

Tactics, 541
Tax, income, 127
Technical performance, 259
Test equipment, 218
Test for outliers, 93
Theoretical first unit (TF), 165
Time-and-materials contract, 513
Time measurement unit (TMU), 439
Time standards, 215
Time study, 433, 434
Time study board, 435
Time value of money, 120
Tooling costs, 221

Transformations, 99
T test, 88
Twelve steps of estimating, 1, 3, 191, 315, 545, 571
Type I and II errors, 89

Unbalanced bids, 397
Uncertainty, 260
Unit costs in CERs, 254
Unit-price contracts, 376

Variable costs, 46, 49, 187
VERT™, 285
Vertical market software, 313
Videotaping, in time study, 435

Wage adjustment factors, 19
Wages, 18
WBS TREE™, 323
Word processing, 311
Work breakdown structure (WBS), 4, 193, 268
Work definition, 192
Work element coding, 10, 312
Work element dictionaries, 11
Work element levels, 9
Work element numbering, 5
Work element pyramid, 5
Work element structure (WES), 4, 193, 231, 268, 315
Work element structure interrelationships, 198
Work element structures:
   arrangements, 8
   typical, 6, 7
Work element structure for software, 466
Work sampling, in time study, 438
Work simplification, 433
Wright learning curve, 159, 162, 163